Lecture Notes in Computer Science     1633
Edited by G. Goos, J. Hartmanis and J. van Leeuwen

Springer

*Berlin*
*Heidelberg*
*New York*
*Barcelona*
*Hong Kong*
*London*
*Milan*
*Paris*
*Singapore*
*Tokyo*

Nicolas Halbwachs   Doron Peled (Eds.)

# Computer Aided Verification

11th International Conference, CAV'99
Trento, Italy, July 6-10, 1999
Proceedings

 Springer

Series Editors

Gerhard Goos, Karlsruhe University, Germany
Juris Hartmanis, Cornell University, NY, USA
Jan van Leeuwen, Utrecht University, The Netherlands

Volume Editors

Nicolas Halbwachs
Vérimag/CNRS
2, avenue de Vignate, F-38610 Gières, France
E-mail: Nicolas.Halbwachs@imag.fr

Doron Peled
Bell Laboratories
600 Mountain Ave., Murray Hill, NJ 07974, USA
and
The Technion, Haifa 32000, Israel
E-mail: doron@cs.technion.ac.il

Cataloging-in-Publication data applied for

Die Deutsche Bibliothek - CIP-Einheitsaufnahme

**Computer aided verification** : 11th international conference ; proceedings / CAV
'99, Trento, Italy, July 6 - 10, 1999. Nicolas Halbwachs ; Doron Peled (ed.). -
Berlin ; Heidelberg ; New York ; Barcelona ; Hong Kong ; London ; Milan ; Paris
; Singapore ; Tokyo : Springer, 1999
 (Lecture notes in computer science ; Vol. 1633)
 ISBN 3-540-66202-2

CR Subject Classification (1998): F.3, D.2.4, D.2.2, F.4.1, B.7.2, C.3, I.2.3

ISSN 0302-9743
ISBN 3-540-66202-2 Springer-Verlag Berlin Heidelberg New York

Typesetting: Camera-ready by author
SPIN: 10703391   06/3142 – 5 4 3 2 1 0    Printed on acid-free paper

# Preface

This volume contains the proceedings of the Eleventh International Conference on Computer-Aided Verification (CAV'99), held at Trento, Italy on July 6–10. The CAV conferences are dedicated to the advancement of the theory and practice of computer-assisted formal analysis methods for software and hardware systems. The conference covers the spectrum from theoretical results to concrete applications and tools and has traditionally drawn contributions from both researchers and practitioners in both academia and industry. This year we received 107 submissions, out of which we accepted 34. We also accepted five short tool presentations.

CAV included a tutorial day this year, with four invited tutorials by Edmund M. Clarke (CMU) on *Symbolic Model Checking*, David Dill (Stanford) on *Alternative Approaches to Hardware Verification*, Joseph Sifakis (VERIMAG) on *The Compositional Specification of Timed Systems*, and Rajeev Alur (UPenn) on *Timed Automata*. The conference also included four invited talks by Gunnar Stålmarck (Prover Technology) on *Stålmarck's Method and QBF Solving*, Zohar Manna (Stanford University) on *Visual Verification of Parameterized Programs (joint with CADE)*, Ed Brinksma (University of Twente) on *Formal Methods for Conformance Testing: Theory Can Be Practical!* and Alain Deutsch (INRIA) on *Abstract Interpretation Applied to the Verification of Ariane 5 Software*.

The conference program included papers on a wide variety of topics, including microprocessor verification, verification and testing of protocols, methods for verification of systems with infinite state spaces, the theory of verification, verification of temporal logic properties, modeling of systems, symbolic model checking, theorem proving, combining theorem proving with model-checking, model-checking techniques based on automata theory and abstraction methods.

Many industrial companies have shown wide interest in CAV, ranging from using the presented technologies to developing and marketing their own techniques and tools. We would like to thank the following generous and forward-looking companies for their sponsorship of CAV'99:

- Intel
- The John von Neumann Minerva Center for Verification of Reactive Systems at the Weizmann Institute
- Lucent Technologies
- Siemens
- ST Microelectronics
- SUN Microsystems

The Steering Committee consists of the conference founders:

Edmund M. Clarke (Carnegie Mellon University), Robert P. Kurshan (Bell Laboratories), Amir Pnueli (The Weizmann Institute of Technology) and Joseph Sifakis (VERIMAG)

The conference program was selected by the program committee, which included this year:

Gerard Berry (Ecole des Mines, France), Ahmed Bouajjani (VER-IMAG, France), Ching-Tsun Chou (Intel, USA), Edmund M. Clarke (CMU, USA), Werner Damm (Oldenburg U., Germany), David Dill (Stanford U., USA), Allen Emerson (Austin U., USA), Javier Esparza (Munich U., Germany), Limor Fix (Intel, Israel), Mike Gordon (Cambridge U., UK), Nicolas Halbwachs (co-chair, VERIMAG, France), Tom Henzinger (Berkeley, USA), Alan Hu (UBC, Canada), Bengt Jonsson (Uppsala U., Sweden), Robert P. Kurshan (Bell Labs, USA), Gavin Lowe (Leicester U., UK), Ken McMillan (Cadence, USA), Doron Peled (co-chair, Bell Labs, USA and Technion, Israel), Carl Pixley (Motorola, USA), A. Prasad Sistla (Chicago U., USA), Fabio Somenzi (Colorado U., USA), Mandayam Srivas (SRI, USA), Antti Valmari (Tampere U. Techn., Finland), Yaron Wolfsthal (IBM, Israel) and Pierre Wolper (Liege U., Belgium).

We would also like to thank the following additional reviewers: Mark Aagaard, Luca de Alfaro, Pascalin Amagbegnon, Simon Ambler, Nina Amla, Flemming Andersen, Eugene Asarin, Landver Avner, Neta Ayzenbood-Reshef, Clark Barrett, Jason Baumgartner, Ilan Beer, Shoham Ben-David, Sergey Berezin, Armin Biere, Roderick Bloem, Juergen Bohn, Bernard Boigelot, Amar Bouali, Marius Bozga, Steve Brookes, Randy Bryant, Gianpiero Cabodi, Paolo Camurati, Ilaria Castellani, Gerard Cece, Pankajkuman Chauhanq, Eve Coste-Maniere, Bruno Courcelle, Sadie Creese, Roy Crole, Eli Dichterman, Jurgend Dingel, Cindy Eisner, Jean-Claude Fernandez, Ranan Fraer, Martin Franzle, Richard Gault, Daniel Geist, Jaco Geldenhuys, Rob Gerth, Boris Ginsburg, Michael Goldsmith, G. Gonthier, Shankar Govindaraju, Susanne Graf, Orna Grumberg, Dilian Gurov, Gary Hachtel, John Harrison, John Havlicek, Nevin Heintze, Keijo Heljanko, Juhana Helovuo, Tamir Heyman, Hiroyuki Higuchi, Pei-Hsin Ho, Gerard Holzmann, Mei Lin Hui, Marten van Hulst, Hardi Hungar, Warren Hunt, Amitai Iron, Jae-Young Jang, Somesh Jha, Robert B. Jones, Bernhard Josko, Tommi Junttila, Gila Kamhi, Konsta Karsisto, Shmuel Katz, Sharon Keidar, Pertti Kellomäki, Astrid Kiehn, Barbara Koenig, Ilkka Kokkarinen, Antonin Kucera, Orna Kupferman, Yassine Lakhnech, Avner Landver, Ranko Lazic, David Lee, Leonid Libkin, Johan Lilius, Zhiming Liu, Yuan Lu, Enrico Macii, Sela Mador-Haim, Will Marrero, Richard Mayr, Jon Millen, Marius Minea, In-Ho Moon, John Moondanos, Laurent Mounier, Anca Muscholl, Kedar Namjoshi, Peter Niebert, Juergen Niehaus, Aletta Nylén, Sven-Olof Nyström, John O'Leary, Atanas Parashkevov, Abelardo Pardo, David Park, D. Stott Parker, Wojciech Penczek, Antoine Petit, Paul Pettersson, Avi Puder, Shaz Qadeer, Stefano Quer, Sriram Rajamani, J-F Raskin, Kavita Ravi, Joy Reed, Eran Rippel, Steven Roberts, Yoav Rodeh, Christine Roeckl, Stefan Roemer, Marco Roveri, Valerie Roy, Harald Ruess, Vlad Rusu, Peter Ryan, Hassan Saidi, Jun Sawada, Rainer Schloer, Steve Schneider, Claus Schroeter, Stefan Schwoon, Ellen Sentovich, Tom Shiple, Robert de Simone, Jens Skakkebaek, Dawn Song, Jeffrey Su, Don Syme, Maciej Szreter, Serdar Tasiran,

Javier Thayer, Horia Toma, Richard Trefler, Stavros Tripakis, Irek Ulidowski, Moshe Vardi, Kimmo Varpaaniemi, Björn Victor, Gopal Vijayan, Heikki Virtanen, Frank Wallner, Howard Wong-Toi, Bwolen Yang, Tali Yatzkar-Haham, Wang Yi, Irfan Zakiuddin, Avi Ziv and Baruch Ziv.

This year, CAV was part of the **Federated Logic Conference (FLoC'99)**, and was organized jointly with CADE (Conference on Automated Deduction), LICS (Logic in Computer Science) and RTA (Rewriting Techniques and Applications). In addition, FLoC included 15 workshops associated with the different conferences, panels and tutorials. We would like to acknowledge the help of the FLOC'99 steering committee: Moshe Y. Vardi (General Chair), Fausto Giunchiglia (Conference Chair), Leonid Libkin (Publicity Chair), Paolo Traverso (CADE), Joseph Sifakis (CAV), Eugenio Moggi (LICS), Simona Ronchi della Rocca (LICS), Andrea Asperti (RTA), Morena Carli, Nadia Oss Papot (Secretariat), Alessandro Tuccio (Treasurer) and Adolfo Villafiorita (National Publicity Chair and Workshops Coordinator).

Finally, we would like to extend special thanks to Richard Gerber for kindly lending us his "START" conference management software — which was of incredible help —, and to Yannick Raoul for installing and adapting the software.

April 1999                                          Nicolas Halbwachs

                                                   Doron Peled

# Table of Contents

## Abstraction

## Tool Presentations

# Alternative Approaches to Hardware Verification

David L. Dill

Computer Systems Laboratory
Stanford University
Stanford, CA 94305
dill@cs.stanford.edu

## Abstract

BDD-based symbolic model checking has received a great deal of attention because of its potential for solving hardware verification problems. However, there are other, qualitatively different, approaches that are also quite promising (which having different strengths and weaknesses). This tutorial surveys a variety of approaches based on symbolic simulation.

Symbolic simulation allows the user to set inputs to variables instead of constants, and propagates expressions containing those variables through the operators and expressions of the circuit. Symbolic simulation is attractive, because it works for large designs and can be made to degrade gracefully when designs become too large. It has the disadvantage that it is difficult or impossible to compute invariants automatically. By comparison, the main strength of model checking is its ability to computer invariants via iterative fixed point computations.

The tutorial discusses different approaches to symbolic simulation and applications that make effective use of it, including abstraction methods and self-comparison.

# The Compositional Specification of Timed Systems — A Tutorial

Joseph Sifakis

VERIMAG, 2 rue Vignate, 38610 Gières, France
Joseph.Sifakis@imag.fr

## Motivation

The analysis of reactive systems requires models representing the system, its interaction with the environment and taking into account features of the underlying execution structure. It is important that such models are timed if analysis concerns performance, action scheduling or in general, dynamic aspects of the behavior. In practice, timed models of systems are obtained by adding timing constraints to untimed descriptions. For instance, given the functional description of a circuit, the corresponding timed model can be obtained by adding timing constraints about propagation delays of the components; to build a timed model of a real-time software, quantitative timing information concerning execution times of the statements and significant changes of the environment must be added.

The construction of timed models of reactive systems raises some important questions concerning their composition and in particular, the way some well-understood constructs for untimed systems can be extended to timed systems.

In this tutorial, we present an overview of existing executable timed formalisms with a global notion of time, by putting emphasis on problems of compositional description. The results on compositionality have been developed in collaboration with S. Bornot, at Verimag.

## Timed Formalisms

Timed formalisms are extensions of untimed ones by adding *clocks*, real-valued variables that can be tested and modified at transitions. Clocks measure the time elapsed at states. Timed automata [AD94,ACH+95], timed process algebras [NS91] and timed Petri nets can be considered as timed formalisms.

The semantics of timed formalisms can be defined by means of transition systems that can perform time steps or (timeless) transitions. A state is a pair $(s, v)$, consisting of a control state $s$ (of the untimed system) and a valuation of the clocks. As a rule, transitions are specified by a guard (predicate) on clocks and an assignment of new values to clocks. They correspond to *actions* of the considered system. *Time progress conditions* are predicates on clocks associated with control states $s$ that specify how time can progress: a time step of duration $d$ can be performed from $s$ only if all the intermediate states satisfy the time progress condition.

An important feature of timed models is the possibility to express *urgency* of an action (transition). An action enabled at a state $(s, v)$, becomes urgent if time cannot progress at $v$. As time cannot advance, the urgent action can be executed. Expressing urgency is essential in modeling the real-time behavior of systems. However, stopping time progress to simulate urgency, can be a source of problems, especially when composing timed models. The independent description of transitions and of time progress conditions may induce undesirable deadlock situations where time cannot progress and no action is enabled.

To avoid timelocks, a class of timed formalisms has been studied where time progress conditions are associated with the transitions in the form of *deadlines* [SY96,BS98,BST97]. The deadline of a transition is a predicate on clocks which implies the associated guard and represents the set of the clock valuations at which the transition becomes urgent. Inclusion of deadlines in the corresponding guards implies *time reactivity* that is, whenever time progress stops, there exists at least one enabled transition. The use of deadlines has another interesting consequence. Each transition with the associated guard, deadline and assignment, corresponds to an elementary timed system, called *timed action*.

We show how a timed transition system can be obtained as the composition of timed actions.

## Composition of Timed Systems

As usual, the behavior of a timed system is obtained by composing the behavior of its components. Most of the work on the composition of timed systems, concerns timed process algebras. Very often it adopts a principle of independence between timed and untimed behavior: transitions and time steps of the system are obtained by composing independently the transitions and time steps of the components. Furthermore, a strong synchrony assumption is adopted for time progress. Time can progress in the system by some amount $d$ only if all the components agree to let time advance by $d$. This leads to elegant *urgency preserving* semantics in the sense that component deadlines are respected. However, this orthogonality between time progress and transitions may easily introduce timelocks, especially when an untimed description with communication allowing waiting, e.g. rendez-vous, is extended into a timed description. In such cases, it is questionable whether the application of a strong synchronization rule for time progress is always appropriate. For instance, if two systems are in states from which they will never synchronize, it may be desirable not to further constrain time progress by the strong synchronization rule.

As an alternative to urgency preserving semantics, *flexible* composition semantics have been studied [BST97,BS98]. This semantics preserve time reactivity. To avoid timelocks, urgency constraints are relaxed in some manner that is shown to be optimal. The main idea behind flexible semantics, is to adjust waiting times of the components so as to achieve a desirable global behavior satisfying by construction, the following two *sanity* properties.

One property is time reactivity which can be guaranteed by construction and is related to absence of timelock. Contrary to other stronger well-timedness properties, time reactivity is very easy to satisfy by construction.

The second property is activity preservation and is related to absence of (local) deadlock. It requires that if some action can be executed after waiting by some time in a component, then some (not necessarily the same) action of the system can be executed, after waiting by some (not necessarily the same) time.

## The Compositional Framework

We show how timed systems can be built from timed actions by preserving both time reactivity and activity of components.

The set of the timed actions on given set of clocks, set of control states and vocabulary of action names, consists of a transition on control states labeled by a tuple $(a, g, d, f)$ where $a$ is an action name, $g$ is a guard, $d$ is a deadline and $f$ is a function on clocks. The guard $g$ and the deadline $d$ are predicates on clocks such that $d$ implies $g$, representing respectively the set of enabling and the set of the urgent states of the timed action. The function $f$ represents the effect of the execution on clock states.

A timed system is a set of timed actions. Following a standard process algebra approach, it can be described in an algebra of terms generated from some constant, representing the idle system, by using timed action prefixing, non deterministic choice and recursion. Equality of terms is the congruence obtained by assuming associativity, commutativity and idempotence of non deterministic choice, that is, the labeled transition structures of the terms are bisimilar, where equality of two labels means identity of their action names and equivalence of the corresponding guards, deadlines and functions.

We define two kinds of operators on timed systems: priority choice operators and parallel composition operators. The operators are timed extensions of untimed operators. We give sufficient conditions for preserving both time reactivity and activity of components.

### Priority choice operators

Priority is a very useful concept for modeling interrupts or preemption in real-time systems. A well-known difficulty with introducing priorities, is that they are badly compatible with compositionality and incrementality of specification [BBK86,CH90,BGL97].

We define priority choice operators, that is choice operators depending on a relation between actions. This relation is an order on action names parameterized by non negative reals representing *degrees of priority*. Roughly speaking, if action $a_2$ has priority over action $a_1$ of degree $d$, then in the priority choice of two timed actions with labels $a_2$ and $a_1$, action $a_1$ will be disabled if action $a_2$ will be enabled within $d$ time units. The main results concerning priority choice are the following:

– Priority choice operators can be expressed in terms of non deterministic choice operators, by restricting appropriately the guard and the deadline of actions of lower priority. The restricted guards and deadlines can be specified in a simple modal language. However, modalities are just a macronotation, as they represent quantification over time which can be eliminated.

- We provide sufficient conditions on the priority order, for the priority operators to be associative, commutative and idempotent. This result allows to consider priority choice operators as basic operators, generalizations of non deterministic choice. The latter can be considered as the choice operator for the empty priority order.
- We show that under these conditions, priority order operators preserve activity in the following sense: for every state, if an action $a$ is enabled under the non deterministic choice then either $a$ or a higher priority action will be enabled under the priority choice.

**Parallel composition operators**

Parallel composition operators for timed systems are considered as extensions of parallel composition operators for untimed systems. We suppose, as usual, that the latter are defined in terms of choice operators and some associative and commutative synchronization operator on actions, by means of an expansion rule [Mil83,Mil89]. Synchronization operators associate with pairs of actions the action resulting from their synchronization. The main results concerning parallel composition operators are the following:

- Parallel composition operators can be expressed in terms of choice operators, by appropriately extending the synchronization operators on timed actions. Synchronization operators are associative and commutative and compose componentwise the guards and the deadlines of the synchronizing actions.
- For the composition of guards, different *synchronization modes* of practical interest are studied. Apart from the usual *and*-synchronization, where the synchronization guard is the conjunction of the guards of the synchronizing actions, are considered *max*-synchronization allowing waiting, and *min*-synchronization allowing interruption by the fasted component.
- Parallel composition operators are associative and commutative if they are extensions of untimed operators satisfying the same properties.
- We show that maximal progress can be achieved in synchronization by using priority choice in the expansion rules. Furthermore, we provide sufficient conditions for activity preservation.

The algebraic framework is completed by studying a simple algebra with synchronization operators for timed actions. We deduce laws for timed systems that take into account the structure of the actions and there properties.

**Typed Actions - A Simplified Framework**

A practically interesting simplification of the theoretical framework comes from the (trivial) remark that any timed action can be expressed as the non deterministic choice between a *lazy* action and an *eager* action. A lazy action is an action whose set of urgent states is empty and an eager action has its deadline equal to its guard. This allows to consider only these two types of actions in specifications and simplifies the rules for synchronization.

Sometimes it is useful in practice, to consider a third type of urgency, *delayable* actions. An action is delayable if its deadline is exactly the falling edge of the guard. That is, it cannot be disabled without becoming urgent. We show that parallel composition of systems with delayable actions yields systems with delayable actions.

## Discussion

The distinction between urgency preserving and flexible approach seems to be an important one and is related to the ultimate purpose of the specification. When a complete specification is sought, in view of analysis and verification, it is reasonable to consider that the violation of component deadlines is an error. On the contrary, if the purpose of the specification is to derive a system which is correct with respect to given criteria, knowing the behavior of its components, the flexible approach is appropriate. This approach provides a basis for constructing timed systems that satisfy the two sanity properties, time reactivity and activity preservation. It is very close to synthesis and can be combined with automatic synthesis techniques.

An important outcome of this work is that composition operators for untimed systems admit different timed extensions due to the possibility of controlling waiting times and "predicting" the future. The use of modalities in guards drastically increases succinctness in modeling and is crucial for compositionality. It does not imply extra expressive power for simple classes of timed systems, where quantification over time in guards can be eliminated.

The definition of different synchronization modes has been motivated by the study of high level specification languages for timed systems, such as Timed Petri nets and their various extensions[SDdSS94,SDLdSS96,JLSIR97]. We have shown that the proposed framework is a basis for the study of the underlying semantics and composition techniques; if they are bounded, then they can be represented as timed systems with finite control.

An outstanding fact is that the combined use of the different synchronization modes, drastically helps keeping the complexity of the discrete state space of the descriptions low [BST97]. Both *max*-synchronization and *min*-synchronization can be expressed in terms of *and*-synchronization but this requires additional states and transitions. Furthermore, this destroys compositionality, in the sense that timed specifications cannot be obtained from untimed specifications by preserving the control structure.

We believe that *max*-synchronization and *min*-synchronization are very powerful primitives for the specification of asynchronously cooperating timed systems. The use of *and*-synchronization is appropriate when a tight synchronization between the components is sought. The other two synchronization modes allow avoiding "clashes" in cooperation, for systems of loosely coupled components. For instance, *max*-synchronization corresponds to timed rendez-vous and can be used to obtain in a straightforward manner, timed extensions of asynchronously communicating untimed systems.

The presented framework requires further validation by examples and practice. We are currently applying the flexible approach to the compositional generation of timed models of real-time applications and in particular, to scheduling.

# References

[ACH+95]  R. Alur, C. Courcoubetis, N. Halbwachs, T. Henzinger, P. Ho, X. Nicollin, A. Olivero, J. Sifakis, and S. Yovine. The algorithmic analysis of hybrid systems. *Theoretical Computer Science*, 138:3–34, 1995.

[AD94]    R. Alur and D.L. Dill. A theory of timed automata. *Theoretical Computer Science*, 126:183–235, 1994.

[BBK86]   J.C.M. Baeten, J.A. Bergstra, and J.W. Klop. Syntax and defining equations for an interrupt mechanism in process algebra. *Fundamenta Informaticae IX (2)*, pages 127–168, 1986.

[BGL97]   P. Bremond-Gregoire and I. Lee. A process algebra of communicating shared resources with dense time and priorities. *Theoretical Computer Science, 189*, 1997.

[BS98]    S. Bornot and J. Sifakis. On the composition of hybrid systems. In *First International Workshop Hybrid Systems : Computation and Control HSCC'98*, pages 49–63, Berkeley, March 1998. Lecture Notes in Computer Science 1386, Spinger-Verlag.

[BST97]   S. Bornot, J. Sifakis, and S. Tripakis. Modeling urgency in timed systems. In *International Symposium: Compositionality - The Significant Difference*, Malente (Holstein, Germany), September 1997. Lecture Notes in Computer Science 1536, Springer Verlag.

[CH90]    R. Cleaveland and M. Hennessy. Priorities in process algebra. *Information and Computation, 87(1/2)*, pages 58–77, 1990.

[JLSIR97] M. Jourdan, N. Layaida, L. Sabry-Ismail, and C. Roisin. An integrated authoring and presentation environment for interactive multimedia documents. In *4th Conference on Multimedia Modeling*, Singapore, November 1997. World Scientific Publishing.

[Mil83]   R. Milner. Calculi for synchrony and asynchrony. *Theoretical Computer Science*, 25:267–310, 1983.

[Mil89]   R. Milner. *Communication and Concurrency*. Prentice Hall, 1989.

[NS91]    X. Nicollin and J. Sifakis. An Overview and Synthesis on Timed Process Algebras. In *Proceedings of CAV'91*. Aalborg, Denmark. LNCS 575, Springer Verlag, July 1991.

[SDdSS94] P. Sénac, M. Diaz, and P. de Saqui-Sannes. Toward a formal specification of multimedia scenarios. *Annals of telecomunications*, 49(5-6):297–314, 1994.

[SDLdSS96] P. Sènac, M. Diaz, A. Léger, and P. de Saqui-Sannes. Modeling logical and temporal synchronization in hypermedia systems. In *Journal on Selected Areas in Communications*, volume 14. IEEE, jan. 1996.

[SY96]    J. Sifakis and S. Yovine. Compositional specification of timed systems. In *13th Annual Symposium on Theoretical Aspects of Computer Science, STACS'96*, pages 347–359, Grenoble, France, February 1996. Lecture Notes in Computer Science 1046, Spinger-Verlag.

# Timed Automata

Rajeev Alur[*]

**Abstract.** Model checking is emerging as a practical tool for automated debugging of complex reactive systems such as embedded controllers and network protocols (see [23] for a survey). Traditional techniques for model checking do not admit an explicit modeling of time, and are thus, unsuitable for analysis of real-time systems whose correctness depends on relative magnitudes of different delays. Consequently, *timed automata* [7] were introduced as a formal notation to model the behavior of real-time systems. Its definition provides a simple way to annotate state-transition graphs with timing constraints using finitely many real-valued *clock variables*. Automated analysis of timed automata relies on the construction of a finite quotient of the infinite space of clock valuations. Over the years, the formalism has been extensively studied leading to many results establishing connections to circuits and logic, and much progress has been made in developing verification algorithms, heuristics, and tools. This paper provides a survey of the theory of timed automata, and their role in specification and verification of real-time systems.

## 1 Modeling

**Transition systems.** We model discrete systems by state-transition graphs whose transitions are labeled with event symbols. A *transition system* $S$ is a tuple $\langle Q, Q^0, \Sigma, \rightarrow \rangle$, where $Q$ is a set of states, $Q^0 \subseteq Q$ is a set of initial states, $\Sigma$ is a set of labels (or events), and $\rightarrow \subseteq Q \times \Sigma \times Q$ is a set of transitions. The system starts in an initial state, and if $q \xrightarrow{a} q'$ then the system can change its state from $q$ to $q'$ on event $a$. We write $q \rightarrow q'$ if $q \xrightarrow{a} q'$ for some label $a$. The state $q'$ is reachable from the state $q$ if $q \rightarrow^* q'$. The state $q$ is a reachable state of the system if $q$ is reachable from some initial state.

A complex system can be described as a product of interacting transition systems. Let $S_1 = \langle Q_1, Q_1^0, \Sigma_1, \rightarrow_1 \rangle$ and $S_2 = \langle Q_2, Q_2^0, \Sigma_2, \rightarrow_2 \rangle$ be two transition systems. Then, the *product*, denoted $S_1 \| S_2$, is $\langle Q_1 \times Q_2, Q_1^0 \times Q_2^0, \Sigma_1 \cup \Sigma_2, \rightarrow \rangle$ where $(q_1, q_2) \xrightarrow{a} (q_1', q_2')$ iff either (i) $a \in \Sigma_1 \cap \Sigma_2$ and $q_1 \xrightarrow{a}_1 q_1'$ and $q_2 \xrightarrow{a}_2 q_2'$, or (ii) $a \in \Sigma_1 \setminus \Sigma_2$ and $q_1 \xrightarrow{a}_1 q_1'$ and $q_2' = q_2$, or (iii) $a \in \Sigma_2 \setminus \Sigma_1$ and $q_2 \xrightarrow{a}_2 q_2'$ and $q_1' = q_1$. Observe that the symbols that belong to the alphabets of both the automata are used for synchronization.

[*] Department of Computer and Information Science, University of Pennsylvania, and Bell Laboratories, Lucent Technologies. Email: alur@cis.upenn.edu. Supported in part by NSF CAREER award CCR-9734115 and by the DARPA grant NAG2-1214.

**Transition systems with timing constraints.** To express system behaviors with timing constraints, we consider finite graphs augmented with a finite set of (real-valued) *clocks*. The vertices of the graph are called *locations*, and edges are called *switches*. While switches are instantaneous, time can elapse in a location. A clock can be reset to zero simultaneously with any switch. At any instant, the reading of a clock equals the time elapsed since the last time it was reset. With each switch we associate a clock constraint, and require that the switch may be taken only if the current values of the clocks satisfy this constraint. With each location we associate a clock constraint called its *invariant*, and require that time can elapse in a location only as long as its invariant stays true. Before we define the timed automata formally, let us consider a simple example.

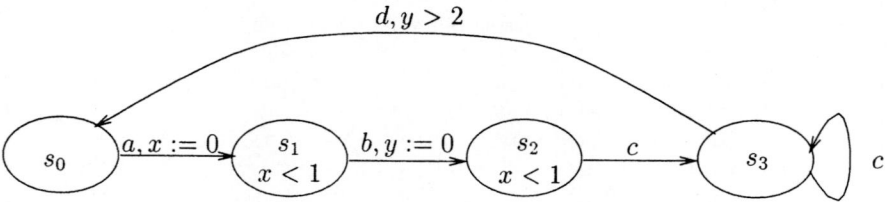

**Fig. 1.** A timed automaton with 2 clocks

Consider the timed automaton of Figure 1 with two clocks. The clock $x$ gets set to 0 each time the system switches from $s_0$ to $s_1$ on symbol $a$. The invariant $(x < 1)$ associated with the locations $s_1$ and $s_2$ ensures that $c$-labeled switch from $s_2$ to $s_3$ happens within time 1 of the preceding $a$. Resetting another independent clock $y$ together with the $b$-labeled switch from $s_1$ to $s_2$ and checking its value on the $d$-labeled switch from $s_3$ to $s_0$ ensures that the delay between $b$ and the following $d$ is always greater than 2. Notice that in the above example, to constrain the delay between $a$ and $c$ and between $b$ and $d$ the system does not put any explicit bounds on the time difference between $a$ and the following $b$, or $c$ and the following $d$. This is an important advantage of having multiple clocks which can be set independently of one another.

**Clock constraints and clock interpretations.** To define timed automata formally, we need to say what type of clock constraints are allowed as invariants and enabling conditions. For a set $X$ of clocks, the set $\Phi(X)$ of *clock constraints* $\varphi$ is defined by the grammar

$$\varphi := x \leq c \mid c \leq x \mid x < c \mid c < x \mid \varphi_1 \wedge \varphi_2,$$

where $x$ is a clock in $X$ and $c$ is a constant in $\mathbb{Q}$. A *clock interpretation* $\nu$ for a set $X$ of clocks assigns a real value to each clock; that is, it is a mapping from $X$ to the set $\mathbb{R}$ of nonnegative reals. For $\delta \in \mathbb{R}$, $\nu + \delta$ denotes the clock interpretation which maps every clock $x$ to the value $\nu(x) + \delta$. For $Y \subseteq X$, $\nu[Y := 0]$ denotes the clock interpretation for $X$ which assigns 0 to each $x \in Y$, and agrees with $\nu$ over the rest of the clocks.

**Syntax and semantics.** A *timed automaton* $A$ is a tuple $\langle L, L^0, \Sigma, X, I, E \rangle$, where

- $L$ is a finite set of locations,
- $L^0 \subseteq L$ is a set of initial locations,
- $\Sigma$ is a finite set of labels,
- $X$ is a finite set of clocks,
- $I$ is a mapping that labels each location $s$ with some clock constraint in $\Phi(X)$, and
- $E \subseteq L \times \Sigma \times 2^X \times \Phi(X) \times L$ is a set of switches. A switch $\langle s, a, \varphi, \lambda, s' \rangle$ represents an edge from location $s$ to location $s'$ on symbol $a$. $\varphi$ is a clock constraint over $X$ that specifies when the switch is enabled, and the set $\lambda \subseteq X$ gives the clocks to be reset with this switch.

The semantics of a timed automaton $A$ is defined by associating a transition system $S_A$ with it. A state of $S_A$ is a pair $(s, \nu)$ such that $s$ is a location of $A$ and $\nu$ is a clock interpretation for $X$ such that $\nu$ satisfies the invariant $I(s)$. The set of all states of $A$ is denoted $Q_A$. A state $(s, \nu)$ is an initial state if $s$ is an initial location of $A$ and $\nu(x) = 0$ for all clocks $x$. There are two types of transitions in $S_A$:

**Elapse of time:** for a state $(s, \nu)$ and a real-valued time increment $\delta \geq 0$, $(s, \nu) \overset{\delta}{\rightarrow} (s, \nu + \delta)$ if for all $0 \leq \delta' \leq \delta$, $\nu + \delta'$ satisfies the invariant $I(s)$.

**Location switch:** for a state $(s, \nu)$ and a switch $\langle s, a, \varphi, \lambda, s' \rangle$ such that $\nu$ satisfies $\varphi$, $(s, \nu) \overset{a}{\rightarrow} (s', \nu[\lambda := 0])$.

Thus, $S_A$ is a transition system with label-set $\Sigma \cup \mathbb{R}$. For instance, for the timed automaton of Figure 1, the state-space of the associated transition system is $\{s_0, s_1, s_2, s_3\} \times \mathbb{R}^2$, the label-set is $\{a, b, c, d\} \cup \mathbb{R}$, and sample transitions are

$$(s_0, 0, 0) \overset{1.2}{\rightarrow} (s_0, 1.2, 1.2) \overset{a}{\rightarrow} (s_1, 0, 1.2) \overset{0.7}{\rightarrow} (s_1, 0.7, 1.9) \overset{b}{\rightarrow} (s_2, 0.7, 0)$$

Note the time-additivity property: if $q \overset{\delta}{\rightarrow} q'$ and $q' \overset{\epsilon}{\rightarrow} q''$ then $q \overset{\delta + \epsilon}{\rightarrow} q''$.

*Remark 1 (Nonzenoness).* We have omitted requirements on the definition necessary for executability. First, when the invariant of a location is violated, some outgoing edge must be enabled. Second, from every reachable state, the automaton should admit the possibility of time to diverge. For example, the automaton should not enforce infinitely many events in a finite interval of time. Automata satisfying this operational requirement are called *nonZeno*. The interested reader is referred to [1, 29, 11]. ∎

**Product construction.** We proceed to define a product construction for timed automata so that a complex system can be defined as a product of component systems. Let $A_1 = \langle L_1, L_1^0, \Sigma_1, X_1, I_1, E_1 \rangle$ and $A_2 = \langle L_2, L_2^0, \Sigma_2, X_2, I_2, E_2 \rangle$ be two timed automata. Assume that the clock sets $X_1$ and $X_2$ are disjoint. Then, the product automaton $A_1 \| A_2$ is $\langle L_1 \times L_2, L_1^0 \times L_2^0, \Sigma_1 \cup \Sigma_2, X_1 \cup X_2, I, E \rangle$, where $I(s_1, s_2) = I(s_1) \wedge I(s_2)$ and the switches are defined by:

1. for $a \in \Sigma_1 \cap \Sigma_2$, for every $\langle s_1, a, \varphi_1, \lambda_1, s_1' \rangle$ in $E_1$ and $\langle s_2, a, \varphi_2, \lambda_2, s_2' \rangle$ in $E_2$, $E$ has $\langle (s_1, s_2), a, \varphi_1 \wedge \varphi_2, \lambda_1 \cup \lambda_2, (s_1', s_2') \rangle$.
2. for $a \in \Sigma_1 \setminus \Sigma_2$, for every $\langle s, a, \varphi, \lambda, s' \rangle$ in $E_1$ and every $t$ in $L_2$, $E$ has $\langle (s, t), a, \varphi, \lambda, (s', t) \rangle$.
3. for $a \in \Sigma_2 \setminus \Sigma_1$, for every $\langle s, a, \varphi, \lambda, s' \rangle$ in $E_2$ and every $t$ in $L_1$, $E$ has $\langle (t, s), a, \varphi, \lambda, (t, s') \rangle$.

Thus, locations of the product are pairs of component-locations, and the invariant of a compound location is the conjunction of the invariants of the component locations. The switches are obtained by synchronizing the switches with identical labels.

**Train-Gate Controller Example.** We consider an example of an automatic controller that opens and closes a gate at a railroad crossing. The system is composed of three components: TRAIN, GATE and CONTROLLER as shown in Figure 2. The safety correctness requirement for the system is that whenever the train is inside the gate, the gate should be closed. This corresponds to establishing that in every reachable state, if the location of TRAIN is $s_2$ then the location of GATE should be $t_2$. Observe that such a location is reachable in the product graph. For example, there is an edge from the initial location $(s_0, t_0, u_0)$ to $(s_1, t_0, u_1)$, and from $(s_1, t_0, u_1)$ to $(s_2, t_0, u_1)$, corresponding to the scenario in which the event *approach* is immediately followed by the event *in*. This is because our product is simply a syntactic operation that annotates product locations with conjunctions of invariants, and product edges with conjunctions of enabling conditions, without any analysis. If we consider the timing information, we can establish that the event *approach* cannot be immediately followed by the event *in*: in the location $(s_1, t_0, u_1)$ both clocks $x$ and $z$ have the same value, and hence the event *lower* with guard $z = 1$ is guaranteed to precede the event *in* with guard $x > 2$. The computational problem in timing verification is to make such deductions by analyzing the timing constraints.

*Remark 2 (Compositionality).* For communication between system components, many competing alternatives to the definition used in this paper exist. The choice of synchronization primitives is somewhat orthogonal to the problem of analysis of timing constraints, and the algorithmic techniques for timed automata can be applied to other models. To model *open* real-time systems (i.e. those interacting with the environment), one needs to make a distinction between which events are controlled by the system and which events are controlled by the environment. Such a compositional framework provides foundations to decompose the analysis problem into simpler problems [44, 11, 43]. Issues pertaining to the impact of timing on synchronization are studied in [19]. ∎

## 2   Reachability Analysis

A location $s$ of the timed automaton $A$ is said to be reachable if some state $q$ with location component $s$ is a reachable state of the transition system $S_A$. The input to the reachability problem consists of a timed automaton $A$ and a set $L^F \subseteq L$

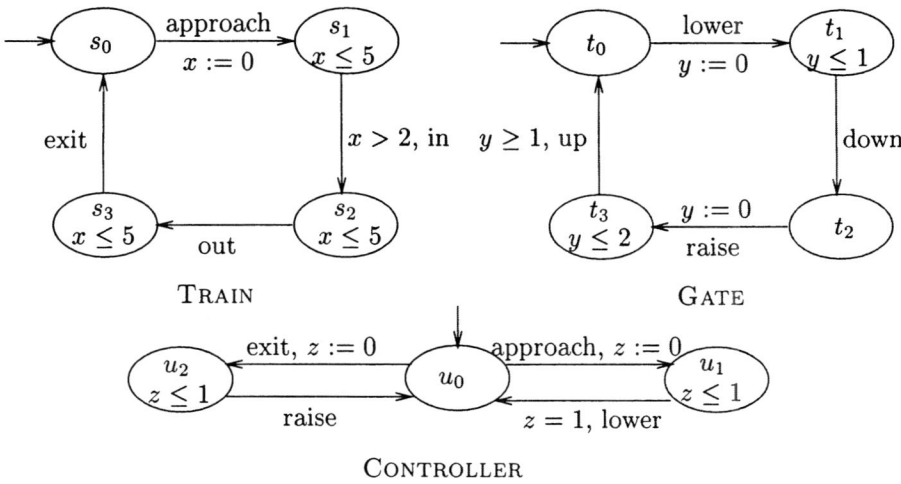

**Fig. 2.** Train-gate controller

of *target* locations of $A$. The reachability problem is to determine whether or not some target location is reachable. Verification of safety requirements of real-time systems can be formulated as reachability problems for timed automata, as illustrated in the train-gate example. Since the transition system $S_A$ of a timed automaton is infinite, our solution to the reachability problem involves construction of finite quotients.

**Time-abstract transition system.** The transition system $S_A$ of a timed automaton $A$ has infinitely many states and infinitely many symbols. As a first step, we define another transition system, called the *time-abstract* transition system and denoted $U_A$, whose transitions are labeled only with the symbols in $\Sigma$ by hiding the labels denoting the time increments. The state-space of $U_A$ equals the state-space $Q_A$ of $S_A$. The set of initial states of $U_A$ equals the set of initial states of $S_A$. The set of labels of $U_A$ equals the set $\Sigma$ of labels of $A$. The transition relation of $U_A$ is the relation $\Rightarrow$: for states $q$ and $q'$ and a label $a$, $q \stackrel{a}{\Rightarrow} q'$ iff there exists a state $q''$ and a time value $\delta \in \mathbb{R}$ such that $q \stackrel{\delta}{\rightarrow} q'' \stackrel{a}{\rightarrow} q'$ holds in the transition system $S_A$. In the reachability problem for timed automata, we wish to determine reachability of target locations. It follows that to solve reachability problems, we can consider the time-abstract transition system $U_A$ instead of $S_A$.

**Stable quotients.** While the time-abstract transition system $U_A$ has only finitely many labels, it still has infinitely many states. To address this problem, we consider equivalence relations over the state-space $Q_A$. An equivalence relation $\sim$ over the state-space $Q_A$ is said to be *stable* iff whenever $q \sim u$ and $q \stackrel{a}{\Rightarrow} q'$, there exists a state $u'$ such that $u \stackrel{a}{\Rightarrow} u'$ and $q' \sim u'$. The *quotient* of $U_A$ with respect to a stable partition $\sim$ is the transition system $[U_A]_\sim$: states of

$[U_A]_\sim$ are the equivalence classes of $\sim$, an equivalence class $\pi$ is an initial state of $[U_A]_\sim$ if $\pi$ contains an initial state of $U_A$, the set of labels is $\Sigma$, and $[U_A]_\sim$ contains an $a$-labeled transition from the equivalence class $\pi$ to the class $\pi'$ if for some $q \in \pi$ and $q' \in \pi'$, $q \overset{a}{\Rightarrow} q'$ holds in $U_A$.

To reduce the reachability problem $(A, L^F)$ to a reachability problem over the quotient with respect to $\sim$, we need to ensure, apart from stability, that $\sim$ does not equate target states with non-target states. An equivalence relation $\sim$ is said to be $L^F$-sensitive, for a set $L^F \subseteq L$ of target locations, if whenever $(s, \nu) \sim (s', \nu')$, either both $s$ and $s'$ belong to $L^F$, or both $s$ and $s'$ do not belong to $L^F$. Consequently, to solve the reachability problem $(A, L^F)$, we search for an equivalence relation $\sim$ that is stable, $L^F$-sensitive, and has only finitely many equivalence classes.

**Region equivalence.** We define an equivalence relation on the state-space of an automaton that equates two states with the same location if they agree on the integral parts of all clock values and on the ordering of the fractional parts of all clock values. The integral parts of the clock values are needed to determine whether or not a particular clock constraint is met, whereas the ordering of the fractional parts is needed to decide which clock will change its integral part first. For example, if two clocks $x$ and $y$ are between 0 and 1 in a state, then a transition with clock constraint $(x = 1)$ can be followed by a transition with clock constraint $(y = 1)$, depending on whether or not the current clock values satisfy $(x < y)$. The integral parts of clock values can get arbitrarily large. But if a clock $x$ is never compared with a constant greater than $c$, then its actual value, once it exceeds $c$, is of no consequence in deciding the allowed switches. Here, we are assuming that all clock constraints involve comparisons with integer constants (if the clock constraints involve rational constants, we can multiply each constant by the least common multiple of denominators of all the constants).

Now we formalize this notion. For any $\delta \in \mathbb{R}$, $fr(\delta)$ denotes the fractional part of $\delta$, and $\lfloor \delta \rfloor$ denotes the integral part of $\delta$; that is, $\delta = \lfloor \delta \rfloor + fr(\delta)$. For each clock $x \in X$, let $c_x$ be the largest integer $c$ such that $x$ is compared with $c$ in some clock constraint appearing in an invariant or a guard. The equivalence relation $\cong$, called the *region equivalence*, is defined over the set of all clock interpretations for $X$. For two clock interpretations $\nu$ and $\nu'$, $\nu \cong \nu'$ iff all the following conditions hold:

1. For all clocks $x \in X$, either $\lfloor \nu(x) \rfloor$ and $\lfloor \nu'(x) \rfloor$ are the same, or both $\nu(x)$ and $\nu'(x)$ exceed $c_x$.
2. For all clocks $x, y$ with $\nu(x) \le c_x$ and $\nu(y) \le c_y$, $fr(\nu(x)) \le fr(\nu(y))$ iff $fr(\nu'(x)) \le fr(\nu'(y))$.
3. For all clocks $x \in X$ with $\nu(x) \le c_x$, $fr(\nu(x)) = 0$ iff $fr(\nu'(x)) = 0$.

A *clock region* for $A$ is an equivalence class of clock interpretations induced by $\cong$. The nature of the equivalence classes can be best understood through an example. Consider a timed transition table with two clocks $x$ and $y$ with $c_x = 2$ and $c_y = 1$. The clock regions are shown in Figure 3. Note that there are only a finite number of regions, at most $k! \cdot 2^k \cdot \Pi_{x \in X}(2c_x + 2)$, where $k$ is the number of clocks. Thus, the number of clock regions is exponential in the encoding of the clock constraints.

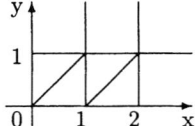

6 Corner points: e.g. $[(0,1)]$

14 Open line segments: e.g. $[0 < x = y < 1]$

8 Open regions: e.g. $[0 < x < y < 1]$

**Fig. 3.** Clock regions

**Region automaton.** Region equivalence relation $\cong$ over the clock interpretations is extended to an equivalence relation over the state-space by requiring equivalent states to have identical locations and region-equivalent clock interpretations: $(s, \nu) \cong (s', \nu')$ iff $s = s'$ and $\nu \cong \nu'$. The key property of region equivalence is its stability. The quotient $[U_A]_{\cong}$ of a timed automaton with respect to the region equivalence is called the *region automaton* of $A$, and is denoted $R(A)$. The number of equivalence classes of $\cong$ is finite, it is stable, and it is $L^F$-sensitive irrespective of the choice of the target locations. It follows that to solve the reachability problem $(A, L^F)$, we can search the finite region automaton $R(A)$.

**Complexity of reachability.** Reachability can be solved in time linear in the number of vertices and edges of the region automaton, which is linear in the number of locations, exponential in the number of clocks, and exponential in the encoding of the constants. Technically, the reachability problem is PSPACE-complete. In fact, in [24], it is established that both sources of complexity, the number of clocks and the magnitudes of the constants, render PSPACE-hardness independently of each other.

*Remark 3 (Choice of timing constraints and decidability).* The clock constraints in the enabling conditions and invariants of a timed automaton compare clocks with constants. Such constraints allow us to express (constant) lower and upper bounds on delays. For any generalization of the constraints, our analysis technique breaks down. In fact, if we allow constraints of the form $x = 2y$ (a special case of linear constraints over clocks), then the reachability problem becomes undecidable [7]. ∎

**Zone automata.** One strategy to improve the region construction is to collapse regions by considering convex unions of clock regions. A *clock zone* $\varphi$ is a set of clock interpretations described by conjunction of constraints each of which puts a lower or upper bound on a clock or on difference of two clocks. If $A$ has $k$ clocks, then the set $\varphi$ is a convex set in the $k$-dimensional euclidean space.

The reachability analysis using zones uses the following three operations:

- For two clock zones $\varphi$ and $\psi$, $\varphi \wedge \psi$ denotes the intersection of the two zones.
- For a clock zone $\varphi$, $\varphi \Uparrow$ denotes the set of interpretations $\nu + \delta$ for $\nu \in \varphi$ and $\delta \in \mathbb{R}$.
- For a subset $\lambda$ of clocks and a clock zone $\varphi$, $\varphi[\lambda := 0]$ denotes the set of clock interpretations $\nu[\lambda := 0]$ for $\nu \in \varphi$.

A key property of the set of clock zones is closure under the above three operations. A *zone* is a pair $(s, \varphi)$ for a location $s$ and a clock zone $\varphi$. We build a transition system whose states are zones. Consider a zone $(s, \varphi)$ and a switch $e = (s, a, \psi, \lambda, s')$ of $A$. Let $succ(\varphi, e)$ be the set of clock interpretations $\nu'$ such that for some $\nu \in \varphi$, the state $(s', \nu')$ can be reached from the state $(s, \nu)$ by letting time elapse and executing the switch $e$. That is, the set $(s', succ(\varphi, e))$ describes the successors of the zone $(s, \varphi)$ under the switch $e$. The set $succ(\varphi, e)$ can be computed using the three operations on clock zones as follows:

$$succ(\varphi, e) \;=\; (((\varphi \wedge I(s)) \Uparrow) \wedge I(s) \wedge \psi)[\lambda := 0]$$

Thus, clock zones are effectively closed under successors with respect to switches. A zone automaton has edges between zones $(s, \varphi)$ and $(s', succ(\varphi, e))$. For a timed automaton $A$, the *zone automaton* $Z(A)$ is a transition system: states of $Z(A)$ are zones of $A$, for every initial location $s$ of $A$, the zone $(s, [X := 0])$ is an initial location of $Z(A)$, and for every switch $e = (s, a, \psi, \lambda, s')$ of $A$ and every clock zone $\varphi$, there is a transition $((s, \varphi), a, (s', succ(\varphi, e)))$.

**Difference-bound matrices.** Clock zones can be efficiently represented using matrices [27]. Suppose the timed automaton $A$ has $k$ clocks, $x_1, \ldots x_k$. Then a clock zone is represented by a $(k + 1) \times (k + 1)$ matrix $D$. For each $i$, the entry $D_{i0}$ gives an upper bound on the clock $x_i$, and the entry $D_{0i}$ gives a lower bound on the clock $x_i$. For every pair $i, j$, the entry $D_{ij}$ gives an upper bound on the difference of the clocks $x_i$ and $x_j$. To distinguish between a strict and a nonstrict bound (i.e. to distinguish between constraints such as $x < 2$ and $x \leq 2$), and allow for the possibility of absence of a bound, define the *bounds-domain* $\mathbb{K}$ to be $\mathbb{Z} \times \{0, 1\} \cup \{\infty\}$. The constant $\infty$ denotes the absence of a bound, the bound $(c, 1)$, for $c \in \mathbb{Z}$, denotes the nonstrict bound $\leq c$, and the bound $(c, 0)$ denotes the strict bound $< c$. A *difference-bound matrix* (DBM) $D$ is a $(k + 1) \times (k + 1)$ matrix $D$ whose entries are elements from $\mathbb{K}$. As an example, consider the clock zone

$$(0 \leq x_1 < 2) \;\wedge\; (0 < x_2 < 1) \;\wedge\; (x_1 - x_2 \geq 0)$$

can be represented by the matrix $D$ as well as by the matrix $D'$:

| | Matrix $D$ | | | Matrix $D'$ | | |
|---|---|---|---|---|---|---|
| | 0 | 1 | 2 | 0 | 1 | 2 |
| 0 | $\infty$ | (0,1) | (0,0) | (0,1) | (0,1) | (0,0) |
| 1 | (2,0) | $\infty$ | $\infty$ | (2,0) | (0,1) | (2,0) |
| 2 | (1,0) | (0,1) | $\infty$ | (1,0) | (0,1) | (0,1) |

Observe that there are many implied constraints that are not reflected in the matrix $D$, while the matrix $D'$ is obtained from the matrix $D$ by "tightening" all the constraints. Such a tightening is obtained by observing that sum of the upper bounds on the clock differences $x_i - x_j$ and $x_j - x_l$ is an upper bound on the difference $x_i - x_l$ (for this purpose, the operations of $+$ and $<$ are extended to the domain $\mathbb{K}$ of bounds). Matrices like $D'$ with tightest possible constraints are called *canonical*. The DBM $D$ is *satisfiable* if it represents a nonempty clock zone. Every satisfiable DBM has an equivalent canonical DBM. We use canonical DBMs to represent clock zones. Given a DBM, using classical algorithms for computing all-pairs shortest paths, we check whether the DBM is satisfiable, and if so, convert it into a canonical form. Two canonical DBMs $D$ and $D'$ are equivalent iff $D_{ij} = D'_{ij}$ for all $0 \leq i, j \leq k$. This test can be used during the search to determine if a zone has been visited earlier. The representation using canonical DBMs supports the required operations of conjunction, $\psi \Uparrow$, and $\psi[\lambda := 0]$ efficiently (cf. [27]).

Theoretically, the number of zones is exponential in the number of regions, and thus, the zone automaton may be exponentially bigger than the region automaton. However, in practice, the zone automaton has fewer reachable vertices, and thus, leads to an improved performance. Furthermore, while the number of clock regions grows with the magnitudes of the constants used in the clock constraints, experience indicates that the number of reachable zones is relatively insensitive to the magnitudes of constants.

**Implementation.** The input to a verification problem consists of a set of component timed automata $A_i$, and the solution demands searching the region automaton $R(\|_i A_i)$ or $Z(\|_i A_i)$. The actual search can be performed by an on-the-fly enumerative engine or a BDD-based symbolic engine. We briefly sketch implementation of the search in timed COSPAN [15]. Suppose the input program $P$ consists of a collection of coordinating timed automata $A_i$. For each $A_i$, let $A'_i$ be the automaton without any timing annotations. A preprocessor generates a new program $P'$ that consists of automata $A'_i$, together with the description of a monitor automaton $A_R$ encoding the region construction or $A_Z$ encoding the DBM-based zone construction. Suppose $\|_i A_i$ has $k$ clocks, and all the constants are bounded by $c$. The automaton $A_R$ has $2k$ variables: $k$ variables ranging over $0..c$ that keep track of the integral parts of the clocks, and $k$ variables ranging over $1..k$ that give the ordering of the fractional parts. The automaton $A_Z$ has $(k+1)^2$ variables ranging over $-c..c$ that keep track of the numerical entries in the DBM and $(k+1)^2$ boolean variables that keep track of the strictness bit for each matrix entry. The update rules for these variables refer to the state-variables of the component automata. Searching the region automaton of $\|_i A_i$ is semantically equivalent to searching the product of $\|_i A'_i$ with $A_R$, while searching the zone automaton of $\|_i A_i$ is semantically equivalent to searching the product of $\|_i A'_i$ with $A_Z$. Following the preprocessing step, the search engine of COSPAN is used to perform the search on the input program $P'$ using BDDs or using on-the-fly enumerative search. Experience shows that for enumerative search the zone construction is preferable, while for symbolic search the region construction is preferable.

*Remark 4 (Dense vs discrete time).* Our choice of time domain is $\mathbb{R}$, the set of nonnegative real numbers. Alternatively, we could choose $\mathbb{Q}$, the set of rational numbers, and all of the results stay unchanged. The key property of the time domain, in our context, is its denseness, which implies that arbitrarily many events can happen at different times in any interval of nonzero length. On the other hand, if we choose $\mathbb{N}$, the set of nonnegative integers, to model time, we have a discrete-time model, and the flavor of the analysis problems changes quite a bit. In the dense-time model, reachability for timed automata is PSPACE, while universality is undecidable; in the discrete-time case, reachability for timed automata is still PSPACE, while universality is EXPSPACE. We believe that discrete-time models, while appropriate for scheduling applications, are inappropriate for modeling asynchronous applications such as asynchronous circuits. For verification of real-time systems using discrete-time models, see, for instance, [28, 21]. In [34], it is established that under certain restrictions the timed reachability problem has the same answer irrespective of choice between $\mathbb{N}$ and $\mathbb{R}$. ∎

*Remark 5 (Minimization).* Suppose we wish to explicitly construct a representation of the state-space of a timed automaton. Then, instead of building the region or the zone automaton, we can employ a minimization algorithm that constructs the coarsest stable refinement of a given initial partition by refining it as needed [4, 54, 37, 50]. ∎

*Remark 6 (Alternative Symbolic Representations).* There have been many attempts to combine BDD-based representation of discrete locations with DBM-based representation of zones. Sample approaches include encoding DBMs using BDDs with particular attention to bit patterns in the variable ordering [20], and variants of BDDs specifically designed to represent clock constraints [18]. ∎

## 3 Discussion

We have summarized the basic techniques for analysis of timed automata (see also [41] for an introduction). We conclude by briefly discussing tools, applications, and theoretical results.

**Tools.** A variety of tools exist for specification and verification of real-time systems. We list three that are most closely related to the approach discussed in this paper. The tool *timed* COSPAN is is an automata-based modeling and analysis tool developed at Bell Labs (see [15, 13]). The tool KRONOS, developed at VERIMAG, supports model checking of branching-time requirements [25]. The UPPAAL toolkit is developed in collaboration between Aalborg University, Denmark and Uppsala University, Sweden [40] and allows checking of safety and bounded liveness properties. All these tools incorporate many additional heuristics for improving the performance.

**Applications.** The methodology described in this paper is suitable for finding logical errors in communication protocols and asynchronous circuits. Examples of analyzed protocols include Philips audio transmission protocol, carrier-sense multiple-access with collision detection, and Bang-Olufsen audio/video protocol (a detailed description of these and other case studies can be obtained from the homepages of KRONOS or UPPAAL). The application of COSPAN to verification of the asynchronous communication on the STARI chip is reported in [49], and to a scheduling problem in telecommunication software is reported in [14].

**Automata-theoretic Verification.** Reachability analysis discussed in Section 2 is adequate to check *safety* properties of real-time systems. To verify *liveness* properties such as "if a request occurs infinitely often, so does the response" we need to consider nonterminating, infinite, executions. Specification and verification of both safety and liveness properties can be formulated in a uniform and elegant way using an automata-theoretic approach [52, 39, 7]. In this approach, a timed automaton, possibly with acceptance conditions (e.g. Büchi), is viewed as a generator of a *timed language* – a set of sequences in which a real-valued time of occurrence is associated with each symbol. Verification corresponds to queries about the timed language defined by the timed automaton modeling the system. If the query is given by a timed automaton that accepts *undesirable* behaviors, then verification question reduces to checking emptiness of the intersection, and can be solved in PSPACE. On the other hand, if the query is given by a timed automaton that accepts all behaviors satisfying the desired property, verification corresponds to testing inclusion of the two timed languages, and is undecidable in general [7]. Decidability of the language-inclusion problem can be ensured by requiring the specification automaton to be *deterministic*, or an *event-clock automaton*.

Since theory of regular (or $\omega$-regular) languages finds many applications including modeling of discrete systems, many attempts have been made to develop a corresponding theory of timed languages. Timed languages defined by timed automata can be characterized using timed version of S1S [53], timed regular expressions [17], and timed temporal logics [36]. The complexity of different types of membership problems for timed automata is studied in [16]. Timed languages definable by timed automata are closed under union and intersection, but not under complementation. This has prompted identification of subclasses such as event-clock automata [9] with better closure properties.

**Equivalence and Refinement Relations.** While timed language equivalence for timed automata is undecidable, stronger equivalences such as timed bisimulation and simulation are decidable. For a timed automaton $A$, a *timed bisimulation* is an equivalence relation $\sim$ on the state-space $Q_A$ such that whenever $q_1 \sim q_2$, if $q_1 \xrightarrow{a} q_1'$ for $a \in \Sigma \cup \mathbb{R}$, then there exists $q_2'$ with $q_2 \xrightarrow{a} q_2'$ and $q_1' \sim q_2'$. While the number of equivalence classes of the maximal timed bisimulation relation is infinite, the problem of deciding whether there exists a timed bisimulation that relates two specified initial states is, surprisingly, decidable [51] (the algorithm involves analysis of the region automaton of the product space $Q(A) \times Q(A)$). The same proof technique is useful to obtain algorithms for checking existence of timed simulation [48] (timed simulation relations are useful for establishing refinement between descriptions at different levels of abstractions). The complexity of deciding timed (bi)simulation is EXPTIME. A hierarchy of approximations to timed bisimulation relation can be defined on the basis of the *number* of clocks that an observer must use to distinguish between two timed automata [6]. The impact of the *precision* of the observer's clocks on the distinguishing ability is studied in [42].

**Linear real-time temporal logics.** Linear temporal logic (LTL) [46] is a popular formalism for writing requirements regarding computations of reactive systems. A variety of real-time extensions of LTL have been proposed for writing requirements of real-time systems [45, 38, 10, 8]. In particular, the real-time temporal logic *Metric Interval Temporal Logic* (MITL) admits temporal connectives such as *always*, *eventually*, and *until*, subscripted with intervals. A typical bounded-response requirement that "every request $p$ must be followed by a response $q$ within 3 time units" is expressed by the MITL formula $\Box( p \rightarrow \Diamond_{\leq 3} q)$. To verify whether a real-time system modeled as a timed automaton $A$ satisfies its specification given as a MITL formula $\varphi$, the model checking algorithm constructs a timed automaton $A_{\neg\varphi}$ that accepts all timed words that violate $\varphi$, and checks whether the product of $A$ with $A_{\neg\varphi}$ has a nonempty language [8]. The definition of MITL requires the subscripting intervals to be nonsingular. In fact, admitting singular intervals as subscripts (e.g. formulas of the form $\Box(p \rightarrow \Diamond_{=1} q)$) makes translation from MITL to timed automata impossible, and the satisfiability and model checking problems for the resulting logic are undecidable. See [31] for a recent survey of real-time temporal logics.

**Branching real-time temporal logics.** Many tools for symbolic model checking employ the branching-time logic CTL [22, 47] as a specification language. The real-time logic *Timed Computation Tree Logic* (TCTL) [3] allows temporal connectives of CTL to be subscripted with intervals. For instance, the bounded response property that "every request $p$ must be followed by a response $q$ within 3 time units" is expressed by the TCTL formula $\forall\Box( p \rightarrow \forall\Diamond_{\leq 3} q)$. It turns out that two states that are region-equivalent satisfy the same set of TCTL-formulas. Consequently, given a timed automaton $A$ and a TCTL-formula $\varphi$, the computation the set of states of $A$ that satisfy $\varphi$, can be performed by a labeling algorithm that labels the vertices of the region automaton $R(A)$ with subformulas of $\varphi$ starting with innermost subformulas [3]. Alternatively, the symbolic model checking procedure computes the set of states satisfying each subformula by a fixpoint routine that manipulates zone constraints [35].

**Probabilistic models.** Probabilistic extensions of timed automata allow modeling constraints such as "the delay between the input event $a$ and the output event $b$ is distributed uniformly between 1 to 2 seconds" (cf. [2]). With introduction of probabilities, the semantics of the verification question changes. Given a probabilistic timed automaton $A$ and a specification automaton $A_S$ that accepts the undesirable behaviors, verification corresponds to establishing that the probability that the run of the system $A$ generates a word accepted by $A_S$ is zero. A modification of the cycle detection algorithm on the region automaton of the product of $A$ and $A_S$ can solve this problem [2]. A similar approach works for verifying TCTL properties of a probabilistic timed automaton. However, if we introduce explicit probabilities in the requirements (e.g. event $a$ will happen within time 2 with probability at least 0.5), then model checking algorithms are known only for a discrete model of time [26].

**Hybrid systems.** The model of timed automata has been extended so that continuous variables other than clocks, such as temperature and imperfect clocks, can be modeled. *Hybrid automata* are useful in modeling discrete controllers embedded within continuously changing environment. Verification of hybrid automata is undecidable in general. For the subclass of *rectangular automata*, analysis is possible via language-preserving translation to timed automata [33], and for the subclass of *linear hybrid automata*, analysis is possible based on symbolic fixpoint computation using polyhedra [12]. See [5] for an introduction to the theory, to [32] for an introduction to the tool HYTECH, and to [30] for a survey.

**Acknowledgements.** My research on timed automata has been in collaboration with Costas Courcoubetis, David Dill, Tom Henzinger, Bob Kurshan, and many others. Many thanks to them, and to Salvatore La Torre for comments on this survey.

# References

1. M. Abadi and L. Lamport. An old-fashioned recipe for real time. In *Real-Time: Theory in Practice, REX Workshop*, LNCS 600, pages 1–27. Springer-Verlag, 1991.
2. R. Alur, C. Courcoubetis, and D. Dill. Model-checking for probabilistic real-time systems. In *Automata, Languages and Programming: Proc. of 18th ICALP*, LNCS 510, pages 115–136, 1991.
3. R. Alur, C. Courcoubetis, and D. Dill. Model-checking in dense real-time. *Information and Computation*, 104(1):2–34, 1993.
4. R. Alur, C. Courcoubetis, N. Halbwachs, D. Dill, and H. Wong-Toi. Minimization of timed transition systems. In *CONCUR '92*, LNCS 630, pages 340–354, 1992.
5. R. Alur, C. Courcoubetis, N. Halbwachs, T. Henzinger, P. Ho, X. Nicollin, A. Olivero, J. Sifakis, and S. Yovine. The algorithmic analysis of hybrid systems. *Theoretical Computer Science*, 138:3–34, 1995.
6. R. Alur, C. Courcoubetis, and T. Henzinger. The observational power of clocks. In *CONCUR '94: Fifth Conference on Concurrency Theory*, LNCS 836, pages 162–177, 1994.
7. R. Alur and D. Dill. A theory of timed automata. *Theoretical Computer Science*, 126:183–235, 1994.
8. R. Alur, T. Feder, and T. Henzinger. The benefits of relaxing punctuality. *Journal of the ACM*, 43(1):116–146, 1996.
9. R. Alur, L. Fix, and T. Henzinger. Event-clock automata: a determinizable class of timed automata. *Theoretical Computer Science*, 211:253–273, 1999.
10. R. Alur and T. Henzinger. A really temporal logic. *Journal of the ACM*, 41(1):181–204, 1994.
11. R. Alur and T. Henzinger. Modularity for timed and hybrid systems. In *CONCUR '97: Eighth Conference on Concurrency Theory*, LNCS 1243, pages 74–88, 1997.
12. R. Alur, T. Henzinger, and P.-H. Ho. Automatic symbolic verification of embedded systems. *IEEE Transactions on Software Engineering*, 22(3):181–201, 1996.
13. R. Alur, A. Itai, R. Kurshan, and M. Yannakakis. Timing verification by successive approximation. *Information and Computation*, 118(1):142–157, 1995.

14. R. Alur, L. Jagadeesan, J. Kott, and J. V. Olnhausen. Model-checking of real-time systems: a telecommunications application. In *Proc. of Intl. Conf. on Software Engineering*, 1997.

15. R. Alur and R. Kurshan. Timing analysis in COSPAN. In *Hybrid Systems III: Control and Verification*, LNCS 1066, pages 220–231. Springer-Verlag, 1996.

16. R. Alur, R. Kurshan, and M. Viswanathan. Membership problems for timed and hybrid automata. In *Proceedings of the 19th IEEE Real-Time Systems Symposium*. 1998.

17. E. Asarin, O. Maler, and P. Caspi. A Kleene theorem for timed automata. In *Proceedings of the 12th IEEE Symposium on Logic in Computer Science*, pages 160–171, 1997.

18. G. Behrmann, K. Larsen, J. Pearson, C. Weise, and W. Yi. Efficient timed reachability analysis using clock difference diagrams. In *Computer Aided Verification*, 1999.

19. S. Bornot, J. Sifakis, and S. Tripakis. Modeling urgency in timed systems. In *Compositionality – the significant difference*, LNCS. Springer-Verlag, 1998.

20. M. Bozga, O. Maler, A. Pnueli, and S. Yovine. Some progress in the symbolic verification of timed automata. In *Computer Aided Verification*, LNCS 1254, pages 179–190. 1997.

21. S. Campos and E. Clarke. Real-time symbolic model checking for discrete time models. In *Theories and experiences for real-time system development*, AMAST series in computing, 1994.

22. E. Clarke and E. Emerson. Design and synthesis of synchronization skeletons using branching time temporal logic. In *Proc. Workshop on Logic of Programs*, LNCS 131, pages 52–71, 1981.

23. E. Clarke and R. Kurshan. Computer-aided verification. *IEEE Spectrum*, 33(6):61–67, 1996.

24. C. Courcoubetis and M. Yannakakis. Minimum and maximum delay problems in real-time systems. In *Third Workshop on Computer-Aided Verification*, LNCS 575, pages 399–409, 1991.

25. C. Daws, A. Olivero, S. Tripakis, and S. Yovine. The tool KRONOS. In *Hybrid Systems III: Verification and Control*, LNCS 1066, pages 208–219. Springer-Verlag, 1996.

26. L. de Alfaro. *Formal verification of probabilistic systems*. PhD thesis, Stanford University, 1997.

27. D. Dill. Timing assumptions and verification of finite-state concurrent systems. In *Automatic Verification Methods for Finite State Systems*, LNCS 407, pages 197–212, 1989.

28. E. Emerson, A. Mok, A. Sistla, and J. Srinivasan. Quantitative temporal reasoning. In *Computer-Aided Verification, 2nd International Conference*, LNCS 531, pages 136–145, 1990.

29. R. Gawlick, R. Segala, J. Sogaard-Andersen, and N. Lynch. Liveness in timed and untimed systems. In *Proc. ICALP'94*, LNCS 820, pages 166–177, 1994.

30. T. Henzinger. The theory of hybrid automata. In *Proceedings of the 11th IEEE Symposium on Logic in Computer Science*, pages 278–293, 1996.

31. T. Henzinger. It's about time: Real-time logics reviewed. In *CONCUR '98: Ninth International Conference on Concurrency Theory*, LNCS 1466, pages 439–454. 1998.

32. T. Henzinger, P. Ho, and H. Wong-Toi. HyTech: the next generation. In *TACAS 95: Tools and Algorithms for the Construction and Analysis of Systems*, LNCS 1019, pages 41–71, 1995.

33. T. Henzinger, P. Kopke, A. Puri, and P. Varaiya. What's decidable about hybrid automata. In *Proceedings of the 27th ACM Symposium on Theory of Computing*, pages 373–382, 1995.

34. T. Henzinger, Z. Manna, and A. Pnueli. What good are digital clocks? In *ICALP 92: Automata, Languages, and Programming*, LNCS 623, pages 545–558. Springer-Verlag, 1992.

35. T. Henzinger, X. Nicollin, J. Sifakis, and S. Yovine. Symbolic model-checking for real-time systems. *Information and Computation*, 111(2):193–244, 1994.

36. T. Henzinger, J. Raskin, and P. Schobbens. The regular real-time languages. In *ICALP 98: Automata, Languages, and Programming*, LNCS 1443, pages 580–593. 1997.

37. I. Kang and I. Lee. State minimization for concurrent system analysis based on state space exploration. In *Proceedings of the Conference On Computer Assurance*, pages 123–134, 1994.

38. R. Koymans. Specifying real-time properties with metric temporal logic. *Journal of Real-Time Systems*, 2:255–299, 1990.

39. R. Kurshan. *Computer-aided Verification of Coordinating Processes: the automata-theoretic approach*. Princeton University Press, 1994.

40. K. Larsen, P. Pettersson, and W. Yi. UPPAAL in a nutshell. *Springer International Journal of Software Tools for Technology Transfer*, 1, 1997.

41. K. Larsen, B. Steffen, and C. Weise. Continuous modeling of real-time and hybrid systems: from concepts to tools. *Software Tools for Technology Transfer*, 1(2):64–85, 1997.

42. K. Larsen and Y. Wang. Time abstracted bisimulation: Implicit specifications and decidability. In *Proceedings of Mathematical Foundations of Programming Semantics*, 1993.

43. N. Lynch. *Distributed algorithms*. Morgan Kaufmann, 1996.

44. M. Merritt, F. Modugno, and M. Tuttle. Time constrained automata. In *Proceedings of Workshop on Theories of Concurrency*, 1991.

45. J. Ostroff. *Temporal Logic of Real-time Systems*. Research Studies Press, 1990.

46. A. Pnueli. The temporal logic of programs. In *Proceedings of the 18th IEEE Symposium on Foundations of Computer Science*, pages 46–77, 1977.

47. J. Queille and J. Sifakis. Specification and verification of concurrent programs in CESAR. In *Proceedings of the Fifth Symposium on Programming*, LNCS 137, pages 195–220, 1982.

48. S. Tasiran, R. Alur, R. Kurshan, and R. Brayton. Verifying abstractions of timed systems. In *CONCUR '96*, LNCS 1119, pages 546–562, 1996.

49. S. Tasiran and R. Brayton. STARI: a case study in compositional and hierarchical timing verification. In *CAV'97*, LNCS 1254, pages 191–201, 1997.

50. S. Tripakis and S. Yovine. Analysis of timed systems based on time-abstracting bisimulations. In *Proceedings of the Eighth Conference on Computer Aided Verification*, LNCS 1102, 1996.

51. K. Čerāns. Decidability of bisimulation equivalence for parallel timer processes. In *CAV'92*, LNCS 663, pages 302–315, 1992.

52. M. Vardi and P. Wolper. An automata-theoretic approach to automatic program verification. In *Proc. of the First IEEE Symp. on Logic in Computer Science*, pages 332–344, 1986.

53. T. Wilke. Specifying state sequences in powerful decidable logics and timed automata. In *FTRTFT'94*, LNCS 863, pages 694–715. Springer-Verlag, 1994.

54. M. Yannakakis and D. Lee. An efficient algorithm for minimizing real-time transition systems. In *CAV'93*, LNCS 697, pages 210–224, 1993.

# Stålmarck's Method with Extensions to Quantified Boolean Formulas

Gunnar Stålmarck

Prover Technology AB
Chalmers University of Technology

**Abstract.** Stålmarck's method is a proof search algorithm, finding proofs of propositional tautologies in a proof system called the *Dilemma proof system* [1,2]. The search procedure is based on a notion of *proof depth* corresponding to the degree of nestings of assumptions in proofs. Stålmarck's algorithm has been successfully used in industrial applications since 1989, for example in verification of railway interlockings and of aircraft control systems [3].
This talk is divided into three parts.

*Part I* We discuss the proof system underlying Stålmarck's method, the Dilemma proof system. We introduce a notion of *refutation graphs* as a framework for proof systems, and then define Dilemma by restrictions on refutation graphs. The various restrictions will be discussed with respect to proof complexity and be compared with restrictions defining other proof systems.
A *closed* refutation graph is a rooted acyclic digraph, starting with a set $\Delta$ of formulas to be refuted and succesive extensions of $\Delta$ with new consequences making all leaves in the refutation explicitly contradictory. Informally, a refutation graph is built up from applications of:

*Propagation* $\qquad \Delta \longrightarrow \Delta \cup \{A\}$

where A is a logical consequence of the formulas in $\Delta$;

*Split*

$$\Delta \Big\langle \begin{array}{c} \Delta \cup \{A_1\} \\ \vdots \\ \Delta \cup \{A_n\} \end{array}$$

where the disjunction $A_1 \vee \ldots \vee A_n$ is a logical consequence of the formulas in $\Delta$;

*Merge*

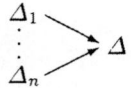

where $\Delta$ is the intersection of $\Delta_1 \ldots \Delta_n$.

Refutation graphs give a sound semantic framework for a variety of proof systems, in that particular proof systems can be characterized in terms of restrictions on refutation graphs.

*Restrictions on refutation graphs*
($i$) Propagations are restricted to instances of predefined schematic rules;
($ii$) split assumptions are restricted to instances of predefined schematic formulas;
($iii$) merge applications are restricted to certain contexts;
($iv$) the set of formulas allowed in proofs is restricted.

*Part II* In the second part we treat the efficiency of the search procedure in Stålmarck's method, the so called *i-saturation* procedure and compare i-saturation with other search procedures such as backtracking.

The i-saturation algorithm is related to the notion of proof depth and the related notion of hardness. Proof depth and hardness are defined for proof systems obeying the so called subformula property and are restricted to series parallel refutation graphs.

*Part III* The third part of this talk concerns the possibiliy to extend Stålmarck's method to more expressive logics, in particular to Quantified Boolean Formulas (QBF). In this part we also discuss applications of the extended algorithm to model checking.

Stålmarck's method is based on a reduction of formulas to sets of definitions, the definitions of all compound subformulas of the original formula. This data stucture is sometimes called triplets.

The extension of Stålmarck's method to QBF is based on a reduction of QBF to QBF triplets and then further from QBF triplets to propositional logic triplets. The reduction combines three ideas of size reduction:

($i$) scope-reduction of quantifiers, that is the application of reversed prenex normal form transforms;
($ii$) use of definitions in order to share common sub-expressions;
($iii$) partial evaluation "on the fly".

# References

[1] G. Stålmarck. A system for determining propositional logic theorems by applying values and rules to triplets that are generated from a formula, 1989. Swedish Patent No. 467 076 (approved 1992), U.S. Patent No. 5 276 897 (approved 1994), European Patent No. 0403 454 (approved 1995).

[2] M. Sheeran and G. Stålmarck. A tutorial on Stålmarck's proof procedure for propositional logic. In *Proceedings of FMCAD'98*, Springer-Verlag LNCS vol. 1522, 1998.

[3] A. Boralv. The industrial success of verification tools based on Stålmarck's method, In *Proceedings of CAV'97*, Springer-Verlag LNCS vol. 1427, 1997.

# Verification of Parameterized Systems by Dynamic Induction on Diagrams *

Zohar Manna and Henny B. Sipma

Computer Science Department
Stanford University
Stanford, CA. 94305-9045
{manna,sipma}@cs.stanford.edu

**Abstract.** In this paper we present a visual approach to proving progress properties of parameterized systems using induction on verification diagrams. The inductive hypothesis is represented by an automaton and is based on a state-dependent order on process indices, for increased flexibility. This approach yields more intuitive proofs for progress properties and simpler verification conditions that are more likely to be proved automatically.

## 1 Introduction

*Verification diagrams* represent a proof that a reactive system satisfies its temporal specification; they were proposed in [MP94] and generalized in [BMS95]. The purpose of a diagram is to provide a high-level proof outline that makes explicit the difficult parts of the proof, while hiding the tedious details.

Parameterized systems are systems that consist of an unbounded number of processes that differ only in their process identifiers (process indices). Proofs of safety properties over parameterized systems introduce universal force quantifiers in the verification conditions. On the other hand, proofs of progress properties for such systems usually introduce both universal force and existential force quantifiers in the verification conditions, making these proofs considerably harder.

The validity of a progress property usually relies on the fairness of certain transitions. In the proof, these transitions must be identified, and they are represented explicitly in a verification diagram. However, for parameterized systems, the validity of a progress property may depend on an unbounded number of distinct fair transitions, so an alternative representation must be used.

One solution, proposed in [MP96], is to assert the existence of such transitions in the diagram without explicitly identifying them. However, this partly defeats

---

* This research was supported in part by the National Science Foundation under grant CCR-98-04100, ARO under grants DAAH04-95-1-0317, DAAH04-96-1-0122 and DAAG55-98-1-0471, ARO under MURI grant DAAH04-96-1-0341, and by Army contract DABT63-96-C-0096 (DARPA).

the purpose of diagrams: the transitions now have to be identified at the theorem-proving level, by instantiating the existential quantifiers. This usually requires a substantial amount of user input at a level where intuition and insight into the program are of little help.

In this paper, we suggest that progress properties can often be proven by induction on the process identifier. In many programs, processes are waiting for each other to achieve their goal in turn. A natural inductive hypothesis is thus that processes with higher priority than the current process will achieve their goal. In some cases, for example in the proof of progress properties for a leader election algorithm presented in [BLM97], standard mathematical induction with a fixed order on the process indices suffices. However, in many cases a more flexible order is required.

The induction principle for diagrams proposed here extends the regular induction principle over the natural numbers by allowing a state-dependent order on the process indices. While in a proof of $\varphi[i]$ by regular induction, $\varphi[j]$ may be assumed only if $j \prec i$, in our diagram induction $\varphi[j]$ may be assumed if for every computation of the system *eventually* always $j \prec i$ holds. In a proof by diagram induction, this condition is incorporated in an automaton for the inductive hypothesis that constrains the set of computations for an arbitrary value of the parameter; this automaton is then conjoined with the main diagram.

We illustrate the diagram induction principle by proving a progress property for a very simple parameterized system. In the last section we demonstrate a more complex application in the proof of accessibility for a fine-grained parameterized algorithm for mutual exclusion.

## 2 Preliminaries

### 2.1 Computational Model

Our computational model is that of *fair transition systems* [MP95]. A fair transition system (FTS) $S : \langle V, \Theta, \mathcal{T}, \mathcal{J} \rangle$ consists of

- $V$: A finite set of typed *system variables*. A *state* is a type-consistent interpretation of the system variables. The set of all states is called the *state space* and is designated by $\Sigma$. A first-order formula with free variables in $V$ is called an *assertion*. We write $s \models p$ if $s$ satisfies $p$.
- $\Theta$: The *initial condition*, an assertion characterizing the initial states.
- $\mathcal{T}$: A finite set of *transitions*. Each transition $\tau \in \mathcal{T}$ is a function $\tau : \Sigma \mapsto 2^{\Sigma}$ mapping each state $s \in \Sigma$ into a (possibly empty) set of $\tau$-successor states, $\tau(s) \subseteq \Sigma$. Each transition $\tau$ is defined by a *transition relation* $\rho_{\tau}(V, V')$, a first-order formula in which the unprimed variables refer to the values in the current state $s$, and the primed variables refer to the values in the next state $s'$. Transitions may be parameterized, thus representing a possibly unbounded set of transitions differing only in their parameter.
- $\mathcal{J} \subseteq \mathcal{T}$: A set of *just* (weakly fair) transitions[1].

---

[1] To simplify the presentation we omit compassion (strong fairness) in this paper.

A *run* of a fair transition system $\mathcal{S} : \langle V, \Theta, \mathcal{T}, \mathcal{J} \rangle$ is an infinite sequence of states $\sigma : s_0, s_1, s_2, \ldots$, such that $s_0 \models \Theta$, and for each $j \geq 0$, $s_{j+1}$ is a $\tau$-*successor* of $s_j$, that is, $s_{j+1} \in \tau(s_j)$ for some $\tau \in \mathcal{T}$. If $s_{j+1}$ is a $\tau$-successor of $s_j$ we say that transition $\tau$ is *taken* at position $j$. The set of runs of $\mathcal{S}$ is written $\mathcal{L}_R(\mathcal{S})$.

A *computation* of a fair transition system $\mathcal{S}$ is a run $\sigma$ of $\mathcal{S}$ that satisfies the *fairness requirement*: for each transition $\tau \in \mathcal{J}$ it is not the case that $\tau$ is continuously enabled beyond some position $j$ in $\sigma$, but not taken beyond $j$. The set of computations of a system $\mathcal{S}$ is denoted by $\mathcal{L}(\mathcal{S})$, called the *language* of $\mathcal{S}$. A state is called $\mathcal{S}$-accessible if it appears in some computation of $\mathcal{S}$.

## Example 1

Figure 1 shows program SIMPLE, parameterized by $M$, written in the SPL language of [MP95]. Its body is the parallel composition of $M$ processes, indexed by $i$. The program has a global array variable $a$ that can be observed by all processes, all of whose elements are initialized to *false*. In addition, each process has a local variable $j$ that cannot be observed by any other process.

It is straightforward to translate this program into an FTS. The system variables are an integer $M$, a boolean array $a$, an integer array $j$, containing the value of the local variable $j$ of each process, and an array $\pi$, containing the label, $\pi[i] \in \{\ell_0, \ell_1, \ell_2, \ell_3\}$, of the current statement of each process. Each program statement can be represented by a parameterized transition. For example, the statement labeled by $\ell_1$ is represented by the parameterized transition with transition relation

$$\rho_{\ell_1}[i] : \ \pi[i] = \ell_1 \wedge \pi'[i] = \ell_0 \wedge (a[j[i]] \vee i \leq j[i]) \wedge a' = a \wedge j' = j$$

The objective of this simple program is for each process $i$ to set $a[i]$ to *true*, but

**in**      $M$ : **integer where** $M > 0$
**local**    $a$   : **array** $[1..M]$ **of boolean where** $a = false$

$\|_{i=1}^{M} P[i] ::$
$\left[\begin{array}{l} \textbf{local } j : \textbf{integer where } j = 1 \\[4pt] \left[\begin{array}{l} \ell_0: \ \textbf{for } j = 1 \textbf{ to } M \textbf{ do} \\ \quad\ \ell_1: \ \textbf{await } a[j] \vee i \leq j \\ \ell_2: \ a[i] := true \\ \ell_3: \end{array}\right] \end{array}\right]$

**Fig. 1.** Program SIMPLE

only after all processes with smaller process indices have done so. We will prove that eventually each process completes its mission. ∎

## 2.2 Specification Language

As specification language we use *linear-time temporal logic* (LTL). LTL formulas are interpreted over infinite sequences of states. A temporal formula [MP95] is constructed out of state formulas and temporal operators. Below we only give the semantics of those operators used in our examples.

For an infinite sequence of states $\sigma : s_0, s_1, \ldots$, an assertion $p$, and temporal formulas $\phi$ and $\psi$,

$$(\sigma, j) \models p \quad \text{iff } s_j \models p \text{ that is, } p \text{ holds on state } s_j$$
$$(\sigma, j) \models \Box \phi \text{ iff } (\sigma, i) \models \phi \text{ for all } i \geq j$$
$$(\sigma, j) \models \Diamond \phi \text{ iff } (\sigma, i) \models \phi \text{ for some } i \geq j$$

An infinite sequence of states $\sigma$ *satisfies* a temporal formula $\phi$, written $\sigma \models \phi$, if $(\sigma, 0) \models \phi$. Given an FTS $\mathcal{S}$, we say that an LTL formula $\varphi$ is $\mathcal{S}$-*valid*, written $\mathcal{S} \models \varphi$, if every computation of $\mathcal{S}$ satisfies $\varphi$.

The *safety closure*[AL90] of a temporal formula $\varphi$, is the smallest safety property, $\varphi_S$ such that $\varphi$ implies $\varphi_S$. For example $(\Box \varphi)_S = \Box \varphi$ and $(\Diamond \varphi)_S = true$.

**Example 2**
The temporal formula

$$\psi[i] : \quad \Box \Diamond \neg \ell_1[i] \;\; \rightarrow \;\; \Diamond \Box a[i] \;,$$

parameterized by $i$, states that if process $i$ is not in location $\ell_1$ infinitely often, then array element $a[i]$ will eventually become *true* and stay *true*. ∎

## 3 Verification Diagrams

A verification diagram $\mathcal{G}$ represents a proof that a possibly infinite-state system $\mathcal{S}$ satisfies a property $\varphi$ if it can be shown that $\mathcal{G}$ is both an overapproximation of the system and an underapproximation of the property. In other words,

$$\mathcal{L}(\mathcal{S}) \subseteq \mathcal{L}(\mathcal{G}) \subseteq \mathcal{L}(\varphi)$$

where $\mathcal{L}(\mathcal{S})$, $\mathcal{L}(\mathcal{G})$, and $\mathcal{L}(\varphi)$ denote the languages of the system, diagram and property, respectively, each of which is a set of infinite sequences of states.

The language inclusion $\mathcal{L}(\mathcal{S}) \subseteq \mathcal{L}(\mathcal{G})$, which states that every computation of $\mathcal{S}$ is a model of the diagram $\mathcal{G}$, is justified by proving a set of first-order verification conditions, using deductive techniques. On the other hand, the inclusion $\mathcal{L}(\mathcal{G}) \subseteq \mathcal{L}(\varphi)$, which states that every model of the diagram satisfies the property, is a decidable language inclusion check that can be established automatically using language-inclusion algorithms for $\omega$-automata. Thus, verification diagrams reduce the proof of an arbitrary temporal property over a system to the proof of a set of first-order verification conditions and an algorithmic check.

## 3.1 Definition

Verification diagrams are $\omega$-automata [Tho90] augmented with an additional node labeling $\mu$, to establish their relation with the FTS that they verify. The diagrams used in this paper are a modified version of those presented in [BMS95] and are described in detail in [MBSU98].

A diagram $\mathcal{G} : \langle N, N_0, E, \mu, \nu, \mathcal{F} \rangle$ over an FTS $\mathcal{S} : \langle V, \Theta, \mathcal{T}, \mathcal{J} \rangle$ and a property $\varphi$ consists of the following components:

- $N$: a finite set of nodes;
- $N_0 \subseteq N$: a set of initial nodes;
- $E \subseteq N \times N$: a set of edges connecting nodes;
- $\mu$: a node labeling function that assigns to each node an assertion over $V$;
- $\nu$: a node labeling function, called the *property labeling*, that assigns to each node a boolean combination of the atomic assertions appearing in $\varphi$;
- $\mathcal{F} \subseteq 2^{2^N}$: a (Müller) acceptance condition given by a set of set of nodes.

A *path* of a diagram is an infinite sequence of nodes $\pi : n_0, n_1, \ldots$, such that $n_0 \in N_0$ and for each $i \geq 0$, $\langle n_i, n_{i+1} \rangle \in E$. Given a path $\pi$, its *limit set*, written $inf(\pi)$, is the set of nodes that occur infinitely often in $\pi$. Note that the limit set of an infinite path must be nonempty since the diagram is finite, and that it must be a strongly connected subgraph (SCS) of the diagram. A path $\pi$ of a diagram is *accepting* if $inf(\pi) \in \mathcal{F}$.

Given an infinite sequence of states $\sigma : s_0, s_1, \ldots$, a path $\pi : n_0, n_1, \ldots$ is called a *trail* of $\sigma$ in the diagram if $s_i \models \mu(n_i)$ for all $i \geq 0$. A sequence of states $\sigma$ is a *run* of a diagram if there exists a trail of $\sigma$ in the diagram. The set of runs of a diagram $\mathcal{G}$ is written $\mathcal{L}_R(\mathcal{G})$. A sequence of states $\sigma : s_0, s_1, \ldots$ is a *model* of a diagram if there exists an accepting trail of $\sigma$ in the diagram. The set of models of a diagram $\mathcal{G}$ is written $\mathcal{L}(\mathcal{G})$.

## 3.2 Verification Conditions

Associated with a diagram is a set of first-order verification conditions that, if valid, prove

$$\mathcal{L}(\mathcal{S}) \subseteq \mathcal{L}(\mathcal{G}) \ .$$

In this case we say that $\mathcal{G}$ is *$\mathcal{S}$-valid*. We use the following notation: For a set of nodes $M = \{n_0, \ldots, n_k\}$, we define

$$\mu(M) \stackrel{\text{def}}{=} \mu(n_0) \vee \ldots \vee \mu(n_k)$$

where $\mu(\{\}) = \textit{false}$. For a node $n$, the set of successor nodes of $n$ is $succ(n)$. We use *Hoare triple* notation to state that a parameterized transition $\tau$ leads from a state satisfying $\varphi$ to a state satisfying $\psi$:

$$\{\varphi\} \, \tau \, \{\psi\} \stackrel{\text{def}}{=} \forall i \, . \, (\varphi \wedge \rho_\tau[i] \ \rightarrow \ \psi')$$

A diagram $\mathcal{G}$ is *$\mathcal{S}$-valid* if it satisfies the following conditions:

- *Initiation*: Every initial state of $S$ must be covered by some initial node of the diagram, that is $\Theta \rightarrow \mu(N_0)$.
- *Consecution*: For every node $n$ and every transition $\tau$, there is a successor node that can be reached by taking $\tau$, that is

$$\{\ \mu(n)\ \}\quad \tau\quad \{\ \mu(succ(n))\ \}\ \ .$$

The Initiation and Consecution conditions, if valid, prove that every run of $S$ is a run of the diagram, that is, $\mathcal{L}_R(S) \subseteq \mathcal{L}_R(\mathcal{G})$

A second set of verification conditions ensures that every computation of the system has an accepting trail in the diagram. Thus, if an SCS $S$ is not accepting, we must show that computations can always leave $S$ or cannot stay in $S$ forever.

We say that an SCS $S$ has a *fair exit transition* $\tau$, if the following verification conditions are valid for every node $m \in S$

$$\mu(m)\ \rightarrow\ enabled(\tau)\quad \text{and}\quad \{\ \mu(m)\ \}\quad \tau\quad \{\ \mu(succ(m) - S)\ \}\ \ ,$$

that is, $\tau$ is enabled on every node in $S$, and from every node in $S$ transition $\tau$ can be taken to leave $S$. Thus if an SCS has a fair exit transition, there is at least one trail of every computation that can leave the SCS.

We say that an SCS $S : \{n_1, \ldots, n_k\}$ is *well-founded* if there exist ranking functions $\{\delta_1, \ldots, \delta_k\}$, mapping the system states into a well-founded domain $(\mathcal{D}, \succ)$, such that the following verification conditions hold: there is a *cut-set*[2] $C$ of edges in $S$ such that for all edges $\langle n_1, n_2 \rangle \in C$ and every transition $\tau$,

$$\mu(n_1) \wedge \rho_\tau \wedge \mu'(n_2)\ \rightarrow\ \delta_1(n_1) \succ \delta_2'(n_2)\ \ ,$$

and for all other edges $\langle n_1, n_2 \rangle \notin C$ in $S$ and for all transitions $\tau$,

$$\mu(n_1) \wedge \rho_\tau \wedge \mu'(n_2)\ \rightarrow\ \delta_1(n_1) \succeq \delta_2'(n_2)\ \ .$$

Thus, if an SCS $S$ is well-founded, no run can have a trail with limit set $S$, since it would violate the well-founded order.

- *Acceptance:* Every nonaccepting SCS $S$ ($S \notin \mathcal{F}$), has a fair exit transition or is well-founded.

The Acceptance condition ensures that every computation of the system has at least one accepting trail in the diagram, that is, $\mathcal{L}(S) \subseteq \mathcal{L}(\mathcal{G})$.

## 3.3 Property Satisfaction

It remains to justify that $\mathcal{L}(\mathcal{G}) \subseteq \mathcal{L}(\varphi)$, which is done using the property labeling $\nu$ of the diagram. Recall that the property labeling assigns to each node of the diagram a boolean combination of atomic assertions appearing in $\varphi$, the property to be proven.

---

[2] A cut-set of an SCS $S$ is a set of edges $C$ such that the removal of $C$ from $S$ results in a subgraph that is not strongly connected.

We say that a path $\pi : n_0, n_1, \ldots$ is a *property trail* of an infinite sequence of states $\sigma : s_0, s_1, \ldots$ if for all $i \geq 0$, $s_i \models \nu(i)$. An infinite sequence of states $\sigma$ is a *property model* of a diagram if it has an accepting property trail in the diagram. The set of property models of $\mathcal{G}$ is written $\mathcal{L}_p(\mathcal{G})$.

Given a property labeling $\nu$, a diagram $\mathcal{G}$ defines a finite-state $\omega$-automaton $\mathcal{A}_{\mathcal{G}}$ by interpreting the atomic assertions of $\nu$ as propositions. Similarly, the property $\varphi$ defines a finite-state $\omega$-automaton $\mathcal{A}_\varphi$. The models of both $\mathcal{A}_{\mathcal{G}}$ and $\mathcal{A}_\varphi$ are infinite sequences of states that assign truth values to these atomic assertions.

The verification conditions to prove Property Satisfaction are

**S1** for every node $n \in N$, $\mu(n) \rightarrow \nu(n)$, which can be shown deductively.

**S2** the language inclusion $\mathcal{L}(\mathcal{A}_{\mathcal{G}}) \subseteq \mathcal{L}(\mathcal{A}_\varphi)$ holds, which can be shown by standard decidable $\omega$-automata techniques.

Condition **S1** proves $\mathcal{L}(\mathcal{G}) \subseteq \mathcal{L}_p(\mathcal{G})$; from **S2** the inclusion $\mathcal{L}_p(\mathcal{G}) \subseteq \mathcal{L}(\varphi)$ follows, and by transitivity we have $\mathcal{L}(\mathcal{G}) \subseteq \mathcal{L}(\varphi)$.

**Example 3**

Returning to program SIMPLE of Figure 1, it is our goal to verify that each process $i$ eventually sets $a[i]$ to true. That is, we want to prove

$$\varphi[i] : \diamondsuit \square \, a[i] \qquad \qquad \text{for all } i \in [1..M] \ .$$

However, we first prove the weaker property

$$\psi[i] : \square \diamondsuit \neg \ell_1[i] \ \rightarrow \ \diamondsuit \square \, a[i] \qquad \qquad \text{for all } i \in [1..M] \ ,$$

given in Example 2.

Figure 2 shows the verification diagram $\mathcal{G}_1[i]$, parameterized by $i$. In the diagram, initial nodes are indicated by a sourceless edge going to the node. The diagram $\mathcal{G}_1[i]$ represents a proof of $\psi[i]$, for all $i \in [1..M]$. That is, for an arbitrary $i \in [1..M]$, $\mathcal{L}(\text{SIMPLE}) \subseteq \mathcal{L}(\mathcal{G}_1[i]) \subseteq \mathcal{L}(\psi[i])$.

The acceptance condition, $\mathcal{F} = \{\{n_1\}, \{n_3\}\}$ states that every trail of a computation must eventually end up in nodes $n_1$ or $n_3$. To justify $\mathcal{L}(\mathcal{G}_1[i]) \subseteq \mathcal{L}(\psi[i])$, we have to show: **S1** the property labeling $\nu$ is implied by the node labeling $\mu$, which is trivial in this case, and **S2** the inclusion $\mathcal{L}(\mathcal{A}_{\mathcal{G}_1[i]}) \subseteq \mathcal{L}(\mathcal{A}_{\psi[i]})$ holds, which is obvious (note that $\psi[i]$ can be rewritten into $\diamondsuit \square \ell_1[i] \vee \diamondsuit \square a[i]$, to make the connection between the acceptance condition and the property more obvious).

To justify $\mathcal{L}(\text{SIMPLE}) \subseteq \mathcal{L}(\mathcal{G}_1[i])$, we have to show Initiation, Consecution and Acceptance. Initiation and Consecution are easily shown. To show Acceptance, we have to show that the three nonaccepting SCSs are well-founded or have a fair exit transition. The SCS $\{n_0, n_1\}$ is shown to be well-founded with the ranking function $\delta : M + 1 - j[i]$ defined on both nodes, and the SCSs $\{n_0\}$ and $\{n_2\}$ have fair exit transitions $\ell_0[i]$ and $\ell_2[i]$ respectively. Therefore $\mathcal{L}(\text{SIMPLE}) \subseteq \mathcal{L}(\psi[i])$ for $i \in [1..M]$.

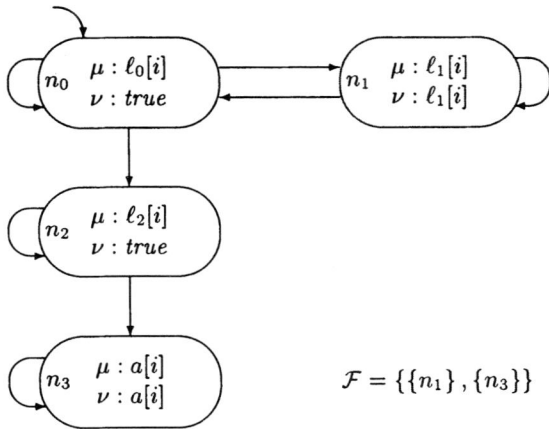

**Fig. 2.** Verification diagram $\mathcal{G}_1[i]$, proving $\psi[i]: \quad \Box \Diamond \neg \ell_1[i] \;\rightarrow\; \Diamond \Box \, a[i]$

Note that we would not have been able to justify a nonaccepting $\{n_1\}$, since transition $\ell_1[i]$ is not guaranteed to be enabled on $n_1$, and therefore is not a fair exit transition. This led us to include $\{n_1\}$ in the acceptance condition, and thus prove the weaker property. ∎

### 3.4 Previously Proven Properties

Diagram verification enables the use of previously proven properties in several ways. As in verification by verification rules, invariants of the program can be added to the antecedents of all verification conditions. However, previously proven temporal properties can be used as well.

Arbitrary temporal properties can be used to relax the Property Satisfaction condition as follows [BMS96]. Let $\mathcal{S} \models \varphi_1, \ldots, \mathcal{S} \models \varphi_n$, and let $\mathcal{G}$ be a diagram for $\mathcal{S}$ and $\varphi$. Then, for Property Satisfaction, it suffices to show

$$\mathcal{L}(\varphi_1) \cap \ldots \cap \mathcal{L}(\varphi_n) \cap \mathcal{L}(\mathcal{G}) \subseteq \mathcal{L}(\varphi) \; ,$$

instead of $\mathcal{L}(\mathcal{G}) \subseteq \mathcal{L}(\varphi)$. To perform this check, additional propositions, appearing in $\varphi_1 \ldots \varphi_n$, may have to be added to the diagram.

Simple temporal properties can also be used to show that a diagram is $\mathcal{S}$-valid. We say that an SCS $S : \{n_1, \ldots, n_k\}$ is *terminating* if

$$\Box \Diamond \neg(\mu(n_1) \; \vee \; \ldots \; \vee \; \mu(n_k))$$

is $\mathcal{S}$-valid, that is every computation will always eventually leave the SCS. The Acceptance condition can now be relaxed to

- *Acceptance:* Every nonaccepting SCS $S$ ($S \notin \mathcal{F}$), has a fair exit transition, is well-founded, or is terminating.

# 4 Diagram Induction

Proofs of progress properties of concurrent systems usually require the explicit identification of the transitions that ensure progress, called *helpful transitions*. For nonparameterized systems the number of distinct helpful transitions is bounded; *ranking functions* are used if these helpful transitions have to be taken an unknown number of times to achieve the goal. Therefore all helpful transitions can be explicitly represented in the diagram.

The situation is different when the system is parameterized. In this case, achieving the goal may depend on an unbounded number of distinct helpful transitions, and thus they cannot be represented explicitly in the diagram. For example, in program SIMPLE, achieving $\Box \Diamond \neg \ell_1[i]$ may require a number of distinct transitions proportional to $M$.

A possible solution in this case is to use *existential diagrams*, which assert the existence of a process index for which the transition guarantees progress. Existence must then be shown as part of the proof of the verification conditions.

**Example 4**
In Example 3 we succeeded in proving

$$\psi[i] : \quad \Box \Diamond \neg \ell_1[i] \rightarrow \Diamond \Box a[i] \qquad \qquad \text{for all } i \in [1..M] \ .$$

If we are able to prove

$$\chi[i] : \quad \Box \Diamond \neg \ell_1[i] \qquad \qquad \text{for all } i \in [1..M] \ ,$$

we can conclude that the desired property, $\varphi[i] : \quad \Diamond \Box a[i]$, holds.

Figure 3 shows the existential diagram $\mathcal{G}_2[i]$, which could be used to prove $\chi[i]$. The diagram uses *encapsulation conventions*: a compound node labeled by an assertion $p$ adds $p$ as a conjunct to all of its subnodes, and an edge arriving at (or departing from) a compound node represents a set of edges that arrive at (or depart from) each of its subnodes.

In the diagram $sup(i)$ stands for the set of process indices for which process $i$ is waiting, that is, those processes that have priority over $i$,

$$sup(i) \stackrel{\text{def}}{=} \{r \mid r < i \wedge \neg a[r]\} \ .$$

The diagram states that as long as $sup(i) \neq \emptyset$, there exists a process $r$ at location $\ell_0$, $\ell_1$ or $\ell_2$, and, if at $\ell_1$, the process is enabled. Proving Initiation for this diagram is straightforward. However, proving Consecution is much harder than for the usual diagrams, due to the existential quantifiers in the verification conditions. For example, using Hoare triple notation, the consecution condition for $n_2$ and transition $\ell_2$ is

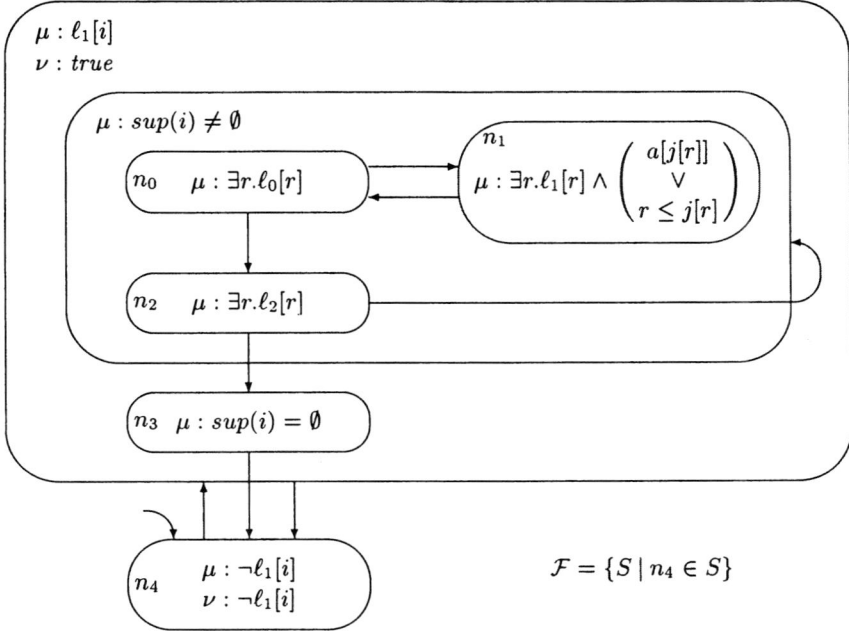

**Fig. 3.** Existential diagram $\mathcal{G}_2[i]$, proving $\chi[i] : \Box \Diamond \neg \ell_1[i]$

$$\{ \exists r.\ell_2[r] \wedge \ell_1[i] \wedge sup(i) \neq \emptyset \}$$

$$\ell_2$$

$$\left\{ \begin{array}{ll} \ell_1[i] \wedge sup(i) \neq \emptyset \wedge \exists r.\ell_0[r] & \vee \\ \ell_1[i] \wedge sup(i) \neq \emptyset \wedge \exists r.\ell_1[r] \wedge (a[j[r]] \vee r \leq j[r]) \vee \\ \ell_1[i] \wedge sup(i) \neq \emptyset \wedge \exists r.\ell_2[r] & \vee \\ \ell_1[i] \wedge sup(i) = \emptyset & \vee \\ \neg \ell_1[i] \end{array} \right\}$$

The proof of this verification condition requires the instantiation of $r$ with the process index of the process that is enabled if $sup(i) \neq \emptyset$.

The verification conditions to justify Acceptance are slightly different from those presented in this paper, to ensure that identity of transitions is preserved for fairness. The full definition of existential diagrams is given in [MP96]. ∎

We now describe our new approach, showing how mathematical induction on a process index can be used to simplify the diagrams and the corresponding verification conditions needed to prove a progress property $\varphi[i]$, over a system $\mathcal{S}$ consisting of $M$ processes.

The standard mathematical induction principle states that to prove $P[i]$ for all natural numbers, it suffices to prove $P[i]$ for an arbitrary $i$, assuming $\forall k < i.P[k]$ holds. This principle is directly applicable to the proof of temporal properties. However, the requirement of a fixed order on the process indices severely limits its applicability. Therefore we introduce a principle of mathematical induction for diagrams that allows a state-dependent order, that is, the truth value of $k \prec i$ may change from state to state in a computation.

Diagram induction requires an *order function* $\prec : \Sigma \mapsto 2^{[1..M] \times [1..M]}$ that maps each state $s$ to a relation $\prec(s)$, such that for every $s \in \Sigma$, the relation $\prec(s)$ is a partial order on $[1..M]$ (that is, $\prec(s)$ is transitive and irreflexive). The order function $\prec$ is incorporated in the inductive hypothesis as follows.

Let $\varphi[i]$ be the property to be proven for all $i \in [1..M]$, let $\prec$ be an order function, and let $\mathcal{A}_{\varphi[i]} : \langle N, N_0, E, \nu, \mathcal{F} \rangle$ be an $\omega$-automaton for $\varphi[i]$. Then the automaton for the inductive hypothesis for $\varphi[i]$ and $\prec$ is the $\omega$-automaton $\mathcal{A}_{\varphi[i]}^{\prec}[k] : \langle N^i, N_0^i, E^i, \nu^i, \mathcal{F}^i \rangle$ obtained from $\mathcal{A}_{\varphi[i]}$ as follows:

$$
\begin{aligned}
N^i &= N \cup \{n_e\} \\
N_0^i &= N_0 \cup \{n_e\} \\
E^i &= E \cup \{(n, n_e) \mid n \in N\} \cup \{(n_e, n) \mid n \in N\} \\
\nu^i(n) &= \nu(n)[k/i] \wedge k \prec i \qquad \text{for } n \in N \\
\nu^i(n_e) &= \neg(k \prec i) \\
\mathcal{F}^i &= \mathcal{F} \cup \{S \mid n_e \in S\}
\end{aligned}
$$

Informally, this *inductive hypothesis automaton* $\mathcal{A}_{\varphi[i]}^{\prec}[k]$ includes those sequences of states that satisfy $\varphi[k]$ or that satisfy $\neg(k \prec i)$ infinitely often.

**Example 5**

Figure 4 shows the $\omega$-automaton and inductive hypothesis automaton for the property $\varphi[i] : \Diamond \square a[i]$ and the order function $\prec$. ∎

**Lemma 1.** *The set of models of the inductive hypothesis of $\varphi[i]$ for $k$ with order function $\prec$ includes all models of $\varphi[k]$, that is,*

$$
\mathcal{L}(\varphi[k]) \subseteq \mathcal{L}(\mathcal{A}_{\varphi[i]}^{\prec}[k])
$$

**Lemma 2.** *For every order function $\prec$, every sequence of states $\sigma \in \mathcal{L}(\varphi[k]_S)$ has a trail in $\mathcal{A}_{\varphi[i]}^{\prec}[k]$.*

With this definition of inductive hypothesis, we can now formulate the induction principle for diagrams:

**Diagram Induction Principle**

Consider a parameterized system $\mathcal{S}$, consisting of $M$ processes, and a property $\varphi[i]$ to be proven for all $i \in [1..M]$. Assume there exists a diagram $\mathcal{G}[i]$, parameterized by $i$, and an order function $\prec$ such that the following conditions hold for all $i \in [1..M]$:

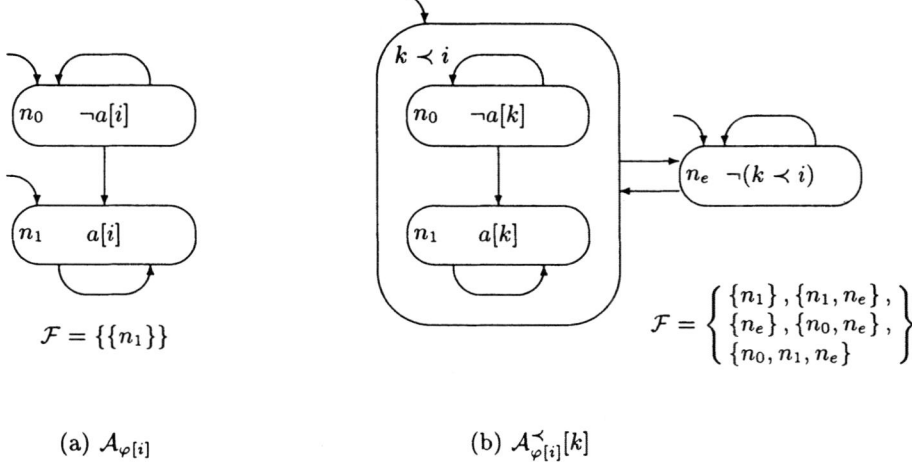

(a) $\mathcal{A}_{\varphi[i]}$                     (b) $\mathcal{A}_{\varphi[i]}^{\prec}[k]$

**Fig. 4.** $\omega$-Automaton and inductive hypothesis automaton for $\varphi[i] : \Diamond \square \, a[i]$

**I1** $\prec(s)$ is a partial order on $[1..M]$ for each $\mathcal{S}$-accessible state $s$;

**I2** $\mathcal{S}$ satisfies the safety closure of $\varphi[i]$, that is, $\mathcal{L}(\mathcal{S}) \subseteq \mathcal{L}(\varphi[i]_S)$;

**I3** $\mathcal{G}[i]$ is $\mathcal{S}$-valid, that is $\mathcal{L}(\mathcal{S}) \subseteq \mathcal{L}(\mathcal{G}[i])$;

**I4** there exists a set of indices $K \subseteq [1..M]$ such that the product of $\mathcal{G}[i]$ and the inductive hypothesis automata $\mathcal{A}_{\varphi[i]}^{\prec}[k]$, for $k \in K$, is included in $\varphi[i]$, that is,

$$\left( \mathcal{L}(\mathcal{G}[i]) \cap \bigcap_{k \in K} \mathcal{L}(\mathcal{A}_{\varphi[i]}^{\prec}[k]) \right) \subseteq \mathcal{L}(\varphi[i]) \qquad \text{for some } K \subseteq [1..M] \ .$$

Then $\mathcal{S} \models \varphi[i]$, for all $i \in [1..M]$.

**Example 6**
Returning to program SIMPLE, we refine diagram $\mathcal{G}_1[i]$ shown in Figure 2 by splitting node $n_1$ into two nodes: $n_{11}$ where $\ell_1[i]$ is guaranteed to be enabled and $n_{12}$ where it is not enabled. The result is the verification diagram $\mathcal{G}_3[i]$, shown in Figure 5. The acceptance condition is $\mathcal{F} = \{\{n_3\}, \{n_{12}\}\}$. Initiation, Consecution and Acceptance are easily shown for this diagram, and thus $\mathcal{L}(\text{SIMPLE}) \subseteq \mathcal{L}(\mathcal{G}_3[i])$. For the property

$$\psi[i] : \square \Diamond a[j[i]] \rightarrow \Diamond \square \, a[i] \qquad \text{for all } i \in [1..M] \ ,$$

Property Satisfaction is also easy to show, and thus $\mathcal{L}(\mathcal{G}_3[i]) \subseteq \mathcal{L}(\psi[i])$, and therefore SIMPLE $\models \psi[i]$ for all $i \in [1..M]$.

However, we claim that by diagram induction diagram $\mathcal{G}_3[i]$ also represents a proof of the desired property

$$\varphi[i] : \Diamond \square \, a[i] \qquad \text{for all } i \in [1..M] \ ,$$

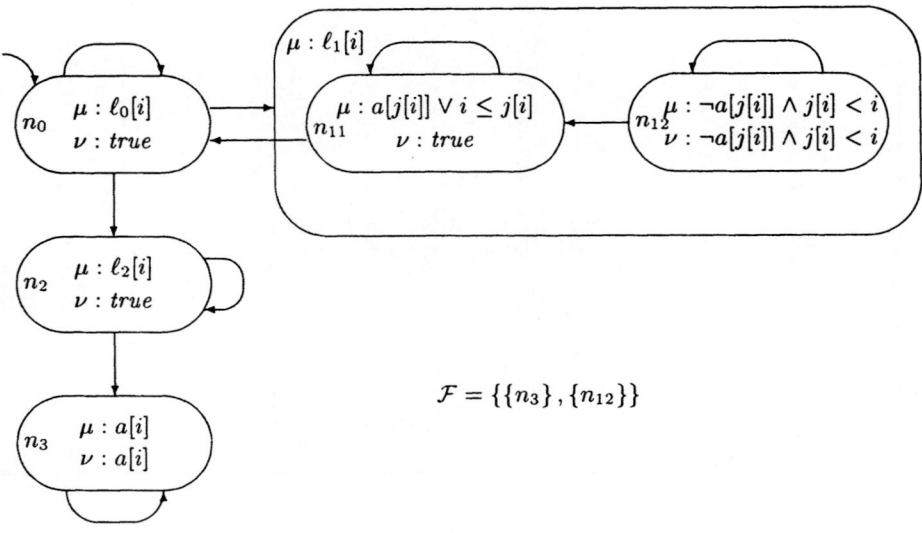

**Fig. 5.** Verification diagram $\mathcal{G}_3[i]$, proving $\phi[i] : \Box \Diamond a[i]$ by diagram induction

using the order function $\prec$ defined as the less-than relation ($<$) on $[1..M]$ at all states. Premise **I1** clearly holds. The safety closure of $\varphi$ is $\varphi_S : true$, so premise **I2** holds trivially. The diagram was shown to be $\mathcal{S}$-valid earlier, thus satisfying premise **I3**. Finally, by taking $K$ to be the singleton set $\{j[i]\}$ the intersection of $\mathcal{G}_3[i]$ of Figure 5 and $\mathcal{A}^{\prec}_{\varphi[i]}[j[i]]$ of Figure 4(b) is included in the property $\Diamond \Box a[i]$ of Figure 4(a), since the inductive hypothesis for $j[i]$ eliminates the SCS $\{n_{12}\}$. Therefore, by the diagram induction principle, we can conclude that SIMPLE$\models \Diamond \Box a[i]$ for all $i \in [1..M]$. ∎

**Theorem 1 (Soundness).** *The Diagram Induction Principle is sound.*

*Proof.* Assume that the premises **I1** through **I4** hold, and suppose, for a contradiction, that $\mathcal{S} \not\models \varphi[k_1]$ for some $k_1 \in [1..M]$. Then there exists a computation $\sigma : s_0, s_1, \ldots$ of $\mathcal{S}$ such that $\sigma \not\models \varphi[k_1]$, that is, $\sigma \notin \mathcal{L}(\varphi[k_1])$. By premise **I3** we have $\mathcal{L}(\mathcal{S}) \subseteq \mathcal{L}(\mathcal{G}[k_1])$, and therefore $\sigma \in \mathcal{L}(\mathcal{G}[k_1])$. But then, by premise **I4**, there must exist some $k_2$ such that $\sigma \notin \mathcal{L}(\mathcal{A}^{\prec}_{\varphi[k_1]}[k_2])$. By premise **I2**, $\sigma \in \mathcal{L}(\varphi[k_2]_S)$, and thus by Lemma 2 the sequence $\sigma$ has a trail in $\mathcal{A}^{\prec}_{\varphi[k_1]}[k_2]$. From the fact that the trail is not accepting we can conclude that the trail eventually has to end up outside the added node $n_e$, since all sets that include this node are accepting. All nodes in $\mathcal{A}^{\prec}_{\varphi[k_1]}[k_2]$ outside $n_e$ are labeled by $k_2 \prec k_1$ and therefore we have $\sigma \models \Diamond \Box (k_2 \prec k_1)$. In addition, by Lemma 1, we know that $\sigma \not\models \varphi[k_2]$.

By the same reasoning we can conclude that there exists some $k_3$ such that $\sigma \notin \mathcal{A}^{\prec}_{\varphi[k_2]}[k_3]$, and that $\sigma \models \Diamond \Box (k_3 \prec k_2)$. Repeating this argument $M$ times we can conclude that

$$\sigma \models \Diamond \Box (k_{M+1} \prec k_M) \ \land \ldots \land \ \Diamond \Box (k_2 \prec k_1) \ ,$$

and therefore

$$\sigma \models \Diamond \Box ((k_{M+1} \prec k_M) \land \ldots \land (k_2 \prec k_1)) \ ,$$

and thus there exists a particular state $s_z$ in $\sigma$ such that

$$s_z \models k_{M+1} \prec k_M \prec \ldots \prec k_1$$

However, some process index $k$ must appear twice in this sequence, violating premise **I1**, that $\prec(s_z)$ is a partial order, a contradiction.

## 5  Example: Accessibility for BAKERY-M

In this section we give an outline of the proof of accessibility for the parameterized system BAKERY-M, shown in Figure 6. This program, taken from [Pnu96], is based on Lamport's bakery algorithm [Lam74,Lam77] for mutual exclusion.

$$
\begin{array}{l}
\textbf{in} \quad\ M \qquad\ : \textbf{integer where } M > 0 \\
\textbf{local}\ \ choosing : \textbf{array}\,[1..M]\ \textbf{of boolean where } choosing = false \\
\qquad\quad number\ \ : \textbf{array}\,[1..M]\ \textbf{of integer where } number = 0 \\[4pt]
\|_{i=1}^{M}\,P[i] ::
\left[
\begin{array}{l}
\textbf{local } j, k, t : \textbf{integer where } j = 0,\ k = 0,\ t = 0 \\[4pt]
\ell_0: \textbf{ loop forever do} \\
\quad
\left[
\begin{array}{l}
\ell_1: \textbf{ noncritical} \\
\ell_2: \ choosing[i] := true \\
\ell_3: \ t := 0 \\
\ell_4: \textbf{ for } k = 1 \textbf{ to } M \textbf{ do} \\
\qquad \ell_5: \ t := \max(t, number[k]) \\
\ell_6: \ number[i] := t + 1 \\
\ell_7: \ choosing[i] := false \\
\ell_8: \textbf{ for } j = 1 \textbf{ to } M \textbf{ do} \\
\qquad
\left[
\begin{array}{l}
\ell_9: \textbf{ await } \neg choosing[j] \\
\ell_{10}: \textbf{ await } \left(
\begin{array}{l}
\quad\ j = i \\
\lor\ number[j] = 0 \\
\lor\ (number[i], i) \prec (number[j], j)
\end{array}
\right)
\end{array}
\right] \\
\ell_{11}: \textbf{ critical} \\
\ell_{12}: number[i] := 0
\end{array}
\right]
\end{array}
\right]
\end{array}
$$

**Fig. 6.** Program BAKERY-M: molecular version

In the program, in statements $\ell_2$ through $\ell_7$, process $i$ determines the maximum ticket number currently held by any other process and assigns it, incremented by 1, to its own ticket number. In the coarser-grained atomic version of the program these statements are replaced by

$$\ell_1^a : number[i] := 1 + max(number) \ .$$

In statements $\ell_8$ through $\ell_{10}$ process $i$ can proceed only if every other process has a ticket number 0 (meaning it is not interested in entering the critical section), or its ticket number is higher than that of process $i$. In the atomic version these statements become

$$\ell_2^a : \textbf{await} \ \forall j : [1..M].(i \neq j \rightarrow number[j] = 0 \vee number[i] \leq number[j]) \ .$$

In [Lam77,Pnu96] it is shown that BAKERY-M guarantees mutual exclusion and accessibility, where in [Pnu96] accessibility is proven using existential diagrams. Here we present an alternative proof of accessibility that uses diagram induction.

The proof of accessibility, specified by

$$acc[i] : \ \square(at\_\ell_2[i] \rightarrow \Diamond \ at\_\ell_{11}[i]) \qquad \text{for all } i \in [1..M] \ ,$$

is represented by four verification diagrams. The $\mathcal{S}$-validity of the diagrams relies on the following invariants, taken from [Pnu96],

$$
\begin{aligned}
&I_0 : choosing[i] \ \leftrightarrow \ at\_\ell_{3...7}[i] \\
&I_1 : at\_\ell_{7...12}[i] \leq number[i] \\
&I_2 : (at\_\ell_4 \rightarrow 1 \leq k \leq M + 1) \wedge (at\_\ell_5 \rightarrow 1 \leq k \leq M) \\
&I_3 : at\_\ell_6 \rightarrow k = M + 1 \\
&I_4 : (at\_\ell_8 \rightarrow 1 \leq j \leq M + 1) \wedge (at\_\ell_{9,10} \rightarrow 1 \leq j \leq M) \\
&I_5 : at\_\ell_{11} \rightarrow j = M + 1 \\
&I_6 : at\_\ell_{10}[i] \wedge choosing[j[i]] \ \rightarrow \ superior[i, j[i]]
\end{aligned}
$$

where

$$superior[i, r] : \begin{pmatrix} at\_\ell_{0...3}[r] \\ \vee \ at\_\ell_{4...6}[r] \wedge (k[r] \leq i \vee number[i] \leq t[r]) \\ \vee \ at\_\ell_{7...12}[r] \wedge (number[i], i) \prec (number[r], r) \end{pmatrix}$$

The first diagram, $\mathcal{G}_4[i]$, shown in Figure 7, proves that accessibility holds provided the program will always leave locations $\ell_9$ and $\ell_{10}$:

$$\phi_4[i] : (\square \Diamond \neg \ell_9[i] \wedge \square \Diamond \neg \ell_{10}[i]) \ \rightarrow \ \square(\ell_2[i] \rightarrow \Diamond \ell_{11}[i])$$

The diagram is a straightforward representation of the path that leads from location $\ell_2$ to $\ell_{11}$. Initiation and Consecution clearly hold for this diagram. To justify the acceptance condition, $\mathcal{F} = \{\{n_7\}, \{n_8\}, \{n_{10}\}\} \cup \{S \mid n_9 \in S\}$, we have to show that all nonaccepting SCSs have a fair exit or are well-founded. It is easy to see that all nonaccepting single-node SCSs have a fair exit transition. The two remaining SCSs, $\{n_2, n_3\}$, and $\{n_6, n_7, n_8\}$ are shown to be well-founded using the ranking functions $\delta(n_2) = \delta(n_3) = M + 1 - k[i]$, and $\delta(n_6) = \delta(n_7) = \delta(n_8) = M + 1 - j[i]$, respectively. The well-foundedness of $M + 1 - k[i]$ and $M + 1 - j[i]$ relies on the invariants $I_2$ and $I_4$ respectively.

It remains to show that the system cannot forever stay in nodes $n_7$ and $n_8$, that is,

$$\psi_1[i] : \square \lozenge \neg at\_\ell_9[i] \qquad\qquad \text{for all } i \in [1..M]$$
$$\psi_2[i] : \square \lozenge \neg at\_\ell_{10}[i] \qquad\qquad \text{for all } i \in [1..M]$$

Two diagrams, not included in this paper, prove that for all $i \in [1..M]$

$$\varphi_5[i] : \square \lozenge \neg choosing[j[i]] \;\rightarrow\; \square \lozenge \neg at\_\ell_9[i]$$

and

$$\varphi_6[i] : \square \lozenge \neg choosing[i]$$

respectively, from which $\psi_1[i]$ can be concluded for all $i \in [1..M]$.

The diagram $\mathcal{G}_7[i]$, shown in Figure 8, represents a proof of $\psi_2[i]$ using diagram induction. Informally, the nodes $n_0, \ldots, n_5$ represent the situation that process $j[i]$ has priority over process $i$ to enter its critical section. In node $n_6$, process $i$ has priority over $j[i]$ and on this node transition $\ell_{10}[i]$ is guaranteed to be enabled, leading to the goal node $n_7$.

Initiation is easily shown for this diagram. Consecution requires several of the invariants. In particular the verification condition

$$\{ \mu(n_6) \} \quad \ell_6 \quad \{ \mu(n_6) \vee \mu(n_7) \}$$

represents a crucial part of the proof, namely that once process $j[i]$ has left its critical section, it will not return with a lower ticket number than process $i$ while process $i$ is at $\ell_{10}$.

To justify the acceptance condition $\mathcal{F} = \{\{n_3\}\} \cup \{S \mid n_7 \in S\}$, all single-node, nonaccepting SCS's, except $\{n_2\}$ are shown to have fair exit transitions; $\{n_2\}$ is shown to be terminating by $\psi_1[j[i]]$; and the SCS $\{n_1, n_2, n_3\}$ is established to be well-founded, with ranking functions $\delta(n_1) = \delta(n_2) = \delta(n_3) = M + 1 - j[j[i]]$, whose well-foundedness relies on the invariant $I_4$.

Without using induction the diagram $\mathcal{G}_7$ represents a proof of

$$\varphi_7[i] : \; \square \lozenge \neg \ell_{10}[j[i]] \;\rightarrow\; \square \lozenge \neg \ell_{10}[i] \;.$$

However, if we apply the diagram induction principle with order function $\prec$, defined by

$$i \prec k \quad \text{iff} \quad (number[i], i) < (number[k], k)$$

at each state, and take $K$ to be the singleton set $\{j[i]\}$, the offending SCS $\{n_3\}$ is eliminated and the diagram represents a proof of $\psi_2[i]$ for all $i \in [1..M]$, as desired. This completes the proof of accessibility for BAKERY-M.

**Acknowledgements**

We thank Anca Browne, Michael Colón and Tomás Uribe for their comments and suggestions.

# References

[AL90]     M. Abadi and L. Lamport. Composing specifications. In *Stepwise Refinement of Distributed Systems: Models, Formalism, Correctness*, vol. 430 of *LNCS*, pages 1–41. Springer-Verlag, 1990.

[BLM97]    N.S. Bjørner, U. Lerner, and Z. Manna. Deductive verification of parameterized fault-tolerant systems: A case study. In *Intl. Conf. on Temporal Logic*. Kluwer, 1997. To appear.

[BMS95]    A. Browne, Z. Manna, and H.B. Sipma. Generalized temporal verification diagrams. In *15th Conference on the Foundations of Software Technology and Theoretical Computer Science*, vol. 1026 of *LNCS*, pages 484–498. Springer-Verlag, 1995.

[BMS96]    A. Browne, Z. Manna, and H.B. Sipma. Hierarchical verification using verification diagrams. In *$2^{nd}$ Asian Computing Science Conf.*, vol. 1179 of *LNCS*, pages 276–286. Springer-Verlag, December 1996.

[Lam74]    L. Lamport. A new solution of Dijkstra's concurrent programming problem. *Communications of the ACM*, 17(8):435–455, 1974.

[Lam77]    L. Lamport. Proving the correctness of multiprocess programs. *IEEE Trans. Software Engin.*, 3:125–143, 1977.

[MBSU98]   Z. Manna, A. Browne, H.B. Sipma, and T.E. Uribe. Visual abstractions for temporal verification. In A. Haeberer, editor, *AMAST'98*, vol. 1548 of *LNCS*, pages 28–41. Springer-Verlag, December 1998.

[MP94]     Z. Manna and A. Pnueli. Temporal verification diagrams. In M. Hagiya and J.C. Mitchell, editors, *Proc. International Symposium on Theoretical Aspects of Computer Software*, vol. 789 of *LNCS*, pages 726–765. Springer-Verlag, 1994.

[MP95]     Z. Manna and A. Pnueli. *Temporal Verification of Reactive Systems: Safety*. Springer-Verlag, New York, 1995.

[MP96]     Z. Manna and A. Pnueli. Temporal verification of reactive systems: Progress. Draft Manuscript, 1996.

[Pnu96]    A. Pnueli. Lecture notes: the Bakery algorithm. Draft Manuscript, Weizmann Institute of Science, Israel, May 1996.

[Tho90]    W. Thomas. Automata on infinite objects. In J. van Leeuwen, editor, *Handbook of Theoretical Computer Science*, vol. B, pages 133–191. Elsevier Science Publishers (North-Holland), 1990.

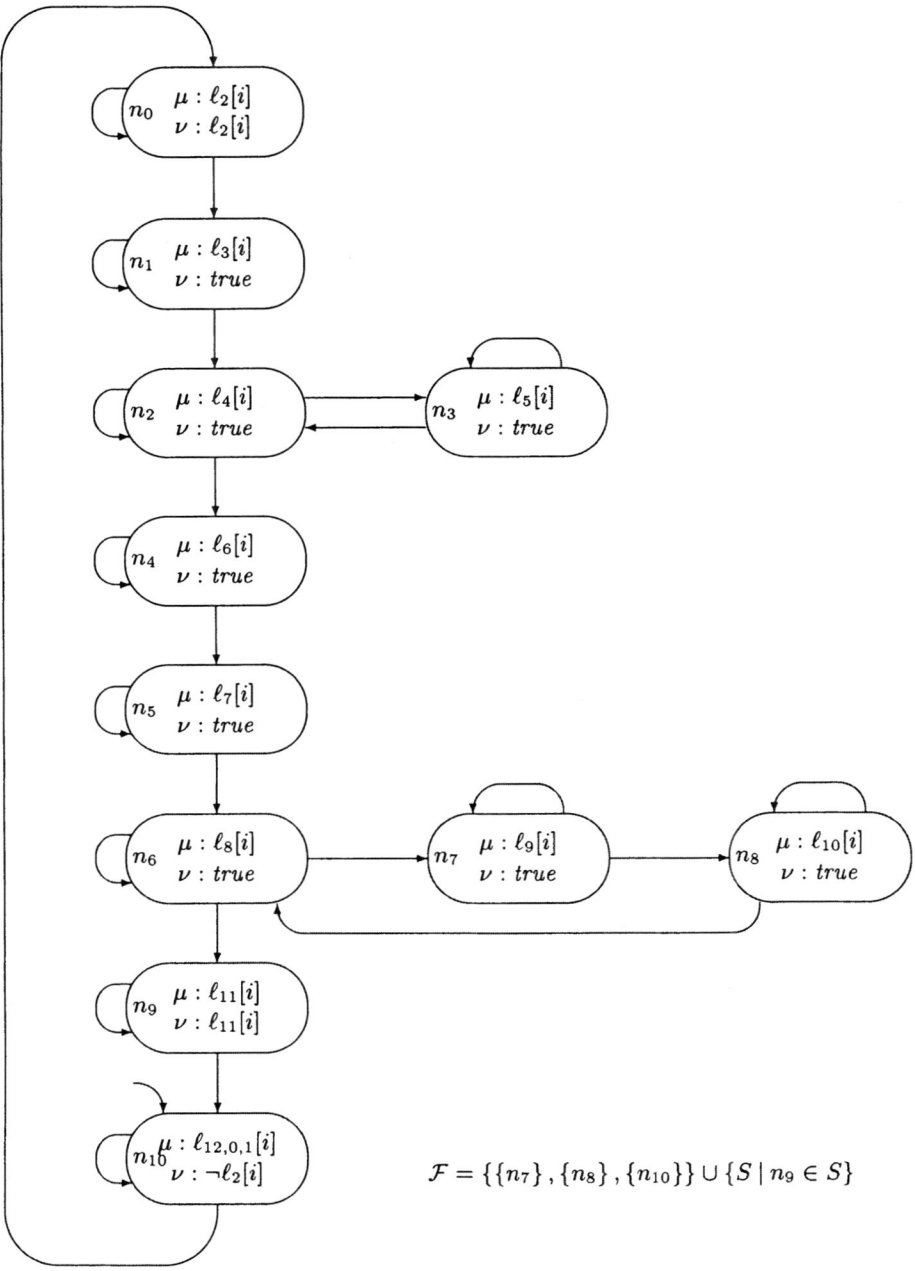

**Fig. 7.** Diagram $\mathcal{G}_4[i]$, proving $(\Box \Diamond \neg \ell_9[i] \wedge \Box \Diamond \neg \ell_{10}[i]) \rightarrow \Box(\ell_2[i] \rightarrow \Diamond \ell_{11}[i])$

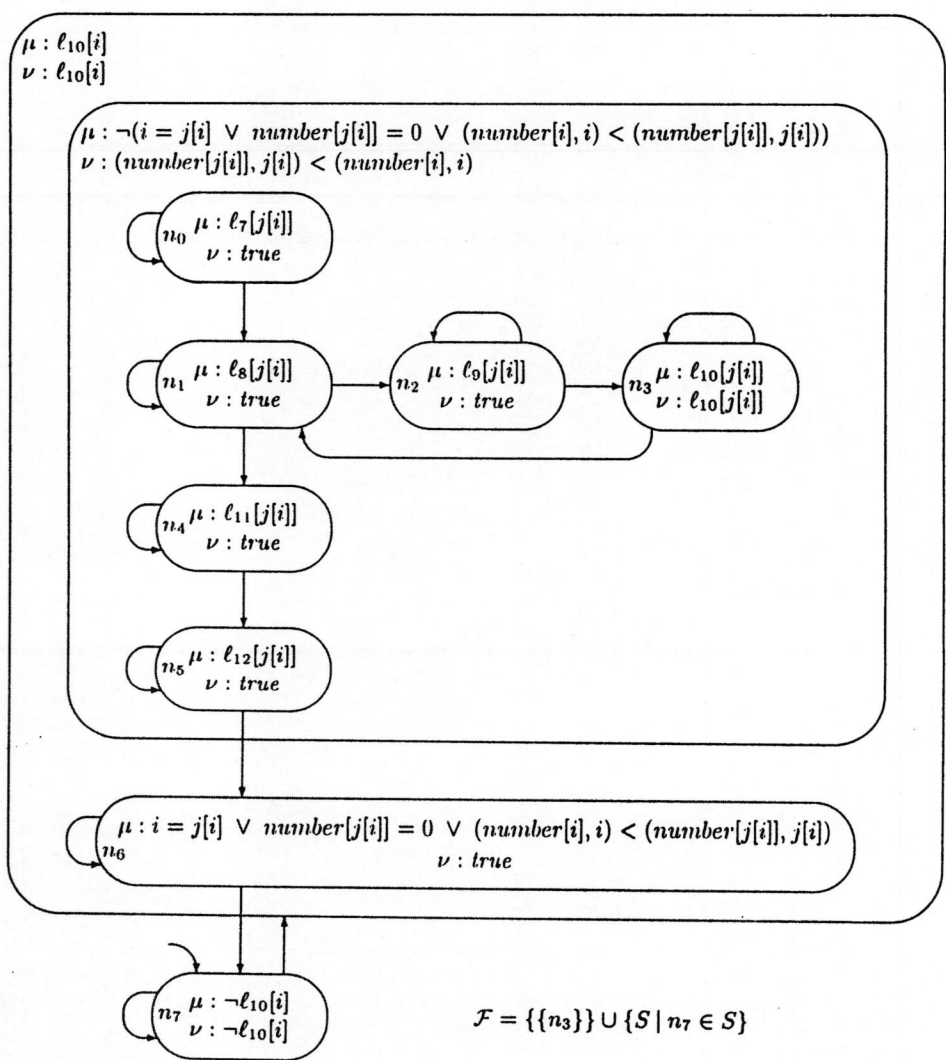

**Fig. 8.** Verification diagram $\mathcal{G}_7[i]$, proving $\phi[i] : \Box \Diamond \neg\ell_{10}[i]$, by diagram induction

# Formal Methods for Conformance Testing: Theory Can Be Practical

Ed Brinksma

Chair of Formal Methods and Tools,
Faculty of Computer Science, University of Twente
P.O. Box 217, 7500 AE Enschede, The Netherlands
brinksma@cs.utwente.nl

## Extended abstract

Although testing is the most widely used technique to control the quality of software systems, it is a topic that, until relatively recently, has received scant attention from the computer research community. Although some pioneering work was already done a considerable time ago [Cho78,GG83,How78,Mye79], the testing of software systems has never become a mainstream activity of scientific research. The reasons that are given to explain this situation usually include arguments to the effect that testing as a technique is inferior to verification – *testing can show only the presence of errors, not their absence* – and that we should therefore concentrate on developing theory and tools for the latter. It has also been frequently said that testing is by its very nature a non-formal activity, where formal methods and related tools are at best of little use.

The first argument is incorrect in the sense that it gives an incomplete picture of the situation. Testing is inferior to verification if the verification model can be assumed to be correct and if its complexity can be handled correctly by the person and or tool involved in the verification task. If these conditions are not fulfilled, which is frequently the case, then testing is often the only available technique to increase the confidence in the correctness of a system. In this talk we will show that the second argument is flawed as well. It is based on the identification of testing with robustness testing, where it is precisely the objective to find out how the system behaves under unspecified circumstances. This excludes the important activity of *conformance testing*, which tries to test the extent to which system behaviour conforms to its specification. It is precisely in this area where formal methods and tools can help to derive tests systematically from specifications, which is a great improvement over laborious, error-prone and costly manual test derivation.

In our talk we show how the process algebraic testing theory due to De Nicola and Hennessy [DNH84,DeN87], originally conceived out of semantic considerations, may be used to obtain principles for test derivation. We will give an overview of the evolution of these ideas over the past ten years or so, starting with the conformance testing theory of simple synchronously communicating reactive systems [Bri88,Lan90] and leading to realistic systems that involve sophisticated asynchronous message passing mechanisms [Tre96,HT97]. Written accounts can be found in [BHT97,He98]. We discuss how such ideas have been used to obtain modern test derivation tools, such as TVEDA and TGV [Pha94,CGPT96,FJJV96], and the tool set that is currently being developed in the Côte-de-Resyste project [STW96]. The advantage of a test theory that is based on well-established process algebraic theory is that in principle there exists a clear link between testing and verification, which allows the areas to share ideas and algorithms [FJJV96,VT98]. Time allowing, we look at some of the methodological differences and commonalities between model checking techniques and testing, one of the differences being that of *state space coverage*, and an important commonality that of *test property selection*.

In recent years the research into the use of formal methods and tools for testing reactive systems has seen a considerable growth. An overview of different approaches and school of thought can be found in [BPS98], reporting on the first ever Dagstuhl seminar devoted to testing. The formal treatment of conformance testing based on process algebra and/or concurrency theory is certainly not the only viable approach. An important school of thought is the FSM-testing theory grown out of the seminal work of Chow [Cho78], of which a good overview is given in [LY96]. Another interesting formal approach to testing is based on abstract data type theory [Gau95,BGM91].

# References

[BGM91]   G. Bernot, M.-C. Gaudel, and B. Marre. Software testing based on formal specifications: a theory and a tool. *Software Engineering Journal*, 1991 (November): 387–405.

[Bri88]   E. Brinksma. A theory for the derivation of tests. In: S. Aggarwal and K. Sabnani, editors, *Protocol Specification, Testing, and Verification VIII*, 63–74, North-Holland, 1988.

[BHT97]   E. Brinksma, L. Heerink, and J. Tretmans. Developments in testing transition systems. In: M. Kim, S. Kang, and K. Hong, editors, *Tenth Int. Workshop on Testing of Communicating Systems*, 143–166, Chapman & Hall, 1997.

[BPS98]   E. Brinksma, J. Peleska, and M. Siegel, editors, *Test Automation for Reactive Systems – Theory and Practice*, Dagstuhl Seminar report 223 (98361), SchloßDagstuhl, Germany, 1998.

[Cho78]   T.S. Chow. Testing software design modeled by finite-state systems. *IEEE Transactions on Software Engineering*, 4(3):178–187, 1978.

[CGPT96]  M. Clatin, R. Groz, M. Phalippou, and R. Thummel. Two approaches linking test generation with verification techniques. In: A. Cavalli and S. Budkowski, editors, *Eighth Int. Workshop on Testing of Communicating Systems*. Chapman & Hall, 1996.

[DeN87]   R. De Nicola. Extensional equivalences for transition systems. *Acta Informatica*, 24:211–237, 1987.

[DNH84]   R. De Nicola and M.C.B. Hennessy. Testing equivalences for processes. *Theoretical Computer Science*, 34:83–133, 1984.

[FJJV96]    J.-C. Fernandez, C. Jard, T. Jéron, and C. Viho. Using on-the-fly verification techniques for the generation of test suites. In: R. Alur and T.A. Henzinger, editors, *Computer Aided Verification CAV'96*. LNCS 1102, Springer-Verlag, 1996.

[Gau95]     M.-C. Gaudel. Testing can be formal, too. In: P.D. Mosses, M. Nielsen, and M.I. Schwarzbach, editors, *TAPSOFT'95: Theory and Practice of Software Development*, 82–96, LNCS 915, Springer -Verlag, 1995.

[GG83]      J.B. Goodenough and S.L. Gerhardt. Toward a theory of test data selection. *IEEE Transactions on Software Engineering*, 9(2), 1983.

[He98]      L. Heerink. *Ins and Outs in Refusal Testing*. Docoral dissertation, University of Twente, The Netherlands, 1998.

[HT97]      L. Heerink and J. Tretmans. Refusal Testing for classes of transition systems with inputs and outputs. In: T. Mizuno, N. Shiratori, T. Higashino, and A Togashi, editors, *Formal Description Techniques and Protocol Specification, Testing, and Verification FORTE X/PSTV XVII*, 23–38, Chapman & Hall, 1997.

[How78]     W.E. Howden. Algebraic program testing. *Acta Informatica*, 10:53–66, 1978.

[Mye79]     G.J. Myers. *The Art of Software Testing*. John Wiley & Sons Inc., 1979.

[Lan90]     R. Langerak. A testing theory for LOTOS using deadlock detection. In: E. Brinksma, G. Scollo, and C.A. Vissers, editors, *Proctocol Specification, Testing, and Verification IX*, 87–98, North-Holland, 1990.

[LY96]      D. Lee and M. Yannakakis. Principles and methods for testing finite state machines. *Proceedings of the IEEE*. August 1996.

[Pha94]     M. Phalippou. *Relations d'implementation et hypothèses de test sur des automates à entrées et sorties*. PhD Thesis, Université de Bordeaux I, France, 1994.

[STW96]     Dutch Technology Foundation STW. *Côte-de-Resyste* – COnformance TEsting of REactive SYSTEms, project TIF.4111. University of Twente, Eindhoven University of Technology, Philips Research, KPN Research, Utrecht, The Netherlands, 1996. URL: http://fmt.cs.utwente.nl/projects/CdR-html/.

[Tre96]     J. Tretmans. Test Generation with inputs, outputs, and quiescence. *Software - Concepts and Tools*, 17(3):103–120, 1996.

[VT98]      R.G. de Vries and J. Tretmans. On-the-fly conformance testing using SPIN. In: G. Holzmann, E. Najm, and A. Serhrouchni, editors, *Fourth Workshop on Automata Theoretic Verification with the SPIN Model Checker*, ENST 98 S 002, 115–128, Paris, France, 1998.

# Proof of Correctness of a Processor with Reorder Buffer Using the Completion Functions Approach*

Ravi Hosabettu[1], Mandayam Srivas[2], and Ganesh Gopalakrishnan[1]

[1] Department of Computer Science, University of Utah, Salt Lake City, UT 84112,
hosabett,ganesh@cs.utah.edu
[2] Computer Science Laboratory, SRI International, Menlo Park, CA 94025,
srivas@csl.sri.com

**Abstract.** The *Completion Functions Approach* was proposed in [HSG98] as a systematic way to decompose the proof of correctness of pipelined microprocessors. The central idea is to construct the abstraction function using completion functions, one per unfinished instruction, each of which specifies the effect (on the observables) of completing the instruction. In this paper, we show that this "instruction-centric" view of the completion functions approach leads to an elegant decomposition of the proof for an out-of-order execution processor with a reorder buffer. The proof does not involve the construction of an explicit intermediate abstraction, makes heavy use of strategies based on decision procedures and rewriting, and addresses both safety and liveness issues with a clean separation between them.

## 1 Introduction

For formal verification to be successful in practice not only is it important to raise the level of automation provided but is also essential to develop methodologies that scale verification to large state-of-the-art designs. One of the reasons for the relative popularity of model checking in industry is that it is automatic when readily applicable. A technology originating from the theorem proving domain that can potentially provide a similarly high degree of automation is one that makes heavy use of decision procedures for the combined theory of boolean expressions with uninterpreted functions and linear arithmetic [CRSS94,BDL96]. Just as model checking suffers from a state-explosion problem, a verification strategy based on decision procedures suffers from a "case-explosion" problem. That is, when applied naively, the sizes of the terms generated and the number of examined cases during validity checking explodes. Just as compositional model checking provides a way of decomposing the overall proof and reducing the effort for an individual model checker run, a practical methodology for decision

* This work was done in part when the first author was visiting SRI International in summer 1998. The work done by the authors at University of Utah was supported in part by NSF through Grant no. CCR-9800928. The work done by the authors at SRI International was supported in part by NASA contract NAS1-20334 and ARPA contract NASA-NAG-2-891 (ARPA Order A721).

procedure-centered verification must prescribe a systematic way to decompose the correctness assertion into smaller problems that the decision procedures can handle.

In [HSG98], we proposed such a methodology for pipelined processor verification called the *Completion Functions Approach*. The central idea behind this approach is to define the abstraction function as a composition of a sequence of completion functions, one for every unfinished instruction, in their program order. A completion function specifies how a partially executed instruction is to be completed in an atomic fashion, that is, desired effect on the observables of completing that instruction. Given such a definition of the abstraction function in terms of completion functions, the methodology prescribes a way of organizing the verification into proving a hierarchy of *verification conditions*. The methodology has the following attributes:

- The verification proceeds incrementally making debugging and error tracing easier.
- The verification conditions and most of the supporting lemmas needed to support the incremental methodology can be generated systematically.
- Every generated verification condition and lemma can be proved, often automatically, using a strategy based on decision procedures and rewriting.

In summary, the completion functions approach strikes a balance between full automation that (if at all possible) can potentially overwhelm the decision procedures, and a potentially tedious manual proof. This methodology is implemented using PVS [ORSvH95] and was applied (in [HSG98]) to three processor examples: DLX [HP90], dual-issue DLX, and a processor that exhibited limited out-of-order execution capability. An attribute common to all these processors was that the maximum number of instructions pending at any time in the pipeline was small and fixed, which made the completion functions approach readily amenable for these examples. It was an open question if the approach would be practical, even if applicable, to verify a truly out-of-order execution processor with a reorder buffer. Such a processor can have scores of pending instructions in the reorder buffer potentially making the task of defining completion functions tedious and possibly exploding the number of generated verification conditions.

In this paper, we demonstrate that the completion functions approach is well-suited to the verification of out-of-order execution processors by verifying an example processor (a simplified model, based on the P6 design) with a reorder buffer and generic execution units and without any data size bounds. We observe that regardless of how many instructions are pending in the reorder buffer, the instructions can only be in one of four distinct states. We exploit this fact to provide a single compact parameterized completion function applicable to all the pending instructions in the buffer. The abstraction function is then defined as a simple recursive function that completes all the pending instructions in the order in which they are stored in the reorder buffer. The proof is organized as a single parameterized verification condition, which is proved using a simple induction on the number of instructions in the buffer. The different cases of the induction are generated on the basis of how an instruction makes a transition from its present state to its next state. We make heavy use of an automatic case-analysis strategy and certain other strategies based on decision procedures and rewriting in discharging these different cases. This same observation about instruction state transitions is used in providing a proof of liveness too.

**Related work**: The problem of verifying the control logic of out-of-order execution processors has received considerable attention in the last couple of years using both theorem proving and model checking approaches. The following yardsticks can be used to evaluate the various approaches: (1) the amount and complexity of information required from the user, (2) the complexity of the manual steps of the methodology (3) the level of automation with which the obligations generated by the methodology can be verified.

Two theorem-proving based verifications of a similar design are described in [JSD98] and [PA98]. The idea in [JSD98] is to first show that for every out-of-order execution sequence that contains as many as $n$ unretired instructions at any time there exists an "equivalent" (*max-1*) execution containing at most 1 unretired instruction by constructing a suitable controller schedule. It then shows the equivalence between a max-1 execution and the ISA level. The induction required in the first step, which was not mechanized, is very complicated. The verifier needs a much deeper insight into the control logic to exhibit a control schedule and to discharge the generated obligations in the first step than that is needed for constructing the completion functions and discharging the generated verification conditions. Whereas our verification makes no assumption on the time taken by the execution units, the mechanized part of their first step bounds the execution time. The proofs mix safety and liveness issues and the verification of liveness issues is not addressed. And the complexity of the reachability invariants needed in their approach and the effort required to discharge them is not clear; few details are provided in the paper.

The verification in [PA98] is based on *refinement* by using "synchronization on instruction retirement" to reduce the complexity of the refinement relations to be proved. Although they do not need any flushing mechanism, there is no systematic method to generate the invariants and obligations needed and hence their mechanization is not as automatic as ours. And they do not address liveness issues needed to complete the proof.

In [SH98], verification of a processor model with a reorder buffer, exceptions, and speculative execution is carried out. Their approach relies on constructing an explicit intermediate abstraction (called MAETT) and expressing invariant properties over this. Our approach avoids the construction of an intermediate abstraction and hence requires significantly less manual effort.

In [McM98], McMillan uses compositional model checking and aggressive symmetry reductions to manually decompose the proof of a processor implementing Tomasulo's algorithm (without a reorder buffer) into smaller correctness obligations via refinement maps. Setting up the refinement maps requires information similar to that provided by the completion functions in addition to some details of the design. An advantage of model checking is that it does not need any reachability invariants to check the refinement maps although the user has to give hints about the environment assumptions to be used.

The rest of the paper is organized as follows: In Section 2, we describe our processor model. Section 3 describes our correctness criteria and provides a brief overview of our approach applied to examples mentioned earlier in [HSG98]. This is followed by the proof of correctness in Section 4 and finally the conclusions.

## 2 Processor Model

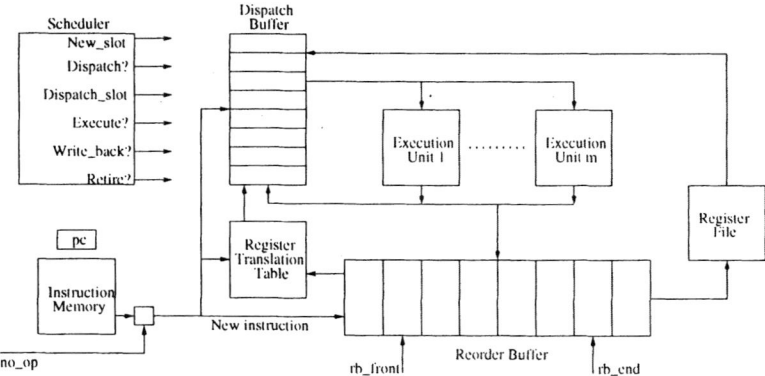

**Fig. 1.** The block diagram model of our implementation

The implementation model of an out-of-order execution processor that we consider in this paper is shown in Figure 1. A reorder buffer is used to maintain the program order of the instructions so that they can be committed in that order to respect the ISA semantics. (rb_end points to the earliest issued instruction and rb_front points to the first available free slot in the buffer). A register translation table (RTT) is maintained to provide the identity of the latest pending instruction writing a particular register. The model has a dispatch buffer (of size z; the dispatch buffer entries are also called "reservation stations" in other literature) where instructions wait before being sent to the execution units. There are m execution units represented by an uninterpreted function (z and m are parameters to our implementation model). A scheduler controls the movement of the instructions through the execution pipeline (such as being dispatched, executed etc.) and its behavior is modeled by axioms (to allow us to concentrate on the processor "core"). Instructions are fetched from the instruction memory (using a program counter which then is incremented); and the implementation also takes a no_op input, which suppresses an instruction fetch when asserted.

An instruction is *issued* by allocating an entry for it at the front of the reorder buffer and a free entry in the dispatch buffer (New_slot). No instruction is issued if the dispatch buffer is full or if no_op is asserted. The RTT entry corresponding to the destination of the instruction is updated to reflect the fact that the instruction being issued is the latest one to write that register. If the source operand is not being written by a previously issued pending instruction (checked using the RTT) then its value is obtained from the register file, otherwise the reorder buffer index of the instruction providing the source operand is maintained (in the dispatch buffer entry). Issued instructions wait in the dispatch buffer for their source operand to become ready, monitoring the execution units if they produce the value they are waiting for. An instruction can be *dispatched* when its source operand is ready and a free execution unit is available. `Dispatch?` and `Dispatch_slot` outputs from the scheduler (each a m-wide vector) determine whether or not to dispatch an instruction to a particular execution unit and the dispatch buffer entry from where to dispatch. As soon as an instruction is dispatched, its dispatch buffer entry is freed. Dispatched instructions get *executed* after a non-deterministic amount of time as determined by the scheduler output `Execute?`. The result of executed instructions are *written back* to their respective reorder buffer entries as well as forwarded to those instructions waiting for this result (at a time determined by the `Write_back?` output of the scheduler). If the instruction at the end of the reorder buffer has written back its result, then that instruction can be retired by copying the result value to the register file (at a time determined by the `Retire?` output of the scheduler). Also, if the RTT entry for the destination of the instruction being retired is pointing to the end, then that entry is updated to reflect the fact that value of that register is in the register file.

Our simplified model does not have memory or branch instructions and does not handle exceptions. For simplicity, multiple instruction issue or retirement is not allowed in a single cycle (but multiple instructions can be simultaneously dispatched or written back). Also, the reorder buffer is implemented as an unbounded buffer as opposed to a circular queue.[1]

At the specification level, the state is represented by a register file, a program counter and an instruction memory. Instructions are fetched from the instruction memory, executed, result written back to the register file and the program counter incremented in one clock cycle.

## 3   Our Correctness Criteria

Intuitively, a pipelined processor is correct if the behavior of the processor starting in a flushed state (i.e., no partially executed instructions), executing a program and terminating in a flushed state is emulated by an ISA level specification machine whose starting and terminating states are in direct correspondence through projection. This criterion is shown in Figure 2(a) where `I_step` is the implementation transition function, `A_step` is the specification transition function, and `projection` extracts those implementation state components visible to the specification (i.e., observables). This criterion can be proved by an easy induction on n once the *commutative diagram* condition shown in Figure 2(b)

---

[1] Using a bounded reorder buffer will not complicate the methodology but makes setting up the induction more involved.

is proved on a single implementation machine transition (and a certain other condition discussed in the next paragraph holds).

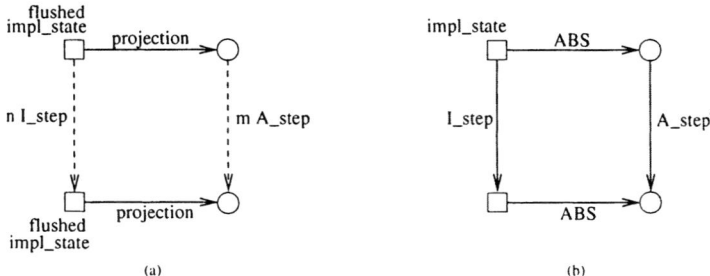

**Fig. 2.** Pipelined microprocessor correctness criteria

The criterion in Figure 2(b) states that if the implementation machine starts in an arbitrary reachable state `impl_state` and the specification machine starts in a corresponding specification state (given by an abstraction function `ABS`), then after executing a transition their new states correspond. Further `ABS` must be chosen so that for all flushed states `fs` the *projection condition* `ABS(fs) = projection(fs)` holds. The commutative diagram uses a modified transition function `A_step'`, which denotes zero or more applications of `A_step`, because an implementation transition from an arbitrary state might correspond to executing in the specification machine zero instruction (*e.g.*, if the implementation machine stalls without fetching an instruction) or more than one instruction (*e.g.*, if multiple instructions are fetched in a cycle). The number of instructions executed by the specification machine is provided by a user-defined *synchronization* function on implementation states. One of the crucial proof obligations is to show that this function does not always return zero (*No_indefinite_stutter* obligation). One also needs to prove that the implementation machine will eventually reach a flushed state if no more instructions are inserted into the machine, to make sure that the correctness criterion in Figure 2(a) is not vacuous (*Eventual_flush* obligation). In addition, the user may need to discover *invariants* to restrict the set of `impl_state` considered in the proof of Figure 2(b) and prove that it is closed under `I_step`.

The completion functions approach suggests a way of constructing the abstraction function. We define a completion function for every unfinished instruction in the processor that directly specifies the intended effect of completing that instruction. The abstraction function is defined as a composition of these completion functions in program order. In the examples in [HSG98], the program order was determined from the structure of the pipeline. This construction of the abstraction function decomposed the proof into proving a series of verification conditions, each of which captured the effect of completing instructions one at a time and that were reused in the proof of the subsequent verification conditions. Since there were a fixed (and small) number of instructions pending in the pipeline, this scheme worked well and the proof was easily accomplished.

However, the number of instructions is unbounded in the present example and the above scheme does not work. But we observe that a pending instruction in the processor can only be in four possible states and provide a parameterized completion function using this fact. The program order is easily determined since the reorder buffer stores it. And we generate a single parameterized verification condition which is proved by an induction on the number of pending instructions in the reorder buffer, where the induction hypothesis captures the effect of completing all the earlier instructions.

## 4  Proof of Correctness

We introduce some notations which will be used throughout this section: q represents the implementation state, s the scheduler output, i the processor input, rf(q) the register file contents in state q and I_step(q,s,i) the "next state" after an implementation transition. Also, we identify an instruction in the processor by its reorder buffer entry index (i.e., instruction rbi means instruction at index rbi). The complete PVS specifications and the proof scripts can be found at [Hos99].

### 4.1  Specifying the completion functions

An instruction in the processor can be in one of the following four possible states inside the processor—issued, dispatched, executed or written back. (A retired instruction is no longer present in the processor). We formulate predicates describing an instruction in each of these states and identify how to complete such an instruction. To facilitate this formulation, we add two auxiliary variables to a reorder buffer entry.[2] The first one maintains the index of the dispatch buffer entry allocated to the instruction while it is waiting to be dispatched. The second one maintains the execution unit index where the instruction executes. The definition of the completion function is shown in 1 .

```
% state_I:impl. state type.   rbindex:reorder buffer index type.        1
Complete_instr(q:state_I,rbi:rbindex):state_I =
  IF written_back_predicate(q,rbi) THEN Action_written_back(q,rbi)
  ELSIF executed_predicate(q,rbi) THEN Action_executed(q,rbi)
  ELSIF dispatched_predicate(q,rbi) THEN Action_dispatched(q,rbi)
  ELSIF issued_predicate(q,rbi) THEN Action_issued(q,rbi)
  ELSE q ENDIF
```

In this implementation, when the instruction is in the written back state, the result value as well as the destination register of the instruction are in its reorder buffer entry. So Action_written_back above completes this instruction by updating the register file by writing the result value to the destination register. An instruction in the issued state is completed (Action_issued) by reading the

---

[2] The auxiliary variables are for specification purposes only. The third auxiliary variable we needed maintained the identity of the source register for a given instruction.

value of the source register from the register file, (this relies on the fact that the completion functions will be composed in the program order in defining the abstraction function; so q for a given instruction will be that state where the instructions ahead of it are completed) computing the result value depending on the instruction operation and then writing this value to the destination register. Similarly `Action_executed` and `Action_dispatched` are specified. None of these "actions" affect the program counter or the instruction memory. The completion function definition is very compact, taking only 15 lines of PVS code.

## 4.2  Constructing the abstraction function

The abstraction function is constructed by flushing the reorder buffer, that is, by completing all the unfinished instructions in the reorder buffer. We define a recursive function `Complete_till` to complete instructions till a given reorder buffer index as shown in ☐2 and then construct the abstraction function by instantiating this definition with the index of the latest instruction in the reorder buffer (i.e., `rb_front(q)-1`). The synchronization function returns zero if `no_op` input is asserted or there is no free dispatch buffer entry (hence no instruction is issued) otherwise returns one.

```
% If the given instr. index is less than the end pointer of the          2
% reorder buffer, do nothing. Else complete that instr. in a state
% where all the previous instructions are completed.
Complete_till(q:state_I,rbi:rbindex): RECURSIVE state_I =
   IF rbi < rb_end(q) THEN q
   ELSE Complete_instr(Complete_till(q,rbi-1),rbi) ENDIF
   MEASURE rbi
% state_A is the specification state type.
ABS(q:state_I):state_A = projection(Complete_till(q,rb_front(q)-1))
```

## 4.3  Proof decomposition

We first prove a single parameterized verification condition that captures the effect of completing all the instructions in the reorder buffer and then use it in the proof of the commutative diagram. We decompose the proof of this verification condition based on how an instruction makes a transition from its present state to its next state.

Consider an arbitrary instruction `rbi`. We claim that the register file contents will be the same whether the instructions till `rbi` are completed in state q or in `I_step(q,s,i)`. This is shown as lemma `same_rf` in ☐3. We prove this by induction on `rbi`.

```
% The single parametrized verification condition.                         3
% valid_rb_entry? predicate tests if rbi is within reorder buffer bounds.
same_rf: LEMMA
    FORALL(rbi:rbindex): valid_rb_entry?(q,rbi) IMPLIES
    rf(Complete_till(q,rbi)) = rf(Complete_till(I_step(q,s,i),rbi))
```

We generate the different cases of the induction argument (as detailed later) based on how an instruction makes a transition from its present state to its next state. This is shown in Figure 3 where we have identified the conditions under which an instruction changes its state. For example, we identify the predicate `Dispatch_trans?(q,s,i,rbi)` that defines the condition under which the instruction `rbi` goes from issued state to dispatched state. In this implementation, this predicate is true when there is an execution unit for which `Dispatch?` output from the scheduler is true and the `Dispatch_slot` output is equal to the dispatch buffer entry index assigned to `rbi`. Similarly other "trans" predicates are defined.

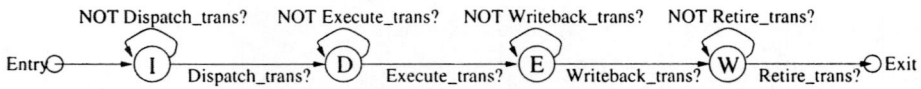

**Fig. 3.** The various states an instruction can be in and transitions between them, I: issued, D: dispatched, E: executed, W: written back.

Having defined these predicates, we prove that they indeed cause instructions to take the transitions shown. Consider a valid instruction `rbi` in the issued state, that is, `issued_predicate(q,rbi)` holds. If `Dispatch_trans?(q,s,i,rbi)` is true, then we show that after an implementation transition, `rbi` will be in the dispatched state (i.e., `dispatched_predicate(I_step(q,s,i),rbi)` is true) and remains valid. This is shown as a lemma in ⟨4⟩. If `Dispatch_trans?(q,s,i,rbi)` is false, we show that `rbi` remains in the issued state in `I_step(q,s,i)` and remains valid. There are five other similar lemmas for the other transitions. In the eighth case, that is, `rbi` in the written back state being retired, the instruction will be invalid (out of reorder buffer bounds) in `I_step(q,s,i)`.

```
issue_to_dispatch: LEMMA                                          4
    FORALL(rbi:rbindex): (valid_rb_entry?(q,rbi) AND
      issued_predicate(q,rbi) AND Dispatch_trans?(q,s,i,rbi)) IMPLIES
    (dispatched_predicate(I_step(q,s,i),rbi) AND
       valid_rb_entry?(I_step(q,s,i),rbi))
```

Now we come back to details of the induction argument for `same_rf` lemma. We do a case analysis on the possible state `rbi` is in and whether or not, it makes a transition to its next state. Assume the instruction `rbi` is in the issued state. We prove the induction claim in the two cases—`Dispatch_trans?(q,s,i,rbi)` is true or false—separately. (The proof obligation for the first case is shown in ⟨5⟩.) We have similar proof obligations for `rbi` being in other states. In all, the proof decomposes into eight very similar proof obligations.

```
% One of the eight cases in the induction argument.                5
issue_to_dispatch_induction: LEMMA
    FORALL(rbi:rbindex): (valid_rb_entry?(q,rbi) AND
      issued_predicate(q,rbi) AND Dispatch_trans?(q,s,i,rbi) AND
      Induction_hypothesis(q,s,i,rbi-1)) IMPLIES
    rf(Complete_till(q,rbi)) = rf(Complete_till(I_step(q,s,i),rbi))
```

We now sketch the proof of `issue_to_dispatch_induction` lemma. (We refer to the goal that we are proving—`rf( ... ) = rf( ... )`—as the consequent.) We expand the definition of the completion function corresponding to

rbi on both sides of the consequent (after unrolling the recursive definition of
Complete_till once). It follows from issue_to_dispatch lemma that since rbi
is in issued state in q, it is in dispatched state in I_step(q,s,i). After rewriting and simplifications in PVS, the left hand side of the consequent simplifies
to rf(Action_issued(Complete_till(q,rbi-1),rbi)) [3] and the right hand
side to rf(Action_dispatched(Complete_till(I_step(q,s,i),rbi-1),rbi))
(Illustrated in Figure 4). Proof now proceeds by expanding the definitions of
Action_issued and Action_dispatched, using the necessary invariants and simplifying. We use many simple PVS strategies during the proof; in particular we
use (apply (then* (repeat (lift-if)) (bddsimp) (ground) (assert))) to
do the simplifications by automatic case-analysis. Observe that when we expand
Action_dispatched, all implementation variables take their "next" values. Also
on the left hand side of the consequent, term rf(Complete_till(q,rbi-1)) appears and on right hand side, term rf(Complete_till(I_step(q,s,i),rbi-1))
appears and these are same by the induction hypothesis.

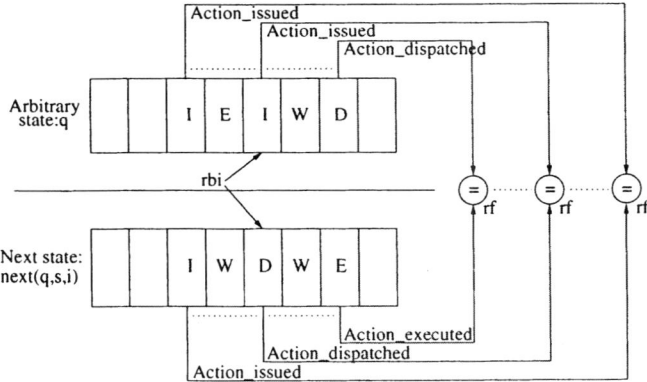

**Fig. 4.** The reorder buffer and the state of the instructions in it before and after an
implementation transition (one possible configuration, empty slot means no instruction
present). Completing a particular instruction reduces to performing the action shown.

We now instantiate the lemma same_rf above with the index of the latest
instruction in the processor (i.e., rb_front(q)-1) and use it in the proof of the
commutative diagram for register file. Assume that no instruction is issued in the
current cycle, that is, the synchronization function returns zero. Then rb_front
remains unchanged after an implementation transition and the proof is trivial. If
indeed a new instruction is issued, then it will be at index rb_front(q) and will
be in issued state, so proving the commutative diagram reduces to establishing
that completing the new instruction (as per Action_issued) has the same effect

---

[3] Observe that issued_predicate(Complete_till(q,rbi-1),rbi) if and only if
issued_predicate(q,rbi). This is because the completion functions affect only the
register file (observables in general) and issued_predicate depends only on the
non-observables.

on the register file as executing a specification machine transition. This proof is similar to the proof of the lemma described above. The commutative diagram proofs for `pc` and the instruction memory are trivial and are omitted.

**Correctness of feedback logic:** The proof presented above requires that the correctness of the feedback logic be captured in the form of a lemma as shown in 6 . This lemma states that if the source operand of an instruction is ready, then its value is equal to the value read from the register file after all the instructions ahead of it are completed. When an instruction `rbi` in the issued state is being dispatched, it uses `src_value(q,rbi)` as the source operand but the `Action_issued` that is used to complete it reads the source value from the register file (see the description of `Action_issued` in Section 4.1) and this lemma establishes that these two values are the same. The proof of this lemma relies on an invariant described later.

```
% select reads from the register file. src_ready?, src_value and        6
% src_reg have their obvious definitions.
Feedback_logic_correct: LEMMA
     FORALL(rbi:rbindex): (valid_rb_entry?(q,rbi) AND
       issued_predicate(q,rbi) AND src_ready?(q,rbi)) IMPLIES
     src_value(q,rbi) = select(rf(Complete_till(q,rbi-1)),src_reg(q,rbi))
```

**Invariants needed:** We now provide a classification of the invariants needed by our approach and describe some of them.

- *Exhaustiveness and Exclusiveness*: Having identified the set of possible states an instruction can be in, we require one to prove that an arbitrary instruction is always in one of these states (exhaustiveness) and never simultaneously in two states (exclusiveness).

- *Instruction state properties*: Whenever an instruction is in a particular state, it satisfies some properties and these are established as invariants. One example is: if an instruction is in issued state, then the dispatch buffer entry assigned to it is valid and has the reorder buffer index of the instruction stored in it.

- *Feedback logic invariant*: Let `rbi` be an arbitrary instruction and let `ptr` be an instruction that is producing its source value. Then this invariant essentially states that all the instructions "in between" `rbi` and `ptr` have the destination different from the source of `rbi`, that `ptr` is in the written back state if and only if the source value of `rbi` is ready and that the source value of `rbi` (when ready) is equal to the result computed by `ptr`.

- *Example specific invariants*: Other invariants needed include characterization about the reorder buffer bounds and the register translation table.

**PVS proof details:** The proofs of all the induction obligations follow the pattern outlined in the sketch of `issue_to_dispatch_induction` lemma. The proofs of certain rewrite rules needed in the methodology [HSG98] and other simple obligations can be accomplished fully automatically. But there is no uniform strategy for proving the invariants. The manual effort involved one week of discussion and planning and then 12 person days of "first time" effort to construct the proofs. The proofs got subsequently cleaned up and evolved as we wrote the paper. The proofs rerun in about 1050 seconds on a 167 MHz Ultra Sparc machine.

### 4.4 Other obligations - liveness properties

We provide a sketch of the proof that the processor eventually gets flushed if no more instructions are inserted into it. The proof that the synchronization function eventually returns a nonzero value is similar. The proofs involve a set of obligations on the implementation machine, a set of fairness assumptions on the inputs to the implementation and a high level argument using these to prove the two liveness properties. All the obligations on the implementation machine are proved in PVS. We now provide a brief sketch (due to space constraints) of the top level argument which is being formalized in PVS.

**Proof sketch**: The processor is flushed if `rb_front(q) = rb_end(q)`.

- First observation: "any instruction in the dispatched state eventually goes to the executed state and then eventually goes to the written back state. It then remains in the written back state until retired". Consider an instruction `rbi` in the dispatched state. If `Execute_trans?(q,s,i,rbi)` is true, then `rbi` goes to the executed state in `I_step(q,s,i)`, otherwise it remains in the dispatched state (refer to Figure 3). We show that when `rbi` is in the dispatched state, the scheduler inputs that determine when an instruction should be executed are enabled and these remain enabled as long as `rbi` is in the dispatched state. By a fairness assumption on the scheduler, it eventually decides to execute the instruction (i.e., `Execute_trans?(q,s,i,rbi)` will be true) and the instruction moves to the executed state. By a similar argument, it moves to the written back state and then remains in that state until retired.
- Second observation: "every busy execution unit eventually becomes free and stays free until an instruction is dispatched on it".
- Third observation: "an instruction in the issued state will eventually go to the dispatched state". Here, the proof is by induction since an arbitrary instruction `rbi` could be waiting for a previously issued instruction to produce its source value. This step also relies on the earlier two observations.
- Final observation: "the processor eventually gets flushed". We know that every instruction eventually goes to the written back state—third and first observations. Also the instructions in the written back state are eventually retired by a fairness assumption on the scheduler. Since `rb_front(q)` remains unchanged when no new instructions are inserted into the processor and `rb_end(q)` is incremented when an instruction is retired, eventually the processor gets flushed.

## 5 Conclusions

We have demonstrated in this paper that the completion functions approach is well-suited for the verification of out-of-order execution processors with a reorder buffer. We have recently extended our approach to be applicable in a scenario where instructions "commit" out-of-order and illustrated it on an example processor implementing Tomasulo's algorithm without a reorder buffer [HGS99]. The proof was constructed in seven person days, reusing lot of the ideas and the machinery developed in this paper. We are currently working on verifying a more detailed out-of-order execution processor involving branches, exceptions and speculative execution. Our approach has been used to handle processors with branch and memory operations [HSG98] and we are investigating how those ideas carry over to this example. We are also developing a PVS theory of the "eventually" temporal operator to mechanize the liveness proofs presented in this paper. Finally, we are investigating how the ideas behind the completion functions approach can be adapted to verify certain "transaction processing systems".

**Acknowledgments:** We would like to thank Abdel Mokkedem and John Rushby for their feedbacks on the earlier drafts of this paper.

# References

[BDL96]    Clark Barrett, David Dill, and Jeremy Levitt. Validity checking for combinations of theories with equality. In Mandayam Srivas and Albert Camilleri, editors, *Formal Methods in Computer-Aided Design, FMCAD '96*, volume 1166 of *LNCS*, pages 187–201. Springer-Verlag, November 1996.

[CRSS94]   D. Cyrluk, S. Rajan, N. Shankar, and M. K. Srivas. Effective theorem proving for hardware verification. In Ramayya Kumar and Thomas Kropf, editors, *Theorem Provers in Circuit Design, TPCD '94*, volume 910 of *LNCS*, pages 203–222. Springer-Verlag, September 1994.

[GW98]     Ganesh Gopalakrishnan and Phillip Windley, editors. *Formal Methods in Computer-Aided Design, FMCAD '98*, volume 1522 of *LNCS*, Palo Alto, CA, USA, November 1998. Springer-Verlag.

[HGS99]    Ravi Hosabettu, Ganesh Gopalakrishnan, and Mandayam Srivas. A proof of correctness of a processor implementing Tomasulo's algorithm without a reorder buffer. 1999. Submitted for publication.

[Hos99]    Ravi Hosabettu. PVS specification and proofs of all the examples verified with the completion functions approach, 1999. Available at http://www.cs.utah.edu/~hosabett/pvs/processor.html.

[HP90]     John L. Hennessy and David A. Patterson. *Computer Architecture: A Quantitative Approach*. Morgan Kaufmann, San Mateo, CA, 1990.

[HSG98]    Ravi Hosabettu, Mandayam Srivas, and Ganesh Gopalakrishnan. Decomposing the proof of correctness of pipelined microprocessors. In Hu and Vardi [HV98], pages 122–134.

[HV98]     Alan J. Hu and Moshe Y. Vardi, editors. *Computer-Aided Verification, CAV '98*, volume 1427 of *LNCS*, Vancouver, BC, Canada, June/July 1998. Springer-Verlag.

[JSD98]    Robert Jones, Jens Skakkebaek, and David Dill. Reducing manual abstraction in formal verification of out-of-order execution. In Gopalakrishnan and Windley [GW98], pages 2–17.

[McM98]    Ken McMillan. Verification of an implementation of Tomasulo's algorithm by compositional model checking. In Hu and Vardi [HV98], pages 110–121.

[ORSvH95]  Sam Owre, John Rushby, Natarajan Shankar, and Friedrich von Henke. Formal verification for fault-tolerant architectures: Prolegomena to the design of PVS. *IEEE Transactions on Software Engineering*, 21(2):107–125, February 1995.

[PA98]     Amir Pnueli and Tamarah Arons. Verification of data-insensitive circuits: An in-order-retirement case study. In Gopalakrishnan and Windley [GW98], pages 351–368.

[SH98]     J. Sawada and W. A. Hunt, Jr. Processor verification with precise exceptions and speculative execution. In Hu and Vardi [HV98], pages 135–146.

# Verifying Safety Properties of a PowerPC™[*] Microprocessor Using Symbolic Model Checking without BDDs[**]

Armin Biere[1,2,3], Edmund Clarke[2,3], Richard Raimi[4,5], and Yunshan Zhu[2,3]

[1] ILKD, University of Karlsruhe, Postfach 6980, 76128 Karlsruhe, Germany
Armin.Biere@ira.uka.de
[2] Computer Science Department, Carnegie Mellon University
5000 Forbes Avenue, Pittsburgh, PA 15213
Edmund.Clarke@cs.cmu.edu, Yunshan.Zhu@cs.cmu.edu
[3] Verysys Design Automation, Inc.
42707 Lawrence Place, Fremont, CA 94538
[4] Motorola, Inc., Somerset PowerPC Design Center
6200 Bridgepoint Pkwy., Bldg. 4, Austin, TX 78759
Richard_Raimi@email.mot.sps.com
[5] Computer Engineering Research Center, University of Texas at Austin
Austin, TX 78730

**Abstract.** In [1] *Bounded Model Checking* with the aid of satisfiability solving (SAT) was introduced as an alternative to symbolic model checking with BDDs. In this paper we show how bounded model checking can take advantage of specialized optimizations. We present a bounded version of the cone of influence reduction. We have successfully applied this idea in checking safety properties of a PowerPC microprocessor at Motorola's Somerset PowerPC design center. Based on that experience, we propose a verification methodology that we feel can bring model checking into the mainstream of industrial chip design.

## 1 Introduction

Model checking has only been partially accepted by industry as a supplement to traditional verification techniques. The reason is that model checking, which, to date, has been based on BDDs or on explicit state graph exploration, has not been robust enough for industry.

Model checking [3, 12] was first proposed as a verification technique eighteen years ago. However, it was not until the discovery of symbolic model checking

---

[*] PowerPC is a trademark of the International Business Machines Corporation, used under license therefrom.
[**] This research is sponsored by the Semiconductor Research Corporation (SRC) under Contract No. 97-DJ-294 and the National Science Foundation (NSF) under Grant No. CCR-9505472. Any opinions, findings and conclusions or recommendations expressed in this material are those of the authors and do not necessarily reflect the views of the SRC, NSF or the United States Government.

techniques based on BDDs [2, 5, 10] around 1990 that it was taken seriously by industry. Unfortunately, BDD based model checkers have suffered from the fact that ordered binary decision diagrams can require exponential space. Recently a new technique called *bounded model checking* [1] has been proposed that uses fast satisfiability solvers instead of BDDs. The advantage of satisfiability solvers like SATO [15], GRASP [13], and Stalmarck's algorithm [14] is that they never require exponential space. In [1], it was shown that this new technique sometimes performed much better than BDD based symbolic model checking. However, the performance was obtained on academic examples, and doubt remained about whether bounded model checking would work well on industrial examples.

In this paper we consider the performance of a bounded model checker, BMC [1], in verifying twenty safety properties on five complex circuits from a PowerPC microprocessor. By any reasonable measure, BMC consistently outperformed the BDD based symbolic model checker, SMV [9]. In part, this performance gain was obtained by utilizing a new *bounded cone of influence reduction* technique which reduces the size of the CNF (conjunctive normal form) formula given to the satisfiability solver.

We believe our new experimental results confirm that bounded model checking can handle industrial examples. Since we, ourselves, are convinced of this, we propose, here, a methodology for using bounded model checking as a supplement to traditional validation techniques in industry. We feel that this represents a significant milestone for formal verification.

## 2 Models, Kripke Structures and Safety Properties

For brevity, we focus on the application of bounded model checking to safety properties. The reader is referred to [1] for a more complete treatment of bounded model checking.

We first consider models that can be represented by a set of initial and next state functions.

**Definition 1 (Model).** *Let* $X = \{x_1, \ldots, x_n, x_{n+1}, \ldots, x_m\}$ *be a set of m Boolean variables, and let* $F = \{f_1, \ldots, f_n\}$ *be a set of* $n \leq m$ *Boolean transition functions, each a function over variables in* $X$. *Finally, let* $R = \{r_1, \ldots, r_n\}$ *be a set of initialization functions, each a function over variables in* $X$. *Then* $M = (X, F, R)$ *is called a* model.

From a model $M$ we can construct a Kripke structure $K = (S, T, I)$ in the following way. The set of states, $S$, is an encoding of the variables in $X$, i.e., $S = \{0, 1\}^m$. A state may also be considered a vector of these $m$ variables, $\bar{x} = (x_1, \ldots, x_n, x_{n+1}, \ldots, x_m)$. Note that we use italic identifiers $s, s_0, \ldots$ for states (elements of $S = \{0, 1\}^m$) and overhead bar identifiers $\bar{s}, \bar{s}_0$ for vectors of Boolean variables. We define present and next state versions of the variables in $X$, denoting the latter with primes, e.g., $x'_j$. The variables in $X$ serve as atomic propositions, and obviate the need for a labeling function. We define the transition relation, $T \subseteq S \times S$ and the set of initial states $I \subseteq S$ via their characteristic functions:

$$T(s, s') := \bigwedge_{j=1}^{n} x'_j \leftrightarrow f_j(x) \qquad \text{and} \qquad I(s) := \bigwedge_{j=1}^{n} x_j \leftrightarrow r_j(x)$$

Here, $f_j$ and $r_j$ are the transition and initialization functions, respectively, of the $j^{th}$ element of the variable vector, $\bar{x}$. Note that transition and initialization functions are not specified for elements $n + 1$ through $m$ of $\bar{x}$. These represent primary inputs (PIs) to an underlying sequential circuit.

In practice, we will often consider a set of propositional constraints imposed on a system. Given a model, $M = (X, F, R)$, a constraint function, $c$, over $X$, and a Kripke structure, $K = (S, T, I)$, derived from $M$, a *constrained Kripke structure*, $K_c = (S, T_c, I_c)$, in which $c$ is an invariant, can be obtained as follows:

$$T_c(s, s') := T(s, s') \wedge c(s) \wedge c(s') \qquad \text{and} \qquad I_c(s) := I(s) \wedge c(s)$$

As a specification logic we use Linear Temporal Logic (LTL). In this paper we consider only the unary temporal operators: *eventually*, **F**, and *globally*, **G**.

A path $\pi = (s_0, s_1, \ldots)$ in a model $M$ is an infinite sequence of states in the corresponding Kripke structure $K$ such that $T(s_i, s_{i+1})$ holds for all $i \in \mathbb{N}$. We call $\pi$ initialized if $I(s_0)$ holds. It is often convenient to discuss the value of a component variable from the underlying vector, $\bar{x}$, in a certain state along a path. The assignment to element $x_j$ of $\bar{x}$ in state $s_i$ along path $\pi$ is written as $s_i(j)$.

We are interested in determining whether $M \models \mathbf{AG}p$ holds, i.e., whether $p$, a propositional formula, holds in every state along every initialized path is some model, $M$. We approach this in two ways: (a) by searching for a finite length counterexample showing $M \models \mathbf{EF}\neg p$, or (b) by proving that $p$ is an inductive invariant for $M$. These have in common that, in both cases, it is not necessary to search unto the *diameter* of the structure, the diameter being that minimal number of transitions sufficient for reaching any state from an initial state.

## 3    Bounded Model Checking for Safety Properties

In bounded model checking [1] the user specifies a number of time steps, $k$, for searching from initial states. A propositional formula is then generated by introducing $k + 1$ vectors of state variables, each representing a state in the prefix of length $k$, $\bar{s}_0, \ldots, \bar{s}_k$. Then the transition relation is unrolled $k$ times, substituting for states the appropriately labeled state variable vectors:

$$[\![ M ]\!]_k := I(\bar{s}_0) \wedge T(\bar{s}_0, \bar{s}_1) \wedge \cdots \wedge T(\bar{s}_{k-1}, \bar{s}_k) \tag{1}$$

Every initialized path of the model $M$ corresponds to an assignment that satisfies (1). When checking a safety property, $\mathbf{G}p$, where $p$ is a propositional formula, we search for a witness to $f = \mathbf{F}q$, where $q = \neg p$. A satisfying assignment to

(1) can be extended to a path that is a witness for $f$ (and a counterexample for $\mathbf{G}p$), iff $q$ holds at one of the $k + 1$ states or equivalently the assignment also satisfies:

$$[\![ f ]\!]_k := q(\bar{s}_0) \vee q(\bar{s}_1) \vee \cdots q(\bar{s}_k) \tag{2}$$

The final step is to translate the conjunction of (1) and (2) into CNF and check it with SAT tools such as [13, 15, 14]. Translation into CNF is described in [11].

## 4  Classical and Bounded Cone of Influence Reduction

The *Cone of Influence Reduction* is a well known technique[1]. For bounded model checking this technique can be specialized to the *Bounded Cone of Influence Reduction*, described below.

The basic idea of COI reduction is to construct a dependency graph of the state variables, rooted at the variables in the specification. The set of state variables in the graph is called the COI of the specification. In this paper, we call this the "classical" COI reduction. Variables not in the classical COI can not influence the validity of the specification and can therefore be removed from the model.

Let $dep(x)$ be the set of successors to variable $x$ in the state variable dependency graph, i.e., the set of variables in the support of the transition function for $x$. The *Bounded Cone of Influence Reduction* is based on the observation that, for any state $s_k$ along a path, the value of an arbitrary state variable, $x$, in the associated state variable vector, $\bar{s}_k$, can depend only on state variables in state variable vector $\bar{s}_j$, with $j < k$. Thus, it is only the copies, in $\bar{s}_{k-1}$, of the variables that are in $dep(x)$ that can determine the value of $x$ in $\bar{s}_k$. Other state variables, and their corresponding transition functions can be removed. If we are looking for violations of a safety property at state $\bar{s}_k$, this argument can be repeated, working backwards, until the initial state is reached.

For instance, consider the following model with five state variables $x_1, \ldots, x_5$ and transition functions

$$f_1 = 1, \quad f_2 = x_1, \quad f_3 = x_2, \quad f_4 = x_3, \quad f_5 = x_4$$

Assume the state variables are initialized to constants:

$$r_1 = 0, \quad r_2 = 1, \quad r_3 = 1, \quad r_4 = 1, \quad r_5 = 1$$

This model has only one execution sequence in which the 0 value is moved from $x_1$ to $x_5$. After the 0 has reached $x_5$ it vanishes, and all state variables stay at 1.

$$01111 \rightarrow 10111 \rightarrow 11011 \rightarrow 11101 \rightarrow 11110 \rightarrow 11111 \rightarrow \cdots$$

---

[1] Cone of influence reduction seems to have been discovered and utilized by a number of people, independently. We note that it can be seen as a special case, of Kurshan's localization reduction [8].

If the property to check is the safety property that $x_4$ is always true, i.e., $\mathbf{G}x_4$, classical COI reduction would remove just $x_5$. Now, a counterexample for this property can be found by unrolling the transition relation three times. Let us assume that we only want to check for a counterexample in the last state, $s_3$. To apply bounded COI we observe that $x_4$ in $\bar{s}_3$ only depends on $x_3$ in $\bar{s}_2$ which in turn depends on $x_2$ in $\bar{s}_1$, which only depends on the initial value of $x_1$. Therefore we can remove all other variables and their corresponding transitions. This application of bounded COI reduction results in the following formula:

$$\bar{s}_0(1) \leftrightarrow 0 \wedge \bar{s}_1(2) \leftrightarrow \bar{s}_0(1) \wedge \bar{s}_2(3) \leftrightarrow \bar{s}_0(2) \wedge \bar{s}_3(4) \leftrightarrow \bar{s}_0(3) \wedge \neg\bar{s}_3(4)$$

This formula is satisfiable, and its only satisfying assignment can be extended to a counterexample for the original formula, $\mathbf{G}x_4$. Without bounded COI, 12 more equalities would have been necessary.

For a formal treatment of the bounded COI reduction we define the *bounded dependency set*, $bdep(\bar{s}_i(j))$, of a component, $\bar{s}_i(j)$, of state variable vector, $\bar{s}_i$, as follows. Here, $\bar{s}_i$ represents a state $s_i$ along a path prefix:

$$bdep(\bar{s}_i(j)) \quad := \quad \text{if } i = 0 \text{ then } \emptyset \text{ else } \{\bar{s}_{i-1}(l) \mid x_l \in dep(x_j)\}$$

The *bounded COI*, $bcoi(\bar{s}_i(j))$, of component $\bar{s}_i(j)$ is defined, recursively, as the least set of variables that includes $\bar{s}_i(j)$, and includes, for each $\bar{s}_{i-1}(l) \in bdep(\bar{s}_i(j))$, if any, the variables in $bcoi(\bar{s}_{i-1}(l))$.

For a fixed $k$, the length of the considered prefix, we define the bounded COI of an LTL formula, $f$, as:

$$\text{bcoi}(k, f) := \{x \in bcoi(\bar{s}_i(j)) \mid \bar{s}_i(j) \in \text{var}(\llbracket\, f \,\rrbracket_k)\}$$

where $\text{var}(\llbracket\, f \,\rrbracket_k)$ is the set of variables of $\llbracket\, f \,\rrbracket_k$.

In (1) we can now remove all factors of the form $\bar{s}_i(j) \leftrightarrow \ldots$ where $\bar{s}_i(j) \notin bcoi(f)$, and derive (for simplicity, we do not remove initial state assignments):

$$\llbracket\, M \,\rrbracket_k^{\text{bcoi}(k,f)} := I(\bar{s}_0) \wedge T_0(\bar{s}_0, \bar{s}_1) \wedge \cdots \wedge T_{k-1}(\bar{s}_{k-1}, \bar{s}_k)$$

where

$$T_{i-1}(\bar{s}_{i-1}, \bar{s}_i) := \bigwedge_{\bar{s}_i(j) \in \text{bcoi}(k,f)} \bar{s}_i(j) \leftrightarrow f_j(\bar{s}_{i-1}) \quad \text{for } i = 1 \ldots k$$

The correctness of the bounded COI reduction is formulated in the following theorem.

**Theorem 1.** *Let $f = \mathbf{F}q$ be an LTL formula with $q$ a propositional formula. Then $\llbracket\, f \,\rrbracket_k \wedge \llbracket\, M \,\rrbracket_k$ is satisfiable iff $\llbracket\, f \,\rrbracket_k \wedge \llbracket\, M \,\rrbracket_k^{\text{bcoi}(k,f)}$ is satisfiable.*

## 5    Experiments

We used the bounded model checker, BMC, on subcircuits from a PowerPC microprocessor under design at Motorola's Somerset design center, in Austin,

Texas. BMC accepts a subset of the input format used by the widely known SMV model checker [9].

When a processor is under design at Somerset, designers insert assertions into the RTL simulation model. These Boolean expressions are important safety properties. The simulator flags an error if these are ever false. We checked, with BMC, 20 assertions chosen from 5 different processor design blocks. For each assertion, $p$, we:

1. Checked whether $p$ was a combinational tautology.
2. Checked whether $p$ was otherwise an inductive invariant.
3. Checked whether $\mathbf{AG}p$ held for various time bounds, $k$, from 0 to 20.

Each circuit latch was represented by a state variable having individual next state and initial state assignments. For the latter, we assigned the 0 or 1 value the latch would have after a designated power-on-reset sequence known to the designer. Primary inputs were modeled as unconstrained state variables, having neither next state nor initial state assignments.

For combinational tautology checking we deleted all initialization statements and ran BMC with $k = 0$, giving the propositional formula, $p$, as the specification. Under these conditions, the specification could hold only if $p$ held for all assignments to the variables in its support.

We then checked whether $p$ was an inductive invariant. A formula is an inductive invariant if it holds in all initial states and is preserved by the transition relation. Leaving all initialization assignments intact, for each design block and each formula $p$, we gave $p$ as the specification and set $k = 0$. This determined whether each $p$ held in the single, valid initial state of each design. Then, for each design block and for each formula, $p$, we removed all initialization assignments and specified $p$ as an initial state predicate. We set $k = 1$ and checked the specification $\mathbf{AG}p$. If the specification held, this meant the successors of every state satisfying $p$, also satisfied $p$. Note that $\mathbf{AG}p$ could fail to hold exclusively due to transitions out of unreachable states. Therefore, this technique can only show that $p$ *is* an invariant, it cannot show that it is not.

The output of BMC is a Boolean formula in CNF that is given to a satisfiability solver. In these experiments, we used both the GRASP [13] and SATO [15] satisfiability solvers. When giving results, we give the best result from the two.

We also ran a recent version of the SMV model checker on each of the 20 $\mathbf{AG}p$ specifications. We used command line options that enabled the early detection, during reachability analysis, of false $\mathbf{AG}p$ properties, so that SMV did not need to compute a fixpoint. This made the comparison to BMC more appropriate. We also enabled dynamic variable ordering when running SMV, and used a partitioned transition relation.

All experiments were run with wall clock time limits. The satisfiability solvers had 15 minutes for each run, while SMV had an hour. BMC was not timed, as the task of translating to CNF is usually done quite quickly. The satisfiability solving and SMV runs were done on RS6000 model 390 workstations, having 256 megabytes of local memory.

We did not model the interfaces between the 5 design blocks and the rest of the microprocessor or the external computer system in which the processor would be placed. This is commonly referred to as "environment modeling". One would ideally like to do environment modeling, since subcircuits usually work correctly only under certain input constraints. However, one will get true positives for safety properties with a totally unconstrained environment. Given Kripke structures $M'$ and $M$, $M'$ representing a design block with an unconstrained environment and $M$ the same block with its real, constrained environment, it is obvious that $M'$ simulates $M$, i.e. $M \leq M'$ in the simulation preorder. It has been shown in [4,6] that if $f$ is an $ACTL$ formula, as are all the properties in these experiments, then $M' \models f$ implies $M \models f$.

Our experiments did result in false negatives. Upon inspection, and after checking with circuit designers, it seems all the counterexamples generated were due to impossible input behaviors. However, our purpose in these experiments was to show the capacity and speed of bounded model checking, and the false negatives did not obscure these results. We discuss, in Section 6, a methodology wherein false negatives could be lessened or eliminated, by incorporating input constraints into the bounded model checking. We certainly feel this would be the way to use bounded model checking in a non-experimental, industrial application. The reader may also want to refer to [7], where input constraints are considered in a BDD based verification environment.

## 5.1 Experimental Results

The 5 design blocks we chose all came from a single PowerPC microprocessor, and were all *control* circuits, having little or no datapath elements. Their sizes were as follows:

| Circuit | Latches | PIs | Gates |
|---------|---------|-----|-------|
| bbc | 209 | 479 | 4852 |
| ccc | 371 | 336 | 4529 |
| cdc | 278 | 319 | 5474 |
| dlc | 282 | 297 | 2205 |
| sdc | 265 | 199 | 2544 |

Before COI

| Circuit | Spec | Latches | PIs |
|---------|------|---------|-----|
| bbc | 1 - 4 | 150 | 242 |
| ccc | 1 - 2 | 77 | 207 |
| cdc | 1 - 4 | 119 | 190 |
| dlc | 1 - 6 | 119 | 170 |
| dlc | 7 | 119 | 153 |
| sdc | 1 - 2 | 113 | 121 |
| sdc | 3 | 23 | 15 |

After (classical) COI

On the left, we report the original size of each circuit, and on the right, the sizes after classical COI reduction. Each specification is given an arbitrary numeric label. These do not relate across design blocks, e.g., specification 2 of *dlc* is in no way related to specification 2 of *sdc*. Many properties involved much the same circuitry on a design block, as can be seen by the large number of cones of influence having identical numbers of latches and PIs. However, these reduced circuits were not identical, though they may have differed only in how the variables in the specification depended, combinationally, upon latches and PIs.

| k | Bounded COI | Classic COI | No COI |
|---|---|---|---|
| 0 | 137 / 449 | 234 / 546 | 376 / 688 |
| 1 | 1023 / 3762 | 1801 / 6790 | 3402 / 12749 |
| 2 | 2330 / 8946 | 3367 / 13025 | 6426 / 24801 |
| 3 | 3755 / 14631 | 4931 / 19259 | 9450 / 36851 |
| 4 | 5259 / 20608 | 6496 / 25492 | 12473 / 48901 |
| 5 | 6820 / 26821 | 8060 / 31725 | 15496 / 60951 |
| 10 | 14643 / 57987 | 15883 / 62891 | 30613 / 121202 |
| 15 | 22466 / 89153 | 23706 / 94057 | 45730 / 181452 |
| 20 | 30288 / 120319 | 31529 / 125223 | 60846 / 241702 |

Average Bounded COI Reduction

| Circuit | Spec | Tautology | Tran Rel'n | Init State |
|---|---|---|---|---|
| bbc | 1 | N | N | Y |
| bbc | 2 | N | Y | N |
| bbc | 3 | N | N | Y |
| bbc | 4 | N | N | Y |
| ccc | 1 | N | N | Y |
| ccc | 2 | N | N | Y |
| cdc | 1 | N | N | Y |
| cdc | 2 | Y | Y | Y |
| cdc | 3 | Y | Y | Y |
| cdc | 4 | Y | Y | Y |
| dlc | 1 | N | N | Y |
| dlc | 2 | N | N | Y |
| dlc | 3 | N | N | Y |
| dlc | 4 | N | N | Y |
| dlc | 5 | N | N | Y |
| dlc | 6 | N | N | Y |
| dlc | 7 | N | N | Y |
| sdc | 1 | N | Y | Y |
| sdc | 2 | N | N | Y |
| sdc | 3 | N | N | N |

Tautology and Invariance Checking

We ran BMC for values of $k$ of $0, 1, 2, 3, 4, 5, 10, 15$ and $20$, on each specification. For each of these, we had BMC create CNF files having no COI reduction, only classical COI, and both classical and bounded COI. In the table labeled "Average Bounded COI Reduction", we give average sizes of all these CNF files. We averaged the number of literals and clauses (a clause is a disjunct of literals) in all the CNF files for each $k$, i.e., for all specifications, for all design blocks, for that $k$. We checked, by hand, that this averaging did not obscure the median case. In the table, we give to the left of a slash, the average number of literals for a $k$ value, and to the right, the average number of clauses. It can be seen that the advantage of bounded COI decreases with increasing $k$. Intuitively, this is because, going out in time, eventually values are computed for all state variables in the classical cone of influence. However, at $k$ up to 10, bounded COI gives distinct benefit. Since bounded model checking seems to be most effective at finding short counterexamples, and, since tautology and invariance checking are run at low $k$, we feel bounded COI augments the system's strengths.

The table labeled "Tautology and Invariance Checking" has columns for tautology checking, for preservation by the transition relation and for preservation in initial states. The last two must both hold for a formula to be an inductive invariant. These runs were done with bounded COI enabled. A "Y" in a column indicates a condition holding, an "N" that it does not. Time and memory usage are not listed, since these were $\leq 1$ second $\leq 5$ megabytes in all but three cases. In the worst case, $sdc$ specification 2, 60 seconds of CPU time and 6.5 megabytes of memory were required, for checking preservation by the transition relation. Clearly, tautology and invariance checking can be remarkably inexpensive. In contrast, these can be quite costly with BDD based methods.

| circuit | spec | long k | vars | clauses | time | mem | holds | fail k |
|---------|------|--------|------|---------|------|-----|-------|--------|
| $bbc$ | 1 | 4 | 7873 | 30174 | 35.4 | NR | Y | |
| $bbc$ | 2 | 15 | 34585 | 93922 | 5.5 | 84 | N | 0 |
| $bbc$ | 3 | 10 | 16814 | 63300 | 58 | NR | Y | |
| $bbc$ | 4 | 5 | 9487 | 35658 | 18 | NR | Y | |
| $ccc$ | 1 | 5 | 9396 | 40450 | 1.3 | 36 | N | 1 |
| $ccc$ | 2 | 5 | 9148 | 38841 | 1.4 | 39 | N | 1 |
| $cdc$ | 1 | 20 | 49167 | 207764 | 128 | 77 | N | 2 |
| $cdc$ | 2 | 20 | 50825 | 213137 | 4.7 | NR | Y | |
| $cdc$ | 3 | 20 | 50571 | 213614 | 4.7 | NR | Y | |
| $cdc$ | 4 | 20 | 50491 | 212406 | 4.8 | NR | Y | |
| $dlc$ | 1 | 20 | 18378 | 71291 | 2.9 | 64 | N | 2 |
| $dlc$ | 2 | 20 | 18024 | 69830 | 2,8 | 63 | N | 2 |
| $dlc$ | 3 | 20 | 17603 | 68333 | 2.6 | 60 | N | 2 |
| $dlc$ | 4 | 20 | 18085 | 69942 | 2.73 | 61 | N | 1 |
| $dlc$ | 5 | 20 | 18378 | 71291 | 2.9 | 60 | N | 2 |
| $dlc$ | 6 | 20 | 17712 | 68714 | 2.7 | NR | N | 2 |
| $dlc$ | 7 | 20 | 16217 | 63781 | 2.4 | 64 | N | 0 |
| $sdc$ | 1 | 4 | 5554 | 20893 | 72 | 14 | Y | |
| $sdc$ | 2 | 4 | 5545 | 20841 | 548 | 21 | Y | |
| $sdc$ | 3 | 20 | 4119 | 15168 | - | 3 | N | 0 |

Highest $k$ Values

The table labeled "Highest $k$ Values" shows the results of increasing $k$. These runs, again, were with bounded COI. We ran to large $k$ regardless of whether we found counterexamples, or determined a property was an invariant, at lower $k$. It was sometimes difficult to obtain memory usage statistics during satisfiability solving; but, this usually does not exceed that needed to store the CNF formula. In the table, NR means not recorded (data unavailable). Time is given in seconds, memory usage in megabytes, with dashes appearing where these were insignificant. The "vars" and "clauses" columns give the number of literals and clauses in the CNF file for the highest value of $k$ on which satisfiability solving completed, the $k$ in the "long k" column. The time and memory usage listings are for satisfiability solving at this highest $k$ value. A "Y" in the "holds" column indicates the property held through all values of $k$ tested, and an "N" indicates a counterexample was found. When these were found, the "fail k" column gives the the first $k$ at which a counterexample appeared. Time and memory consumption are not listed for the runs giving counterexamples, because the satisfiability solving took less than a second, and no more than 5 megabytes of memory, in each case!

Lastly, the BDD-based model checker, SMV, completed only one of the 20 verifications it was given. The 19 others all timed out at one hour of wall clock time, with SMV unable to build the BDDs for the partitioned transition relation. SMV was only able to complete the verification of $sdc$, specification 3. Classical COI for this specification gave a very small circuit, having only 23 latches and 15 PIs. SMV found the specification false in the initial state, in approximately 2 minutes. Even this, however, can be contrasted to BMC needing 2 seconds to translate the specification to CNF, and the satisfiability solver needing less than 1 second to check it!

## 6 A Verification Methodology

Our experimental results lead us to propose an automated methodology for checking safety properties on industrial designs. In what follows, we assume a design divided up into separate blocks, as is the norm with hierarchical VLSI designs. Our methodology is as follows:

1. Annotate each design block with Boolean formulae required to hold at all time points. Call these the block's *inner assertions*.
2. Annotate each design block with Boolean formulae describing constraints on that block's inputs. Call these the block's *input constraints*.
3. Use the procedure outlined in Section 6.1 to check each block's inner assertions under its input constraints, using bounded model checking with satisfiability solving.

This methodology could be extended to include *monitors* for satisfaction of sequential constraints, in the manner described in [7], where input constraints were considered in the context of BDD based model checking.

### 6.1 Safety Property Checking Procedure

Let us consider a Kripke structure, $K$, for a design block having input constraints, $c$. A *constrained Kripke structure*, $K_c$, can be derived from $K$ as in

Section 2. To check whether an inner block assertion, $p$, is an invariant in $K_c$, we need not work with $K_c$ directly. Unrolling the transition relation of $K_c$, as per formula (1) of Section 3, is entirely equivalent to unrolling the transition relation of $K$, and conjoining each term with the constraint function, $c$:

$$[\![ M ]\!]_k := I(\bar{s}_0) \wedge c(\bar{s}_0) \wedge T(\bar{s}_0, \bar{s}_1) \wedge c(\bar{s}_1) \wedge \cdots \wedge T(\bar{s}_{k-1}, \bar{s}_k) \wedge c(\bar{s}_k) \qquad (3)$$

The steps for checking whether a block's inner assertion, $p$, is an invariant under input constraints, $c$, are:

1. Check whether $p$ is a combinational tautology in $K$. If it is, exit.
2. Check whether $p$ is an inductive invariant for $K$. If it is, exit.
3. Check whether $p$ is a combinational tautology in $K_c$. If it is, go to step 6.
4. Check whether $p$ is an inductive invariant for $K_c$. It it is, go to step 6.
5. Check if a bounded length counterexample exists to $\mathbf{AG}p$ in $K_c$. If one is found, there is no need to examine $c$, since the counterexample would exist without input constraints[2]. If a counterexample is not found, go to step 6. The input constraints may need to be reformulated and this procedure repeated from step 3.
6. Check the input constraints, $c$, on pertinent design blocks, as explained below.

Inputs that are constrained in one design block, $A$, will, in general, be outputs of another design block, $B$. To check $A$'s input constraints, we turn them into inner assertions for $B$, and check them with the above procedure. One must take precautions, however, against circular reasoning. Circular reasoning can be detected automatically, however, and should not, therefore, be a barrier to this methodology.

The ease with which we carried out tautology and invariance checking indicates the above is entirely feasible. Searching for a counterexample, step 5, may become costly at high $k$ values; however, this can be arbitrarily limited. It is expected that design teams would set limits for formal verification, and would complement its use with simulation, for the remainder of available resources.

## 7 Conclusion

In this paper, we have outlined a specialized version of cone of influence reduction for bounded model checking. The present set of experiments, on a large and complex PowerPC microprocessor, are compelling. They tell us that, for some applications, the efficiency of model checking has increased by orders of magnitude. The fact that the BDD-based SMV model checker failed to complete on all but one of 20 examples, underscores this point. We still believe, however, that BDD-based model checking fills important needs. Certainly, it seems to be the

---

[2] This is implied by the theorems for ACTL formulae in [4, 6], which we referred to in Section 5

only technique that can presently find long counterexamples, though, of course, this can be done only for designs that fall within its capacity limitations.

We feel that new verification methodologies can now be introduced in industry, to take advantage of bounded model checking. We have outlined one such procedure here, for checking safety properties. Our hope is that the widened use of model checking will illuminate further possibilities for optimization.

## References

1. A. Biere, A. Cimatti, Edmund M. Clarke, and Y. Zhu. Symbolic model checking without BDDs. In *TACAS'99*, 1999. to appear.
2. J. R. Burch, E. M. Clarke, K. L. McMillan, D. L. Dill, and L. J. Hwang. Symbolic model checking: $10^{20}$ states and beyond. *Information and Computation*, 98(2):142–170, June 1992. Originally presented at the 1990 Symposium on Logic in Computer Science (LICS90).
3. E. M. Clarke and E. A. Emerson. Design and synthesis of synchronization skeletons using branching time temporal logic. In *Logic of Programs: Workshop, Yorktown Heights, NY*, volume 131 of *Lecture Notes in Computer Science*. Springer-Verlag, May 1981.
4. E. M. Clarke, O. Grumberg, and D. E. Long. Model checking and abstraction. In *Proc. 19th Ann. ACM Symp. on Principles of Prog. Lang.*, Jan., 1992.
5. O. Coudert, J. C. Madre, and C. Berthet. Verifying temporal properties of sequential machines without building their state diagrams. In *Proc. 10th Int'l Computer Aided Verification Converence*, pages 23–32, 1990.
6. O. Grumberg and D. E. Long. Model checking and modular verification. *ACM Transactions on Programming Languages and Systems*, 16:843–872, May, 1994.
7. M. Kaufmann, A. Martin, and C. Pixley. Design constraints in symbolic model checking. In *Proc. 10th Int'l Computer Aided Verification Converence*, June, 1998.
8. R. P. Kurshan. *Computer-Aided Verification of Coordinating Processes: The Automata-Theoretic Approach*, pages 170–172. Princeton University Press, Princeton, New Jersey, 1994.
9. K. L. McMillan. *Symbolic Model Checking: An Approach to the State Explosion Problem*. Kluwer Academic Publishers, 1993.
10. C. Pixley. Verifying temporal properties of sequential machines without building their state diagrams. In *Proc. 10th Int'l Computer Aided Verification Converence*, pages 54–64, 1990.
11. D. Plaisted and S. Greenbaum. A structure-preserving clause form translation. *Journal of Symbolic Computation*, 2:293–304, 1986.
12. J. P. Quielle and J. Sifakis. Specification and verification of concurrent systems in CESAR. In *Proc. 5th Int. Symp. in Programming*, 1981.
13. J. P. M. Silva. Search algorithms for satisfiability problems in combinational switching circuits. *Ph.D. Dissertation, EECS Department, University of Michigan*, May 1995.
14. G. Stalmarck and M. Säflund. Modeling and verifying systems and software in propositional logic. In B. K. Daniels, editor, *Safety of Computer Control Systems (SAFECOMP'90)*, pages 31–36. Pergamon Press, 1990.
15. H. Zhang. A decision procedure for propositional logic. *Assoc. for Automated Reasoning Newsletter*, 22:1–3, 1993.

# Model Checking the IBM Gigahertz Processor: An Abstraction Algorithm for High-Performance Netlists

Jason Baumgartner[1], Tamir Heyman[2], Vigyan Singhal[3], and Adnan Aziz[4]

[1] IBM Corporation, Austin, Texas 78758, USA,
jasonb@austin.ibm.com
[2] IBM Haifa Research Laboratory, Haifa, Israel,
tamirh@vnet.ibm.com
[3] Cadence Berkeley Labs, Berkeley, California 94704, USA,
vigyan@cadence.com
[4] The University of Texas at Austin, Austin, Texas 78712, USA,
adnan@ece.utexas.edu

**Abstract.** A common technique in high-performance hardware design is to intersperse combinatorial logic freely between level-sensitive latch layers (wherein one layer is transparent during the "high" clock phase, and the next during the "low"). Such logic poses a challenge to verification – unless the two-phase netlist $N$ may be abstracted to a full-cycle model $N'$ (wherein each memory element may sample every cycle), model checking of $N$ requires at least twice as many state variables as would be necessary to obtain equivalent coverage for $N'$. We present an algorithm to automatically obtain such an abstraction by selectively eliminating latches from both layers. The abstraction is valid for model checking CTL* formulae which reason solely about latches of a single phase. This algorithm has been implemented in IBM's model checker, RuleBase, and has been used to enable model checking of IBM's Gigahertz Processor, which may not have been feasible otherwise. This abstraction has furthermore allowed verification engineers to write properties and environments more efficiently.

## 1 Introduction

A *latch* is a hardware memory element with two Boolean inputs – data and clock – and one Boolean output. A behavioral definition for latches is provided in [1]. High performance netlists often must use level-sensitive latches [2]. For such a latch, when its clock input is a certain value (e.g., a logical "1"), the value at its data input will be propagated to its data output (i.e., transparent mode); otherwise, its last propagated value is held at its output.

The clock is modeled as a signal which alternates between 0 and 1 at every time-step. A latch which samples when the clock is a 1 will be denoted as an L1 latch; one which samples when the clock is a 0 will be denoted as an L2 latch. Hardware design rules, arising from timing constraints, require any logic path between two L1 latches to pass through an L2 latch, and vice-versa. An elementary design style requires each L1 latch to feed directly to an L2 latch (called a master-slave latch pair), and allow only L2 to drive combinatorial logic. However, a common high-performance hardware development technique involves utilizing combinatorial logic freely between L1 and L2 latches to better utilize each half-cycle. It should be noted that such designs are typically explicitly implemented in this manner; this topology is not the byproduct of a synthesis tool.

There are two major problems with the verification of such netlists. First, because of the larger number of latches, the verification tool requires much more time and memory. Additionally, the manual modeling of environments and properties is more complicated in that they must be written in terms of the less abstract half-cycle model, and an oscillating clock must be explicitly introduced.

Most hardware compilers will allow automatic translations of a master-slave latch pair into a single flip-flop; retiming algorithms [3] may be used to retime the netlist such that L1-L2 layers become adjacent and one-to-one. However, retiming adds complexity in that the specification, the environment, and any witnesses / counterexamples (all of which may "observe" the netlist), may need to be retimed as well to match the retimed, full-cycle model.

We develop an efficient algorithm for abstracting a half-cycle netlist $N$ to a full-cycle model $N'$, which may be utilized for enhanced verification in any FSM-based verification framework (e.g., simulation and model checking). We will achieve this by selectively eliminating some latches. We will use a notion of dual-phase-bisimulation equivalence between the abstracted and unabstracted models. This equivalence ensures that specification and environment written in terms of L2 latch outputs need not be modified other than a conversion to full-cycle format (as will be discussed in Sect. 3). Our algorithm performs maximum such reductions, and thus provides an important model reduction step which may greatly augment existing techniques (such as retiming, cone-of-influence, etc.). As we show, this reduction alone reduces the number of state variables by at least one-half, and has greatly enhanced the model checking of IBM's Gigahertz Processor, which may not have been feasible otherwise (as demonstrated by our experimental evidence). This abstraction is now part of the model checker RuleBase [4]. Additionally, designers and verification engineers prefer to reason about the full-cycle models.

The optimality of the algorithm results from the identification of *minimal dependent layers (MDL)* of latches, and removing all L1s or all L2s per MDL.

**Definition 1.** *A dependent layer is a set of L1 and L2 latches L1' and L2', such that L2' is a superset of all latches in the transitive fanout of L1', and L1' is a superset of all latches in the transitive fanin of L2'.*

**Definition 2.** *A dependent layer is termed* minimal *if and only if there does not exist a nonempty set of L1 and L2 latches L' which may be removed from that layer and still result in a nonempty dependent layer.*

74

Consider the netlist in Fig. 1 (the triangles denote combinatorial logic, and the rectangles denote latches). The L1 latches are shaded. The two unique MDLs are marked with dotted boxes. Merely removing all L1s or all L2s will not yield an optimum reduction in this case; the L1s of layer A, and the L2s of layer B should be removed to yield an optimum solution for this netlist, which removes four of the six latches.

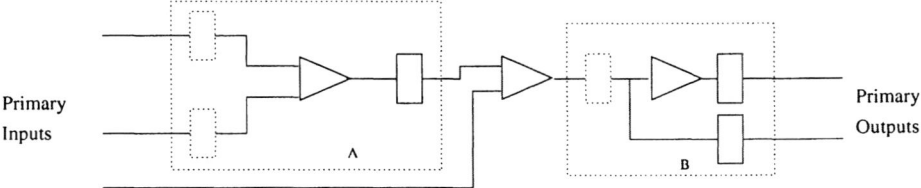

**Fig. 1.** Sample Netlist with Two Minimal Dependent Layers

In Sect. 2 we introduce a half-cycle netlist, and two different abstracted full-cycle models of this netlist. In Sect. 3 we study the state space of the netlist and its two abstracted models to demonstrate the validity of the abstraction for CTL* formulae which reason solely about latches of a single type (L1 or L2). In Sect. 4 we introduce the algorithm used to perform the netlist reduction, and demonstrate its optimality. In Sect. 5 we give some experimental results of the use of this algorithm as implemented in RuleBase [4] for application to IBM's Gigahertz Processor.

## 2  Half-Cycle versus Full-Cycle Models

Consider the half-cycle netlist, denoting an MDL, shown in Fig. 2. All nets and primitives may be vectors.

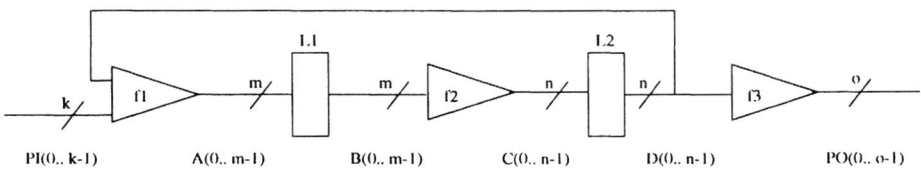

**Fig. 2.** Half-Cycle Netlist $N$

**Definition 3.** *A* netlist is *dual-phase (DP)* if and only if:

*1. All latches in the transitive fanouts of L1 latches are L2 latches, and*

2. *All latches in the transitive fanin of L2 latches are L1 latches, and*
3. *No primary inputs exist in the transitive fanin of any L2 latch, and*
4. *No primary outputs exist in the transitive fanout of any L1 latch.*

The first two rules are enforced by hardware timing constraints. Note that, at the periphery of a design, there may be some inputs which have L2 latches in their transitive fanout, and outputs which are in the transitive fanout of L1 latches (thus violating rules 3 and 4). While the analysis presented in this paper disallows such connectivity for simplicity, these cases are supported by our implementation; for ease of reasoning, we have found it beneficial to preserve all L2 latches which violate rule 3, and to remove all L1 latches which violate rule 4.

The notion of MDLs (Defn. 2) allows us to partition the design under test into a maximum number of partitions such that each is DP. Next, we propose two abstractions for DP netlists. For each DP partition of the original design, one of these two abstractions may be applied independently of the other partitions, thus yielding an overall abstraction which has a globally minimum number of latches (refer to Theorem 5). This minimum would, in general, be less than removing either all of the L1 or all of the L2 latches.

In this paper, we assume that properties may only refer to the L2 nets (which we term $L2 - visible$ properties). In our actual implementation, we also handle the case where the properties refer only to L1 nets. Furthermore, by forcing our tool to remove only L1 or only L2 latches (i.e., restricting its freedom to choose which type to remove), each property may refer to both types of nets. However, we skip these generalizations in this paper.

## 2.1 The Abstracted Models

The values of the nets in Fig. 2 are specified for time-steps $i \geq 0$. The pre-specified initial values of the latches are $B_0(0..m - 1)$ and $D_0(0..n - 1)$. Let $c$ denote the clock input, which initializes to 1, and alternates between 1 and 0 at every time step, indicating whether the L1 or L2 latches (respectively) are presently transparent. The subscript $i$ means "at time $i$".

For $i > 0$, if $(c_i = 1)$, $B_i(0..m - 1) = A_{i-1}(0..m - 1)$, else $B_i(0..m - 1) = B_{i-1}(0..m - 1)$. Similarly, for $i > 0$, if $(c_i = 1)$, $D_i(0..n - 1) = D_{i-1}(0..n - 1)$, else $D_i(0..n - 1) = C_{i-1}(0..n - 1)$. For the combinatorial nets, $A_i(0..m - 1) = f1(PI_i(0..k - 1), D_i(0..n - 1))$; $C_i(0..n - 1) = f2(B_i(0..m - 1))$; and $PO_i(0..o - 1) = f3(D_i(0..n - 1))$.

Either layer of latches may be removed (and the remaining layer transformed to flip-flops which may be clocked every cycle – not by an alternating clock), and the resulting abstracted model will be shown to be bisimilar to the original netlist. Fig. 3 shows the first abstraction with layer L2 removed. We need a new variable, labeled $f$, whose initial value is 1, and thereafter is 0. This latch ensures that the initial value $D_0$ from the original netlist $N$ (which need not be deterministic) is applied to the combinatorial nets $D$ in $N'$. $B_0(0..m - 1)$ is still the initial value of the remaining latches. For $i > 0$, $B_i(0..m-1) = A_{i-1}(0..m-1)$.

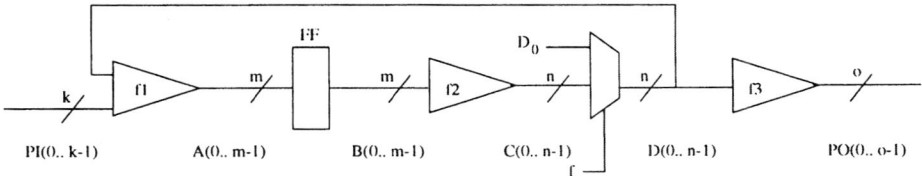

**Fig. 3.** Abstracted Model $N'$

If $(f_i = 1)$, $D_i(0..n - 1) = D_0(0..n - 1)$, else $D_i(0..n - 1) = C_i(0..n - 1)$. For the other combinatorial nets, $A_i(0..m - 1) = f1(PI_i(0..k - 1), D_i(0..n - 1))$; $C_i(0..n - 1) = f2(B_i(0..m - 1))$; and $PO_i(0..o - 1) = f3(D_i(0..n - 1))$.

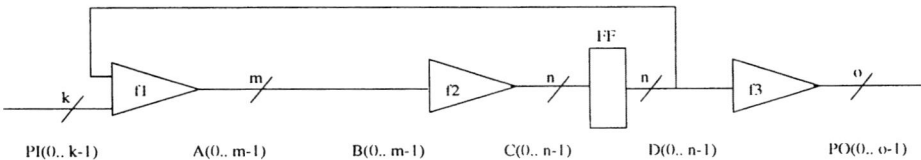

**Fig. 4.** Alternate Abstracted Model $N''$

Fig. 4 illustrates the second abstraction, which removes the L1s. $D_0(0..n - 1)$ is the initial value of the remaining latches; $D_i(0..n-1) = C_{i-1}(0..n-1)$. For the combinatorial nets, $A_i(0..m-1) = f1(PI_i(0..k-1), D_i(0..n-1))$; $B_i(0..m-1) = A_i(0..m-1)$; $C_i(0..n-1) = f2(B_i(0..m-1))$; and $PO_i(0..o-1) = f3(D_i(0..n-1))$. Note that the $f$ variable is unnecessary for this abstraction; the initial value of the removed latch does not propagate.

It is noteworthy that either one of the two abstractions may be chosen; since the layers may be of differing width ($m \neq n$), the removal of one layer may result in a smaller state space than the other. We term both of the above reductions as dual-phase (DP) reductions.

## 3 Validity of Abstraction

We define a notion of dual-phase-bisimulation relation (inspired by Milner's bisimulation relations [5]); this notion is preserved for composition of Moore machines. Further, if two structures are related by a dual-phase-bisimulation relation, we show that $L2-visible$ CTL* properties are preserved (modulo a simple transformation). We show the existence of a dual-phase-bisimulation relation for both abstractions presented in the previous section.

We will relate our designs to Kripke structures, which are defined as follows.

**Definition 4.** *A Kripke structure* $\mathcal{K} = \langle S, S_0, \mathcal{A}, \mathcal{L}, R \rangle$, *where* $S$ *is a set of states,* $S_0 \subseteq S$ *is the set of initial states,* $\mathcal{A}$ *is the set of atomic propositions,* $\mathcal{L} : S \rightarrow 2^{\mathcal{A}}$ *is the labeling function, and* $R : S \times S$ *is the transition relation.*

Our designs are described as Moore machines (using Moore machines, instead of the more general Mealy machines [6], simplifies the exposition for this paper, though our implementation is able to handle Mealy machines). We use the following definitions for a Moore machine and its associated structure (similar to Grumberg and Long [7]).

**Definition 5.** *A* Moore machine $\mathcal{M} = \langle L, S, S_0, I, O, V, \delta, \gamma \rangle$, *where $L$ is the set of state variables (latches), $S : 2^L$ is the set of states, $S_0 \subseteq S$ is the set of initial states, $I$ is the set of input variables, $O$ is the set of output variables, $V \subseteq L$ is the set of property visible nets, $\delta : S \times 2^I \times S$ is the transition relation, and $\gamma : S \rightarrow 2^O$ is the output function.*

**Definition 6.** *The* structure *of a Moore machine $\mathcal{M} = \langle L, S, S_0, I, O, V, \delta, \gamma \rangle$ is denoted by $K(M) = \langle S^K, S_0^K, \mathcal{A}, \mathcal{L}, R \rangle$, where $S^K = 2^L \times 2^I$, $S_0^K = S_0 \times 2^I$, $\mathcal{A} = V$, $\mathcal{L} = S^K \rightarrow 2^V$, and $R((s, x), (t, y))$ iff $\delta(s, x, t)$.*

In the sequel we will use $M$ to denote the Moore machine as well as the structure for the machine. We now define our notion of dual-phase-bisimilarity, which characterizes our proposed abstraction.

**Definition 7.** *Let $M$ and $M'$ be two structures. A relation $G \subseteq S \times S'$ is a* dual-phase-bisimulation *relation if $G(s, s')$ implies:*

1. $\mathcal{L}(s) = \mathcal{L}'(s')$.
2. *for every $t, v \in S$, such that $R(s, v)$ and $R(v, t)$, we have $\mathcal{L}(s) = \mathcal{L}(v)$, and there exists $t' \in S'$ such that $R'(s', t')$ and $G(t, t')$.*
3. *for every $t' \in S'$, such that $R'(s', t')$, there exist $t, v \in S$ such that $\mathcal{L}(v) = \mathcal{L}'(s')$, $R(s, v)$, $R(v, t)$, and $G(t, t')$.*

*We say that a dual-phase-bisimulation exists from $M$ to $M'$ (denoted by $M \prec M'$) iff there exists a dual-phase-bisimulation relation $G$ such that for all $s \in S_0$ and $t' \in S_0'$, there exist $t \in S_0$ and $s' \in S_0'$ such that $G(s, s')$ and $G(t, t')$.*

Notice that, in the above definition, such a dual-phase-bisimulation relation may exist only if $M$ has a dual-phase nature – i.e., for all $i$, the visible labels of states $s_{2i}$ and $s_{2i+1}$ are equivalent.

An infinite path $\pi = (s_0, s_1, s_2, \ldots)$ is a sequence of states ($s_0 \in S_0$) such that any two successive states are related by the transition relation (i.e., $R(s_i, s_{i+1})$). Let $\pi^i$ denote the suffix path $(s_i, s_{i+1}, s_{i+2}, \ldots)$. We say that the dual-phase-bisimulation relation exists between two infinite paths $\pi = (s_0, s_1, s_2, \ldots)$ and $\pi' = (s_0', s_1', s_2', \ldots)$, denoted by $G(\pi, \pi')$, iff for every $i$, $G(s_{2i}, s_i')$.

The composition of Moore machines ($M_1 \parallel M_2$) is defined in the standard way [7], by allowing the outputs of one design to become inputs of the other. The following result is shown similarly as the proof that simulation precedence is preserved under composition [7].

**Theorem 1.** *If $M_1 \prec M_1'$ and $M_2 \prec M_2'$, then a dual-phase-bisimulation exists from the Moore composition $M_1 \parallel M_2$ to the Moore composition $M_1' \parallel M_2'$ (i.e., $M_1 \parallel M_2 \prec M_1' \parallel M_2'$).*

The set of dual-phase-reducible CTL* formulae is a subset of CTL* formulae [8], and is a set of state and path formulae given by the following inductive definition. We also define the dual-phase reduction for such formulae:

**Definition 8.** *A* dual-phase-reducible (DPR) *CTL\* formula* $\phi$, *and its dual-phase reduction,* *denoted by* $\Omega(\phi)$, *are defined inductively as:*

- *every atomic proposition p is a DPR state formula* $\phi = p$; $\Omega(\phi) = p$.
- *if p is a DPR state formula, so is* $\phi = \neg p$; $\Omega(\phi) = \neg\Omega(p)$.
- *if p, q are DPR state formulae, so is* $\phi = p \wedge q$; $\Omega(\phi) = \Omega(p) \wedge \Omega(q)$.
- *if p is a DPR path formula, then* $\phi = \mathsf{E}p$ *is a DPR state formula;* $\Omega(\phi) = \mathsf{E}\Omega(p)$.
- *each DPR state formula* $\phi$ *is also a DPR path formula* $\phi$.
- *if p is a DPR path formula, so is* $\phi = \neg p$; $\Omega(\phi) = \neg\Omega(p)$.
- *if p, q are DPR path formulae, so is* $\phi = p \wedge q$; $\Omega(\phi) = \Omega(p) \wedge \Omega(q)$.
- *if p is a DPR path formula, so is* $\phi = \mathsf{XX}p$; $\Omega(\phi) = \mathsf{X}\Omega(p)$.
- *if p, q are DPR path formulae, so is* $\phi = p\mathsf{U}q$; $\Omega(\phi) = \Omega(p)\mathsf{U}\Omega(q)$.

Note that $XX$ is transformed to $X$ through the reduction; intuitively, this is due to the "doubling of the clock frequency", or the replacement of the oscillating clock with an "always active" clock, enabled by the abstraction. As an example, if $\phi = \mathsf{AG}(rdy \rightarrow (\mathsf{AXAX}(req \rightarrow \mathsf{AF}(ack))))$, then $\Omega(\phi) = \mathsf{AG}(rdy \rightarrow (\mathsf{AX}(req \rightarrow \mathsf{AF}(ack))))$ (note that $\mathsf{AXAXp}$ is equivalent to $\mathsf{AXXp}$). $L2 - visible$ properties may be readily expressed utilizing DPR CTL*, since latches of any given type may only toggle every second time-step; there is no need to express such a property with a single $X$, which is the only restriction we impose upon full CTL* expressibility.

**Theorem 2.** *Let s and s' be states of M and M', and* $\pi = (s_0, s_1, s_2, \ldots)$ *and* $\pi' = (s_0', s_1', s_2', \ldots)$ *be infinite paths of M and M', respectively. If G is a dual-phase-bisimulation relation such that* $G(s, s')$ *and* $G(\pi, \pi')$, *then*

1. *for every dual-phase-reducible CTL\* state formula* $\phi$, $s \models \phi$ *iff* $s' \models \Omega(\phi)$.
2. *for every dual-phase-reducible CTL\* path formula* $\phi$, $\pi \models \phi$ *iff* $\pi' \models \Omega(\phi)$.

We describe the Moore specifications (Defn. 5) for the abstractions presented in Sect. 2. Refer to Figs. 2-4. Let $c$ be the clock variable which alternates between 1 and 0, indicating whether the L1 or L2 latches are presently transparent, respectively. The original netlist $N = \langle L^N, S^N, S_0^N, PI, PO, V^N, \delta^N, \lambda^N \rangle$ has $L^N = B \cup D \cup \{c\}$, $V^N = D$, and the transition and output functions, $\delta^N$ and $\lambda^N$, are given by the formulae in Sect. 2.1. The state space of $N$ is denoted by $(b, d, v, x)$, comprising of the values of latches $B$, $D$, $c$, and the input $PI$, respectively.

As presented here, the properties cannot refer to inputs – $V^N$ does not contain inputs. This restriction is due to the requirement that visible labels of states $s_{2i}$ and $s_{2i+1}$ are identical (Defn. 7), and is not necessary if the inputs to the design do not change values between $s_{2i}$ and $s_{2i+1}$. This assumption is typically sound; except for clock inputs (which no longer need to be modeled), synthesis timing constraints enforce this requirement (since the partition will ultimately be composed with other partitions, or occur at chip boundaries). After our abstraction, the environment is no longer constrained from toggling only once every two time-steps, but may toggle every time-step – this reflects a conversion of the environment from half-cycle to full-cycle, and (along with the synthesis requirements reflected in rules 1 and 2 of Defn. 3, and the synthesis requirement that the design be free from combinatorial loops) allows applicability of this abstraction to Mealy machines.

The first abstraction $N' = \langle L^{N'}, S^{N'}, S_0^{N'}, PI, PO, V^{N'}, \delta^{N'}, \lambda^{N'} \rangle$, which we denote the "remove-L2" abstraction, has $L^{N'} = B \cup \{f\}$, $S_0^{N'} = (B_0, 1)$, $V^{N'} = D$. Again, the transition and output functions, $\delta^{N'}$ and $\lambda^{N'}$, are given by the formulae in Sect. 2.1. The state space of $N'$ is denoted by $(b, w, x)$, comprising of the values of latches $B$, $f$, and the input $PI$, respectively. The second abstraction $N''$, which we denote the "remove-L1" abstraction, has $L^{N''} = D$, $S_0^{N''} = D_0$, $V^{N''} = D$. The state space of $N''$ is denoted by $(d, x)$, comprising of the values of latches $D$ and the input $PI$, respectively. Note that we define $V$ in all cases as $D$, the L2 latch outputs, as necessary for arbitrary $L2 - visible$ properties, and to enable the dual-phase-bisimulation.

**Theorem 3.** *If $N'$ is a "remove-L2" abstraction of $N$, then $N \prec N'$.*

*Proof.* The following relation $G$ between states of $N$ and $N'$ is a dual-phase-bisimulation relation. $G$ is defined so that it is 1 only for the following two cases:

- for any $x$, $G((B_0, D_0, 1, x), (B_0, 1, x))$ is 1
- for any $(b, d, 1, x)$ reachable from the initial state of $N$ after at least one transition, $G((b, d, 1, x), (b, 0, x))$ is 1

**Theorem 4.** *If $N''$ is a "remove-L1" abstraction of $N$, then $N \prec N''$.*

*Proof.* The following relation $G$ between states of $N$ and $N''$ is a dual-phase-bisimulation relation. $G$ is defined so that it is 1 only for the following two cases:

- for any $x$, $G((B_0, D_0, 1, x), (D_0, x))$ is 1
- for any $(b, d, 1, x)$ reachable from the initial state of $N$ after at least one transition, $G((b, d, 1, x), (d, x))$ is 1

Theorems 1, 2, 3 and 4 allow us to apply the two abstractions independently on each dependent layer, and still show the validity of model checking $L2 - visible$ CTL* formulae on the composition of the abstractions:

**Corollary 1.** *If $D'$ is obtained from $D$ by applying either the "remove-L2" abstraction or the "remove-L1" abstraction, independently, on each of its minimal dependent layers, $D \prec D'$.*

# 4 Algorithm for the Abstraction of DP Netlists

The algorithm picks a primary input at random – a *while* loop ensures that every primary input is chosen. It then finds the latches in the transitive fanout of this input – this set is called $L1''$, and must consist solely of L1 latches (except for inputs connected to L2s, which are treated specially). It places these elements of $L1''$ one-at-a-time into the set $L1'$. For each latch in $L1'$ not previously considered, it finds all L2 latches in the transitive fanout of $L1'$ – this set is denoted $L2'$. It then looks for any latches in the transitive fanin of $L2'$ – these must be L1s – and adds them to $L1'$. It then iteratively ping-pongs between the L1s and L2s for this MDL until no new latches are found. These latches are now labeled with their type and layer identifier (which is then incremented), and a record kept as to the number of L1 and L2 latches in that layer. It then continues iteratively with the next element of the set $L1''$.

The algorithm then looks for L1 latches in the transitive fanout of the L2s encountered in the previous layers. If it finds any, these new MDLs are explored iteratively as above until no new latches are encountered. The outer *while* loop then begins traversing from the next primary input.

If the algorithm encounters a previously-marked L1 latch while looking for an L2 latch (or vice-versa), it flags this violation. If no violation has been reported during the analysis, the netlist is DP, and reduction may proceed.

After the above analysis, either the L1 or the L2 set may be removed per layer; these layers are minimal by construction. A simple iteration over every MDL will yield optimum reductions; if the given layer has more L2s than L1s, the L2s of that layer should be replaced with multiplexors as discussed in Sect. 2.1. If not, the L1s of that layer should be replaced with wires.

If the type of all latches is provided (L1 versus L2), an alternate algorithm may simply iterate over each latch within the netlist, and calculate its MDL given its type. When this abstraction was initially deployed, no such type data was automatically available; the inputs provided a convenient point of reference.

**Theorem 5.** *This algorithm performs optimum DP reductions.*

*Proof.* By construction, each latch will be a member of exactly one MDL. Furthermore, the MDLs are of minimum size, resulting in a maximum number of dependent layers in the netlist. Since each MDL is independent of the others, the locally optimal solutions yield a globally optimum result.

Note that along any input - output path within a single MDL, exactly one flip-flop must exist after abstraction – if zero or two exist, the bisimulation is clearly broken. Take any latch from any MDL which which was removed by the abstraction – assume that it is an L1 latch $L1'$. All L2s $L2'$ in the fanout of $L1'$ must remain. All L1s in the fanin of $L2'$ must have been removed, and so on until we are left with the case that (within this MDL) all of the L1s are removed, and all of the L2s remain, if this is a correct abstraction (similar reasoning applies to consideration of a removed L2 latch). This demonstrates optimality of reduction of each MDL.

The algorithm may be optimized to ensure that each combinatorial gate (or net) is only considered once in fanout traversal, and once in fanin traversal, to ensure that its complexity is $O(netlist\ size^2)$. However, in practice, we have found that the complexity of this algorithm grows roughly linearly with model size and takes a matter of seconds for even the largest designs we have considered for model checking (more than 8,000 latches). This near-linearity is not surprising for synthesizable high-performance netlists, since the depth of combinatorial logic between latches and the number of sinks of a net are restricted to ensure that the netlist meets timing constraints.

## 5  Experimental Results

The above algorithm was implemented into the model checker RuleBase [4], developed in IBM Haifa Research Lab as an extension to SMV [9]. It is utilized as a first-pass netlist reduction technique; the reduced full-cycle model is saved and used as the basis for further optimizations before being passed to SMV for model checking.

This algorithm was deployed for use on many components of IBM's Gigahertz Processor. The reduction results obtained by this step are given in Table 1 below. These numbers do not reflect the results of any other reduction techniques. We recommend, due to the speed of this algorithm ($O(n^2)$ in theory, but roughly $O(n)$ in practice) and its global preservation of $L2 - visible$ properties, that it be used as a first-pass reduction technique upon design compilation. The resulting abstracted design may then be analyzed for formula-specific reductions (e.g., cone-of-influence, constant propagations, retiming), which are likely to proceed faster upon the abstracted design due to the fewer number of latches and simpler transition relation (the clock is no longer in the support of the transition relation).

| Logic Function | State Bits Before Reduction | State Bits After Reduction |
|---|---|---|
| Load Serialization Logic | 8096 | 2586 |
| L1 Reload Logic | 3102 | 1418 |
| Instruction Flushing Logic | 138 | 69 |
| Instruction-Fetch Address Generation Logic | 4891 | 2196 |
| Branch Logic | 6918 | 3290 |
| Instruction Issue Logic | 6578 | 3249 |
| Tag Management Logic | 578 | 289 |
| Instruction Decode Logic | 1980 | 978 |
| Load / Store Control | 821 | 409 |

Table 1. DP Reduction Results

During the initial stages of model checking, this abstraction was not available. Once the abstraction became available, properties which previously took many hours to complete would finish in several minutes. More encompassing properties became feasible on the abstracted model which would not otherwise complete.

As a small example, a property run on the Load Serialization Logic which took 25.6 seconds, 36 MB of memory on the abstracted model (with 81 variables) took 450.2 seconds, 92 MB of memory for the unabstracted netlist (with 116 variables) on the same machine (an IBM RS/6000 Workstation Model 590 with 2 GB main memory), with no initial BDD order. This time includes that necessary to perform the netlist analysis and reduction. As a larger example, a property run on the Instruction Flushing Logic took 852 seconds of user time, 48 MB on the abstracted model (with 96 variables). This same property did not complete on the unabstracted netlist (with 162 variables) within 72 hours.

While it may seem surprising that the number of variables after abstraction is more than half that before abstraction, this is due to two phenomena. First, some of these variables are used for environment and specification; these are modeled directly as flip-flops (rather than L1-L2 latches). Second, in some cases, RuleBase was able to exploit some redundancy among these variables through other model reduction techniques (e.g., constant simulation).

The benefits obtained by this algorithm extend beyond a mere reduction in state depth, which reduces the time and memory consumed by reachability calculations. BDD variable reordering time is often greatly reduced (since the BDDs tend to be smaller, and since with less variables a "good ordering" tends to be faster to compute). The reduction to full-cycle models also reduces the number of image calculations necessary to reach a fixed-point or on-the-fly failure – the diameter of the model is halved. Further, since fewer state variables require evaluation, it is possible that the above reduction may be exploited to "collapse" adjacent functions to a single function, which may be represented on the same BDD. However, this risks blowing up the BDD size; the functions may thus remain distinct and implicitly conjoined [10] to ensure proper evaluation.

With this abstraction available, as demonstrated above, model checking was enabled to verify much "larger" and more meaningful properties in less time. Users of our tool have found that writing specifications and environments for the full-cycle abstracted models is much less complex than for the corresponding half-cycle netlists (as is viewing traces). All RuleBase users quickly converted to running exclusively with this abstraction. There have been many hundreds of formulae written and model checked to date on this project, which collectively have exposed on the order of 200 bugs at various design stages. We have not encountered any properties we wished to specify which became impossible on the abstracted model. This algorithm thus provided an efficient and necessary means by which to free ourselves from the verification burdens imposed by the low level of the implementation.

It is noteworthy that roughly 70 HDL bugs were isolated due to violations of L1-L2 connectivity during this work. While algorithms for detecting such problems are simple (and other tools implementing such checks became available later in the design cycle), the many benefits resulting from this reduction provided strong motivation for quickly correcting these errors. Due to the nature of logic interpretation in simulation and model checking frameworks, the logic flawed in such a manner typically behaved "properly" for verification – these platforms assume zero combinatorial delay, but no combinatorial "flow-through" for two adjacent level-sensitive latches even if both are simultaneously in the transparent phase.

## 6 Conclusions

We have developed an efficient algorithm for identifying and abstracting dual-phase L1-L2 netlists. The algorithm performs netlist graph traversal, rather than FSM analysis, hence is CPU-efficient – $O(n^2)$ in theory, but roughly $O(n)$ in practice due to timing constraints imposed upon synthesizable netlists. The benefits obtained by the abstraction include much smaller verification time and memory requirements (through "shallower" state depth – often less than one-half that necessary without the abstraction – which reduces complexity of the transition relation and simplifies BDD reordering, and a halving of the diameter of the model), as well as more abstract specification and environment definitions. A bisimulation relation is established between the unreduced and reduced models. This reduction is optimum, and is valid for model checking CTL* formulae which reason solely about latches of a given phase. Experimental results from the deployment of this algorithm (as implemented in the model checker Rule-Base) upon IBM's Gigahertz Processor are provided, and illustrate its extreme practical benefit.

## References

1. S. Mador-Haim and L. Fix. Input Elimination and Abstraction in Model Checking. In G. Gopalakrishnan and P. Windley, editor, *Proc. Conf. on Formal Methods in Computer-Aided Design*, volume 1522, pages 304–320. Springer, November 1998.
2. K. Nowka and T. Galambos. Circuit Design Techniques for a Gigahertz Integer Microprocessor. In *Proc. Intl. Conf. on Computer Design*, October 1998.
3. C. E. Leiserson and J. B. Saxe. Optimizing Synchronous Systems. *Journal of VLSI and Computer Systems*, 1(1):41–67, Spring 1983.
4. I. Beer, S. Ben-David, C. Eisner, and A. Landver. RuleBase: an Industry-Oriented Formal Verification Tool. In *Proc. Design Automation Conf.*, June 1996.
5. R. Milner. *Communication and Concurrency*. Prentice Hall, New York, 1989.
6. Z. Kohavi. *Switching and Finite Automata Theory*. Computer Science Series. McGraw-Hill Book Company, 1970.
7. O. Grumberg and D. E. Long. Module Checking and Modular Verification. *ACM Transactions on Programming Languages and Systems*, 16(3):843–871, 1994.
8. E. M. Clarke, E. A. Emerson, and A. P. Sistla. Automatic Verification of Finite-State Concurrent Systems Using Temporal Logic Specifications. *ACM Transactions on Programming Languages and Systems*, 8(2):244–263, 1986.
9. K. L. McMillan. *Symbolic Model Checking*. Kluwer Academic Publishers, 1993.
10. A. J. Hu, G. York, and D. L. Dill. New Techniques for Efficient Verification with Implicitly Conjoined BDDs. In *Proc. Design Automation Conf.*, June 1994.

# Validation of Pipelined Processor Designs Using Esterel Tools: A Case Study* (Extended Abstract)

S. Ramesh[1] and Purandar Bhaduri[2] **

[1] Department of Computer Science and Engineering
Indian Institute of Technology Bombay
Powai, Mumbai 400 076, INDIA
Email: ramesh@cse.iitb.ernet.in
[2] Applied Technology Group, Tata Infotech Ltd
Seepz, Andheri (E), Mumbai 400 096, INDIA
Email: purandar.bhaduri@tatainfotech.com

**Abstract.** The design of control units of modern processors is quite complex due to many speed-up techniques like pipelining and out-of-order execution. The existing approaches to formal verification of processor designs are applicable to very high level descriptions that ignore timing details of control signals. In this paper, we propose an approach for verification of detailed design of processors. Our approach suggests the use of Esterel language which has rich constructs for succinct and modular description of control. The Esterel simulation tool Xes and verification tools Xeve and FcTools can be used effectively to catch minor bugs as well as subtle timing errors. As an illustration, we have developed an Esterel implementation of DLX pipeline control and verified certain crucial properties.

## 1 Introduction

Modern processors employ many techniques like pipelining, branch prediction and out-of-order execution to enhance their performance. The design and validation of these processors, especially their control circuitry, is a challenging task [6, 7].

Formal verification techniques, emerging as a viable approach to validation [10], are still inadequate in verification of large systems like processors. Recently many new techniques have been proposed specifically for processor verification [1, 7, 6, 9, 11]. These techniques verify that the given implementation is equivalent to a simpler sequential model of execution, as described by the instruction set architecture. But in these approaches, the implementation is at

---

* Partial support for this work came from the Indo-US Project titled Programming Dynamical Real-time systems and Tata Infotech Research Laboratory, IIT Bombay.
** This author's current address: TRDDC, 54 B, Hadapsar Industrial Estate, Pune 411 013, INDIA. Email: pbhaduri@pune.tcs.co.in

a very high level of abstraction ignoring details of finer timing constraints on control signals. These details are to be introduced to arrive at the final implementation that can be realized in hardware. Even if the design at the higher level of abstraction is proved to be equivalent to a sequential model, later refinements may introduce timing errors.

The aim of this paper is to propose a verification method for detailed processor implementations containing timing constraints of control signals. We suggest the use of Esterel language [3, 2] and its associated verification tools for describing the implementations and verifying their properties. Esterel has a number of attractive features that come in handy for our purpose. It provides a nice separation between data and control. It offers a rich set of high level constructs, like preemption, interrupts and synchronous parallelism, that are natural for hardware systems and that enable modular and succinct description of complex controllers. Besides simulation, Esterel descriptions can be rigorously verified using the tools Xeve [4] and FcTools [5]. Finally, Esterel programs can be directly translated into hardware.

In this paper we illustrate our approach by developing an Esterel model of the DLX pipelined processor control unit [8]. The model has been debugged using the simulator tool Xes and has been verified to satisfy a number of desired properties using the verification tools.

## 2  Esterel Specification of Pipelined Control Unit

The specification is based upon the informal description of DLX processor given in [8]. We confine ourselves to the control unit specification; the data path specification can be trivially given using a host language like C.

### 2.1  The Main Controller

The execution of an instruction in the DLX processor goes through five stages: *Instruction Fetch (IF)*, *Instruction Decode/Register Fetch (ID)*, *Execution/Effective Address Calculation (EX)*, *Memory Access/Branch Completion (MEM)* and *Write-Back (WB)*. The introduction of pipelining leads to increased complexity in design in terms of additional registers and control logic due to various *hazards*. *Pipeline registers* are required to store the intermediate values produced by different stages. DLX uses the *branch-not-taken* prediction scheme and hence to handle the control hazard that occurs when a branch is taken (determined in the EX stage), the instruction in the ID stage must be squashed; the handling of interrupts requires even more complex control logic. Appropriate actions like data forwarding or *stalling* have to be taken to handle *data hazards*, for instance when an instruction updates a register or memory location that is read by a subsequent instruction.

Figure 1 gives an Esterel module that models a generic pipeline stage of the DLX controller. An Esterel program in general consists of one or more modules. Each module has an input-output interface and reactive code that is executed

```
module XXUnit:
input GoPrev, Stall, Restart;
output GoNext, StallPrev, RestartPrev;

loop  % execute the 'loop' body repeatedly
 do % the 'body' of the 'do-watching' statement starts here
  signal Go in  %Go is a local signal
    [
      suspend  % stop execution
      [
       loop
         await immediate Go; %wait till the other component emits 'Go'
         emit GoNext;   % generate the signal GoNext
         run XX; % execute the module named XX
         await tick % wait for one reaction
       end loop
       ||
       loop
         await immediate GoPrev; %wait till 'GoPrev' is present in the input
         await tick; % wait one reaction step
         emit Go % generate 'Go' signal
       end loop
       ]
       when immediate Stall  % stop execution of the 'suspend' body when 'Stall'
                             % is present
     ||
      loop
        await  tick;
        await immediate Stall;
        emit StallPrev
      end
    ]
  end signal % end of scope of local signal declaration
  watching Restart; % abort the 'watching' body when 'Restart' is present
  emit RestartPrev
 end loop % end of the outermost loop

end module % end of the module
```

**Fig. 1.** A pipeline stage in Esterel

periodically at the phase of the built-in signal tick. Every time a module is executed, it reads input signals and depending upon the state of the module generates appropriate output signals and changes the state. Every such execution is called a *reaction*. A reaction is assumed to be instantaneous so that there is no time delay between input consumption and output generation. All Esterel statements are instantaneous excepting the 'halt' statement which does not terminate at all. The control of an Esterel program resides at one or more halt statements (more than one when there are concurrent components) which decide the state of the program. A reaction, besides generating outputs, results in a change of state with the movement of control points from one set of halt statements to another.

Esterel possesses a rich set of constructs for describing control. Here we give a very brief explanation of some of these constructs. The statement await S is a simple 'wait construct' that delays termination until the signal S is present in the input; await immediate S is a variant which can terminate even in the very first instant when control reaches the construct. The statement do watching stat S continues to execute stat as long as the signal S is not present; the moment S appears on the input, the whole statement terminates aborting the computation inside stat. The statement suspend stat till S suspends the execution of stat in all reactions in which S is present; execution continues where it got suspended when S is not present.

Now we will describe the behavior of the module in Figure 1. For the sake of simplicity, we have taken the tick signal to define the clock of the processor. Suppose the signals Stall and Restart are not present in a reaction, corresponding to the uninterrupted flow of an instruction through the pipeline stages. Then the submodule XX (in the first branch of the parallel operator within the suspend statement) is executed in the cycle when the local signal Go is present; the Go signal is present in this cycle provided the GoPrev signal was present in the previous cycle (in the second branch of the parallel operator within the suspend statement). At the end of execution of XX, which is assumed to be instantaneous, the module generates GoNext.

Suppose that Stall is present in a cycle, representing a hazard in the pipeline stage XX. Then the execution of XX is suspended by the suspend statement and the signal GoNext is not generated; the signal StallPrev is generated (in the second branch of the outer parallel operator). If on the other hand the Restart signal is present, representing an interrupt or a taken branch, then the body of the outer watchdog primitive is killed and the execution is restarted because of the presence of the outer loop construct. This results in the loss of information about the presence of the GoPrev signal in the previous cycle. Also a Restart triggers a RestartPrev signal.

Thus, XXUnit executes the submodule XX in every cycle in which GoPrev is present and generates GoNext, as long as Stall or Restart are not present. A Stall in a cycle suspends the execution of XX while a Restart restarts the execution of whole module afresh resetting its internal state, i.e., it squashes the execution of XX.

```
module CONTROL:
input IssueNextInstr;
output InstrCompleted;
output WritePCn : integer,WritePCb: integer;
inputoutput Restart0, RestartIF, RestartID,
          RestartEX, RestartMEM, RestartWB;
inputoutput Stall0, StallIF, StallID, StallEX, StallMEM, StallWB;

signal GoIF, GoID, GoEX, GoMEM
in

  [
    run IFUnit [ signal  IssueNextInstr / GoPrev, GoIF / GoNext,
                         StallIF / Stall, Stall0 / StallPrev,
                         RestartIF / Restart, Restart0 / RestartPrev]
      ||
    run IDUnit [ signal  GoIF / GoPrev, GoID / GoNext,
                         StallID / Stall, StallIF / StallPrev,
                         RestartID / Restart, RestartIF / RestartPrev]
      ||
    run EXUnit [ signal  GoID / GoPrev, GoEX / GoNext,
                         StallEX / Stall, StallID / StallPrev,
                         RestartEX / Restart, RestartID / RestartPrev]
      ||
    run MEMUnit [ signal GoEX / GoPrev, GoMEM / GoNext,
                         StallMEM / Stall, StallEX / StallPrev,
                         RestartMEM / Restart, RestartEX / RestartPrev]
      ||
    run WBUnit [ signal  GoMEM / GoPrev, InstrCompleted / GoNext,
                         StallWB / Stall, StallMEM / StallPrev,
                         RestartWB / Restart, RestartMEM / RestartPrev]
    end signal

end module
```

**Fig. 2.** The control unit for the DLX pipeline stages

The Esterel module in Figure 2 models the behavior of the entire pipeline controller. Each pipeline stage is an instantiation of the generic module XXUnit given in Figure 1; for example, IFUnit is obtained from XXUnit by replacing the command run XX by run IF where the module IF, shown in Figure 3, describes the behavior of the instruction fetch stage.

In the module CONTROL, the renaming of the Go, Stall and Restart signals leads to the establishment of a forward Go-chain and two reverse Stall and Restart-chains. When there is no Stall signal (none of StallIF,···,StallWB is present), the input IssueNextInstr signal triggers the execution of the five stages, with the execution of each stage in a cycle triggering via the Go-chain the execution of the next stage in the next cycle. When StallXX is present, it stalls the pipeline up to stage XX; this is achieved by the instantaneous transmission of the various Stall signals to the preceding stages via the Stall-chain. The succeeding stages are not affected by this stall. Similarly, a Restart signal triggers the restart of all the earlier stages up to the current stage using the Restart-chain.

## 2.2 The Pipeline Stages

The Esterel specification of the various pipe stages which instantiate XX in Figure 1 can now be described. Because of space constraints, we describe only the IF and EX stages.

```
module IF:
input ReadPC : integer, BranchTaken;
output WritePCn: integer, IfOut : integer;
function FetchInstr (integer) : integer;
function IncrPC (integer) : integer;

  emit IfOut(FetchInstr(?ReadPC));
  present BranchTaken
  else
    emit WritePCn(IncrPC(?ReadPC))
  end present;
end module
```

**Fig. 3.** IF Stage

The module IF in Figure 3 emits a signal IfOut with a value representing the current instruction and a signal WritePCn whose value indicates the new value of PC. The signal BranchTaken indicates a taken branch, and the IF stage writes a PC value only if this signal is absent, indicating a normal flow of execution. If the BranchTaken signal is present the PC value is written by the EX stage, shown in Figure 4, through a signal called WritePCb to indicate a branch in instruction execution. The external functions `FetchInstr` and `IncrPC` abstract the actions corresponding to fetching an instruction and incrementing the PC.

```
module EX:
input BranchTaken, Bypass, MemInAdr:integer, MemInVal : integer,
     ExInOpcode : integer, ExInOpnd : integer;
output ExOutAdr : integer, ExOutVal : integer, WritePCb:integer;
function AluOpAdr (integer, integer) : integer;
function AluOpVal (integer, integer) : integer;

  present Bypass then
    emit ExOutAdr(AluOpAdr(?ExInOpcode, ?MemInVal));
    emit ExOutVal(AluOpVal(?ExInOpcode, ?MemInVal))
  else
    emit ExOutAdr(AluOpAdr(?ExInOpcode, ?ExInOpnd));
    emit ExOutVal(AluOpVal(?ExInOpcode, ?ExInOpnd))
  end present;

  present BranchTaken then
    emit WritePCb(AluOpAdr(?ExInOpcode, ?ExInOpnd))
  end present
end module
```

**Fig. 4.** EX Stage

The module `EX` in Figure 4 emits two signals `ExOutAdr` and `ExOutVal`, corresponding to the address and value computed by the ALU by operations abstracted by the external functions `AluOpAdr` and `AluOpVal`. The presence of the input signal `Bypass` indicates that there is a data hazard and hence that the inputs to ALU are to be taken through a forwarding process from the output of the EX/MEM pipe stage; in the absence of this signal, the inputs come from the ID/EX pipe stage. The `BranchTaken` signal indicates a taken branch and triggers the signal `WritePCb` which writes the new branch address into PC.

The above Esterel model of the DLX processor has abstracted away details about the data path, instruction decoding, alternative actions based on various types of instructions (such as load/store) and hazard detection. This is the reason that the signals `Bypass`, `Restart`, `BranchTaken` and `Stall` have been modeled as external input signals, rather than being generated internally (by hazard detection units).

## 3  Validation using Esterel tools

In this section we outline the validation of the design of the DLX processor control unit using the Esterel simulation tool Xes and verification tools Xeve and FcTools. We focus on the micro-properties of the control unit, such as smooth flow of instructions through the pipeline, absence of deadlock, proper issuing of stall and restart instructions, and correct behavior of the pipeline with respect to these signals. We are able to verify that for example, in case of a taken branch (determined in the EX stage) the instruction following the branch (in its ID stage) is restarted or aborted. Similarly, we can verify that a stall signal sent to some stage propagates as a bubble through the pipeline.

The properties verified by us are finer than the macro-property verified in [7], namely that the pipelined machine has the same effect on visible state as the sequential one for the same input. The latter property, in its full glory, cannot be verified using existing Esterel tools because they deal with only control states. However, the property restricted to control states is still verifiable (see the paragraph titled Stall in Section 3.1).

## 3.1 Verification

The simple properties of the DLX pipeline controller mentioned above can be verified using the Esterel tools Xeve [4] and FcTools [5]. They are verification environments for Esterel programs modeled as *finite state machines* (FSMs) with a user-friendly graphical interface.

The Esterel compiler generates FSMs implicitly in the form of boolean equations with latches. One of the verification tasks performed by Xeve is to take an implicit FSM and perform a state minimization using the notion of bisimulation equivalence. Before minimization a set of input /output signals can be hidden. This results in a nondeterministic FSM where some transitions may be labeled by $\tau$, a hidden internal action. Xeve generates minimized FSMs, that can be further reduced using some abstraction criterion by FcTools and can be graphically explored using the tool ATG.

FcTools is a verification tool set for networks of communicating FSMs. Its capabilities include graphical depiction of automata, reduction of automata and verification of simple modal properties by observers, counterexample production and visualization.

In our verification process the original FSM produced by Xeve had about 1500 states, which after making some irrelevant interface signals local got reduced to 543 reachable states. This was reduced to 16 states and 72 transitions after applying the observational equivalence minimization procedure available in FcTools. Still the automaton could not be inspected due to the large number of transitions. So we used the powerful abstraction technique available in FcTools to further reduce the size of the automaton. An *abstraction criterion* defines a new set of action symbols that are regular expressions on the action symbols in the original automaton. The reduction involves abstraction of sequences of old actions into new actions so that the reduced automaton contains only new action symbols; further, certain paths in the original automaton are eliminated, thereby resulting in a small automaton that can be checked easily.

Depending upon the property to be checked, we applied different criteria to get small automata which we verified with respect to appropriate properties.

| Criterion | States | Transitions |
|---|---|---|
| Initial | 16 | 72 |
| Smooth Flow | 8 | 12 |
| Stall | 16 | 32 |
| Branch | 1 | 1 |

**Table 1.** Sizes of Reduced Automata

Table 1 summarizes the sizes of the various reduced automata obtained for different criteria. The details about the criteria 'Smooth Flow' and 'Stall' are given below. The criterion 'Branch' checks for proper updation of the PC value at any cycle by abstracting paths into two abstract actions 'success' and 'failure'. The reduced automaton has only one transition with the label 'success'.

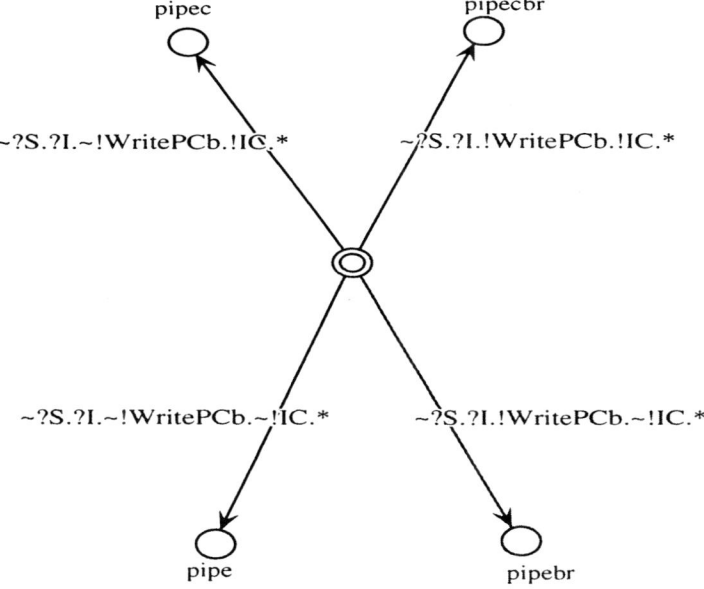

**Fig. 5.** Abstraction Criterion for Smooth Flow

**Smooth flow of instructions** This criterion verifies that every instruction issued is completed after four cycles in the absence of stalls and branches. The criterion depicted in Figure 5, defines four abstract actions `pipe`, `pipec`, `pipebr` and `pipecbr` which rename the edges satisfying the corresponding regular expressions, eg., `pipebr` renames any edge in which a branch has been taken and no instruction is completed; in the regular expressions, . denotes synchronous product of input and output events (prefixed by ? and ! respectively) and their

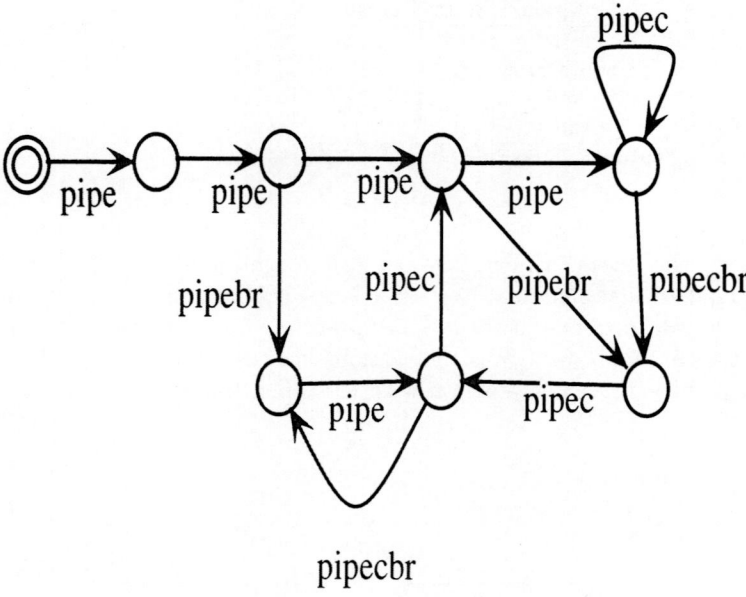

**Fig. 6.** Reduced Automaton for Smooth Flow

negations (prefixed by ~); the event * matches any event. Figure 6 gives the reduced automaton which can be verified with respect to the desired property by inspection.

For the sake of clarity in the figures, the signals StallIF, IssueNextInstr, and InstrCompleted of the original automaton are renamed as S, I and IC respectively; further the WritePCb signal is treated as being synonymous with BranchTaken for technical reasons.

**Stall** The property verified here is that the StallIF signal stalls the IF stage for a cycle: no instruction is completed four cycles after a StallIF assuming later stages are not stalled or squashed in the intervening period. The abstraction criterion for this is shown in Figure 7 and the reduced automaton in Figure 8. In the reduced automaton there is no path of length five starting with a stall or a stallc that ends with a ic or stallc edge. Another interesting thing to note from this automaton is that from every state there is a sequence of 'stalls' that leads to the initial state; this property corresponds to the sequential equivalence property of [7] for control states.

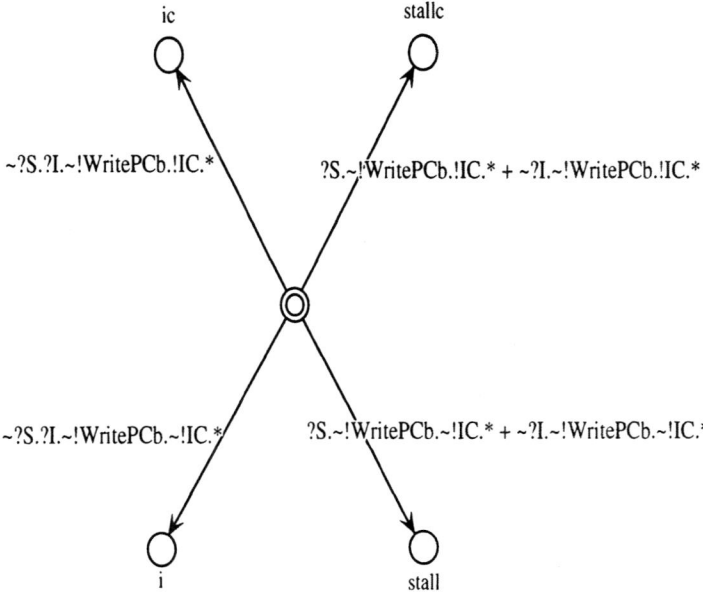

**Fig. 7.** Abstraction Criterion for Stall

# 4 Conclusion

We have proposed the use of Esterel language and tools for verification of modern processors. Esterel can be used to describe, in sufficient detail and in a modular and succinct way, control units of processors using its rich set of constructs. Complex timing properties of Esterel descriptions can be verified using powerful tools.

We have illustrated the use of Esterel tools for the description of DLX processor. The initial results are encouraging. The verification tools Xes, Xeve and FcTools were found to be quite useful in detecting anomalies ranging from simple bugs to complex timing errors. We plan to extend our investigation to more complex processors involving superscalar features like out-of-order executions. We also plan to investigate, in greater detail, the relative merits of Esterel for describing control units of processors with respect to the traditional HDLs.

# References

1. S. Berezin, A. Biere, Ed. Clarke, and Y. Zhu. Combining symbolic model checking with uninterpreted functions for out of order processor verification. In G. Gopalakrishnan and P. Windley, editors, *FMCAD'98, LNCS 1522*. Springer Verlag, 1998.

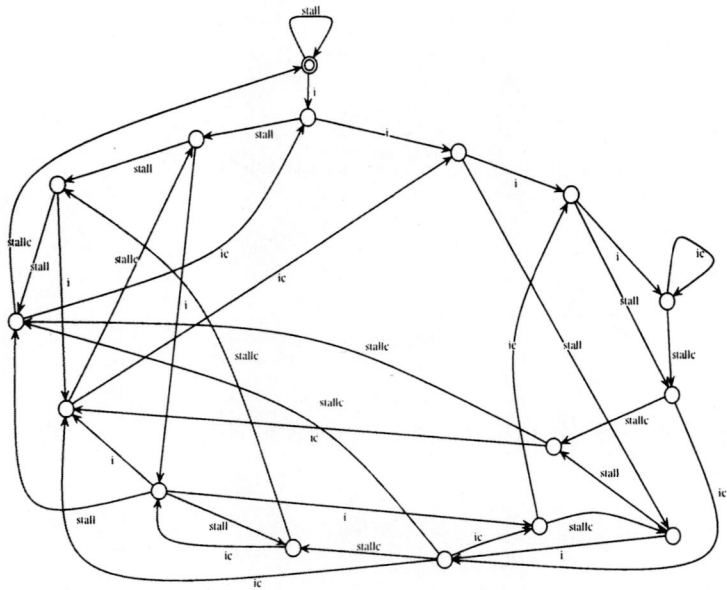

**Fig. 8.** Reduced Automaton for Stall

2. G. Berry. The Foundations of Esterel. In G. Plotkin, C. Stirling, and M. Tofte, editors, *Proof, Language and Interaction: Essays in Honour of Robin Milner*. MIT Press, 1998.

3. G. Berry and G. Gonthier. The Esterel synchronous programming language: Design, semantics, implementation. *Science Of Computer Programming*, 19(2), 1992.

4. A. Bouali. XEVE: An Esterel Verification Environment. Available by ftp from `ftp-sop.inria.fr` as file `/meije/verif/xeve-doc.ps.gz`.

5. A. Bouali, A. Ressouche, R. de Simone, and V. Roy. The FcTools User Manual. Available by ftp from `ftp-sop.inria.fr` as file `/meije/verif/fc2userman.ps`.

6. R. E. Bryant. Formal Verification of Pipelined Processors. In *Proc. TACAS 98, LNCS 1384*. Springer Verlag, March-April 1998.

7. J. R. Burch and D. L. Dill. Automatic Verification of Pipelined Microprocessor Control. In *Proc. CAV'94, LNCS 818*. Springer Verlag, June 1994.

8. J. Hennessy and D. Patterson. *Computer Architecture: A Quantitative Approach, Second Edition*. Morgan Kaufman Publishers Inc., 1995.

9. R. Hosabettu, M. Srivas, and G. Gopalakrishnan. Decomposing the Proof of Correctness of Pipelined Microprocessors. In *Proc. CAV'98, LNCS 1427*. Springer Verlag, June/July 1998.

10. T. Kropf, editor. *Formal Hardware Verification, LNCS 1287*. Springer Verlag, 1997.

11. J. U. Skakkebaek, R. B. Jones, and D. L. Dill. Formal Verification of Out-of-order Execution using Incremental Flushing. In *Proc. CAV'98, LNCS 1427*. Springer Verlag, June 1998.

# Automated Verification of a Parametric Real-Time Program: The ABR Conformance Protocol

Béatrice Bérard and Laurent Fribourg *

LSV – Ecole Normale Supérieure de Cachan & CNRS
61 av. Pdt. Wilson - 94235 Cachan - France
email: {berard,fribourg}@lsv.ens-cachan.fr

**Abstract.** The ABR conformance protocol is a real-time program developed at France Telecom, that controls dataflow rates on ATM networks. A crucial part of this protocol is the dynamical computation of the expected rate of data cell emission. We present here a modelization of the corresponding program, using parametric timed automata. In this framework, a fundamental property of the service provided by the protocol to the user is expressed as a reachability problem. The tool HyTech is then used for computing the set of reachable states of the model, and automatically proving the property. This case study gives additional evidence of the importance of the model of parametric timed automata and the practical usefulness of symbolic analysis tools.

## 1 Introduction

Over the last few years, an extensive amount of research has been devoted to the formal verification of real-time concurrent systems. Among the various approaches to the analysis of timed models, one of the most successful is based on timed automata. Since its first introduction in [3], this model was extended with many different features, leading to the general notion of hybrid automata [1,2,15]. Although hybrid automata have an infinite number of states, the fixpoint computation of reachable states often terminates in practice, thus allowing the verification of "safety" properties. This explains the increasing success of the development of tools for the analysis of real-time systems [5,8,12], as well as the numerous industrial case studies which have already been presented. In this paper, we propose an automated verification of correctness for the *Available Bit Rate* (ABR) conformance protocol, developed by France Telecom at CNET (Centre National d'Etudes des Télécommunications, Lannion, France) in the context of network communications with *Asynchronous Transfer Mode* (ATM).

**The ABR conformance protocol.** ATM is a flexible packet-switching network architecture, where several communications can be multiplexed over a

---

* Supported by Action *FORMA* (Programme DSP-STTC/CNRS/MENRT)

same physical link, thus providing better performances than traditional circuit-switching networks. Different types of ATM connections are possible at the same time, according to the dataflow rate asked (and paid) for by the service user [9]. A contract with ABR connection makes it possible for a source to emit at any time with a rate depending on the load of the network: according to the available bandwidth, the ABR protocol dynamically computes the highest possible dataflow rate and sends this information, via so called *Resource Management* (RM) cells, to the user, who has to adapt his transfer rate of *data* (D) cells.

The service provider has to control the conformance of emission with respect to the currently allowed rate, and filter out D cells emitted at an excessive rate. This is achieved by a program located at an interface between the user and the network, which receives RM cells on their way to the user as well as D cells from the user to the network (see Figure 1). This program has two parts: the easy task

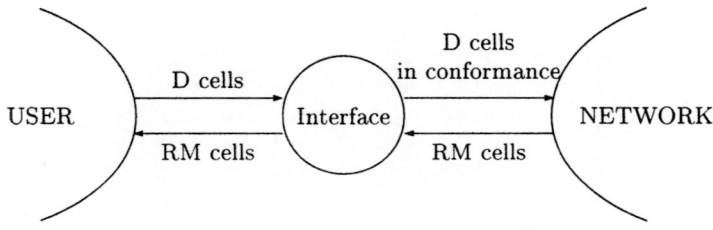

**Fig. 1.** Schematic view of cells traffic

is to compare the emission rate of D cells with the rate value currently allowed, while the difficult problem is to dynamically compute (or update) the rate values expected for future D cells. The program must take into account the delays introduced by the transit of cells from the interface to the user and back, but the exact value of this delay is not known: only lower and upper bounds, denoted $a$ and $b$, are given. A simple algorithm called $\mathcal{I}$ computes, from a sequence of rate values carried by previously arrived RM cells, the *ideal (expected) rate* $E_t$ for emission of D cells which will arrive at future time $t$. However, since the value of $t$ is not known in advance, an implementation of $\mathcal{I}$ would require to store a huge number of rate values. A more realistic algorithm, called $\mathcal{B}'$, due to C. Rabadan, has been adopted by CNET. It stores only two RM cell rates, and dynamically updates an estimated value $A$ of ideal rate $E_t$.

**Correctness of program $\mathcal{B}'$.** Before being accepted as an international standard (norm ITU I-371.1), this protocol had to be proved correct: it was necessary to ensure that the flow control of D cells by comparison with $A$ rather than $E_t$ is never disadvantageous to the user. This means that when some D cell arrives at time $t$, $A$ is an *upper* approximation of $E_t$. In other words, $A \geq E_t$ when current time reaches $t$. This property $U$ was proved by hand by Monin and Klay, using a classical method of invariants [14]. However, since this proof was quite difficult to obtain, CNET felt the need for using formal methods and tools to verify $\mathcal{B}'$ in a more mechanical way, as well as future versions of $\mathcal{B}'$ currently under development.

This paper presents a modelization of algorithms $\mathcal{I}$ and $\mathcal{B}'$ as *parametric timed automata* [4], and an automated proof of property $U$ (viewed as a reachability problem) via tool HYTECH [12].

**Plan of the paper.** Section 2 presents the model of parametric timed automata. Section 3 describes algorithms $\mathcal{I}$ and $\mathcal{B}'$, and correctness property $U$ within this framework. Section 4 gives the experimental results obtained with HYTECH and a comparison with previous work. Section 5 concludes with final remarks.

## 2 Parametric timed automata

We use here a model of parametric timed automata, called p-automata for short, which are extensions of timed automata [3] with parameters. A minor difference with the classical parametric model of Alur-Henzinger-Vardi [4] is that we have only one clock variable $S$ and several "discrete" variables $w_1, ..., w_n$ while, in [4], there are several clocks and no discrete variable. One can retrieve (a close variant of) Alur-Henzinger-Vardi parametric timed automata by changing our discrete variable $w_i$ into $S - w_i$ (see [10]). Alternatively, our parametric automata can simply be viewed as particular cases of *linear hybrid automata* [1,2,15].

**P-automata.** In addition to a finite set of locations, p-automata have a finite set $P$ of *parameters*, a finite set $W$ of *discrete variables* and a *universal clock* $S$. These are all real-valued variables which differ only in the way they evolve when time increases. Parameter values are fixed by an initial constraint and never evolve later on. Discrete variables values do not evolve either, but they may be changed through instantaneous updates. A universal clock is a variable whose value increases uniformly with time (without reset).

Formally, a *parametric term* is an expression of the form $w + \sum_{i=1}^{k} p_i + c$, $S + \sum_{i=1}^{k} p_i + c$ or $\sum_{i=1}^{k} p_i + c$, where $w \in W$, $p_i \in P$ and $c \in \mathbb{N}$. (As usual, by convention, a term without parameter corresponds to the case where $k = 0$.) An *atomic constraint* is an expression $term_1 \# term_2$, where $term_1, term_2$ are parametric terms and $\# \in \{<, \leq, =, \geq, >\}$. A *constraint* is a conjunction of atomic constraints. The formulas used in p-automata are *location invariants*, *guards* and *update relations*. A location invariant is a conjunction of atomic constraints. A guard is a conjunction of atomic constraints with possibly the special expression *asap*. An update relation is a conjunction of formulas of the form $w' \# term$ where $w'$ belongs to a primed copy of $W$, $term$ is a parametric term and $\# \in \{<, \leq, =, \geq, >\}$. As usual $w' = w$ is implicit if $w'$ does not appear in the update relation.

A *p-automaton* $\mathcal{A}$ is a tuple $\langle L, \ell_{init}, P, W, S, I, \Sigma, T \rangle$, where

- $L$ is a finite set of locations, with *initial location* $\ell_{init} \in L$,
- $P$ and $W$ are respectively the sets of parameters and discrete variables, $S$ is the universal clock,
- $I$ is a mapping that labels each location $\ell$ in $L$ with some location invariant, simply written $I_\ell$ instead of $I(\ell)$ in the following,
- $\Sigma$ is a finite set of *labels* partitioned into *synchronization* labels and *internal* labels,
- $T$ is a set of *action transitions* of the form $\langle \ell, \varphi, \sigma, \theta, \ell' \rangle$, where $\ell$ and $\ell'$ belong to $L$, $\varphi$ is a guard, $\sigma \in \Sigma$ is a label and $\theta$ an update relation. The transition is *urgent* if its guard $\varphi$ contains the symbol *asap*.

**Semantics of p-automata.** We briefly and informally recall the semantics of timed automata (see [4] for details), described in terms of transition systems. For a p-automaton $\mathcal{A}$, the (global) state space of the transition system is the set $Q_{\mathcal{A}} = L \times \mathbb{R}^P \times \mathbb{R}^W \times \mathbb{R}$ of tuples $(\ell, \gamma, v, s)$, where $\ell$ is a location of $\mathcal{A}$, $\gamma : P \mapsto \mathbb{R}$ is a *parameter valuation*, $v : W \mapsto \mathbb{R}$ is a data valuation and $s$ is a real value of the clock $S$. A *region* is a subset of states of the form $\{(\ell, \gamma, v, s) \mid \varphi \text{ holds for } (\gamma, v, s)\}$, for some location $\ell$ and some constraint $\varphi$, written $\ell \times \varphi$.

The set $Q_{init}$ of *initial states* is the region $\ell_{init} \times \varphi_{init}$, for some constraint $\varphi_{init}$: the automaton starts in its initial location, with some given initial constraint. (From this point on, the parameter values are not modified.)

A state $q = (\ell, \gamma, v, s)$ is *urgent* if there exists some action transition $e$, with source location $\ell$ and a guard of the form $\varphi \wedge asap$, such that $\varphi$ holds for $(\gamma, v, s)$: some urgent transition is enabled. From a non urgent state $q = (\ell, \gamma, v, s)$, the automaton can spend some time $\varepsilon \geq 0$ in a location $\ell$, providing the invariant $I_\ell$ remains true. This *delay move* results in state $q' = (\ell, \gamma, v, s + \varepsilon)$ (nothing else is changed during this time). Since location invariants are convex formulas, if $I_\ell$ is satisfied for $s$ and $s + \varepsilon$, then it is also satisfied for any $\alpha$, $0 \leq \alpha \leq \varepsilon$.

From a state $q = (\ell, \gamma, v, s)$, the automaton can also apply some action transition $\langle \ell, \varphi, \sigma, \theta, \ell' \rangle$, providing guard $\varphi$ is true for the current valuations $(\gamma, v, s)$. In an instantaneous *action move*, the valuation of discrete variables is modified from $v$ to $v'$ according to update relation $\theta$ and the automaton switches to target location $\ell'$, resulting in state $q' = (\ell', \gamma, v', s)$.

A *successor* of a state $q$ is a state obtained either by a delay or an action move. For a subset $Q$ of states, $Post^*(Q)$ is the set of iterated successors of the states in $Q$. Similarly, the notions of predecessor and set $Pre^*(Q)$ can be defined.

**Synchronized product of p-automata.** Let $\mathcal{A}_1$ and $\mathcal{A}_2$ be two p-automata with a common universal clock $S$. The *synchronized product* (or parallel composition, see e.g. [12]) $\mathcal{A}_1 \times \mathcal{A}_2$ is a p-automaton with $S$ as universal clock and the union of sets of parameters (resp. discrete variables) of $\mathcal{A}_1$ and $\mathcal{A}_2$ as sets of parameters (resp. discrete variables). Locations of the product are pairs $(\ell_1, \ell_2)$ of locations from $\mathcal{A}_1$ and $\mathcal{A}_2$ respectively. Constraints associated with locations (invariants, initial constraint) are obtained by the conjunction of the components constraints. The automata move independently, except when transitions from $\mathcal{A}_1$ and $\mathcal{A}_2$ have a common synchronization label. In this case, both automata perform a synchronous action move, the associated guard (resp. update relation) being the conjunction of both guards (resp. update relations). For simplicity we suppose here that synchronized transitions are non urgent.

**Parametric verification.** For a given automaton, $Post^*(Q_{init})$ represents the set of reachable states. For p-automata, we have the following *closure* property: if $Q$ is a finite union of regions, also called *zone*, then the successor of $Q$ is also a zone. Hence, the output of the computation of $Post^*(Q_{init})$ (if it terminates) is a zone. Consider now some property $U$, such that the set of states violating $U$ can be characterized by a zone $Q_{\neg U}$. Proving that $U$ holds for the system reduces to prove the emptiness of zone $Post^*(Q_{init}) \cap Q_{\neg U}$. Alternatively it suffices to prove: $Pre^*(Q_{\neg U}) \cap Q_{init} = \emptyset$. Note that we are interested here in proving that property $U$ holds for *all* the valuations of parameters satisfying the initial constraint. The problem is known to be undecidable in general [4]: there is no guarantee of termination for the computation of $Post^*$ (or $Pre^*$).

## 3 Description and modelization of the system

Recall that algorithms $\mathcal{I}$ and $\mathcal{B}'$ use rate values carried by RM cells to dynamically compute the rate expected by the network for the conformance test of future D cells. In order to verify the correctness of $\mathcal{B}'$ with respect to $\mathcal{I}$, we introduce a snapshot action taking place at an arbitrary time t, which will be a parameter of the model. For our purpose of verification, it is enough to consider the snapshot as a final action of the system.

We first give p-automata as models for the environment and algorithms $\mathcal{I}$ and $\mathcal{B}'$. Then, in the complete system obtained as a synchronized product of the three automata, we explain how to check the correctness property. All these p-automata share a universal clock S, the value of which is the current time $s$. Without loss of understanding (context will make it clear), we will often use S instead of $s$.

### 3.1 A model of environment and observation

The p-automaton $\mathcal{A}_{env}$ modeling environment (see Figure 2) involves the parameter t (snapshot time) and a discrete variable R representing the rate value carried by the last received RM cell. In the initial location $Wait$, a loop with label *newRM* simulates the reception of a new RM cell: the rate R is updated to a non deterministic value (R' > 0). The *snapshot* action has S=t as a guard, and location $Wait$ is assigned invariant S $\leq$ t in order to "force" the switch to location $EndE$.

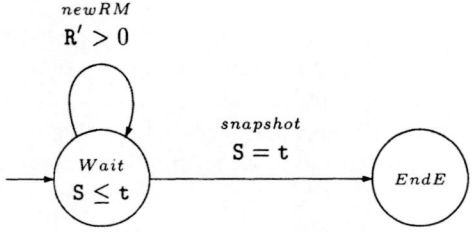

**Fig. 2.** Automaton $\mathcal{A}_{env}$ modeling arrivals of RM cells and snapshot

## 3.2 Algorithm $\mathcal{I}$

**Definition of Ideal Rate.** As already mentioned, transmissions are not instantaneous and parameters $a$ and $b$ represent respectively a lower and an upper bound of the delay. Recall that $s$ is the current time and $t$ the date of the snapshot. An RM cell received from the network is relevant to the computation of the "ideal rate" only if it has been received before $s$ and (1) either it is the last received before or at time $t - b$, or (2) it arrived inside the time interval $]t - b, t - a]$. The *ideal rate* $E_t(s)$, estimated at current time $s$ for time $t$, is the highest value among these RM cells. In other words, if $n \geq 0$ and $r_0, r_1, \ldots, r_n$ are the successive arrival times (before $s$) of RM cells, such that $r_0 \leq t - b < r_1 \leq r_2 \leq \cdots \leq r_n \leq t - a$, and if $R_0, R_1, \ldots, R_n$ are the corresponding rate values, then the expected rate is $E_t(s) = Max\{R_i, 0 \leq i \leq n\}$. The case where $n = 0$ is obtained when no new RM cell arrived between $t - b$ and $t - a$. Note that in [14], RM cell arrival times $r_1, r_2, \ldots, r_n$ are additionally assumed to form a *strictly* increasing sequence (see section 4.2).

**Incremental algorithm $\mathcal{I}$.** The following algorithm $\mathcal{I}$ proceeds in an incremental way, by updating a variable E at each reception of an RM cell, until current time $s$ becomes equal to $t$. It is easy to see that, at this time, the value of E is equal to the ideal rate $E_t(s)$ defined above. More precisely, algorithm $\mathcal{I}$ involves variable R and parameter t (in common with $\mathcal{A}_{env}$) and, in addition:
- the two parameters a and b (representing the lower and upper bounds of the transit time from the interface to the user and back),
- the specific variable E (which will be equal to the ideal rate $E_t(s)$ when the value of the universal clock S reaches $t$).
Initially, E and R are equal. Algorithm $\mathcal{I}$ reacts to each arrival of a new RM cell with rate value R by updating E. There are three cases, according to the position of its arrival time S with respect to t-b and t-a:

1. If S $\leq$ t-b (case $n = 0$ above), E is updated to the new value of R:
   [I1] if t >= S+b then E'= R
2. If t-b < S $\leq$ t-a, the new ideal rate becomes E'=$Max$(E,R) (from the definition and the associativity of $Max$). To avoid using function $Max$, this computation is split into two subcases:

102

```
[I2a] if S+a <= t < S+b and E < R then E'= R
[I2b] if S+a <= t < S+b and E >= R then E'= E
```

3. If S > t-a, the rate E is left unchanged:
   `[I3] if t < S+a then E'= E`

Algorithm $\mathcal{I}$ terminates when the snapshot takes place (S=t).

**Remark.** A program of conformance control based on $\mathcal{I}$ would need to store at each instant $s$ all the rate values of the RM cells received during interval $]s-b, s]$, which may be in huge number on an ATM network with large bandwidth.

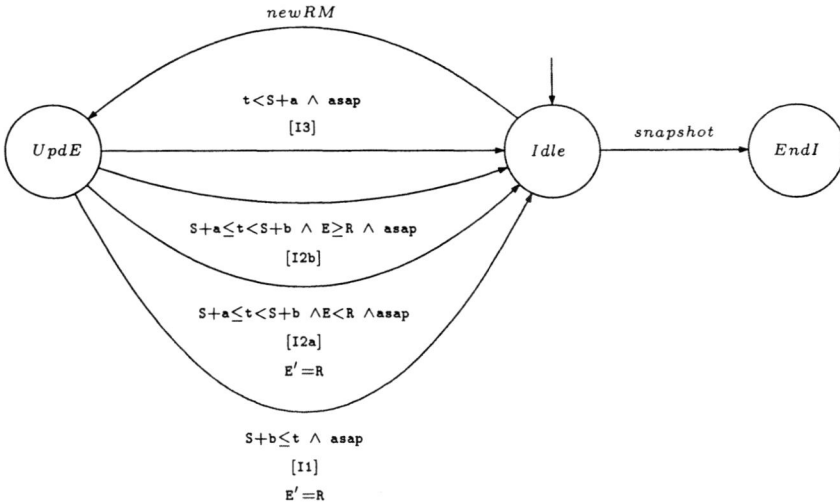

**Fig. 3.** Automaton $\mathcal{A_I}$

**Automaton $\mathcal{A_I}$.** Algorithm $\mathcal{I}$ is naturally modeled as p-automaton $\mathcal{A_I}$ (see Figure 3). Initial location is *Idle*, with initial constraint E = R. The reception of an RM cell is modeled as a transition *newRM* from location *Idle* to location *UpdE*. This transition is followed by an urgent (*asap*) transition from *UpdE* back to *Idle*, which updates E depending on the position of S w.r.t. t-b and t-a, as explained above. Without loss of understanding, transitions from *UpdE* to *Idle* are labeled [I1],[I2a],[I2b],[I3] as the corresponding operations. Observation of the value E corresponds to the transition *snapshot* from *Idle* to final location *EndI*.

## 3.3 Algorithm $\mathcal{B}'$: computation of an approximation

Like $\mathcal{I}$, algorithm $\mathcal{B}'$ involves parameters a and b (but not t), and variable R. In addition, it has six specific variables:
- tfi and tla, which play the role of fi-rst and la-st deadline respectively,
- ACR, for "Approximate Current Rate" , which corresponds to $A(s)$,
- FR, for "First Rate", which is the value taken by ACR when current time S reaches tfi,
- LR, for "Last Rate", which is the value taken by ACR when current time S reaches tla. It stores the rate value R carried by the last received RM cell.
- Emx is just a convenient additional variable, intended to be equal to Max(FR, LR).

Initially, S=tfi=tla, and the other variables are all equal. Algorithm $\mathcal{B}'$ reacts to two types of events: "receiving an RM cell" and "reaching tfi".

**Receiving an RM cell.** When, at current time S, a new RM cell with value R arrives, the variables are updated according to the relative positions of S+a and S+b with respect to tfi and tla, and those of R with respect to Emx and ACR. Among the eight cases (from [1] to [8]), we omit operations [1] to [5] for lack of space, but they are similar to [6]:

```
[6] if S < tfi and Emx > R and R >= LR then
        LR' = R, FR' = Emx.
[7] if S >= tfi and  ACR <= R then
        LR' = R, FR' = R, Emx'= R, tfi'= S+a, tla'= S+a.
[8] if S >= tfi and  ACR > R then
        LR' = R, FR' = R, Emx' = R, tfi' = S+b, tla' = S+b.
```

**Reaching tfi.** When the current time S becomes equal to tfi, the approximate current rate ACR is updated to FR while FR is updated to LR. Moreover, tfi is updated to tla. There are two cases depending on whether tfi was previously equal to tla (operation [9a]) or not (operation [9b]). In the first case, current time S will go beyond tfi (= tla), while in the second case, S will stay beneath the updated value tla of tfi. We have:

```
[9a] if tfi = tla then
         ACR' = FR, FR' = LR, Emx' = LR.
[9b] if tfi < tla then
         ACR' = FR, tfi' = tla, FR' = LR, Emx' = LR.
```

When the events "reaching tfi" (S=tfi) and "receiving an RM cell" simultaneously occur, operation [9a] (case tfi=tla) or [9b] (case tfi<tla) must be performed before operation [1],...,[8] (accounting for the RM cell reception).

Like $\mathcal{I}$, algorithm $\mathcal{B}'$ terminates at snapshot time (S=t). If the snapshot occurs simultaneously with reaching tfi, operation [9a] or [9b] must be performed before termination of $\mathcal{B}'$.

**Automaton $\mathcal{A}_{\mathcal{B}'}$.** Algorithm $\mathcal{B}'$ is modeled as p-automaton $\mathcal{A}_{\mathcal{B}'}$, represented in Figure 4 with only the most significant guards and no update information. Like before, the same labels are used for automaton transitions and corresponding program operations.

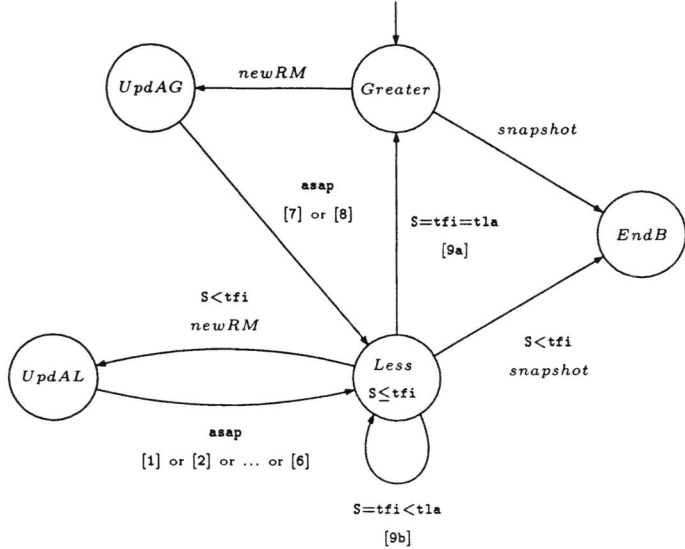

**Fig. 4.** Approximation automaton $\mathcal{A}_{\mathcal{B}'}$

Event "reaching tfi" (S=tfi) is simulated by introducing two locations *Less* and *Greater* in $\mathcal{A}_{\mathcal{B}'}$. Initially $\mathcal{A}_{\mathcal{B}'}$ is in *Greater*, with constraint: S=tfi=tla ∧ ACR=FR=LR=Emx=R. Location *Less* has S≤tfi as an invariant, in order to force execution of transition [9b] (if tfi<tla) or [9a] (if tfi=tla) when S reaches tfi. From *Less*, transition [9b] goes back to *Less* (since, after update, S<tfi=tla) while transition [9a] switches to *Greater* (since S≥tfi=tla as time increases).

The reception of an RM cell corresponds to a transition *newRM*. There are two cases depending on whether the source location is *Less* or *Greater*. From *Less* (resp. *Greater*), transition *newRM* goes to location *UpdAL* (resp. *UpdAG*). This transition is followed by an urgent transition from *UpdAL* (resp. *UpdAG*) back to *Less*, which updates the discrete variables according to operations [1],...,[6] (resp. [7],[8]), as explained above. Note that transition *newRM* from *Less* to *UpdAL* has an additional guard S<tfi in order to prevent an execution of *newRM* before [9a] or [9b] when S=tfi (which is forbidden when "reaching tfi" and *newRM* occur simultaneously).

Like before, observation is modeled as a transition *snapshot* from location *Less* or *Greater* to *EndB*. Also note that transition *snapshot* from *Less* to *EndB* has guard S<tfi in order to prevent its execution before [9a] or [9b] when S=tfi (which is forbidden when "reaching tfi" and the snapshot occur simultaneously).

### 3.4 Synchronized product and property $U$

The complete system is obtained by the product automaton $\mathcal{T} = \mathcal{A}_{env} \times \mathcal{A}_\mathcal{I} \times \mathcal{A}_{\mathcal{B}'}$ of the three p-automata above, synchronized by the labels $newRM$ and $snapshot$. In order to mechanically prove property $U$, we have to compute $Post^*$ for the product automaton $\mathcal{T}$, starting from its initial region
$$Q_{init} = (Wait, Idle, Greater) \times \varphi_{init},$$
where $\varphi_{init}$ is the constraint S=tfi=tla $\wedge$ R=E=ACR=FR=LR=Emx $\wedge$ 0<a<b.
We then have to check that $Post^*(Q_{init})$ does not contain any state where the property $U$ is violated. Recall that property $U$ expresses in terms of the ideal rate $E_t(s)$ computed by $\mathcal{I}$, and the approximate value $A(s)$ computed by $\mathcal{B}'$, by: For all $t$, when $s$ reaches $t$, $A(s) \geq E_t(s)$. In our model $\mathcal{T}$, E corresponds to $E_t(s)$, ACR to $A(s)$ and snapshot (at S=t) makes the automaton switch to its final state, hence property $U$ translates as:

when $\mathcal{T}$ is in location $(EndE, EndI, EndB)$, ACR $\geq$ E.

The set of states where $U$ does not hold is therefore the region
$$Q_{\neg U} = (EndE, EndI, EndB) \times \text{ACR<E}.$$
As explained in Section 2, we have to check $Post^*(Q_{init}) \cap Q_{\neg U} = \emptyset$ or, alternatively, $Pre^*(Q_{\neg U}) \cap Q_{init} = \emptyset$.

## 4 Verification of correctness

### 4.1 Verification with HyTech

Automata $\mathcal{A}_{env}$, $\mathcal{A}_\mathcal{I}$ and $\mathcal{A}_{\mathcal{B}'}$ can be directly implemented into HyTech [12], which automatically computes the synchronization product $\mathcal{T}$. The forward computation of $Post^*(Q_{init})$ requires 23 iteration steps and its intersection with $Q_{\neg U}$ is checked to be empty. This takes 487 sec. on a SUN station ULTRA-1 with 64 Megabytes of RAM memory. Alternatively, the backward computation of $Pre^*(Q_{\neg U})$ requires 15 iteration steps and its intersection with $Q_{init}$ is checked to be empty in 90 sec. The automated proof of correctness of $\mathcal{B}'$ is thus achieved. Recall that these automata (with 3 parameters $a$, $b$ and $t$) belong to an undecidable class [4], so termination was not guaranteed a priori.

### 4.2 Comparison with previous work

**Verification at CNET.** Ideal rate algorithm $\mathcal{I}$ and correctness property $U$ (S=t$\Rightarrow$ E$\leq$ ACR) have been formalized by J.-F. Monin and F. Klay at CNET. In [14], they give the first manual proof of $U$, using the classical method of invariants. They first split $U$ into a conjunction of two properties:
$U_1$ : tfi $\leq$ S $\leq$ t $\Rightarrow$ E $\leq$ ACR and $U_2$ : S $\leq$ t < tfi $\Rightarrow$ E $\leq$ ACR.
The proof of $U_1 \wedge U_2$ is then done in two steps. First, $U_1 \wedge U_2$ is in turn strengthened into $V \equiv U_1 \wedge U_2 \wedge U_3 \wedge \cdots \wedge U_{10}$, where $U_3, \ldots, U_{10}$ are nontrivial auxiliary properties of $\mathcal{B}'$. Second, $V$ is proved to be an invariant (true initially and remaining true after each event). The invariance proof for $V$ has been mechanically checked with the proof assistant COQ [13]. The auxiliary properties $U_3, \ldots, U_{10}$

can be seen as "lemmas" necessary to achieve the proof of $U_1 \wedge U_2$ by (fixpoint) induction.

With respect to our approach, property $V$ can be seen as a fixpoint of $Post$ and, as such, is an overall approximation of $Post^*$ (since $Post^*$ is the *least* fixpoint). The main advantage of our approach, is that no auxiliary property ("lemma") such as $U_3, \cdots, U_{10}$ has to be manually discovered: $U$ is mechanically verified in its original form. Note that one of the $U_i$ (tfi= tla $\Rightarrow$ FR=LR) is not true in our model but should be replaced by tfi= tla $\Rightarrow$ FR $\geq$ LR. This is a consequence of the slightly more general hypothesis $r_1 \leq r_2 \leq \cdots \leq r_n$ instead of $r_1 < r_2 < \cdots < r_n$. Another advantage here is that $Post^*$ characterizes *all* the properties of the system, and not only $U$. Therefore $Post^*$ can be immediately reused for proving any other property $P$ of the system by testing that $Post^*$ does not contain any state violating $P$. Finally our modelization is likely to be reusable for modeling and verifying enhanced versions of $\mathcal{B}'$, which are currently under development at CNET.

**Verification with GAP.** In [10], we achieved a first mechanical proof of $U$ by encoding the successor relation of the system as a logic program with arithmetical constraints, and computing a fixed-point of the program through the bottom-up evaluation procedure of Revesz [16]. The encoding required an approximation of the successor relation, so that only an upper approximation of $Post^*$ was generated. Nevertheless this approximation was sufficient to prove $U$, because it did not contain any state violating $U$.

With respect to that approach, we used here HYTECH [12], a sophisticated and widely spread analysis tool for hybrid systems [2], rather than GAP, a specific prototype implementation of Revesz's procedure [11]. Therefore our results are now easily reproducible. Besides, with respect to GAP, we reach an exact fixed-point rather than an approximation, and the execution time is much (about 10 times) faster. On the other hand, termination of fixpoint computation was guaranteed with GAP by Revesz's decidability result.

## 5 Final Remarks

Our modelization is a direct translation without any simplification of the real algorithm $\mathcal{B}'$ described in the international norm ITU I-371. We automatically proved the basic correctness property $U$ of algorithm $\mathcal{B}'$ using HYTECH [12] (the full HYTECH code is given in [6]). The proof is parametric in the sense that $U$ holds for all values of the two parameters $a$ and $b$ (with $0 < a < b$) involved by $\mathcal{B}'$. A third parameter $t$ was used for specifying property $U$ itself. Such a proof is *a priori* impossible to do with other analysis tools of real-time systems such as UPPAAL [5] or KRONOS [8] due to this use of parameters. Our analysis contributes to improve the comprehension of the correctness proof for the ABR conformance protocol, in particular in relaxing some unnecessary assumptions. It paves the way for the verification of enhanced versions of $\mathcal{B}'$ currently under development at CNET. This case study gives additional evidence of the importance of (variants of) *parametric timed automata* [4] as a means for modeling and analysing real industrial applications. Other successful verifications of parametric concurrent systems using HYTECH can be found in [7].

# References

1. R. Alur, C. Courcoubetis, N. Halbwachs, T.A. Henzinger, P.-H. Ho, X. Nicollin, A. Olivero, J. Sifakis and S. Yovine. "The Algorithmic Analysis of Hybrid Systems". *Theoretical Computer Science 138:3*, 1995, pp. 3–34.
2. R. Alur, C. Courcoubetis, T.A. Henzinger and P.-H. Ho. "Hybrid Automata: An Algorithmic Approach to the Specification and Verification of Hybrid Systems". *Hybrid Systems I*, LNCS 736, 1993, pp. 209–229.
3. R. Alur and D. Dill. "Automata for Modeling Real-Time Systems". *Proc. 17th ICALP*, LNCS 443, 1990, pp. 322–335.
4. R. Alur, T.A. Henzinger, M. Vardi. "Parametric real-time reasoning". *Proc. 25th Annual ACM Symp. on Theory of Computing (STOC)*, 1993, pp. 592–601.
5. J. Bengtsson, K.G. Larsen, F. Larsson, P. Pettersson and W. Yi. "UPPAAL – a Tool Suite for Automatic Verification of Real-Time Systems". *Hybrid Systems III*, LNCS 1066, 1996, pp. 232-243.
6. B. Bérard and L. Fribourg. "Automated verification of a parametric real-time program: the ABR conformance protocol". *Technical Report LSV-98-12*, CNRS & Ecole Normale Supérieure de Cachan, Dec. 1998 (http://www.lsv.ens-cachan.fr/Publis/).
7. B. Bérard and L. Fribourg. "Reachability Analysis of (Timed) Petri Nets Using Real Arithmetic". *Technical Report LSV-99-3*, CNRS & Ecole Normale Supérieure de Cachan, March 1999 (http://www.lsv.ens-cachan.fr/Publis/).
8. C. Daws, A. Olivero, S. Tripakis and S. Yovine. "The Tool KRONOS". *Hybrid Systems III*, LNCS 1066, 1996, pp. 208-219.
9. P. Felix et al.. "Compréhension de l'étude de cas ABR". *Internal Note*, LaBRI, University of Bordeaux, France, 1997.
10. L. Fribourg. "A Closed-Form Evaluation for Extended Timed Automata". *Technical Report LSV-98-2*, CNRS & Ecole Normale Supérieure de Cachan, March 1998. (http://www.lsv.ens-cachan.fr/Publis/)
11. L. Fribourg and J. Richardson. "Symbolic Verification with Gap-Order Constraints". *Proc. 6th Intl. Workshop on Logic Program Synthesis and Transformation (LOPSTR)*, LNCS 1207, 1996, pp. 20–37.
12. T. Henzinger, P.-H. Ho and H. Wong-Toi. "A User Guide to HYTECH". *Proc. TACAS'95*, LNCS 1019, 1995, pp. 41–71.
13. J.F. Monin. "Proving a real time algorithm for ATM in Coq". *Types for Proofs and Programs*, LNCS 1512, 1998, pp. 277–293.
14. J.-F. Monin and F. Klay. "Formal specification and correction of I.371.1 algorithm for ABR conformance". *Internal Report NT DTL/MSV/003*, CNET, 1997.
15. X. Nicollin, A. Olivero, J. Sifakis and S. Yovine. "An Approach to the Description and Analysis of Hybrid Systems". *Hybrid Systems I*, LNCS 736, 1993, pp. 149–178.
16. P.Z. Revesz. "A Closed-Form Evaluation for Datalog Queries with Integer (Gap)-Order Constraints", *Theoretical Computer Science*, 1993, vol. 116, pp. 117-149.

# Test Generation Derived from Model-Checking *

Thierry Jéron and Pierre Morel

IRISA / INRIA Rennes, Campus de Beaulieu, F-35042 Rennes, France,
{Thierry.Jeron, Pierre.Morel}@irisa.fr

**Abstract.** Model-checking and testing are different activities, at least conceptually. While model-checking consists in comparing two specifications at different abstraction levels, testing consists in trying to find errors or gain some confidence in the correctness of an implementation with respect to a specification by the execution of test cases. Nevertheless, there are also similarities in models and algorithms. We argue for this by giving a new on-the-fly test generation algorithm which is an adaptation of a classical graph algorithm which also serves as a basis of some model-checking algorithms. This algorithm is the Tarjan's algorithm which computes the strongly connected components of a digraph.

## 1 Introduction

Conformance testing aims at applying test cases to an implementation under test ($IUT$) in order to detect errors or increase ones confidence in the fact that the $IUT$ is correct with respect to its specification. It is a black box testing: the source of the $IUT$ is unknown but its behavior is known by its interactions with the environment. Conformance testing is applied in several domains and especially in the domain of protocols where its activity is standardized but not well formalized by [1]. [16] partly bridges this gap by defining a formal framework but does not instantiate it into a precise test generation algorithm.

Nevertheless, a lot of theoretical work has been done on test generation algorithms. Some syntactical methods exist but we will limit our discussion to semantical ones. Semantical methods can be divided into two classes which differ on the models, theories and algorithms. Techniques based on automata theory (see e.g. [20] for a survey) use Mealy machines (automata with each transition labelled with an input and an output) as models. They theoretically have a powerful fault coverage but make strong asumptions on specifications and $IUT$ and are limited to small specifications. The other class of semantical techniques uses the model of labelled transition systems ($LTS$). They stem from fundamental studies on testing theory [8, 2, 5]. Originally defined for general $LTS$, their applicability was not clear. But they were the starting points for more realistic theories based on $LTS$ with differentiated input and output transitions named $IOSM$, $IOTS$ or $IOLTS$ [25, 21]. The central point is a conformance relation relating specifications to correct implementations. These methods at least insure

---

* This work has been partially supported by the french action Forma.

unbias (only non conformant implementations can be rejected by a test case) and "theoretical" exhaustiveness (under some assumptions on implementations, all non conformant implementations can be rejected by a test suite).

In [12] we proposed a first on-the-fly test generation algorithm and we completed the picture in [17]. These algorithms have been implemented in our prototype tool TGV and gave good results on industrial experiments [13]. The main algorithm was based on a traversal of the synchronous product of a test purpose automaton with an $IOLTS$ representing the observable behavior of the specification. We thought that test cases should be acyclic in order to ensure the finiteness of their execution on the $IUT$, so the algorithm was cutting loops. But test practitioners and standardized test suite showed us that this was not always the case. It is the reason why we started to investigate a way for producing test cases with loops.

Some model-checking algorithms for CTL [6] or LTL [23], in particular local or on-the-fly ones also have to tackle with loops. Some of these algorithms (see e.g. [7, 26]) are adaptations of the classical Tarjan's algorithm which computes strongly connected components (SCCs) of a digraph during a depth first search (DFS). For on-the-fly model-checking, this algorithm has the advantage to provide a diagnostic sequence in the stack as soon as a violation of the property is detected. This facility has been used for test generation [10] as the negation of the checked property can be seen as a test selection criterion, i.e. a test purpose.

In our opinion, this is not sufficient as diagnostic sequences have to be further transformed into test sequences by taking into account output freedom of the specification, thus giving test sequences with possibly a lot of *Inconclusive* verdicts [1]. These verdicts should be reduced to the minimum in generating more adaptative test cases. We believe that test generation can benefit from model-checking algorithms but they need some adaptations to the testing framework. We present here such algorithms.

The paper is organized as follows. We first present in Section 2 the models used for test generation. Section 3 then gives an iterative formulation of the Tarjan's algorithm and present it as a framework for the derivation of all other algorithms presented in the paper. The three subsequent sections present instantiations of this framework for test generation. Section 4 describes an algorithm computing the subgraph of all sequences leading to *Accept* states of the test purpose and can be seen as a complete diagnosis for the CTL property $AG\neg Accept$ (or a complete explanation of $EF\,Accept$). In Section 5 we extract one test case from this subgraph. Section 6 improves the first algorithm for on-the-fly generation by anticipating operations of the second algorithm. Section 7 then describes how these algorithms are integrated into our tool TGV. We conclude with a comparison with other works and perspectives.

---

[1] *Inconclusive* verdicts are given to correct outputs of the $IUT$ which do not lead to the satisfaction of the test purpose.

## 2 Conformance Testing

In this section we introduce the models used for test case generation and how they are used to describe specifications, implementations, test cases and test purposes. These models are based on the classical model of labelled transition systems with distinguished inputs and outputs. We report to [25] for a precise definition of the testing theory used.

**Definition 1.** *An IOLTS is an LTS $M = (Q^M, A^M, \rightarrow_M, q_0^M)$ with $Q^M$ a finite set of states, $A^M$ a finite alphabet partitioned into three distinct sets $A^M = A_I^M \cup A_O^M \cup I^M$ where $A_I^M$ and $A_O^M$ are respectively inputs and outputs alphabets and $I^M$ is an alphabet of unobservable, internal actions, $\rightarrow_M \subset Q^M \times A^M \times Q^M$ is the transition relation and $q_0^M$ is the initial state.*

We will use the classical following notations of $LTS$ for $IOLTS$.
Let $q, q', q_{(i)} \in Q^M, Q \subseteq Q^M, a_{(i)} \in A_I^M \cup A_O^M, \tau_{(i)} \in I^M$, and $\sigma \in (A_I^M \cup A_O^M)^*$.
$q \overset{\epsilon}{\Rightarrow}_M q' \equiv (q = q' \vee q \overset{\tau_1...\tau_n}{\rightarrow}_M q')$ and $q \overset{a}{\Rightarrow}_M q' \equiv \exists q_1, q_2 : q \overset{\epsilon}{\Rightarrow}_M q_1 \overset{a}{\rightarrow}_M q_2 \overset{\epsilon}{\Rightarrow}_M q'$
which generalizes in $q \overset{a_1...a_n}{\Rightarrow}_M q' \equiv \exists q_0, ...q_n : q = q_0 \overset{a_1}{\Rightarrow}_M q_1... \overset{a_n}{\Rightarrow}_M q_n = q'$.
$Trace_M(q) \equiv \{\sigma | q \overset{\sigma}{\Rightarrow}_M\}$ and $Trace_M(M) = Trace_M(q_0^M)$.
We note $q \textbf{ after}_M \sigma \equiv \{q' | q \overset{\sigma}{\Rightarrow}_M q'\}$ and $Q \textbf{ after}_M \sigma \equiv \cup_{q \in Q} q \textbf{ after}_M \sigma$. We define $Out_M(q) \equiv \{a \in A_O^M | q \overset{a}{\Rightarrow}_M\}$ and $Out_M(Q) \equiv \{Out_M(q) | q \in Q\}$. We will not always distinguish between an $IOLTS$ and its initial state and note $M \Rightarrow_M$ instead of $q_0^M \Rightarrow_M$. We will omit the subscript $_M$ when it is clear from the context.

A specification is given in a formal description language (e.g. SDL, LOTOS or Estelle) which semantics allows to describe the behavior of the specification by an $IOLTS$ $S = (Q^S, A^S, \rightarrow^S, q_0^S)$ [2]. The $IOLTS$ $S$ and intermediate $IOLTS$ defined from S are not effectively built but we need to define them for reasonning. As usually, we will assume that the behavior of the $IUT$ can also be described by an $IOLTS$ which can never refuse an input: $IUT = (Q^{IUT}, A^{IUT}, \rightarrow^{IUT}, q_0^{IUT})$ with $A^{IUT} = A_I^{IUT} \cup A_O^{IUT} \cup I^{IUT}$ and $A_I^S \subseteq A_I^{IUT}$ and $A_O^S \subseteq A_O^{IUT}$. We use a conformance relation which says that an $IUT$ conforms to $S$ if and only if after a trace of $S$, outputs of the $IUT$ are outputs of $S$:
$IUT \textbf{ ioconf } S \iff \forall \sigma \in Trace(S), Out(IUT \textbf{ after}_{IUT} \sigma) \subseteq Out(S \textbf{ after}_S \sigma)$
For the sake of clarity, we took the definition of **ioconf** but all results also apply to **ioco** [25] which considers quiescence (i.e. deadlock and output quiescence) as an observable event. In [17] we also treat livelocks. The relation **ioco** is obtained from **ioconf** by adding loops labelled with a particular output $\delta$ to quiescent states of $S$ and $IUT$.

In practice, test purposes are used as test selection criteria. We formalize them by automata i.e $IOLTS$ with selected marked states. A test purpose is a deterministic $IOLTS$ $TP = (Q^{TP}, A^{TP}, \rightarrow_{TP}, q_0^{TP})$ equipped with two sets of sink states $Accept^{TP}$ which defines $Pass$ verdicts and $Reject^{TP}$ which allows to limit the exploration of the graph $S$. We suppose that $A^{TP} = A^S$ (this authorizes

---

[2] LOTOS does not distinguishes between inputs and outputs and a renaming is necessary for test generation.

actions of $TP$ to be internal actions of $S$ which is useful for testing in context) and $TP$ is complete ($\forall q \in Q^{TP}, a \in A^{TP} q \xrightarrow{a}_{TP}$ ).

The synchronous product of $S$ and $TP$ is an $IOLTS$ $SP = (Q^{SP}, A^{SP}, \rightarrow_{SP}, q_0^{SP})$ with $Q^{SP} = Q^S \times Q^{TP}$, $A^{SP} = A^S$, $(p,q) \xrightarrow{a}_{SP} (p',q') \iff p \xrightarrow{a}_S p'$ and $q \xrightarrow{a}_{TP} q'$, $q_0^{SP} = (q_0^S, q_0^{TP})$. It can be understood as an automaton with sets of sink states defined by $Accept^{SP} = Q^S \times Accept^{TP}$ and $Reject^{SP} = Q^S \times Reject^{TP}$.

As test generation only considers the observable behavior of $S$, a first step is to replace in $SP$ all internal actions by $\tau$, to reduce $\tau$ actions (while adding $\delta$ loops for **ioco**) and to determinize the result.

This defines an $IOLTS$ $SP_{VIS} = (Q^{VIS}, A^{VIS}, \rightarrow_{VIS}, q_0^{VIS})$ with $Q^{VIS} \subseteq 2^{Q^{SP}}$, $A^{VIS} = A_I^{VIS} \cup A_O^{VIS}$ with $A_O^{VIS} = A_O^{SP}$ and $A_I^{VIS} = A_I^{SP}$, $q_0^{VIS} = q_0^{SP}$ **after**$_{SP}$ $\epsilon$,

# 3 Tarjan's Algorithm as a Framework

In this section we present an iterative version of the algorithm "StrongConnect" [24] computing the SCCs of a given digraph $G = (Q^G, A^G, \rightarrow_G, q_0^G)$ as a framework to derive other algorithms. First, we introduce all the notions and results used to describe this framework and following algorithms. Finally, we show the framework "StrongConnect" and its resulting graph.

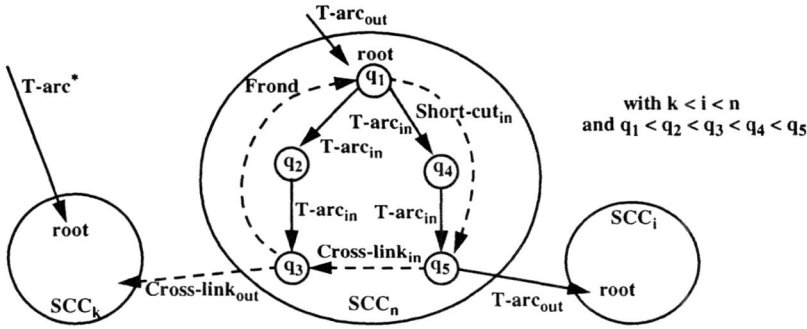

**Fig. 1.** Partition of edges defined by a DFS

Recall that a graph is strongly connected if for each pair of states (v,w) there is a path from v to v containing w. The SCCs of a graph $G$ are the maximal strongly connected subgraphs of $G$. A DFS applied to $G$ defines a spanning forest F by considering edges leading to unvisited states (tree-arcs). We suppose that states are numbered in the order in which they are reached during the search (field "number" of a state). Inspired from [24] a DFS defines a partition of edges (see Figure 1) : edges leading to a new state (not yet numbered) of the same (resp. distinct) SCC(s) are called "tree-arcs$_{in}$" (resp. "tree-arcs$_{out}$"); "fronds" are edges running from descendants to ancestors in the tree; "short-cuts$_{in}$" (resp. "short-cuts$_{out}$") are edges running from ancestors to descendants of the same (resp. distinct) SCC(s); edges in a SCC (resp. between two SCCs) running from one subtree to another subtree of F are called "cross-links$_{in}$" (resp. "cross-links$_{out}$"). For any frond (resp. short-cut) between two states v and u (resp. u and v), there exists a path of tree-arcs from u leading to v. A root of a SCC is the first reached state of this SCC and thus the smallest numbered state. The field "lowlink" of a state allows to detect the root of each SCC synthesizing the smallest state which is in the same component and is reachable by traversing zero or more tree-arcs followed by at most one frond or cross-link$_{in}$. A state is a root of a SCC if and only if its number and its lowlink are equal. The following framework is the well-known algorithm "StrongConnect" of Tarjan, where some sections (Start state, New state, Old state, State of a new SCC, Tree-arc backtrack) are left empty for derived algorithms. This algorithm identifies the set of SCCs of a graph $G$. The stack "Dfs_Stack" stores the current exploration sequence during the search and the stack "Scc_Stack" keeps all the visited states which SCC is still not completed. The field "act" of a state q is the label of the tree-arc leading to q.

The function Adjacency_Set gives fireable transitions from a given state q, so:

Adjacency_Set $(q) := \{(a, q') \mid (q, a, q') \in \rightarrow_G\}$

**Procedure** StrongConnect (**state** : $q_{start}$);

**state** : $q_{source}$, $q_{target}$, $q_{pred}$, $q$; **adjacency_set** : $Adj_{source}$, $Adj_{target}$, $Adj_{pred}$;

**BEGIN**

    Creation of $Dfs\_Stack$; Creation of $Scc\_Stack$;

    $q_{start}.number := q_{start}.lowlink := i := i + 1$; $q_{start}.act := \epsilon$;

    [**Start state**]

    Push $(q_{start}, Adjacency\_Set(q_{start}))$ in $Dfs\_Stack$; Push $q_{start}$ in $Scc\_Stack$;

    **while** not empty $Dfs\_Stack$ **do begin**

        $(q_{source}, Adj_{source}) := Top(Dfs\_Stack)$;

      **if** not empty $Adj_{source}$ **then begin**

          Remove $(m, q_{target})$ from $Adj_{source}$;

          **if** $q_{target}$ is not yet numbered **then begin** (*$(q_{source}, m, q_{target})$ is a tree-arc*)

              $q_{target}.number := q_{target}.lowlink := i := i + 1$; $q_{target}.act := m$;

              Push $(q_{target}, Adjacency\_Set(q_{target}))$ in $Dfs\_Stack$; Push $q_{target}$ in $Scc\_Stack$;

              [**New state**]

          **else begin** (* $(q_{source}, m, q_{target})$ is not a tree-arc *)

              **if** $q_{target}.number < q_{source}.number$ and $q_{target}$ in $Scc\_Stack$ **then**

              (* $(q_{source}, m, q_{target})$ is a frond or a cross-link$_{in}$ (in same SCC) *)

                  $q_{source}.lowlink := min(q_{source}.lowlink, q_{target}.number)$;

              [**Old state**]

          **end**

      **else begin** (* $Adj_{source}$ is empty *)

          Pop $(q_{source})$ from $Dfs\_Stack$;

          **if** $q_{source}.lowlink = q_{source}.number$ **then begin** (*$q_{source}$ is root of SCC*)

              **while** $q := top(Scc\_Stack)$ satisfies $q.number \geq q_{source}.number$ **do**

              **begin** (* creation of a new component *)

                  Pop $(q)$ from $Scc\_Stack$ and put $q$ in current component;

                  [**State of a new SCC**]

              **end**

          **end**

          **if** not empty Dfs_Stack **then begin** (* backtracking *)

              $(q_{pred}, Adj_{pred}) := top(Dfs\_Stack)$;

              $q_{pred}.lowlink := min(q_{pred}.lowlink, q_{source}.lowlink)$;

              [**Tree-arc backtrack**]

          **end**

        **end**

      **end**

    **end**

**END;**

**Procedure** MAIN (G);
**BEGIN**
    integer : i := 0;
    for $q_{start}$ in $Q^G$ if $q_{start}$ not yet numbered **then** StrongConnect ($q_{start}$);
**END**;

We can interpret the result of this program as the reduced directed acyclic graph (DAG) where a node is a SCC of $G$ and where edges are either tree-arc$_{out}$, cross-link$_{out}$, or short-cut$_{out}$. This algorithm is linear in both space and time. Notice that if the input graph $G$ is rooted, a call to StrongConnect with the root will visit all states.

## 4   Computation of the Complete Test Graph

Notice that if the controllability condition defined in Section 2 is suppressed and in condition 3 we redefine *Pass* by $Pass = Accept_{VIS}$, the resulting set of properties uniquely defines a subgraph of $SP_{VIS}$ called *Complete Test Graph* (*CTG*) as it defines all potential test cases w.r.t. $TP$. Even if it does not define a test case, it is sometimes interesting to produce $CTG$ and then to seperate it into a set of test cases. The following algorithm instantiating the undefined parts of StrongConnect framework computes the subgraph of the graph $SP_{VIS}$ composed of all sequences leading to states in $Accept^{VIS}$. Moreover, as **ioco** forces to take into account all outputs of the specification, those not leading to $Accept^{VIS}$ have to be kept. Target states are put in the *Inconclusive* set.

$$Trace(CTG) = \{\sigma \mid SP_{VIS} \textbf{ after } \sigma \subseteq Accept^{VIS}\}$$
$$\cup \{\sigma.a \in Trace(SP_{VIS}) \mid a \in A_O^{VIS} \wedge \exists\sigma'(SP_{VIS} \textbf{ after } \sigma.\sigma' \subseteq Accept^{VIS})\}$$

The problem of finding this subgraph reduces to the problem of finding the reduced DAG of SCCs which lead to an *Accept* state and thus reduces to find the roots of SCCs leading to an *Accept* state. For a DAG, a simple DFS allows to correctly synthesize the reachability to an *Accept* state along tree-arcs$_{out}$, cross-links$_{out}$ and short-cuts$_{out}$ (there is no other type of edge in such a graph). This property is used to prove the correctness of the synthesis for each root of SCC using the underlying DAG structure of SCCs. Notice that a short-cut$_{out}$ between u and v does not give additional information regarding reachability in u w.r.t. v because there exists another path of tree-arcs from u leading to v. A root of a SCC leads to an *Accept* state if and only if it is an *Accept* state or a state of its SCC can reach another SCC, by a tree-arc$_{out}$ or cross-link$_{out}$, which leads to an *Accept* state. The field "*L2A*" of a state meaning "Leads to an Accept state" is used to synthesize this reachability information. Moreover, $L2A$ is also used for garbage collection of unnecessary parts of the graph.

When we reach a state for the first time, its $L2A$ field is initialized to true if and only if it is an *Accept* state. So:

**[Start state]**

$q_{\text{start}}.L2A := q_{\text{start}} \in Accept^{\text{VIS}}$;

**if** $q_{\text{start}} \in Reject^{\text{VIS}} \cup Accept^{\text{VIS}}$ **then**

remove all $(q_{\text{start}}, a, q')$ from $\rightarrow_{\text{VIS}}$;

**[New state]**

$q_{\text{target}}.L2A := q_{\text{target}} \in Accept^{\text{VIS}}$;

**if** $q_{\text{target}} \in Reject^{\text{VIS}} \cup Accept^{\text{VIS}}$ **then**

remove all $(q_{\text{target}}, a, q')$ from $\rightarrow_{\text{VIS}}$;

When a state is reached again, only cross-link$_{out}$ transitions add more information about reachability to an *Accept* state to the root of a strongly connected component. An input short-cut$_{out}$ or cross-link$_{out}$ to a SCC not leading to *Accept* is pruned. So:

**[Old state]**

**if** $q_{\text{target}}$ not in Scc_Stack **then begin**

(* It is a short-cut$_{out}$ or cross-link$_{out}$ *)

**if** $q_{\text{target}}.number < q_{\text{source}}.number$

**then** (* It is a cross-link$_{out}$ *)

$q_{\text{source}}.L2A := q_{\text{source}}.L2A \vee q_{\text{target}}.L2A$;

**if** $\neg q_{\text{target}}.L2A \wedge \text{m} \in A_{\text{I}}^{\text{VIS}}$ **then**

remove $(q_{\text{source}}, \text{m}, q_{\text{target}})$ from $\rightarrow_{\text{VIS}}$;

**end**

When a root of a SCC is found, its $L2A$ field is correct. All the states of this SCC update their $L2A$ field w.r.t. their root and the part of the graph which cannot lead to *Accept* is pruned.

**[State of a new SCC]**

$q.L2A := q_{\text{source}}.L2A$;

**if** $\neg q.L2A$ **then**

remove all $(q, a, q')$ from $\rightarrow_{\text{VIS}}$;

We have to synthesize the reachability information along tree-arcs. An input tree-arc$_{out}$ leading to a state not in $CTG$ is pruned. So:

**[Tree-arc backtrack]**

$q_{\text{pred}}.L2A := q_{\text{pred}}.L2A \vee q_{\text{source}}.L2A$;

**if** $q_{\text{source}}.number = q_{\text{source}}.lowlink \wedge \neg q_{\text{source}}.L2A \wedge m' := q_{\text{source}}.act \in A_{\text{I}}^{\text{VIS}}$

**then**

remove $(q_{\text{pred}}, \text{m'}, q_{\text{source}})$ from $\rightarrow_{\text{VIS}}$;

Let $CTG$ be the subgraph obtained by this algorithm from $SP_{\text{VIS}}$ and reduced to the accessible part from its initial state. $CTG = (Q^{\text{CTG}}, A^{\text{CTG}}, \rightarrow_{\text{CTG}}, q_0^{\text{CTG}})$, with two sets of marked states $Pass^{\text{CTG}}$ and $Inconc^{\text{CTG}}$ such that:

$A^{\text{CTG}} = A_{\text{O}}^{\text{CTG}} \cup A_{\text{I}}^{\text{CTG}}$ with $A_{\text{O}}^{\text{CTG}} \subseteq A_{\text{O}}^{\text{VIS}}$ and $A_{\text{I}}^{\text{CTG}} = A_{\text{I}}^{\text{VIS}}$ (mirror image),
$\rightarrow_{\text{CTG}} = \{(v, a, w) \in \rightarrow_{\text{VIS}} \mid v.L2A \wedge (w.L2A \vee a \in A_{\text{I}}^{\text{CTG}})\}$, $q_0^{\text{CTG}} = q_0^{\text{VIS}}$,
$Q^{\text{CTG}} = \{v \in Q^{\text{VIS}} \mid q_0^{\text{CTG}} \xrightarrow{*}_{\text{CTG}} v\}$, $Pass^{\text{CTG}} = Accept^{\text{VIS}} \cap Q^{\text{CTG}}$,
$Inconc^{\text{CTG}} = \{v \in Q^{\text{CTG}} \backslash Pass^{\text{CTG}} \mid \forall a \in A^{\text{CTG}} \wedge w \in Q^{\text{CTG}}, (v, a, w) \notin \rightarrow_{\text{CTG}}\}$.

The graph $CTG$ contains all the behaviors a test case might have. According to the test case definition, now we have to deal with controllability.

## 5 Extraction of a Controllable Test Graph

We present here an algorithm based on the StrongConnect framework and computing a subgraph of the accepted subgraph $CTG$, controllable and where each state can reach *Pass* state or is an *Inconclusive* state. Informally, the adaptation of StrongConnect consists in a DFS starting from each *Pass* state of $CTG$ and using the predecessor transition relation. A correction of possibly controllability conflicts is done for all new reached state by pruning conflicting actions with the current action. This may modify the reachability from the initial state which is synthesized in order to determine the set of states of the resulting controllable test case. This is based on the same scheme as the synthesis of $L2A$ (field "$rfis$" for "Reachable From the Initial State").

The function Adjacency_Set takes into account the backward sight of the new algorithm.

$Adjacency\_Set(q) :=$
$\quad \{(a, q')|(q', a, q) \in \rightarrow_{\text{CTG}}\}$

The procedure Pruning allows to prune transitions of $CTG$ causing controllability conflicts with the current transition of a given state.

**Procedure** Pruning (q, m)

**Begin**

if $m \in A_O^{\text{CTG}}$ then (* remove all others *)

$\forall\, m' \neq m$, remove $(q, m', q')$ from $\rightarrow_{\text{CTG}}$;

**else** (* remove all the outputs *)

$\forall m' \in A_O^{\text{CTG}}$, remove $(q, m', q')$ from $\rightarrow_{\text{CTG}}$;

**End**

The initialization and synthesis of the $rfis$ field are based on the $L2A$ field scheme. We prune conflicting transitions when a new state is reached.

[Start state]

$q_{\text{start}}.rfis := (q_{\text{start}} = q_0^{\text{CTG}});$

[**New state**]

$q_{\text{target}}.rfis := (q_{\text{target}} = q_0^{\text{CTG}});$

Pruning $(q_{\text{target}}, m);$

[**Old State**]

$q_{\text{source}}.rfis := q_{\text{source}}.rfis \lor q_{\text{target}}.rfis;$

if $\neg q_{\text{target}}.rfis \land m \in A_O^{\text{CTG}}$ then

$\quad$ remove $(q_{\text{target}}, m, q_{\text{source}})$ from $\rightarrow_{\text{CTG}}$

[State of a new SCC]

$q.rfis := q_{\text{source}}.rfis;$

if $\neg q.rfis$ then

$\quad$ remove all $(q, a, q')$ from $\rightarrow_{\text{CTG}};$

[Tree-arc backtrack]

$q_{\text{pred}}.rfis := q_{\text{pred}}.rfis \lor q_{\text{source}}.rfis;$

if $q_{\text{source}}.number = q_{\text{source}}.lowlink \land$
$\neg q_{\text{source}}.rfis \land m' := q_{\text{source}}.act \in A_O^{\text{CTG}}$
then

$\quad$ remove $(q_{\text{source}}, m', q_{\text{pred}})$ from $\rightarrow_{\text{CTG}};$

Let $TC = (Q^{\text{TC}}, A^{\text{TC}}, \rightarrow_{\text{TC}}, q_0^{\text{TC}})$, with two sets $Pass^{\text{TC}}$ and $Inconc^{\text{TC}}$ such that : $A^{\text{TC}} = A_O^{\text{TC}} \cup A_I^{\text{TC}}$ with $A_O^{\text{TC}} = A_O^{\text{CTG}}$ and $A_I^{\text{TC}} = A_I^{\text{CTG}}$,
$\rightarrow_{\text{TC}} = \{(v, a, w) \rightarrow_{\text{CTG}} | v.rfis \land (w.rfis \lor a \in A_I^{\text{TC}})\}$, $q_0^{\text{TC}} = q_0^{\text{CTG}}$,
$Q^{\text{TC}} = \{v \in Q^{\text{CTG}} \mid q_0^{\text{TC}} \xrightarrow{*}_{\text{TC}} v\}$, $Pass^{\text{TC}} = Pass^{\text{CTG}} \cap Q^{\text{TC}}$,
$Inconc^{\text{TC}} = \{v \in Q^{\text{TC}} \backslash Pass^{\text{TC}} \mid \forall a \in A^{\text{TC}} \land w \in Q^{\text{TC}}, (v, a, w) \notin \rightarrow_{\text{TC}}\}$.

**Remark:** The order in which we apply "controllable" StrongConnect to $Pass$ states of $CTG$ influences the resulting test case. Breadth-first search starting from the set of $Pass$ states could give shortest test cases, but StrongConnect allows to interleave garbage collection. The graph $CTG$ represents all the behavior to be tested w.r.t. a test purpose. We can derive from this graph sequential, arborescent, or looping test cases. We could even apply some automata based methods such as UIO to each SCC of $CTG$.

# 6 Solving Controllability Conflicts during Forward Search

In the previous section, we have shown an algorithm resolving all the controllability conflicts of the graph $CTG$. In fact some conflicts can be solved during the forward DFS as will be shown in this section.

Notice that in the complete algorithm, we attempt to synthesize in an efficient way the information of reachability to an $Accept$ state on all the roots of SCC of $SP_{\text{VIS}}$. First, we prone that a controllability conflict in a state can be removed during this algorithm in the case where we know that this state leads to an *Accept* state. This is done while backtracking a transition m between a source state such that its *L2A* is still false and a target state such that its *L2A* is true. In this case, we can prune all the transitions from the source state in conflict with m. This assumption leads us to synthesize *L2A* not only for a root of a SCC but also for all the states of this SCC which can get the information earlier and then to prune parts of the initial graph earlier and thus saving time. In this algorithm refined from the *CTG* computation, the synthesis of *L2A* information is done along tree-arcs, cross-links and fronds and possible pruning actions are done earlier. As seen before, short-cut transitions give redundant information.

The function "pruning" not only prune conflicting already synthesized transitions but also conflicting transitions not already treated.

**Procedure** Pruning $(q, m, Adj)$

**Begin**

**if** $m \in A_I^{VIS}$ **then**

**begin** (*remove all other transitions*)

$Adj := \emptyset$;

$\forall m' \neq m$, remove all $(q, m', q')$ from $\rightarrow_{VIS}$;

**else begin** (* remove all the inputs *)

$\forall m' \in A_I^{VIS}$, remove all $(q, m', q')$ from $\rightarrow_{VIS}$;

$\forall m' \in A_I^{VIS}$, remove all $(m', q')$ from $Adj$;

**end**

**End**

[**Start state**], [**New state**] and [**State of a new SCC**] are identical to parts of the complete test graph computation. The synthesis of *L2A* is done along cross-links, short-cuts, fronds and tree-arcs. Now, pruning actions are done earlier when backtracking to a state which knows that it leads to *Accept*.

[**Old State**]

**if** $q_{target}.L2A \wedge \neg q_{source}.L2A$ **then**

Pruning $(q_{source}, m, Adj_{source})$;

**else if** $q_{target} \notin Scc\_Stack \wedge \neg q_{target}.L2A$

$\wedge\ m \in A_I^{VIS}$ **then**

remove $(q_{source}, m, q_{target})$ from $\rightarrow_{VIS}$;

$q_{source}.L2A := q_{source}.L2A \vee q_{target}.L2A$;

[**Tree-arc backtrack**]

**if** $q_{source}.L2A \wedge \neg q_{pred}.L2A$ **then**

Pruning $(q_{pred}, q_{source}.act, Adj_{pred})$;

**else if** $q_{source} \notin Scc\_Stack \wedge \neg q_{source}.L2A$

$\wedge\ m' := q_{source}.act \in A_I^{VIS}$ **then**

remove $(q_{pred}, m', q_{source})$ from $\rightarrow_{VIS}$;

$q_{pred}.L2A := q_{pred}.L2A \vee q_{source}.L2A$;

**Remark:** The resulting graph is a subgraph of *CTG*. Some controllability conflicts persist in some states which have synthesized the *L2A* information w.r.t. their root only. We have to apply to this resulting graph the algorithm of the previous section to correct persistent conflicts.

# 7 Tool

**Architecture and Algorithms:** The algorithms presented in the paper are the basis of our prototype tool TGV developed in collaboration with IRISA/INRIA Rennes and Verimag Grenoble [12, 13, 17, 4]. In Section 2 we have presented all *IOLTS* considered for the test cases generation: $S$, $TP$, $SP$, $SP_{VIS}$. As TGV works on-the-fly, only necessary parts of these *IOLTS* are constructed on demand in a lazy way. This imposes that *IOLTS* are implicit and accessed through APIs giving the functions for their construction: the initial state, the transition relation and comparison of states. TGV also uses an API of CADP [11] to store parts of all intermediate $IOLTS$. TGV is interfaced with several different simulators which provide the API for S. In particular it is interfaced with the SDL simulator ObjectGeode from Verilog [3] and the LOTOS simulator from CADP.

Another central algorithm is the algorithm which computes $SP_{\mathrm{VIS}}$ from $SP$ already presented in [17]. It combines several aspects: addition of $\delta$ actions in the case of quiescence, $\tau$-reduction and determinization. All this is done on-the-fly with again an adaptation of StrongConnect interleaved with a classical subset construction for determinization (see e.g. [15]). In this case StrongConnect is applied to the subgraph of $SP$ composed of $\tau$-actions. Meanwhile, observable actions and target states are synthesized on top of the subgraphs and a subset construction is applied for determinization. StrongConnect starts from the initial state of $SP$ and creates new initial states for subsequent calls to StrongConnect each time an observable action reaches a new state until no new initial state is created. Links from states to their SCCs are stored avoiding to explore an already computed SCC. The application of Tarjan algorithm has linear complexity in time and space but the subset construction involves an exponential blow up in the size of the resulting graph. Nevertheless as TGV is applied on-the-fly we have been able to tackle examples with a lot of internal actions (specifications describing services for example) where determinization was the bottleneck for methods with complete state graph generation.

**Case Studies:** The first experiment of TGV [13] was done on an SDL specification of an ISDN protocol named DREX. Even with this embryonic version implementing the algorithm of [12] which did not completely work on the fly, TGV proved its efficiency and the quality of generated test cases compared to manual ones. TGV now works on-the-fly with the algorithms presented here and has been experimented on two industrial size case studies. The first one is an SDL specification of the SSCOP protocol of the ATM which served for many other case studies. This study allowed us to combine static analysis techniques in prelude to test generation and to use TGV on a multi-process specification in an asynchronous environment [4]. The second one is a LOTOS specification of a cache coherency protocol of a multiprocessor architecture of Bull [18]. Produced test cases have been executed on the real architecture and improved the test practice in a domain to which it was not originally dedicated. For these two case studies, on-the-fly generation proved its utility as it was impossible to generate the complete state graphs.

**Comparison with other Techniques:** Compared to TGV, methods based on automata theory (see e.g. [20]) have serious drawbacks. They need the construction of complete state graphs which limits their use to small specifications. As in TGV, they need abstraction and reduction of internal actions, determinization and often minimization, but on the whole state graph of the specification. They need the construction of identifying sequences (UIO for example) and quite complex algorithms to build test cases while TGV is linear in this phase. Their advantage is the complete coverage of a fault model but, as other methods, this needs assumptions on the implementation such as fairness. Often determinism is required but this is not realistic. A test suite is a monolithic sequence and does not correspond to hand-written test cases. Observable non-determinism (possible responses of the implementation to an input) is not really taken into account because output divergence of the specification w.r.t. the test sequence directly leads to an *Inconclusive* verdict . Nevertheless, test suites written by hand sometimes have identifying sequences that automatic tools should be able to produce. These sequences do not identify states of the state graph but control states of the specification. An idea is to use these methods on more abstract specifications (only the control part) in order to generate test purposes for control state identification.

This leads us to the comparison with TVEDA. TGV and TVEDA are complementary tools. TVEDA can produce automatically test purposes that can be used by TGV. But generating test purposes automatically is in general not sufficient to cover all interesting behaviors. So users will still have to specify some test purposes by hand.

In some aspects, TGV seems similar to Samstag [14] which uses test purposes specified by MSCs. But there are important differences. The first one is that the theory underlying Samstag is not clear. Nothing refers to any conformance relation or fault model which prevent from any proof on the correctness of generated test cases. Non-determinism is not taken into account because if a test purpose MSC does not define a "unique observable", it is rejected. A test purpose specified by an MSC must describe a complete sequence of observable events which makes it difficult to write and prevents for any abstraction. Finally, the algorithm is almost limited to checking that the MSC describes a (non-deterministic) behavior of the specification and completing the MSC with inputs leading to *Inconclusive*.

Trojka [9] has common points with TGV. It is based on the same theoretical background [25]. It performs on-the-fly test case generation in the sense that it can simultaneously execute them on the IUT. Trojka does not use test purposes as TGV but randomly chooses outputs of the test case among possible ones and checks the validity of inputs according to the observable behavior of the specification. This necessitates a function similar to $\tau$-reduction and determinization . This has been implemented by a breadth traversal which prevents the detection of livelocks and may duplicate some work, problems which are solved by TGV with the computation of SCCs.

## 8   Conclusion

We have presented a new on-the-fly test case generation algorithm based on a classical graph algorithm also used in some local and on-the-fly model-checkers. This algorithm has complexity linear in the size of the observable behavior of the product of a test purpose and a specification. It produces test cases of high quality and very similar to those written by hand with choices and loops. This algorithm and those sketched in Section 7 are being transfered into the Object-

Geode tool from Verilog [3]. They will serve as the test generation engine which will accept test purposes either written by hand or obtained by simulation or automatically computed by a method derived from TVeda with a coverage strategy [19]. However, what is lacking in TGV is a clever treatment of data. For the moment, the stress has been put on control and data values are enumerated by the underlying simulation tools which may lead to a state explosion for specifications with large value domains. But we have started to study the possibility to combine the algorithms of TGV with a constraint solver and abstract interpretation techniques with the ambition to generate symbolic test cases with parameters and variables. Some ideas from previous works on TVEDA for example [22] could also be helpful.

# References

1. ISO/IEC International Standard 9646-1/2/3. OSI-Open Systems Interconnection, Information Technology - Open Systems Interconnection Conformance Testing Methodology and Framework, 1992.
2. S. Abramsky. Observational equivalence as a testing equivalence. *Theoretical Computer Science*, 53(3), 1987.
3. B. Algayres, Y. Lejeune, F. Hugonnet, and F. Hantz. The AVALON project : A VALidatiON Environment For SDL/MSC Descriptions. In *6th SDL Forum, Darmstadt*, 1993.
4. M. Bozga, J.-C. Fernandez, L. Ghirvu, C. Jard, T. Jéron, A. Kerbrat, P. Morel, and L. Mounier. Verification and test generation for the SSCOP protocol. *Journal of Science of Computer Programming, Special Issue on The Application of Formal Methods in Industrial Critical Systems*, To appear, 1999.
5. E. Brinskma. A theory for the derivation of tests. In *Protocol Specification, Testing and Verification VIII*, pages 63–74. North-Holland, 1988.
6. E.M. Clarke, E.A. Emerson, and A.P. Sistla. Automatic verification of finite state concurrent systems using temporal logic specification. *ACM Transactions on Programming Languages and Systems*, 2(8):244–263, 1986.
7. C. Courcoubetis, M. Vardi, P. Wolper, and M. Yannakakis. Memory efficient algorithms for the verification of temporal properties. In *Workshop on Computer Aided Verification*. LNCS 531, June 1990.
8. R. De Nicola and M. Henessy. Testing equivalences for processes. *Theoretical Computer Science*, 34:83–133, 1984.
9. R.G. De Vries and J. Tretmans. On-the-Fly Conformance Testing using SPIN. In G. Holzmann, E. Najm, and A. Serhrouchni, editors, *Fourth Workshop on Automata Theoretic Verification with the SPIN Model Checker*, ENST 98 S 002, pages 115–128, Paris, France, November 2 1998.
10. A. Engels, L. Feijs, and S. Mauw. Test generation for intelligent networks using model checking. In *Third Workshop TACAS, Enschede, The Netherlands*, LNCS 1217. Springer-Verlag, 1997.
11. J.-C. Fernandez, H. Garavel, A. Kerbrat, R. Mateescu, L. Mounier, and M. Sighireanu. CADP: A Protocol Validation and Verification Toolbox. In Rajeev Alur and Thomas A. Henzinger, editors, *Proc. of CAV'96 (New Brunswick, New Jersey, USA)*. LNCS 1102, August 1996.

12. J.-C. Fernandez, C. Jard, T. Jéron, and C. Viho. Using On-the-fly Verification Techniques for the Generation of Test Suites. In R. Alur and T.A. Henzinger, editors, *Proc. of CAV'96, (New Brunswick, New Jersey, USA)*. LNCS 1102, August 1996.

13. J.-C. Fernandez, C. Jard, T. Jéron, and C. Viho. An Experiment in Automatic Generation of Test Suites for Protocoles with Verification Technology. *Science of Computer Programming*, 29, 1997.

14. J. Grabowski, D. Hogrefe, and R. Nahm. Test case generation with test purpose specification by MSCs. In O. Færgemand and A. Sarma, editors, *6th SDL Forum*, pages 253–266, Darmstadt (Germany), 1993. Elsevier Science B.V. (North-Holland).

15. J.E. Hopcroft and J.D. Ullman. *Introduction to automata theory, languages, and computation*. Addison-Wesley series in computer science, 1979.

16. ITU-T SG 10/Q.8 ISO/IEC JTC1/SC21 WG7. Information retrieval, transfer and management for OSI; framework: Formal Methods in Conformance Testing. CD 13245-1, ITU-T proposed recommendation Z500. ISO/ITU-T, 1996.

17. T. Jéron and P. Morel. Abstraction, $\tau$-réduction et déterminisation à la volée: application à la génération de test. In G. Leduc, editor, *CFIP'97 : Ingénierie des Protocoles*. Hermes, September 1997.

18. H. Kahlouche, C. Viho, and M. Zendri. An industrial experiment in automatic generation of executable test suites for a cache coherency protocol. In A. Petrenko and N. Yevtushenko, editors, *IFIP TC6 $11^{th}$ International Workshop on Testing of Communicating Systems*. Chapman & Hall, September 1998.

19. A. Kerbrat, T. Jéron, and R. Groz. Automated Test Generation from SDL Specifications. In *Proc. $9^{th}$ SDL FORUM (Montréal, Quebec, Canada)*, June 1999.

20. D. Lee and M. Yannakakis. Principles and methods of testing finite state machines - a survey. *Proc. of the IEEE*, 84(8):1090–1123, August 1996.

21. M. Phalippou. *Relations d'implantations et Hypothèses de test sur les automates à entrées et sorties*. PhD thesis, Université de Bordeaux, 1994.

22. M. Phalippou. Test sequence generation using Estelle or SDL structure information. In *FORTE'94*, Berne, October 1994.

23. A. Pnueli. The temporal logic of programs. In *Proc. of the 18th Symposium on the Foundations of Computer Science*. ACM, November 1977.

24. R. Tarjan. Depth-first search and linear graph algorithms. *SIAM Journal Computing*, 1(2):146–160, June 1972.

25. J. Tretmans. Test generation with inputs, outputs and repetitive quiescence. *Software—Concepts and Tools*, 17(3):103–120, 1996.

26. B. Vergauwen and J. Lewi. A linear local model checking algorithm for CTL. In E. Best, editor, *CONCUR '93*, LNCS 715, pages 447–461. Springer-Verlag, 1993.

# Latency Insensitive Protocols

Luca P. Carloni[1], Kenneth L. McMillan[2], and
Alberto L. Sangiovanni-Vincentelli[1]

[1] University of California at Berkeley, Berkeley, CA 94720-1772
{lcarloni,alberto}@ic.eecs.berkeley.edu
[2] Cadence Berkeley Laboratories, Berkeley, CA 94704-1103
mcmillan@cadence.com

**Abstract.** *The theory of latency insensitive design is presented as the foundation of a new correct by construction methodology to design very large digital systems by assembling blocks of Intellectual Properties. Latency insensitive designs are synchronous distributed systems and are realized by assembling functional modules exchanging data on communication channels according to an appropriate protocol. The goal of the protocol is to guarantee that latency insensitive designs composed of functionally correct modules, behave correctly independently of the wire delays. A latency-insensitive protocol is presented that makes use of relay stations buffering signals propagating along long wires. To guarantee correct behavior of the overall system, modules must satisfy weak conditions. The weakness of the conditions makes our method widely applicable.*

## 1 Introduction

The level of integration available today with Deep Sub-Micron (DSM) technologies ($0.1 \mu m$ and below) is so high that entire systems can now be implemented on a single chip. Designs of this kind expose problems that were barely visible at previous levels of integration: the dominance of wire delays on the chip and the strong effects created by the clock skew [2]. It is predicted that a signal will need more than five (and up to more than ten!) clock ticks to traverse the entire chip area. Thus it will be very important to limit the distance traveled by critical signals to guarantee the performance of the design. However, precise data on wire-lengths are available late in the design process and several costly re-designs may be needed to change the placement or the speed of the components of the design to satisfy performance and functionality constraints. We believe that, for deep sub-micron designs where millions of gates are customary, a design method that guarantees by construction that certain properties are satisfied is the only hope to achieve correct designs in short time. In particular, we focus on methods that allow a designer to compose pre-designed and verified components so that the composition formally satisfies certain properties.

In this paper, we present a theory for the design of digital systems that maintains the inherent simplicity of synchronous designs and yet does not suffer of the "long-wire" problem. According to our methodology, the system can be thought as completely synchronous, i.e. just as a collection of modules that communicate by means of channels having a latency of one clock cycle. Unfortunately, the final layout may require more than one clock cycle to transmit the appropriate signals. Our methodology does not require costly re-design cycles or to slow down the clock. The key idea is borrowed from pipelining: partition the long wires into segments whose lengths satisfy the timing requirements imposed by the clock by inserting logic blocks called *relay stations*, which have a function similar to the one of latches on a pipelined data-path. The timing requirements imposed by the real clock are now met by construction. However, the latency of a channel connecting two modules is generally equal to more than one real clock cycle. If the functionality of the design is based on the sequencing of the output signals and not on their exact timing, then this modification of the design does not change functionality provided that the components of the design are *latency insensitive*, i.e., the behavior of each module does not depend on the latency of the communication channels. We have essentially traded off latency for throughput by not slowing down the clock and by inserting relay stations. In this paper, we introduce these concepts formally and prove the properties outlined above. Classical works on trace theory [3, 7] and delay insensitive circuits could be used to address our problem, but these approaches imply that the delay between two events on a communication channel is completely arbitrary, while in our case we obtain stronger results by assuming that this arbitrary delay is a *multiple of the clock period*.

The paper is organized as follows: in Section 2 we give the foundation of latency insensitive design by presenting the notion of patient processes. In Section 3 we discuss how in a system of patient processes communication channels can be segmented by introducing *relay stations*. Section 4 illustrates the overall design methodology and discusses under which assumption a generic system can be transformed in a patient one.

## 2 Latency Insensitivity

To cast our methodology in a formal framework, we use the approach of Lee and Sangiovanni-Vincentelli to represent signals and processes [5].

### 2.1 The Tagged-Signal Model

Given a set of *values* $V$ and a set of *tags* $T$, an *event* is a member of $V \times T$. Two events are *synchronous* if they have the same tag. A *signal* $s$ is a set of events. Two signals are synchronous if each event in one signal is synchronous with an event in the other signal and vice versa. Synchronous signals must have the same set of tags.

The set of all $N$-tuples of signals is denoted $S^N$. A *process* $P$ is a subset of $S^N$. A particular $N$-tuple $\mathbf{s} \in S^N$ satisfies the process if $\mathbf{s} \in P$. A $N$-tuple $\mathbf{s}$ that satisfies a process is called a *behavior* of the process. Thus a process is a set of possible behaviors [1]. A *composition of processes* (also called a *system*) $\{P_1, \ldots, P_M\}$, is a process defined as the intersection of their behaviors $P = \bigcap_{m=1}^{M} P_m$. Since processes can be defined over different signal sets, to form the composition we need to extend the set of signals over which each process is defined to contain all the signals of all processes. Note that the extension changes the behavior of the processes only formally.

Let $J = (j_1, \ldots, j_h)$ be an ordered set of integers in the range $[1, N]$, the projection of a behavior $b = (s_1, \ldots, s_N) \in S^N$ onto $S^h$ is $proj_J(b) = (s_{j_1}, \ldots, s_{j_h})$. The projection of a process $P \subseteq S^N$ onto $S^h$ is $proj_J(P) = (\mathbf{s}' \mid \exists \mathbf{s} \in P \wedge proj_J(\mathbf{s}) = \mathbf{s}')$. A *connection* $C$ is a particularly simple process where two (or more) of the signals in the $N$-tuple are constrained to be identical: for instance, $C(i, j, k) \subset S^N : (s_1, \ldots, s_N) \in C(i, j, k) \Leftrightarrow s_i = s_j = s_k$, with $i, j, k \in [1, N]$.

In a *synchronous system* every signal in the system is synchronous with every other signal. In a *timed system* the set $T$ of tags, also called *timestamps*, is a totally ordered set. The ordering among the timestamps of a signal $s$ induces a natural order on the set of events of $s$.

### 2.2 Informative Events and Stalling Events

A latency insensitive system is a synchronous timed system whose set of values $V$ is equal to $\Sigma \cup \{\tau\}$, where $\Sigma$ is the set of *informative symbols* which are exchanged among modules and $\tau \notin \Sigma$ is a special symbol, representing the absence of an informative symbol. From now on, all signals are assumed to be synchronous. The set of timestamps is assumed to be in one-to-one correspondence with the set $\mathbb{N}$ of natural numbers. An event is called *informative* if it has an informative symbol $\iota_i$ as value [2]. An event whose value is a $\tau$ symbol is said a *stalling event* (or $\tau$ *event*).

---

[1] For $N \geq 2$, processes may also be viewed as a relation between the $N$ signals in $\mathbf{s}$.
[2] We use subscripts to distinguish among the different informative symbols of $\Sigma : \iota_1, \iota_2, \iota_3, \cdots$

**Definition 1.** $\mathcal{E}(s)$ *denotes the set of events of signal $s$ while $\mathcal{E}_i(s)$ and $\mathcal{E}_\tau(s)$ are respectively the set of informative events and the set of stalling events of $s$. The $k$-th event $(v_k, t_k)$ of a signal $s$ is denoted $e_k(s)$. $\mathcal{T}(s)$ denotes the set of timestamps in signal $s$, while $\mathcal{T}_i(s)$ is the set of timestamps corresponding to informative events.*

Processes exchange "useful" data by sending and receiving informative events. Ideally only informative events should be communicated among processes. However, in a latency insensitive system, a process may not have data to output at a given timestamp thus requiring the output of a stalling event at that timestamp.

**Definition 2.** *The set of all sequences of elements in $\Sigma \cup \{\tau\}$ is denoted by $\Sigma_{lat}$. The length of a sequence $\sigma$ is $|\sigma|$ if it is finite, otherwise is infinity. The empty sequence is denoted as $\epsilon$ and, by definition, $|\epsilon| = 0$. The $i$-th term of a sequence $\sigma$ is denoted $\sigma_i$.*

**Definition 3.** *Function $\sigma : S \times \mathcal{T}^2 \to \Sigma_{lat}$ takes a signal $s = \{(v_0, t_0), (v_1, t_1), ..\}$ and an ordered pair of timestamps $(t_i, t_j)$, $i \leq j$, and returns a sequence $\sigma_{[t_i, t_j]} \in \Sigma_{lat}$ s.t. $\sigma_{[t_i, t_j]}(s) = v_i, v_{i+1}, \dots, v_j$. The sequence of values of a signal is denoted $\sigma(s)$. The infinite subsequence of values corresponding to an infinite sequence of events, starting from $t_i$ is denoted $\sigma_{[t_i, \infty]}(s)$.*

For example, considering signal $s = \{(\iota_1, t_1), (\iota_2, t_2), (\tau, t_3), (\iota_2, t_4), (\iota_1, t_5), (\tau, t_6)\}$ we have [3] $\sigma(s) = \iota_1 \ \iota_2 \ \tau \ \iota_2 \ \iota_1 \ \tau$, $\sigma_{[t_2, t_4]}(s) = \iota_2 \ \tau \ \iota_2$, $\sigma_{[t_5, t_5]}(s) = \iota_1$, and respectively, $|\sigma(s)| = 6$, $|\sigma_{t_2, t_4}(s)| = 3$, $|\sigma_{t_5, t_5}(s)| = 1$. To manipulate sequences of values we define the following filtering operators.

**Definition 4.** $\mathcal{F}_\iota : \Sigma_{lat} \to \Sigma^\star$ *returns a sequence $\sigma' = \mathcal{F}_\iota[\sigma]$ s.t.*

$$\sigma_i' = \begin{cases} \sigma_{[t_i, t_i]}(s) & \text{if } \sigma_{[t_i, t_i]}(s) \in \Sigma \\ \epsilon & \text{otherwise} \end{cases}$$

**Definition 5.** $\mathcal{F}_\tau : \Sigma_{lat} \to \{\tau\}^\star$ *returns a sequence $\sigma' = \mathcal{F}_\tau[\sigma]$ s.t.*

$$\sigma_i' = \begin{cases} \sigma_{[t_i, t_i]}(s) & \text{if } \sigma_{[t_i, t_i]}(s) = \tau \\ \epsilon & \text{otherwise} \end{cases}$$

For instance, if $\sigma(s) = \iota_1 \ \iota_2 \ \tau \ \iota_2 \ \iota_1 \ \tau$, then $\mathcal{F}_\iota[\sigma(s)] = \iota_1 \ \iota_2 \ \iota_2 \ \iota_1$ and $\mathcal{F}_\tau[\sigma(s)] = \tau \ \tau$. Obviously, $|\sigma(s)| = |\mathcal{F}_\iota[\sigma(s)]| + |\mathcal{F}_\tau[\sigma(s)]|$. Latency insensitive systems are assumed to have a finite horizon over which informative events appear, i.e., for each signal $s$ there is a greatest timestamp $T \in \mathcal{T}_i(s)$ which corresponds to the "last" informative event. However, to build our theory we need to extend the set of signals of a latency insensitive system over an infinite horizon by adding a set of timestamps such that all events with timestamp greater than $T$ have $\tau$ values.

**Definition 6.** *A signal $s$ is strict if and only if (iff) all informative events precede all stalling events, i.e., iff there exists a $k \in \mathbb{N}$ s.t. $|\mathcal{F}_\tau[\sigma_{[t_0, t_k]}(s)]| = 0$ and $|\mathcal{F}_\iota[\sigma_{[t_k, t_\infty]}(s)]| = 0$. A signal which is not strict is said to be* delayed *(or stalled).*

## 2.3 Latency Equivalence

Two signals are latency equivalent if they present the same sequence of informative events, i.e., they are identical except for different delays between two successive informative events. Formally:

---

[3] In this paper we assume that for all timestamps $t_i, t_j \in \mathcal{T}(s)$, $t_i \leq t_j \Leftrightarrow i \leq j$.

**Definition 7.** *Two signals $s_1$, $s_2$ are latency equivalent $s_1 \equiv_r s_2$ iff $\mathcal{F}_i[\sigma(s_1)] = \mathcal{F}_i[\sigma(s_2)]$.*

The *reference signal* $s_{ref}$ of a class of latency equivalent signals is a strict signal obtained by assigning the sequence of informative values that characterizes the equivalence class to the first $|\mathcal{F}_i[\sigma(s_1)]|$ timestamps. For instance, signals $s_1$ and $s_2$ presenting the following sequences of values

$$\sigma(s_1) = \iota_1 \; \iota_2 \; \tau \; \iota_1 \; \iota_2 \; \iota_3 \; \tau \; \iota_1 \; \iota_2 \; \tau \; \tau \; \tau \; \ldots$$
$$\sigma(s_2) = \iota_1 \; \iota_2 \; \tau \; \tau \; \iota_1 \; \tau \; \iota_2 \; \iota_3 \; \tau \; \iota_1 \; \tau \; \iota_2 \; \tau \ldots$$

are latency equivalent. Their reference signal $s_{ref}$ is characterized by the sequence of values $\sigma(s_{ref}) = \iota_1 \; \iota_2 \; \iota_1 \; \iota_2 \; \iota_3 \; \iota_1 \; \iota_2 \; \tau \; \tau \; \tau \ldots$

Latency equivalent signals contain the same sequences of informative values, but with different timestamps. Hence, it is useful to identify their informative events with respect to the common reference signal: the *ordinal* of an informative event coincides with its position in the reference signal.

**Definition 8.** *The ordinal of an informative event $e_k = (v_k, t_k) \in \mathcal{E}_i(s)$ is defined as $ord(e_k) = |\mathcal{F}_i[\sigma_{[t_0, t_k]}](s)| - 1$. Let $s_1$ and $q_1$ be two latency equivalent signals: two informative events $e_k(s_1) \in \mathcal{E}_i(s_1)$ and $e_l(q_1) \in \mathcal{E}_i(q_1)$ are said* corresponding *events iff $ord(e_k(s_1)) = ord(e_l(q_1))$. The slack between two corresponding events is defined as $slack(e_k(s_1), e_l(q_1)) = |k - l|$.*

We extend the notion of latency equivalence to behaviors, in a component-wise manner:

**Definition 9.** *Two behaviors $(s_1, \ldots, s_N)$ and $(s'_1, \ldots, s'_N)$ are equivalent iff $\forall i \; (s_i \equiv_r s'_i)$. A behavior $b = (s_1, \ldots, s_N)$ is strict iff every signal $s_i \in b$ is strict. Every class of latency equivalent behaviors contains only one strict behavior: this is called the* reference behavior.

**Definition 10.** *Two processes $P_1$ and $P_2$ are latency equivalent, $P_1 \equiv_r P_2$, if every behavior of one is latency equivalent to some behavior of the other. A process $P$ is strict iff every behavior $b \in P$ is strict. Every class of latency equivalent processes contains only one strict process: the* reference process.

**Definition 11.** *A signal $s_1$ is latency dominated by $s_2$, $s_1 \leq_r s_2$ iff $s_1 \equiv_r s_2$ and $T_1 \leq T_2$, with $T_k = \max \{t \mid t \in \mathcal{T}_i(s_k)\}, k = 1, 2$.*

Hence, referring to the previous example, signal $s_1$ is dominated by signal $s_2$ since $T_1 = 9$ while $T_2 = 12$. Notice that a reference signal is latency dominated by every signal belonging to its equivalence class. Latency dominance is extended to behaviors and processes as in the case of latency equivalence. A total order among events of a behavior is necessary to develop our theory. In particular, we introduce an ordering among events that is motivated by causality: events that have smaller ordinal are ordered before the ones with larger ordinal (think of a strict process where the ordinal is related to the timestamp; the order implies that past events do not depend on future events). In addition, to avoid cyclic behaviors created by processing events with the same ordinal, we assume that there is an order among signals. This order in real-life designs corresponds to input-output dependencies. We cast this consideration in the most general form possible to extend maximally the applicability of our method.

**Definition 12.** *Given a behavior $b = (s_1, \ldots, s_N)$, $\leq_c$ denotes a well-founded order on its set of signals. The well-founded order induces a lexicographic order $\leq_{lo}$ over the set of informative events of $b$, s.t. for all pairs of events $(e_1, e_2)$ with $e_1 \in \mathcal{E}_i(s_i)$ and $e_2 \in \mathcal{E}_i(s_j)$*

$$e_1 \leq_{lo} e_2 \; \Leftrightarrow \; [\, (ord(e_1) < ord(e_2)) \vee (\, (\, ord(e_1) = ord(e_2) \,) \wedge (s_i \leq_c s_j) \,) \,]$$

The following function returns the first informative event (in signal $s_j$ of behavior $b$) following an event $e \in b$ with respect to the lexicographic order $\leq_{lo}$.

**Definition 13.** *Given a behavior* $b = (s_1, \ldots, s_N)$ *and an informative event* $e(s_i) \in \mathcal{E}_i(s_i)$, *the function* nextEvent *is defined as:* $nextEvent(s_j, e(s_i)) = \min_{e_k(s_j) \in \mathcal{E}_i(s_j)} \{e(s_i) \leq_{lo} e_k(s_j)\}$

A *stall move* postpones an informative event of a signal of a given behavior by one timestamp. The stall move is used to account for long delays along wires and to add delays where needed to guarantee functional correctness of the design.

**Definition 14.** *Given a behavior* $b = (s_1, \ldots, s_j, \ldots, s_N)$ *and an informative event* $e_k(s_j) = (v_k, t_k)$, *a stall move* returns *a behavior* $b' = stall(e_k(s_j)) = (s_1, \ldots, s'_j, \ldots, s_N)$, *s.t. for all* $l \in \mathbb{N}$: $\sigma_{[t_0, t_{k-1}]}(s'_j) = \sigma_{[t_0, t_{k-1}]}(s_j)$, $\sigma_{[t_k, t_k]}(s'_j) = \tau$, $\sigma_{[t_{k+l+1}, t_{k+l+1}]}(s'_j) = \sigma_{[t_{k+l}, t_{k+l}]}(s_j)$.

A *procrastination effect* represents the "effect" of a stall move $stall(e_k(s_j))$ on other signals of behavior $b$ in correspondence of events following $e_k(s_j)$ in the lexicographic order. The processes will "respond" to the insertion of stalls in some of their signals "delaying" other signals that are causally related to the stalled signals.

**Definition 15.** *A* procrastination effect *is a* point-to-set map *which takes a behavior* $b' = (s'_1, \ldots, s'_N) = stall(e_k(s_j))$ *resulting from the application of a stall move on event* $e_k(s_j)$ *of behavior* $b = (s_1, \ldots, s_N)$ *and returns a set of behaviors* $\mathcal{PE}[stall(e_k(s_j))]$ *s.t.* $b'' = (s''_1, \ldots, s''_N) \in \mathcal{PE}[b']$ *iff*

 - $s''_j = s'_j$;
 - $\forall i \in [1, N], i \neq j, s''_i \equiv_\tau s'_i$ *and* $\sigma_{[t_0, t_{l-1}]}(s''_i) = \sigma_{[t_0, t_{l-1}]}(s'_i)$, *where* $t_l$ *is the timestamp of event* $e_l(s_i) = nextEvent(s_i, e_k(s_j))$;
 - $\exists K$ *finite s.t.* $\forall i \in [1, N], i \neq j, \exists k_i \leq K, \sigma_{[t_{l+k_i}, \infty]}(s''_i) = \sigma_{[t_l, \infty]}(s'_i)$.

Each behavior in $\mathcal{PE}[b']$ is obtained from $b'$ by possibly inserting other stalling events in any signal of $b'$, but only at "later" timestamps, i.e. to postpone informative event which follow $e_k(s_j)$ with respect to the lexicographic order $\leq_{lo}$. Observe that a procrastination effect returns a behavior that latency dominates the original behavior.

## 2.4 Patient Processes

We are now ready to define the notion of patient process: a patient process can take stall moves on any signal of its behaviors by reacting with the appropriate procrastination effects. Patience is the key condition for the IP blocks to be combinable according to our method. The following theorems [4] guarantee that, for patient processes, the notion of latency equivalence of processes is compositional.

**Definition 16.** *A* process $P$ *is* patient *iff*

$$\forall b = (s_1, \ldots, s_N) \in P, \ \forall j \in [1, N], \ \forall e_k(s_j) \in \mathcal{E}_i(s_j), \ (\mathcal{PE}[stall(e_k(s_j))] \cap P \neq \emptyset)$$

Hence, the result of a stall move on one of the events of a patient process may not satisfy the process, but one of the behaviors of the procrastination effect corresponding to the stall move does satisfy the process, i.e., if we stall a signal on an input to a functional block, the block will be forced to delay some of its outputs or if we request an output signal to be delayed then an appropriate delay has to be added to the inputs.

**Lemma 1.** *Let* $P_1$ *and* $P_2$ *be two patient processes. Let* $b_1 \in P_1$, $b_2 \in P_2$ *be two behaviors with the same lexicographic order s.t.* $b_1 \equiv_\tau b_2$. *Then, there exists a behavior* $b' \in (P_1 \cap P_2)$, $b_1 \equiv_\tau b' \equiv_\tau b_2$.

**Theorem 1.** *If* $P_1$ *and* $P_2$ *are patient processes then* $(P_1 \cap P_2)$ *is a patient process.*

---

[4] The proofs of the lemmas and the theorems presented in this paper can be found in [1].

**Theorem 2.** *For all patient processes $P_1, P_2, P_1', P_2'$, if $P_1 \equiv_\tau P_1'$ and $P_2 \equiv_\tau P_2'$ then $(P_1 \cap P_2) \equiv_\tau (P_1' \cap P_2')$*

Therefore, we can replace any process in a system of patient processes by a latency equivalent process, and the resulting system will be latency equivalent. A similar theorem holds for replacing strict processes with patient processes.

**Theorem 3.** *For all strict processes $P_1, P_2$ and patient processes $P_1', P_2'$, if $P_1 \equiv_\tau P_1'$ and $P_2 \equiv_\tau P_2'$ then $(P_1 \cap P_2) \equiv_\tau (P_1' \cap P_2')$*

This means that we can replace all processes in a system of strict processes by corresponding patient processes, and the resulting system will be latency equivalent. This is the core of our idea: take a design based on the assumption that computation in one functional block and communication among blocks "take no time" (synchronous hypothesis) [5], i.e., the processes corresponding to the functional blocks and their composition are strict, and replace it with a design where communication does take time (more than one clock cycle) and, as a result, signals are delayed, but without changing the sequence of informative events observed at the system level, i.e., with a set of patient processes.

## 3 Latency Insensitive Design

As explained in Section 1, one of the goal of the latency insensitive design methodology is to be able to "pipeline" a communication channel by inserting an arbitrary amount of memory elements. In the framework of our theory, this operation corresponds to adding some particular processes, called *relay stations*, to the given system. In this section, we first show how patient systems (i.e. systems of patient processes) are insensitive to the insertion of relay stations and, then, we discuss under which assumption a generic system can be transformed into a patient system.

### 3.1 Channels and Buffers

A *channel* is a connection [6] constraining two signals to be identical.

**Definition 17.** *A channel $C(i, j) \subset \mathcal{S}^N, i, j \in [1, N]$ is a process s.t. $b = (s_1, ..., s_N) \in C(i, j) \Leftrightarrow s_i = s_j$.*

**Lemma 2.** *A channel $C(i, j) \subset \mathcal{S}^N$ is not a patient process.*

**Definition 18.** *A buffer $B_{l_f, l_b}^c(i, j)$ with capacity $c \geq 0$, minimum forward latency $l_f \geq 0$ and minimum backward latency $l_b \geq 0$ is a process s.t. $\forall i, j \in [1, N]$: $b = (s_1, ..., s_N) \in B_{l_f, l_b}^c(i, j)$ iff $(s_i \equiv_\tau s_j)$ and $\forall k \in \mathbb{N}$*

$$0 \leq |\mathcal{F}_i [\sigma_{[t_0, t_{(k-l_f)}]}(s_i)]| \ - \ |\mathcal{F}_i [\sigma_{[t_0, t_k]}(s_j)]| \tag{1}$$

$$c \geq |\mathcal{F}_i [\sigma_{[t_0, t_k]}(s_i)]| \ - \ |\mathcal{F}_i [\sigma_{[t_0, t_{(k-l_b)}]}(s_j)]| \tag{2}$$

By definition, given a pair of indexes $i, j \in [1, N]$, for all $l_b, l_f, c \geq 0$, all buffers $B_{l_f, l_b}^c(i, j)$ are latency equivalent. Observe also that buffer $B_{0,0}^0(i, j)$ coincides with channel $C(i, j)$. In particular, we are interested in buffers having unitary latencies and we want to establish under which conditions such buffers are patient processes.

**Theorem 4.** *Let $l_b = l_f = 1$. For all $c \geq 1$, $B_{1,1}^c(i, j)$ is patient iff $s_i \leq_c s_j$.*

---

[5] In other words, communication and computation are completed in one clock cycle.
[6] See section 2.1 for the definition of connection.

Consider a strict system $P_{strict} = \bigcap_{m=1}^{M} P_m$ with $N$ strict signals $s_1, \ldots, s_N$. As explained in section 2.1, processes can be defined over different signal sets and to compose them we may need to formally extend the set of signals of each process to contain all the signals of all processes. However, without loss of generality, consider the particular case of composing

$$B_{1,1}^1 \begin{cases} s_1 = l_1 \; \tau \; l_2 \; \tau \; l_3 \; \tau \; l_4 \; \tau \; \tau \; \tau \; l_5 \; \tau \; l_6 \; \tau \; l_7 \; \tau \; l_8 \; \tau \; l_9 \; \tau \; \tau \; \tau \; l_{10} \; \tau \; \cdots \\ s_2 = \tau \; l_1 \; \tau \; l_2 \; \tau \; l_3 \; \tau \; l_4 \; \tau \; \tau \; \tau \; l_5 \; \tau \; l_6 \; \tau \; l_7 \; \tau \; l_8 \; \tau \; \tau \; \tau \; l_9 \; \tau \; l_{10} \; \tau \; \cdots \end{cases}$$

$$B_{1,1}^2 \begin{cases} s_1 = l_1 \; l_2 \; l_3 \; \tau \; \tau \; l_4 \; l_5 \; l_6 \; \tau \; \tau \; \tau \; l_7 \; \tau \; l_8 \; l_9 \; l_{10} \; \cdots \\ s_2 = \tau \; l_1 \; l_2 \; l_3 \; \tau \; \tau \; l_4 \; \tau \; \tau \; \tau \; l_5 \; l_6 \; l_7 \; \tau \; l_8 \; l_9 \; l_{10} \; \cdots \end{cases}$$

**Fig. 1.** Comparing two possible behaviors of finite buffers $B_{1,1}^1$ and $B_{1,1}^2$.

$M$ processes which are already defined on the same $N$ signals. Hence, any generic behavior $b_m = (s_{m_1}, \ldots, s_{m_N})$ of $P_m$ is also a behavior of $P_{strict}$ iff for all $l \in [1, M], l \neq m$ process $P_l$ contains a behavior $b_l = (s_{l_1}, \ldots, s_{l_N})$ s.t. $\forall n \in [1, N]$ $(s_{l_n} = s_{m_n})$. In fact, we may assume to derive system $P_{strict}$ by connecting the $M$ processes with $(M - 1) \cdot N$ channel processes $C(l_n, (l+1)_n)$, where $l \in [1, (M-1)]$ and $n \in [1, N]$. Further, we may also assume to "decompose" any channel process $C(m_n, l_n)$ with an arbitrary number $X$ of channel processes $C(m_n, x_1), C(x_1, x_2), \ldots, C(x_{X-1}, l_n)$, by adding $X - 1$ auxiliary signals, each of them forced to be equal to $m_n = l_n$. The theory developed in section 2 guarantees that if we replace each process $P_m \in P_{strict}$ with a latency equivalent patient process and each channel $C(i,j)$ with a patient buffer $B_{1,1}^1(i,j)$ we obtain a system $P_{patient}$ which is patient and latency equivalent to $P_{strict}$. In fact, *"having a patient buffer in a patient system is equivalent to having a channel in a strict system"*. Since "decomposing" a channel $C(i,j)$ has no observable effect on a strict system, we are therefore free to add an arbitrary number of patient buffers into the corresponding patient system to replace this channel. Since we use patient buffers with unitary latencies, we can distribute them along that long wire on the chip which implements $C(i,j)$, in such a way that the wire gets decomposed in segments whose physical lengths can be spanned in a single physical clock cycle.

### 3.2 Relay Stations

The following Lemma 3 proves that no behaviors in $B_{1,1}^1(i,j)$ may contain two informative events of $s_i, s_j$ which are synchronous: this implies that the maximum achievable throughput across such a buffer is 0.5, which may be considered suboptimal. Instead, buffer $B_{1,1}^2(i,j)$ is the minimum capacity buffer which is able to "transfer" one informative unit per timestamp, thus allowing, in the best case, to communicate with maximum throughput equal to 1. Figure 1 compares two possible behaviors of these buffers.

**Lemma 3.** $B_{1,1}^2(i,j)$ *is the minimum capacity buffer with* $l_f = l_b = 1$ *s.t.*

$$\exists b^\star = (s_1^\star, \ldots, s_N^\star) \in B_{1,1}^2(i,j) \; \wedge \; \exists k \in \mathbb{N}, \; (e_k(s_i^\star) \in \mathcal{E}_\iota(s_i^\star) \; \wedge \; e_k(s_j^\star) \in \mathcal{E}_\iota(s_j^\star))$$

**Definition 19.** *The buffer* $B_{1,1}^2$ *is called a* relay station *RS.*

## 4 Latency Insensitive Design Methodology

In this section, we move towards the implementation of the theory introduced in the previous sections. To do so, we assume that:

- the pre-designed functional blocks are synchronous processes;
- there is a set of signals for each process that can be considered as inputs to the process and a set of signals that can be considered as outputs of the process, i.e., the processes are *functional*;
- the processes are strictly causal (a process is *strictly causal* if two outputs can only be different at timestamps that strictly follow the timestamps when the inputs producing these outputs show a difference [7]).
- the processes belong to a particular class of processes called *stallable*, a weak condition to ask the processes to obey.

The basic ideas are as follows. Composing a set of pre-designed synchronous functional blocks in the most efficient way is fairly straightforward if we assume that the synchronous hypothesis holds. This composition corresponds to a composition of strict processes since there is a priori no need of inserting stalling events. However, as we have argued in the introduction, it is very likely that the synchronous hypothesis will not be valid for communication. If indeed the processes to be composed are patient, then adding an appropriate number of relay stations yields a process that is latency equivalent to the strict composition. Hence, if we use as the definition of correct behavior the fact that the sequences of informative events do not change, the addition of the relay stations solves the problem. However, requiring processes to be patient at the onset is quite strong. Still, in practice, a patient system can be *derived* from a strict one as follows: first, we take each strict process $P_m$ and we compose it with a set of auxiliary processes to obtain an equivalent patient process $P'_m$. To be able to do so, all processes $P_m$ must satisfy a simple condition (the processes must be stallable) specified in the next section. Then, we put together all patient processes by connecting them with relay stations. The set of auxiliary processes implements a "queuing mechanism" across the signal of $P_m$ in such a way that informative events are buffered and reordered before being passed to $P_m$: informative events having the same ordinal are passed to $P_m$ synchronously.

In the sequel, we first introduce the formal definition of functional processes. Then, we present the simple notion of stallable processes and we prove that every stallable process can be encapsulated into a wrapper process which acts as an interface towards a latency insensitive protocol.

## 4.1 Stallable Processes

An *input* to a process $P \subseteq S^N$ is an externally imposed constraint $P_I \subseteq S^N$ such that $P_I \cap P$ is the total set of acceptable behaviors. Commonly, one considers processes having input signals and output signals: in this case, given process $P$, the set of signals can be partitioned into three disjoint subsets by partitioning the index set as $\{1, \ldots, N\} = I \cup O \cup R$, where $I$ is the ordered set of indexes for the input signals of $P$, $O$ is the ordered set of indexes for the output signals and $R$ is the ordered set of indexes for the remaining signals (also called irrelevant signals with respect to $P$). A process is *functional* with respect to $(I, O)$ if for all behaviors $b \in P$ and $b' \in P$, $proj_I(b) = proj_I(b')$ implies $proj_O(b) = proj_O(b')$.

In the sequel, we consider only strictly causal processes and for each of them we assume that the well founded order $\leq_c$ of definition 12 subsumes the causality relations among its signals, i.e. formally: $\forall i \in I, \forall j \in O, (s_i \leq_c s_j)$.

$$
\begin{array}{lcl}
s_1 & = & \iota_1\ \iota_3\ \iota_1\ \tau\ \iota_3\ \tau\ \tau \ \cdots \\
s_2 & = & \tau\ \iota_4\ \tau\ \iota_7\ \iota_8\ \tau\ \iota_8 \ \cdots \\
s_3 & = & \tau\ \iota_5\ \iota_5\ \tau\ \iota_9\ \tau\ \iota_6 \ \cdots
\end{array}
\quad \rightarrow \quad
\begin{array}{lcl}
s_4 & = & \tau\ \iota_1\ \tau\ \iota_3\ \iota_1\ \tau\ \iota_3 \ \cdots \\
s_5 & = & \tau\ \iota_4\ \tau\ \iota_7\ \iota_8\ \tau\ \iota_8 \ \cdots \\
s_6 & = & \tau\ \iota_5\ \tau\ \iota_5\ \iota_9\ \tau\ \iota_6 \ \cdots
\end{array}
$$

**Fig. 2.** Example of a behavior of an equalizer $E$ with $I = \{1, 2, 3\}$ and $O = \{4, 5, 6\}$.

---

[7] For a more formal definition see [5].

**Definition 20.** *A process $P$ with $I = \{1, \ldots, Q\}$ and $O = \{Q+1, \ldots, N\}$ is stallable iff for all $b = (s_1, \ldots, s_Q, s_{Q+1}, \ldots, s_N) \in P$ and for all $k \in \mathbb{N}$ :*

$$\forall i \in I \ (\sigma_{[t_k, t_k]}(s_i) = \tau) \ \Leftrightarrow \ \forall j \in O \ (\sigma_{[t_{k+1}, t_{k+1}]}(s_j) = \tau)$$

Hence, while a patient process tolerates arbitrary distributions of stalling events among its signals (as long as causality is preserved), a stallable process demands more regular patterns: $\tau$ symbols can only be inserted synchronously (i.e., with the same timestamp) on all input signals and this insertion implies the synchronous insertion of $\tau$ symbols on all output signals at the following timestamp. To assume that a functional process is stallable is quite reasonable with respect to a practical implementation. In fact, most hardware systems can be stalled: for instance, consider any sequential logic block that has a *gated clock* or a Moore finite state machine $M$ with an extra input, that, if equal to $\tau$, forces $M$ to stay in the current state and to emit $\tau$ at the next cycle.

### 4.2 Encapsulation of Stallable Processes

Now, our goal is to define a group of functional processes that can be composed with a stallable process $P$ to derive a patient process which is latency equivalent to $P$. We start considering a process that aligns all the informative events across a set of channels.

**Definition 21.** *An equalizer $E$ is a process, with $I = \{1, \ldots, Q\}$ and $O = \{Q+1, \ldots, 2 \cdot Q\}$, s.t. for all behaviors $b = (s_1, \ldots, s_Q, s_{Q+1}, \ldots, s_{2 \cdot Q}) \in E$: $\forall i \in I, (s_i \equiv_\tau s_{Q+i})$ and $\forall k \in \mathbb{N}$*

$$\forall i, j \in O \ ( (\sigma_{[t_k, t_k]}(s_i) = \tau) \Rightarrow (\sigma_{[t_k, t_k]}(s_j) = \tau) \ )$$
$$\min_{i \in I} \{ \ | \ \mathcal{F}_\iota \ [\sigma_{[t_0, t_k]}(s_i)] \ | \ \} - \max_{j \in O} \{ \ | \ \mathcal{F}_\iota \ [\sigma_{[t_0, t_k]}(s_j)] \ | \ \} \ \geq 0$$

The first relation forces the output signals to have stalling events only synchronously, while the second guarantees that at every timestamp the number of informative events occurred at any input is always greater than the number of informative events occurred at any output. In particular, the presence of a stalling event at any input at a given timestamp forces the presence of a stalling event on all outputs at the same timestamp. Figure 2 illustrates a possible behavior of an equalizer.

**Definition 22.** *An extended relay station $\mathcal{ERS}$ is a process with $I = \{i\}$ and $O = \{j, l\}$, $i \neq j \neq l$ s.t. signals $s_q, s_2$ are related by inequalities (1) and (2) of definition 18 (with $l_f = l_b = 1$ and $c = 2$) and $\forall k \in \mathbb{N}$:*

$$\sigma_{[t_k, t_k]}(s_l) = \begin{cases} 1 \ if \ | \ \mathcal{F}_\iota \ [\sigma_{[t_0, t_k]}(s_i)] \ | \ - \ | \ \mathcal{F}_\iota \ [\sigma_{[t_0, t_{k-1}]}(s_j)] \ | \ = 2 \\ 0 \ otherwise \end{cases}$$

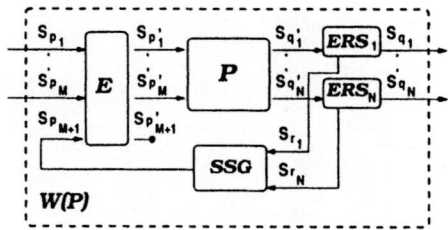

**Fig. 3.** Encapsulation of a stallable process $P$ into a wrapper $W(P)$.

**Definition 23.** *A stalling signal generator $SSG$ is a process with $I = \{1, \dots, Q\}$ and $O = \{Q+1\}$ s.t. $\forall b = (s_1, \dots, s_{Q+1}), \forall k \in \mathbb{N}, \forall i \in [1, Q], (\mathcal{F}_i\, [\sigma_{[t_k, t_k]}(s_i)] \in [0, 1])$ and*

$$\sigma_{[t_k, t_k]}(s_{Q+1}) = \begin{cases} \tau \text{ if } \exists j \in [1, Q] \ ( \ \mathcal{F}_i\, [\sigma_{[t_k, t_k]}(s_j)] = 1 \ ) \\ 0 \text{ otherwise} \end{cases}$$

As illustrated in Figure 3, any stallable process $P$ can be composed with an equalizer, a stalling signal generator and some extended relay stations to derive a patient process which is latency equivalent to $P$.

**Definition 24.** *Let $P$ be a stallable process with $I_P = \{p'_1, \dots, p'_M\}$ and $O_P = \{q'_1, \dots, q'_N\}$. A wrapper process (or, shell process) $W(P)$ of $P$ is the process with $I_W = \{p_1, \dots, p_M\}$ and $O_W = \{q_1, \dots, q_N\}$ which is obtained composing $P$ with the following processes:*

- *an equalizer $E$ with $I_E = \{p_1, \dots, p_M, p_{M+1}\}$ and $O_E = \{p'_1, \dots, p'_M, p'_{M+1}\}$,*
- *$N$ extended relay stations $\mathcal{ERS}_1, \mathcal{ERS}_2, \dots, \mathcal{ERS}_N$ s.t. $I_j = \{q'_j\}$ and $O_j = \{q_j, r_j\}$, with $j \in [1, N]$*
- *a stalling signal generator $SSG$ with $I_G = \{r_1, \dots, r_N\}$ and $O_G = \{p_{M+1}\}$.*

**Theorem 5.** *Let $W(P)$ be the wrapper process of def. 24. Process $W = proj_{I_W \cup O_W}(W(P))$ is a patient process that is latency equivalent to $P$.*

In conclusion, our latency insensitive design methodology can be summarized as follows:

1. Begin with a system of $M$ stallable processes and $N$ channels.
2. Encapsulate each stallable process to yield a wrapper process.
3. Using relay stations decompose each channel in segments whose physical length can be spanned in a single physical clock cycle.

This approach clearly "orthogonalizes" computation and communication: in fact, we can build systems by putting together hardware cores (which can be arbitrarily complex as far as they satisfy the stalling assumption) and wrappers (which interface them with the channels, by "speaking" the latency insensitive protocol). While the specific functionality of the system is distributed in the cores, the wrappers can be automatically generated around them [8]. Finally, the validation of the system can now be efficiently decomposed based on assume-guarantee reasoning [4, 6]: each wrapper is verified assuming a given protocol, and the protocol is verified separately.

## 5  Conclusions and Future Work

A new design methodology for large digital systems implemented in DSM technology has been presented. The methodology is based on the assumption that the design is built by assembling blocks of Intellectual Properties (IPs) that have been designed and verified previously. The main goal is to develop a theory for the composition of the IP blocks that *ensures* the correctness of the overall design. The focus is on timing properties since DSM designs suffer (and will continue to suffer even more for the foreseeable future) from delays on long wires that often cause costly redesigns. Designs carried out with our methodology are called latency insensitive design. Latency insensitive designs are synchronous distributed systems and are realized by assembling functional modules exchanging data on communication channels according to a latency-insensitive protocol. The protocol guarantees that latency insensitive designs composed of functionally correct modules, behave correctly independently of the wire delays. This allow us to pipeline long wires by inserting special memory elements called relay stations. The protocol works on the assumption that the functional blocks satisfy certain weak properties.

---

[8] This is the reason why wrappers are also called *shells*: they just "protect" the intellectual property (*the pearl*) they contain from the "troubles" of the external communication architecture.

The method trades-off latency for throughput, hence it is important to optimize the amount of latency that we must allow to obtain correct designs. This optimization leads to the concept of speculative latency insensitive protocols which will be the subject of a future paper.

## 6   Acknowledgments

We wish to acknowledge the discussions with Luciano Lavagno and Alex Saldanha that led to the theory of latency insensitive designs. Patrick Scaglia gave us strong support based on his experience as a designer of highly complex digital systems and continuous encouragement. This research has been partially sponsored by Cadence Design Systems, SRC and by CNR.

## References

1. L. P. Carloni, K. L. McMillan, and Alberto L. Sangiovanni-Vincentelli. Latency-Insensitive Protocols. Technical Report UCB/ERL M99/11, Electronics Research Lab, University of California, Berkeley, CA 94720, February 1999.
2. D. Matzke. Will Physical Scalability Sabotage Performance Gains? *IEEE Computer*, 8(9):37–39, September 1997.
3. D.L. Dill. *Trace Theory for Automatic Hierarchical Verification of Speed-Independent Circuits*. The MIT Press, Cambridge, Mass., 1988. An ACM Distinguished Dissertation 1988.
4. T.A. Henzinger, S. Qadeer, and R.K. Rajamani. You Assume, We Guarantee: Methodology and Case Studies. In *Proceedings of the 10th International Conference on Computer-Aided Verification*, Vancouver, Canada, July 1998.
5. E. A. Lee and A. Sangiovanni-Vincentelli. A Framework for Comparing Models of Computation. *IEEE Transactions on Computer-Aided Design*, 17(12):1217–1229, December 1998.
6. K. L. McMillan. A Compositional Rule for Hardware Design Refinement. In *Proceedings of the 9th International Conference on Computer-Aided Verification*, Haifa, Israel, July 1997.
7. J. L. A. van de Snepscheut. *Trace Theory and VLSI Design*, volume 200 of *Lecture Notes in Computer Science*. Springer Verlag, Berlin, 1985.

# Handling Global Conditions in Parameterized System Verification

Parosh Aziz Abdulla[1], Ahmed Bouajjani[2], Bengt Jonsson[1], and Marcus Nilsson[1]

[1] Dept. of Computer Systems, P.O. Box 325, S-751 05 Uppsala, Sweden
{parosh, bengt, marcusn}@docs.uu.se
[2] VERIMAG, Centre Equation, 2 av. de Vignate, 38610 Gieres, France
Ahmed.Bouajjani@imag.fr

**Abstract.** We consider symbolic verification for a class of parameterized systems, where a system consists of a linear array of processes, and where an action of a process may in general be guarded by both *local conditions* restricting the state of the process about to perform the action, and *global conditions* defining the *context* in which the action is enabled. Such actions are present, e.g., in idealized versions of mutual exclusion protocols, such as the bakery and ticket algorithms by Lamport, Burn's protocol, Dijkstra's algorithm, and Szymanski's algorithm. The presence of both local and global conditions makes the parameterized versions of these protocols infeasible to analyze fully automatically, using existing model checking methods for parameterized systems. In all these methods the actions are guarded only by local conditions involving the states of a finite set of processes.

We perform verification using a standard symbolic reachability algorithm enhanced by an operation to accelerate the search of the state space. The acceleration operation computes the effect of an arbitrary number of applications of an action, rather than a single application. This is crucial for convergence of the analysis e.g. when applying the algorithm to the above protocols.

We illustrate the use of our method through an application to Szymanski's algorithm.

## 1 Introduction

Much attention has recently been paid to extending the applicability of model checking to infinite-state systems. One reason why a program may have an infinite state space is that it operates on unbounded data structures. Examples of such systems include timed automata [ACD90], data-independent systems [Wol86], relational automata [Čer94], pushdown processes [BS95], and lossy channel systems [AJ96]. Another reason is that the program has an infinite control part. This is the case e.g. in Petri nets [Esp95,Jan90], and parameterized systems, in which the topology of the system is parameterized by the number of processes inside the system. In verification of parameterized systems, we are often interested in proving the correctness of the system regardless of the number of processes. Verification algorithms for systems consisting of an unbounded number of similar or identical finite-state processes include [GS92,AJ98,KMM+97], and (using a manually supplied induction hypothesis) [CGJ95,KM89,WL89].

In this paper we consider algorithmic verification of a class of parameterized systems, intended to capture at least the behaviours of several mutual-exclusion algorithms that can be found in the literature. Examples of mutual exclusion algorithms that work for an arbitrary number of processes are: the bakery and ticket algorithms by Lamport, Burn's protocol, Dijkstra's algorithm, and Szymanski's algorithm. These algorithms are implemented on systems with an arbitrary number of processes with linearly ordered identities. The ordering of the processes may reflect the actual physical ordering (e.g. Szymanski's algorithm), or the values assigned to local variables inside processes (e.g. the ticket given to each process during the execution of Lamport's bakery protocol). A configuration of the system can be described as a string representing the local states of the processes. A common feature which places these protocols outside the scope of existing model checking methods, is that an action of a process is in general guarded by both *local* and *global* conditions on the processes. Local conditions restrict the state of the process which is about to perform the action. Global conditions define the *context* in which the action is allowed to occur. A *context* is typically stated as a formula which is quantified over the set of processes inside the system. Examples of contexts are "all processes with lower identities should have local states belonging to given set", or "there should be at least one process with a higher identity which has a local state included in a given set", etc. We propose a model which combines both types of conditions. An action involves the change of local state of a process, and may be conditioned on both the local state, and the context in which the action is performed.

To verify our protocols we perform a standard symbolic forward reachability analysis, using regular expressions to represent (possibly infinite) sets of configurations. It is well-known that checking most safety properties (including satisfiability of mutual exclusion) can be reduced to checking the reachability of a set of "bad" configurations (in our case specified as a regular expression). However, the presence of both local and global guards implies that the standard reachability algorithm will not terminate when applied to any of the earlier mentioned protocols. A main contribution of this paper is that we define an operation to accelerate the search through the state space. The acceleration operator computes the effect of an arbitrary number of applications of an action, rather than the effect of only a single application. This is crucial for obtaining termination during the analysis of any of the above protocols. Notice that the algorithm is incomplete and may in general still fail to terminate.

**Related Work** There are several results on verification of parameterized systems [GS92,AJ98,CGJ95,KMM+97]. In all these works the actions are guarded only by local conditions involving the states of a finite set of processes. A work, which is close in spirit to ours is [KMM+97]. The authors propose to use regular sets of strings to represent states of parameterized arrays of processes, and to represent the effect of performing an action by a predicate transformer (transducer). However, the work in [KMM⁺97] considers only transducers that represent the effect of a single application of a transition. This means that their approach will not terminate if applied to reachability analysis for the protocols we consider in this paper. In contrast, we introduce a acceleration operator for actions with both local and global contexts, meaning that reachability analysis will terminate. Applications of acceleration operations are reported in the context of communicating finite state automata [BG96,BGWW97,BH97,ABJ98]. The acceleration operation is applied to transitions of different types than in our work, namely those that iterate a single loop in the control part of a program, rather than repetitive applications of a transition to different processes in the system. There has also been a number of case studies in verification of mutual exclusion protocols such as Burn's protocol [JL98] and Szymanski's algorithm [GZ98,MAB⁺94,MP90]. The verification in each case is dependent on abstraction functions or lemmas explicitly provided by the user.

**Outline** In the next section, we define the class of system models that we consider and illustrate it by an idealized version of Szymanski's mutual exclusion algorithm. In Sect. 3 we define composition and acceleration of actions. In Sect. 4 we show how they can be used in verification of safety properties, illustrated by a verification of Szymanski's algorithm. Section 5 contains conclusions and some non-resolved problems.

## 2   Preliminaries

In this section, we will introduce a generic system model which is intended to capture the behaviour of idealized versions of many existing mutual exclusion protocols, e.g. Dijkstra's mutual exclusion problem, Lamport's bakery algorithm, Burn's protocol, Szymanski's algorithm. In our model, a program consists of an arbitrary number of identical processes, ordered in a linear array. The process behaviours are defined through a finite set of *actions*. An action represents a change of local state of a process. An action may be conditioned on both the local state of the process, and the *context* in which it may take place. The context represents a global condition on the local states of the rest of processes inside the system. The ordering of the processes may reflect the actual physical ordering (e.g. Szymanski's algorithm), or the values assigned to local variables inside processes (e.g. the ticket given to each process during the execution of Lamport's bakery protocol).

An idealized version of Szymanski's mutual exclusion algorithm can be given as follows. In the algorithm, an arbitrary number of processes compete for a critical section. The local state of each process $i$ consists of a control state ranging over the integers from 1 to 7 and of two boolean flags, $w_i$ and $s_i$. A process is in the critical section when the control state is 7. A pseudo-code version of the actions of any process $i$ could look as follows:

1 :     **await** $\forall j : j \neq i : \neg s_j$

2 :     $w_i, s_i := true, true$

3 :     **if** $\exists j : j \neq i : (pc_j \neq 1) \wedge \neg w_j$

          **then** $s_i := false$; goto 4

          **else** $w_i := false$; goto 5

4 :     **await** $\exists j : j \neq i : s_j \wedge \neg w_j$ **then** $w_i, s_i := false, true$

5 :     **await** $\forall j : j \neq i : \neg w_j$

6 :     **await** $\forall j : j < i : \neg s_j$

7 :     $s_i := false$, goto 1

For instance, according to the code at line 6, if the control state of a process $i$ is 6, and the value of $s$ is *false* in all processes to the left, i.e. for all processes $j < i$, then the control state of $i$ may be changed to 7. In a similar manner, according to the code at line 4, if the control state of a process $i$ is 4, and if the context is that there is at least another process $j$ (either to the right or to the left of $i$) where the value of $s_j$ is *true* and the value of $w_j$ is *false*, then the control state, $w_i$ and $s_i$ in $i$ may be changed to 5, *false*, and *true*, respectively. In fact in almost all the protocols that we have considered, contexts are defined by existentially or universally quantified formulas restricting the local states of processes to the left or to the right. In our model we work with a particular subclass of regular languages, which can capture such contexts.

A *left context* is a regular language which can be accepted by a deterministic finite-state automaton with a unique accepting state, and where all outgoing transitions from the accepting state are self-loops. (transitions with identical source and target states). A *right context* is a language such that the language of reversed strings is a left context. The *tail* of a left context is the set of symbols that label self-loops from the accepting state. The tail of a right context is the tail of the left context which is its reverse language.

Examples of left contexts are regular expressions of the form

$$e_1 f_1 e_2 f_2 \cdots e_n f_n e_{n+1}$$

where each $e_i$ is of form $(a_1 + \cdots + a_m)^*$, where each $f_i$ is of form $(b_1 + \cdots + b_k)$ such that $b_j$ does not occur in the expression $e_i$, for any $j = 1, \ldots, k$.

Now, we give the formal definition of our model. We use a finite set $C$ of *colours* to model the local states of processes. A *program* is a triple $\mathcal{P} = \langle C, \phi_I, \mathcal{A} \rangle$ where

$C$ is a finite set of colours,

$\phi_I$ is a regular expression denoting a set of *initial configurations* over $C$, and

$\mathcal{A}$ is a finite set of *actions*. An *action* is a triple of the form

$$\phi_L \; ; \; \tau(c, c') \; ; \; \phi_R$$

where $\phi_L$ is a left context, $\phi_R$ is a right context, and $\tau(c, c')$ is a an idempotent binary relation on $C$.

A *configuration* $\gamma$ of $\mathcal{P}$ is a string $\gamma[1]\ \gamma[2]\ \cdots\ \gamma[n]$ over $C$, where $\gamma[i]$ denotes the local state of process $i$. For a regular expression $\phi$, we use $\gamma \in \phi$ to denote that $\gamma$ is a string in the language denoted by $\phi$. For $i, j : 1 \le i \le j \le n$, we use $\gamma[i\mathbin{..}j]$ to denote the substring $\gamma[i]\ \gamma[i+1]\ \cdots\ \gamma[j]$. An action

$$\alpha = \phi_L \ ; \ \tau(c, c') \ ; \ \phi_R$$

defines a relation $\alpha$ on configurations such that $\alpha(\gamma, \gamma')$ holds if $\gamma$ and $\gamma'$ are of equal length $n$, and there is an $i$ with $1 \le i \le n$ such that $\tau(\gamma[i], \gamma'[i])$ holds, $\gamma[1\mathbin{..}i-1] = \gamma'[1\mathbin{..}i-1] \in \phi_L$, and $\gamma[i+1\mathbin{..}n] = \gamma'[i+1\mathbin{..}n] \in \phi_R$. Thus, an action corresponds to a (possibly nondeterministic) program statement in which the colour at one position $i$ can be changed from some colour $c$ to some colour $c'$, provided that $\tau(c, c')$ holds and that the string to the left of $i$ is in $\phi_L$ and that the string to the right of $i$ is in $\phi_R$. We write $\gamma_1 \longrightarrow \gamma_2$ to denote that $\alpha(\gamma_1, \gamma_2)$ for some action $\alpha \in \mathcal{A}$. We use $\alpha^*$ and $\overset{*}{\longrightarrow}$ to denote the transitive closures of $\alpha$ and $\longrightarrow$ respectively. A configuration $\gamma$ is said to be *reachable* if there is a configuration $\gamma_I \in \phi_I$ such that $\gamma_I \overset{*}{\longrightarrow} \gamma$.

The *reachability problem* is defined as follows.

**Instance** A program $\mathcal{P}$ and a set of configurations of $\mathcal{P}$ represented by a regular expression $\phi_F$.

**Question** Is any $\gamma \in \phi_F$ reachable?

In Fig. 1 we represent Szymanski's algorithm as a program in our framework. To simplify the notation, we introduce the following syntactical notations. We let a colour be a triple $\langle pc, w, s \rangle$, where $pc \in \{1, \ldots, 7\}$, and $w$ and $s$ are boolean. We use predicates to define colours. For example, the predicate $(\neg s)$ denotes the set of colours where the value of $s$ is equal to *false*, that is the set $\{\langle pc, w, \mathit{false}\rangle : pc \in \{1, \ldots, 7\}$ and $w \in \{\mathit{true}, \mathit{false}\}\}$. We use the predicate *true* to denote the set of all colours. We use guarded commands to represent binary relations on colours. For instance, the command $(pc = 1) \longrightarrow pc := 2$ represents the relation $\{\langle\langle pc_1, w, s\rangle, \langle pc_2, w, s\rangle\rangle : (pc_1 = 1) \text{ and } (pc_2 = 2)\}$. Notice that e.g. at line 3 the left context $((pc = 1) \lor w)^*((pc \ne 1) \land \neg w)\mathit{true}^*$ is equivalent to $\mathit{true}^*((pc \ne 1) \land \neg w)\mathit{true}^*$; however, we use the previous expression in order to be consistent with the definition of a left context.

## 3 Acceleration of Actions

In this section we define an operation which computes the effect of an unbounded number of executions of an action.

For an action $\alpha$, let $\alpha^*$ be the action constructed by repeating the action $\alpha$ an arbitrary number of times. More precisely, $\alpha^*$ denotes the set of pairs $(\gamma, \gamma')$ of configurations such that there exists a sequence $\gamma_0 \gamma_1 \gamma_2 \cdots \gamma_n$ of configurations with $n \ge 0$ such that $\gamma = \gamma_0$, $\gamma' = \gamma_n$, and such that $\alpha(\gamma_i, \gamma_{i+1})$ for $i = 0, 1, \ldots, n-1$. Similarly, we let $\alpha^+$ be the action constructed by repeating the action $\alpha$ one or more times.

$$
\begin{array}{ll}
1: & (\neg s)^* \ ; \ (pc = 1) \longrightarrow pc := 2 \ ; \ (\neg s)^* \\
2: & true^* \ ; \ (pc = 2) \longrightarrow pc, w, s := 3, true, true \ ; \ true^* \\
3: & ((pc = 1) \lor w)^*((pc \neq 1) \land \neg w)true^* \ ; \ (pc = 3) \longrightarrow pc, s := 4, false \ ; \ true^* \\
4: & true^* \ ; \ (pc = 3) \longrightarrow pc, s := 4, false \ ; \ true^*((pc \neq 1) \land \neg w)((pc = 1) \lor w)^* \\
5: & ((pc = 1) \lor w)^* \ ; \ (pc = 3) \longrightarrow pc, w := 5, false \ ; \ ((pc = 1) \lor w)^* \\
6: & (\neg s \lor w)^*(s \land \neg w)true^* \ ; \ (pc = 4) \longrightarrow pc, w, s := 5, false, true \ ; \ true^* \\
7: & true^* \ ; \ (pc = 4) \longrightarrow pc, w, s := 5, false, false \ ; \ true^*(s \land \neg w)(\neg s \lor w)^* \\
8: & (\neg w)^* \ ; \ (pc = 5) \longrightarrow pc := 6 \ ; \ (\neg w)^* \\
9: & (\neg s)^* \ ; \ (pc = 6) \longrightarrow pc := 7 \ ; \ true^* \\
10: & true^* \ ; \ (pc = 7) \longrightarrow pc, s := 1, false \ ; \ true^*
\end{array}
$$

**Fig. 1.** Actions for Modelling Szymanski's Algorithm

We shall now characterize $\alpha^+$ for any action $\alpha$. A characterization of $\alpha^*$ can be obtained from a characteriztion of $\alpha^+$ by taking the union with the identity relation.

**Theorem 1.** *Let $\alpha$ be an action of the form*

$$
\alpha = \phi_L \ ; \ \tau(c, c') \ ; \ \phi_R
$$

*where $\tau(c, c')$ is idempotent, and where $\Sigma_L$ ($\Sigma_R$) is the tail of $\phi_L$ ($\phi_R$). Then $\alpha^+$ consists of the set of pairs $(\gamma, \gamma')$ of configurations of equal length (say $n$), such that there are indices $i, j$ with $1 \leq i \leq j \leq n$ such that*

1. *$\gamma[1..i-1] = \gamma'[1..i-1] \in \phi_L$,*
2. *$\gamma[j+1..n] = \gamma'[j+1..n] \in \phi_R$,*
3. *$\tau(\gamma[i], \gamma'[i])$, $\tau(\gamma[j], \gamma'[j])$ and for each $k$ with $i < k < j$ we have $\gamma[k] = \gamma'[k]$ or $\tau(\gamma[k], \gamma'[k])$.*
4. *For each $k$ with $i < k \leq j$ we have $\gamma[k] \in \Sigma_R$ or $\gamma'[k] \in \Sigma_R$.*
5. *For each $k$ with $i \leq k < j$ we have $\gamma[k] \in \Sigma_L$ or $\gamma'[k] \in \Sigma_L$.*
6. *For all indices $k_1, k_2$ with $i \leq k_1 < k_2 \leq j$ we have $\gamma[k_1] \in \Sigma_L \lor \gamma[k_2] \in \Sigma_R$ and $\gamma'[k_1] \in \Sigma_L \lor \gamma'[k_2] \in \Sigma_R$.* $\square$

In the symbolic reachability analysis (described in Sect. 4), we use regular expressions as representations of sets of configurations. The characterization of Theorem 1 can be used to model the effect of (repetitive applications of) actions on regular sets by using *finite-state transducers*. This approach is proposed in [KMM+97], where however acceleration is not considered.

We recall that an action $\alpha$ denotes a set of pairs $(\gamma, \gamma')$ of configurations. Equivalently, we can represent the action as a set of finite strings over $C \times C$, namely as the strings $(c_1, c'_1) (c_2, c'_2) \cdots (c_n, c'_n)$ such that $(c_1 c_2 \cdots c_n, c'_1 c'_2 \cdots c'_n) \in \alpha$. It is easy to see that each action can be represented by a finite-state transducer.

More importantly, for any action $\alpha$ the characterization of Theorem 1 can be used to find a representation of $\alpha^+$ in a straight-forward way, since $\alpha^+$ can be represented as a regular language over $C \times C$. As an example, in Fig. 2 we show the transducer which accepts $\alpha^+$ where $\alpha$ is the action at line 3 in Fig.1. We note that the transducer in Fig. 2 need not use the full generality of the characterization of Theorem 1, since the alphabets $\Sigma_L$ and $\Sigma_R$ both are equal to the set of all colours.

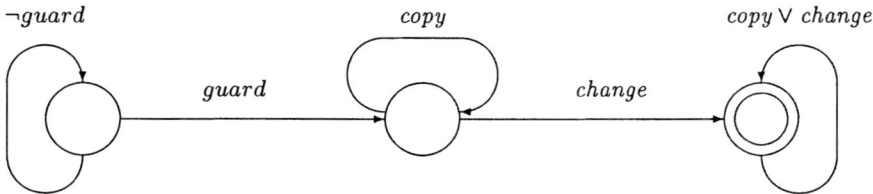

**Fig. 2.** Transducer for $\alpha^+$ from line 3 of Fig. 1.

In the figure we use $\neg guard$ to denote pairs $\{(\langle pc, w, s \rangle, \langle pc, w, s \rangle) \; : \; pc \neq 1 \wedge \neg w\}$, we use $guard$ to denote pairs $\{(\langle pc, w, s \rangle, \langle pc, w, s \rangle) \; : \; pc = 1 \vee w\}$, we use $copy$ to denote pairs $(\langle pc, w, s \rangle, \langle pc, w, s \rangle)$ of identical tuples, and $change$ to denote pairs $\{(\langle pc, w, s \rangle, \langle pc', w', s' \rangle) \; : \; pc = 3 \wedge pc' = 4 \wedge w' = w \wedge s' = false\}$ that represent a change of local control state.

For a regular expression $\phi$ and an action $\alpha$, we use $\alpha^*(\phi)$ to denote the regular expression we get by computing (in the usual way) the product of $\phi$ and the transducer corresponding to $\alpha^*$.

In order to illustrate that the conditions in Theorem 1 characterize a regular relation between configurations, we show a representation of this relation in terms of a finite-state transducer. We show the part which is inserted between the accepting state $q_L$ of an automaton that copies strings in $\phi_L$ and the initial state $q_R$ of an automaton that copies strings in $\phi_R$. In Fig. 3, we show the general construction. Edges are labeled by predicates on pairs $(c, c')$ of colours that are read. We use the abbreviations $c_L$ for $c \in \Sigma_L$, $c'_L$ for $c' \in \Sigma_L$, $c_R$ for $c \in \Sigma_R$, and $c'_R$ for $c' \in \Sigma_R$. In addition to the transitions in the figure, there are self-loop at states $q_1$, $q_2$, $q_3$, and $q_4$ labeled $c = c' \in \Sigma_L \cap \Sigma_R$. Informally, the states correspond to the following situations.

- $q_1$ corresponds to a state when the transducer has read an index where some change has occurred, but where so far there has been no index with change at which $c \notin \Sigma_L \vee c' \notin \Sigma_L$.
- $q_2$ corresponds to a state when the transducer has read an index where some change has occurred where $c \notin \Sigma_L$, but where so far there has been no index with change at which $c' \notin \Sigma_L$.
- $q_3$ corresponds to a state when the transducer has read an index where some change has occurred where $c' \notin \Sigma_L$, but where so far there has been no index with change at which $c \notin \Sigma_L$.

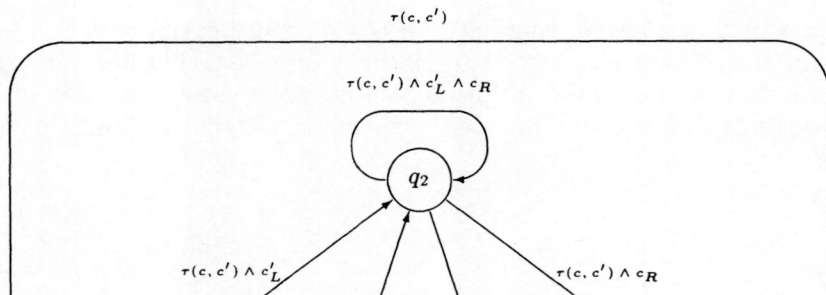

current set. We use regular expressions to represent (potentially infinite) sets of configurations. As we shall illustrate later in the section, this algorithm will not terminate when applied to any of the protocols mentioned in the introduction. To solve this problem, we use the operation $\alpha^*$ (defined in Sect. 3) to accelerate the exploration of the state space. We recall that $\alpha^*$ computes the set of successors corresponding to an arbitrary number of applications of an action (rather than a single application).

Suppose we are given a program $\mathcal{P} = \langle C, \phi_I, \mathcal{A} \rangle$ and a regular expression $\phi_F$, and that we want to check whether some configuration $\gamma_F \in \phi_F$ is reachable in $\mathcal{P}$. For the current discussion, let us represent the set of configurations maintained by the algorithm by a set $V$ of regular expressions. The set $V$ represents the union of the sets denoted by all regular expressions in $V$. Initially, $V = \{\phi_I\}$. The algorithm will now for each regular expression $\phi$ in $V$ and each action $\alpha$ compute $\alpha^*(\phi)$ represented as a finite union of regular expressions. When a new expression $\phi$ is generated, it is compared with those which are already in $V$. If $\phi \subseteq \phi'$ for some $\phi' \in V$, then $\phi$ is discarded, since it will not add new configurations to the explored state space (it is actually sufficient that $\phi \subseteq \sum_{\phi' \in V} \phi'$ for $\phi$ to be safely discarded). In fact, we can also discard all $\phi' \in V$ with $\phi' \subseteq \phi$. It is also checked whether $\phi$ has a non-empty intersection with $\phi_F$. If the intersection is non-empty, the algorithm terminates, reporting that some configuration in $\phi_F$ is reachable. Otherwise, the algorithm terminates when no new regular expressions can be generated. Obviously, our algorithm is incomplete in the sense that while it will always find reachable configurations in $\phi_F$, it will not necessarily terminate if all configurations in $\phi_F$ are unreachable.

We illustrate this algorithm through an application to Szymanski's protocol. To simplify the notation we use the coding of colours shown in Table 1, so e.g. $c_2$ corresponds to the colour $\langle 2, false, false \rangle$. The set of initial configurations is represented by $\phi_0 = c_1^*$.

First, we observe that the above standard reachability algorithm will run into an infinite loop as follows. By applying action 1 to $\phi_0$ we get $c_1^* \, c_2 \, c_1^*$. Applying action 1 again gives $c_1^* \, c_2 \, c_1^* \, c_2 \, c_1^*$, etc.

Although the standard algorithm fails, using the acceleration operation leads to termination. In Table 2 we describe a simulation of our algorithm. We start from the set of initial configurations $\phi_0$. For each regular expression $\phi_i$ and action $\alpha$, we compute $\alpha^*(\phi_i)$ or $\alpha^+(\phi_i)$ and add the resulting regular expressions to the set of existing expressions. For instance, from $\phi_0$, only action 1 is enabled, resulting in the configurations denoted by $\phi_1$. Whenever an expression is entailed by another one (e.g. $\phi_7 \subseteq \phi_0$), we indicate that in the table. In such a case, the constraint (in this case $\phi_7$) is discarded and not explored further. At $\phi_2$, we pursue both $\alpha_3^+$ and $\alpha_4^+$, denoted $\alpha_3^+ \cup \alpha_4^+$, in one step. The algorithm terminates in 19 steps.

| | |
|---|---|
| $c_1$ | $\langle 1, false, false \rangle$ |
| $c_2$ | $\langle 2, false, false \rangle$ |
| $c_3$ | $\langle 3, true, true \rangle$ |
| $c_4$ | $\langle 4, true, false \rangle$ |
| $c_5$ | $\langle 5, false, true \rangle$ |
| $c_6$ | $\langle 6, false, true \rangle$ |
| $c_7$ | $\langle 7, false, true \rangle$ |

**Table 1.** Coding of colours in analysis of Szymanski's algorithm

## 5   Conclusions

In the paper, we have presented techniques for reachability analysis of parameterized systems where a configuration of the system can be described by a string representing the local states of the processes. We have found that naive symbolic reachability analysis does not converge for such systems, and propose to use acceleration of actions to obtain termination. We showed that using acceleration, symbolic reachability analysis terminates for an idealized version of Szymanski's algorithm. We have also analyzed corresponding versions of other mutual exclusion algorithms, including Burn's and Dijkstra's mutual exclusion algorithms, and the bakery and ticket algorithms by Lamport. For some of these algorithms, we use variants of the acceleration operation presented in this paper: we perform the acceleration on the action obtained by sequentially composing two actions, and we also define an acceleration operation on actions that involve two adjacent processes which can be guarded by left and right contexts.

We further note that we have considered idealized versions of the mutual exclusion algorithms. In most implementations of these algorithms, a global guard (such as e.g., $\forall j : j < i : \neg s_j$) is not atomic: in a more refined description of the algorithm this is a loop which checks the states of other processes. We have not considered how to treat the non-atomic versions of statements such as this one.

## References

[ABJ98]   Parosh Aziz Abdulla, Ahmed Bouajjani, and Bengt Jonsson. On-the-fly analysis of systems with unbounded, lossy fifo channels. In *Proc. $10^{th}$ Int. Conf. on Computer Aided Verification*, volume 1427 of *Lecture Notes in Computer Science*, pages 305–318, 1998.

[ACD90]   R. Alur, C. Courcoubetis, and D. Dill. Model-checking for real-time systems. In *Proc. $5^{th}$ IEEE Int. Symp. on Logic in Computer Science*, pages 414–425, Philadelphia, 1990.

[AJ96]   Parosh Aziz Abdulla and Bengt Jonsson. Verifying programs with unreliable channels. *Information and Computation*, 127(2):91–101, 1996.

[AJ98]   Parosh Aziz Abdulla and Bengt Jonsson. Verifying networks of timed processes. In Bernhard Steffen, editor, *Proc. TACAS '98, $7^{th}$ Int. Conf. on Tools and Algorithms for the Construction and Analysis of Systems*, volume 1384 of *Lecture Notes in Computer Science*, pages 298–312, 1998.

| $\phi_0$ | $c_1^*$ | $\alpha_1^*$ | $\phi_1$ |
|---|---|---|---|
| $\phi_1$ | $(c_1+c_2)^*$ | $\alpha_2^*$ | $\phi_2$ |
| $\phi_2$ | $(c_1+c_2+c_3)^*$ | $\alpha_3^+ \cup \alpha_4^+$ $\alpha_5^+$ | $\phi_3$ $\phi_4$ |
| $\phi_3$ | $(c_1+c_2+c_3)^* c_2(c_1+c_2+c_3+c_4)^* c_4(c_1+c_2+c_3+c_4)^*$ $+$ $(c_1+c_2+c_3+c_4)^* c_4(c_1+c_2+c_3+c_4)^* c_2(c_1+c_2+c_3)^*$ | $\alpha_3^*$ | $\phi_8$ |
| $\phi_4$ | $(c_1+c_3)^* c_5(c_1+c_3)^*$ | $\alpha_8^+$ | $\phi_5$ |
| $\phi_5$ | $c_1^* c_6 c_1^*$ | $\alpha_9^+$ | $\phi_6$ |
| $\phi_6$ | $c_1^* c_7 c_1^*$ | $\alpha_{10}^+$ | $\phi_7$ |
| $\phi_7$ | $c_1^* c_1 c_1^*$ | | Subs $\phi_0$ |
| $\phi_8$ | $(c_1+c_2+c_3)^* c_2(c_1+c_2+c_3+c_4)^* c_4(c_1+c_2+c_3+c_4)^*$ $+$ $(c_1+c_2+c_3+c_4)^* c_4(c_1+c_2+c_3+c_4)^* c_2(c_1+c_2+c_3+c_4)^*$ | $\alpha_4^*$ | $\phi_9$ |
| $\phi_9$ | $(c_1+c_2+c_3+c_4)^* c_2(c_1+c_2+c_3+c_4)^* c_4(c_1+c_2+c_3+c_4)^*$ $+$ $(c_1+c_2+c_3+c_4)^* c_4(c_1+c_2+c_3+c_4)^* c_2(c_1+c_2+c_3+c_4)^*$ | $\alpha_2^*$ | $\phi_{10}$ |
| $\phi_{10}$ | $(c_1+c_2+c_3+c_4)^* (c_2+c_3)(c_1+c_2+c_3+c_4)^* c_4(c_1+c_2+c_3+c_4)^*$ $+$ $(c_1+c_2+c_3+c_4)^* c_4(c_1+c_2+c_3+c_4)^* (c_2+c_3)(c_1+c_2+c_3+c_4)^*$ | $\alpha_5^+$ | $\phi_{11}$ |
| $\phi_{11}$ | $(c_1+c_3+c_4)^* c_5(c_1+c_3+c_4)^* c_4(c_1+c_3+c_4)^*$ $+$ $(c_1+c_3+c_4)^* c_4(c_1+c_3+c_4)^* c_5(c_1+c_3+c_4)^*$ | $\alpha_6^*$ | $\phi_{12}$ |
| $\phi_{12}$ | $(c_1+c_3+c_4)^* c_5(c_1+c_3+c_4+c_5)^* (c_4+c_5)(c_1+c_3+c_4+c_5)^*$ $+$ $(c_1+c_3+c_4+c_5)^* (c_4+c_5)(c_1+c_3+c_4+c_5)^* c_5(c_1+c_3+c_4)^*$ | $\alpha_7^*$ | $\phi_{13}$ |
| $\phi_{13}$ | $(c_1+c_3+c_4+c_5)^* c_5(c_1+c_3+c_4+c_5)^* (c_4+c_5)(c_1+c_3+c_4+c_5)^*$ $+$ $(c_1+c_3+c_4+c_5)^* (c_4+c_5)(c_1+c_3+c_4+c_5)^* c_5(c_1+c_3+c_4+c_5)^*$ | $\alpha_8^+$ | $\phi_{14}$ |
| $\phi_{14}$ | $(c_1+c_5+c_6)^* c_6(c_1+c_5+c_6)^* (c_5+c_6)(c_1+c_5+c_6)^*$ $+$ $(c_1+c_5+c_6)^* (c_5+c_6)(c_1+c_5+c_6)^* c_6(c_1+c_5+c_6)^*$ | $\alpha_9^+$ | $\phi_{15}$ |
| $\phi_{15}$ | $c_1^* c_7(c_1+c_5+c_6)^* (c_5+c_6)(c_1+c_5+c_6)^*$ | $\alpha_{10}$ | $\phi_{16}$ |
| $\phi_{16}$ | $c_1^* c_1(c_1+c_5+c_6)^* (c_5+c_6)(c_1+c_5+c_6)^*$ | $\alpha_9$ | $\phi_{17}$ |
| $\phi_{17}$ | $c_1^* c_1 c_7(c_1+c_5+c_6)^*$ | $\alpha_{10}$ | $\phi_{18}$ |
| $\phi_{18}$ | $c_1^* c_1 c_1(c_1+c_5+c_6)^*$ | $\alpha_9^+$ | $\phi_{19}$ |
| $\phi_{19}$ | $c_1^* c_1 c_1 c_7(c_1+c_5+c_6)^*$ | | Subs $\phi_{17}$ |

**Table 2.** Reachability Analysis of Szymanski's Algorithm

[BG96]     B. Boigelot and P. Godefroid. Symbolic verification of communication protocols with infinite state spaces using QDDs. In Alur and Henzinger, editors, *Proc. $8^{th}$ Int. Conf. on Computer Aided Verification*, volume 1102 of *Lecture Notes in Computer Science*, pages 1–12. Springer Verlag, 1996.

[BGWW97] B. Boigelot, P. Godefroid, B. Willems, and P. Wolper. The power of QDDs. In *Proc. of the Fourth International Static Analysis Symposium*, Lecture Notes in Computer Science. Springer Verlag, 1997.

[BH97]     A. Bouajjani and P. Habermehl. Symbolic reachability analysis of fifo-channel systems with nonregular sets of configurations. In *Proc. ICALP '97*, number 1256 in Lecture Notes in Computer Science, 1997.

[BS95]     O. Burkart and B. Steffen. Composition, decomposition, and model checking of pushdown processes. *Nordic Journal of Computing*, 2(2):89–125, 1995.

[Čer94]    K. Čerāns. Deciding properties of integral relational automata. In Abiteboul and Shamir, editors, *Proc. ICALP '94*, volume 820 of *Lecture Notes in Computer Science*, pages 35–46. Springer Verlag, 1994.

[CGJ95]    E. M. Clarke, O. Grumberg, and S. Jha. Verifying parameterized networks using abstraction and regular languages. In Lee and Smolka, editors, *Proc. CONCUR '95, $6^{th}$ Int. Conf. on Concurrency Theory*, volume 962 of *Lecture Notes in Computer Science*, pages 395–407. Springer Verlag, 1995.

[Esp95]    J. Esparza. Petri nets, commutative context-free grammers, and basic
           parallel processes. In *Proc. Fundementals of Computation Theory*, number
           965 in Lecture Notes in Computer Science, pages 221–232, 1995.

[GS92]     S. M. German and A. P. Sistla. Reasoning about systems with many
           processes. *Journal of the ACM*, 39(3):675–735, 1992.

[GZ98]     E.P. Gribomont and G. Zenner. Automated verification of Szymanski's
           algorithm. In *Proc. TACAS '98, 7$^{th}$ Int. Conf. on Tools and Algorithms
           for the Construction and Analysis of Systems*, number 1384 in Lecture
           Notes in Computer Science, pages 424–438, 1998.

[Jan90]    P. Jančar. Decidability of a temporal logic problem for Petri nets. *Theo-
           retical Computer Science*, 74:71–93, 1990.

[JL98]     E. Jensen and N. A. Lynch. A proof of Burn's n-process mutual exclusion
           algorithm using abstraction. In *Proc. TACAS '98, 7$^{th}$ Int. Conf. on Tools
           and Algorithms for the Construction and Analysis of Systems*, number 1384
           in Lecture Notes in Computer Science, pages 409–423, 1998.

[KM89]     R.P. Kurshan and K. McMillan. A structural induction theorem for pro-
           cesses. In *Proc. 8$^{th}$ ACM Symp. on Principles of Distributed Computing,
           Canada*, pages 239–247, Edmonton, Alberta, 1989.

[KMM$^{+}$97] Y. Kesten, O. Maler, M. Marcus, A. Pnueli, and E. Shahar. Symbolic
           model checking with rich assertional languages. In O. Grumberg, editor,
           *Proc. 9$^{th}$ Int. Conf. on Computer Aided Verification*, volume 1254, pages
           424–435, Haifa, Israel, 1997. Springer Verlag.

[MAB$^{+}$94] Z. Manna, A. Anuchitanukul, N. Bjørner, A. Browne, E. chang, M. Colón,
           L. de Alfaro, H. Devarajan, H. Sipma, and T. Uribe. STEP: the stanfor
           temporal prover. Draft Manuscript, June 1994.

[MP90]     Z. Manna and A. Pnueli. An exercise in the verification of multi – process
           programs. In W.H.J. Feijen, A.J.M van Gasteren, D. Gries, and J. Misra,
           editors, *Beauty is Our Business*, pages 289–301. Springer-Verlag, 1990.

[WL89]     P. Wolper and V. Lovinfosse. Verifying properties of large sets of pro-
           cesses with network invariants (extended abstract). In Sifakis, editor, *Proc.
           Workshop on Computer Aided Verification*, number 407 in Lecture Notes
           in Computer Science, pages 68–80, 1989.

[Wol86]    Pierre Wolper. Expressing interesting properties of programs in proposi-
           tional temporal logic (extended abstract). In *Proc. 13$^{th}$ ACM Symp. on
           Principles of Programming Languages*, pages 184–193, Jan. 1986.

# Verification of Infinite-State Systems by Combining Abstraction and Reachability Analysis*

Parosh Aziz Abdulla[1]    Aurore Annichini[2]    Saddek Bensalem[2]
Ahmed Bouajjani[2]    Peter Habermehl[3]    Yassine Lakhnech[4]

[1] Dept. of Computer Systems, P.O. Box 325, 75105 Uppsala, Sweden.
[2] VERIMAG, Centre Equation, 2 av. de Vignate, 38610 Gières, France.
[3] LIAFA - Case 7014, 2 place Jussieu, 75251 Paris Cedex 05, France.
[4] Institut für Informatik und Praktishe Mathematik,
Christian-Albrechts-Universität zu Kiel, Preußerstr. 1-9, 24105 Kiel, Germany.

**Abstract.** We address the problem of verifying systems operating on different types of variables ranging over infinite domains. We consider in particular systems modeled by means of extended automata communicating through unbounded fifo channels. We develop a general methodology for analyzing such systems based on combining automatic generation of abstract models (not necessarily finite-state) with symbolic reachability analysis. Reachability analysis procedures allow to verify automatically properties at the abstract level as well as to generate auxiliary invariants and accurate abstraction functions that can be used at the concrete level. We propose a realization of this approach in a framework which extends PVS with automatic invariant checking strategies, automatic procedures for generating abstract models, as well as automata-based decision procedures and reachability analysis procedures for fifo channels systems.

## 1 Introduction

Communication protocols can be naturally modeled by automata communicating through fifo queues. However, in the modeling of such systems, we often need, besides queues, additional variables and data structures such as counters (for instance to memorize the number of messages sent) and timers (to check timeouts and introduce synchrony between processes). Hence, to reason about protocols, we need in general to analyze *extended automata* operating on variables which may range over several different domains. Moreover, the relevant domains may in general be infinite (e.g., in the case of counters, unbounded fifo channels, etc). We are here interested in *automatic* analysis of such *heterogeneous* infinite-state models, especially of extended automata with fifo channels. We develop a general analysis methodology for these models based on combining abstraction and symbolic reachability analysis. We show a realization of this methodology

* This work was partially funded by the National Science Foundation under grant CCR-9509931 to SRI International and has been done while S. Bensalem and P. Habermehl were visiting SRI International.

in a framework which extends the tool InVeSt [6] by automata-based decision procedures and reachability analysis techniques in order to deal with unbounded fifo channels.

Several approaches can be adopted to analyze infinite-state systems. One of them is *abstraction*. It consists in finding an abstraction function allowing to construct a faithful abstract model which can be automatically analyzed [13, 12, 23]. The problem is then how to find a suitable abstraction function and how to derive automatically the abstract model from the concrete one. Several frameworks that provide assistance for performing these tasks [18, 15, 19, 5] have been proposed. However, finding abstraction functions remains in general a non trivial problem which requires a deep understanding of the behavior of the system. In some extreme cases, knowledge of the set of reachable configurations of the system is needed.

Another approach is *symbolic reachability analysis*. It consists in computing a finite representation of the set of all reachable configurations of the system. If such a computation can be done, this approach allows to solve verification problems that are reducible to reachability problems (e.g., verification of safety properties). Moreover, the generation of the set of reachable configurations allows to get for free, and fully automatically, finite abstractions of the system. These abstractions are usually finite transition graphs (called symbolic graphs) where nodes represent sets of configurations. This approach has been applied for several kind of extended automata: timed automata and hybrid automata [4], counter automata [14, 8], pushdown automata [9, 17], fifo-channel automata [3, 7, 10, 2], etc. However, the existing symbolic techniques concern in general *homogeneous* models, i.e., models with one kind of variables ranging over unbounded data domains. So, in order to apply these techniques to communication protocols, we need in general an abstraction step allowing to get homogeneous models from heterogeneous ones.

From the descriptions above of the two approaches, it appears that they are complementary. In this work, we propose to combine these two approaches:

1. Using abstraction and automatic techniques for generating abstract models in order to obtain homogeneous models from heterogeneous ones. Notice that we need here methods allowing to generate automatically abstract extended automata that are not necessarily finite-state.
2. Using symbolic reachability analysis techniques in order to verify automatically properties at the abstract level, as well as to generate auxiliary invariants and abstraction functions that can be used at the concrete level.

Let $\mathcal{A}$ be an extended automaton with variables of two different types $T_1$ and $T_2$. To verify a property on $\mathcal{A}$, the ideal situation is that we are able to provide an abstraction function $\rho$ on the whole state space of $\mathcal{A}$, to construct a corresponding finite-state abstract model $\mathcal{A}_\rho$ which simulates $\mathcal{A}$, i.e., that contains for each behavior of $\mathcal{A}$ a corresponding behavior, and to check that the property holds on $\mathcal{A}_\rho$. As we mentioned above, it is in general hard to find such a $\rho$. However, it is often the case that we have a way to define an abstraction function on the variables of type $T_1$ (for instance by taking systematically a partition of their space of values according to the predicates appearing in the model), whereas the set of all reachable values of variables of type T2 must still be analyzed precisely.

In such a case, we can start in a first step by applying an abstraction $\rho_1$ on the variables of type $T_1$ and obtain a model $\mathcal{A}_{\rho_1}$ where all variables are of type $T_2$. Then, in a second step, we apply to $\mathcal{A}_{\rho_1}$ a symbolic reachability analysis procedure which is specific to extended automata of type $T_2$. This procedure computes a representation of $Reach(\mathcal{A}_{\rho_1})$ which is the set of all reachable configurations in $\mathcal{A}_{\rho_1}$. Then, the result of this computation can be used in different ways:

- Generation of invariants and verification of invariance properties: To show that every reachable configuration of $\mathcal{A}$ satisfies a property $\varphi$, we can show that $Reach(\mathcal{A}_{\rho_1}) \subseteq \rho_1(\varphi)$ at the abstract level. Moreover, $\rho_1^{-1}(Reach(\mathcal{A}_{\rho_1}))$ is an invariant of the concrete model $\mathcal{A}$ which can help in establishing invariance properties at the concrete level.
- Construction of finite abstractions of $\mathcal{A}_{\rho_1}$: we can consider the partition of $Reach(\mathcal{A}_{\rho_1})$ according to control states, or any finer partition $\pi$, and construct the corresponding symbolic graph $(\mathcal{A}_{\rho_1}/\pi)$. This graph can be used to check properties in the universal fragments of temporal logics (in particular, linear-time properties).
- Generation of abstraction functions: Verifying a safety property on $\mathcal{A}$ can be reduced to checking a reachability property on a system $\mathcal{A} \times \mathcal{O}$ where $\mathcal{O}$ is an *observer* (finite automaton expressing the property). Then, each time we consider a new observer $\mathcal{O}$, we need to define an abstraction function on $\mathcal{A} \times \mathcal{O}$. The knowledge of the possible contents of the variables of $\mathcal{A}$ (considered separately) can help in constructing such an abstraction function.

Clearly, in order to apply this methodology, we should have for each type of variables we consider a symbolic representation allowing to represent and manipulate infinite sets of configurations: These structures must allow to perform some basic operations such as boolean operations and the computation of successors and predecessors. We also need decision procedures on these representations for solving emptiness, membership, and entailment problems. These procedures are needed during the symbolic reachability analysis, as well as during the construction of the abstract models for given abstraction functions. Furthermore, since we must reason at the concrete level on heterogeneous models and combine the results of analysis of several kinds of variables, we need a general and uniform framework where all the representation structures we consider can be embedded. In this paper, we consider a framework based on InVeSt-PVS, and we show how this framework is extended in order to support the methodology we describe above for extended automata with fifo queues.

The original framework we consider offers the logical language of PVS [26] which is based on higher order logic, where extended automata can be specified. Also, various decision procedures are available in this framework, in particular for linear arithmetics. The tool InVeSt [6] provides strategies for checking invariants, as well as an automatic procedure for constructing in a compositional manner abstract models for given abstraction functions [5]. During the construction of abstract models, the existing implementation of this procedure in InVeSt invokes PVS (and its decision procedures) in order to decide the existence of the transitions between abstract states. This procedure is reasonably efficient as long as the considered data structures in the models can be described in theories for which PVS provides decision procedures. For instance, this procedure can be applied efficiently in the case of integer counters with linear operations. However, when we consider sequence variables like fifo channels, the use of the PVS-based implementation of this procedure becomes ad-hoc and cumbersome. This is due to the lack in PVS of decision procedures on regular languages. Indeed, sets of contents of sequence variables can be naturally represented by means of finite-state automata or regular expressions, and many of the proof goals concerning these variables could be solved as emptiness or entailment problems of regular languages.

A contribution of this work is to propose an embedding of regular languages in InVeSt-PVS. This embedding consists of a theory of regular expressions allowing to express in the PVS language constraints like $x \in L$ where $x$ is of type sequence and $L$ is a regular language, a connection to the tool AMORE [24] (which provides a library of procedures on finite-state automata), and an automatic procedure for computing abstract models using automata-based decision procedures.

Another contribution of this work is an extension of InVeSt by an automatic reachability analysis procedure for (lossy) fifo-channel systems. This extension is made through a connection to the tool LCS [1] which allows to compute the set of reachable configurations of a lossy fifo-channel system by means of a regular expressions-based symbolic representation, following the procedure introduced in [2]. The tool LCS allows also to generate automatically finite abstract models as symbolic graphs.

We illustrate the use of our framework on the examples of the Alternating Bit Protocol and the Bounded Retransmission Protocol.

## 2  Extended Fifo-Channel Automata

We consider in this paper *untimed* models of protocols that are parallel compositions of extended automata communicating through unbounded lossy queues.

An extended fifo-channel automaton $\mathcal{A}$ consists of a set of control locations $Q$, a vector of typed variables $\vec{x}$, an initial control location $q_{init} \in Q$, a set $V_{init}$ of initial vectors of values, and a set of transitions $\delta$ between control locations. Each transition is labelled by a *guarded command*. The guard is a predicate on the variables and defines an enabling condition of the transition. The command is a transformation (assignment) of the variables.

Among the variables, we distinguish fifo channels. We suppose that messages in these channels are in a finite alphabet $\Gamma$, and we consider the following operations: the emptyness test $empty(c)$ (true if the channel $c$ is empty), $c!a$ (*send $a$ to channel $c$*), and $c?a$ (*receive $a$ from $c$ provided $a$ is the first symbol in $c$*), for any $a \in \Gamma$. We do not fix the types of the other variables. They may range over finite or infinite domains (boolean, integers, etc).

A configuration of the system is a tuple $\langle q, \vec{v} \rangle$ where $q \in Q$ is a control location, $\vec{v}$ is a valuation of the variables. Notice that the valuation of each channel is a word on the alphabet $\Gamma$. Let $\Sigma_{\mathcal{A}}$ be the set of configurations of $\mathcal{A}$. The set of the *initial configurations* of $\mathcal{A}$ is $Init_{\mathcal{A}} = \{q_{init}\} \times V_{init}$.

The semantics of the model is defined by means of a transition relation $R_{\mathcal{A}} \subseteq \Sigma_{\mathcal{A}} \times \Sigma_{\mathcal{A}}$ between configurations. We assume that the channels are lossy in the sense that they can lose messages at any time. Hence, in the definition of $R_{\mathcal{A}}$, the execution of a transition in $\delta$ can be preceded and followed by losses of messages (contents of channels may decrease according to the subsequence ordering). The formal definition of $R_{\mathcal{A}}$ is standard and is omitted here. Then, we associate with $\mathcal{A}$ the transition system $S_{\mathcal{A}} = (\Sigma_{\mathcal{A}}, Init_{\mathcal{A}}, R_{\mathcal{A}})$.

We consider the two usual functions $post_{\mathcal{A}}, pre_{\mathcal{A}} : 2^{\Sigma_{\mathcal{A}}} \to 2^{\Sigma_{\mathcal{A}}}$ such that, for any set of configurations $X \subseteq \Sigma_{\mathcal{A}}$, $post_{\mathcal{A}}(X)$ (resp. $pre_{\mathcal{A}}(X)$) is the set of immediate successors (resp. predecessors) of $X$ in $S_{\mathcal{A}}$. We denote by $\widetilde{post}$ and $\widetilde{pre}$ the dual functions of $post$ and $pre$, i.e., $\tilde{\phi} = \neg\phi\neg$, for $\phi \in \{post, pre\}$. We denote by $post^*$ and $pre^*$ the reflexive-transitive closures of $post$ and $pre$. The set of all *reachable configurations* of $\mathcal{A}$ is defined by $Reach(\mathcal{A}) = post^*(Init_{\mathcal{A}})$.

## 3 Abstractions and Invariants

*Invariants* Let $S = (\Sigma, Init, R)$ be a transition system. We say that $\varphi \subseteq \Sigma$ is an *invariant* of $S$, if $Reach(S) \subseteq \varphi$. Checking that $\varphi$ is an invariant of $S$ consists in finding an *auxiliary invariant* $\psi$ such that $post_R(\psi) \subseteq \psi$, $Init \subseteq \psi$, and $\psi \subseteq \varphi$.

Of course, one possible $\psi$ is the set $Reach(S)$ itself. However, it is not always possible to have an effective way to construct a representation of $Reach(S)$ in a theory where $Reach(S) \subseteq \varphi$ can be checked effectively. Alternatively, one can use abstractions to prove invariance properties on abstract models for which the set of reachable configurations can be computed in such a theory. This set can also be used to define an auxiliary invariant at the concrete level.

*Abstractions* Consider two transition systems $(\Sigma_i, Init_i, R_i)$ with $i = 1, 2$. A *Galois connection*[5] between $\Sigma_1$ and $\Sigma_2$ is a pair $(\alpha, \gamma)$ of functions $\alpha : 2^{\Sigma_1} \to 2^{\Sigma_2}$ and $\gamma : 2^{\Sigma_2} \to 2^{\Sigma_1}$ such that $\alpha(X_1) \subseteq X_2$ iff $X_1 \subseteq \gamma(X_2)$, for every $X_i \subseteq \Sigma_i$. We call $\alpha$ the *abstraction function* and $\gamma$ its *concretization*.

Given a Galois connection $(\alpha, \gamma)$, we say that $S_2$ is an *abstraction* of $S_1$, denoted by $S_1 \sqsubseteq_{(\alpha,\gamma)} S_2$, if $\alpha(Init_1) \subseteq Init_2$ and $\alpha \circ post_{R_1} \circ \gamma \subseteq post_{R_2}$. We say also in this case that $S_2$ $(\alpha, \gamma)$-*simulates* $S_1$. We write $S_1 \sqsubseteq S_2$ ($S_2$ simulates $S_1$) if there exists a Galois connection $(\alpha, \gamma)$ such that $S_1 \sqsubseteq_{(\alpha,\gamma)} S_2$.

An efficient way to describe Galois connections consists in giving a total relation $\rho \subseteq \Sigma_1 \times \Sigma_2$. Indeed, it is shown in [23] that such a relation induces the Galois connection $(post_\rho, \widetilde{pre}_\rho)$. It is easy to check that in case $\rho$ is a function, the concretization $\widetilde{pre}_\rho$ coincides with $pre_\rho$, which we will tacitly denote by $\rho^{-1}$. In the sequel, we will write $S \sqsubseteq_\rho S_A$ instead of $S \sqsubseteq_{(post_\rho, \widetilde{pre}_\rho)} S_A$. Moreover, we will also refer to $\rho \subseteq \Sigma_1 \times \Sigma_2$ as the *abstraction relation (function)* as the distinction between $\rho$ and $post_\rho$ is easily made from the context.

---

[5] The use of Galois connections and abstract interpretation as a general and unifying framework for abstraction techniques has been first proposed in [13].

*Checking invariance properties under abstraction* It can be shown that if $S_1 \sqsubseteq_{(\alpha,\gamma)}$ $S_2$ then $Reach(S_1) \subseteq \gamma(Reach(S_2))$. Hence, if $S_1 \sqsubseteq_{(\alpha,\gamma)} S_2$ and $Reach(S_2) \subseteq \varphi_2$, then $Reach(S_1) \subseteq \gamma(\varphi_2)$. Therefore, in order to check that $Reach(S_1) \subseteq \varphi_1$, for some $\varphi_1 \subseteq \Sigma_1$, it suffices to find a Galois connection $(\alpha, \gamma)$ and a system $S_2$ such that $S_1 \sqsubseteq_{(\alpha,\gamma)} S_2$, and to check $post_{R_1}(\gamma(Reach(S_2)) \cap \varphi_1) \subseteq \varphi_1$. Notice, that the last condition holds immediately in case $\gamma(Reach(S_2)) \subseteq \varphi_1$, since $S_1 \sqsubseteq_{(\alpha,\gamma)} S_2$ implies $post_{R_1}(\gamma(Reach(S_2))) \subseteq \gamma(Reach(S_2))$. This is the standard preservation result concerning invariance properties [12, 23]. Notice also, that in case $\varphi_1$ is an invariant of $S_1$, there must exist $S_2$ and $(\alpha, \gamma)$ which fulfill the conditions above.

Since function composition is monotone and $\subseteq$ is transitive, $S_1 \sqsubseteq_{(\alpha,\gamma)} S_2$ and $S_2 \sqsubseteq_{(\alpha',\gamma')} S_3$ implies $S_1 \sqsubseteq_{(\alpha'\circ\alpha,\gamma\circ\gamma')} S_3$. Then, we can consider a hierarchy of abstractions, that is, a sequence $S_1 \sqsubseteq_{(\alpha_1,\gamma_1)} S_2 \cdots \sqsubseteq_{(\alpha_n,\gamma_n)} S_{n+1}$ with $n \geq 1$, in order to check properties at different levels of abstraction, and derive auxiliary invariants (for every $i$, $\gamma_1 \circ \cdots \circ \gamma_i(Reach(S_i))$ is an invariant of $S_1$).

## 4 Computing Abstract Models

Given a system of extended automata $\mathcal{A} = \mathcal{A}_1 \parallel \cdots \parallel \mathcal{A}_n$ and an abstraction relation $\rho \subseteq \Sigma \times \Sigma_A$, we want to construct an abstract system $\mathcal{A}_\rho = \mathcal{A}_1^\rho \parallel \cdots \parallel \mathcal{A}_n^\rho$, such that $S_{\mathcal{A}} \sqsubseteq_\rho S_{\mathcal{A}_\rho}$. For that, we adopt the method presented in [5], which consists in considering separately each concrete transition $\tau_c$, and construct its corresponding abstract transitions $\tau_a$. This is achieved by starting from the universal relation between abstract states and eliminating transitions that do not correspond to concrete ones. Given two abstract states $a_1$ and $a_2$ and a concrete transition $\tau_c$ of $\mathcal{A}$, if the condition

$$\rho^{-1}(a_1) \Rightarrow \widetilde{pre}_{\tau_c}(\neg\rho^{-1}(a_2)) \tag{1}$$

holds, then the transition $\tau_a$ between $a_1$ and $a_2$ is removed. In the existing implementation of this method in the InVeSt tool, condition (1) is checked using PVS. In order to enhance the efficiency of the method, it is safe to partition the abstract variables and to compute an abstraction transition for each partition separately. The global abstract transition is then obtained by conjunctively composing these abstract transitions. An interesting property of this technique is that it allows to deal with variables from different types separately, and use for each of these types specific methods and decision procedures to check Condition (1). Moreover, it allows to deal with abstract relations that behave as the identity on variables that range over infinite domains. This is necessary if we want to abstract for instance an extended automaton with counters and fifo channels, without abstracting the channels (we abstract counters and get an unbounded fifo-channels system).

Now, to compute abstract transitions, we need to compute abstractions of concrete guards, as well as concretizations of abstract states. In case the abstraction relation is given by a predicate, these operations involve quantifier elimination which can be computationally costly, when possible. Therefore, we only consider abstraction functions which are given by an expression of the form: $\bigwedge_{i=1}^{n} \bigwedge_{j=1}^{k_i}(\varphi_{i,j} \rightarrow a_i = exp_{i,j})$ where $a_1, \cdots, a_n$ are the abstract variables and the $\varphi_{i,j}$'s partition $\Sigma$, for every $i = 1, \cdots, n$, and the $\varphi_{i,j}$'s and $exp_{i,j}$'s only involve concrete variables. Moreover, we require that for every literal $l$ occurring in a guard of some transition of the concrete system there exist $i$ and $j$ such that $\varphi_{i,j}$ is $l$. This ensures that we can compute an over-approximation of the abstraction of a guard simply by substituting every literal by its corresponding function $a_i = exp_{i,j}$.

Let us now consider the concretization function. If the abstraction relation $\rho$ is given in the form above, then it is a total function and $\widetilde{pre}_\rho(\varphi_A) = pre_\rho(\varphi_A) = \rho^{-1}(\varphi_A)$ is easily computed by $\bigwedge_{i=1}^{n} \bigwedge_{j=1}^{k_i} (\varphi_{i,j} \rightarrow \varphi_A[exp_{i,j}/a_i])$.

Now, given a concrete model, we can compute an abstraction function $\rho$ which satisfies the requirements above by introducing an abstract boolean variable $a_l$ for each literal $l$ occurring in some guard and defining $\rho$ by the formula $\bigwedge_l a_l = l$. In order to avoid an explosion in the number of abstract variables, literals that refer to the same set of concrete variables are checked whether they build a partitioning of $\Sigma$. In case $n$ literals $l_1, \cdots, l_n$ build such a partitioning, a single abstract variable ranging over $\{1, \cdots, n\}$ is introduced instead of $n$ boolean variables. Moreover, it is also possible to consider the predicates occurring in the assignments to obtain a finer abstraction function.

## Abstracting queues

The accuracy of the abstract model obtained by applying the method presented above strongly depends on the proof strategy used to check condition (1). In our experience, the use of the decision procedures and proof strategies of PVS leads to reasonable results unless recursive functions and recursive data types are used. Now, since queues range over lists of values, it seems to be natural to encode them using lists and define abstractions on them using recursive functions. This, however, may lead to unnecessarily cumbersome definitions and require ad-hoc proof strategies as is the case for the Alternating Bit Protocol (ABP) and the clever abstraction used by Müller and Nipkow [25].

This abstraction is based on the observation that the content of the channels is always of the form $m_1^* m_2^*$. Hence, if a finite alphabet of messages is considered, one can obtain a finite state abstraction of the ABP by merging adjacent identical messages.

We have specified the ABP in the specification language of PVS. We specified channels as variables of type list over *Mes*, where *Mes* is a finite set of messages. Sending and receiving messages are then specified using list operations as *car*, *cdr*, and *cons*. Müller and Nipkow's abstraction can then be specified using a recursively defined function. Using InVeSt and the proof strategies of PVS, we have computed a finite abstraction of ABP for $Mes = \{0, 1\}$. The difficulty in this exercise has been to find a suitable proof strategy that handles the involved lists and the recursively defined functions. If we had used regular expressions, we could have specified the abstraction function very easily and we could have constructed the abstract system fully automatically without providing any particular strategy using decision procedures on regular languages.

# 5 Embedding Regular Languages in InVeSt-PVS

To be able to efficiently handle in InVeSt systems with fifo-channels we introduce PVS-theories for queues and regular languages, and we embed automata-based decision procedures. These extensions allow us to naturally represent sets of contents (sequences of messages) of fifo channels by means of regular expressions, which simplifies the definition of abstractions functions on queues as well as the construction of the corresponding abstract models.

## 5.1 Extending the specification language of PVS

A theory for queues is introduced on the theory of finite sequences which is predefined in PVS. This new theory includes the definition of a polymorphic type $queue[Mes]$ and the definitions of the polymorphic functions $add$, $front$ and $remove$. Using these functions, sending a message (resp. receiving a message) can be specified by the guarded commands $true \rightarrow c := add(m, c)$ (resp. $front(c) = m \rightarrow c := remove(c)$).

Then, we introduce a theory to deal with extended regular expressions with the standard operations (Kleene star, concatenation, union), as well as positive Kleene star ($\cdot^+$), intersection, complementation and right-quotient ($\cdot^{-1}$). This theory allows to express language constraints like $c \in L$ where $c$ is a queue variable and $L$ a language given by an extended regular expression on the set of message symbols $Mes$. Using this theory, we can specify abstraction functions on queues by a formula of the form: $\bigwedge_{i=1}^{n} c \in L_i \Rightarrow c_A = a_i$, where $Chcont^a = \{a_1, \ldots, a_n\}$ is a finite set of abstract values, $c_A$ is the abstract variable associated with the queue $c$, and $L_1, \cdots, L_n$ are regular expressions which form a partition of $Mes^*$. For example, the Müller-Nipkow abstraction function on the channels of the ABP (see section 4) can be defined straightforwardly using this theory ($c \in 0^+ \cdot 1^+ \Rightarrow c_A = 01 \wedge c \in 1^+ \cdot 0^+ \Rightarrow c_A = 10 \wedge \cdots$). Notice that our PVS theory on regular expressions is also useful for the representation of sets of reachable states calculated symbolically (see Section 6).

## 5.2 Calculating the abstract operations on a fifo-channel

Let $Mes$ be a set of messages, let $c$ be a queue variable, and let $\rho$ be its abstraction function defined by a formula as above. Following the method described in Section 4, given an operation $op$ on $c$ (i.e., $op \in \{c!m, c?m \mid m \in Mes\}$), we compute the abstract operation $op_A$ by checking conditions of the form (1), which is equivalent to check the complementation-free condition $\rho^{-1}(c_A = a_i) \cap pre_{op}(\rho^{-1}(c_A = a_j)) = \emptyset$. By definition of $\rho$, $\rho^{-1}(c_A = a_i)$ corresponds to $L_i$ (represented in our PVS theory by the predicate $c \in L_i$). Hence, the condition above is equivalent to $L_i \cap pre_{op}(L_j) = \emptyset$. It easy to see that $pre_{op}$ can be defined in terms of basic operations on regular languages: $pre_{c!m}(L) = L \cdot m^{-1}$ and $pre_{c?m}(L) = m \cdot L$. Hence, checking the condition above consists in checking emptiness problems on regular languages, which can be done automatically by invoking decision procedures for extended regular expressions. For that, we have connected InVeSt to the tool AMORE [24] which can handle regular expressions and decide problems like emptiness, inclusion, etc.

We repeated the ABP example using our PVS theories on queues and regular expressions, and the InVeSt-AMORE connection. Not only writing the abstraction function is significantly simpler within this framework, but also the time for computing the abstract models reduced from $\sim$ 45 minutes to 11 seconds.

# 6 Reachability Analysis: The tool Lcs (Lossy Channel Systems)

## 6.1 Computing reachability sets

The set $Reach(\mathcal{A})$ of any lossy fifo-channel automaton is recognizable but not effectively constructible (there is no algorithm allowing to compute a representation of this set for any $\mathcal{A}$) [11]. Hence, we adopt a semi-algorithmic approach based on computing successively representations of an increasing sequence of (lower) approximations of $Reach(\mathcal{A})$, by adding at each step the immediate successors (*post*-images) of the configurations computed so far, and using *acceleration* techniques [22, 13] in order to enhance the chance of convergence. When our procedure terminates, it delivers a structure representing precisely the set $Reach(\mathcal{A})$. The acceleration principle we adopt is based on computing in one step the effect of executing a control loop an arbitrary number of times (control loops are considered as *meta-transitions* [8, 7]).

To realize this approach, we need symbolic representation structures of sets of configurations which allow *finite* representations of the infinite sets we are interested in, which are effectively closed under union and *post*, which have a decidable entailment problem, and moreover, which allow the computation and representation of images by meta-transitions (the effects of control loops). Another important feature of such a representation structure is to be *normalizable* formal, i.e., for every representable set, there is a unique normal (or canonical) representation which can be derived from any alternative representation. Indeed, all operations (e.g., entailment testing) are often easier to perform on normal forms. Furthermore, normality (canonicity) often corresponds to a notion of minimality, which is crucial for practical reachability analysis procedures.

In [2], we have introduced a symbolic representation structure based on a class of regular expressions called SRE's, for use in the computation of the sets of reachable configurations of lossy fifo-channels automata. An SRE is either the empty set $\emptyset$ or a finite union of products, each of these products is either an empty string $\epsilon$ or a finite concatenation $e_1 \cdots e_n$ of atomic expressions which can be either of the form $(a + \epsilon)$, or $(a_1 + \cdots + a_n)^*$. We showed in [2] that SRE's satisfy all the needed features mentioned above: they characterize exactly the class of reachability sets of lossy channels automata, and there are simple and efficient procedures (polynomial) for normalization, for entailment testing, for computing *post*-images, and for computing the effect of *any* control loop.

Based on the results of [2], we have implemented in a tool called Lcs [1] a procedure for computing reachability sets using the following principle: Given a parallel composition of a set of fifo-channel automata, the procedure starts from the initial configurations and constructs the set of all reachable configurations by applying a depth-first-search strategy through a symbolic transition graph. The nodes of this graph are *symbolic states*, i.e., representations of sets of configurations as pairs of the form $\langle q, E \rangle$, where $q$ is a control location and $E$ is an SRE-based representation of the contents of the channels: If the system has $n$ channels, $E$ is a finite set $\{(e_1^1, \ldots, e_n^1), \ldots, (e_1^m, \ldots, e_n^m)\}$ of $n$-dim vectors of SRE's representing the set $[\![E]\!] = \bigcup_{i=1}^m [\![e_1^i]\!] \times \cdots \times [\![e_n^i]\!]$, where $[\![e]\!]$ denotes the language described by the expression $e$. At each step, the procedure computes the immediate successors (post-images) of the current symbolic state by all possible transitions of the automaton, and considers them according to the depth-first-search ordering. When a control loop is detected, an acceleration is performed by computing the effect of iterating the considered control loop on the current symbolic state. The set of encountered configurations is memorized progressively. After computing the post-image of a symbolic state, the procedure checks whether the obtained symbolic state is covered by the set of configurations computed so far. If this is the case, the successors of this symbolic state are not generated. Notice that this procedure can also be used for *on-the-fly* verification of safety or invariance properties.

## 6.2 Constructing Finite Abstract Models

Computing the set of reachable configurations can be used to generate finite abstract models. Let $\mathcal{A}$ be a fifo-channel automaton. Let $\Phi$ be a finite set of symbolic states of $\mathcal{A}$ (see definition in the previous paragraph). Then, the symbolic graph associated with $\Phi$ is the finite-state transition system $\mathcal{G}_\Phi = (\Phi, Init_\Phi, R_\Phi)$ such that $Init_\Phi$ is the set of all symbolic states containing the initial configuration $init_\mathcal{A}$, and $\forall \phi_1, \phi_2 \in \Phi.\ \phi_1 R_\Phi \phi_2$ iff $\exists \sigma_1 \in \phi_1, \sigma_2 \in \phi_2.\ \sigma_1 R_\mathcal{A} \sigma_2$.

The *canonical symbolic graph* of $\mathcal{A}$ corresponds to the partition of $Reach(\mathcal{A})$ according to the control states, i.e., $\Phi_\mathcal{A} = \{\langle q_1, E_1 \rangle, \ldots, \langle q_m, E_m \rangle\}$ where $Q = \{q_1, \ldots, q_m\}$ and $Reach(\mathcal{A}) = \bigcup_{i=1}^m \{q_i\} \times [\![E_i]\!]$. It is easy to see that for every set of symbolic states which covers $Reach(\mathcal{A})$, i.e., $Reach(\mathcal{A}) \subseteq \bigcup_{\phi \in \Phi} \phi$, we have $S_\mathcal{A} \sqsubseteq \mathcal{G}_\Phi$ ($\mathcal{G}_\Phi$ simulates $S_\mathcal{A}$). This fact holds in particular for the canonical symbolic graph $\mathcal{G}_{\Phi_\mathcal{A}}$, as well as for all the symbolic graphs obtained from refinements of the partition $\Phi_\mathcal{A}$.

The tool Lcs allows the automatic construction of the canonical symbolic graph of a given fifo-channel system. The construction of this graph is done during the construction of the reachability set.

*Example:* The Alternating Bit Protocol can be modeled by two automata, a sender and a receiver, communicating through two lossy channels $K$ and $L$. We applied to the ABP the procedure of the Lcs tool which has terminated and generated the set of reachable configurations given in the table 1, as well as the canonical symbolic graph. The execution time is 0.07 seconds (UltraSparc). This symbolic graph is then reduced after hiding all internal actions to a cyclic graph with two transitions, a **SND** followed by a **RCV**, which shows that the protocol behaves as a one-place buffer.

| Sender | Receiver | Chan. K | Chan. L | Sender | Receiver | Chan. K | Chan. L |
|--------|----------|---------|---------|--------|----------|---------|---------|
| 0 | 0 | $1^*$ | $1^*$ | 2 | 2 | $0^*$ | $0^*$ |
| 1 | 0 | $1^*0^*$ | $1^*$ | 3 | 2 | $0^*1^*$ | $0^*$ |
| 1 | 1 | $0^*$ | $1^*$ | 3 | 3 | $1^*$ | $0^*$ |
| 1 | 2 | $0^*$ | $1^*0^*$ | 3 | 0 | $1^*$ | $0^*1^*$ |

**Table 1.** Reachability set of the ABP

# 7 Combining Abstraction and Reachability Analysis

## 7.1 From the Concrete to the Abstract $\cdots$

The first possible combination of abstraction and reachability analysis is to apply these two techniques sequentially. Given an heterogeneous model $\mathcal{A}$ of a system, say a parallel composition of extended automata with counters and fifo-channels, the first step consists in applying an abstraction $\mathcal{A}_\rho$ in order to get a (unbounded) fifo-channels system, and then the second step consists in applying the symbolic reachability analysis method in order to, either check directly (on-the-fly) an invariance property on the abstract fifo-channel model $\mathcal{A}_\rho$, or to generate a finite abstraction of this model which can be used for finite-state model-checking.

We illustrate this approach on the example of the Bounded Retransmission Protocol (BRP). Detailed descriptions of the BRP can be found in [21, 20, 16]. The BRP is a data link protocol whose service consists in transmitting large files (sequences of data of arbitrary lengths) from one client to another one. Each datum is transferred in a separate frame. Both clients, the sender and the receiver, obtain an indication whether the whole file has been delivered successfully or not. We model this protocol by means of two automata, a sender and a receiver, communicating through two lossy channels $K$ and $L$. The BRP can be seen as an extended version of the ABP. However, one of the specific features of the BRP is that the model of the sender uses integer counters: First, it has a counter which gives the index $i$ of the current frame in the considered file. This counter allows to know whether the current frame is the first one, the last one, or some intermediate frame. When the sender does not receive an acknowledgment, it may resend the same message up to a maximal number of retransmissions MAX which is a parameter of the protocol. Hence, the sender uses a counter CR for counting retransmissions.

Starting from this model, we use InVeSt-PVS to generate automatically an abstract model which is an unbounded fifo-channel system. For that, we consider an abstraction function on the integer variables and parameters. This abstraction function is defined *automatically* from the guards appearing in the model (as shown in section 4). Then, the corresponding abstract unbounded fifo-channel model is computed automatically and compositionally. The execution times for computing the abstract sender and receiver are 64.71 and 10.47 sec.

Then, in a second step, we apply the Lcs tool to the obtained abstract fifo-channel model. The Lcs tool constructs automatically the set of reachable configurations and the canonical symbolic graph. The execution time for these operations is 0.56 seconds (UltraSparc). After hiding internal actions and minimization, we obtain a finite transition system (5 states and 10 transitions) which is used to model-check service properties of the BRP such as: between two consecutive requests, the sender and the receiver must deliver indications of success or failure to their clients, the receiver delivers a failure indication only if an abortion (by the sender) has occurred, etc.

## 7.2 · · · and Back

*Strengthening of Invariants* Suppose that we want to show that all configurations of $\mathcal{A}$ satisfy a property $\varphi$ expressed as a predicate on the variables of $\mathcal{A}$. Then, given an abstraction function $\rho$, we can consider the corresponding abstract model $\mathcal{A}_\rho$ and compute $Reach(\mathcal{A}_\rho)$. Since, $\rho^{-1}(Reach(\mathcal{A}_\rho))$ is an invariant of $\mathcal{A}$ (see Section 3), to solve our verification problem on $\mathcal{A}$ it suffices to show that $post_\mathcal{A}(\rho^{-1}(Reach(\mathcal{A}_\rho)) \wedge \varphi) \Rightarrow \varphi$.

Let $Reach(\mathcal{A}_\rho)) = \{\langle q_i, e_1^i, \ldots, e_n^i \rangle \mid i = 1, \ldots, m\}$. Notice that the $e_i^j$'s may be empty sets (when the $q_i$'s are not reachable). Notice also that control locations in $\mathcal{A}_\rho$ correspond to finite abstractions of variables (e.g., counters) in $\mathcal{A}$. Then, the concretization $\rho^{-1}(Reach(\mathcal{A}_\rho))$ is given by the formula $\bigwedge_{i=1}^m (\rho^{-1}(q_i) \Rightarrow \bigwedge_{j=1}^n c_j \in e_j^i)$, which can be written in PVS using our theory on regular expressions. Now, it is worth to notice that in general the formula $\varphi$ we want to check does not constrain the contents of the channels. The conjunction of the formula above with $\varphi$ allows to strengthen this formula according to the fact that some control locations in $\mathcal{A}_\rho$ are not reachable and expresses constraints on the variables of $\mathcal{A}$ that are not channels.

*Generating and Reusing Abstraction Functions* Safety properties can be expressed by means of observers. An observer $\mathcal{O}$ is an extended automaton which runs in parallel with the system and observes its behaviors without interfering with them. Then, invariance properties can be checked on the synchronous parallel composition $\mathcal{A} \times \mathcal{O}$ of the system and its observer. In general, we may consider the same system $\mathcal{A}$ with several observers. Then, it is interesting to compute informations about $\mathcal{A}$ that can be reused each time we consider a composed system $\mathcal{A} \times \mathcal{O}$. In particular, we can use our symbolic reachability analysis of fifo-channel systems in order to derive informations on the contents of the channels of $\mathcal{A}$ (notice that usually, observers are not fifo-channel systems since they represent service properties. However, they may have unbounded local variables like counters). If $\mathcal{A}$ is itself an heterogeneous system, to obtain the information about the contents of the channels of $\mathcal{A}$, we start by applying an abstraction in order to get a fifo-channel system $\mathcal{A}_\rho$ and we compute $Reach(\mathcal{A}_\rho)$. Then, the information we compute allows to define once and for all an abstraction function on the channels which can be used, each time we consider an observer $\mathcal{O}$, in the definition of a finite abstraction of the system $\mathcal{A} \times \mathcal{O}$.

Indeed, given a description of the set of reachable configurations of a fifo-channel systems $\mathcal{A}_\rho$, we can define systematically an abstraction function on its channels: Let $Reach(\mathcal{A}_\rho)) = \{\langle q_i, e_1^i, \ldots, e_n^i \rangle \mid i = 1, \ldots, m\}$. Then, for each $i = 1, \ldots n$, let $\mathcal{C}_i = \{e_i^1, \ldots, e_i^m\}$, and let $\mathcal{R}_i = \bigcup_{j=1}^m e_i^j$ (the set of all possible contents of $c_i$). We let $P_i$ denote the coarsest partition of $\mathcal{R}_i$ which is compatible with the collection $\mathcal{C}_i$ (i.e., $\forall e \in \mathcal{C}_i. \exists p_1, \ldots, p_k \in P_i. e = p_1 \cup \ldots \cup p_k$) and we consider a finite set of *abstract contents* $A_i = \{a_p \mid p \in P_i\}$. Then, we define the abstraction function $\rho_i : \Gamma^* \to A_i \cup \{\bot\}$ such that: $\forall w \in \Gamma^*. (\bigwedge_{p \in P_i} w \in p \Rightarrow \rho_i(w) = a_p) \land w \notin \mathcal{R}_i \Rightarrow \rho_i(w) = \bot$.

Notice that the abstraction functions we generate this way can be written in the PVS language using our theory on regular expressions, and hence, they can be composed with other abstraction functions concerning other variables.

As an illustration, consider again the example of the ABP. Starting from the set of reachable configurations given in Table 1 which was computed by the Lcs tool, we generate using the definition above abstraction functions $\rho_K$ and $\rho_L$ for the channels $K$ and $L$. These two functions are equal and coincide exactly with the Müller-Nipkow abstraction function (see Sections 4 and 5). Based on this abstraction function, we can define an abstraction function of the ABP composed with an observer which checks that the input and output streams coincide.

## 8 Conclusion

We have developed a methodology for verifying infinite-state systems by combining automatic abstraction techniques and symbolic reachability analysis procedures. We have illustrated the application of this methodology on the case of extended fifo-channels systems. For that, we have extended the tool InVeSt by automata-based decision procedures and reachability analysis techniques for fifo-channels systems.

The method we propose for combining abstractions and reachability analysis can be applied for any type of variables or combination of (interdependent) types corresponding to decidable (mixed) theories, and for which there are symbolic representations and procedures for reachability analysis. Hence a crucial issue is to identify such decidable theories and the corresponding representation structures, and to design efficient symbolic reachability analysis procedures based on these representations. Indeed, improving the power and the efficiency of these procedures allows to simplify the needed abstraction steps.

## References

1. P. Abdulla, A. Annichini, and A. Bouajjani. Symbolic Verification of Lossy Channel Systems: Application to the Bounded Retransmission Protocol. In *TACAS'99*. LNCS 1579, 1999.
2. P. Abdulla, A. Bouajjani, and B. Jonsson. On-the-fly Analysis of Systems with Unbounded, Lossy Fifo Channels. In *CAV'98*. LNCS 1427, 1998.
3. P.A. Abdulla and B. Jonsson. Verifying Programs with Unreliable Channels. *Inform. and Comput.*, 127(2):91–101, 1996.
4. R. Alur, C. Courcoubetis, N. Halbwachs, T. Henzinger, P. Ho, X. Nicollin, A. Olivero, J. Sifakis, and S. Yovine. The Algorithmic Analysis of Hybrid Systems. *TCS*, 138, 1995.

5. S. Bensalem, Y. Lakhnech, and S. Owre. Computing Abstractions of Infinite State Systems Compositionally and Automatically. In *CAV'98*. LNCS 1427, 1998.

6. S. Bensalem, Y. Lakhnech, and S. Owre. InVeSt : A Tool for the Verification of Invariants. In *CAV'98*. LNCS 1427, 1998.

7. B. Boigelot and P. Godefroid. Symbolic Verification of Communication Protocols with Infinite State Spaces using QDDs. In *CAV'96*. LNCS 1102, 1996.

8. B. Boigelot and P. Wolper. Symbolic Verification with Periodic Sets. In *CAV'94*. LNCS 818, 1994.

9. A. Bouajjani, J. Esparza, and O. Maler. Reachability Analysis of Pushdown Automata: Application to Model Checking. In *CONCUR'97*. LNCS 1243, 1997.

10. A. Bouajjani and P. Habermehl. Symbolic Reachability Analysis of FIFO-Channel Systems with Nonregular Sets of Configurations. In *ICALP'97*. LNCS 1256, 1997.

11. Gérard Cécé, Alain Finkel, and S. Purushothaman Iyer. Unreliable Channels Are Easier to Verify Than Perfect Channels. *Inform. and Comput.*, 124(1):20–31, 1996.

12. E.M. Clarke, O. Grumberg, and D.E. Long. Model checking and abstraction. *ACM TOPLAS*, 16(5), 1994.

13. P. Cousot and R. Cousot. Static Determination of Dynamic Properties of Recursive Procedures. In *IFIP Conf. on Formal Description of Programming Concepts*. North-Holland Pub., 1977.

14. P. Cousot and N. Halbwachs. Automatic Discovery of Linear Restraints among Variables of a Program. In *POPL'78*. ACM, 1978.

15. D. Dams, R. Gerth, and O. Grumberg. Generation of Reduced Models for Checking Fragments of CTL. In *CAV'93*. LNCS 697, 1993.

16. P. D'Argenio, J-P. Katoen, T. Ruys, and G.J. Tretmans. The Bounded Retransmission Protocol must be on Time. In *TACAS'97*. LNCS 1217, 1997.

17. A. Finkel, B. Willems, and P. Wolper. A Direct Symbolic Approach to Model Checking Pushdown Systems. In *Infinity'97*, 1997.

18. S. Graf and C. Loiseaux. A Tool for Symbolic Program Verification and Abstraction. In *CAV'93*. LNCS 697, 1993.

19. S. Graf and H. Saidi. Construction of Abstract State Graphs with PVS. In *CAV'97*, volume 1254 of *LNCS*, 1997.

20. J-F. Groote and J. Van de Pol. A Bounded Retransmission Protocol for Large Data Packets. In *AMAST'96*. LNCS 1101, 1996.

21. L. Helmink, M.P.A. Sellink, and F. Vaandrager. Proof checking a Data Link Protocol. In *Types for Proofs and Programs*. LNCS 806, 1994.

22. R.M. Karp and R.E. Miller. Parallel Program Schemata: A Mathematical Model for Parallel Computation. In *Switch. and Automata Theory Symp.* IEEE, 1967.

23. C. Loiseaux, S. Graf, J. Sifakis, A. Bouajjani, and S. Bensalem. Property Preserving Abstractions for the Verification of Concurrent Systems. *FMSD*, 6(1), 1995.

24. Oliver Matz, Axel Miller, Andreas Potthoff, Wolfgang Thomas, and Erich Valkema. Report on the Program AMoRE. Technical Report 9507, Inst. f. Informatik u. Prakt. Math., CAU Kiel, 1995.

25. O. Müller and T. Nipkow. Combining Model Checking and Deduction for I/O-Automata. In *TACAS'95*. LNCS 1019, 1995.

26. S. Owre, J. Rushby, N. Shankar, and F. von Henke. Formal verification for fault-tolerant architectures: Prolegomena to the design of PVS. *IEEE Transactions on Software Engineering*, 21(2):107–125, Feb. 1995.

# Experience with Predicate Abstraction *

Satyaki Das[1], David L. Dill[1], and Seungjoon Park[2]

[1] Computer Systems Laboratory, Stanford University, Stanford, CA 94305
[2] RIACS, NASA Ames Research Center, Moffett Field, CA 94035

**Abstract.** This reports some experiences with a recently-implemented prototype system for verification using predicate abstraction, based on the method of Graf and Saïdi [9]. Systems are described using a language of iterated guarded commands, called $Mur\phi^{--}$ (since it is a simplified version of our $Mur\phi$ protocol description language). The system makes use of two libraries: SVC [1] (an efficient decision procedure for quantifier-free first-order logic) and the CMU BDD library. The use of these libraries increases the scope of problems that can be handled by predicate abstraction through increased efficiency, especially in SVC, which is typically called thousands of times. The verification system also provides limited support for quantifiers in formulas. The system has been applied successfully to two nontrivial examples: the Flash multiprocessor cache coherence protocol, and a concurrent garbage collection algorithm. Verification of the garbage collector algorithm required proving properties simple of graphs, which was also done using predicate abstraction.

## 1 Introduction

Abstraction is emerging as the key to formal verification of large designs, especially designs that are not finite-state. *Predicate abstraction,* first described by Graf and Saïdi [9], provides a means for combining theorem proving and model checking techniques by automatically mapping an unbounded system (called the *concrete system*) to a finite state system (called the *abstract system*). The states of the abstract system correspond to truth assignments to a set of predicates. The user must supply the predicates and properties to be proven. The system automatically model checks the properties on the abstract system defined by the predicates. The abstraction is *conservative*, meaning that if a property is shown to hold on the abstract system, there is a concrete version of the property that holds on the concrete system; however, if the property fails to hold on the abstract system, it may or may not hold on the concrete system.

We have recently implemented a prototype system for efficient verification of invariants by predicate abstraction, to discover how far predicate abstraction can take us towards the goal of formal verification of real systems. Results have

---

* This work was supported by DARPA/NASA contract DABT63-96-C-0097-P00002 and NASA contract NASI-98139. The content of this paper does not necessarily reflect the position or the policy of the Government and no official endorsement should be inferred.

been encouraging. Systems are described using a language of iterated guarded commands, which we call $Mur\phi^{--}$ (since it is a simplified version of our $Mur\phi$ protocol description language). The system makes use of two libraries: an efficient decision procedure for quantifier-free first-order logic, called SVC [1], and the CMU BDD library written by David Long. The use of these libraries increases the scope of problems that can be handled by predicate abstraction through increased efficiency, especially in SVC, which is typically called thousands of times. The prototype verifier is written in Common Lisp, and the libraries (which are written in C and C++) are called via the "foreign function" interface.

We have applied it successfully to two nontrivial examples: the Flash multiprocessor cache coherence protocol, and a concurrent garbage collection algorithm. In verification, discovering strategies for effective use of a tool is often as important as the design of the tool. We quickly found that we needed limited support for quantifiers, for expressing properties of unbounded numbers of processes and data. For the garbage collection algorithm, it was necessary to prove some properties of a recursive function. Interestingly, some recursive algorithms can be verified by translating them to $Mur\phi^{--}$ and using predicate abstraction.

The more detailed description below has programs written in a syntax other than $Mur\phi^{--}$, and logical formulas in a syntax other than SVC. The benefits of readability were deemed to outweigh the possibility of translation errors.

## Related work

Our work is derived from the Graf/Saïdi abstraction scheme [9]. However, the original implementation represented the abstract state space as a set of *monomials* (a monomial is a product of Boolean variables and negated variables). Instead, we use BDDs, which usually represent Boolean functions more efficiently. However, Graf and Saidi also sacrificed some accuracy by representing the image of a monomial under a transition rule as a single monomial which must cover all of the states in the image of the transition rule. Our method has no such restriction. So, our verifier is more accurate, but may require more computation (which is performed more efficiently).

Our approach to handling parameterized systems uses quantified formulas, (similar to [17] and [13]), which differs from the method presented in [12]. They used linear systems of equations to deal with state transitions. The basic idea is that for each state there is an abstract variable which keeps track of the number of processes in that state. So if a process moves from $q$ to $q'$ then the value of $X_q$ is decremented by one while $X_{q'}$ is incremented by one. We have handled reasoning about parameterized systems by introducing formulas quantified over the replicated processes as abstract state variables. This is similar to what was proposed in [8] and [7].

Another approach to generating abstract state graphs is to abstract the concrete rules [3]. This has the advantage of requiring fewer validity checks (as they are required when constructing the abstract transitions). However, abstracting the rules may also lose more information about the concrete system, and so might be unable to prove the invariant of interest.

# 2 Predicate abstraction

This section summarizes the theory of predicate abstraction and its implementation in the prototype verifier. The notation is somewhat different from Graf and Saïdi's, but everything is very similar until the details of the computation of the successors of a set of abstract states (the recursive decomposition).

### The concrete and abstract descriptions

As with previous work in this area, the concrete system is modeled as a collection of iterated nondeterministic commands. There is a single global state variable $X$ that represents the complete state of the system. Multiple state variables can be represented by making them fields of a variable of record type. The initial state of the concrete system is generated by an assignment $X := init(X)$ [1]

There is a set of transition rules. Each rule defines a transition function $f$ which maps states to states (the input language has guarded commands, but the guards are not necessary since the transition functions can be defined to leave state variables unchanged when their guards are not satisfied).

An *execution* of the system is a sequence of states, $q_0, \ldots q_n, q_{n+1}, \ldots$, where $q_0 = init(q_{-1})$ for some arbitrary state $q_{-1}$ (note that $q_{-1}$ does not occur in the execution sequence) and $q_{n+1} = f(q_n)$ for some transition function $f$. A concrete state $q$ is reachable if it appears in some execution sequence. We are interested in whether predicates on the state variables are *invariants*, meaning that they hold for every reachable state of a concrete system.

An abstract system is defined by a concrete system and a set of $N$ predicates, $\phi_1, \phi_2, \ldots \phi_N$. Each state $q_A$ of the abstract state space is a truth assignment to the indices 1 through $N$ (so the set of states is finite). The predicates define an *abstraction function*, $\alpha$, which maps concrete states to abstract states. In particular, $q_A = \alpha(q_C)$ whenever $\forall i : q_A(i) = \phi_i(q_C)$. An abstract state $q_A$ is *reachable* if it is an abstraction of a reachable concrete state $q_C$.

The reachable state space can be used to check invariants. If the user knows what invariants he or she wants to prove, these invariants are supplied as some of the predicates $\phi_i$ (actually, the invariant may sometimes be decomposed into a conjunction of simpler properties). If $q_A(i)$ is true in all reachable abstract states, the invariant has been proven. In addition, a BDD describing the abstract reachable state space can be converted into an invariant for the concrete state space by *concretizing* it, as described below.

### Approximating the abstract reachable state space

Sets of abstract or concrete states are represented using logical formulas. Abstract states are represented using BDDs, which can be regarded as propositional

---

[1] Initialization depends on the values of the state variables, which are unconstrained, so as to allow nondeterministic choice of start states. The initialization rule is also conveniently similar to the transition rules of the system.

formulas, by associating Boolean variables $B_1, \ldots, B_n$ with the truth values of the corresponding predicates. The concrete domain is not necessarily finite, so the concrete state space is represented using first-order formulas.

If $s_C$ is a set of concrete states, $\alpha(s_C)$ will be taken to be $\{\alpha(q_C) \mid q_C \in s_C\}$. The *concretization function* $\gamma$ is the inverse image of $\alpha$: $\gamma(s_A) = \{q_C \mid \alpha(q_C) \in s_A\}$. Note that $\forall s_C : s_C \subseteq \gamma(\alpha(s_C))$. If $\psi_A$ is a propositional formula (e.g., a BDD) over the variables $B_i$ representing the set $s_A$, a first-order formula $\psi_C$ representing $\gamma(s_A)$ can be computed by substituting each predicate $\phi_i$ for $B_i$ in $\psi_A$.

An approximation of the reachable state space of the abstract system is computed by (the usual) breadth-first symbolic traversal. At any time, the algorithm has a BDD representing the current abstract reachable set. Initially, this formula represents an abstraction of the initial states of the concrete system. Then, the algorithm iteratively computes an over-approximation of the set of all successors of the current reachable set. At the end of the next iteration, the formula is the logical disjunction of the formula for the current reachable set and the formula for its successor set.

The key step in this procedure is how to find the formula for the set of successors. Given a BDD $\psi_A$ which characterizes $s_A$, find a BDD $\psi'_A$ characterizing the successors of $s_A$ in the abstract system. It is sufficient to compute the successors contributed by each concrete transition function $f$, since the set of abstract successors is the union of the successors contributed by the individual functions. The formula for the initial abstract states is computed by finding the possible successors of the entire state space under the "transition function" *init* (in other words, finding the formula for the successors of *true* under *init*).

The abstract successors are computed by a method similar to that of Graf and Saïdi, but using recursive subdivision of the concrete state space. The first step computes $\psi_C = \gamma(\psi_A)$ by substitution (as described above). $\psi_C$ represents the set of all states that could abstract to a state in $s_A$.

We assume that each transition function $f$ can be written as a first-order term, which is also name $f$. Predicates $\phi'_i(x)$ that characterize the sets $\{q_C \mid \phi_i(f(q_C))\}$ can be pre-computed by substituting the term $f(X)$ for $X$ in $\phi$. Intuitively, $\phi'_i(x)$ means "$x$ is a predecessor of a state that can satisfy $\phi_i$."

We compute $\psi'_A$ by recursive case splitting on each bit $B_i$ in the abstract formula, in ascending order of $i$.

$$H(\psi, m) = \begin{cases} \begin{aligned} B_m \wedge H(\psi \wedge \phi'_m, m+1) \\ \vee \ \neg B_m \wedge H(\psi \wedge \neg\phi'_m, m+1) \end{aligned} & \text{if } 0 < m \le N \\ true & \text{if } m = N+1 \wedge \psi \text{ is satisfiable} \\ false & \text{if } m = N+1 \wedge \psi \text{ is unsatisfiable} \end{cases}$$

The formula $\psi$ is a Boolean combination of predicates $\phi_i$ for $m \le i \le N+1$. If $s$ is the set of concrete states represented by $\psi$, the function $H$, below, computes a logical formula representing the set of abstract states $\alpha(f(s))$. If $m \le N$, it splits $s$ into two parts, $s'$ and $s''$, by conjoining $\psi$ with $\phi_i$ and then $\neg\phi_i$; $H$ is then called recursively to compute $\alpha(f(s'))$ and $\alpha(f(s''))$. When $m = N+1$, every $\phi_i$ has been assumed *true* or *false* in $\psi$, so $\psi$ is equivalent to one of these values.

Several important optimizations are not shown. First, $H(false, m)$ is always *false*, so we check whether $\psi$ is satisfiable at each step, using SVC. Second, $H(\psi, m)$ is saved in a table the first time it is computed; this table is checked to see if the needed value is available before computing $H$ recursively. Finally, the propositional operations are performed using a BDD library, so common subexpressions are shared.

### Dealing with indexed sets of transitions

$Mur\phi^{--}$, like Mur$\phi$ before it, allows the user to define a set of transition rules that vary over an index variable. There is a construct called a "ruleset," which declares a index variable that can be used in the code for transition rules contained in the ruleset. This feature is useful for describing collections of nearly identical processes.

Ruleset parameters are encoded as accesses to an infinite array, indexed by the natural numbers, whose entries are rule indices. The contents of the array are unconstrained, so it serves as a source of nondeterministic choices. The $i$th element of the array is looked up to determine the choice of the transition rule to execute in the $i$th step of a computation.

Stating properties of parameterized systems requires quantified formulas, but SVC can only decide quantifier-free formulas. The prototype verifier copes with quantifiers using some simple heuristics:

- In parameterized processes, the concrete variables associated with each process are frequently stored in an array, so quantified variables are instantiated with all array index expressions.
- Since SVC checks validity, variables that are universally quantified outside of the scope of an existential quantifier can be replaced by a fresh symbolic constant (which is distinct from all other names in the formula). Instantiation of quantifiers with these fresh variables is also useful.
- As a last resort, the system allows the user to supply hints about how to instantiate (and not instantiate) variables.

These measures are barely adequate; more sophisticated handling of quantifiers is required in the future.

## 3 FLASH cache coherence protocol example

One advantage of predicate abstraction is that it can be used to strengthen invariants, automatically. This is potentially valuable, since finding appropriate invariants is one of the most difficult aspects of verifying a design using a theorem prover.

This technique was evaluated on a protocol that was previously verified by several methods: the Stanford FLASH multiprocessor cache coherence protocol.

The model of the cache coherence protocol consists of a set of nodes, each of which contains a processor, caches, and a portion of global memory of the system. Each cache line-sized block in memory is associated with a directory header which keeps information about the line. The state of a cached copy is in either *invalid, shared* (readable), or *exclusive* (readable and writable). The distributed nodes communicate using asynchronous messages through a point-to-point network.

This protocol has been verified using an aggregation abstraction with help of a theorem prover. This proof required many lemmas that showed that various pairs of actions commute (produce the same state, regardless of execution order). However, the lemmas don't hold in arbitrary system states; instead, it is necessary to prove an invariant that characterizes the reachable states, then prove that the lemma holds given the invariant. Finding this invariant was the most difficult part of the proof. A more detailed description of the protocol and the proof can be found in [14].

To prove the invariants, it is necessary to strengthen them until they are inductive (strengthening them is equivalent to finding an induction hypothesis). In practice, strengthening an invariant is a trial-and-error process involving repeated failed proofs, from which new properties must be manually extracted. This usually requires many iterations, and each iteration is difficult.

Predicate abstraction makes invariant strengthening easier. The user supplies plausible properties that might be useful in strengthening the invariant, and the system automatically tries various Boolean combinations of these conditions until it is able to prove the property (or not). This saves the effort of trying Boolean combinations by hand. When the abstract reachability analysis generates a state where the candidate invariant does not hold, it is possible to report an abstract state, along with a concrete transition that enters the state. This information may suggest additional predicates that should be added.

To use predicate abstraction for invariant strengthening, the user starts with a description of the system and some (relatively simple) invariants that are sufficient conditions to prove the verification conditions of interest. For example, a desired property of FLASH was that there be at most one exclusive copy of a memory line in the system. To prove this, two predicates were supplied initially:

- There are no exclusive copies.
- There is a single exclusive copy

The invariants discovered using these properties are not strong enough, so two more properties were added about the PUTX message, which is a message from the directory to the cache that wants an exclusive copy.

- There are no PUTX replies in the network.
- There is a single PUTX reply in the network

The $Mur\phi^{--}$ description of the protocol used in this test was somewhat different from the PVS description used in the aggregation proof. The first simplification was modeling the memory as a separate node in the machine, when in fact memory is stored in processing nodes. This simplification was necessitated by the inefficient treatment of quantifiers in the current $Mur\phi^{--}$ prototype. The second simplification was the result of a limitation of $Mur\phi^{--}$: In the PVS description, the directory entry for a memory block maintained a count of sharers (read-only cached copies of the memory block). There was no easy way to count the number of actual sharers in $Mur\phi^{--}$, so this was changed to be the set of sharing nodes, instead of a count. [2] In spite of these compromises, we believe that the problem of invariant strengthening for the modified FLASH protocol is quite difficult, and the ability to solve it with $Mur\phi^{--}$ indicates that predicate abstraction is an effective approach to this problem.

One of the interesting challenges presented by the FLASH protocol is finding invariants for an unknown number of processes. As with the original description, the protocol description is parameterized for unknown number of processes. The caches are modeled as an unbounded array indexed by node indices. This tends to lead to predicates and properties to prove that are quantified over all process indices. For instance, the property that there should be no write-back request when there exists any exclusive copy of the memory line in the whole system can be specified with a universal quantifier as

$$\forall p : (\ cache[p].state = exclusive \Rightarrow net_{WB} = empty\ ).$$

As explained in Section 2, $Mur\phi^{--}$ is able to handle quantified predicates, albeit sub-optimally, by trying many instantiations without human interaction. This capability was critical for completing the proof with reasonable effort.

Overall, we estimate that finding the invariants with predicate abstraction was at least an order-of-magnitude easier than finding them by trial and error with PVS. It required no more than five days of user time and two hours of CPU time to strengthen the invariants.

## 4 Garbage collection example

The most ambitious example we have attempted is the on-the-fly garbage collection algorithm, which was first proposed by Dijkstra, et al. [4]. The algorithm is widely acknowledged to be difficult to get right, and difficult to prove. A more detailed discussion of the subtlety of this algorithm and subsequent variations can be found in a paper by Havelund and Shankar [11].

An extended version of this algorithm which can handle multiple concurrent mutators was used as the garbage collector of Concurrent Caml Light. The proof of the safety property required 58 invariants to be proved. Details of the modified algorithm and its proof are discussed in [6] and [5].

The original algorithm was simplified by Ben-Ari [2] to involve two colors instead of three. This also led to a simpler argument of correctness. Alternative

---

[2] This problem could possibly have been addressed by writing a recursive function to count the sharing nodes, then verifying some properties of it as in the proof of the garbage collection algorithm. We haven't tried this yet.

justifications of Ben-Ari's algorithm were also given by Van de Snepscheut [18] and Pixley [15]. However, these proofs were informal *pencil and paper* proofs.

Later, this modified algorithm was mechanically proved by Russinoff [16] using the Boyer-Moore theorem prover. A formulation of the same algorithm was also proved by Havelund and Shankar in PVS [10] and [11]. The proofs of both [10] and [11] were of approximately the same size. The proofs needed 19 invariant lemmas and 57 function lemmas and [11] took about two months. So far as we know, no one has mechanically proved the original algorithm of Dijkstra, et al.

In the garbage collection algorithm, the *collector* and the *mutator* (which models the behavior of the user program by nondeterministically changing pointers) run concurrently with both processes accessing a shared memory. The memory is abstractly modeled as a directed graph with each node having at most two outgoing edges. A subset of these nodes are called *roots*; they are special in the sense that they are always accessible (our proof of the algorithm assumes without loss of generality that there is only one root node). Any node that can be reached from one of the roots by following edges is also accessible. The mutator is allowed to choose an arbitrary node and redirect one of its edges to an arbitrarily chosen accessible node. Each memory node also has a *color* field which the collector uses to keep track of the accessible nodes. The collector adds nodes that are not accessible to the mutator, so-called *garbage* nodes, to a *free-list* for recycling.

The mutator, which is described in pseudo-code in Figure 1, first redirects an edge of an arbitrarily selected accessible node towards an arbitrary accessible node ($acc(j)$ says $j$ is accessible). It then colors the second node gray if it was white, or otherwise does nothing. Part of the subtlety of the algorithm is that the collector can mark nodes between these two steps of the mutator.

The collector finds the nodes that are not reachable from the roots, so they can be added to the free list. It begins by coloring the root nodes gray ("coloring a node gray" is called *shading*, from now on). Then it iterates through all the nodes; whenever it finds a gray node, it shades its successors and colors the node black. After this the collector starts this iteration again. The collector algorithm is presented in Figure 1.

The basic property to prove is that the collector does not free an accessible node. An extra state variable called *error* was added to the collector, which is set to *true* if the collector ever frees an accessible node, reducing the desired property to an invariant that *error* is never true.

Most of the predicates were simply guards from the $Mur\phi^{--}$ description of the algorithm or derived directly from the invariant to be proved. Some required insight, however. Two predicates are needed because, when the collector is in the *marking phase*, the mutator can change the color of a node to gray, in which case there must already exist a gray node yet to be examined by the collector.

$$\forall x \in [i, M) : color[x] \neq gray$$
$$\exists y \in [0, M) : color[y] = gray$$

```
/* mutator */
while(true)
    choose n, k ∈ [0, M),
        s.t. acc(k) = true
    /* choose to change left or right */
    [   left[n] := k; q := k
    □  right[n] := k; q := k]
    if color[q] = white →
        color[q] := gray; fi
end /* while */
```

```
/* collector */
shade all roots;
error := false;
i := 0; k := M;
/* marking phase */
do (k > 0) →
    c := color[i];
    if c = gray →
        k := M;
        shade left[i], right[i];
        color[i] := black;
    □c ≠ gray → k := k − 1
    fi;
    i := (i + 1) mod M
od
/* collecting phase */
j := 0;
do  (j < M) →
    c := color[j];
    if c = white →
        if acc(j) → error := true fi
        append j to free list
    □c ≠ white → color[j] := white
    fi;
    j := j + 1
od
```

**Fig. 1.** Mutator and Collector Algorithms

The correctness of the algorithm also depends on the invariant that a black node never has a white successor (except in the transitory case where the mutator is about to shade the white successor).

$$\forall x \in [0, M) : (color[x] = black \Rightarrow (color[left[x]] \neq white \vee q = left[x]))$$
$$\forall x \in [0, M) : (color[x] = black \Rightarrow (color[right[x]] \neq white \vee q = right[x]))$$

## Verifying properties of graphs

A major difficulty with verifying the garbage collection algorithm using predicate abstraction is that its correctness depends on some simple properties of graphs that are not easy to prove by simple instantiation of quantifiers (induction is actually needed). These properties are given as axioms to the verifier when verifying the algorithm, and are proved by using predicate abstraction on "auxiliary" $Mur\phi^{--}$ programs that compute the graph properties.

For example, the following property about the function *acc* is necessary:

$$
\begin{aligned}
&(color[0] = black) \\
&\wedge(\forall p \in [0, M) : color[p] = black \\
&\qquad\qquad\qquad \Rightarrow (color[left[p]] = black \wedge color[right[p]] = black)) \\
&\Rightarrow (\forall q \in [0, M) : acc(left, right)(q) \Rightarrow (color[q] = black))
\end{aligned} \tag{1}
$$

(The function *acc* is actually a function of the graph structure of the nodes, so *left* and *right* are its arguments.)

Another axiom is says that redirecting an edge to point to an already accessible node never makes a previously inaccessible node accessible. In the following, *write*(*left*, *q*, *p*) represents an array which is the same as *left* except that it has the value *p* at index *q*. There is a similar equation for redirecting the right side.

$$
\begin{aligned}
\forall p, q, r \in [0, M) : (acc(left, right)(p) \wedge acc(write(left, q, p), right)(r)) \\
\Rightarrow acc(left, right)(r)
\end{aligned} \tag{2}
$$

The most difficult property required some insight. It states that if the root node of the graph is gray in color and all other nodes are either gray or white then, for every accessible white node, there exists a path from a gray node to it, entirely through white nodes.

$$
\begin{aligned}
&(color[0] = gray \wedge \forall x \in [0, M) : color[x] = white \wedge acc(left, right)(x)) \\
&\Rightarrow \exists y \in [0, M) : color[y] = gray \wedge reachable\_white(left, right)(y, x)
\end{aligned} \tag{3}
$$

where *reachable_white* is a similarly recursive definition that says there is a path of all white nodes from *left* to *right*.

It is frequently possible to write an auxiliary $Mur\phi^{--}$ program that computes a graph property, then verify some predicates on this algorithm. The verified properties are then used as axioms in the main verification effort. These auxiliary programs are not tricky to write, because they do not require concurrency. Although this method is currently *ad hoc*, it seems that the properties we encountered, and many others, could be written as simple recursive definitions and then translated by some provably correct algorithm to a $Mur\phi^{--}$ program that computes the same property.

For example, starting with a simple recursive definition of accessibility,

$$
acc(0) \wedge (\forall x \in [0, M) : acc(x) \Rightarrow (acc(left(x)) \wedge acc(right(x)))),
$$

it is simple to write a $Mur\phi^{--}$ program that sets the entries of an array $acc[i]$ to true or false depending on whether node $i$ is accessible.

To prove property 1, we assume that the array *color* is initialized so that

$$
\begin{aligned}
&(color[0] = black) \\
&\wedge(\forall p \in [0, M) : color[p] = black \\
&\qquad\qquad\qquad \Rightarrow (color[left[p]] = black \wedge color[right[p]] = black))
\end{aligned}
$$

and then check the abstract state space with the predicate $\forall x : acc[x] \Rightarrow color[x] = black$.

A similar approach was used to prove property 2. This property was slightly more complex, since the function needed to be computed twice: once on the original memory structure and once after the mutator has redirected an edge in the memory graph.

As might be expected from its complexity, property 3 was somewhat more difficult to prove. We provided an auxiliary $Mur\phi^{--}$program that, given a white accessible node, finds the witness to the existential quantifier in the consequent.

We were able to prove this algorithm correct in about seven days. The machine time required to prove the final version of the garbage collection algorithm is about three hours. Finding appropriate abstraction predicates took much of the time, and required an understanding of the algorithm. Typically we would start with some invariants which seemed should hold in the system as part of the abstract state. More often than not, the proof process would generate traces where the candidate invariant would fail. This mostly happened because of two reasons:

– We left out some "obvious" axiom about *acc*.
– The invariant does not hold under some situations and needed to be tweaked to get it right. This either needed changing the predicate or adding other predicates.

During the proof process we also discovered some bugs which were accidentally added while coding the algorithm. Of course, much of the human time was spent figuring out what the axioms should be and how to prove them.

## 5    Conclusions

Based on the experiences reported here, we believe that predicate abstraction can be a very cost-effective verification technique for non-finite problems such as parameterized systems.

Predicate abstraction could be regarded as an infinite-state alternative to model checking. However, we believe it would be most valuable in as a method for checking or strengthening invariants in a larger verification effort involving other tools, especially interactive theorem provers.

The $Mur\phi^{--}$ verifier is a prototype for evaluating ideas, not a polished tool. To be generally useful, every aspect of the $Mur\phi^{--}$ system needs additional work (including a name change). In particular, there is a need for better support for quantifiers, and more generally efficient and powerful decision procedures.

## 6    Acknowledgments

We are grateful to Mahadevan Subramaniam for suggesting the use of predicate abstraction, Hassen Saïdi for his help in understanding the abstraction methodology, Klaus Havelund for telling us about the concurrent garbage collection algorithm, Clark Barrett for his help in integrating SVC libraries, and Shankar Govindraju for his help with the CMU-BDD package.

# References

1. C. Barrett, D. Dill, and J. Levitt. Validity checking for combinations of theories with equality. In M. Srivas and A. Camilleri, editors, *Formal Methods In Computer-Aided Design*, volume 1166 of *Lecture Notes in Computer Science*, pages 187–201. Springer-Verlag, November 1996. Palo Alto, California, November 6–8.

2. M. Ben-Ari. Algorithms for on-the-fly garbage collection. *ACM Transactions on Programming Languages and Systems*, 6(3):333–344, July 1984.

3. M. A. Colón and T. E. Uribe. Generating finite-state abstractions of reactive systems using decision procedures. In *Conference on Computer-Aided Verification*, volume 1427 of *Lecture Notes in Computer Science*, pages 293–304. Springer-Verlag, 1998.

4. E. W. Dijkstra, L. Lamport, A. Martin, C. S. Scholten, and E. F. M. Steffens. On-the-fly garbage collection: An exercise in cooperation. *Communications of the ACM*, 21(11):966–75, November 1978.

5. D. Doligez and G. Gonthier. Portable, unobtrusive garbage collection for multiprocessor systems. *Proc. ACM Symp. on Principles of Programming Languages*, January 1994.

6. D. Doligez and X. Leroy. A concurrent, generational garbage collector for a multithreaded implementation of ML. *Proc. ACM Symp. on Principles of Programming Languages*, January 1993.

7. E. A. Emerson and K. S. Namjoshi. Reasoning about rings. *Proc. ACM Symp. on Principles of Programming Languages*, 1995.

8. S. M. German and A. P. Sistla. Reasoning about systems with many processes. *Journal of the ACM*, 39(3), July 1992.

9. S. Graf and H. Saïdi. Construction of abstract state graphs with PVS. In O. Grumberg, editor, *Conference on Computer Aided Verification*, volume 1254 of *Lecture notes in Computer Science*, pages 72–83. Springer-Verlag, 1997. June 1997, Haifa, Israel.

10. K. Havelund. Mechanical verification of a garbage collector. Unpublished manuscript, 1996.

11. K. Havelund and N. Shankar. A mechanized refinement proof for a garbage collector. Unpublished manuscript, 1997.

12. D. Lessens and H. Saïdi. Automatic verification of parameterized networks of processes by abstraction. *Electronic Notes of Theoretical Computer Science (ENTCS)*, 1997.

13. Z. Manna and A. Pnueli. *Temporal Verification of Reactive Systems: Safety*. Springer-Verlag, 1995.

14. S. Park and D. L. Dill. Verification of cache coherence protocols by aggregation of distributed transactions. *Theory of Computing Systems*, 31(4):355–376, 1998.

15. C. Pixley. An incremental garbage collection algorithm for multi-mutator systems. *Distributed Computing*, 3(1):41–50, 1988.

16. D. M. Russinoff. A mechanically verified incremental garbage collector. *Formal Aspects of Computing*, 6(4):359–390, 1994.

17. A. P. Sistla and S. M. German. Reasoning with many processes. *Symp. on Logic in Computer Science, Ithaca*, pages 138–152, June 1987.

18. J. van de Snepscheut. Algorithms for on-the-fly garbage collection revisited. *Information Processing Letters*, 24(4):211–16, March 1987.

# Model Checking of Safety Properties

Orna Kupferman[1]* and Moshe Y. Vardi[2]**

[1] Hebrew University, The institute of Computer Science, Jerusalem 91904, Israel
Email: orna@cs.huji.ac.il,  URL: http://www.cs.huji.ac.il/~orna
[2] Rice University, Department of Computer Science, Houston, TX 77251-1892, U.S.A.
Email: vardi@cs.rice.edu,  URL: http://www.cs.rice.edu/~vardi

**Abstract.** Of special interest in formal verification are safety properties, which assert that the system always stays within some allowed region. A computation that violates a general linear property reaches a bad cycle, which witnesses the violation of the property. Accordingly, current methods and tools for model checking of linear properties are based on a search for bad cycles. A symbolic implementation of such a search involves the calculation of a nested fixed-point expression over the system's state space, and is often very difficult. Every computation that violates a safety property has a finite prefix along which the property is violated. We use this fact in order to base model checking of safety properties on a search for finite bad prefixes. Such a search can be performed using a simple forward or backward symbolic reachability check. A naive methodology that is based on such a search involves a construction of an automaton (or a tableau) that is doubly exponential in the property. We present an analysis of safety properties that enables us to prevent the doubly-exponential blow up and to use the same automaton used for model checking of general properties, replacing the search for bad cycles by a search for bad prefixes.

## 1 Introduction

Today's rapid development of complex and safety-critical systems requires reliable verification methods. In formal verification, we verify that a system meets a desired property by checking that a mathematical model of the system meets a formal specification that describes the property. Of special interest are properties asserting that observed behavior of the system always stays within some allowed set of finite behaviors, in which nothing "bad" happens. For example, we may want to assert that every message received was previously sent. Such properties of systems are called *safety properties*. Intuitively, a property $\psi$ is a safety property if every violation of $\psi$ occurs after a finite execution of the system. In our example, if in a computation of the system a message is received without previously being sent, this occurs after some finite execution of the system.

In order to define safety properties formally, we refer to computations of a nonterminating system as infinite words over an alphabet $\Sigma$. Typically, $\Sigma = 2^{AP}$, where $AP$ is the set of the system's atomic propositions. Consider a language $L$ of infinite words over $\Sigma$. A finite word $x$ over $\Sigma$ is a *bad prefix* for $L$ iff for all infinite words $y$ over $\Sigma$, the concatenation $x \cdot y$ of $x$ and $y$ is not in $L$. Thus, a bad prefix for $L$ is a finite word that cannot be

---

* Part of this work was done when this author was visiting Cadence Berkeley Laboratories.
** Supported in part by the NSF grants CCR-9628400 and CCR-9700061, and by a grant from the Intel Corporation. Part of this work was done when this author was a Varon Visiting Professor at the Weizmann Institute of Science.

extended to an infinite word in $L$. A language $L$ is a *safety language* if every word not in $L$ has a finite bad prefix. For example, $L = \{0^\omega, 1^\omega\} \subseteq \{0,1\}^\omega$ is a safety language: every word not in $L$ contains 01 or 10, and a prefix that ends in one of these sequences cannot be extended to a word in $L$. The definition of safety we consider here is given in [AS85], it coincides with the definition of limit closure defined in [Eme83], and is different from the definition in [Lam85], which also refers to the property being closed under stuttering.

Linear properties of nonterminating systems are often specified using Büchi automata on infinite words or linear temporal logic (LTL) formulas. We say that an automaton $\mathcal{A}$ is a safety automaton if it recognizes a safety language. Similarly, an LTL formula is a safety formula if the set of computations that satisfy it form a safety language. Sistla shows that the problem of determining whether a nondeterministic Büchi automaton or an LTL formula are safety is PSPACE-complete [Sis94] (see also [AS87]). From the results in [KV97], it follows that the problem is in PSPACE even when the Büchi automaton is alternating. On the other hand, when the Büchi automaton is deterministic, the problem can be solved in linear time [MP92]. Sistla also describes sufficient syntactic requirements for safe LTL formulas. For example, a formula (in positive normal form) whose only temporal operators are $G$ (always) and $X$ (next), is a safety formula [Sis94]. Suppose that we want to verify the correctness of a system with respect to a safety property. Can we use the fact that the property is known to be a safety property in order to improve general verification methods? The positive answer to this question is the subject of this paper.

Much previous work on verification of safety properties follow the *proof-based* approach to verification [Fra92]. In the proof-based approach, the system is annotated with assertions and proof rules are used to verify the assertions. In particular, Manna and Pnueli consider verification of reactive systems with respect to safety properties in [MP92,MP95]. The definition of safety formulas considered in [MP92,MP95] is syntactic: a safety formula is a formula of the form $G\varphi$ where $\varphi$ is a past formula. The syntactic definition is equivalent to the definition discussed here [MP92]. While proof-rules approaches are less sensitive to the size of the state space of the system, they require a heavy user support. Our work here considers the *state-exploration* approach to verification, where automatic *model checking* [CE81,QS81] is performed in order to verify the correctness of a system with respect to a specification. Previous work in this subject considers special cases of safety properties such as invariance checking [GW91,McM92,Val93,MR97], or assume that a general safety property is given by the set of its bad prefixes [GW91].

General methods for model checking of linear properties are based on a construction of a tableau or an automaton $\mathcal{A}_{\neg\psi}$ that accepts exactly all the infinite computations that violate the property $\psi$ [LP85,VW94]. Given a system $M$ and a property $\psi$, verification of $M$ with respect to $\psi$ is reduced to checking the emptiness of the product of $M$ and $\mathcal{A}_{\neg\psi}$ [VW86]. This check can be performed on-the-fly and symbolically [CVWY92,GPVW95,TBK95]. When $\psi$ is an LTL formula, the size of $\mathcal{A}_\psi$ is exponential in the length of $\psi$, and the complexity of verification that follows is PSPACE, with a matching lower bound [SC85].

Consider a safety property $\psi$. Let $pref(\psi)$ denote the set of all bad prefixes for $\psi$. Recall that every computation that violates $\psi$ has a prefix in $pref(\psi)$. We say that an automaton on finite words is *tight* for a safety property $\psi$ if it recognizes $pref(\psi)$. Since every system that violates $\psi$ has a computation with a prefix in $pref(\psi)$, an automaton tight for $\psi$ is practically more helpful than $\mathcal{A}_{\neg\psi}$. Indeed, reasoning about automata on finite words is easier than reasoning about automata on infinite words (cf. [HKSV97]). In particular, when the words are finite, we can use backward or forward symbolic reachability analysis [BCM⁺92,IN97]. In addition, using an automaton for bad prefixes, we can return to the user a finite error trace, which is a bad prefix, and which is often more helpful than an infinite error trace.

Given a safety property $\psi$, we construct an automaton tight for $\psi$. We show that the construction involves an exponential blow-up in the case $\psi$ is given as a nondeterministic Büchi automaton, and involves a doubly-exponential blow-up in the case $\psi$ is given in LTL. These results are surprising, as they indicate that detection of bad prefixes with a nondeterministic automaton has the flavor of determinization. The tight automata we construct are indeed deterministic. Nevertheless, our construction avoids the difficult determinization of the Büchi automaton for $\psi$ (cf. [Saf88]) and just uses a subset construction.

Our construction of tight automata reduces the problem of verification of safety properties to the problem of *invariance checking* [Fra92,MP92]. Indeed, once we take the product of a tight automaton with the system, we only have to check that we never reach an accepting state of the tight automaton. Invariance checking is amenable to both model checking techniques [BCM⁺92,IN97] and deductive verification techniques [BM83,SOR93,MAB⁺94]. In practice, the verified systems are often very large, and even clever symbolic methods cannot cope with the state-explosion problem that model checking faces. The way we construct tight automata also enables, in case the BDDs constructed during the symbolic reachability test get too large, an analysis of the intermediate data that has been collected. The analysis can lead to a conclusion that the system does not satisfy the property without further traversal of the system.

In view of the discouraging blow-ups described above, we release the requirement on tight automata and seek, instead, an automaton that need not accept all the bad prefixes, yet must accept at least one bad prefix of every computation that does not satisfy $\psi$. We say that such an automaton is *fine* for $\psi$. For example, an automaton that recognizes $p^* \cdot (\neg p) \cdot (p \vee \neg p)$ does not accept all the words in $pref(Gp)$, yet is fine for $Gp$. In practice, almost all the benefit that one obtain from a tight automaton can also be obtained from a fine automaton. We show that for natural safety formulas $\psi$, the construction of an automaton fine for $\psi$ is as easy as the construction of $\mathcal{A}_\psi$. In order to formalize the notion of "natural safety formulas", we partition safety properties into *intentionally*, *accidentally*, and *pathologically* safe properties. While most safety properties are intentionally safe, accidentally safe and especially pathologically safe properties contain some redundancy, and we do not expect to see them often in practice. We show that the automaton $\mathcal{A}_{\neg\psi}$, which accepts exactly all infinite computations that violate $\psi$, can easily (and with no blow-up) be modified to an automaton $\mathcal{A}_{\neg\psi}^{true}$ on finite words, which is tight for $\psi$ that is intentionally safe, and is fine for $\psi$ that is accidentally safe. We present a methodology for model checking of safety properties that is based on the above classification, uses $\mathcal{A}_{\neg\psi}^{true}$ instead of $\mathcal{A}_{\neg\psi}$, and thus replaces the search for bad cycles by a search for bad prefixes.

## 2 Preliminaries

### 2.1 Safety languages and formulas

Consider a language $L \subseteq \Sigma^\omega$ of infinite words over the alphabet $\Sigma$. A finite word $x \in \Sigma^*$ is a *bad prefix* for $L$ iff for all $y \in \Sigma^\omega$, we have $x \cdot y \notin L$. A language $L$ is a *safety* language iff every $w \notin L$ has a finite bad prefix. For a safety language $L$, we denote by $pref(L)$ the set of all bad prefixes for $L$. We say that a set $X \subseteq pref(L)$ is a *trap* for a safety language $L$ iff every word $w \notin L$ has at least one prefix in $X$. We denote all the traps for $L$ by $trap(L)$.

For a language $L \subseteq \Sigma^\omega$, we use $comp(L)$ to denote the complement of $L$; i.e., $comp(L) = \Sigma^\omega \setminus L$. We say that a language $L \subseteq \Sigma^\omega$ is a *co-safety* language iff $comp(L)$ is a safety language. (The term used in [MP92] is *guarantee* language.) Equivalently, $L$ is co-safety iff every $w \in L$ has a *good prefix* $x \in \Sigma^*$ such that for all $y \in \Sigma^\omega$, we have $x \cdot y \in L$. For a co-safety language $L$, we denote by $co\text{-}pref(L)$ the set of good prefixes for $L$. Note that $co\text{-}pref(L) = pref(comp(L))$.

For an LTL formula $\psi$ over a set $AP$ of atomic propositions, let $\|\psi\|$ denote the set of computations in $(2^{AP})^\omega$ that satisfy $\psi$. We say that $\psi$ is a safety formula iff $\|\psi\|$ is a safety language. Also, $\psi$ is a co-safety formula iff $\|\psi\|$ is a co-safety language or, equivalently, $\|\neg\psi\|$ is a safety language.

## 2.2 Word automata

Given an alphabet $\Sigma$, an *infinite word over* $\Sigma$ is an infinite sequence $w = \sigma_1 \cdot \sigma_2 \cdots$ of letters in $\Sigma$. We denote by $w^l$ the suffix $\sigma_l \cdot \sigma_{l+1} \cdot \sigma_{l+2} \cdots$ of $w$. An automaton on infinite words is $\mathcal{A} = \langle \Sigma, Q, \delta, Q_0, F \rangle$, where $\Sigma$ is the input alphabet, $Q$ is a finite set of states, $\delta$ is a transition function, $Q_0 \subseteq Q$ is a set of initial states, and $F \subseteq Q$ is an acceptance condition. When $\mathcal{A}$ is *deterministic*, the size of $Q_0$ is 1, and $\delta : Q \times \Sigma \to Q$ maps each state and letter to a single successor state. When $\mathcal{A}$ is *nondeterministic*, $\delta : Q \times \Sigma \to 2^Q$ maps each state and letter to a possible set of successor states. Since the choice of a successor state is existential, we can regard a transition $\rho(q, \sigma) = \{q_1, q_2, q_3\}$ as a disjunction $q_1 \vee q_2 \vee q_3$. Transitions of *alternating* automata can be arbitrary positive formulas over $Q$. We can have, for instance, a transition $\delta(q, \sigma) = (q_1 \wedge q_2) \vee (q_3 \wedge q_4)$, meaning that the automaton accepts from state $q$ a suffix $w^l$, starting by $\sigma$, of $w$, if it accepts $w^{l+1}$ from both $q_1$ and $q_2$ or from both $q_3$ and $q_4$. Such a transition combines existential and universal choices. Runs of an alternating automaton are infinite trees, where branches corresponds to universal choices of the automaton. For example, if $\mathcal{A}$ is an automaton with an initial state $q_0$ and $\delta(q_{in}, \sigma_0) = (q_1 \vee q_2) \wedge (q_3 \vee q_4)$, then possible runs of $\mathcal{A}$ on $w$ have a root labeled $q_{in}$, have one node in level 1 labeled $q_1$ or $q_2$, and have another node in level 1 labeled $q_3$ or $q_4$. When $\mathcal{A}$ is a *Büchi* automaton on infinite words, a run is *accepting* iff it visits infinitely many states from $F$ along each of its branches. The automaton $\mathcal{A}$ can also run on finite words in $\Sigma^*$. Then, a run over a word in $\Sigma^n$ is accepting if it visits states in $F$ in it all its nodes of level $n$. A word (either finite or infinite) is accepted by $\mathcal{A}$ iff there exists an accepting run on it. The language of $\mathcal{A}$, denoted $\mathcal{L}(\mathcal{A})$, is the set of words that $\mathcal{A}$ accepts. Deterministic and nondeterministic automata can be viewed as special cases of alternating automata. Formally, an alternating automaton is deterministic if for all $q$ and $\sigma$, we have $\delta(q, \sigma) \in Q \cup \{false\}$, and it is nondeterministic if $\delta(q, \sigma)$ is always a disjunction. For a detailed definition of alternating automata see [Var96].

We define the *size* of an alternating automaton $\mathcal{A} = \langle \Sigma, Q, \delta, Q_0, F \rangle$ as the sum of $|Q|$ and $|\delta|$, where $|\delta|$ is the sum of the lengths of the formulas in $\delta$. We say that the automaton $\mathcal{A}$ over infinite words is a safety (co-safety) automaton iff $\mathcal{L}(\mathcal{A})$ is a safety (co-safety) language. We use $pref(\mathcal{A})$, $co\text{-}pref(\mathcal{A})$, $trap(\mathcal{A})$, and $comp(\mathcal{A})$ to abbreviate $pref(\mathcal{L}(\mathcal{A}))$, $co\text{-}pref(\mathcal{L}(\mathcal{A}))$, $trap(\mathcal{L}(\mathcal{A}))$, and $comp(\mathcal{L}(\mathcal{A}))$, respectively. For an automaton $\mathcal{A}$ and a set of states $S$, we denote by $\mathcal{A}^S$ the automaton obtained from $\mathcal{A}$ by defining the set of initial states to be $S$. We say that an automaton $\mathcal{A}$ over infinite words is *universal* iff $\mathcal{L}(\mathcal{A}) = \Sigma^\omega$.

When $\mathcal{A}$ runs on finite words, it is universal iff $\mathcal{L}(\mathcal{A}) = \Sigma^*$. An automaton is *empty* iff $\mathcal{L}(\mathcal{A}) = \emptyset$. A set $S$ of states is *universal* (resp., *rejecting*), when $\mathcal{A}^S$ is universal (resp., empty). Note that the universality problem for nondeterministic automata is known to be PSPACE-complete [MS72,Wol82].

## 3 Detecting Bad Prefixes

Linear properties of nonterminating systems are often specified using automata on infinite words or linear temporal logic (LTL) formulas. Given an LTL formula $\psi$, one can build a nondeterministic Büchi automaton $\mathcal{A}_\psi$ that recognizes $\|\psi\|$. The size of $\mathcal{A}_\psi$ is, in the worst case, exponential in $\psi$ [GPVW95,VW94]. In practice, when given a property that happens to be safe, what we want is a nondeterministic automaton on finite words that detects bad prefixes. As we discuss in the introduction, such an automaton is easier to reason about. In this section we construct, from a given safety property, an automaton for its bad prefixes.

We first study the case where the property is given by a nondeterministic Büchi automaton. When the given automaton $\mathcal{A}$ is deterministic, the construction of an automaton $\mathcal{A}'$ for $pref(\mathcal{A})$ is straightforward. Indeed, we can obtain $\mathcal{A}'$ from $\mathcal{A}$ by defining the set of accepting states to be the set of states $s$ for which $\mathcal{A}^s$ is empty. Theorem 1 below shows that when $\mathcal{A}$ is a nondeterministic automaton, things are not that simple. While we can avoid a difficult determinization of $\mathcal{A}$ [Saf88], we cannot avoid an exponential blow-up.

**Theorem 1.** *Given a safety nondeterministic Büchi automaton $\mathcal{A}$ of size $n$, the size of an automaton that recognizes $pref(\mathcal{A})$ is $2^{\Theta(n)}$.*

*Proof.* We start with the upper bound. Let $\mathcal{A} = \langle \Sigma, Q, \delta, Q_0, F \rangle$. Recall that $pref(\mathcal{L}(\mathcal{A}))$ contains exactly all prefixes $x \in \Sigma^*$ such that for all $y \in \Sigma^\omega$, we have $x \cdot y \notin \mathcal{L}(\mathcal{A})$. Accordingly, the automaton for $pref(\mathcal{A})$ accepts a prefix $x$ iff the set of states that $\mathcal{A}$ could be in after reading $x$ is rejecting. Formally, we define the (deterministic) automaton $\mathcal{A}' = \langle \Sigma, 2^Q, \delta', \{Q_0\}, F' \rangle$, where $F'$ contains all the rejecting sets of $\mathcal{A}$, and $\delta'$ follows the subset construction induced by $\delta$; that is, for every $S \in 2^Q$ and $\sigma \in \Sigma$, we have $\delta'(S, \sigma) = \bigvee_{s \in S} \delta(s, \sigma)$.

We now turn to the lower bound. Essentially, it follows from the fact that $pref(\mathcal{A})$ refers to words that are not accepted by $\mathcal{A}$, and hence, it has the flavor of complementation. Complementing a nondeterministic automaton on finite words involves an exponential blow-up [MF71]. In fact, one can construct a nondeterministic automaton $\mathcal{A} = \langle \Sigma, Q, \delta, Q_0, Q \rangle$, in which all states are accepting, such that the smallest nondeterministic automaton that recognizes $comp(\mathcal{A})$ has $2^{\Theta(|Q|)}$ states. (To see this, consider the language $L_n$ consisting all all words $w$ such that either $|w| < 2n$ or $w = uvz$, where $|u| = |v| = n$ and $u \neq v$.) Given $\mathcal{A}$ as above, let $\mathcal{A}'$ be $\mathcal{A}$ when regarded as a Büchi automaton on infinite words. It is not hard to see that $pref(\mathcal{A}') = comp(\mathcal{A})$.

The lower bound in Theorem 1 is not surprising, as complementation of nondeterministic automata involves an exponential blow-up, and, as we demonstrate in the lower-bound proof, there is a tight relation between $pref(\mathcal{A})$ and $comp(\mathcal{A})$. We could hope, therefore, that when properties are specified in a negative form (that is, they describe the forbidden behaviors of the system) or are given in LTL, whose formulas can be negated, detection of bad prefixes would not be harder than detection of bad computations. In Theorems 2 and 3 we refute this hope.

**Theorem 2.** *Given a co-safety nondeterministic Büchi automaton $A$ of size $n$, the size of an automaton that recognizes co-pref($\mathcal{L}(A)$) is $2^{\Theta(n)}$.*

*Proof.* The upper bound is similar to the one in Theorem 1, only that now we define the set of accepting states in $A'$ as the set of all the universal sets of $A$. We prove a matching lower bound. For $n \geq 1$, let $\Sigma_n = \{1, \ldots, n, \&\}$. We define $L_n$ as the language of all words $w \in \Sigma_n^\omega$ such that $w$ contains at least one $\&$ and the letter after the first $\&$ is either $\&$ or it has already appeared somewhere before the first $\&$. The language $L_n$ is a co-safety language. Indeed, each word in $L_n$ has a good prefix (e.g., the one that contains the first $\&$ and its successor). We can recognize $L_n$ with a nondeterministic Büchi automaton with $O(n)$ states (the automaton guesses the letter that appears after the first $\&$). Obvious good prefixes for $L_n$ are 12&&, 123&2, etc. We can recognize these prefixes with a nondeterministic automaton with $O(n)$ states. But $L_n$ also has some less obvious good prefixes, like $1234 \cdots n\&$ (a permutation of $1 \ldots n$ followed by $\&$). These prefixes are indeed good, as every suffix we concatenate to them would start in either $\&$ or a letter in $\{1, \ldots, n\}$ that has appeared before the $\&$. To recognize these prefixes, a nondeterministic automaton needs to keep track of subsets of $\{1, \ldots, n\}$, for which it needs $2^n$ states. Consequently, a nondeterministic automaton for co-pref($L_n$) must have at least $2^n$ states.

We now extend the proof of Theorem 2 to get a doubly-exponential lower bound for going from a safety LTL formula to a nondeterministic automaton for its bad prefixes. The idea is similar: while the proof in Theorem 2 uses the exponential lower bound for going from nondeterministic to deterministic Büchi automata, the proof for this case is a variant of the doubly exponential lower bound for going from LTL formulas to deterministic Büchi automata [KV98].

**Theorem 3.** *Given a safety LTL formula, the size of a nondeterministic Büchi automaton for pref($\psi$) is doubly exponential in the length of $\psi$.*

In order to get the upper bound in Theorem 3, we apply the exponential construction in Theorem 1 to the exponential Büchi automaton $A_\psi$ for $\|\psi\|$. The construction in Theorem 1 is based on a subset construction for $A_\psi$, and it requires a check for the universality of sets of states $Q$ of $A_\psi$. Such a check corresponds to a validity check for a DNF formula in which each disjunct corresponds to a state in $Q$. While the size of the formula can be exponential in $|\psi|$, the number of distinct literals in the formula is at most linear in $|\psi|$, implying that the the universality of $Q$ can be checked using space polynomial in $|\psi|$.

Given a safety formula $\psi$, we say that a nondeterministic automaton $A$ over finite words is *tight* for $\psi$ iff $\mathcal{L}(A) = pref(\|\psi\|)$. In view of the lower bounds proven above, a construction of tight automata may be too expensive. We say that a nondeterministic automaton $A$ over finite words is *fine* for $\psi$ iff there exists $X \in trap(\|\psi\|)$ such that $\mathcal{L}(A) = X$. Thus, a fine automaton need not accept all the bad prefixes, yet it must accept at least one bad prefix of every computation that does not satisfy $\psi$. In practice, almost all the benefit that one obtain from a tight automaton can also be obtained from a fine automaton (we will get back to this point in Section 6). It is an open question whether there are feasible constructions of fine automata for general safety formulas. In Section 5 we show that for natural safety formulas $\psi$, the construction of an automaton fine for $\psi$ is as easy as the construction of an automaton for $\psi$.

# 4 Symbolic Verification of Safety Properties

Our construction of tight automata reduces the problem of verification of safety properties to the problem of invariance checking, which is amenable to a large variety of techniques. In particular, backward and forward symbolic reachability analysis have proven to be effective techniques for checking invariant properties on systems with large state spaces [BCM+92,IN97]. In practice, however, the verified systems are often very large, and even clever symbolic methods cannot cope with the state-explosion problem that model checking faces. In this section we describe how the the way we construct tight automata enables, in case the BDDs constructed during the symbolic reachability test get too big, an analysis of the intermediate data that has been collected. The analysis solves the model-checking problem without further traversal of the system.

Consider a system $M = \langle AP, W, R, W_0, L \rangle$, where $W$ is the set of states, $R \subseteq W \times W$ is a transition relation, $W_0$ is a set of initial states, and $L : W \to 2^{AP}$ maps each state to the sets of atomic propositions that hold in it. Let $fin(M)$ be an automaton that accepts all finite computations of $M$. Given $\psi$, let $\mathcal{A}_{\neg\psi}$ be the nondeterministic co-safety automaton for $\neg\psi$, thus $\mathcal{L}(\mathcal{A}_{\neg\psi}) = \|\neg\psi\|$. In the proof of Theorem 2, we construct an automaton $\mathcal{A}'$ such that $\mathcal{L}(\mathcal{A}') = pref(\psi)$ by following the subset construction of $\mathcal{A}_{\neg\psi}$ and defining the set of accepting states to be the set of universal sets in $\mathcal{A}_{\neg\psi}$. Then, one needs to verify the invariance that the product $fin(M) \times \mathcal{A}'$ never reaches an accepting state of $\mathcal{A}'$. In addition to forward and backward symbolic reachability analysis, one could use a variety of recent techniques for doing semi-exhaustive reachability analysis [RS95,YSAA97], including standard simulation techniques [LWA98]. Note, however, that if $\mathcal{A}'$ is doubly exponential in $|\psi|$, the BDD representation of $\mathcal{A}'$ will use exponentially (in $|\psi|$) many Boolean variables.

Another approach is to apply forward reachability analysis to the product $M \times \mathcal{A}_{\neg\psi}$ of the system $M$ and the automaton $\mathcal{A}_{\neg\psi}$. Formally, let $\mathcal{A}_{\neg\psi} = \langle 2^{AP}, Q, \delta, Q_0, F \rangle$, and let $M$ be as above. The product $M \times \mathcal{A}_{\neg\psi}$ has state space $W \times Q$, and the successors of a state $\langle w, q \rangle$ are all pairs $\langle w', q' \rangle$ such that $R(w, w')$ and $q' \in \delta(q, L(w))$. Forward symbolic methods use the predicate $post(S)$, which, given a set of $S$ of states (represented symbolically) returns the successor set of $S$, that is, the set of all states $t$ such that there is a transition from some state in $S$ to $t$. Starting from the initial set $S_0 = W_0 \times Q_0$, forward symbolic methods iteratively construct, for $i \geq 0$, the set $S_{i+1} = post(S_i)$. The calculation the $S_i$'s proceeds symbolically, and they are represented by BDDs. Doing so, forward symbolic methods actually follow the subset construction of $M \times \mathcal{A}_{\neg\psi}$. Indeed, for each $w \in W$ the set $Q_i^w = \{q : \langle w, q \rangle \in S_i\}$ is the set of states that $\mathcal{A}_{\neg\psi}$ that can be reached via a path of length $i$ in $M$ from a state in $W_0$ to the state $w$. Note that this set can be exponentially (in $|\psi|$) large resulting possibly in a large BDD; on the other hand, the number of Boolean variables used to represent $\mathcal{A}_{\neg\psi}$ is linear in $|\psi|$.

The discussion above suggests the following technique for the case we encounter space problems. Suppose that at some point the BDD for $S_i$ gets too big. We then check whether there is a state $w$ such that the set $Q_i^w$ is universal. As discussed in Section 3, we can check the universality of $Q_i^w$ in space polynomial in $|\psi|$. Note that we do not need to enumerate all states $w$ and then check $Q_i^w$. We can enumerate directly the sets $Q_i^w$, whose number is at most doubly exponential in $|\psi|$. It can be shown that $M \times \mathcal{A}_{\neg\psi}$ is nonempty iff $Q_i^w$ is universal for some $w \in W$ and $i > 0$, thus this check solves the model-checking problem without further traversal of the system.

Note that it is possible to use semi-exhaustive reachability techniques also when analyzing $M \times A_{\neg \psi}$. That is, instead of taking $S_{i+1}$ to be $post(S_i)$ we can take it to be a subset $S'_{i+1}$ of $post(S_i)$ [RS95,YSAA97]. We have to ensure, however, that $S'_{i+1}$ is *saturated* with respect to states of $A_{\neg \psi}$ [LWA98]. Informally, we are allowed to drop states of $M$ from $S_{i+1}$, but we are not allowed to drop states of $A_{\neg \psi}$. Formally, if $\langle w, q \rangle \in S'_{i+1}$ and $\langle w, q' \rangle \in S_{i+1}$, then $\langle w, q' \rangle \in S'_{i+1}$. This ensures that if the semi-exhaustive analysis follows a bad prefix of length $i$ in $M$, then $Q'^w_i = \{q : \langle w, q \rangle \in S'_i\}$ will be universal. In the extreme case, we follow only one trace of $M$, i.e., we simulate $M$. In that case, we have that $S'_{i+1} = \{w\} \times Q'^w_i$. For a related approach see [CES97].

## 5 Classification of Safety Properties

Consider the safety LTL formula $Gp$. A bad prefix $x$ for $Gp$ must contain a state in which $p$ does not hold. If the user gets $x$ as an error trace, he can immediately understand why $Gp$ is violated. Consider now the LTL formula $\psi = G(p \vee (Xq \wedge X\neg q))$. The formula $\psi$ is equivalent to $Gp$ and is therefore a safety formula. Moreover, the set of bad prefixes for $\psi$ and $Gp$ coincide. Nevertheless, a minimal bad prefix for $\psi$ (e.g., a single state in which $p$ does not hold) does not tell the whole story about the violation of $\psi$. Indeed, the latter depends on the fact that $Xq \wedge X\neg q$ is unsatisfiable, which (especially in more complicated examples), may not be trivially noticed by the user. This intuition, of a prefix that "tells the whole story", is the base for a classification of safety properties into three distinct safety levels. We first formalize this intuition in terms of *informative prefixes*. We assume that LTL formulas are given in positive normal form, where negation is applied only to propositions (when we write $\neg \psi$, we refer to its positive normal form). In the positive normal form, we use the operator $V$ as dual to the operator $U$, and use $cl(\psi)$ to denote the closure of $\psi$, namely, the set of $\psi$'s subformulas.

For an LTL formula $\psi$ and a finite computation $\pi = \sigma_1 \cdot \sigma_2 \cdots \sigma_n$, with $\sigma_i \in 2^{AP}$, we say that $\pi$ is *informative for* $\psi$ iff there exists a mapping $L : \{1, \ldots, n+1\} \to 2^{cl(\psi)}$ such that the following hold: (1) $\neg \psi \in L(1)$. (2) $L(n+1)$ is empty. (3) For all $1 \leq i \leq n$ and $\varphi \in L(i)$, the following hold.

- If $\varphi$ is a propositional assertion, it is satisfied by $\sigma_i$.
- If $\varphi = \varphi_1 \vee \varphi_2$ then $\varphi_1 \in L(i)$ or $\varphi_2 \in L(i)$.
- If $\varphi = \varphi_1 \wedge \varphi_2$ then $\varphi_1 \in L(i)$ and $\varphi_2 \in L(i)$.
- If $\varphi = X\varphi_1$, then $\varphi_1 \in L(i+1)$.
- If $\varphi = \varphi_1 U \varphi_2$, then $\varphi_2 \in L(i)$ or $[\varphi_1 \in L(i)$ and $\varphi_1 U \varphi_2 \in L(i+1)]$.
- If $\varphi = \varphi_1 V \varphi_2$, then $\varphi_2 \in L(i)$ and $[\varphi_1 \in L(i)$ or $\varphi_1 V \varphi_2 \in L(i+1)]$.

Note that the emptiness of $L(n+1)$ guarantees that all the requirements imposed by $\neg \psi$ are fulfilled along $\pi$. For example, while the finite computation $\{p\} \cdot \emptyset$ is informative for $Gp$ (with $L(1) = \{F\neg p\}, L(2) = \{F\neg p, \neg p\}$, and $L(3) = \emptyset$), it is not informative for $\psi = G(p \vee (Xq \wedge X\neg q))$. Indeed, as $\neg \psi = F(\neg p \wedge (X\neg q \vee Xq))$, an informative prefix for $\psi$ must contain at least one state after the first state in which $\neg p$ holds.

We distinguish between three types of safety formulas.

- A safety formula $\psi$ is *intentionally safe* iff all the bad prefixes for $\psi$ are informative. For example, the formula $Gp$ is intentionally safe.

- A safety formula $\psi$ is *accidentally safe* iff not all the bad prefixes for $\psi$ are informative, but every computation that violates $\psi$ has an informative bad prefix. For example, the formulas $G(q \vee XGp) \wedge G(r \vee XG\neg p)$ and $G(p \vee (Xq \wedge X\neg q))$ are accidentally safe.
- A safety formula $\psi$ is *pathologically safe* if there is a computation that violates $\psi$ and has no informative bad prefix. For example, the formula $[G(q \vee GFp) \wedge G(r \vee GF\neg p)] \vee Gq \vee Gr$ is pathologically safe.

Sistla has shown that all temporal formulas in positive normal form constructed with the temporal connectives $X$ and $V$ are safety formulas [Sis94]. We call such formulas *syntactically safe*. The following strengthens Sistla's result.

**Theorem 4.** *If $\psi$ is syntactically safe, then $\psi$ is intentionally or accidentally safe.*

Given an LTL formula $\psi$ in positive normal form, one can build an alternating Büchi automaton $\mathcal{A}_\psi = \langle 2^{AP}, Q, \delta, Q_0, F \rangle$ such that $\mathcal{L}(\mathcal{A}_\psi) = \|\psi\|$. Essentially, each state of $\mathcal{L}(\mathcal{A}_\psi)$ corresponds to a subformula of $\psi$, and its transitions follow the semantics of LTL [Var96]. We define the alternating Büchi automaton $\mathcal{A}_\psi^{true} = \langle 2^{AP}, Q, \delta, Q_0, \emptyset \rangle$ by redefining the set of accepting states to be the empty set. So, while in $\mathcal{A}_\psi$ a copy of the automaton may accept by either reaching a state from which it proceed to *true* or visiting states of the form $\varphi_1 V \varphi_2$ infinitely often, in $\mathcal{A}_\psi^{true}$ all copies must reach a state from which they proceed to *true*. Accordingly, $\mathcal{A}_\psi^{true}$ accepts exactly these computations that have a finite prefix that is informative for $\psi$. To see this, note that such computations can be accepted by a run of $\mathcal{A}_\psi$ in which all the copies eventually reach a state that is associated with propositional assertions that are satisfied. Now, let $fin(\mathcal{A}_\psi^{true})$ be $\mathcal{A}_\psi^{true}$ when regarded as an automaton on finite words.

**Theorem 5.** *For every safety formula $\psi$, the automaton $fin(\mathcal{A}_{\neg\psi}^{true})$ accepts exactly all the prefixes that are informative for $\psi$.*

**Corollary 1.** *Consider a safety formula $\psi$. If $\psi$ is intentionally safe, then $fin(\mathcal{A}_{\neg\psi}^{true})$ is tight for $\psi$. Also, if $\psi$ is accidentally safe, then $fin(\mathcal{A}_{\neg\psi}^{true})$ is fine for $\psi$.*

**Theorem 6.** *Deciding whether a given formula is pathologically safe is PSPACE-complete.*

*Proof.* Consider a formula $\psi$. Recall that the automaton $\mathcal{A}_\psi^{true}$ accepts exactly these computations that have a finite prefix that is informative for $\psi$. Hence, $\psi$ is not pathologically safe iff every computation that does not satisfy $\psi$ is accepted by $\mathcal{A}_{\neg\psi}^{true}$. Accordingly, checking whether $\psi$ is pathologically safe can be reduced to checking the containment of $\mathcal{L}(\mathcal{A}_{\neg\psi})$ in $\mathcal{L}(\mathcal{A}_{\neg\psi}^{true})$. Since the size of $\mathcal{A}_\psi$ is linear in the length of $\psi$ and containment for alternating Büchi automata can be checked in polynomial space [KV97], we are done. For the lower bound, we do a reduction from the problem of deciding whether a given formula is a safety formula. Consider a formula $\psi$, and let $p$, $q$, and $r$ be atomic propositions not in $\psi$. The formula $\varphi = [G(q \vee GFp) \wedge G(r \vee GF\neg p)] \vee Gq \vee Gr$ is pathologically safe. It can be shown that $\psi$ is a safety formula iff $\psi \wedge \varphi$ is pathologically safe.

Note that the lower bound in Theorem 6 implies that the reverse direction of Theorem 4 does not hold.

# 6 A Methodology

In Section 5, we partitioned safety formulas into three safety levels and showed that for some formulas, we can circumvent the blow-up involved in constructing a tight automaton for the bad prefixes. In particular, we showed that the automaton $fin(\mathcal{A}^{true}_{\neg\psi})$, which is linear in the length of $\psi$, is tight for $\psi$ that is intentionally safe and is fine for $\psi$ that is accidentally safe. In this section we describe a methodology for efficient verification of safety properties that is based on these observations. Consider a system $M$ and a safety LTL formula $\psi$. Let $fin(M)$ be a nondeterministic automaton on finite words that accepts the prefixes of computations of $M$, and let $\mathcal{U}^{true}_{\neg\psi}$ be the nondeterministic automaton on finite words equivalent to the alternating automaton $fin(\mathcal{A}^{true}_{\neg\psi})$ [CKS81]. The size of $\mathcal{U}^{true}_{\neg\psi}$ is exponential in the size of $fin(\mathcal{A}^{true}_{\neg\psi})$, hence it is exponential in the length of $\psi$. Given $M$ and $\psi$, we suggest to proceed as follows (see the figure below).

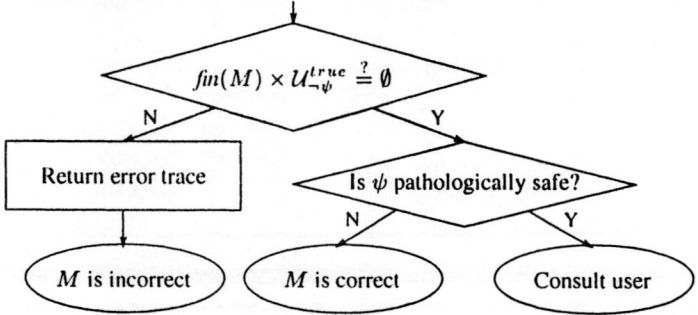

Instead of checking the emptiness of $M \times \mathcal{A}_{\neg\psi}$, verification starts by checking $fin(M)$ with respect to $\mathcal{U}^{true}_{\neg\psi}$. Since both automata refer to finite words, this can be done using finite forward reachability analysis. If the product $fin(M) \times \mathcal{U}^{true}_{\neg\psi}$ is not empty, we return a word $w$ in the intersection, namely, a bad prefix for $\psi$ that is generated by $M$[1]. If the product $fin(M) \times \mathcal{U}^{true}_{\neg\psi}$ is empty, then, as $\mathcal{U}^{true}_{\neg\psi}$ is fine for intentionally and accidentally safe formulas, there may be two reasons for this. One, is that $M$ satisfies $\psi$, and the second is that $\psi$ is pathologically safe. Therefore, we next check whether $\psi$ is pathologically safe. (Note that for syntactically safe formulas this check is unnecessary, by Theorem 4.) If it is not pathologically safe, we conclude that $M$ satisfies $\psi$. Otherwise, we tell the user that his formula is pathologically safe, indicating that his specification is needlessly complicated (accidentally and pathologically safe formulas contain redundancy). At this point, the user would probably be surprised that his formula was a safety formula (if he had known it is safety, he would have simplified it to an intentionally safe formula – a feasible automatic simplification of such formulas is an open problem). If the user wishes to continue with this formula, we give up using the fact that $\psi$ is safety and proceed with usual LTL model checking, thus we check the emptiness of $M \times \mathcal{A}_{\neg\psi}$. (Recall that the symbolic algorithm for emptiness of Büchi automata is in the worst case quadratic [HKSV97,TBK95].) Note that at this point, the error trace that the user gets if $M$ does not satisfy $\psi$ consists of a prefix and a cycle, yet since the user does not want to change his formula, he probably has no idea why it is a safety formula and a finite non-informative error trace would not

---

[1] Note that since $\psi$ may not be intentionally safe, the automaton $\mathcal{U}^{true}_{\neg\psi}$ may not be tight for $\psi$, thus while $w$ is a minimal informative bad prefix, it may not be a minimal bad prefix.

help him). If the user prefers, or if $M$ is very large (making the discovery of bad cycles infeasible), we can build an automaton for $pref(\psi)$, hoping that by learning it, the user would understand how to simplify his formula or that, in spite of the potential blow-up in $\psi$, finite forward reachability would work better.

**Acknowledgement.** The second author is grateful to Avner Landver for stimulating discussions.

## References

[AS85]    B. Alpern and F.B. Schneider. Defining liveness. *Information processing letters*, 21:181–185, 1985.

[AS87]    B. Alpern and F.B. Schneider. Recognizing safety and liveness. *Distributed computing*, 2:117–126, 1987.

[BCM$^+$92] J.R. Burch, E.M. Clarke, K.L. McMillan, D.L. Dill, and L.J. Hwang. Symbolic model checking: $10^{20}$ states and beyond. *Information and Computation*, 98(2):142–170, June 1992.

[BM83]    R.S. Boyer and J.S. Moore. Proof-checking, theorem-proving and program verification. Technical Report 35, Institute for Computing Science and Computer Applications, University of Texas at Austin, January 1983.

[CE81]    E.M. Clarke and E.A. Emerson. Design and synthesis of synchronization skeletons using branching time temporal logic. In *Proc. Workshop on Logic of Programs*, LNCS 131, pp. 52–71, 1981.

[CES97]   W. Canfield, E.A. Emerson, and A. Saha. Checking formal specifications under simulation. In *Proc. International Conference on Computer Design*, pp. 455–460, 1997.

[CKS81]   A.K. Chandra, D.C. Kozen, and L.J. Stockmeyer. Alternation. *Journal of the Association for Computing Machinery*, 28(1):114–133, January 1981.

[CVWY92] C. Courcoubetis, M.Y. Vardi, P. Wolper, and M. Yannakakis. Memory efficient algorithms for the verification of temporal properties. *Formal Methods in System Design*, 1:275–288, 1992.

[Eme83]   E.A. Emerson. Alternative semantics for temporal logics. *Theoretical Computer Science*, 26:121–130, 1983.

[Fra92]   N. Francez. *Program verification*. International Computer Science. Addison-Weflay, 1992.

[GPVW95] R. Gerth, D. Peled, M.Y. Vardi, and P. Wolper. Simple on-the-fly automatic verification of linear temporal logic. In *Protocol Specification, Testing, and Verification*, pp. 3–18. Chapman & Hall, August 1995.

[GW91]    P. Godefroid and P. Wolper. Using partial orders for the efficient verification of deadlock freedom and safety properties. In *Proc. 3rd CAV*, LNCS 575, pp. 332–342, 1991.

[HKSV97] R.H. Hardin, R.P. Kurshan, S.K. Shukla, and M.Y. Vardi. A new heuristic for bad cycle detection using BDDs. In *Proc. 9th CAV*, LNCS 1254, pp. 268–278, 1997.

[IN97]    H. Iwashita and T. Nakata. Forward model checking techniques oriented to buggy designs. In *Proc. IEEE/ACM ICCAD*, pp. 400–404, 1997.

[KV97]    O. Kupferman and M.Y. Vardi. Weak alternating automata are not that weak. In *Proc. 5th ISTCS*, pp. 147–158. IEEE Computer Society Press, 1997.

[KV98]    O. Kupferman and M.Y. Vardi. Freedom, weakness, and determinism: from linear-time to branching-time. In *Proc. 13th LICS*, pp. 81–92, June 1998.

[Lam85]   L. Lamport. Logical foundation. In *Distributed systems - methods and tools for specification*, LNCS 190, 1985.

[LP85]    O. Lichtenstein and A. Pnueli. Checking that finite state concurrent programs satisfy their linear specification. In *Proc. 12th POPL*, pp. 97–107, 1985.

[LWA98] Y. Luo, T. Wongsonegoro, and A. Aziz. Hybrid techniques for fast functional simulation. In *Proc. 35th DAC.* IEEE Computer Society, 1998.

[MAB+94] Z. Manna, A. Anuchitanukul, N. Bjorner, A. Browne, E. Chang, M. Colon, L. De Alfaro, H. Devarajan, H. Sipma, and T. Uribe. STeP: The Stanford Temporal Prover. Technical Report STAN-CS-TR-94-1518, Dept. of Computer Science, Stanford University, 1994.

[McM92] K. McMillan. Using unfolding to avoid the state explosion problem in the verification of asynchronous circuits. In *Proc. 4th CAV*, LNCS 663, pp. 164–174, 1992.

[MF71] A.R. Meyer and M.J. Fischer. Economy of description by automata, grammars, and formal systems. In *Proc. 12th IEEE Symp. on Switching and Automata Theory*, pp. 188–191, 1971.

[MP92] Z. Manna and A. Pnueli. *The Temporal Logic of Reactive and Concurrent Systems: Specification.* Springer-Verlag, Berlin, January 1992.

[MP95] Z. Manna and A. Pnueli. *The Temporal Logic of Reactive and Concurrent Systems: Safety.* Springer-Verlag, New York, 1995.

[MR97] S. Melzer and S. Roemer. Deadlock checking using net unfoldings. In *Proc. 9th CAV*, LNCS 1254, pp. 364–375, 1997.

[MS72] A.R. Meyer and L.J. Stockmeyer. The equivalence problem for regular expressions with squaring requires exponential time. In *Proc. 13th IEEE Symp. on Switching and Automata Theory*, pp. 125–129, 1972.

[QS81] J.P. Queille and J. Sifakis. Specification and verification of concurrent systems in Cesar. In *Proc. 5th International Symp. on Programming*, LNCS 137, pp. 337–351, 1981.

[RS95] K. Ravi and F. Somenzi. High-density reachability analysis. In *Proc. CAD*, pp. 154–158, 1995.

[Saf88] S. Safra. On the complexity of ω-automata. In *Proc. 29th FOCS*, pp. 319–327, White Plains, 1988.

[SC85] A.P. Sistla and E.M. Clarke. The complexity of propositional linear temporal logic. *Journal ACM*, 32:733–749, 1985.

[Sis94] A.P. Sistla. Satefy, liveness and fairness in temporal logic. *Formal Aspects of Computing*, 6:495–511, 1994.

[SOR93] R.E. Shankar, S. Owre, and J.M. Rushby. The PVS proof checker: A reference manual (beta release). Technical report, Computer Science laboratory, SRI International, Menlo Park, California, March 1993.

[TBK95] H.J. Touati, R.K. Brayton, and R. Kurshan. Testing language containment for ω-automata using BDD's. *Information and Computation*, 118(1):101–109, April 1995.

[Val93] A. Valmari. On-the-fly verification with stubborn sets. In *Proc. 5nd CAV*, LNCS 697, 1993.

[Var96] M.Y. Vardi. An automata-theoretic approach to linear temporal logic. In F. Moller and G. Birtwistle, editors, *Logics for Concurrency: Structure versus Automata*, LNCS 1043, pp. 238–266, 1996.

[VW86] M.Y. Vardi and P. Wolper. An automata-theoretic approach to automatic program verification. In *Proc. 1st LICS*, pp. 322–331, 1986.

[VW94] M.Y. Vardi and P. Wolper. Reasoning about infinite computations. *Information and Computation*, 115(1):1–37, November 1994.

[Wol82] P. Wolper. *Synthesis of Communicating Processes from Temporal Logic Specifications.* PhD thesis, Stanford University, 1982.

[YSAA97] J. Yuan, J. Shen, J. Abraham, and A. Aziz. On combining formal and informal verification. In *Proc 9th CAV*, LNCS 1254, pp. 376–387, 1997.

# A Complete Finite Prefix for Process Algebra

Rom Langerak and Ed Brinksma

University of Twente, Department of Computer Science, PO Box 217, 7500 AE
Enschede, The Netherlands, {langerak,brinksma}@cs.utwente.nl

**Abstract.** In this paper we show how to use McMillan's complete finite
prefix approach for process algebra. We present the model of component
event structures as a semantics for process algebra, and show how to
construct a complete finite prefix for this model. We present a simple
adequate order (using an order on process algebra expressions) as an
optimization to McMillan's original algorithm.

## 1 Introduction

A major problem in the verification of distributed systems is the state explosion
problem. This problem results when the modelling a system consisting of parallel
subsystems causes the model to have a number of states that is of the same order
of magnitude as the product of the states of the subsystems.

In process algebra (e.g. [Hoa85,BB87,BW90] state explosion may occur when using the standard interleaving semantics. In order to deal with this problem one
line of research has been to look for alternative semantic models based on partial
orders, of which event structures [Win89,BC94,Lan92] are a prominent example.
Event structures can be used as a semantics for process algebra and are easily extended with timing, probabilistic and stochastic information [BKLL98,KLL⁺98].
A problem though with event structures is that recursion leads to infinite structures, whereas for techniques like model checking it is important to have finite
representations of infinite behaviour.

An interesting direction of research has been initiated by McMillan, originally for
finite state Petri nets [McM92,McM95a,McM95b]. He has presented an algorithm
for constructing an initial part of the occurrence net [NPW81,Eng91] of a Petri
net which contains all information on reachable states and transitions. This
so-called complete finite prefix can be used as the basis for model checking
[Esp94,Gra97,Wal98].

In this paper we explore how this McMillan complete finite prefix approach
can be used in giving an event structure semantics to process algebra. Using a
translation of process algebra into Petri nets (as has been done in [Old91]) would
pose severe complications when calculating a prefix. The translation there makes
use of a trick for dealing with the choice operator; this has as a side effect that
not all reachable markings correspond in a clear way to reachable process algebra
expressions. This would greatly complicate the computation of a finite prefix.
Therefore we directly translate a process algebra expression into a model similar
to an occurrence net in which choice can be modelled in a natural way.

The paper is organized as follows. In section 2 we present a process algebra and a model called *component event structures* which is to process algebra what occurrence nets are to Petri nets. In section 3 we use this model as a semantics for process algebra and in section 4 we show how to construct a complete finite prefix for this model. In section 5 we present an optimization to the McMillan algorithm which has the same advantages as a proposal in [ERV97] but profits from the process algebra setting. Section 6 is for conclusions.

An extended version of this paper (containing all proofs) can be found in [LB99].

## 2 Process algebra and component event structures

This paper uses a simple process algebra with a parallel operator similar to the one from CSP [Hoa85] or LOTOS [BB87]. The syntax is given by the following grammar:

$$B ::= \textbf{stop} \mid a; B \mid B + B \mid B \mid_A B \mid P$$

The *inaction* process **stop** cannot do anything. *Action prefix* is denoted by $a; B$ where $a \in Act$, with $Act$ a set of *actions* (a distinction between observable and invisible actions plays no role in this paper). The *choice* between $B_1$ and $B_2$ is denoted by $B_1 + B_2$. *Parallel composition* is denoted by $B_1 \mid_A B_2$ where $A$ is the set of synchronizing actions; $B_1 \mid_\emptyset B_2$ is abbreviated to $B_1 | B_2$. Finally, $P$ denotes *process instantiation* where a behaviour expression is assumed to be in the context of a set of process definitions of the form $P := B$ with $B$ possibly containing process instantiations of $P$.

A process algebra expression can be decomposed into so-called components, which are action prefix expressions together with information about the synchronization context. This approach has been inspired by the Petri net semantics for process algebra presented in [Old91].

**Definition 1.** A *component* $s$ is defined by
$S ::= \textbf{stop} \mid a; B \mid S \mid_A \mid \mid_A S$ with $B$ a process algebra expression; the universe of all components is denoted by $Comp$.

Convention: let $S = \{S_1, \ldots, S_n\}$ be a set of components, then we use the notation $S \mid_A = \{S_1 \mid_A, \ldots, S_n \mid_A\}$, and similarly for $\mid_A S$.

Components can be in a *choice* relation which will be used to model the effect of the process algebra choice operator.

**Definition 2.** A *state* is a tuple $(S, R)$ with $S$ a set of components, and $R$ an irreflexive and symmetric relation between components (so $R \subset S \times S$) called the *choice* relation.

Convention: let $R = \{(S_1, S_1'), \ldots, (S_n, S_n')\}$ be a choice relation, then we use the notation $R \mid_A = \{(S_1 \mid_A, S_1' \mid_A), \ldots, (S_n \mid_A, S_n' \mid_A)\}$ and similarly for $\mid_A R$. Components (and the choice relation between them) can be obtained by *decomposing* a process algebra expression.

**Definition 3.** The decomposition function *dec*, which maps a process algebra expression on a state, is recursively defined by $dec(B) = (\mathcal{S}(B), \mathcal{R}(B))$ with

$dec(\mathbf{stop}) = (\{\mathbf{stop}\}, \emptyset)$

$dec(a_x; B) = (\{a_x; B\}, \emptyset)$

$dec(B \mid_A B') = (\mathcal{S}(B)\mid_A \cup \mid_A \mathcal{S}(B'), \mathcal{R}(B)\mid_A \cup \mid_A \mathcal{R}(B'))$

$dec(B + B') = (\mathcal{S}(B) \cup \mathcal{S}(B'), \mathcal{R}(B) \cup \mathcal{R}(B') \cup (\mathcal{S}(B) \times \mathcal{S}(B')))$

$dec(P_\Phi) = dec(\Phi(B))$ if $P := B$

In order to avoid that the decomposition of a process instantiation leads to an infinite chain of substitutions, we have to adopt the constraint that all process definitions are guarded (see e.g. [BW90]).

We define an event structure model which is very similar to a type of Petri nets called *occurrence* nets [NPW81,Eng91]; the main difference is that there are no tokens, and conditions can be in a binary *choice* relation.

**Definition 4.** A *condition event structure* is a 4-tuple $(D, E, \sharp, \prec)$ with:
- $D$ a set of conditions
- $E$ a set of events
- $\sharp \subset D \times D$, the choice relation (symmetric and irreflexive)
- $\prec \subseteq (D \times E) \cup (E \times D)$ the *flow* relation

We adopt some Petri net terminology: a *marking* is a set of conditions. A *node* is either a condition or an event. The *preset* of a node $x$, denoted by ${}^\bullet x$, is defined by ${}^\bullet x = \{y \in D \cup E \mid y \prec x\}$, and the *postset* $x^\bullet$ by $x^\bullet = \{y \in D \cup E \mid x \prec y\}$. The *initial marking* $M_0$ is defined by $M_0 = \{d \in D \mid {}^\bullet d = \emptyset\}$.

**Definition 5.** The transitive and reflexive closure of $\prec$ is denoted by $\leq$.
The *conflict* relation on nodes, denoted by $\#$, is defined by: let $x_1$ and $x_2$ be two different nodes, then $x_1 \# x_2$ iff there are two nodes $y_1$ and $y_2$, such that $y_1 \leq x_1$ and $y_2 \leq x_2$, with
- either $y_1$ and $y_2$ are two conditions in the choice relation, i.e. $y_1 \sharp y_2$
- or $y_1$ and $y_2$ are two events with ${}^\bullet y_1 \cap {}^\bullet y_2 \neq \emptyset$

**Definition 6.** A condition event structure is *well-formed* if the following properties hold:
1. $\leq$ is anti-symmetric, i.e. $x \leq x' \wedge x' \leq x \Rightarrow x = x'$
2. finite precedence, i.e. for each node $x$ the set $\{y \in E \cup D \mid y \leq x\}$ is finite
3. no self-conflict, i.e. for each node $x$: $\neg(x \# x)$
4. for each event $e$: ${}^\bullet e \neq \emptyset$ and $e^\bullet \neq \emptyset$
5. for each condition $d$: $|{}^\bullet d| \leq 1$
6. for all conditions $d_1$ and $d_2$: $d_1 \sharp d_2 \Rightarrow {}^\bullet d_1 = {}^\bullet d_2$

Let $d$ be a condition, then we define $\sharp(d)$, the set of conditions in choice with $d$, by $\sharp(d) = \{d' \mid d \sharp d'\}$. Similarly for a set of conditions $\mathcal{D}$, $\sharp(\mathcal{D}) = \{d' \mid \exists d \in \mathcal{D} : d \sharp d'\}$.

**Definition 7.** Suppose we have a condition event structure, with $e$ an event, and $M$ and $M'$ markings, then we say there is an *event transition* $M \xrightarrow{e} M'$ iff $\bullet e \subseteq M$ and $M' = (M \cup e^\bullet) \setminus (\bullet e \cup \sharp(\bullet e))$ (note there are no loops in well-formed condition event structures).

An *event sequence* is a sequence of events $e_1 \ldots e_n$ such that there are markings $M_1, \ldots, M_n$ with $M_0 \xrightarrow{e_1} M_1 \rightarrow \ldots \xrightarrow{e_n} M_n$. We call $C = \{e_1, \ldots, e_n\}$ a configuration of the condition event structure.

**Definition 8.** Two nodes $x$ and $x'$ are said to be independent, notation $x \asymp x'$, iff $\neg(x \leq x') \wedge \neg(x' \leq x) \wedge \neg(x \# x')$.

**Definition 9.** A *cut* is a marking $M$ such that for each pair of different conditions $d$ and $d'$ in $M$ holds: $d \asymp d'$ or $d \sharp d'$, and that is maximal (w.r.t. set inclusion).

**Theorem 1.** *Let $C$ be a configuration and $M$ a cut. Define*
$Cut(C) = (M_0 \cup C^\bullet) \setminus (\bullet C \cup \sharp(\bullet C))$ *and* $Conf(M) = \{e \in E \mid \exists d \in M : e \leq d\}$.
*Then: $Cut(C)$ is a cut, $Conf(M)$ is a configuration, $Conf(Cut(C)) = C$, and $Cut(Conf(M)) = M$.*

**Definition 10.** A condition event structure $\mathcal{E} = (D, E, \sharp, \prec)$ with mappings
$\qquad l_C : D \rightarrow Comp$ (mapping conditions to components)
$\qquad l_E : E \rightarrow Act$ (mapping events to actions)
is called a *component event structure*.

We will often be sloppy and denote a condition by its component label (but note that different conditions may be labelled with the same component).

# 3 Component event structures as semantics for process algebra

In this section we define a component event structure as a semantics for a process algebra expression with the help of a derivation system for transitions (again inspired by [Old91]). This derivation system will allow derivations of transitions of the form $\mathcal{S} \xrightarrow{a} (\mathcal{S}', \mathcal{R}')$, where $\mathcal{S}$ and $\mathcal{S}'$ are sets of components, and $\mathcal{R}'$ is a choice relation over components $\mathcal{S}'$. The rules are given in table 1.

**Definition 11.** Let $\mathcal{E}$ be a component event structure. The *possible extensions* of $\mathcal{E}$, denoted by $PE(\mathcal{E})$, is the set of all pairs $(\mathcal{D}, \mathcal{S} \xrightarrow{a} (\mathcal{S}', \mathcal{R}'))$ such that:
- $\mathcal{D}$ is a set of pairwise independent conditions of $\mathcal{E}$, with $l_D(\mathcal{D}) = \mathcal{S}$
- $\mathcal{S} \xrightarrow{a} (\mathcal{S}', \mathcal{R}')$ can be derived from the rules in table 1
- $\mathcal{E}$ does not already contain an event $e$ with $l_E(e) = a$ and $\bullet e = \mathcal{D}$

For component event structures it is easy to check that if two conditions have the same component label they are in conflict; this means that a set of pairwise independent conditions is labelled by a set of components with the same cardinality.

$$\{a_x; B\} \xrightarrow{a} dec(B)$$

$$\frac{S \xrightarrow{a} (S', \ \mathcal{R}')}{S|_A \xrightarrow{a} (S'|_A, \ \mathcal{R}'|_A)} \ (a \notin A) \qquad \frac{S \xrightarrow{a} (S', \ \mathcal{R}')}{|_A S \xrightarrow{a} (|_A S', \ |_A \mathcal{R}')} \ (a \notin A)$$

$$\frac{S_1 \xrightarrow{a} (S_1', \ \mathcal{R}_1') \quad S_2 \xrightarrow{a} (S_2', \ \mathcal{R}_2')}{S_1|_A \cup |_A S_2 \xrightarrow{a} (S_1'|_A \cup |_A S_2', \ \mathcal{R}_1'|_A \cup |_A \mathcal{R}_2')} \ (a \in A)$$

**Table 1.** Derivation system for component transitions

We can *add* a possible extension $(\mathcal{D}, \ S \xrightarrow{a} (S', \ \mathcal{R}')) \in PE(\mathcal{E})$ to $\mathcal{E}$ by adding a new event $e$ labelled $a$ and new conditions $\mathcal{D}'$ with labels from $S'$, such that ${}^\bullet e = \mathcal{D}$ and $e^\bullet = \mathcal{D}'$, and a choice relation over the conditions $\mathcal{D}'$ induced by the relation $\mathcal{R}'$ over $S'$.

**Algorithm 1.** Let $B$ be a process algebra expression, with $dec(B) = (S_0, \mathcal{R}_0)$. The *unfolding* of $B$, denoted $Unf(B)$, is generated by the following algorithm:

> Let $\mathcal{E}$ be the component event structure with conditions $M_0$,
> $l_D(M_0) = S_0$, choice relation $\mathcal{R}_0$, and no events;
> $pe := PE(\mathcal{E})$;
>
> **while** $pe \neq \emptyset$
> **do** select a pair $(\mathcal{D}, \ S \xrightarrow{a} (S', \ \mathcal{R}'))$ from $pe$;
>     add it to $\mathcal{E}$;
>     $pe := PE(\mathcal{E})$
> **od**;
> $Unf(B) = \mathcal{E}$ $\hfill\square$

The algorithm only terminates for expressions with finite behaviour. For expressions with infinite behaviour, the above algorithm produces arbitrarily large unfolding approximations (under the fairness assumption that each pair in $pe$ is eventually added to $\mathcal{E}$). In that case we define $Unf(B)$ as the limit of these approximations. It is easy to prove that $Unf(B)$ is a well-formed component event structure, i.e. the properties of definition 6 hold.

Notation: let $\mathcal{R} \subseteq S \times S$, and $S' \subseteq S$, then $\mathcal{R}\lceil S' = \mathcal{R} \cap (S' \times S')$. Note that if $\sharp$ is the choice relation of $Unf(B)$, and $dec(B) = (M, \ \mathcal{R})$, then by the definition of unfolding $\mathcal{R} = \sharp\lceil M$.

In [Lan92] it is shown how by slightly adapting the standard operational semantics it is possible to derive event sequences. In [LB99] this idea has been adapted to component event structures and the following result has been proven there.

**Theorem 2.** *Let $B$ be a process algebra expression, $Unf(B)$ its unfolding and $M_0$ the initial marking of $Unf(B)$. Let $\sigma$ be an event trace. Then:*

$$B \xrightarrow{\sigma} B' \Leftrightarrow M_0 \xrightarrow{\sigma} M' \qquad \text{with } dec(B') = (M', \sharp\lceil M')$$

In the last section we saw that there is a one-to-one correspondence between cuts and configurations via the mappings *Cut* and *Conf*. In [Lan92] it has been proven (Theorem 7.4.1) that there is also a one-to-one correspondence between configurations and reachable states (where each reachable state is a process algebra expression). It follows that there is a one-to-one correspondence between cuts and states of some unfolding $Unf(B)$; therefore given a cut $M'$, there is a process algebra expression $B'$ such that $dec(B') = (M', \sharp\lceil M')$. So given an unfolding $Unf(B)$, we define a mapping $St$ from cuts to process algebra expressions by $St(M') = B'$ where $B'$ is the reachable state corresponding to $Conf(M')$, so $dec(B') = (M', \sharp\lceil M')$. If $C$ is a configuration, we will also write $St(C)$ for $St(Cut(C))$.

## 4    A complete finite prefix for component event structures

In the last section we have defined the component event structure $Unf(B)$ for a process algebra expression $B$. This representation may be infinite for recursive processes; we would like to have a finite representation of such behaviour.

Therefore in this section we will look at McMillan's so-called *complete finite prefix* of an unfolding, which is an initial part of the unfolding that is complete in the following sense:

For each cut $M$ of $Unf(B)$ there is a cut $M'$ of the finite prefix such that:

- $St(M) = St(M')$, so the prefix contains all reachable states
- if $M \xrightarrow{e}$ in $Unf(B)$ with $l_E(e) = a$ then $M' \xrightarrow{e'}$ and $l_E(e') = a$, so the prefix contains all transitions

The complete finite prefix and McMillan's algorithm for computing it have originally been defined in the context of Petri nets (see [McM95b,Esp94,ERV97]). However, the approach (using the concepts of event, configuration and cut) can be transferred completely to the setting of component event structures, as we show here. For details and proofs we refer to [McM95b,Esp94,ERV97].

The complete finite prefix approach only works for finite state processes, i.e. processes with a finite number of reachable states. It is in general undecidable whether a process algebra expression is finite state. However, there exist syntactical restrictions that are sufficient to guarantee that an expression is finite state (see [FGM92] for discussion and overview). In the following we simply assume that all process algebra expressions are finite state.

We first need some preliminary definitions where we closely follow [ERV97].

Let $E$ be a set of events and let $C$ be a configuration of a component event structure. If $C \cup E$ is a configuration, and $C \cap E = \emptyset$, then we denote $C \cup E$ by $C \oplus E$, the *extension* of $C$ by $E$.

Let $M$ be a marking of a (well-formed) component event structure. Define the successor nodes of $M$ by $N = \{x \in E \cup D \mid \exists y \in M : y \leq x\}$. We define $\Uparrow M = (D \cap N, E \cap N, \sharp\lceil N, \prec \lceil N)$. It is easy to check that $\Uparrow M$ is a well-formed component event structure.

It is easy to check that for a configuration $C$ the unfolding $Unf(St(C))$ is isomorphic to $\Uparrow Cut(C)$. So if $C_1$ and $C_2$ are two configurations such that $St(C_1) = St(C_2)$, then $\Uparrow Cut(C_1)$ and $\Uparrow Cut(C_2)$ are isomorphic. So there is an isomorphism $I_{C_1}^{C_2}$ from $\Uparrow Cut(C_1)$ to $\Uparrow Cut(C_2)$; this induces a mapping from the extensions of $C_1$ onto the extensions of $C_2$, so $C_1 \oplus E$ is mapped onto $C_2 \oplus I_{C_1}^{C_2}(E)$.

The following definition presents an important technical aspect of the calculation of a complete finite prefix.

**Definition 12.** A (strict) partial order $\sqsubset$ on the finite configurations of an unfolding is an *adequate order* iff:

1. $\sqsubset$ is well-founded, i.e. there is no infinite sequence $C_1 \sqsupset C_2 \sqsupset \ldots$
2. $\sqsubset$ refines $\subset$, i.e. $C_1 \subset C_2$ implies $C_1 \sqsubset C_2$
3. $\sqsubset$ is preserved by finite extensions, which means that if $C_1 \sqsubset C_2$ and $St(C_1) = St(C_2)$, then $C_1 \oplus E \sqsubset C_2 \oplus I_{C_1}^{C_2}(E)$.

The original algorithm by McMillan uses as adequate order the order $\sqsubset_m$ defined by $C_1 \sqsubset_m C_2 \Leftrightarrow |C_1| < |C_2|$. This order is intuitively easy to understand but can be very inefficient. An improvement has been given in [ERV97]; in the next section we present an adequate order that is very suitable for a process algebra prefix.

Let $e$ be an event of a component event structure, then the *local configuration* $[e]$ is defined by $[e] = \{e' \in E | e' \le e\}$ (it is very easy to prove that $[e]$ is indeed a configuration).

**Definition 13.** Let $Unf(B)$ be an unfolding and let $\sqsubset$ be the selected adequate partial order on the configurations of $Unf(B)$. An event $e$ is a *cut-off event* if $Unf(B)$ has a local configuration $[e']$ such that $St([e]) = St([e'])$ and $[e'] \sqsubset [e]$

**Definition 14.** Let $X$ be the set of nodes of $Unf(B)$ such that $x \in X$ iff no event causally preceding $x$ is a cut-off event. Then the *finite prefix* $Fp(B)$ of $Unf(B) = (D, E, \sharp, \prec)$ is defined by $Fp(B) = (D \cap X, E \cap X, \sharp \lceil X, \prec \lceil X)$

So $Fp(B)$ contains all local configurations, and stops at cut-off events since their local configuration has been encountered already. The nice result (originally proven by McMillan for Petri nets [McM95b]) is that this is enough to guarantee completeness, so the prefix contains also all non-local configurations; $Fp(B)$ is finite and complete.

Conceptually a finite prefix is obtained by taking an unfolding and cutting away all successor nodes of cut-off events. This is not a practical recipe; the next algorithm shows how to obtain directly the complete finite prefix, without first creating the (possibly infinite) unfolding. First we redefine the set of possible extensions, to make sure that no successors of cut-off events are created.

**Definition 15.** Let $\mathcal{E}$ be a labelled component event structure with a set of cut-off events *cut*. The *possible non-cut-off extensions* of $\mathcal{E}$, denoted by $PE'(\mathcal{E}, cut)$, is the set of all pairs $(\mathcal{D}, \mathcal{S} \xrightarrow{a} (\mathcal{S}', \mathcal{R}'))$ such that $(\mathcal{D}, \mathcal{S} \xrightarrow{a} (\mathcal{S}', \mathcal{R}')) \in PE(\mathcal{E})$ and $\forall d \in \mathcal{D} : {}^{\bullet}d \notin cut$

**Algorithm 2.** Let $B$ be a process algebra expression, with $dec(B) = (\mathcal{S}_0, \mathcal{R}_0)$. Then the finite prefix $Fp(B)$, is generated by the following algorithm:

> Let $\mathcal{E}$ be the component event structure with components $M_0$, $l_D(M_0) = \mathcal{S}_0$, choice relation $\mathcal{R}_0$, and no events;
> $cut := \emptyset$;
> $pe := PE'(\mathcal{E}, cut)$;
>
> **while** $pe \neq \emptyset$
> **do** select a pair $(\mathcal{D}, \mathcal{S} \xrightarrow{a} (\mathcal{S}', \mathcal{R}'))$ from $pe$ such that adding it
>        leads to a new $e$ with $[e]$ minimal w.r.t. $\sqsubset$;
>        add it to $\mathcal{E}$;
>        if $e$ is a cut-of event then $cut := cut \cup \{e\}$;
>        $pe := PE'(\mathcal{E}, cut)$
> **od**;
> $Fp(B) = \mathcal{E}$                                                                          $\square$

It is easy to check that $Fp(B)$ as generated by algorithm 2 contains all nodes of $Unf(B)$ that are not causally preceded by a cut-off event, so it is indeed the finite prefix defined by definition 14.

*Example 1.* Consider $B = P \mid_b Q$ with $P = a; b; P$ and $Q = c; b; (e; P + d; Q)$. Then the unfolding is given in figure 1; cut-off events are indicated by a box.

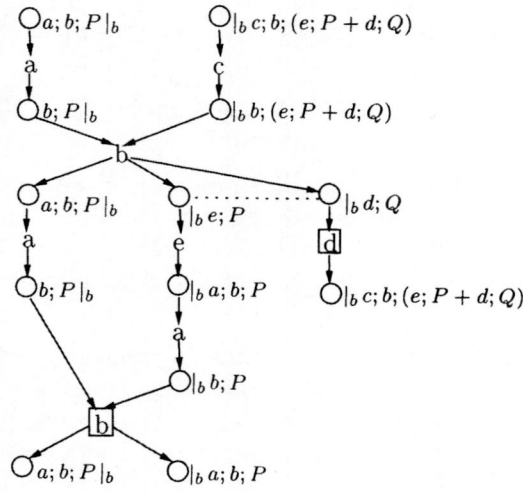

**Fig. 1.** Example of a complete finite prefix

## 5 An adequate order for process algebra

As already noted in [ERV97], the original McMillan ordering $\sqsubset_m$ defined by $C_1 \sqsubset_m C_2$ iff $|C_1| < |C_2|$ can be quite inefficient. Consider e.g. the expression $a; P + b; P$. Now although both $a$ and $b$ lead to the same state, it is not possible to make one of them a cut-off event as $[a]$ and $[b]$ have the same number of events. This makes it possible to find examples in which the finite prefix has a size that is exponential in the number of reachable states of the process algebra expression.

In [ERV97] an adequate order has been defined that does not suffer from this problem. This order is total on all configurations, so whenever two local configurations have the same state this leads to a cut-off. This is an important improvement on the original McMillan order, but an adequate order does not need to be total on all configurations, in order to have this property. The order in [ERV97] is rather complicated as it requires operations on configurations like subtracting the set of minimal events of a configuration (in fact this order is defined on suffixes of configurations).

In this section we define an adequate order which differs from $\sqsubset_m$ only for configurations having the same state and the same number of events. This order is easy to implement as it is defined syntactically as a kind of lexicographical order on process algebra expressions. The order orders each pair of configurations with the same state, so local configurations having the same state always lead to a cut-off.

We assume that initially process instantiations in an expressions are indexed with *simple process indices* (denoted by Greek letters) and actions are indexed by *action indices*. We furthermore assume an operation $\Phi(B)$ that takes an indexed expression $B$ and prefixes all indices with $\Phi$. We change the operational rule for process instantiation into $(\Phi(B) \overset{a}{\longrightarrow} B', P := B) \Rightarrow P_\Phi \overset{a}{\longrightarrow} B')$. This means that the process index of an instantiation $P_\Phi$ has the effect of prefixing all indices in the defining expression of $P$ with $\Phi$, leading to process indices that are strings of simple process indices; for details we refer to [LB99].

We assume there is an order on simple process indices; this order is arbitrary but we have (for technical reasons) the constraint that the order should respect the left to right order of the indices in the indexed process algebra expression that we are interested in (so if $\alpha$ is ordered before $\beta$, it will occur as a process index to the left of the occurrence of $\beta$). Remember that a proces index is a string of simple process indices; so the order on simple process indices induces a lexicographical order on process indices. This lexicographical order is not well-founded but can be used to define a well-founded order on process indices:

**Definition 16.** Let $\Phi_1$ and $\Phi_2$ be two process indices. We define $\Phi_1 \ll \Phi_2$ iff either $|\Phi_1| < |\Phi_2|$, or $|\Phi_1| = |\Phi_2|$ and $\Phi_1$ is lexicographically smaller than $\Phi_2$.

With this order we can define an order on process algebra expressions that are equal modulo process identifiers; $B_1$ and $B_2$ are equal modulo process indentifier, notation $B_1 =_p B_2$, iff after removing all process indices they are equal.

A component is of the form $\mathbf{stop}_{\Phi}$ or $a_{\Phi i}; B$, with $\Phi$ a process index and $i$ a simple action index, possibly decorated with strings of parallel operators to the left and right. In these cases we call $\Phi$ the process index of the component.

**Definition 17.** Let $B_1$ and $B_2$ be two different process algebra expressions with $B_1 =_p B_2$. Then to each component of $B_1$ corresponds a component of $B_2$ that is equal modulo process identifiers. We define $B_1 \ll B_2$ iff for the leftmost first two corresponding components of $B_1$ respectively $B_2$ that have different process indices $\Phi_1$ respectively $\Phi_2$ holds: $\Phi_1 \ll \Phi_2$.

*Example 2.* Suppose $\alpha$ comes before $\beta$ in the order on simple process indices, then $\alpha_{\alpha 1}; P_{\alpha\phi} \mid_G b_{\alpha 2}; Q_{\alpha\psi} \ll \alpha_{\alpha 1}; P_{\alpha\phi} \mid_G b_{\beta 2}; Q_{\beta\psi}$ and
$\mathbf{stop}_{\alpha} \mid_G a_1; P_{\phi} \ll \mathbf{stop}_{\beta} \mid_G a_1; P_{\phi}$

With the help of $\ll$ we define the *state* order $\sqsubset_s$ on the configurations of $Unf(B)$:

**Definition 18.** Let $C_1$ and $C_2$ be two configurations of $Unf(B)$. Then $C_1 \sqsubset_s C_2$ iff $|C_1| < |C_2|$ or: $|C_1| = |C_2|$, $St(C_1) =_p St(C_2)$ and $St(C_1) \ll St(C_2)$.

**Theorem 3.** $\sqsubset_s$ *is an adequate order on the configurations of* $Unf(B)$.

Just like the adequate order presented in [ERV97] (denoted $\prec_r$ there) our order has the property that for each pair of events $e$ and $e'$ with $St([e]) = St([e'])$: either $[e] \sqsubset_s [e']$ or $[e'] \sqsubset_s [e]$. This has two desirable consequences:

- the number of non-cut-off events in a complete finite prefix cannot exceed the number of local states (i.e. states of local configurations)
- since events are generated in accordance with $\sqsubset_s$ in algorithm 2, we need for each newly added event $e$ only to check if there is already an event $e'$ with $St([e]) = St([e'])$ in order to check that $e$ is a cut-off event.

We think that in comparison with the adequate order of [ERV97] our order is easier to understand as it is based on a syntactical lexicographical order on process algebra expressions. For the same reason we expect it to be easy to implement. This will be checked in an implementation of our algorithm that is currently under construction.

## 6 Conclusions

We have presented component event structures which are similar to both prime event structures and occurrence nets. The advantage of component event structures over Petri nets is that the choice operator can be modelled naturally with the choice relation. When using Petri nets to model process algebra (as has been done in [Old91]) extra places have to be introduced, using a technical trick, to model the effect of choice. This trick leads to markings that do not directly correspond to process algebra expressions (only after a kind of garbage collection) which would greatly complicate the construction of a complete finite prefix. Our component event structures do not suffer from these complications. In addition, they are very similar to prime event structures which can be obtained by just deleting the components.

We have shown how McMillans approach can be used for obtaining a finite complete prefix. We have presented an optimization that has the same effect as the one in [ERV97] but profits from the process algebra context in such a way that it is less complex.

Our current research is concentrating on how the complete prefix can be transformed into a kind of graph grammar that produces the infinite behavior. This graph grammar representation can then be used for simulation and model checking. Furthermore, using timed, probabilistic and stochastic extensions similar to [KLL+98,BKLL98] we will investigate how the graph grammar can be used for performance modelling. We are also working on an implementation which we hope to finish soon.

## Acknowledgements

Many thanks to Joost-Pieter Katoen, Diego Latella and Mieke Massink for extensive discussions and many suggestions for improvement.

# References

[BB87]     T. Bolognesi and E. Brinksma. Introduction to the ISO specification language LOTOS. *Computer Networks and ISDN Systems*, 14:25–59, 1987.

[BC94]     G. Boudol and I. Castellani. Flow models of distributed computations: three equivalent semantics for CCS. *Information and Computation*, 114:247–314, 1994.

[BKLL98]  E. Brinksma, J.-P. Katoen, D. Latella, and R. Langerak. Partial-order models for quantitative extensions of LOTOS. *Computer Networks and ISDN Systems*, 30(9/10):925–950, 1998.

[BW90]     J.C.M. Baeten and W.P. Weijland. *Process Algebra*, volume 18 of *Cambridge Tracts in Theoretical Computer Science*. Cambridge University Press, 1990.

[Eng91]    J. Engelfriet. Branching processes of Petri nets. *Acta Informatica*, 28:575–591, 1991.

[ERV97]    J. Esparza, S. Römer, and W. Vogler. An improvement of McMillan's unfolding algorithm. In *Proc. TACAS '96*, volume 1055 of *Lecture Notes in Computer Science*, pages 87–106. Springer-Verlag, 1997.

[Esp94]    J. Esparza. Model checking using net unfoldings. *Science of Computer Programming*, 23(2):151–195, 1994. Also appeared in *Proc. TAPSOFT '93*, volume 668 of *Lecture Notes in Computer Science*, pages 613–628. Springer-Verlag, 1993.

[FGM92]   A. Fantechi, S. Gnesi, and G. Mazzarini. The expressive power of LOTOS behaviour expressions. Nota Interna I.E.I. B4-43, I.E.I (Pisa), October 1992.

[Gra97]    B. Graves. Computing reachability properties hidden in finite net unfoldings. *Lecture Notes in Computer Science*, 1055:327–342, 1997.

[Hoa85]    C.A.R. Hoare. *Communicating Sequential Processes*. Prentice-Hall, 1985.

[KLL+98]  J.-P. Katoen, D. Latella, R. Langerak, E. Brinksma, and T. Bolognesi. A consistent causality-based view on a timed process algebra including urgent interactions. *Journal on Formal Methods for System Design*, 12(2):189–216, 1998.

[Lan92]  R. Langerak. *Transformations and Semantics for LOTOS*. PhD thesis, University of Twente, 1992.

[LB99]  R. Langerak and E. Brinksma. A complete finite prefix for process algebra. Technical report, University of Twente, January 1999.

[McM92]  K. McMillan. Using unfoldings to avoid the state explosion problem in the verification of asynchronous circuits. In *Proc. CAV '92, Fourth Workshop on Computer-Aided Verification*, volume 663 of *Lecture Notes in Computer Science*, pages 164–174, 1992.

[McM95a]  K. McMillan. Trace theoretic verification of asynchronous circuits using unfoldings. In *Proc. CAV '95, 7th International Conference on Computer-Aided Verification*, volume 939 of *Lecture Notes in Computer Science*, pages 180–195. Springer-Verlag, 1995.

[McM95b]  K.L. McMillan. A technique of state space search based on unfolding. *Formal Methods in System Design*, 6:45 – 65, 1995.

[NPW81]  M. Nielsen, G.D. Plotkin, and G. Winskel. Petri nets, event structures and domains, part 1. *Theoretical Computer Science*, 13(1):85–108, 1981.

[Old91]  E.-R. Olderog. *Nets, terms and formulas*. Cambridge University Press, 1991.

[Wal98]  F. Wallner. Model-checking LTL using net unfoldings. In *Proc. CAV '98, 10th International Conference on Computer-Aided Verification*, volume 1427 of *Lecture Notes in Computer Science*, pages 207–218, Vancouver, Canada, 1998.

[Win89]  G. Winskel. An introduction to event structures. In J.W. de Bakker, W.-P. de Roever, and G. Rozenberg, editors, *Linear Time, Branching Time and Partial Order in Logics and Models for Concurrency*, Lecture Notes in Computer Science, pages 364–397. Springer-Verlag, 1989.

# The Mathematical Foundation of Symbolic Trajectory Evaluation

Ching-Tsun Chou*
⟨ctchou@mipos2.intel.com⟩

Intel Corporation
3600 Juliette Lane, SC12-401
Santa Clara, CA 95052, U.S.A.

**Abstract.** In this paper we elucidate the mathematical foundation underlying both the *basic* and the *extended* forms of *symbolic trajectory evaluation* (STE), with emphasis on the latter. The specific technical contributions we make to the theory of STE are threefold. First, we provide a satisfactory answer to the question: what does it mean for a circuit to satisfy a trajectory assertion? Second, we make the observation that STE is a form of *data flow analysis* and, as a corollary, propose a conceptually simple algorithm for extended STE. Third, we show that the theory of *abstract interpretation* based on Galois connections is the appropriate framework in which to understand STE.

## 1 Introduction

In BDD-based formal verification, *symbolic trajectory evaluation* (STE) [8,3] is the main alternative to *symbolic model checking* (SMC) [5]. Compared with SMC, STE has the advantage that it can be applied to very large circuits directly, without the need to abstract the circuits before verification. This is made possible by a pleasant property of STE: the number of BDD variables needed in an STE run depends only on the assertion being checked, not on the circuit under analysis. Thus one can use STE to verify a collection of assertions against the same circuit without having to invent a different abstraction of the circuit for each assertion, as one often has to do when doing SMC. On the other hand, what STE can verify is more restricted than what SMC can. In its basic form [8], STE can only verify assertions over bounded intervals of time, possibly iterated by non-nested loops. But in its extended form [3][1], STE can verify assertions expressed as arbitrary state-transition graphs, thus enabling STE to verify any safety properties. As far as we know, STE has not been generalized to reason about liveness properties.

Unfortunately, STE seems to be much less well-known than SMC, certainly less than it deserves to be. Partly in the hope of generating more interests in STE, we elucidate in this paper the mathematical foundation underlying both

---

* The author is grateful to Pascalin Amagbegnon, John Mark Bouler, Pei-Hsin Ho, Marten van Hulst, Victor Konrad, Carl Seger, and the reviewers for comments and encouragements, and to his wife and children for love and tolerance.

[1] According to Carl Seger, the basic ideas of *extended* (a.k.a. *generalized*) STE came out of an e-mail brainstorming session in 1994 among Derek Beatty, Randy Bryant, and Seger on a note written by Beatty, which unfortunately was never published.

the basic [8] and the extended [3] forms of STE, with emphasis on the latter. The main mathematical theories used in this paper—data flow analysis [4, 6] and abstract interpretation [1, 7]—are not new. And it is quite possible that the basic ideas of this paper were already known at an intuitive level in the STE research community. But, to the best of our knowledge, these theories and ideas have never been brought together to form a coherent framework in which to understand (especially the extended form of) STE. The specific technical contributions we make to the theory of STE are threefold.

First, we clarify the semantics of STE by providing a satisfactory answer to the following question:

- What does it mean for a circuit to satisfy a trajectory assertion?

More precisely, we propose to define the satisfaction relation for extended STE [3], in which trajectory assertions can have arbitrary state-transition graphs, as a universally quantified generalization of the form of basic STE [8] in which trajectory assertions are bounded sequences of states. This is not how the satisfaction relation for extended STE was originally defined in [3], which uses a definition containing both universal and existential quantifiers. To justify our definition, we show that it guarantees that a circuit satisfies a trajectory assertion iff (if and only if) the set-theoretic STE algorithm returns a positive answer, and that this is not the case for the definition in [3]. Another advantage of our definition is that it does not require us to make the distinction of whether a trajectory assertion is "oblivious" (which basically means "deterministic"), whereas the definition in [3] does.

Second, we make the following observation:

- STE is a form of *data flow analysis* (DFA).

More precisely, we show that, when properly formulated, what an STE algorithm computes is exactly the solution of a data flow equation in the classic format [4, 6]. Though perhaps obvious in retrospect, this point seems to have never been noticed before. As a corollary of this DFA formulation, we propose a BDD-based, completely implicit algorithm for extended STE that is very easy to understand and, we hope, can lead to efficient implementations of STE. (Of course, this hope can be confirmed or disproved only through experimentation, which is beyond the scope of this paper.)

Third, we propose an appropriate framework in which to address the following question:

- How is the ternary model of circuits that STE algorithms use related to the ordinary boolean model of circuits?

Specifically, we show that the ternary model is an *abstract interpretation* in the classic sense [1, 7] of the boolean model via a *Galois connection* [2, 7]. We also point out a relationship between the two models (namely, the Galois connection should be a *simulation* from the boolean model to the ternary model) that seems to have never been articulated in the existing literature on STE [8, 3].

The rest of this paper is organized as follows. Section 2 presents STE from a set-theoretic viewpoint, in which circuits are modeled as functions operating on sets of boolean vectors. Section 3 presents STE from a lattice-theoretic viewpoint, in which circuits are modeled as functions operating on ternary vectors, which form a lattice. Section 4 presents the conceptually simple algorithm for extended STE mentioned above. The proofs of all theorems and the reviews of some mathematical machineries are relegated to the Appendices.

## 2 Set-Theoretic STE

Following [3], we start with set-theoretic STE, which manipulates sets of configurations of circuits. As will be seen, set-theoretic STE is impractical except on small circuits. But it provides an easy-to-understand semantic foundation by which STE can be related to symbolic model checking, which takes a set-theoretic view of circuits. Furthermore, the development of lattice-theoretic STE in the next section closely parallels that of set-theoretic STE.

### 2.1 Set-Theoretic Models of Circuits

Consider a digital circuit $M$ operating in discrete time. A *configuration* of $M$ is an assignment of "values" to "signals" in $M$, representing a snapshot of $M$ at a discrete point in time. In this section, exactly what "values" and "signals" are, is not important. All we need to assume is that the set of all configurations of $M$, denoted by $C$, is nonempty and finite.

**Circuits as Relations.** The conceptually simplest model of $M$ is a *transition relation*, $M_{\mathrm{Rel}} \subseteq C \times C$, where $(c, c') \in M_{\mathrm{Rel}}$ means that $M$ can in one step move from configuration $c$ to configuration $c'$. Note that since $M$ cannot control its input signals, $M_{\mathrm{Rel}}$ is in general a relation rather than a function.

**Circuits as Functions.** The power set of $C$, denoted by $\mathcal{P}(C)$, can be viewed as the set of *predicates* on configurations, where $\cap$, $\cup$, and $\subseteq$ correspond to conjunction, disjunction, and implication, respectively. For any $Q \subseteq \mathcal{P}(C)$, we denote by $\cap Q$ and $\cup Q$ the intersection and union of all members of $Q$, respectively.

Using the relational image operation, the transition relation $M_{\mathrm{Rel}}$ induces a *predicate transformer* $M_{\mathrm{Fun}} \in \mathcal{P}(C) \to \mathcal{P}(C)$ in a natural way:

$$M_{\mathrm{Fun}}(p) \;=\; \{c' \in C \mid \exists\, c \in p : (c, c') \in M_{\mathrm{Rel}}\} \tag{1}$$

for all $p \in \mathcal{P}(C)$. Intuitively, if $M$ is in one of the configurations in $p$, then in one step it must be in one of the configurations in $M_{\mathrm{Fun}}(p)$. It is easy to show from (1) that $M_{\mathrm{Fun}}$ distributes over arbitrary union:

$$M_{\mathrm{Fun}}(\cup Q) \;=\; \cup\{M_{\mathrm{Fun}}(q) \mid q \in Q\} \tag{2}$$

for all $Q \subseteq \mathcal{P}(C)$. Conversely, for any $M_{\mathrm{Fun}} \in \mathcal{P}(C) \to \mathcal{P}(C)$ that satisfies (2), the equivalence: $(c, c') \in M_{\mathrm{Rel}} \Leftrightarrow c' \in M_{\mathrm{Fun}}(\{c\})$, where $c, c' \in C$, defines a $M_{\mathrm{Rel}} \subseteq C \times C$ that satisfies (1). Thus there is no loss of information in going from $M_{\mathrm{Rel}}$ to $M_{\mathrm{Fun}}$ and vice versa.

In the remainder of this paper we will use the functional model of circuits exclusively and drop the subscript $_{\mathrm{Fun}}$. Note that it follows from distributivity (2) that $M$ $(= M_{\mathrm{Fun}})$ both preserves $\emptyset$ (i.e., $M(\emptyset) = \emptyset$) and is monotonic (i.e., $p \subseteq q \Rightarrow M(p) \subseteq M(q)$ for all $p, q \in \mathcal{P}(C)$).

## 2.2   Set-Theoretic Trajectory Assertions

From now on we focus on a fixed, but arbitrary, circuit $M \in \mathcal{P}(C) \to \mathcal{P}(C)$, where $C$ is nonempty and finite, such that (2) is true.

**Definition of Trajectory Assertions.** A *trajectory assertion* for $M$ is a quintuple $A = (S, s_0, R, \pi_a, \pi_c)$, where $S$ is a finite set of *states*, $s_0 \in S$ is an *initial state*, $R \subseteq S \times S$ is a *transition relation*, and $\pi_a \in S \to \mathcal{P}(C)$ and $\pi_c \in S \to \mathcal{P}(C)$ label each state $s$ with an *antecedent* $\pi_a(s)$ and a *consequent* $\pi_c(s)$. Furthermore, we assume $\forall s \in S : (s, s_0) \notin R$, for the technical reason that in formulating data flow algorithms, it is convenient to have a unique source node whose flow value never needs changing. No generality is lost by making this assumption.

**Satisfaction of a Trajectory Assertion by a Circuit.** What does it mean for the circuit $M$ to satisfy the trajectory assertion $A = (S, s_0, R, \pi_a, \pi_c)$? Roughly speaking, it means that for every trajectory $\tau$ of $M$ and every run $\rho$ of $A$, as long as $\tau$ satisfies the antecedents in $\rho$, $\tau$ satisfies the consequents in $\rho$. To state this precisely, we have to introduce some terminologies. (Also, see Appendix A.1 for notations about sequences.)

A *trajectory* of $M$ is a nonempty sequence of configurations, $\tau \in C^+$, such that $\forall i \in \mathbf{N} : 0 < i < |\tau| \Rightarrow \tau[i] \in M(\{\tau[i-1]\})$; the set of trajectories of $M$ is denoted by $Traj(M)$. A *run* of $A$ is a nonempty sequence of states, $\rho \in S^+$, such that $\rho[0] = s_0$ and $\forall i \in \mathbf{N} : 0 < i < |\rho| \Rightarrow (\rho[i-1], \rho[i]) \in R$; the set of runs of $A$ is denoted by $Runs(A)$. Note that both $Traj(M)$ and $Runs(A)$ are prefix-closed. For any $\tau \in Traj(M)$ and $\rho \in Runs(A)$ such that $|\tau| = |\rho|$, we say $\tau$ *a-satisfies* (resp., *c-satisfies*) $\rho$, denoted by $\tau \models_a \rho$ (resp., $\tau \models_c \rho$), iff $\tau[i] \in \pi_a(\rho[i])$ (resp., $\tau[i] \in \pi_c(\rho[i])$) for each $i < |\tau| = |\rho|$. Finally, we say the circuit $M$ *satisfies* the trajectory assertion $A$, denoted by $M \models A$, iff:

$$\forall \tau \in Traj(M) : \forall \rho \in Runs(A) : |\tau| = |\rho| \Rightarrow (\tau \models_a \rho \Rightarrow \tau \models_c \rho) \quad (3)$$

**Comparison with Another Definition of Satisfaction.** It is instructive to compare (3) with the definition used in [3]:

$$\forall \tau \in Traj(M) :$$
$$(\exists \rho \in Runs(A) : |\tau| = |\rho| \wedge \tau \models_a \rho \wedge \tau \models_c \rho) \vee \quad (4)$$
$$(\forall \tau' \preceq \tau : \forall \rho' \in Runs(A) : |\tau'| = |\rho'| \Rightarrow (\tau' \models_a \rho' \Rightarrow \tau' \models_c \rho'))$$

Note that (3) implies (4), because $Traj(M)$ is prefix-closed. The converse is not true; but if its first disjunct were removed, (4) would indeed be equivalent to (3). That first disjunct, which contains an existential quantifier, makes (4) harder to implement than (3). Intuitively, the existential quantifier requires backtracking to implement. Formally, we will show in the next subsection that (3) holds iff the set-theoretic STE algorithm returns a positive answer, and that (4) lacks this nice property.

To get around this difficulty, [3] introduces the notion of oblivious trajectory assertions. A trajectory assertion $A = (S, s_0, R, \pi_a, \pi_c)$ is *oblivious* iff for any

$s, s', s'' \in S$ such that $(s, s') \in R$ and $(s, s'') \in R$, it must be the case that $\pi_a(s') \cap \pi_a(s'') = \emptyset$. Consequently, given any trajectory $\tau$, there is at most one run $\rho$ of $A$ such that $\tau$ $a$-satisfies $\rho$. It is not hard to see that for an oblivious trajectory assertion, (4) implies (3), which then implies that (4) is equivalent to the set-theoretic STE algorithm returning a positive answer. With our definition (3), there is no need to introduce the notion of obliviousness.

### 2.3 Set-Theoretic STE as DFA

In this subsection we show that the checking of $M \models A$ can be formulated as a DFA problem [4, 6].

Define $F \in S \to (\mathcal{P}(C) \to \mathcal{P}(C))$ such that $F(s)(p) = M(\pi_a(s) \cap p)$ for all $s \in S$ and $p \in \mathcal{P}(C)$. It follows from (2) that for all $s \in S$, $F(s)$ preserves $\emptyset$ (i.e., $F(s)(\emptyset) = \emptyset$), is monotonic (i.e., $p \subseteq q \Rightarrow F(s)(p) \subseteq F(s)(q)$ for all $p, q \in \mathcal{P}(C)$), and distributes over arbitrary union (i.e., $F(s)(\cup Q) = \cup\{F(s)(q) \mid q \in Q\}$ for all $Q \subseteq \mathcal{P}(C)$). Next, define $\mathcal{F} \in (S \to \mathcal{P}(C)) \to (S \to \mathcal{P}(C))$ such that:

$$\mathcal{F}(\varPhi)(s) \;=\; \text{if } (s = s_0) \text{ then } C \text{ else } \cup\{F(s')(\varPhi(s')) \mid (s', s) \in R\}$$

for all $\varPhi \in S \to \mathcal{P}(C)$ and $s \in S$. Since $F(s)$ is monotonic for all $s \in S$, $\mathcal{F}$ is monotonic as well, where the function space $S \to \mathcal{P}(C)$ is ordered as follows: $\varPhi \sqsubseteq \varPhi' \Leftrightarrow \forall s \in S : \varPhi(s) \subseteq \varPhi'(s)$ for all $\varPhi, \varPhi' \in S \to \mathcal{P}(C)$. Hence, by Knaster-Tarski Fixpoint Theorem [2], the fixpoint equation $\varPhi = \mathcal{F}(\varPhi)$ has a least solution $\varPhi_* \in S \to \mathcal{P}(C)$. Furthermore, since both $S$ and $C$ are finite, $\varPhi_*$ is the limit of the sequence $\langle \varPhi_n \in S \to \mathcal{P}(C) \mid n \in \mathbf{N} \rangle$ defined by:

$$\varPhi_n \;=\; \text{if } (n = 0) \text{ then } (\lambda s \in S : \emptyset) \text{ else } \mathcal{F}(\varPhi_{n-1}) \tag{5}$$

in the sense that there exists a sufficiently large $k \in \mathbf{N}$ such that $\varPhi_n = \varPhi_*$ for all $n \geq k$.

We say the circuit $M$ *satisfies* the trajectory assertion $A$ *by set-theoretic STE*, denoted by $M \models_{\text{Set}} A$, iff $\forall s \in S : \varPhi_*(s) \cap \pi_a(s) \subseteq \pi_c(s)$. Now we are ready to state our first main result:

**Theorem 1.** $M \models_{\text{Set}} A \Leftrightarrow M \models A$

*Proof.* See Appendix A.4.

Had we used the definition adopted in [3] for $M \models A$ (viz., (4) above), the $\Rightarrow$ direction of Theorem 1 would still be true (furthermore, obliviousness is not needed in this part of the proof; see Appendix A.4), but the $\Leftarrow$ direction would be false, as the following example shows.[2] Consider a trivial circuit $M$ with only one signal whose value is either 0 or 1 (i.e., $C = \{0, 1\}$); this signal is the output of a constant source 1 (i.e., $M(p) = \{1\}$ for $\emptyset \neq p \subseteq \{0, 1\}$). Suppose that the trajectory assertion $A$ has only three states $S = \{s_0, s_1, s_2\}$ and two transitions $R = \{(s_0, s_1), (s_0, s_2)\}$ such that $\pi_a(s_0) = \pi_a(s_1) = \pi_a(s_2) = \pi_c(s_0) = \{0, 1\}$ and $\pi_c(s_1) = \{1\}$ and $\pi_c(s_2) = \{0\}$. Then (4) is satisfied, because for any trajectory $\tau$ of $M$ with $|\tau| = 2$, the run $\rho = \langle s_0, s_1 \rangle$ satisfies both $\tau \models_a \rho$ and $\tau \models_c \rho$. But $M \not\models_{\text{Set}} A$, since $\varPhi_*(s_2) = \{1\}$, $\pi_a(s_2) = \{0, 1\}$, but $\pi_c(s_2) = \{0\}$.

---

[2] Space limitations prevent us from including state-transition diagrams for this and subsequent examples, but the reader should have no trouble drawing his own.

# 3 Lattice-Theoretic STE

The definition (5) of the sequence $\langle \Phi_n \,|\, n \in \mathbf{N} \rangle$ above yields a simple method for computing the least fixpoint solution $\Phi_*$: just compute $\Phi_0, \Phi_1, \Phi_2, \dots$ one by one until a fixpoint, which must be $\Phi_*$, is reached. Then, by Theorem 1, $M \models A$ can be checked by checking $M \models_{\mathsf{Set}} A$. Since all objects involved are finite, this scheme for checking $M \models A$, which we call the *set-theoretic STE algorithm*, is clearly effective.

Unfortunately, the set-theoretic STE algorithm is not practical except for small circuits. For, if the circuit $M$ has $m$ boolean signals, then its set of configurations is $\mathbf{B}^m$, where $\mathbf{B} = \{0, 1\}$ is the set of boolean values. Even with state-of-the-art BDD technologies, manipulating subsets of $\mathbf{B}^m$ is impractical for even moderately large $m$, say several hundred signals. But interesting circuits in the real world often contain thousands of (if not more!) signals, for which set-theoretic STE is powerless.

In this section we will describe what may be regarded as the key insight of the STE paradigm. Namely, instead of manipulating subsets of $\mathbf{B}^m$ directly, we approximate them with ternary vectors, whose sizes are only linear in $m$. But, to compensate for possible loss of information in the approximation process, we may have to complicate the trajectory assertion, or use a family of trajectory assertions, or both. Yet, in both cases, the number of BDD variables depends only on the trajectory assertion(s) and *not* on the circuit under analysis. This makes it possible to do STE on very large circuits without first abstracting them.

We will use many concepts and notations from the theory of partial orders and lattices [2]. In particular, the notions of *complete lattices* and *Galois connections* are reviewed in Appendices A.2 and A.3, respectively.

## 3.1 Lattice-Theoretic Models of Circuits

Recall that $M \in \mathcal{P}(C) \to \mathcal{P}(C)$ represents a circuit such that (2) is true, and that the set $C$ of configurations of $M$ is nonempty and finite. What exactly $C$ is, is not important until Section 4.

Let $(\hat{P}, \sqsubseteq)$ be a finite complete lattice of *abstract predicates* such that there is a Galois connection $\ll \; \subseteq \mathcal{P}(C) \times \hat{P}$. An abstract predicate transformer $\hat{M} \in \hat{P} \to \hat{P}$ is an *abstract interpretation* [1,7] of $M \in \mathcal{P}(C) \to \mathcal{P}(C)$ iff $\hat{M}$ preserves bottom (i.e., $\hat{M}(\hat{\bot}) = \hat{\bot}$), $\hat{M}$ is monotonic (i.e., $\hat{p} \sqsubseteq \hat{q} \Rightarrow \hat{M}(\hat{p}) \sqsubseteq \hat{M}(\hat{q})$ for all $\hat{p}, \hat{q} \in \hat{P}$), and $\ll$ is a *simulation relation* from $\mathcal{P}(C)$ to $\hat{P}$ (i.e., $p \ll \hat{p} \Rightarrow M(p) \ll \hat{M}(\hat{p})$ for all $p \in \mathcal{P}(C)$ and $\hat{p} \in \hat{P}$). That the Galois connection $\ll$ is a simulation relation can also be stated in terms of its abstraction function $\alpha : \mathcal{P}(C) \to \hat{P}$ (viz., $\alpha(M(p)) \sqsubseteq \hat{M}(\alpha(p))$ for all $p \in \mathcal{P}(C)$) or in terms of its concretization function $\gamma : \hat{P} \to \mathcal{P}(C)$ (viz., $M(\gamma(\hat{p})) \subseteq \gamma(\hat{M}(\hat{p}))$ for all $\hat{p} \in \hat{P}$). Although this notion of simulation is standard in the literature on abstract interpretation [1,7], it seems to have never been used in the literature on STE [8,3]. It would be interesting to check whether actual implementations of STE satisfy this condition.

We do not require of $\hat{M}$ the counterpart of (2): $\hat{M}(\sqcup \hat{Q}) = \sqcup \{\hat{M}(\hat{q}) \,|\, \hat{q} \in \hat{Q}\}$, because it is not true in general. For example, suppose $\hat{M}$ abstracts a unit-delay two-input AND-gate using ternary values. Then it is reasonable to require:

$$\hat{M}(\langle 0,1,\mathsf{X}\rangle \sqcup \langle 1,0,\mathsf{X}\rangle) \;=\; \hat{M}(\langle \mathsf{X},\mathsf{X},\mathsf{X}\rangle) \;=\; \langle \mathsf{X},\mathsf{X},\mathsf{X}\rangle$$
$$\hat{M}(\langle 0,1,\mathsf{X}\rangle) \sqcup \hat{M}(\langle 1,0,\mathsf{X}\rangle) \;=\; \langle \mathsf{X},\mathsf{X},0\rangle \sqcup \langle \mathsf{X},\mathsf{X},0\rangle \;=\; \langle \mathsf{X},\mathsf{X},0\rangle$$

where the first two vector components correspond to the two inputs and the last the output. Intuitively, the join operation $\langle 0,1,\mathsf{X}\rangle \sqcup \langle 1,0,\mathsf{X}\rangle = \langle \mathsf{X},\mathsf{X},\mathsf{X}\rangle$ throws away the information that one of the inputs is 0, so $\hat{M}$ can no longer assign 0 to the output. Note, however, that the inequality $\hat{M}(\sqcup \hat{Q}) \sqsupseteq \sqcup\{\hat{M}(\hat{q}) \mid \hat{q} \in \hat{Q}\}$ does hold, since it is implied by the monotonicity of $\hat{M}$.

## 3.2  Lattice-Theoretic Trajectory Assertions

A trajectory assertion for $\hat{M}$ is a quintuple $\hat{A} = (S, s_0, R, \hat{\pi}_a, \hat{\pi}_c)$, where the assumptions on $S$, $s_0$, and $R$ are the same as in Section 2.2, and $\hat{\pi}_a \in S \to \hat{P}$ and $\hat{\pi}_c \in S \to \hat{P}$ are the antecedent and consequent labeling functions, respectively. Define $\gamma(\hat{A}) = (S, s_0, R, \gamma(\hat{\pi}_a), \gamma(\hat{\pi}_c))$, where $\gamma(\hat{\pi}_a) = \lambda s \in S : \gamma(\hat{\pi}_a(s))$ and $\gamma(\hat{\pi}_c) = \lambda s \in S : \gamma(\hat{\pi}_c(s))$. Note that $\gamma(\hat{A})$ is a trajectory assertion for $M$.

## 3.3  Lattice-Theoretic STE as DFA

Define $\hat{F} \in S \to (\hat{P} \to \hat{P})$ such that $\hat{F}(s)(\hat{p}) = \hat{M}(\hat{\pi}_a(s) \sqcap \hat{p})$ for all $s \in S$ and $\hat{p} \in \hat{P}$. For any $s \in S$, since $\hat{M}$ preserves bottom and is monotonic, $\hat{F}(s)$ also preserves bottom (i.e., $\hat{F}(s)(\hat{\bot}) = \hat{\bot}$) and is monotonic (i.e., $\hat{p} \sqsubseteq \hat{q} \Rightarrow \hat{F}(s)(\hat{p}) \sqsubseteq \hat{F}(s)(\hat{q})$ for all $\hat{p}, \hat{q} \in \hat{P}$). Next, define $\hat{\mathcal{F}} \in (S \to \hat{P}) \to (S \to \hat{P})$ such that:

$$\hat{\mathcal{F}}(\hat{\Phi})(s) \;=\; \texttt{if } (s = s_0) \texttt{ then } \hat{\top} \texttt{ else } \sqcup \{\,\hat{F}(s')(\hat{\Phi}(s')) \mid (s',s) \in R\,\}$$

for all $\hat{\Phi} \in S \to \hat{P}$ and $s \in S$. Since $\hat{F}(s)$ is monotonic for all $s \in S$, $\hat{\mathcal{F}}$ is monotonic as well, where the function space $S \to \hat{P}$ is ordered as follows: $\hat{\Phi} \sqsubseteq \hat{\Phi}' \Leftrightarrow \forall s \in S : \hat{\Phi}(s) \sqsubseteq \hat{\Phi}'(s)$ for all $\hat{\Phi}, \hat{\Phi}' \in S \to \hat{P}$. Hence, by Knaster-Tarski Fixpoint Theorem [2], the fixpoint equation $\hat{\Phi} = \hat{\mathcal{F}}(\hat{\Phi})$ has a least solution $\hat{\Phi}_* \in S \to \hat{P}$. Furthermore, since both $S$ and $\hat{P}$ are finite, $\hat{\Phi}_*$ is the limit of the sequence $\langle \hat{\Phi}_n \in S \to \hat{P} \mid n \in \mathbf{N}\rangle$ defined by:

$$\hat{\Phi}_n \;=\; \texttt{if } (n = 0) \texttt{ then } (\lambda s \in S : \hat{\bot}) \texttt{ else } \hat{\mathcal{F}}(\hat{\Phi}_{n-1}) \tag{6}$$

in the sense that there exists a sufficiently large $k \in \mathbf{N}$ such that $\hat{\Phi}_n = \hat{\Phi}_*$ for all $n \geq k$.

We say the abstract circuit $\hat{M}$ *satisfies* the abstract trajectory assertion $\hat{A}$ *by lattice-theoretic STE*, denoted by $\hat{M} \models_{\mathrm{Lat}} \hat{A}$, iff $\forall s \in S : \hat{\Phi}_*(s) \sqcap \hat{\pi}_a(s) \sqsubseteq \hat{\pi}_c(s)$. Now we are ready to state our second main result:

**Theorem 2.** *If $\hat{M}$ is an abstract interpretation of $M$, then:*

$$\hat{M} \models_{\mathrm{Lat}} \hat{A} \;\;\Rightarrow\;\; M \models_{\mathrm{Set}} \gamma(\hat{A})$$

*Proof.* See Appendix A.5.

The converse of Theorem 2 is not true. For example, consider a circuit with five signals $\langle i_1, i_2, j_1, j_2, o \rangle$, where $j_1$ (resp., $j_2$) is $i_1$ ($i_2$) delayed by one unit of time and $o$ is the unit-delayed AND of $j_1$ and $j_2$. Suppose that the trajectory assertion has five states $\{s_0, s_1, s_1', s_2, s_3\}$ and five transitions $\{(s_0, s_1), (s_0, s_1'), (s_1, s_2), (s_1', s_2), (s_2, s_3)\}$ and the labeling: $\pi_a(s_1) = \langle 0, 1, X, X, X \rangle$, $\pi_a(s_1') = \langle 1, 0, X, X, X \rangle$, $\pi_c(s_3) = \langle X, X, X, X, 0 \rangle$; all other labels are $\langle X, X, X, X, X \rangle$. Intuitively, the antecedent at $s_1$ (resp., $s_1'$) assumes that $i_1 = 0$ and $i_2 = 1$ (resp., $i_1 = 1$ and $i_2 = 0$) at time 1, and the consequent at $s_3$ checks that at time 3, $o = 0$ regardless of which assumption was used. It is easy to verify that for this example, $M \models_{\text{Set}} \gamma(\hat{A})$ but $\hat{M} \not\models_{\text{Lat}} \hat{A}$. And the reason is simple: at time 2, when the information from $s_1$ and $s_1'$ is merged at $s_2$, we have:

$$\{\langle 0, 1 \rangle\} \cup \{\langle 1, 0 \rangle\} = \{\langle 0, 1 \rangle, \langle 1, 0 \rangle\} \quad \text{but} \quad \langle 0, 1 \rangle \sqcup \langle 1, 0 \rangle = \langle X, X \rangle$$

the latter of which loses information. Clearly, this merge could be avoided by duplicating $s_2$ and $s_3$, so that there is a separate copy of them to deal with each of the assumptions $\pi_a(s_1)$ and $\pi_a(s_1')$. But then the number of states in the trajectory assertion increases. This kind of trade-offs between complexity and precision is typical of STE.

## 4  An Implicit Algorithm for Lattice-Theoretic STE

Up to this point, except in a few examples, we have not needed to specify what exactly the set $C$ of configurations is, except that $C$ should be nonempty and finite. This makes our theory more general. But in order to have a BDD-based implementation, we have to make up our mind now as to what $C$ is. Thus, in this section, we shall assume that $C = \mathbf{B}^m$ for some $m \in \mathbf{N}$. In other words, $M$ is a boolean circuit with $m$ signals. Furthermore, we assume that the abstract circuit $\hat{M}$ operates on ternary vectors, i.e., $\hat{P} = \mathbf{T}_\perp^m$. How sets of boolean vectors can be approximated by ternary vectors is explained in Appendix A.3.

Similar to the set-theoretic case, the definition (6) of the sequence $\langle \hat{\Phi}_n \mid n \in \mathbf{N} \rangle$ yields a simple algorithm for checking $\hat{M} \models_{\text{Lat}} \hat{A}$: compute $\hat{\Phi}_0, \hat{\Phi}_1, \hat{\Phi}_2, \ldots$ one by one until a fixpoint, which must be $\hat{\Phi}_*$, is reached; then check $\hat{M} \models_{\text{Lat}} \hat{A}$ using its definition. Note that since the converse of Theorem 2 is not true, this algorithm, which we call the *lattice-theoretic STE algorithm*, can give falsely negative answers (i.e., when $\hat{M} \not\models_{\text{Lat}} \hat{A}$ but $M \models \gamma(\hat{A})$). But, by virtue of Theorems 1 and 2, it can never produce falsely positive answers (i.e., $\hat{M} \models_{\text{Lat}} \hat{A}$ does imply $M \models \gamma(\hat{A})$). We now argue that the lattice-theoretic STE algorithm can be implemented using BDDs in a straightforward manner.

First, notice that every ternaray value $t \in \mathbf{T}$ can be encoded with two boolean values: $B_0(t) = (0 \sqsubseteq t)$ and $B_1(t) = (1 \sqsubseteq t)$. With this encoding, join and meet are implemented by: $B_i(t \sqcup t') = B_i(t) \vee B_i(t')$ and $B_i(t \sqcap t') = B_i(t) \wedge B_i(t')$, where $i \in \mathbf{B}$. For any $m \in \mathbf{N}$, this encoding and the associated join and meet operations can be extended component-wise to $\mathbf{T}_\perp^m$. Note that $\perp$ has multiple encodings (viz., all $m$-tuples of boolean pairs in which at least one of the pairs is such that $B_0 = B_1 = 0$).

Without loss of generality, suppose the state space $S$ of the trajectory assertion is $\mathbf{B}^k$, for some $k \in \mathbf{N}$. With the above encoding of ternary values, the objects manipulated by the lattice-theoretic STE algorithm have the following types: $R \in \mathbf{B}^k \times \mathbf{B}^k \to \mathbf{B}$ and $\hat{\pi}_a, \hat{\pi}_c, \hat{\Phi}_n, \hat{\Phi}_* \in \mathbf{B}^k \to (\mathbf{B} \times \mathbf{B})^m$, for all $n \in \mathbf{N}$. It is not hard to see that these objects can all be represented by BDDs on at most $2k$ variables, and that $\hat{\mathcal{F}}$ and the checking of $\hat{M} \models_{\text{Lat}} \hat{A}$ can be implemented by BDD operations on these BDDs, *provided that* the output of the abstract circuit $\hat{M} \in \mathbf{T}_\perp^m \to \mathbf{T}_\perp^m$ for any given input can be computed without ever having to represent $\hat{M}$ itself as BDDs (which would require $2m$ variables). Real-world STE implementations amply demonstrate that this proviso is practical.

We emphasize again that the maximum number of boolean variables needed by our algorithm, $2k$, depends only on the trajectory assertion and *not* on the circuit. Of course, this independence is somewhat illusory, since the possible loss of information in the approximation by ternary vectors may necessitate more complex state-transition structure in the trajectory assertion, which would increase $k$. Furthermore, note that our formulation so far has been "unparameterized" in the sense that the antecedents and consequents are simple ternary vectors without parameters. In fact, they can be parameterized by boolean variables, so that a single run of the parameterized algorithm is equivalent to multiple runs of the unparameterized algorithm, one for each truth assignment to the boolean parameters. Needless to say, such parameters increase further the total number of boolean variables.

Despite its simplicity, the STE algorithm outlined above does not seem to have ever been implemented. Can it be as efficient in practice as, or even more so than, current implementations of extended STE? We do not know, but it would be interesting to find out.

# A  Appendices

## A.1  Sequences

Let $\mathbf{N} = \{0, 1, 2, \cdots\}$ be the set of natural numbers. For any set $V$ and any $n \in \mathbf{N}$, $V^n$ (resp., $V^+$ and $V^*$) denotes the set of all finite sequences of length $n$ (resp., positive and nonnegative lengths) over $V$. Let $\sigma, \tau \in V^*$. The length of $\sigma$ is denoted by $|\sigma|$, the concatenation of $\sigma$ followed by $\tau$ by $\sigma \,\hat{}\, \tau$, and $\sigma$ being a prefix of $\tau$ by $\sigma \preceq \tau$. A set $S \subseteq V^*$ is *prefix-closed* iff $\sigma \in S$ and $\tau \preceq \sigma$ imply $\tau \in S$. For any $i \in \mathbf{N}$ with $0 \le i < |\sigma|$, the $i$-th element of $\sigma$ is denoted by $\sigma[i]$. (Note that we index sequence elements starting from 0 instead of 1.) The last element of $\sigma$ is denoted by $last(\sigma)$, i.e., $last(\sigma) = \sigma[|\sigma| - 1]$. The empty sequence (i.e., the sequence whose length is 0) is denoted by $\langle \rangle$. A sequence consisting of elements $v_0, v_1, v_2, \cdots, v_{n-1} \in V$ (in that order) is written as $\langle v_0, v_1, v_2, \cdots, v_{n-1} \rangle$. We use the terms "sequences" and "vectors" interchangeably; the elements of vectors are sometimes referred to as "components".

## A.2  Complete Lattices

A *complete lattice* is a poset $(P, \sqsubseteq)$ in which the meet and join of elements of any subset $Q \subseteq P$, denoted by $\sqcap Q$ and $\sqcup Q$ respectively, always exist. Intuitively, we think of the elements of a complete lattice as "predicates", so that $\sqcap$, $\sqcup$, and $\sqsubseteq$ corresponds to "conjunction", "disjunction", and "implication", respectively.

For any set $V$, its power set $\mathcal{P}(V)$, ordered by set inclusion $\subseteq$, forms a complete lattice. Here $\sqcap$, $\sqcup$, and $\sqsubseteq$ are $\cap$, $\cup$, and $\subseteq$, respectively.

Let $\mathbf{T} = \{0, 1, \mathsf{X}\}$ be the set of *ternary values*, where $\mathsf{X}$ denotes an unknown value. Intuitively, $\mathsf{X}$ signifies a lack of information: it could be 0, it could be 1; we simply don't know. We partially order $\mathbf{T}$ as follows:[3] $0 \sqsubseteq \mathsf{X}$ and $1 \sqsubseteq \mathsf{X}$. For any $m \in \mathbf{N}$, this order on $\mathbf{T}$ is extended component-wise to $\mathbf{T}^m$. But $(\mathbf{T}^m, \sqsubseteq)$ is not a complete lattice, because it lacks a bottom. We fix this by introducing a special bottom element, $\perp$, such that $\perp \sqsubseteq t$ and $\perp \neq t$ for all $t \in \mathbf{T}^m$. Now $\mathbf{T}^m_\perp = \mathbf{T}^m \cup \{\perp\}$, ordered by $\sqsubseteq$, is indeed a complete lattice. We denote the top element $\langle \mathsf{X}, \cdots, \mathsf{X} \rangle$ of $\mathbf{T}^m_\perp$ by $\top$.

## A.3  Galois Connections

**Galois Connections as Relations.** Let $(P^\flat, \sqsubseteq^\flat)$ and $(P^\sharp, \sqsubseteq^\sharp)$ be complete lattices of "concrete predicates" and "abstract predicates", respectively. (Below we will drop $^\flat$ and $^\sharp$ from $\sqsubseteq^\flat$ and $\sqsubseteq^\sharp$ and the meet and join operations they induce, since they will always be clear from the context.) A *Galois connection* [2, 7] from $P^\flat$ to $P^\sharp$ is a binary relation $\ll \subseteq P^\flat \times P^\sharp$, where $p^\flat \ll p^\sharp$ reads: "$p^\flat$ can be approximated by $p^\sharp$", such that for all $Q^\flat \subseteq P^\flat$ and $Q^\sharp \subseteq P^\sharp$:

$$Q^\flat \ll Q^\sharp \;\Leftrightarrow\; \sqcup Q^\flat \ll \sqcap Q^\sharp \tag{7}$$

where we define: $Q^\flat \ll Q^\sharp \Leftrightarrow \forall p^\flat \in Q^\flat : \forall p^\sharp \in Q^\sharp : p^\flat \ll p^\sharp$. Intuitively, (7) says that the approximation relation $\ll$ is an extension of the partial orders *inside* $P^\flat$ and $P^\sharp$ to *between* $P^\flat$ and $P^\sharp$.

**Galois Connections as Functions.** The usual definitions of Galois connections in the literature [2, 7] are in terms of an *abstraction* function $\alpha : P^\flat \to P^\sharp$ and a *concretization* function $\gamma : P^\sharp \to P^\flat$, which in our framework can be derived from $\ll$ as follows:

$$\alpha(p^\flat) = \sqcap \{p^\sharp \in P^\sharp \mid p^\flat \ll p^\sharp\} \qquad \gamma(p^\sharp) = \sqcup \{p^\flat \in P^\flat \mid p^\flat \ll p^\sharp\} \tag{8}$$

for all $p^\flat \in P^\flat$ and $p^\sharp \in P^\sharp$. Intuitively, $\alpha(p^\flat)$ (resp., $\gamma(p^\sharp)$) is the most precise approximation of $p^\flat$ ($p^\sharp$) in $P^\sharp$ ($P^\flat$). Conversely, the relation $\ll$ can be derived from $\alpha$ or $\gamma$ as follows:

$$p^\flat \ll p^\sharp \;\Leftrightarrow\; \alpha(p^\flat) \sqsubseteq p^\sharp \qquad\qquad p^\flat \ll p^\sharp \;\Leftrightarrow\; p^\flat \sqsubseteq \gamma(p^\sharp) \tag{9}$$

for all $p^\flat \in P^\flat$ and $p^\sharp \in P^\sharp$. It is easy to see from (8) and (9) how $\alpha$ and $\gamma$ can be derived from each other. It is not hard to show that $\gamma$ preserves top (i.e., $\gamma(\top^\sharp) = \top^\flat$), is monotonic (i.e., $p^\sharp \sqsubseteq q^\sharp \Rightarrow \gamma(p^\sharp) \sqsubseteq \gamma(q^\sharp)$ for all $p^\sharp, q^\sharp \in P^\sharp$), and distributes over arbitrary meet (i.e., $\gamma(\sqcap Q^\sharp) = \sqcap\{\gamma(q^\sharp) \in P^\flat \mid q^\sharp \in Q^\sharp\}$ for all $Q^\sharp \subseteq P^\sharp$). Similarly, $\alpha$ preserves bottom, is also monotonic, and distributes over arbitrary join.

**Galois Connection from $\mathcal{P}(\mathbf{B}^m)$ to $\mathbf{T}^m_\perp$.** For any $m \in \mathbf{N}$, there is a natural Galois connection $\ll$ from $\mathcal{P}(\mathbf{B}^m)$ to $\mathbf{T}^m_\perp$, which is most conveniently defined by specifying its concretization function $\gamma : \mathbf{T}^m_\perp \to \mathcal{P}(\mathbf{B}^m)$:

$$\gamma(\langle t_0, \cdots, t_{m-1} \rangle) = \{ \langle b_0, \cdots, b_{m-1} \rangle \in \mathbf{B}^m \mid \forall i < m : t_i \neq \mathsf{X} \Rightarrow b_i = t_i \}$$
$$\gamma(\perp) = \emptyset$$

for all $\langle t_0, \cdots, t_{m-1} \rangle \in \mathbf{T}^m$. In other words, for any ternary vector $t \in \mathbf{T}^m$, $\gamma(t)$ is the set of all boolean vectors $\in \mathbf{B}^m$ that agree with $t$ on all non-$\mathsf{X}$ components (so $\mathsf{X}$'s can

---

[3] Our ordering of $\mathbf{T}$ is the reverse of that used in [8, 3]. We do so because we want to make clear that the ordering of $\mathbf{T}$ is an abstraction of set inclusion.

be thought of as "wild cards"). Note that $\gamma$ is in fact a bijection from $\mathbf{T}_\perp^m$ to those subsets of $\mathbf{B}^m$ that are (hyper)cubes. From $\gamma$, the Galois connection $\ll \subseteq \mathcal{P}(\mathbf{B}^m) \times \mathbf{T}_\perp^m$ and the abstraction function $\alpha : \mathcal{P}(\mathbf{B}^m) \to \mathbf{T}_\perp^m$ can be easily derived using (8) and (9). Intuitively, $b \ll t$ iff the cube corresponding to $t$ contains $b$, and $\alpha(b)$ is the element of $\mathbf{T}_\perp^m$ that corresponds to the smallest cube in $\mathbf{B}^m$ that contains $b$.

## A.4 Proof of Theorem 1

We prove the two directions of $\Leftrightarrow$ separately.

The $\Rightarrow$ direction: Suppose this is not true, i.e., $M \models_{\mathrm{Set}} A$ but $M \not\models A$. Then $M \not\models A$ implies that there exist $\tau \in \mathit{Traj}(M)$ and $\rho \in \mathit{Runs}(A)$ such that $|\tau| = |\rho|$, $\tau \models_a \rho$, and $\tau' \models_c \rho'$, but $last(\tau) \notin \pi_c(last(\rho))$, where $\tau'$ and $\rho'$ are the prefixes of $\tau$ and $\rho$ respectively such that $|\tau'| = |\tau| - 1$ and $|\rho'| = |\rho| - 1$. We claim that for all $i \in \mathbf{N}$ with $0 \leq i < |\tau|$, $\tau[i] \in \Phi_*(\rho[i])$. This is proved by induction on $i$. The base case $i = 0$ is trivial, since $\Phi_*(s_0) = C$. For the induction step, assume the claim is true for $i < |\tau| - 1$. Then $\tau[i] \in \Phi_*(\rho[i]) \cap \pi_a(\rho[i])$, since $\tau \models_a \rho$. So $\tau[i+1] \in F(\rho[i])(\Phi_*(\rho[i]))$, since $\tau \in \mathit{Traj}(M)$. But, since $\Phi_* = \mathcal{F}(\Phi_*)$, $F(\rho[i])(\Phi_*(\rho[i])) \subseteq \Phi_*(\rho[i+1])$. This completes the induction step, so the claim is true. But the claim implies that $last(\tau) \in \Phi_*(last(\rho)) \cap \pi_a(last(\rho))$, which implies $last(\tau) \in \pi_c(last(\rho))$ because $M \models_{\mathrm{Set}} A$. So $last(\tau) \in \pi_c(last(\rho))$ and $last(\tau) \notin \pi_c(last(\rho))$, a contradiction.

The $\Leftarrow$ direction: Since $F(s)$ is distributive over arbitrary union for all $s \in S$, a well-known result from DFA [4] states that the least fixpoint solution $\Phi_*$ of the equation $\Phi = \mathcal{F}(\Phi)$ is identical to the union-over-all-runs solution. More precisely, $\Phi_*$ must satisfy the following equation:

$$\Phi_*(s) = \text{if } (s = s_0) \text{ then } C \text{ else } \cup \{G(\rho') \mid \rho' \in \mathit{Runs}(A) \wedge (last(\rho'), s) \in R\}$$

for all $s \in S$, where $G : \mathit{Runs}(A) \cup \{\langle\rangle\} \to \mathcal{P}(C)$ is defined inductively by $G(\langle\rangle) = C$ and $G(\rho^\frown \langle s \rangle) = F(s)(G(\rho))$. Let $c \in C$ and $s \in S$. Using the definitions of $G$, $F$, and $M$, the equation above can be rephrased as:

$$c \in \Phi_*(s) \Leftrightarrow \exists \tau \in \mathit{Traj}(M) : \exists \rho \in \mathit{Runs}(A) :$$
$$|\tau| = |\rho| \wedge last(\tau) = c \wedge last(\rho) = s \wedge$$
$$\forall i \in \mathbf{N} : 0 \leq i < |\tau| - 1 \Rightarrow \tau[i] \in \pi_a(\rho[i])$$

Conjoining $c \in \pi_a(s)$ to both sides, we get:

$$c \in \Phi_*(s) \cap \pi_a(s) \Leftrightarrow \exists \tau \in \mathit{Traj}(M) : \exists \rho \in \mathit{Runs}(A) :$$
$$|\tau| = |\rho| \wedge last(\tau) = c \wedge last(\rho) = s \wedge \tau \models_a \rho$$

Now the definition of $M \models A$ shows that the $\Leftarrow$ direction is indeed true.

## A.5 Proof of Theorem 2

Throughout this proof, we will freely use the right half of (9): $p \ll \hat{p} \Leftrightarrow p \subseteq \gamma(\hat{p})$ for all $p \in \mathcal{P}(C)$ and $\hat{p} \in \hat{P}$. For set-theoretic STE, the notations are exactly the same as in Section 2.3 and Appendix A.4, except that the (concrete) trajectory assertion is $\gamma(\hat{A}) = (S, s_0, R, \gamma(\hat{\pi}_a), \gamma(\hat{\pi}_c))$ instead of $A$.

Claim 1: $p \ll \hat{p} \Rightarrow F(s)(p) \ll \hat{F}(s)(\hat{p})$ for all $p \in \mathcal{P}(C)$, $\hat{p} \in \hat{P}$, and $s \in S$. This is proved as follows:

$$\gamma(\hat{F}(s)(\hat{p})) \; = \; \gamma(\hat{M}(\hat{\pi}_a(s) \sqcap \hat{p})) \qquad \{\, \text{definition of } \hat{F} \,\}$$
$$\sqsupseteq \; M(\gamma(\hat{\pi}_a(s) \sqcap \hat{p})) \qquad \{\, \ll \text{ is a simulation relation} \,\}$$
$$= \; M(\gamma(\hat{\pi}_a(s)) \cap \gamma(\hat{p})) \qquad \{\, \text{distributivity of } \gamma \,\}$$
$$\sqsupseteq \; M(\gamma(\hat{\pi}_a(s)) \cap p) \qquad \{\, p \ll \hat{p} \text{ and monotonicity of } M \,\}$$
$$= \; F(s)(p) \qquad \{\, \text{definition of } F \,\}$$

where $\{\cdots\}$'s give the justifications of proof steps.

**Claim 2:** $\Phi_*(s) \ll \hat{\Phi}_*(s)$ for all $s \in S$. Since $\Phi_*(s) = \lim \Phi_n(s)$ and $\hat{\Phi}_*(s) = \lim \hat{\Phi}_n(s)$, it suffices to prove that $\Phi_n(s) \ll \hat{\Phi}_n(s)$ for all $s \in S$ and $n \in \mathbf{N}$. This is proved by induction on $n$. The base case is trivial, since a Galois connection always relates the two bottoms. For the induction step, assume $\Phi_n(s) \ll \hat{\Phi}_n(s)$ for all $s \in S$. That $\Phi_{n+1}(s_0) \ll \hat{\Phi}_{n+1}(s_0)$ is also trivial, since a Galois connection always relates the two tops. For any $s_0 \neq s \in S$, we have:

$$\gamma(\hat{\Phi}_{n+1}(s)) \; = \; \gamma(\sqcup \{ \hat{F}(s')(\hat{\Phi}_n(s')) \mid (s',s) \in R \}) \qquad \{\, (6) \,\}$$
$$\sqsupseteq \; \cup \{ \gamma(\hat{F}(s')(\hat{\Phi}_n(s'))) \mid (s',s) \in R \} \qquad \{\, \text{monotonicity of } \gamma \,\}$$
$$\sqsupseteq \; \cup \{ F(s')(\Phi_n(s')) \mid (s',s) \in R \} \qquad \{\, \Phi_n(s) \ll \hat{\Phi}_n(s) \text{ and claim 1} \,\}$$
$$= \; \Phi_{n+1}(s) \qquad \{\, (5) \,\}$$

This completes the induction step, so the claim is true.

Finally, suppose $\hat{M} \models_{\text{Lat}} \hat{A}$. Then, for all $s \in S$, we have:

$$\gamma(\hat{\pi}_c(s)) \; \sqsupseteq \; \gamma(\hat{\Phi}_*(s) \sqcap \hat{\pi}_a(s)) \qquad \{\, \hat{M} \models_{\text{Lat}} \hat{A} \text{ and monotonicity of } \gamma \,\}$$
$$= \; \gamma(\hat{\Phi}_*(s)) \cap \gamma(\hat{\pi}_a(s)) \qquad \{\, \text{distributivity of } \gamma \,\}$$
$$\sqsupseteq \; \Phi_*(s) \cap \gamma(\hat{\pi}_a(s)) \qquad \{\, \text{claim 2} \,\}$$

Therefore, $M \models_{\text{Set}} \gamma(\hat{A})$.

# References

1. P. Cousot and R. Cousot, "Abstract Interpretation: A Unified Lattice Model for Static Analysis of Programs by Construction or Approximation of Fixpoints", pp.238–252 of *Conf. Rec. of 4th ACM Symp. on Principles of Programming Languages (POPL '77)*, Oct. 1977.
2. B.A. Davey and H.A. Priestley, *Introduction to Lattices and Order*, Cambridge University Press, 1990.
3. A. Jain, "Formal Hardware Verification by Symbolic Trajectory Evaluation", Ph.D. Thesis supervised by R.E. Bryant, Carnegie-Mellon University, July 1997.
4. G.A. Kildall, "A Unified Approach to Global Program Optimization", pp.194–206 of *Conf. Rec. of 1st ACM Symp. on Principles of Programming Languages (POPL '73)*, Oct. 1973.
5. K.L. McMillan, *Symbolic Model Checking*, Kluwer Academic Publishers, 1993.
6. S.S. Muchnick, *Advanced Compiler Design and Implementation*, Morgan Kaufmann Publishers, 1997.
7. D.A. Schmidt and B. Steffen, "Data-Flow Analysis as Model Checking of Abstract Interpretations", invited tutorial paper, *Proc. 5th Static Analysis Symposium*, G. Levi (ed.), Pisa, Sep. 1998, Springer LNCS 1503.
8. C.-J.H. Seger and R.E. Bryant, "Formal Verification by Symbolic Evaluation of Partially-Ordered Trajectories", *Formal Methods in System Designs*, Vol. 6, No. 2, pp. 147–189, March 1995.

# Assume-Guarantee Refinement
# Between Different Time Scales *

Thomas A. Henzinger **     Shaz Qadeer ***     Sriram K. Rajamani [†]

{tah,shaz,sriramr}@eecs.berkeley.edu

**Abstract.** Refinement checking is used to verify implementations against more abstract specifications. Assume-guarantee reasoning is used to decompose refinement proofs in order to avoid state-space explosion. In previous approaches, specifications are forced to operate on the same time scale as the implementation. This may lead to unnatural specifications and inefficiencies in verification. We introduce a novel methodology for decomposing refinement proofs of temporally abstract specifications, which specify implementation requirements only at certain sampling instances in time. Our new assume-guarantee rule allows separate refinement maps for specifying functionality and timing. We present the theory for the correctness of our methodology, and illustrate it using a simple example. Support for sampling and the generalized assume-guarantee rule have been implemented in the model checker MOCHA and successfully applied to verify the VGI multiprocessor dataflow chip with 6 million transistors.

## 1 Introduction

Formal verification is a systematic approach for detecting logical errors in designs. The design is first described in a language with a mathematical semantics and then analyzed for correctness with respect to a specification. We refer to the design being analyzed as the implementation. The verification problem is called *refinement checking* when the specification is a more abstract design. The refinement-checking problem is PSPACE-hard in the size of the implementation description. Not surprisingly, algorithms for refinement checking are exponential in the size of the implementation description. This is the so-called *state-explosion* problem in verification.

Specifications are typically less detailed than the implementation. For example, the specification of an adder might simply state that the output is the sum of the two inputs, whereas the implementation might be a gate-level adder circuit, which operates at the detail of individual bits. Nonetheless, common notions of correctness require specifications to operate in "lock-step" with the

---

\* This research was supported in part by the DARPA/NASA grant NAG2-1214, by the SRC contract 97-DC-324.041, by the NSF CAREER award CCR-9501708, by the ARO MURI grant DAAH-04-96-1-0341, and by an SRC fellowship of the third author.

\*\* EECS Department, University of California, Berkeley, USA, and Max-Planck Institute for Computer Science, Saarbrücken, Germany

\*\*\* EECS Department, University of California, Berkeley, USA

[†] EECS Department, University of California, Berkeley, USA

implementation: every possible computation step of the implementation must be matched by an admissible computation step of the specification. If the natural time scale of the specification is less detailed than that of the implementation —for example, if the gate-level adder requires several clock cycles to compute a sum— then the specification often is "slowed down" by stuttering, even for perfectly synchronous designs. A prominent example of this occurs in pipeline verification, where the Instruction Set Architecture (ISA) specification usually is slowed down by introducing a nondeterministic *stall* signal to stretch its time scale to match that of the pipeline [HQR98,McM98]. Instead of slowing down the specification, we pursue the alternative of "speeding up" the implementation. For this purpose, we use an operator called *Sample*, which samples the behavior of the implementation at appropriately defined sampling instants.[1]

Our motivation for sampling arose specifically from the attempt of verifying a 96-processor V(ideo) G(raphics) I(mage) chip designed by the Infopad project at the University of California, Berkeley [STUR98]. There, the specification consists of ISAs for the individual processors and FIFO buffers that abstract the point-to-point communication protocols, which interact subtly with the processor pipelines. Since the implementation contains level-sensitive latches and different parts of the circuit are active at high vs. low phases of the clock, sampling must be used to match the implementation time scale with the specification time scale. While the computational advantages of sampling in state-space exploration have been demonstrated in [AHR98], the VGI is still far beyond the scope of exhaustive search. Hence, we needed to generalize a compositional verification methodology to accommodate the *Sample* operator.

Scalable approaches to refinement checking make use of the compositional structure of both implementation and specification, and divide the verification task at hand into simpler subtasks. Suppose we have a refinement-checking problem of the form $P_1 \| P_2 \preceq Q_1 \| Q_2$, and the state space of the implementation $P_1 \| P_2$, even when sampled, is too large to be handled by exhaustive search algorithms. A naive compositional approach would attempt to prove both $P_1 \preceq Q_1$ and $P_2 \preceq Q_2$, and then conclude that $P_1 \| P_2 \preceq Q_1 \| Q_2$. Though sound, the naive approach often fails in practice, because $P_1$ usually refines $Q_1$ only in a suitable constraining environment, and so does $P_2$. The constraining environments are taken into account by the *assume-guarantee* approach, which concludes $P_1 \| P_2 \preceq Q_1 \| Q_2$ from the two proof obligations $P_1 \| Q_2 \preceq Q_1$ and $Q_1 \| P_2 \preceq Q_2$ (the apparent circularity in such proofs is resolved by an induction over time) [Sta85,Kur94,AL95,AH96,McM97,HQR98]. Note that the assume-guarantee approach avoids constructing $P_1 \| P_2$. With assume-guarantee reasoning, the difficulty in refinement checking shifts from the sizes of the involved state spaces to the "semantic gap" between implementation and specification. To bridge this gap, one writes witness modules that map implementation sig-

---

[1] The *Sample* operator is similar, but not identical, to the *Next* operator of Reactive Modules [AH96]: while *Next* changes the time scale of a module *and* its environment, *Sample* does not constrain the environment, which therefore may offer multiple inputs between sampling instances.

nals to specification signals, and refinement constraints that relate specification signals to implementation signals [HQR98].

In this paper, we generalize the assume-guarantee method to accommodate the sampling operator. If implementation and specification operate at the same time scale, witness modules generate values for hidden specification variables at each step. However, if a single macro-step of the specification corresponds to several micro-steps of the implementation, it is necessary to provide witness modules that operate at the micro-step level. The purpose of such a witness is to generate the correct value for the specification signal to be witnessed and to maintain that value until the next sampling instance. Dually, if implementation and specification operate at the same time scale, refinement constraints provide abstract definitions for implementation variables at each step. If one specification step corresponds to several implementation steps, then it no longer suffices for the refinement constraints to supply values for the implementation variables at the rate of the specification —at sampling instances— but additional constraints need to be provided between sampling instances. Providing different refinement constraints at the macro and micro levels enables a separation of concerns: while macro-level constraints (at sampling instances) tend to describe the functional behavior of an implementation variable, micro-level constraints (between sampling instances) tend to describe its timing behavior. This separation of functionality and timing is particularly natural for collections of synchronous blocks that communicate asynchronously.

We develop the theory and methodology to carry out assume-guarantee reasoning when specifications are abstract in both space (fewer variables/components) and time (fewer observation points). The crux of the theory lies in the ability to distribute the *Sample* operator over the parallel composition of implementation components using micro-level refinement constraints. The resulting assume-guarantee proof rule produces refinement obligations both at the macro level and at the micro level, which are then discharged by our model checker MOCHA [AHM+98]. While micro-level refinement obligations can be handled using traditional model checking, we had to enhance MOCHA to discharge macro-level refinement obligations. We have used this methodology successfully in the verification of the VGI chip. We found several subtle bugs which were unknown to the designers. The case study describing this effort can be found in [HLQR99].

Speeding up the implementation using *Sample* has significant computational advantages when compared to earlier approaches that slow down the specification using stuttering. The sampled implementation typically has a smaller state space than the original implementation. If the refinement checking uses explicit state enumeration, we can use a secondary stack to explore and discard the implementation states between two sampling instances. If we use symbolic search using binary decision diagrams (BDDs), the sampled state space can be typically represented using a smaller BDD [AHR98].

**Outline of the paper.** Since the VGI is too complex for the purpose of exposing our methodology, we present a simple GCD example in Section 2. MOCHA operates in the heterogeneous modeling framework of Reactive Modules [AH96].

In order to introduce sampling, we have to generalize modules to so-called *transition constraints*, which need not be executable. This is done in Section 3. The *Sample* operator and its properties are introduced in Section 4. The assume-guarantee methodology of [McM97,HQR98,McM98] is generalized in Section 5 to accommodate the *Sample* operator, and the generalized methodology is applied in Section 6 to the GCD example. Finally, in Section 7, the VGI verification is described briefly.

## 2 Example

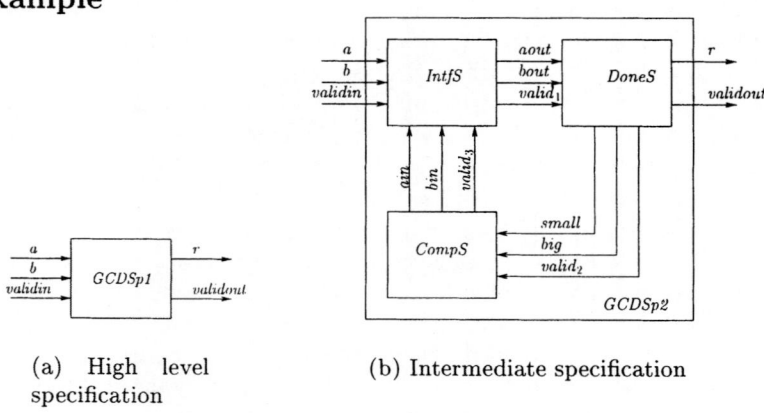

(a) High level specification

(b) Intermediate specification

**Fig. 1.** GCD Specification

We consider a design that computes the Greatest Common Divisor (*GCD*) of two numbers. We will start with a synchronous specification shown in Figure 1(a). Given two inputs $a$ and $b$, the module *GCDSp1* computes the *GCD* of $a$ and $b$ and places the result in the output $r$. The boolean input *validin* asserts that the inputs are valid in the current round and the boolean output *validout* asserts that the output is valid in the current round. Module *GCDSp1* operates synchronously, with a delay of one round. If inputs $a$ and $b$ are given in the current round, then the output is available at $r$ in the next round.

We refine our specification and add more spatial and temporal detail on how the *GCD* is computed. We use Euclid's algorithm to compute the *GCD*:

GCD ($a,b$)
{Given positive non-zero integers $a$ and $b$, compute $GCD(a, b)$ }
    (1) **if** ($a = b$) **return** ($a$);
    (2) **if** (($a = 1$) or ($b = 1$)) **return** (1);
    (3) *small* := **min**($a$, $b$);
    (4) *big* := **max**($a$, $b$);
    (5) **return** ($GCD(small, big - small)$);

The resulting refinement *GCDSp2* (Figure 1(b)) has three modules: *IntfS*, *DoneS*, and *CompS*. Given two numbers, the *DoneS* module decides if the *GCD* is computed trivially (if the numbers are equal, or one of the numbers is 1). If so,

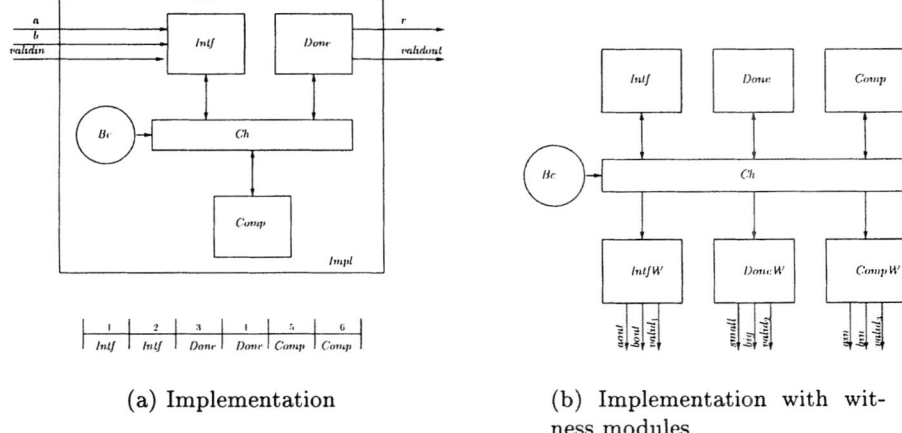

(a) Implementation

(b) Implementation with witness modules

**Fig. 2.** GCD Implementation

it sends the result, otherwise, it resends the numbers in increasing order. Suppose *small* and *big* are sent by the *DoneS* module. The *CompS* module responds by sending *small* and *big* − *small*. The *IntfS* module takes data inputs from both *CompS* and the environment and feeds the data to the *DoneS* module. The modules *IntfS*, *DoneS*, and *CompS* communicate with each other using point-to-point communication links. Valid bits ($valid_1$, $valid_2$ and $valid_3$) are used to validate the presence of meaningful data on these links. For instance, if *IntfS* wants to send two numbers to *DoneS*, it places the numbers in *aout* and *bout*, and sets $valid_1$ to TRUE. Each of these communications is assumed to complete in one round.

While *GCDSp1* requires only one round to compute the *GCD*, the module *GCDSp2* requires multiple rounds depending on the data inputs. We add an additional variable *inprogress* in module *GCDSp2* and set it to TRUE whenever a *GCD* computation is in progress. Using this variable and the *Sample* operator in Section 4, we will formally state how *GCDSp2* refines *GCDSp1*.

Our final level of refinement uses a single physical broadcast channel for communication between the modules. Time-division multiplexed access (TDMA) is used to share the channel. Communication in the channel is conducted in units called *frames*. A frame is divided, in time, into several *time-slots*. Each module is allocated one or more time-slots to send data. There is a beacon module *Bc*, that signals the beginning of a frame. Each module has its local counter that is synchronized on the *Bc* module's signal. Once the frame starts, each module sends data in its allocated time-slots. A valid bit sent on the channel indicates if the data being sent in the current time-slot is valid. The allocation of time-slots to modules is done statically at configuration time, and stays fixed thereafter. Thus, every module knows the identity of the sender in each time-slot. Figure 2(a) shows the block digram of the implementation *Impl*. In our example, a frame is divided into 6 slots. The figure also shows the allocation of time-slots within the frame to individual modules —the first two time-slots are given to the *Intf* module, the next two to the *Done* module, and the last two to the *Comp* module. The *Intf*, *Done*, and *Comp* modules are intended to have the same functionality as the specification modules *IntfS*, *DoneS*, and *CompS* from *GCDSp2*. However, while the communication between modules in *GCDSp2* happens in a single round through point-to-point links, the communication between modules in *Impl* is through a shared channel, and takes several rounds. Let *sync* be a variable of the module *Bc* that is set to TRUE whenever the *Bc* module sends the synchronizing signal. We will use *sync* and the *Sample* operator to relate *Impl* to *GCDSp2* in Section 4.

## 3 Transition Constraints and Modules

**Transition constraints.** Reactive Modules is a formalism for the modular description of systems with heterogeneous components. The definition of reactive modules can be found in [AH96]. In this paper, we generalize modules to transition constraints. A *transition constraint* is a temporal constraint on a set of variables. The state of a transition constraint is determined by values of two kinds of variables, namely, *observable variables* and *private variables*. The state of a transition constraint changes in a sequence of rounds. The first round is called the *initial round*, and determines initial values for all variables. Each subsequent round is called an *update round*, and determines new values for all variables. A sequence of states such that the first state results from an initial round, and each successive state in the sequence results from the previous state from an update round is called a *trajectory*. The projection of a trajectory to the observable variables is called a *trace*. The semantics of a transition constraint is its set of traces.

A state of a transition constraint $A$ is a valuation for all its variables. We use primed variables to denote the new value in a round, and unprimed variables to denote the old value. Formally, the transition constraint $A$ contains two predicates, namely, an *initial predicate* and *update predicate*. The initial predicate is a boolean function over the primed variables of $A$. A state $s$ of $A$ is *initial* if it satisfies the initial predicate of $A$. The update predicate is a boolean function over both the primed and unprimed variables of $A$. Given two states $s$ and $t$, we write $s \rightarrow_A t$ if the update predicate of $A$ evaluates to TRUE, when its unprimed variables are assigned values from $s$ and its primed variables are assigned values from $t$. A *trajectory* of $A$ is a finite sequence $s_0, \ldots, s_n$ of states such that (1) $s_0$ is an initial state of $A$, and (2) for $i \in \{0, 1, \ldots, n-1\}$, we have $s_i \rightarrow_A s_{i+1}$. The states that lie on trajectories are called *reachable*. An *observation* of $A$ is a valuation for the observable variables of $A$. If $s$ is a valuation to a set of variables, we use $[s]_A$ to denote the valuation restricted to the observable variables of $A$. For a state sequence $\bar{s} = s_0, \ldots, s_n$, we write $[\bar{s}]_A = [s_0]_A, \ldots, [s_n]_A$ for the corresponding observation sequence. If $\bar{s}$ is a trajectory of $A$, then the projection $[\bar{s}]_A$ is called a *trace* of $A$. Sometimes there is a need to effect a transition constraint only for a fixed number of update steps. We use $A^\tau$ to denote the transition constraint with the same variables as $A$, which restricts their valuations only up to $\tau$ update rounds. Formally, a state sequence $\bar{s} = s_0, \ldots, s_n$ is a trajectory of $A^\tau$ if (1) $n \le \tau$ and $\bar{s}$ is a trajectory of $A$, or (2) $n > \tau$ and $s_0, \ldots, s_\tau$ is a trajectory of $A$. Note that if $\tau < 0$, then every state sequence is a trajectory of $A^\tau$.

**Modules.** Modules are a special class of transition constraints with two special properties: (1) differentiation between inputs and outputs, and (2) executable non-blocking semantics. The observable variables of a module are partitioned into *external variables* and *interface variables*. External variables are updated by the environment and can be read by the module, and interface variables are updated by the module and can be read by the environment. The interface and private variables of a module are called *controlled variables*.

The state of a reactive module changes again in a sequence of rounds. For the external variables, the values in the initial and update rounds are left unspecified (i.e., chosen nondeterministically). For the controlled variables, the values in the initial and update rounds are specified by (possibly nondeterministic) guarded commands. A formal description of modules can be found in [AH96].

**Parallel composition.** The composition operation combines two transition constraints into a single transition constraint whose behavior captures the interaction between the two components. Two transition constraints $A$ and $B$ are *compatible* if their sets of private variables is disjoint. Given two compatible transition constraints $A$ and $B$, the *composition* $A\|B$ is a transition constraint. The observable variables of $A\|B$ are the union of the observable variables of $A$ and $B$. The private variables of $A\|B$ are the (disjoint) union of the private variables of $A$ and $B$. The initial predicate of $A\|B$ is the conjunction of the initial predicates of $A$ and $B$, and the update predicate of $A\|B$ is the conjunction of the update predicates of $A$ and $B$.

**Refinement.** The notion that two transition constraints describe the same system at different levels of detail is captured by the refinement relation between transition constraints. The transition constraint $B$ is *refinable* by transition constraint $A$ if every observable variable of $B$ is an observable variable of $A$. The transition constraint $A$ *refines* the transition constraint $B$, written $A \preceq B$, if (1) $B$ is refinable by $A$, and (2) for every trajectory $\bar{s}$ of $A$, the projection $[\bar{s}]_B$ is a trace of $B$.

## 4  The Sample Operator

Let $A$ be a transition constraint and $\varphi$ be a predicate on the primed and unprimed observable variables of $A$. We define $B = (Sample\ A\ at\ \varphi)$ to be a transition constraint. The private and observable variables of $B$ are the private and observable variables of $A$. The initial predicate of $B$ is equal to the initial predicate of $A$. The update predicate of $B$ is TRUE at the pair of states $(s, t)$ iff there is a sequence of states $s_0, s_1, \ldots, s_n$, such that (1) $s = s_0$, (2) $t = s_n$, (3) $s_i \rightarrow_A s_{i+1}$ for $i = 0, 1, \ldots, n-1$, and (4) $\varphi(s_i, s_{i+1})$ is FALSE for $i = 0, 1, \ldots, n-2$ and TRUE for $i = n-1$. Informally, $B$ updates from state $s$ to $t$ if there exists a sequence of rounds of $A$ starting at $s$ and ending at $t$, such that the final round satisfies $\varphi$, and none of the intermediate rounds satisfy

$\varphi$. Given a trajectory of $A$, we use the term *sampling instants* to refer to the instants in the trajectory where $\varphi$ is true.

We note that the *Sample* operator differs from the *Next* operator of [AH96] in two ways: (1) *Sample* operates on transition constraints, whereas *Next* operates on modules, and (2) *Sample* does not constrain the environment between sampling instants, whereas *Next* constrains the environment to not change between sampling instants. In the rest of this paper, whenever we write $B = (Sample\ A\ at\ \varphi)$, we assume that $\varphi$ is a predicate on the primed and unprimed observable variables of $A$.

**Example.** Recall the *GCD* computation example from Section 2. The module *GCDSp1* is the high-level specification. The intermediate-level specification and implementation modules are composed as follows:

$$GCDSp2 = IntfS \| DoneS \| CompS$$
$$Impl = Bc \| Ch \| Intf \| Done \| Comp$$

We wish to relate the intermediate specification *GCDSp2* to the high level specification *GCDSp1*. Recall that *GCDSp1* computes *GCD* in one round, whereas *GCDSp2* takes multiple rounds. Also recall that *inprogress* is a variable of *GCDSp2* that is set to TRUE when *GCDSp2* is doing the *GCD* computation. If we sample the behaviors of *GCDSp2* during the instances where *inprogress* is FALSE, the sampling should conform to the behaviors allowed by *GCDSp1*. Using the *Sample* operator, we can express this requirement as:

$$(Sample\ GCDSp2\ at\ (\neg inprogress')) \preceq GCDSp1$$

We also wish to relate *GCDSp2* to the final implementation *Impl*. Recall that every communication in *GCDSp2* happens in a single round, whereas every communication in *Impl* takes several rounds (as many rounds it takes to transmit a frame) to complete. Recall that the *Bc* module has a variable *sync* that is set to TRUE when it sends the synchronization signal. Though *Impl* and *GCDSp2* operate at different time scales, if we consider any trace of *Impl* and sample only the instants where *sync* is TRUE, the resulting subsequence should be a trace of *GCDSp2*. Using the *Sample* operator, we can express this requirement as:

$$(Sample\ Impl\ at\ sync') \preceq GCDSp2$$

**Properties of Sample.** The following proposition asserts the distributivity of *Sample* with respect to the parallel-composition operator.

**Proposition 1.** *[Distributivity of Sample] If $A$, $B$ are any two transition constraints and $\varphi$ is a predicate on the observable variables common to $A$ and $B$, then $(Sample\ (A\|B)\ at\ \varphi) \preceq (Sample\ A\ at\ \varphi) \| (Sample\ B\ at\ \varphi)$.*

In practice, the traces of $(Sample\ A\ at\ \varphi) \| (Sample\ B\ at\ \varphi)$ form a large superset of the traces of $(Sample\ (A\|B)\ at\ \varphi)$. It is desirable to constrain the observable variables of $A$ and $B$ while distributing the *Sample* operator over parallel composition. We can strengthen the above proposition in the presence of suitable transition constraints $T_A$ and $T_B$ on the observable variables of $A$ and $B$, respectively. The resulting proposition, given below, will be used in the next section to carry out assume-guarantee reasoning between different time scales.

**Proposition 2.** *[Constrained distributivity of Sample] Consider transition constraints $A$, $B$, $T_A$ and $T_B$, such that every variable of $T_A$ is an observable variable of $A$, and every variable of $T_B$ is an observable variable of $B$. If $A\|B \preceq T_A\|T_B$ and $\varphi$ is a predicate on the observable variables common to $A$ and $B$, then $(Sample\ (A\|B)\ at\ \varphi) \preceq (Sample\ (A\|T_A)\ at\ \varphi)\ \|\ (Sample\ (B\|T_B)\ at\ \varphi)$.*

## 5 Refinement Checking Methodology

We generalize the methodology for assume-guarantee style refinement checking given in [HQR98] to accommodate the *Sample* operator.

**Witness modules.** The problem of checking if $A \preceq B$ is PSPACE-hard in the state space of $B$. However, the refinement check is simpler in the special case in which all variables of $B$ are observable. The transition constraint $A$ is *projection refinable* by transition constraint $B$ if (1) $B$ is refinable by $A$, and (2) $B$ has no private variables. If $B$ is projection refinable by $A$, then every variable of $B$ is observable in both $B$ and $A$. Therefore, checking if $A \preceq B$ reduces to checking if for every trajectory $\overline{s}$ of $A$, the projection $[\overline{s}]_B$ is a *trajectory* of $B$. This can be done by a transition-invariant check [HQR98], whose complexity is linear in the state spaces of both $A$ and $B$. If $B$ is projection refinable by $A$, then $A \preceq B$ iff (1) if $s$ is an initial state of $A$, then $[s]_B$ is an initial state of $B$, and (2) if $s$ is a reachable state of $A$ and $s \to_A t$, then $[s]_B \to_B [t]_B$.

Suppose that $B$ is refinable by $A$, but not projection refinable. This means that there are some private variables in $B$. Define $B^u$ to be the transition constraint obtained by making every private variable of $B$ an observable variable. If we compose $A$ with a module $W$ whose observable variables include the private variables of $B$, then $B^u$ is projection refinable by the composition $A\|W$. Moreover, if $W$ does not constrain any observable variables of $A$, then $A\|W \preceq B^u$ implies $A \preceq B$ (in fact, $A$ is simulated by $B$). Such a module $W$ is called a *witness* to the refinement $A \preceq B$. We require $W$ to be a module, because we need to enforce that $W$ does not constrain the observable variables of $A$, and that it does not deadlock. In order to check refinement, it is sufficient to first find a witness module and then check projection refinement. If the sample operator needs to be applied to the implementation to relate it to the specification, the witness could be composed either before or after applying the *Sample* operator.

**Proposition 3.** *[Sampled Witnesses] Consider two transition constraints $A$ and $B$, and a predicate $\varphi$ on the variables of $A$ such that $B$ is refinable by $A$. Let $W$ be a module such that the interface variables of $W$ include the private variables of $B$, and are disjoint from the observable variables of $A$. Then (1) $B^u$ is projection refinable by $(Sample\ (A\|W)\ at\ \varphi)$, and (2) $(Sample\ (A\|W)\ at\ \varphi) \preceq B^u$ implies $(Sample\ A\ at\ \varphi) \preceq B$.*

Proposition 3 is a generalization of a proposition from [HQR98]. The latter can be obtained by setting $\varphi$ to TRUE in Proposition 3.

**Assume-guarantee reasoning.** The state space of a transition constraint may be exponential in the size of its description. Consequently, even checking projection refinement may not be feasible. However, typically both the implementation

$A$ and the specification $B$ consist of the parallel composition of several transition constraints, in which case it may be possible to reduce the problem of checking if $A \preceq B$ to several subproblems that involve smaller state spaces. The assume-guarantee rules allows us to conclude $A \preceq B$ as long as each component of the specification $B$ is refined by the corresponding components of the implementation $B$ within a suitable environment. The apparent circularity in the environment assumptions is resolved by an induction over time. If we operate with modules, the acyclic await dependencies of legal modules breaks this circularity. Since our purpose in this paper is to carry out assume-guarantee reasoning with the *Sample* operator, which gives transition constraints, not modules, we impose a well-founded order on the specification components [McM98] to break the circularity.

**Proposition 4.** *[Assume-Guarantee [McM98]] Let* $A = A_1 \| A_2 \| \ldots \| A_n$ *and* $B = B_1 \| B_2 \| \ldots \| B_m$ *be transition constraints. Let* $\prec$ *be a well-founded order on the components of* $B$, *let* $Z(B_i) = \{B_j | B_j \prec B_i\}$, *and let* $Z^C(B_i) = \{B_j | B_j \notin Z(B_i)\}$. *For each* $B_i$, *let* $C_i$ *be some composition of transition constraints from* $A$, *let* $D_i$ *be some composition of transition constraints from* $Z(B_i)$, *and let* $E_i$ *be some composition of transition constraints from* $Z^C(B_i)$. *If* $C_i^\tau \| D_i^\tau \| E_i^{\tau-1} \preceq B_i^\tau$ *for all* $1 \leq i \leq m$ *and* $\tau \in \mathbb{N}$, *then* $A \preceq B$.

Proposition 4 produces proof obligations of the form $C_i^\tau \| D_i^\tau \| E_i^{\tau-1} \preceq B_i^\tau$. For each specification component $B_i$, the corresponding implementation component that is intended to implement the functionality specified by $B_i$ is $C_i$, and the constraining environments are $D_i$ and $E_i$. This obligation can be discharged by a reachability computation on $C_i \| D_i \| E_i$. At each stage of the reachability one has to merely check that every transition possible in $C_i \| D_i$ is also allowable in $B_i$. Note that while the transition constraint $E_i$ is used to constrain the reachable states of $C_i \| D_i$, it is not used to constrain the transition invariant check at each step.

While discharging the obligation for $B_i$ according to Proposition 4, we would like to keep the state spaces to be small. Thus, it is preferable to choose most components of the constraining environment from the specification. Unfortunately, due to lack of detail, the specification does not have sufficiently abstract definitions of internal variables of the implementation. For all transition constraints $A$, $B$, and $F$, if $A \preceq B \| F$ and $B$ is refinable by $A$, then $A \preceq B$. Thus, we can arbitrarily "enrich" the specification by composing it with new transition constraints. Before applying the assume-guarantee rule, we may add components to the specification and prove $A \preceq B \| F_1 \| \cdots \| F_k$ instead of $A \preceq B$. The new transition constraints $F_1, \ldots, F_k$ are called *abstract constraints*, and they usually give high-level descriptions for some implementation variables, in order to provide a sufficient supply of abstract components while applying Proposition 4. While witness modules are introduced "on the left" of a refinement relation, abstract constraints are introduced "on the right."

Suppose the left side of a refinement relation is of the form *Sample*$(A \| B)$ at $\varphi$. It is not directly possible to apply the assume-guarantee rule from Proposition 4 in such cases. However, we can distribute the *Sample* operator with respect to parallel composition using Proposition 1. In practice, Proposition 1 tends to provide abstractions that are too coarse to be useful. To see why, imagine $A$ and $B$ as modules, each constraining the other's inputs. By distributing the *Sample* inside the parallel composition, $B$ is allowed to constrain the inputs to $A$ only at the sampling instants. The inputs to $A$ are essentially unconstrained between sampling instants. Symmetrically, the inputs to $B$ are constrained at sampling instants by $A$ and left unconstrained between sampling instants. In several common situations, the interactions between $A$ and $B$ can be orthogonalized into (1) functionality, and (2) timing of the communication protocol used for the interaction. The functionality determines values at the sampling instants, whereas the timing determines how these values propagate between sampling instants.

Suppose $T_A$ and $T_B$ are transition constraints that specify how the inputs to $A$ and $B$ behave between sampling instants. Then, we can use Proposition 2 to distribute the *Sample* operator, while constraining the inputs to $A$ by $T_A$ and the inputs to $B$ by $T_B$. Thus, we get the following generalization of the assume-guarantee rule, with the *Sample* operator.

**Theorem 1.** *[Assume-Guarantee with Sample] Let $A = A_1 \| A_2 \| \ldots \| A_n$ and $B = B_1 \| B_2 \| \ldots \| B_m$ be transition constraints. Let $T_i$ be a transition constraint on the observable variables of $A_i$, for $1 \leq i \leq n$. Let $\prec$ be a well-founded order on the components of $B$, and let $T$, $Z$ and $Z^C$ be defined as follows: $T = \{T_1, \ldots, T_n\}$, $Z(B_i) = \{B_j | B_j \prec B_i\}$, and $Z^C(B_i) = \{B_j | B_j \notin Z(B_i)\}$. For each $B_i$, let $C_i$ be some composition of transition constraints from $A$, let $U_i$ be some composition of transition constraints from $T$, let $D_i$ be some composition of transition constraints from $Z(B_i)$, and let $E_i$ be some composition of transition constraints from $Z^C(B_i)$. If $A \preceq T_1 \| \ldots \| T_n$, and $\psi$ is any predicate such that $(Sample \ (C_i \| U_i) \ at \ \psi)^\tau \| D_i^\tau \| E_i^{\tau-1} \preceq B_i^\tau$ for all $1 \leq i \leq m$ and $\tau \in \mathbb{N}$, then $(Sample \ A \ at \ \psi) \preceq B$.*

In the above theorem, note that the antecedent $A \preceq T_1 \| \ldots \| T_n$ can itself be discharged by traditional assume-guarantee reasoning (Proposition 4).

## 6 Refinement Proof

Recall the high-level specification *GCDSp1*, intermediate specification *GCDSp2*, and implementation *Impl* from the previous sections. As stated in Section 4, the refinements we would like to verify are:

$$(Sample \ GCDSp2 \ at \ (\neg inprogress')) \preceq GCDSp1$$
$$(Sample \ Impl \ at \ sync') \preceq GCDSp2$$

In this section, we will focus on how to carry out the second refinement, which relates the intermediate specification *GCDSp2* to the implementation *Impl*. We first observe that *GCDSp2* is not projection refinable by *Impl*, due to the presence of private variables in *GCDSp2* that represent point-to-point communication channels. The module *Impl* has a single channel that is shared by all modules using TDMA. The specification, while more abstract in time, provides individual point-to-point channels for communication. Each round of *GCDSp2* corresponds to multiple rounds of *Impl*, during which a frame is transmitted. It is possible to relate the values that appear on the shared implementation channel, at particular time-slots during the communication of a frame, to values that appear on particular point-to-point channels in the specification. For instance, the values of the specification variables *aout* and *bout* at the end of each round are expected to be equal to the values occurring in time-slots 1 and 2 of the frame. We can write a witness module *IntfW* that looks at the implementation channel during the transmission of the frame, collects the values at time-slots 1 and 2, and assigns them to *aout* and *bout*, respectively. If the values in time-slots 1 and 2 are valid, then $valid_1$ is set to TRUE. Further, the values assigned to *aout*, *bout*, and $valid_1$ are retained till the end of the frame. Similar witness modules *DoneW* and *CompW* can be written. All these witnesses take inputs from the channel as shown in Figure 2(b). Let *ImplW* be the module given by

$$ImplW = Impl \| IntfW \| DoneW \| CompW.$$

Note that the witnesses do not interfere with the channel —they merely observe the values on the channel. Due to Proposition 3, it suffices to check that $(Sample\ ImplW\ at\ sync') \preceq GCDSp2$. Recall $GCDSp2 = IntfS \| DoneS \| CompS$. We use the order $DoneS \prec CompS \prec IntfS$ and apply Theorem 1. Let us consider the component *CompS* of *GCDSp2*. The component of *Impl* that is intended to implement the functionality of *CompS* is *Comp*. We wish to check if:

$$(Sample\ Comp\ at\ sync')^\tau \| DoneS^\tau \preceq CompS^\tau.$$

This check fails because the outputs of module *CompS*, namely, *ain*, *bin* and $valid_3$ are not present in module *Comp*. Adding the witness module and appropriately constraining it, we obtain the obligation:

$$(Sample\ (Comp \| CompW \| Ch \| Bc)\ at\ sync')^\tau \preceq CompS^\tau.$$

This still fails, because we have not constrained the inputs of *Comp*. In this obligation, the specification *CompS* looks at the inputs *small*, *big*, and $valid_2$ in every round and produces corresponding outputs *ain*, *bin* and $valid_3$ in the next round. The implementation *Comp* anticipates two values at time-slots 3 and 4 (which correspond to *small* and *big*, respectively) of every frame. If these inputs are valid, then *Comp* generates values in time-slots 5 and 6 (which correspond to *ain* and *bin* respectively) of the next frame. The module *Comp* makes the following assumptions: (1)the inputs are available at time-slots 3 and 4, (2)either both inputs are available at a given frame, or none of the inputs are available, and (3)if both inputs are available, the first input (from time-slot 3) is smaller than the second input (from time-slot 4). In our refinement obligation, the inputs to *Comp* have to be constrained both at the sampling instants and between sampling instants, in order to satisfy the above assumptions. The specification component *DoneS* supplies the constraint at sampling instants, which ensures that assumptions 2 and 3 are satisfied. The timing assumption *DoneW* constrains the inputs between sampling instants and ensures that assumption 1 is satisfied. Thus we get the proof obligation

$$(Sample\ (Comp \| CompW \| Ch \| Bc \| DoneW)\ at\ sync')^\tau \| DoneS^\tau \preceq CompS^\tau.$$

Similarly, we can verify the correctness of modules *Done* and *Intf* separately. The complete refinement proof, which is a direct application of Theorem 1, uses the ordering $DoneS \prec CompS \prec IntfS$:

$$(Sample\ (Done\|DoneW\|Ch\|Bc\|IntfW)\ at\ sync')^\tau \qquad\qquad \preceq DoneS^\tau$$
$$(Sample\ (Comp\|CompW\|Ch\|Bc\|DoneW)\ at\ sync')^\tau\|DoneS^\tau \qquad \preceq CompS^\tau$$
$$(Sample\ (Intf\|IntfW\|Ch\|Bc\|CompW)\ at\ sync')^\tau\|CompS^\tau\|DoneS^\tau \preceq IntfS^\tau$$

$$(Sample\ (ImplW)\ at\ sync') \qquad\qquad\qquad\qquad\qquad \preceq GCDSp2$$

Each of the obligations above the line involves a single implementation component, possibly along with specification components, witnesses and abstract constraints to constrain the inputs. They can be automatically discharged by MOCHA. We thus conclude that $(Sample\ Impl\ at\ sync') \preceq GCDSp2$.

# 7 VGI Processor Verification

The approach described in this paper has been used in a case study [HLQR99] to verify a large parallel DSP processor. The VGI chip [STUR98] is an array of DSP processors designed to be part of a system for web-based image processing [SR97]. The VGI chip contains a total of 96 processors and has approximately 6M transistors. Of the 96 processors, 64 are 3-stage pipelined compute processors. Each compute processor has about 30,000 logic gates. Data is communicated between the processors by means of FIFO queues. No assumptions are made about the relative speeds at which data is produced and consumed in the processors. Hence, to transfer data reliably, an elaborate handshake mechanism is used between the sender and the receiver. In addition, the interaction between the control of the pipeline and the control of the communication unit is quite complex. The details of the VGI processor verification can be found in [HLQR99]. Here, we only discuss the role the *Sample* operator in the verification of VGI.

The implementation has a clock signal clk with activity on both the HIGH and LOW phases in different parts of the design. For instance, in the execute phase of the pipeline a bus carries an operand when clk is HIGH and the result when clk is LOW. But the specification does not mention clk at all. In fact, the whole computation happens in just one step. Thus, one round of the specification is equal to two rounds of the implementation, one with clk = HIGH and one with clk = LOW. Therefore, we sample the implementation whenever clk is low and check if the sampled behavior is present in the specification.

In the remainder of this section, we use $\varphi$ to refer to clk = LOW. Our goal is to verify that an arbitrary network of compute processors implements its corresponding ISAs(instruction set architectures), using refinement checking. Let $P_1, P_2, \ldots, P_n$ be the compute processors, and let $Q_1, Q_2, \ldots, Q_n$ be their respective ISAs. The verification problem is to check that

$$Sample\ (P_1\|P_2\|\cdots\|P_n)\ at\ \varphi \preceq (Q_1\|Q_2\|\cdots\|Q_n).$$

For the correct functioning of a processor it is essential that all input signals change only when clk is HIGH. Let $T_i$ be a module that says that all input signals of $P_i$ change only when clk is HIGH. We use Theorem 1 to decompose this proof as follows:

$$\frac{(Sample(P_i\|T_i)\ at\ \varphi) \preceq Q_i\ \text{for all}\ 1 \leq i \leq n \qquad P_1\|P_2\|\cdots\|P_n \preceq T_1\|T_2\|\cdots\|T_n}{Sample(P_1\|P_2\|\cdots\|P_n)\ at\ \varphi \preceq Q_1\|Q_2\|\cdots\|Q_n}$$

The second antecedent says that the inputs of any processor in the network change only when clk is HIGH. Since any input to a processor has to be the output of some other processor, this antecedent can be discharged easily by proving that for all $1 \leq i \leq n$, the outputs of $P_i$ change only when clk is HIGH. This is an easy proof local to each processor. In the first antecedent, there are $n$ symmetric proof obligations, one for each $P_i$. Each $P_i$ can be in any one of a finite number of configurations. Moreover, if $P_j$ and $P_k$ are in the same configuration, then the $j$th and $k$th proofs are identical except for variable renaming. In this way, we decompose the proof of a 64 processor network to proofs about individual processor configurations that have 800 latches each. This is still beyond the scope of monolithic model checking. We use Theorem 1 again, to decompose the proof for a single processor configuration into about 35 proof obligations and check them using MOCHA. None of the individual lemmas require more than a few minutes on a 625 MHz DEC Alpha 21164. We found and fixed several subtle bugs that were unknown to the designers. Most bugs were in the interaction between the pipeline and the communication protocol.

# References

[AH96] R. Alur and T.A. Henzinger. Reactive modules. In *Proc. 11th Annual Symposium on Logic in Computer Science*, pp 207–218, 1996.

[AHM+98] R. Alur, T.A. Henzinger, F.Y.C. Mang, S. Qadeer, S.K. Rajamani, and S. Tasiran. MOCHA : Modularity in model checking. In *CAV 98: Computer Aided Verification*, Springer LNCS 1427, pp 521–525, 1998.

[AHR98] R. Alur, T.A. Henzinger, and S.K. Rajamani. Symbolic exploration of transition hierarchies. In *TACAS 98: Tools and Algorithms for Construction and Analysis of Systems*, Springer LNCS 1384, pp 330–344, 1998.

[AL95] M. Abadi and L. Lamport. Conjoining specifications. *ACM Transactions on Programming Languages and Systems*, 17(3):507–534, 1995.

[HLQR99] T. A. Henzinger, X. Liu, S. Qadeer, and S. K. Rajamani. Formal specification and verification of a dataflow processor array. Technical Report M99/14, ERL, University of California, Berkeley, 1999.

[HQR98] T.A. Henzinger, S. Qadeer, and S.K. Rajamani. You assume, we guarantee: methodology and case studies. In *CAV 98: Computer Aided Verification*, Springer LNCS 1427, pp 440–451, 1998.

[Kur94] R.P. Kurshan. *Computer-aided Verification of Coordinating Processes*. Princeton University Press, 1994.

[McM97] K.L. McMillan. A compositional rule for hardware design refinement. In *CAV 97: Computer-Aided Verification*, Springer LNCS 1254, pp 24–35, 1997.

[McM98] K.L. McMillan. Verification of an implementation of Tomasulo's algorithm by compositional model checking. In *CAV 98: Computer-Aided Verification*, Springer LNCS 1427, pp 110-121, 1998.

[SR97] V.P. Srini and J.M. Rabaey. An architecture for web-based image processing. In *Proc. SPIE Conference 3166*, pp 90–101, 1997.

[Sta85] E.W. Stark. A proof technique for rely/guarantee properties. In *Proc. 5th Conference on Foundations of Software Technology and Theoretical Computer Science*, Springer LNCS 206, pp 369–391, 1985.

[STUR98] V.P. Srini, J. Thendean, S.Z. Ueng, and J.M. Rabaey. A parallel DSP with memory and I/O processors. In *Proc. SPIE Conference 3452*, pp 2–13, 1998.

# Efficient Decision Procedures for Model Checking of Linear Time Logic Properties*

Roderick Bloem[1], Kavita Ravi[2], and Fabio Somenzi[1]

[1] Department of Electrical and Computer Engineering
University of Colorado, Boulder, CO, 80309-0425
{Roderick.Bloem,Fabio}@Colorado.EDU
[2] Cadence Design Systems
New Providence, NJ, 07974-1143
kravi@cadence.com

**Abstract.** We propose an algorithm for LTL model checking based on the classification of the automata and on guided symbolic search. Like most current methods for LTL model checking, our algorithm starts with a tableau construction and uses a model checker for CTL with fairness constraints to prove the existence of fair paths. However, we classify the tableaux according to their structure, and use efficient decision procedures for each class. Guided search applies hints to constrain the transition relation during fixpoint computations. Each fixpoint is thus translated into a sequence of fixpoints that are often much easier to compute than the original one. Our preliminary experimental results suggest that the new algorithm for LTL is quite efficient. In fact, for properties that can be expressed in both CTL and LTL, the algorithm is competitive with the CTL model checking algorithm.

## 1 Introduction

Successful application of model checking requires strategies to bridge the gap between the size of the models and the capacity of the model checkers. Abstraction closes the gap from above by eliminating unnecessary detail from the models and decomposing complex proofs into sequences of simpler ones. Abstraction is fundamental to the practical use of model checking. It is important, however, to close the gap also from below—by increasing the capacity of the model checkers. Indeed, too much reliance on abstraction inevitably means too much reliance on manual intervention, which in turns entails low productivity and exposure to errors.

The symbolic approach to model checking (BDD-based [4, 26] and, more recently, SAT-based [2]) addresses the complexity issue by representing models, sets of states, and paths as solutions to equations. Though not uniformly superior to the approach based on the explicit representation of states, symbolic model checking can deal with many more states and transitions. On the other hand, it has proved hard to predict whether a model will exceed the memory and time limits imposed on a given experiment: Whereas models with as many as 5000 state variables have been analyzed successfully without any abstraction, other models with 30 state variables turn out to be

---

* This work was supported in part by SRC contract 98-DJ-620.

intractable. In this paper we propose techniques that improve the performance and robustness of BDD-based model checking algorithms for linear time properties [24, 34].

Model checking for Linear Time Logic (LTL) is usually based on converting the property into a Büchi automaton (or tableau), composing the automaton and the model, and finally checking for emptiness of the language of the composed system. The last step can be performed by CTL model checking with fairness constraints [6]. In the context of this general strategy, our contribution is twofold: First, we propose a classification of the automata obtained by translation of the properties; our classification refines the one proposed in [20] to three types: general, weak, and terminal automata. We show that applying a specific decision procedure to each class results in an algorithm that is superior to the standard one both in theory and in practice. Different tableau constructions produce automata that may differ according to our classification. We adopt the procedure of [15] because it tends to produce automata that are amenable to more efficient decision procedures.

Converting properties into automata and applying specialized decision procedures based on the structure of the automaton tends to reduce the number of fixpoints that must be computed by the model checker. If the number of fixpoints is reduced to one, on-the-fly model checking can be easily applied [1]. In Section 5 we show that this sometimes produces substantial savings in memory and CPU time, even when comparing to CTL model checking. In general, our experiments confirm and strengthen the observation of [20] about the efficiency of LTL model checking.

Our second contribution is the extension of guided symbolic search from reachability analysis [32] to LTL model checking. Guided symbolic search applies constraints to the transition relation of the model to make the computation of fixpoints more efficient. The constraints are eventually lifted, so that the result of the computation does not differ from the the one of the conventional approach. However, by exploring the state space not in strict breadth-first fashion, guided search can be substantially more efficient than conventional fixpoint computations. The constraints can be seen as *hints* on the order in which transitions should be explored. Effective hints can be derived with only a limited understanding of the behavior of the model subjected to verification. In this paper we show how to apply hints to both least and greatest fixpoint computations. The asymmetry in the two computations is another reason for reducing the number of fixpoints when translating LTL properties.

The rest of this paper is organized as follows. Section 2 reviews the background material. Section 3 discusses the classification of the automata derived from LTL properties and the decision procedures for each class, while Section 4 deals with the application of guided symbolic search to model checking. Section 5 presents our preliminary experimental results, and Section 6 summarizes, outlines future work, and concludes.

## 2 Preliminaries

### 2.1 Linear Time Model Checking

We adopt the positive normal form (a.k.a. negation normal form) for the specification of LTL. Given a set of atomic propositions $A$, the standard boolean connectives, and the temporal operators X (*next time*), U (*until*) and R (*releases*), LTL formulae in positive normal form are defined as follows:

- **true, false**, the atomic propositions, and their negations are formulae;
- if $\varphi$ and $\psi$ are formulae, then so are $\varphi \vee \psi$, $\varphi \wedge \psi$, $X \varphi$, $\varphi \cup \psi$, and $\varphi R \psi$.

It is customary to define two additional operators: $F \varphi$ abbreviates **true** $\cup \varphi$ and $G \varphi$ abbreviates **false** $R \varphi$. The boolean connectives $\rightarrow$ and $\leftrightarrow$ are also defined as abbreviations in the usual way.

We define the semantics of LTL with respect to a Kripke structure $\langle S, T, S_0, A, L \rangle$, where $S$ is the set of states, $T \subseteq S \times S$ is the transition relation, $S_0 \subseteq S$ is the set of initial states, $A$ is the set of atomic propositions $A$, and $L : S \rightarrow 2^A$ is the labeling function. The transition relation is assumed to be *complete*; that is, every state has at least one successor. An infinite path $\pi$ in $M$ is an infinite sequence $s_0, s_1, \ldots$ such that $(s_i, s_{i+1}) \in T$ for $i \geq 0$. We denote by $\pi^i$ the suffix of $\pi$ starting at $s_i$. The satisfaction of an LTL formula along path $\pi$ of $M$ is defined as follows.

$\pi \models$ **true**

$\pi \models \varphi$ iff $\varphi \in L(s_0)$ for $\varphi \in A$

$\pi \models \varphi \vee \psi$ iff $\pi \models \varphi$ or $\pi \models \psi$

$\pi \models X \varphi$ iff $\pi^1 \models \varphi$

$\pi \models \varphi \cup \psi$ iff there exists $i \geq 0$ such that $\pi^i \models \psi$, and for all $j$, $0 \leq j < i$, $\pi^j \models \varphi$

$\pi \not\models$ **false**

$\pi \models \neg\varphi$ iff $\varphi \notin L(s_0)$ for $\varphi \in A$

$\pi \models \varphi \wedge \psi$ iff $\pi \models \varphi$ and $\pi \models \psi$

$\pi \models \varphi R \psi$ iff for all $i \geq 0$ $\pi^i \models \psi$, or there exists $j$, $0 \leq j < i$, such that $\pi^j \models \varphi$

A formula is *satisfied* in a Kripke structure $M$ if it is satisfied along a path of $M$ such that $s_0 \in S_0$. A formula is *valid* in a Kripke structure $M$ if it is satisfied along all paths of $M$ such that $s_0 \in S_0$. Given an LTL formula in positive normal form, its negation can be computed by recursively applying De Morgan's Laws and the following identities: $\neg X \varphi = X \neg\varphi$, and $\neg(\varphi \cup \psi) = \neg\varphi R \neg\psi$. Writing the negation in positive normal form does not change the length of the formula $|\varphi|$, if one assumes that for an atomic proposition $p$, $|p| = |\neg p|$.[1] Therefore we can efficiently solve the validity problem for $\varphi$ by checking the satisfiability of $\neg\varphi$. This is the approach that we adopt in the sequel.

Model checking of linear time property $\varphi$ is usually accomplished by constructing a Büchi automaton $B_{\neg\varphi}$ from the formula $\neg\varphi$. This automaton is often referred to as the *tableau* of the formula; it accepts runs that visit sets of *fair states* infinitely often. The product of the automaton $B_{\neg\varphi}$ and the model $M$ is then analyzed to see if it contains a so-called *fair cycle*. A fair cycle reachable from the initial states signals satisfaction of $\neg\varphi$; hence, it is a counterexample to the validity of $\varphi$ in $M$. When explicit enumeration is used, the run time of the model checking algorithm is linear in the size of the model and exponential in the length of the formula.

In the rest of this paper we shall have occasion to refer to logics other than LTL. Computational Tree Logic (CTL) is a branching time logic. Temporal operators are always preceded by universal or existential path quantifiers in CTL formulae. The expressiveness of CTL is not comparable to that of LTL: Properties like AG EF $p$ have no equivalent in LTL, while F G $p$ (fairness) is not expressible in CTL. Model checkers for

---

[1] This assumption is valid for BDD-based model checkers.

CTL usually allow the user to specify fairness constraints separately from the property. Both LTL and CTL are subsumed by CTL*, which is in turn subsumed by the $L\mu_2$ fragment of the $\mu$-calculus. The reader interested in the formal definition and a detailed analysis of these logics is referred to [12].

## 2.2 Symbolic Model Checking

The main difficulty to model checking comes from the size of the state space $S$. This is typically true also of LTL model checking, in spite of the exponential dependence of the runtime on the length of the formula, because the formulae of interest are usually short. *Symbolic model checking* [6, 26, 2] addresses this concern by representing sets of states *implicitly* via their *characteristic functions*. In this paper we consider BDD-based symbolic model checking, in which Binary Decision Diagrams [4] are used to represent the characteristic functions. Although almost all boolean functions have exponentially sized BDDs [27], symbolic model checkers have been successful on problems that vastly exceed the capacity of explicit enumeration algorithms. BDDs can be manipulated efficiently; in particular, algorithms have been devised for the computation of all the successors (*image* computation) or predecessors (*pre-image* computation) of a set of states according to a given transition relation [10, 5, 14, 31].

Symbolic model checking algorithms for various logics are based on the computation of fixpoints by repeated image or pre-image computations. In the relational $\mu$-calculus (see, for instance, [26]), the computation of the states reachable from $S_0$ is expressed by the formulae

$$\mathsf{EY}\, p = \lambda y.\exists x.T(x,y) \wedge p(x)$$
$$\mathsf{Rch}\, S_0 = \mu Z.S_0 \vee \mathsf{EY}\, Z \ ,$$

which prescribe a sequence of image computations. Symbolic LTL model checking, on the other hand, is normally based on the algorithm of Emerson and Lei [13] for the $L\mu_2$ fragment of $\mu$-calculus. If the acceptance condition of the automaton is described by a set of fair states, $C$, the set of states from which a fair cycle can be reached, Fair, is given by:

$$\mathsf{EX}\, p = \lambda x.\exists y.T(x,y) \wedge p(y)$$
$$\mathsf{E}p\, \mathsf{U}\, q = \mu Z.q \vee (p \wedge \mathsf{EX}\, Z)$$
$$\mathsf{Fair} = \nu Z.\mathsf{EX}\, \mathsf{E}(Z\, \mathsf{U}\, (Z \wedge C)) \ .$$

If Fair $\cap\, S_0 \neq \emptyset$ for $M \times B_{\neg\varphi}$, then there is a fair path, and the LTL formula $\varphi$ is not valid in $M$. The observation that Fair is the set of states that satisfy the CTL [9] formula **EG true** under the fairness constraint $C$ has led to the use of symbolic model checkers for fair CTL in LTL model checking [6, 8].

Many fixpoint computations used in symbolic model checking, including the two just mentioned, can be formulated both in terms of image computations (forward traversal of the state space) and in terms of pre-image computations (backward traversal). In recent times considerable attention has been devoted to the relative efficiency of the alternative formulations [19, 18, 17, 28].

Besides the direction of traversal of the state space, an important factor affecting the efficiency of symbolic model checking algorithms is the presence of multiple fixpoints, especially if nested. Thus, the computation of fair states is intrinsically more difficult than the computation of reachable states.

# 3   Classification of Tableaux

As outlined in Section 2.1, a linear time property can be checked by converting its negation into a Büchi automaton called the tableau of the property, composing the tableau with the model, and checking language emptiness. The last step of this procedure involves the computation of nested fixpoints and is therefore potentially expensive. The question naturally arises as to whether LTL model checkers can compete with CTL model checkers for those properties that can be expressed in both logics. Kupferman and Vardi [20, 21] call these properties *branchable* and observe that many of them translate into tableaux with special structure. They claim that an appropriate variant of the LTL model checking algorithm can then achieve efficiency comparable to that of CTL model checkers. In this section we recall the classification of [20] and refine it in a natural yet effective way.

Different tableau construction procedures have been proposed in the literature [24, 34, 6, 8, 15]. Even though the automata produced by these procedures for a given formula obviously accept the same language, they have different structures, and therefore are not equivalent from the point of view of the classification we propose. We discuss this issue at the end of this section.

A Büchi automaton is a quintuple $\langle \Sigma, Q, Q_0, \delta, F \rangle$, where $\Sigma$ is the input alphabet, $Q$ is the finite set of states, $Q_0 \subseteq Q$ is the set of initial states, $\delta : Q \times \Sigma \to 2^Q$ is the transition function, and $F \subseteq Q$ is the acceptance condition. An input word is accepted iff there is a run of the automaton on that word that visits $F$ infinitely often. We assume that the transition function is complete, that is $\delta(q, \sigma) \neq \emptyset$ for all $q \in Q$ and $\sigma \in \Sigma$.

A Büchi automaton is *weak* [20, 29] iff there exists a partition of $Q$ into $Q_1, \ldots, Q_n$ such that each $Q_i$ is either contained in $F$ or disjoint from it; in addition, the blocks of the partition are partially ordered so that the transitions of the automaton never move from $Q_i$ to $Q_j$ unless $Q_i \leq Q_j$.

**Theorem 1.** *The language of a weak Büchi automaton $\mathcal{A}$ is empty iff $\mathcal{A} \models \neg\mathsf{EFEG}\, F$.*

*Proof.* A run of a weak Büchi automaton that leaves a block $Q_i$ of the partition cannot enter it again. Hence, the only way for a run to visit a fair state infinitely often is to eventually be confined inside one $Q_i \subseteq F$. Such a run therefore is a witness for $\mathsf{EFEG}\, F$. Conversely, if $\mathcal{A}, s_0 \models \mathsf{EFEG}\, F$ for some $s_0 \in S_0$, then there is a fair run in $\mathcal{A}$ and its language is not empty. □

A Büchi automaton is *terminal* iff it is weak and the blocks of the partition contained in $F$ are maximal elements of the partial order.

**Theorem 2.** *The language of a terminal Büchi automaton $\mathcal{A}$ is empty iff $\mathcal{A} \models \neg\mathsf{EF}\, F$.*

*Proof.* An accepting run in a terminal Büchi automaton must reach a maximal block $Q_i$ of the partition, otherwise no fair state is visited. Conversely, a run that reaches a maximal block can always be extended to a fair run, because $\delta$ is complete. It is therefore necessary and sufficient for a fair run to reach a fair state. □

Theorems 1 and 2 provide the foundation for our model checking strategy. The CTL model checker is used to prove $\neg \text{EG true}$ under the fairness constraint $F$, $\neg \text{EFEG}\,F$, or $\neg \text{EF}\,\neg F$, depending on the classification of the automaton. Correctness follows from the fact that the composition of the model and a terminal Büchi automaton is a terminal Büchi automaton, and the composition of the model and a weak Büchi automaton is weak. Checking whether an automaton is weak or terminal can be done in polynomial time. The checking of the properties can be carried out by either backward or forward analysis. Forward analysis applied to terminal automata corresponds to reachability analysis.

As pointed out in [16], the Emerson-Lei algorithm, which is quadratic in the size of the state space, is often much slower in practice than reachability analysis and CTL model checking, which are linear. Our classification has the desirable effect of using the more efficient algorithms when possible.

Several variants of the tableau construction have been proposed in the literature. All are based on the identity $\varphi\,\text{U}\,\psi = \psi \vee (\varphi \wedge \text{X}\,(\varphi\,\text{U}\,\psi))$, but they differ in the details. Figure 1 shows the tableaux produced by the procedures of [8] (left) and [15] (center) for the formula $f = p\,\text{U}\,q$. It also shows a variant of the tableau of [15] (right) that has labels on the arcs instead of the states and a complete transition function.

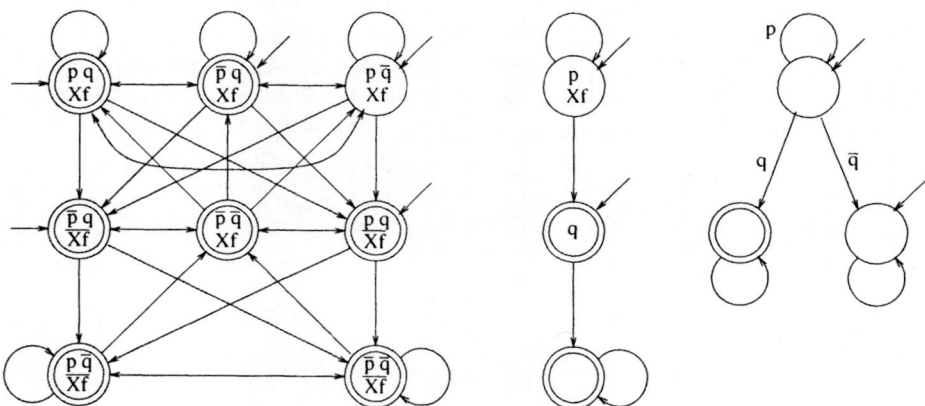

**Fig. 1.** Tableaux for $p\,\text{U}\,q$. Fair states are indicated by double circles, initial states have an extra incoming arrow, and negation is indicated by an overbar.

The construction of [8] identifies the elementary subformulae of the given formula $f$ ($p$, $q$, and $\text{X}\,f$ in our example) and creates one state in the tableau for each combination of elementary subformulae of $f$. It then adds a transition $(s, s')$ if, for all elementary subformulae $g$, either $X g$ holds in $s$ and $g$ holds in $s'$, or $X g$ does not hold in $s$ and $g$ does not hold in $s'$.

The procedure of [15] creates states of the tableau on the fly, starting with a node that represents $f$ and adding nodes according to the syntactic structure of the the formula.

The disparity in number of states is the most visible difference between the results of the two constructions, but it is of little consequence on the efficiency of symbolic model checking. In fact, since every atomic proposition appearing in $f$ also appears— possibly negated—in the label of each state, the left tableau shares the state variables for $p$ and $q$ with the model and only requires one additional bit for $X f$. The other two automata need two extra bits.

Another difference between the two constructions is of greater import for the efficiency of the model checker. The automaton on the left of Fig. 1 is not weak, unlike the other two (which are indeed terminal). The approach of adding all possible transitions to the automaton at once, instead of adding them as they become needed tends to create more paths in the tableau; hence, it tends to prevent the partial ordering of the states required for weakness.

Therefore, we use the construction of [15] modified to yield automata with labels on the arcs and complete transition functions as in [20]. These modifications allow us to easily express the automata in Verilog that we use as input language for our experiments. It should be noted that our choice is not optimal from the point of view of the number of state variables and transitions of the composition of the model and the property automaton.

# 4 Guided Search in Model Checking

## 4.1 Guided Search for the Computation of Least Fixpoints

In [32] it is shown that symbolic reachability analysis, and hence invariant checking, can be substantially sped up by applying *hints*. The hints are predicates on the inputs or state variables of the model. Their effect is to inhibit some transitions; it is obtained by conjoining the hints and the transition relation. Several hints may be applied in sequence. Therefore the computation of the reachable states is decomposed in the computation of a sequence of fixpoints—one for each hint.

**Theorem 3.** *Given a sequence of monotonic functionals* $\tau_1, \tau_2, \ldots, \tau_k$ *such that* $\tau_i \leq \tau_k$ *for* $0 < i < k$, *the sequence* $\rho_0, \rho_1, \ldots, \rho_k$ *of least fixpoints defined by*

$$\rho_0 = 0$$
$$\rho_i = \mu X . \rho_{i-1} \vee \tau_i(X), \quad 0 < i \leq k$$

*monotonically converges to* $\rho = \mu X . \tau_k(X)$; *that is,* $\rho_0 \leq \rho_1 \leq \cdots \leq \rho_k = \rho$.

*Proof.* We prove by induction that $\rho_i \leq \rho$. The basis is trivially established ($\rho_0 = 0 \leq \rho$). For the inductive step we have:

$$\rho_i = \mu X . \rho_{i-1} \vee \tau_i(X) \leq \mu X . \rho_{i-1} \vee \tau_k(X) = \mu X . \tau_k(X) ,$$

where the last equality follows from the inductive hypothesis and the properties of fix-points. The sequence is clearly monotonic, and for $i = k$ the inductive step shows that $\rho_k = \rho$. □

Decomposing the computation of a least fixpoint may have two main advantages; both are based on the fact that an appropriately chosen $\tau_i$ (i.e., a properly chosen hint) may make the computation of $\rho_i$ orders of magnitude faster than the direct computation of $\rho$ [32]. The first advantage is that one may not need to compute the whole sequence of fixpoints. For instance, a state that violates an invariant may be contained in $\rho_1$, in which case the rest of the computation can be avoided. The second advantage applies also to cases in which the computation of $\rho$ must be carried to completion. Indeed, it may be much more efficient to compute $\rho$ from $\rho_{k-1}$ than to compute it directly. In this latter respect symbolic guided search differs from explicit guided search [35], in which guidance is only used to accelerate the detection of states where invariants do not hold.

In [32] evidence is presented in support of the claim that finding good hints requires understanding of the system to be verified at a level comparable to that required to write functional tests for it. In this paper we extend the use of hints from invariant checking to LTL.

### 4.2   Guided Search for the Computation of Greatest Fixpoints

The method presented in [32] applies to the computation of least fixpoints. Least fix-points suffice to check invariants, but not for the properties of more expressive logics. In this section we therefore describe the extension of guided symbolic search to the computation of greatest fixpoints. Hints produce underapproximations of the transition relation; therefore, guided symbolic search can complement known methods [22, 25, 7, 23], when both lower bounds and upper bounds are required [30].

The main objective of the works just cited is to prove the desired property of the system on a simplified model. Our objective is complementary: We want to speed up the computation of the fixpoints for a given model, by addressing the computational bottlenecks; for instance, image computations that are too slow and memory consuming because of poor quantification schedule [14, 31].

Another possible reason for using underapproximations in greatest fixpoints is to deal with nested fixpoints. If a greatest fixpoint is nested in a least fixpoint, or vice versa, then by using underapproximations for both computations, one obtains an under-approximation of the result if either computation is restricted to a prefix of the sequence. (For instance, $\rho_0, \ldots, \rho_j$ for $j < k$ in the case of a least fixpoint.)

**Theorem 4.** *Given a sequence of monotonic functionals* $\tau_1, \tau_2, \ldots, \tau_k$ *such that* $\tau_i \leq \tau_k$ *for* $0 < i < k$, *the sequence* $\eta_0, \eta_1, \ldots, \eta_k$ *defined by*

$$\eta_0 = 0$$
$$\eta_i = \nu X.\eta_{i-1} \vee \tau_i(X), \quad 0 < i \leq k$$

*monotonically converges to* $\eta = \nu X.\tau_k(X)$; *that is,* $\eta_0 \leq \eta_1 \leq \cdots \leq \eta_k = \eta$.

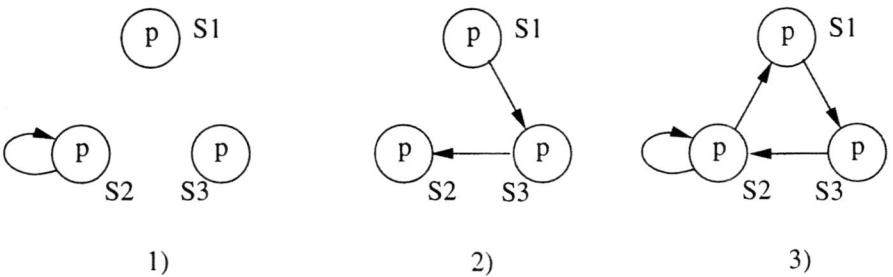

**Fig. 2.** Greatest fixpoint computation illustrating $\eta_i > \eta_{i-1} \vee \nu X.\tau_i(X)$.

The proof is along the lines of the proof of Theorem 3. It should be observed that $\eta_i \geq \eta_{i-1} \vee \nu X.\tau_i(X)$, and that the inequality can be strict, as shown in the example of Fig. 2. In the example $k = 3$. The rightmost graph can be though of as the original system, and the other two graphs as the systems obtained by applying hints. Let $\mathsf{EX}_i X$ compute the predecessors of the states in $X$ in the graph shown in Part $i$ of Fig. 2. Let $\tau_i = \lambda X.p \wedge \mathsf{EX}_i X$. With these definitions, $\eta$ is the set of states along infinite paths where $p$ always holds. One can verify that $\eta_2 = \{S1, S2, S3\} = \eta > \{S2\} = \eta_1 \vee \nu X.\tau_2(X)$.

Theorem 4 can speed up model checking in two ways. If the greatest fixpoint being computed is the outermost fixpoint, as in $\mathsf{EG\,true}$, then we may not have to compute all $k$ fixpoints in the sequence if there is indeed a fair cycle. In these cases, a procedure that yields a large subset of the fixpoint at a small fraction of the computational cost is desirable. This application of Theorem 4 is complementary to the approach of [16], which works best when there are no fair cycles.

In cases where convergence must be proved, Theorem 4 can still speed up computation if $R^+$ and $\eta^+$ are given upper bounds on the reachable states and the greatest fixpoint, and $\eta_i \geq R^+ \wedge \eta^+$ for $i < k$. This case occurs in the example of Fig. 2, in which $\eta_2$ equals the trivial upper bound on $\eta$ given by $S$ itself; hence, $\eta_3$ needs not be computed. Finally, if $R^+ \wedge \eta^+ > \eta_i$ for all $i < k$, it may still be that $\eta_{k-1} = \eta$. In this case, the last iteration of the computation of $\eta_k$ can be skipped because $\eta_{i-1}$ is a lower bound on $\eta_i$.

Comparing Theorems 3 and 4, the following observations are in order. First of all, Theorem 3 can be extended by not insisting on the convergence of all the fixpoints except the last. This is possible because the $j$-th iterate of the computation of $\rho_i$ contains $\rho_{i-1}$ and is contained in $\rho_i$. However, this is not the case of the greatest fixpoint computation. Another important difference is that knowledge of $\rho_{k-1}$ helps the computation of $\rho_k$ more than knowledge of $\eta_{k-1}$ helps the computation of $\eta_k$. In practice, application of Theorem 3 tends to be more effective than application of Theorem 4 when convergence must be reached.

# 5 Experimental Results

In this section we present preliminary experimental results that we have obtained with VIS 1.3 [3], extended to accept hints. CPU times are measured on an IBM Intellistation running Linux with an Intel Pentium II 400 MHz CPU and 1 GB of RAM.

We consider properties that can be expressed in both LTL and CTL. This gives us a means to contrast our decision procedure against the CTL decision procedure. The results can be found in Table 1. The leftmost column gives the model and the type of property. *Soap* is a model of a token-passing algorithm for distributed mutual exclusion [11]. The token is passed along a spanning tree of a network of processors. For this model we checked a liveness property of the form $G\,(p \to F\,q)$ and two safety properties of the form $G\,(p \to X\,(q\,R\,r))$ expressing the requirement that access to the resource is not granted to a processor unless the processor has requested it. The first of these two properties fails (error in the specification), while the second passes. *Gcd* is a model of a circuit computing the greatest common divisor of two integers; *Pcell* is a model of a production cell; *Palu* is a three-stage pipeline with an ALU and a register file; *Fpmult* is a floating point multiplier; finally, *NullModem* is a circuit to check the correctness of a simple UART and of the handshaking between the UART and a processor.

We ran all the applicable algorithms for each formula and compared CPU time and memory requirements. The table also reports the number of pre-images (EX) and images (EY) computed by each approach. These numbers indicate whether model checking used pure forward analysis (0 pre-images), pure backward analysis (0 images) or a combination of the two: reachability analysis followed by backward model checking. For each formula we checked, one of these three methods was clearly superior to the other two. Results are reported for that method. Some of the results could have been improved by using forward CTL [19], but for uniformity all experiments have been conducted using backward CTL only.

The importance of choosing the right algorithm is underlined by the results of Table 1, which were obtained with the same fixed variable order for all the runs of a given model and without hints. They confirm the observation of [20] about the comparable efficiency of CTL and LTL model checkers when the right algorithms are used for the latter. Notice, however, that experiments performed with dynamic variable reordering enabled may yield quite different results, simply because the orders end up being different. For formulae that fail, the ability to check the property on-the-fly may result in a substantial advantage to our algorithm.

*Nullmodem* is a special case. The property $G\,F\,p \lor F\,G\,q$ is not expressible in CTL without using fairness constraints. All three approaches used for that example use a fairness constraint and compute nested fixpoints. The example is included to show that there are cases in which the LTL model checking algorithm that uses an extra automaton is faster than the standard fair CTL algorithm.

We next examine the effects of applying hints. Results for invariant checking are reported in [32]; hence here we only consider properties of other types. Our current implementation only supports hints for properties that translate into terminal automata. Therefore Table 2 has results only for a subset of the experiments shown in Table 1.

The hint used in the two model checking experiments for the *Soap* model is to prevent some of the processors from issuing requests. In the case of the property that fails,

**Table 1.** Comparing model checking approaches for various LTL properties.

| experiment | procedure | time (sec) | EXs+ EYs | memory (MB) | peak BDD nodes |
|---|---|---|---|---|---|
| Soap (140 latches) | CTL | 580 | 55+45 | 635 | 19.4M |
| $G\,(p \to F\,q)$ | ¬EF EG fair | 639 | 56+45 | 644 | 18.8M |
| | ¬EG fair **true** | 9598 | 311+45 | 637 | 19.3M |
| Soap | CTL | 42 | 16+45 | 146 | 3.4M |
| $G\,(p \to X\,(q\,R\,r))$ | ¬EF fair | 8 | 0+13 | 43 | 0.8M |
| (failing) | ¬EF EG fair | 260 | 17+53 | 570 | 15.4M |
| | ¬EG fair **true** | 288 | 32+53 | 571 | 15.4M |
| Soap | CTL | 29 | 4+45 | 99 | 2.1M |
| $G\,(p \to X\,(q\,R\,r))$ | ¬EF fair | 78 | 0+45 | 300 | 6.0M |
| (passing) | ¬EF EG fair | 80 | 3+45 | 233 | 6.0M |
| | ¬EG fair **true** | 77 | 3+45 | 233 | 6.0M |
| Gcd (45 latches) | CTL | 1131 | 19+0 | 639 | 21.2M |
| $G\,(p \to X\,F\,q)$ | ¬EF EG fair | 291 | 19+0 | 591 | 15.0M |
| | ¬EG fair **true** | 8831 | 186+11 | 659 | 19.8M |
| Pcell (61 latches) | CTL | 3 | 47+66 | 23 | 120k |
| $G\,(p \to p\,U\,q)$ | ¬EF EG fair | 4 | 45+80 | 25 | 195k |
| | ¬EG fair **true** | 56 | 1252+80 | 73 | 973k |
| Palu (99 latches) | CTL | 2 | 5+0 | 23 | 228k |
| $G\,(p \to F\,q)$ | ¬EF EG fair | 3 | 6+0 | 25 | 285k |
| | ¬EG fair **true** | 3 | 12+0 | 26 | 394k |
| Fpmult (60 latches) | CTL | 0.2 | 5+0 | 14 | 12.0k |
| $G\,(p \to X\,X\,X\,q)$ | ¬EF fair | 2.9 | 0+6 | 15 | 53.9k |
| | ¬EF EG fair | 0.2 | 6+0 | 14 | 13.6k |
| | ¬EG fair **true** | 0.2 | 10+0 | 14 | 13.7k |
| NullModem (53 latches) | CTL | 1143 | 28800+388 | 49 | 387k |
| $G\,F\,p \lor F\,G\,q$ | ¬EF EG fair | 1225 | 28623+388 | 42 | 310k |
| | ¬EG fair **true** | 797 | 17250+388 | 91 | 1120k |

**Table 2.** Effects of guided search. The lines without hints are taken from Table 1.

| experiment | procedure | time (sec) | EXs+ EYs | memory (MB) | peak BDD nodes |
|---|---|---|---|---|---|
| Soap $G\,(p \to X\,(q\,R\,r))$ | no | 7.5 | 0+13 | 43 | 773k |
| (failing) | yes | 1.0 | 0+13 | 17 | 39k |
| Soap $G\,(p \to X\,(q\,R\,r))$ | no | 78 | 0+45 | 300 | 6.0M |
| (passing) | yes | 27 | 0+60 | 90 | 2.0M |
| Fpmult $G\,(p \to X\,X\,X\,q)$ | no | 2.9 | 0+6 | 15 | 53.9k |
| | yes | 1.9 | 0+15 | 15 | 53.6k |

it is indeed possible to generate a counterexample when requests from one processor only are enabled. Considerable speed-up was obtained with a generic hint not specifically targeted at the property. Conversely, the hint that is optimal for the property that fails (only one processor is enabled) is not optimal for the property that passes, but still improves runtime with respect to the standard algorithm. The time to devise the hint was small compared to the time required to formulate the properties. Still, larger test cases than those presented in Table 2 will be required to assess the practical impact of guided search in symbolic model checking.

## 6 Conclusions and Future Work

In this paper we have presented an efficient algorithm for BDD-based LTL model checking based on guided search and specialized decision procedures for classes of automata. Our algorithm improves on the standard approach in both theory and practice: The selection of the most appropriate decision procedure for an LTL property decreases the asymptotic complexity of the model checking algorithm from quadratic in the size of the state space to linear in many cases, while our preliminary experimental results show that both classification of the automata and the use of hints can have large impacts on the runtime and memory requirements.

Considerable work remains to be done besides the completion of the experimental evaluation of our algorithm. We outline a few of the issues that we plan to explore.

Given an algorithm for CTL model checking with fairness constraints and a tableau construction procedure, a model checker for CTL* is readily available. Also, given the ability to compute least and greatest fixpoints, a $\mu$-calculus model checker can be built. Therefore, our guided search approach can be applied to the logics most commonly used in model checking.

We have seen that LTL model checking may be faster than CTL model checking for the same property, because of the reduction in the number and alternation depth of fixpoints. The opposite may also occur, due to the additional state variables brought by the automaton that may increase the sizes of the BDDs manipulated by the model checker. Direct translation to $\mu$-calculus [17] should therefore be considered as an alternative to composition with the automaton. A better understanding of the relation between different tableau construction procedures is also desirable.

The use of hints is not restricted to BDD-based approaches, but should apply to SAT-based model checking as well [2]. Finally, partial automation of the extraction of hints from the model and the property appears as a worthwhile research goal.

## References

1. I. Beer, S. Ben-David, and A. Landver. On-the-fly model checking of RCTL formulas. In A. J. Hu and M. Y. Vardi, editors, *Tenth Conference on Computer Aided Verification (CAV'98)*, pages 184–194. Springer-Verlag, Berlin, 1998. LNCS 1427.
2. A. Biere, A. Cimatti, E. Clarke, and Y. Zhu. Symbolic model checking without BDDs. Unpublished manuscript, October 1998.

3. R. K. Brayton et al. VIS: A system for verification and synthesis. In T. Henzinger and R. Alur, editors, *Eigth Conference on Computer Aided Verification (CAV'96)*, pages 428–432. Springer-Verlag, Rutgers University, 1996. LNCS 1102.

4. R. E. Bryant. Graph-based algorithms for boolean function manipulation. *IEEE Transactions on Computers*, C-35(8):677–691, August 1986.

5. J. R. Burch, E. M. Clarke, and D. E. Long. Representing circuits more efficiently in symbolic model checking. In *Proceedings of the Design Automation Conference*, pages 403–407, San Francisco, CA, June 1991.

6. J. R. Burch, E. M. Clarke, K. L. McMillan, D. L. Dill, and L. J. Hwang. Symbolic model checking: $10^{20}$ states and beyond. In *Proceedings of the Fifth Annual Symposium on Logic in Computer Science*, June 1990.

7. H. Cho, G. D. Hachtel, E. Macii, B. Plessier, and F. Somenzi. Algorithms for approximate FSM traversal based on state space decomposition. *IEEE Transactions on Computer-Aided Design*, 15(12):1465–1478, December 1996.

8. E. Clarke, O. Grumberg, and K. Hamaguchi. Another look at LTL model checking. In D. L. Dill, editor, *Sixth Conference on Computer Aided Verification (CAV'94)*, pages 415–427. Springer-Verlag, Berlin, 1994. LNCS 818.

9. E. M. Clarke and E. A. Emerson. Design and synthesis of synchronization skeletons using branching time temporal logic. In *Proceedings Workshop on Logics of Programs*, pages 52–71, Berlin, 1981. Springer-Verlag. LNCS 131.

10. O. Coudert, C. Berthet, and J. C. Madre. Verification of sequential machines using boolean functional vectors. In L. Claesen, editor, *Proceedings IFIP International Workshop on Applied Formal Methods for Correct VLSI Design*, pages 111–128, Leuven, Belgium, November 1989.

11. J. Desel and E. Kindler. Proving correctness of distributed algorithms using high-level Petri nets: A case study. In *International Conference on Application of Concurrency to System Design*, Aizu, Japan, March 1998.

12. E. A. Emerson. Temporal and modal logic. In van Leeuwen [33], chapter 16, pages 995–1072.

13. E. A. Emerson and C.-L. Lei. Efficient model checking in fragments of the propositional mu-calculus. In *Proceedings of the First Annual Symposium of Logic in Computer Science*, pages 267–278, June 1986.

14. D. Geist and I. Beer. Efficient model checking by automated ordering of transition relation partitions. In D. L. Dill, editor, *Sixth Conference on Computer Aided Verification (CAV'94)*, pages 299–310, Berlin, 1994. Springer-Verlag. LNCS 818.

15. R. Gerth, D. Peled, M. Y. Vardi, and P. Wolper. Simple on-the-fly automatic verification of linear temporal logic. In *Protocol Specification, Testing, and Verification*, pages 3–18. Chapman & Hall, 1995.

16. R. H. Hardin, R. P. Kurshan, S. K. Shukla, and M. Y. Vardi. A new heuristic for bad cycle detection using BDDs. In O. Grumberg, editor, *Ninth Conference on Computer Aided Verification (CAV'97)*, pages 268–278. Springer-Verlag, Berlin, 1997. LNCS 1254.

17. T. A. Henzinger, O. Kupferman, and S. Qadeer. From *pre*-historic to *post*-modern symbolic model checking. In A. J. Hu and M. Y. Vardi, editors, *Tenth Conference on Computer Aided Verification (CAV'98)*, pages 195–206. Springer-Verlag, Berlin, 1998. LNCS 1427.

18. H. Iwashita and T. Nakata. Forward model checking techniques oriented to buggy designs. In *Proceedings of the International Conference on Computer-Aided Design*, pages 400–405, San Jose, CA, November 1997.

19. H. Iwashita, T. Nakata, and F. Hirose. CTL model checking based on forward state traversal. In *Proceedings of the International Conference on Computer-Aided Design*, pages 82–87, San Jose, CA, November 1996.

20. O. Kupferman and M. Y. Vardi. Freedom, weakness, and determinism: From linear-time to branching-time. In *Proc. 13th IEEE Symposium on Logic in Computer Science*, June 1998.

21. O. Kupferman and M. Y. Vardi. Relating linear and branching model checking. In *IFIP Working Conference on Programming Concepts and Methods*, New York, June 1998. Chapman & Hall.

22. R. P. Kurshan. *Computer-Aided Verification of Coordinating Processes*. Princeton University Press, Princeton, NJ, 1994.

23. W. Lee, A. Pardo, J. Jang, G. Hachtel, and F. Somenzi. Tearing based abstraction for CTL model checking. In *Proceedings of the International Conference on Computer-Aided Design*, pages 76–81, San Jose, CA, November 1996.

24. O. Lichtenstein and A. Pnueli. Checking that finite state concurrent programs satisfy their linear specification. In *Proceedings of the Twelfth Annual ACM Symposium on Principles of Programming Languages*, New Orleans, January 1985.

25. D. E. Long. *Model Checking, Abstraction, and Compositional Verification*. PhD thesis, Carnegie-Mellon University, July 1993.

26. K. L. McMillan. *Symbolic Model Checking*. Kluwer Academic Publishers, Boston, MA, 1994.

27. C. Meinel and T. Theobald. *Algorithms and Data Structures in VLSI Design*. Springer, Berlin, 1998.

28. I.-H. Moon, J.-Y. Jang, G. D. Hachtel, F. Somenzi, C. Pixley, and J. Yuan. Approximate reachability don't cares for CTL model checking. In *Proceedings of the International Conference on Computer-Aided Design*, pages 351–358, San Jose, CA, November 1998.

29. D. E. Muller, A. Saoudi, and P. E. Schupp. Weak alternating automata give a simple explanation of why most temporal and dynamic logics are decidable in exponential time. In *Proceedings of the 3rd IEEE Symposium on Logic in Computer Science*, pages 422–427, Edinburgh, UK, July 1988.

30. A. Pardo and G. D. Hachtel. Incremental CTL model checking using BDD subsetting. In *Proceedings of the Design Automation Conference*, pages 457–462, San Francisco, CA, June 1998.

31. R. K. Ranjan, A. Aziz, R. K. Brayton, B. F. Plessier, and C. Pixley. Efficient BDD algorithms for FSM synthesis and verification. Presented at IWLS95, Lake Tahoe, CA., May 1995.

32. K. Ravi. *Adaptive Techniques to Improve State Space Search in Formal Verification*. PhD thesis, University of Colorado, Department of Electrical and Computer Engineering, 1999.

33. J. van Leeuwen, editor. *Handbook of Theoretical Computer Science*. The MIT Press/Elsevier, Amsterdam, 1990.

34. M. Y. Vardi and P. Wolper. An automata-theoretic approach to automatic program verification. In *Proceedings of the First Symposium on Logic in Computer Science*, pages 322–331, Cambridge, UK, June 1986.

35. C. H. Yang and D. L. Dill. Validation with guided search of the state space. In *Proceedings of the Design Automation Conference*, pages 599–604, San Francisco, CA, June 1998.

# Stutter-Invariant Languages, $\omega$-Automata, and Temporal Logic

Kousha Etessami

Bell Labs
Murray Hill, NJ 07974
kousha@research.bell-labs.com

**Abstract.** Temporal logic and $\omega$-automata are two of the common frameworks for specifying properties of reactive systems in modern verification tools. In this paper we unify these two frameworks in the linear time setting for the specification of stutter-invariant properties, which are used in the context of partial-order verification.

We will observe a simple variant of linear time propositional temporal logic (LTL) for expressing exactly the stutter-invariant $\omega$-regular languages. The complexity of, and algorithms for, all the relevant decision procedures for this logic remain essentially the same as with ordinary LTL. In particular, satisfiability remains PSPACE-complete and temporal formulas can be converted to at most exponential sized $\omega$-automata. More importantly, we show that the improved practical algorithms for conversion of LTL formulas to automata, used in model-checking tools such as SPIN, which typically produce much smaller than worst-case output, can be modified to incorporate this extension to LTL with the same benefits. In this way, the specification mechanism in temporal logic-based tools that employ partial-order reduction can be extended to incorporate all stutter-invariant $\omega$-regular properties.

## 1 Introduction

Today, $\omega$-automata and $\omega$-regular languages are used in verification tools to both describe the models of reactive systems as well as to specify the properties being verified. While $\omega$-automata typically form the basis for describing the system, a popular alternative for specifying properties is temporal logic [16], which offers an intuitive language for describing relationships between the occurrence of events over time. Linear time temporal logic, which we deal with in this paper, is used as a specification language in tools including SPIN [6], as well as more recent versions of SMV [12]. Standard linear time propositional temporal logic (LTL) can only express a strict subset of the $\omega$-regular properties. To correct this, various remedies have been proposed (see [23]).

Stutter-invariant languages ([9]) are used in the context of partial-order verification [21, 5, 7, 14]. In order to take full advantage of partial-order reduction, the properties that are specified need to be *stutter-invariant* (formal definitions will be supplied later). One way to assure that only stutter-invariant properties are specified is to restrict linear temporal logic, LTL, to only those formulas without the "next" operator. This is precisely the approach currently employed in the tool SPIN [6], which exploits partial-order reduction, and uses "next"-free LTL to specify properties.

LTL without "next" has been shown to accept all stutter-invariant LTL expressible properties [15]. However, the fact remains that LTL can not express all $\omega$-regular properties, and similarly, LTL without "next" can not specify all stutter-invariant $\omega$-regular properties.

In this paper we provide a simple variant of LTL for expressing all the stutter-invariant $\omega$-regular languages, based on an equally simple temporal logic for all $\omega$-regular languages. Significantly, the complexity of the relevant decision procedures remain the same as with ordinary LTL. In particular, satisfiability remains PSPACE-complete, as does model checking for negated formulas. Equally important, a practical algorithm for converting LTL formulas to automata ([4]), used in the tool SPIN [6], which typically produces much smaller than worst-case output, can be converted to incorporate this extension to LTL with basically the same benefits. As described in the conclusion, a preliminary version of this translation has been implemented with satisfactory results.

The logics we will describe are variants of Existential Quantified Linear Propositional Temporal Logic (EQLTL). Wolper [23] considered extensions of LTL with operators based on automata and right-linear grammars. He showed that this extended logic defines exactly the $\omega$-regular languages and has the desired complexity. However, the syntax of a logic augmented with grammars is cumbersome and more akin to automata specifications. Sistla, Vardi, and Wolper, [19], considered variants of Wopler's logic as well as Quantified Propositional Linear Temporal Logic (QLTL), where they provided complexity bounds for the satisfiability problem for formulas in the quantifier alternation hierarchy, including EQLTL. They showed, as part of this hierarchy, that QLTL satisfiability has non-elementary complexity and EQLTL satisfiability is PSPACE-complete. Kupferman, [8], studied branching time temporal logics with existentially quantified propositions.

It follows from Büchi's original theorem ([1]) that EQLTL already captures the $\omega$-regular languages, and hence also all of QLTL. The properties of EQLTL as a logic, in particular the complexity of decision procedures for the logic as well as its simple syntactic normal forms, make it worthy of closer examination.

The main subject of this paper is a *stutter-invariant* version of EQLTL, which we call SI-EQLTL. We will show that SI-EQLTL expresses precisely the stutter-invariant $\omega$-regular languages. In proving this, we will also provide a simple normal form for $\omega$-automata that accept stutter-invariant languages. We will then describe an efficient translation algorithm from the logic into automata.

Formal definitions of all the mentioned notions are provided in the next section. Section 3 overviews EQLTL and its correspondence to the $\omega$-regulars, preparing the way for section 4, where SI-EQLTL and stutter-invariant languages are considered. Section 5 covers the improved translation algorithm to automata, and in section 6 we conclude and describe an implementation of this translation.

**Note:** After publication of this paper as a technical report ([3]), I have been informed by D. Peled that in [17] A. Rabinovich has independently obtained a characterization of the stutter-invariant $\omega$-regular languages in terms of Lamport's Temporal Logic of Actions ([10]). Although TLA semantics generally differ substantially from LTL, his results appear to amount to the fact that SI-QLTL captures the stutter-invariant languages. But the complexity of the critical decision procedures for SI-QLTL remain non-elementary because of nested negation, and entire the reason we focus on SI-EQLTL is because of the complexity of these procedures.

## 2 Definitions and Background

Let $\mathcal{L}_{LTL}^P$ denote the set of LTL formulas over propositional symbols $P = \{p_1, \ldots, p_r\}$. These are defined according to the following inductive rules:

- $p_i \in \mathcal{L}_{LTL}^P$ for each $p_i \in P$.
- $\neg\varphi$, $\varphi \vee \psi$, $\Diamond\varphi$, $\bigcirc\varphi$, $\varphi\mathcal{U}\psi \in \mathcal{L}_{LTL}^P$, for $\varphi, \psi \in \mathcal{L}_{LTL}^P$.

We extend LTL by allowing quantification over new propositions $q_1, q_2, \ldots$. We define both the existential and universal fragment of *Quantified (propositional) Linear Temporal Logic (QLTL)*. Formulas in $\mathcal{L}_{EQLTL}^P$, and $\mathcal{L}_{AQLTL}^P$, are defined, respectively, by the following additional rule:

- $\exists q_1 \ldots \exists q_k \varphi \in \mathcal{L}_{EQLTL}^P$, for $\varphi \in \mathcal{L}_{LTL}^{P \cup Q}$, $k \in \mathbb{N}$.
- $\forall q_1 \ldots \forall q_k \varphi \in \mathcal{L}_{AQLTL}^P$, for $\varphi \in \mathcal{L}_{LTL}^{P \cup Q}$, $k \in \mathbb{N}$.

We define the semantics of EQLTL and AQLTL, over $\omega$-words and over Kripke structures. Let our alphabet be $\Sigma_P = 2^P$. An $\omega$-**word** $w = w_0 w_1 w_2 \ldots \in \Sigma_P^\omega$ is a sequence of characters $w_i \in \Sigma_P$, where $i$ ranges over $\mathbb{N} = \{0, 1, 2, \ldots\}$. Since we allow quantification over new propositional variables, we will also allow enlargement of our alphabet. Given $P'$, such that $P \subseteq P'$, and given a character $a \in \Sigma_{P'}$, we define $a|_P \doteq \{p_i \in P \mid p_i \in a\}$. Let $w$ and $w'$ be $\omega$-words over the alphabets $\Sigma_P$ and $\Sigma_{P'}$, respectively. We say that $w'$ is an *extension* of $w$ iff $w_i = w_i'|_P$ for all $i \in \mathbb{N}$.

Given a word $w = w_0 w_1 w_2 \ldots$, and given a position $i \in \mathbb{N}$, we let $(w, i) \models \varphi$ denote the fact that $\varphi$ is true on $w$ at position $i$, defined inductively as usual, with the following semantics for propositional quantification:

1. $(w, i) \models \exists q \varphi$ if there is an extension $w' \in (\Sigma_{P \cup \{q\}})^\omega$ of $w$ such that $(w', i) \models \varphi$.
2. $(w, i) \models \forall q \varphi$ if for all extensions $w' \in (\Sigma_{P \cup \{q\}})^\omega$ of $w$, $(w', i) \models \varphi$.

A *language* over $\Sigma$ is a set $L \subseteq \Sigma^\omega$. A formula $\varphi$ is said to *express* the language $L(\varphi) = \{w \mid (w, 0) \models \varphi\}$. We let **EQLTL** stand for the languages $\bigcup_P \{L(\psi) \mid \psi \in \mathcal{L}_{EQLTL}^P\}$, and we assume analogous definitions for the other logics.

We will define a variant of EQLTL that captures precisely the *stutter-invariant* $\omega$-regular languages. Before we define what stutter-invariance means, let us define the logic. A word $w'$ is a **harmonious** extension of the word $w$, if $w'$ is an extension of $w$ such that, for all $i \in \mathbb{N}$, if $w_i = w_{i+1}$ then $w'_i = w'_{i+1}$. We define a restricted quantifier $\exists^h q\varphi$, which differs from ordinary quantification in the following way:

1. $(w, i) \models \exists^h q\varphi$ iff there is a harmonious extension $w' \in (\Sigma_{P\cup\{q\}})^\omega$ of $w$ such that $(w', i) \models \varphi$.
2. $(w, i) \models \forall^h q\varphi$ if for all harmonious extensions $w' \in (\Sigma_{P\cup\{q\}})^\omega$ of $w$, $(w', i) \models \varphi$.

We define *stutter-invariant* EQLTL (AQLTL), denoted **SI-EQLTL (SI-AQLTL)**, by replacing existential (universal) quantification of propositions with the harmonious quantification defined by $\exists^h$ ($\forall^h$), and by disallowing the use of the $\bigcirc$ operator in formulas. Thus, SI-EQLTL formulas are those of the form: $\exists^h q_1, \ldots, q_k \varphi$ where $\varphi$ is a $\bigcirc$-free LTL formula.

A *Kripke structure* $\mathcal{K} = (S, R, \kappa)$ over the alphabet $2^P$ is a set S of states, together with a transition relation $R \subseteq S \times S$, and a labeling function $\kappa : S \to 2^P$. Let $\pi = s_0 s_1, \ldots \in S^\omega$ be a sequence of states of $\mathcal{K}$. Extending the definition of $\kappa$ to sequences, the sequence $\pi$ defines an $\omega$-word $\kappa(\pi) \doteq \kappa(s_0)\kappa(s_1) \ldots \in \Sigma_P^\omega$. Given an initial state $s_{init}$, we will say that a sequence $\pi$ is a *proper sequence* with respect to $(\mathcal{K}, s_{init})$ if $s_0 = s_{init}$ and $(s_i, s_{i+1}) \in R$, for all $i$. We now define what it means for a formula $\varphi$ to be satisfied by a Kripke structure, given an initial state $s_{init}$:

- $(\mathcal{K}, s_{init}) \models \varphi$ if for every proper sequence $\pi$ of $(\mathcal{K}, s_{init})$, $(\kappa(\pi), 0) \models \varphi$.

We now briefly recall the terminology for $\omega$-regular languages and $\omega$-automata. A *Büchi automaton* is $A = (Q, \Sigma, \delta, F, Q_{start})$, where $Q$ is a set of states, $\Sigma$ an alphabet, $\delta \subseteq Q \times \Sigma \times Q$ is a transition relation, $F \subseteq Q$ a set of final states, and $Q_{start} \subseteq Q$ is a set of start states. Given a word $w$, a *run* $r$ of $A$ on $w$ is a sequence of states $q_0, q_1, \ldots$, such that $q_0 \in Q_{start}$, $q_i \in Q$, and $(q_i, w_i, q_{i+1}) \in \delta$, for all $i$. Let $inf(r)$ denote the set of states that occur infinitely often in $r$. $A$ is said to *accept* an $\omega$-word $w$ from the alphabet $\Sigma$ if there is a run $r$ of $A$ on $w$, such that there is some state $q \in F$ which occurs infinitely often on this run, i.e. $F \cap inf(r) \neq \emptyset$. This is called the *Büchi acceptance condition*. Let $\mathbf{L}(\mathbf{A})$ be the the set of $\omega$-words accepted by $A$. The $\omega$-**regular** languages are the class of languages $\{L(A) | A$ a Büchi automaton $\}$.

Another acceptance criterion defines a *Muller automaton* $A = (Q, \Sigma, \delta, \mathcal{F}, Q_{start})$. Here, instead of one set $F$ of final states, we are given a collection $\mathcal{F} \subseteq 2^Q$, and the Muller acceptance condition states that there exists a run $r$ of $A$ on $w$ such that $inf(r) \in \mathcal{F}$. It is easy to convert Büchi acceptance to Muller acceptance, and, conversely, it is a well known theorem of McNaughton [13] that Muller automata accept precisely the $\omega$-regular languages.

Given a word $w = w_0 w_1 \ldots$, and given function $f : \mathbb{N} \mapsto \mathbb{N}^+$ from the natural numbers to the positive natural numbers, let:

$$w[f] \doteq w_0^{f(0)} w_1^{f(1)} w_2^{f(2)} \ldots$$

Here, $w_i^n$ is shorthand for the concatenation of $n$ copies of the character $w_i$. A language $L$ is **stutter-invariant**[1] if, for any $\omega$-words $w = w_0 w_1 \ldots w_i \ldots$, and for any $f$

$$w \in L \iff w[f] \in L$$

An $\omega$-word $w$ is *stutter-free* if for all $i \geq 0$, $w_i \neq w_{i+1}$ or $w_i = w_j$ for all $j \geq i$.

**Proposition 1.** *Let $L$ and $L'$ be stutter-invariant languages. Then $L' = L$ iff they contain exactly the same stutter-free words.*

The stutter-invariant $\omega$-regular languages are a strictly larger class than the stutter-invariant LTL definable languages:

**Proposition 2.** *The stutter-invariant language, over $\Sigma = \{a, b\}$:*

$$L = \{w \mid \text{the substring } ab \text{ occurs an odd number of times in } w\}$$

*is not LTL definable, but is $\omega$-regular.*

## 3  EQLTL and the $\omega$-regular languages

It follows from the proof of Büchi's theorem and known results about LTL, that EQLTL captures exactly the $\omega$-regular languages. In this section we will look carefully at this correspondence. This will facilitate our proof in the next section that a variant of this logic captures the stutter-invariant $\omega$-regular languages.

**Theorem 1.** *(follows [1] & [18]. See also [19].) EQLTL defines exactly the $\omega$-regular languages.*

*Proof.* $\Leftarrow$. Given an automaton $A = (Q = \{q_1, \ldots, q_k\}, \Sigma_P, \delta, F, s)$, we write an $EQLTL$ formula that expresses $L(A)$. This is just the easy direction of Büchi's theorem: we "guess" an accepting run, and verify it, using temporal logic instead of first-order logic. We modify things slightly to facilitate the stutter-invariant version of this translation.

$$\varphi \equiv \exists q_1, \ldots, q_k (\Box(\bigwedge_{i \neq j} \neg(q_i \wedge q_j)) \wedge \tag{1}$$

$$(\bigvee_{\{(q_i, a, q_j) \in \delta \mid q_i \in Q_{start}\}} (\bigwedge_{p_l \in a} p_l \wedge \bigwedge_{p_r \notin a} \neg p_r) \wedge q_j) \wedge \tag{2}$$

$$\Box(\bigvee_{(q_i, a, q_j) \in \delta} (q_i \wedge \bigcirc(\bigwedge_{p_l \in a} p_l \wedge \bigwedge_{p_r \notin a} \neg p_r) \wedge \bigcirc q_j) \wedge \tag{3}$$

$$\bigvee_{q_j \in F} \Box\Diamond q_j \tag{4}$$

---

[1] This definition differs slightly from previous definitions in the literature, e.g., in [15], but is equivalent, and perhaps somewhat simpler conceptually because we avoid introducing the notion of stutter equivalence in order to get at the notion of stutter invariance.

$\Rightarrow$. Given an EQLTL formula $\varphi = \exists q_1, \ldots, q_k \psi$, let $A_\psi$ be a Büchi automaton for $\psi$ (see [18, 22, 2]). We construct $A_\varphi$, with the same set of states, by projection from $A_\psi$: for any edge $(Q, a, Q') \in \delta_{A_\psi}$, where $a = \{p_{i_1}, \ldots, p_{i_r}, q_{i_1}, \ldots, q_{i_l}\}$, put the edge $(Q, a', Q')$ in $\delta_{A_\varphi}$, where $a' = \{p_{i_1}, \ldots, p_{i_r}\}$. $\square$

**Corollary 1.** *(see [20]) Every EQLTL formula $\varphi$ is equivalent to one in the following normal form (note only one quantified proposition):*

$$\varphi' = \exists q \, \psi$$

*where $\psi$ is an LTL formula without the "Until" operator $\mathcal{U}$.*

*Moreover, there is a polynomial $p$, such that for an automaton $A$, there is a normal form formula $\varphi_A$, $L(\varphi_A) = L(A)$, such that $|\varphi_A| = p(|A|)$.*

The proof is an adaptation of [20]. We can readily eliminate the $\mathcal{U}$ operator because the formula $\varphi$ in the proof of Theorem 1 contains none. Next we observe the computation complexity of the associated decision procedures.

**Corollary 2.**

1. *([19]) The satisfiability problem for EQLTL is PSPACE-complete.*
2. *An EQLTL formula $\varphi$ can be translated to an equivalent Büchi automaton of size $2^{O(|\varphi|)}$, in time proportional to the size of the output.*
3. *Model checking, given a Kripke structure $K$ and the negation of an EQLTL formula, or given an AQLTL formula, is PSPACE-complete.*

## 4  Stutter-invariant $\omega$-regular languages and SI-EQLTL

Now we prove a result analogous to Theorem 1 for SI-EQLTL. First, we provide a normal form for automata that accept a stutter-invariant language.

**Definition 1.** *A Muller automaton $A' = (Q', \delta', \{q'_{start}\}, \mathcal{F}')$ is a **stutter-invariant (SI) automaton** if every state is reachable from $q'_{start}$, and all of the following syntactic properties are satisfied, for each state $q$ of $A'$, $q \neq q'_{start}$:*

1. *All incoming edges to $q$ are labeled with the same character, $a_q$.*
2. *$(q, a_q, q) \in \delta'$, and $(q, b, q) \notin \delta'$ for $b \neq a_q$.*
3. *$(q, a_q, q') \notin \delta'$ for $q' \neq q$.*
4. *Moreover, the exceptional start state $q'_{start}$ has no incoming edges.*

A cleaner, equivalent, way to view such automata is as Kripke structures with (Muller) acceptance conditions, and a given set of start states. Viewed this way, an SI automaton then amounts to a Kripke structure with the following two additional properties:

1. Every state $s$ has a self loop, i.e., $\forall s \in S, R(s, s)$.
2. $\forall s \neq s' \in S$, if $R(s, s')$ then $\kappa(s) \neq \kappa(s')$.

**Proposition 3.** *An SI automaton accepts a stutter-invariant language.*

**Lemma 1.** *If $L(A)$ is stutter-invariant then $L(A) = L(A')$, where $A'$ is a SI automaton. Moreover, we can pick $A'$ such that $|A'| \leq O(|A| \times |\Sigma|)$.*

*Proof.* We define $A'$ to mimic $A$, except that a state of $A'$ remembers the last-seen character. In addition, we need some extra surgery in order not to allow both arrival and departure from a state using the same character.

Given $A = (Q, \delta, Q_{start}, F)$, we define $A' = ((Q \times \Sigma) \cup \{q'_{start}\} \cup \{q_a^{new} \mid a \in \Sigma\}, \delta', \{q'_{start}\}, \mathcal{F}')$:

1. $((q, a), b, (q', c)) \in \delta'$ iff ($b = c \neq a$ and $(q, b, q') \in \delta$) or ($b = c = a$ and $q = q'$)
2. $((q, a), b, q_c^{new}) \in \delta'$ iff ($b = c \neq a$ and starting at state $q$ in $A$ there exists an accepting run on the word $b^\omega$).
3. $(q_a^{new}, b, q_c^{new}) \in \delta'$ iff $a = b = c$.
4. $(q'_{start}, a, (q_2, b)) \in \delta'$ iff $a = b$ and $(q_1, a, q_2) \in \delta$ for some $q_1 \in Q_{start}$.

Now, the accepting sets are given by: $\mathcal{F}' = \{F' \subseteq Q \times \Sigma \mid |F'| > 1 \wedge \exists (q, a) \in F' \text{ s.t. } q \in F\} \cup \{\{(q, a)\} \mid q \in F \wedge (q, a, q) \in \delta\} \cup \{\{q_a^{new}\} \mid a \in \Sigma\}$.

By inspection, $A'$ is an SI automaton. By Proposition 3 and Proposition 1 we need only show that $L(A)$ and $L(A')$ contain the same stutter-free words.

*Claim.* For any stutter-free word $w$, there is an accepting run $r$ of $A$ on $w$ if and only if there is an accepting run $r'$ of $A'$ on $w$.

We must omit the proof of the claim, which splits things into two cases: either (1) $w = w_0 w_1, \ldots w_i^\omega$, or (2) $w = w_0 w_1, \ldots$, where there are never two consecutive occurrences of the same character. The claim concludes the lemma, as $A'$ satisfies all the required conditions. $\square$

**Theorem 2.** *SI-EQLTL defines exactly the stutter-invariant $\omega$-regular languages.*

*Proof.* $\subseteq$: First, a SI-EQLTL formula $\psi = \exists^h q_1, \ldots, q_k \varphi$ can only express a stutter-invariant language. To see this, consider $w$ and $w[f]$ for any $f : \mathbb{N} \mapsto \mathbb{N}^+$.

*Claim.* $w \in L(\psi)$ if and only if $w[f] \in L(\psi)$.

*Proof.* $\Rightarrow$. Suppose $w \in L(\psi)$, then there is a harmonious extension $v$ of $w$ such that $v \in L(\varphi)$. But the $\bigcirc$-free LTL formula, $\varphi$, accepts a stutter-invariant language ([15]), and thus since $v[f]$ is a harmonious extension of $w[f]$, and $v[f] \in L(\varphi)$, it follows that $w[f] \in L(\psi)$.

$\Leftarrow$. Suppose $w[f] \in L(\psi)$. Thus there is a harmonious extension $v[f]$ of $w[f]$ such that $v[f] \in L(\varphi)$. But, since $L(\varphi)$ is stutter-invariant, it must again be the case that $v$ is a harmonious extension of $w$ such that $v \in L(\varphi)$, and hence $w \in L(\psi)$. $\square$

Now, to see that $L(\psi)$ is $\omega$-regular: Let $A_{guess} = (Q_{guess} = 2^{P \cup \{q_1, \ldots, q_k\}} \cup \{q_{start}\}, \delta_{guess}, \{q_{start}\}, Q_{guess})$ be an automaton which has a transition $\delta_{guess}(q, a, q')$ if and only if

1. $q' = a$, (note: states, as well as transition labels, are denoted by sets of propositions).
2. If $a|_P = q|_P$ then $a = q$. (this insures the harmonious nature of the guess).

Let the automaton $A_\varphi$ for $\varphi$ be derived from the tableau construction ([18, 22]). We construct the automaton $A_\psi \subseteq A_\varphi \times A_{guess}$, where the states are $Q_\psi = \{(g, f) \mid g \in Q_\varphi \land f \in Q_{guess}\}$, where moreover $g$ and $f$ are *consistent*, meaning that, for $q_i \in cl(\varphi)$, $q_i \in g \iff q_i \in f$. The transition relation $\delta((g, f), a, (g', f'))$ holds iff $\delta_\varphi(g, a, g')$ and $\delta_{guess}(f, a, f')$, the start states $Q_{\psi start} = \{(g, f) \mid \varphi \in g\}$, and $F_\psi = F_\psi \times F_{guess}$. It can be verified that the automaton $A_\psi$ accepts $L(\psi)$, with $A_{guess}$ basically used to insure that we only "guess" harmonious extensions.

$\supseteq$. Given $L(A)$, a stutter-invariant language, our objective is to write an SI-EQLTL formula expressing the language $L(A)$. By Lemma 1, we can assume that $A$ is a stutter-invariant automaton. We will use the fact ([15]) that $\bigcirc$-free LTL captures precisely the stutter-invariant subset of LTL.

Consider an EQLTL formula $\psi = \exists q_1, \ldots, q_k \phi$ expressing the language L(A). The crucial point is that because $A$ has the syntactic normal form, there exists an accepting run $r$ of $A$ on $w$ iff there exists a harmonious extension $w'$ of $w$, such that $w'$ is satisfied by the LTL formula. Thus, it suffices to convert the quantification to $\exists^h q_1, \ldots, q_k$.

It only remains to remove the $\bigcirc$ operators from the expression. This can be done by extending the proof of [15]. Let **SI-EQLTL($\bigcirc$)** be the logic where we *do* allow the ($\bigcirc$) operator to occur in the LTL part of the formula.

*Claim.* Any SI-EQLTL($\bigcirc$) formula, $\psi$, that accepts a stutter-invariant language can be converted to an SI-EQLTL formula $\psi'$ such that $L(\psi) = L(\psi')$.

The proof is as [15]. The only new observation needed is that any harmonious extension of a stutter-free word is also stutter-free. That concludes the theorem.

□

To prove a normal form result for SI-EQLTL analogous to EQLTL, which eliminates the use of the binary $\mathcal{U}$ operator, we will need the following stutter-invariant version of the $\bigcirc$ operator, $\bigcirc^\star$, which intuitively means "at the next distinct character". Formally, let $\bigcirc^\star \phi$ be defined as follows:

- $(w, i) \models \bigcirc^\star \phi$ if $(\exists j > i w_j \neq w_i \land \forall i', i \leq i' < j w_i = w_{i'}) \to (w, j) \models \phi$.

Let SI-EQLTL($\bigcirc^\star$, $\mathcal{U}$) denote the variant of SI-EQLTL where the $\mathcal{U}$ operator is disallowed, but $\bigcirc^\star$ is allowed. It can be shown that

**Corollary 3.** *SI-EQLTL expresses the same languages as SI-EQLTL($\bigcirc^\star$, $\mathcal{U}$).*

We are unable to provide a normal form where only one existential quantification is necessary, because Thomas's elimination argument [20] doesn't work in the stutter-invariant setting. It will be interesting to establish whether such a normal form exists. Finally, we address the costs and complexities involved in the mentioned translations and results above. They are, as one would expect, basically the same as for EQLTL.

**Corollary 4.**

1. *The satisfiability problem for SI-EQLTL is PSPACE-complete.*
2. *An SI-EQLTL formula $\varphi$ can be translated to an equivalent Büchi automaton of size $2^{O(|\varphi|)}$, in time proportional to the size of the output.*
3. *Model-checking, given a Kripke structure $K$ and* the negation *of an SI-EQLTL formula, or given an SI-AQLTL formula, is PSPACE-complete.*

## 5 Improved algorithm for SI-EQLTL conversion to Automata

In translating from LTL formulas to automata, a naive implementation of the tableau construction always incurs the worst-case exponential blow-up. In [4] an algorithm is provided which in practice behaves much better. A version of this algorithm for $\bigcirc$-free LTL has been implemented in the SPIN tool.

For our purposes, it is important to know that, rather than a standard Büchi automaton $A = (Q, \delta, \mathcal{F}, s)$ over $\Sigma_P = 2^P$, the automaton produced by the algorithm of [4] actually has the following **special form**: for every state $q \in Q$, there is a unique *term* (a conjunction of literals) from $P$, such that every "edge" from another state to $q$ has the label $\sigma_q$; this term is a symbolic shorthand for all the characters consistent with it, meaning the actual edge $(q', a, q)$ exists iff $a$ is consistent with the term $\sigma_q$. In practice, this shorthand can be much more concise than the ordinary notation for automata. Later, we will need another important fact about the output of the [4] algorithm, namely, a monotonicity which it preserves.

We now describe how to modify the [4] algorithm to work for translating from both EQLTL and SI-EQLTL to automata. For EQLTL, modifying the algorithm is trivial. The only observation necessary is that existential quantification corresponds to projection, even on term-labeled edges:

**Proposition 4.** *Given an EQLTL formula $\varphi = \exists q_1 \ldots q_k \, \psi$, and given a special form automaton $A_\psi$, such that $L(\psi) = L(A_\psi)$, the special form automaton $A_\varphi$ derived from $A_\psi$ by removing all literals over $\{q_1, \ldots, q_k\}$ from the terms labeling the edges of $A_\psi$, defines precisely the language defined by $\varphi$, i.e., $L(A_\varphi) = L(\varphi)$.*

Note that the automaton generated for $\exists q_1 \ldots q_k \psi$ is never bigger that the one generated for $\psi$. The case of SI-EQLTL is more interesting and complicated. In particular, it is not in general possible to obtain an automaton for $\exists^h t_1 \ldots t_k \psi$ which is no bigger than the automaton for $\psi$ produced by the [4] algorithm.

The following theorem gives an algorithm that incurs exponential blow-up in terms of $k$ and quadratic blow-up in terms of the number of unquantified propositions in $\psi$. We then give a modification of this algorithm which in practice behaves much better.

**Theorem 3.** *Given a formula $\varphi = \exists^h t_1 \ldots t_k \psi$, where $\psi$ is a formula over the propositions $p_1 \ldots, p_r, t_1, \ldots, t_k$, there is a special form automaton $A_\varphi$, such that*

$L(A_\varphi) = L(\varphi)$, *and such that*

$$|A_\varphi| \leq O(2^k \times r^2 \times |A_\psi|)$$

*where $A_\psi$ is a special form automaton for the formula $\psi$ (as produced by the [4] algorithm).*

*Proof.* Let $T = \{t_1, \ldots, t_k\}$. Given the set $P = \{p_1, \ldots, p_r\}$ of propositions, let $\neg P$ denote the set $\{\neg p_1, \ldots, \neg p_r\}$ of negations of these propositions. Given a special form automaton $A_\psi = (Q, \delta, \mathcal{F}, q_{start})$ for $\psi$, we would like to obtain an automaton for $\varphi$.

We now define an automaton $A'$ which will be central to the definition of $A_\varphi$.

$$A' = (Q' \subseteq (Q \times 2^{\{t_1, \ldots, t_k\}} \times (P \cup \neg P)^2) \cup \{s_{start}\}, \delta', \mathcal{F}', s_{start})$$

The states $Q'$ of $A'$, other than the start state $s_{start}$, consist of those triplets $(q, \theta, \tau)$, where $q \in Q$ is a state of $A_\psi$, $\theta$ is a subset of $T$ and defines a *full* valuation of all the variables in $T$, and $\tau$ specifies two elements of the set $P \cup \neg P$, where these two elements are consistent with each other, i.e., it is not the case that one is the negation of the other. Furthermore, for $(q, \theta, \tau)$ to qualify as a state in $Q'$ it must also satisfy the following extra condition: we view $\tau$ as specifying a partial valuation of $P$, namely, the two literals specified in $\tau$ must hold. Now, the extra condition that must be satisfied by $(q, \theta, \tau)$ is that the unique term $\sigma_q$, which labels all edges in $A_\psi$ which enter the state $q$, must be consistent with the valuation (full on $T$ and partial on $P$) specified by $\theta$ and $\tau$. $A'$ will also be a special form automaton, in that all edges into a state $s = (q, \theta, \tau)$ will be labeled with the same term $\sigma_s$.

The transition $\delta'(s' = (q', \theta', \tau'), \sigma_s, s = (q, \theta, \tau))$ will exist if and only if all of the following conditions hold:

1. $\sigma_s$ is consistent with the valuation defined by $\theta$, and the partial valuation on the pair of $p_j$'s defined by $\tau$.
2. There is a transition $\delta(q', \sigma_q, q)$ in $A_\psi$, such that the term $\sigma_q$ is a *subterm* of the term $\sigma_s$, meaning that every literal of $\sigma_q$ is also a literal of $\sigma_s$.
3. If the valuations $\theta'$ and $\theta$ on the $t_i$'s are inconsistent, then the partial valuations defined by $\tau'$ and $\tau$ must also be inconsistent.

The transitions out of the exceptional start state $s_{start}$ are defined as follows $\delta'(s_{start}, \sigma_s, (q, \theta, \tau))$ holds if and only if the first two condition above hold, with $q_{start}$ substituted for $q'$ in the statement of the second condition. Next we define the acceptance condition $\mathcal{F}'$ in $A'$. For each set $F = \{q_{i_1}, \ldots, q_{i_r}\} \in \mathcal{F}$, we put the set $F' = \{s = (q_{i_j}, \theta, \tau) \mid j \in \{1, \ldots, r\} \wedge s \in Q'\}$ in $\mathcal{F}'$.

From the automaton $A'$ we will now obtain the automaton $A_\varphi$, by "projecting out" the $q_i$'s as we normally would for regular existential quantification. More formally: for each transition $\delta'(s', \sigma_s, s)$ of $A'$ the term $\sigma_s$ is replaced in $A_\varphi$ by a term $\sigma_s^{new}$ with all the literals over the $q_i$'s removed, obtaining the transition $\delta_\varphi(s', \sigma_s^{new}, s)$. It remains to show that $A_\varphi$ defines the language we are after.

**Lemma 2.** *Given* $\exists^h t_1, \ldots, t_r \psi$, *and given* $A_\varphi$ *obtained from* $\varphi$ *via the above construction:*

$$L(A_\varphi) = L(\varphi)$$

We have to omit the proof, which is a bit technical, but the reason we need only remember two literals from $(P \cup \neg P)$ is that we can "guess" the literals over $P$ which will distinguish distinct consecutive characters, and we need two literals rather than one per character because we use one to distinguish it from its predecessor and the other to distinguish it from its successor. This concludes our theorem. □

The construction of $A'$ was the crucial step in Theorem 3, and it is there that a $2^k \times r^2$ blow-up occurs. As it stands, $A'$ *always* suffers from this blow-up. However, with an important observation, we can modify the algorithm so that the blow-up in $k$ need not be worst-case.

In going from $A_\psi$ to $A'$, for every state $q$ of $A_\psi$, and every $\tau$, we built the states $(q, \theta, \tau)$ for every *full* valuation $\theta$ of $T$. The observation is that these $\theta$'s need not be full valuations of $T$. In fact, the only condition we need is that, for any run of $A_\psi$, the domains of the sequence of expansions $\theta_i$'s in our new automaton form a *monotonic* (non-increasing) sequence of partial valuations of $T$, by which we mean that the domains form a monotonic sequence of sets. This assures us that, if there is any accepting run in the resulting automaton, then an accepting run can be constructed where the "guessed" variables form a harmonious extension. The reason, intuitively, is that we can safely extend a partial valuation of $T$ that is consistent with a predecessor to fully match this predecessor valuation, without forcing an inconsistency with future valuations, because future valuations can evaluate at most the same or fewer variables and can thus be extended likewise if they are consistent with their predecessor.

But how are we to come up with such a monotonically decreasing sequence of partial-valuations to satisfy the condition? It turns out that we are in a rather fortuitous situation. The output of [4]'s algorithm already provides us with such a sequence. Each state of that output is marked by a set of subformulas of the original temporal logic formula being translated, and here is where we find our monotonic sequence: on any path in the automaton the set of $t_i$'s that occur in the set of subformulas in each node form a monotonic (non-increasing) sequence. We can thus simply use these sets as our monotonic sequence directly from the [4] algorithm. Using this observation, we can reduce the state space of $A'$ by only evaluating the $t_i's$ that need to be evaluated for each given state $q$ of $A_\psi$. We have to omit details.

## 6 Conclusions

We have provided a simple temporal logic, SI-EQLTL, for expressing the stutter-invariant $\omega$-regular languages. We have shown that the basic algorithms for, e.g., satisfiability and conversion to automata, for LTL, can be modified to the setting of SI-EQLTL without any substantial penalty in computational complexity.

Along the way, we have defined stutter-invariant automata, a syntactic normal form for automata which captures the stutter-invariant $\omega$-regular languages.

The purpose of such a logic is to close the gap, in a natural way, between systems like COSPAN where properties are specified as $\omega$-automata, and those such as SPIN, where properties are specified in the weaker LTL formalism, and where, moreover, only stutter-invariant properties are allowed in order to enable partial-order verification.

One potential criticism for both SI-EQLTL and EQLTL is that, although both logics are semantically closed under complementation, they are not *syntactically* so. Indeed, complementation of a formula is, in the worst case, costly: incurring an exponential blow-up. As a result, in order to perform model checking with the same complexity as LTL, we need to work with the *negation* of SI-EQLTL formulas or with SI-AQLTL formulas. Although this is undesirable, it is a situation no different than the behavior of non-deterministic $\omega$-automata, for which complementation is similarly costly. This was the reason behind [11]'s advocacy of ∀-automata. In other words, in either formalism one has to deal with the cost of complementation, but the benefits of a more succinct logical representation make these temporal logics an attractive alternative to automata.

We have implemented the translation algorithm of section 5 in the programming language ML, extending an implementation due to Doron Peled of the [4] algorithm. Preliminary experiments indicate that the translation produces very reasonable sized automata. The intention has been to ultimately incorporate the extended logic, using the translation, in Gerard Holzmann's tool SPIN in order to supply it with the extra expressive power.

*Acknowledgment.* Thanks to Mihalis Yannakakis for several important comments. Thanks to Doron Peled for allowing me to use his ML implementation of the [4] algorithm. Thanks to Gerard Holzmann, Orna Kupferman, Bob Kurshan, Doron Peled, Moshe Vardi, and Thomas Wilke for helpful comments.

# References

1. J. R. Büchi. On a decision method in restricted second-order arithmetic. In *Proceedings of the International Congress on Logic, Methodology, and Philosophy of Science*, 1960. Stanford University Press, 1962.
2. E. A. Emerson. Temporal and modal logics. In J. van Leeuwen, editor, *Handbook of Theoret. Comput. Sci.*, volume B, pages 995–1072. Elsevier, Amsterdam, 1990.
3. K. Etessami. Stutter-invariant languages, $\omega$-automata, and temporal logic. Technical Report BL011272-980611-07TM, Bell Laboratories, June 11 1998.
4. R. Gerth, D. Peled, M. Y. Vardi, and P. Wolper. Simple on-the-fly automatic verification of linear temporal logic. In *PSTV95, Protocol Specification Testing and Verification*, pages 3–18, 1995.
5. P. Godefroid and P. Wolper. A partial approach to model checking. In *Proc. 6th Ann. IEEE Symp. on Logic in Computer Science*, pages 406–415, 1991.
6. G. J. Holzmann. The model checker spin. *IEEE Transactions on Software Engineering*, 23(5):279–295, 1997.

7. G. J. Holzmann and D. Peled. An improvement in formal verification. In *7th International Conference on Formal Description Techniques*, pages 177–194, 1994.

8. O. Kupferman. Augmenting branching temporal logics with existential quantification over atomic propositions. *Journal of Logic and Computation*, 7:1–14, 1997.

9. L. Lamport. What good is temporal logic. In R. E. A. Mason, editor, *Information Processing '83: Proc. IFIP 9th World Computer Congress*, pages 657–668, 1983.

10. L. Lamport. The temporal logic of actions. *ACM Transactions on Programming Languages and Systems*, pages 872–923, 1994.

11. Z. Manna and A. Pnueli. Specification and verification of concurrent programs by ∀-automata. In *Proc. 14th Ann. ACM Symp. on Principles of Programming Languages*, pages 1–12, 1987.

12. K. McMillan, 1998. See http://www-cad.eecs.berkeley.edu/kenmcmil for recent versions of SMV and its documentation.

13. R. McNaughton. Testing and generating infinite sequences by a finite automaton. *Information and Control*, 9:521–530, 1966.

14. D. Peled. Combining partial order reductions with on-the-fly model checking. *Formal Methods in System Design*, 8:39–64, 1996.

15. D. Peled and T. Wilke. Stutter-invariant temporal properties are expressible without the next-time operator. *Information Processing Letters*, 63:243–246, 1997.

16. A. Pnueli. The temporal logic of programs. In *Proc. 18th Symp. on Foundations of Computer Science*, pages 46–57, 1977.

17. A. Rabinovich. Expressive completeness of temporal logic of actions. In *Mathematical Foundations of Computer Science*, pages 229–238, August 1998.

18. A. P. Sistla and E. M. Clarke. The complexity of propositional linear temporal logics. *Journal of the ACM*, 32(3):733–749, 1985.

19. A. P. Sistla, M. Y. Vardi, and P. Wolper. The complementation problem for büchi automata with applications to temporal logic. *Theoretical Computer Science*, 49:217–237, 1987.

20. Thomas, W. Classifying regular events in symbolic logic. *Journal of Computer and System Sciences*, 25:360–376, 1982.

21. A. Valmari. A stubborn attack on state explosion. *Formal Methods in System Design*, 1:297–322, 1992.

22. M. Y. Vardi and P. Wolper. Reasoning about infinite computation. *Information and Computation*, 115:1–37, 1994.

23. Pierre Wolper. Temporal logic can be more expressive. *Information and Control*, 56:72–99, 1983.

# Improved Automata Generation for Linear Temporal Logic[*]

Marco Daniele[1,2], Fausto Giunchiglia[3,2], and Moshe Y. Vardi[4]

[1] Dipartimento di Informatica e Sistemistica
Università di Roma "La Sapienza", 00198 Roma, Italy
[2] Istituto Trentino di Cultura
Istituto per la Ricerca Scientifica e Tecnologica
38050 Povo, Trento, Italy
[3] Dipartimento di Informatica e Studi Aziendali
Università di Trento, 38100 Trento, Italy
[4] Department of Computer Science
Rice University, Houston TX 77251, USA

**Abstract.** We improve the state-of-the-art algorithm for obtaining an automaton from a linear temporal logic formula. The automaton is intended to be used for model checking, as well as for satisfiability checking. Therefore, the algorithm is mainly concerned with keeping the automaton as small as possible. The experimental results show that our algorithm outperforms the previous one, with respect to both the size of the generated automata and computation time. The testing is performed following a newly developed methodology based on the use of randomly generated formulas.

## 1 Introduction

This paper focuses on the explicit-state automata-based approach to model checking of linear temporal logic specifications [VW86,VW94,Hol97]. In this approach, both the system and the *negation* of the specifications are turned into automata on infinite words [Tho90]. The former automaton recognizes the system execution sequences, while the latter one comprises all the execution sequences (models) violating the specifications. Verification amounts then to checking whether the language recognized by the synchronous product of the above automata is empty. Similarly, satisfiability checking amounts to checking that the language recognized by the automaton built for the formula to be checked is non-empty. Satisfiability also plays an important role in model checking, for avoiding model checking unsatisfiable or valid specifications.

The automaton for the specifications can have as many as $2^{O(n)}$ states, where $n$ is the number of subformulas of the specifications [VW94]. Therefore, the size of

[*] Supported in part by NSF grants CCR-9628400 and CCR-9700061, and by a grant from the Intel Corporation. Part of this work was done while the first author was a visiting student and the third author was a Varon Visiting Professor at the Weizmann Institute of Science.

the product automaton, which determines the overall complexity of the method, is proportional to $N \cdot 2^{O(n)}$, where $N$ is the number of reachable system states. For these reasons, it is clearly desirable to keep the specification automaton as small as possible, and to work on-the-fly, that is, to detect that a system violates its specifications by constructing and visiting only some part of the search space containing the bug. Note that even though in practice the assertions being verified are typically expressed by short formulas, it is often impossible to verify these properties without making some assumptions on the environment of the system being verified. Thus, in practice, one typically model checks formulas of the form $\phi \to \psi$, where the assertion $\psi$ may be quite simple, but the assumption $\phi$ may be rather complicated.

The state-of-the-art on-the-fly algorithms for turning specifications into automata and performing the emptiness check can be found in [CVWY91] and [GPVW95]. Such algorithms define the kernel of the model checker SPIN [Hol97]. We refer to the algorithm described in [GPVW95] as GPVW. That paper also discusses several possible improvements. We refer to the improved algorithm as GPVW+. An alternative automata construction for temporal specifications [KMMP93] starts with a two-state automaton that is repeatedly "refined" until all models of the specifications are realized. Due to this refinement process, however, this algorithm can not be used in an on-the-fly fashion. Another approach could be turning the on-the-fly decision procedure presented in [Sch98] into a procedure for automata construction. It is not clear, however, whether and how this modification could be done, for that procedure is geared towards finding and representing one model, but not all models.

In this paper we present, and describe experiments with, an algorithm for building an automaton from a linear temporal logic formula. Our algorithm, hereafter LTL2AUT, though being based on GPVW+, is geared towards building smaller automata in less time. Our improvements are based on simple syntactic techniques, carried out on-the-fly when states are processed, that allow us to eliminate the need of storing some information. Experimental results demonstrate that GPVW+ significantly outperforms GPVW and show that LTL2AUT further outperforms GPVW+, with respect to both the size of the generated automata and computation time. The testing has been performed following a newly developed methodology, which, inspired by the methodologies proposed in [MSL92] and [GS96] for propositional and modal $K$ logics, is based on randomly generated formulas.

The rest of the paper is structured as follows. Section 2 introduces linear temporal logic and automata on infinite words. Section 3 presents the core underlying GPVW, GPVW+, and LTL2AUT, and Section 4 shows how GPVW, GPVW+, and LTL2AUT can be obtained by suitably instantiating such core. The test is divided between Section 5, where our test method is discussed, and Section 6, where a comparison of the three algorithms is given. Finally, we make some concluding remarks in Section 7.

## 2 Preliminaries

The set of Linear Temporal Logic formulas (LTL) is defined inductively starting from a finite set $\mathcal{P}$ of *propositions*, the standard Boolean operators, and the temporal operators $X$ ("next time") and $\mathcal{U}$ ("until") as follows:

- each member of $\mathcal{P}$ is a formula,
- $\neg\mu_1$, $\mu_1 \vee \mu_2$, $\mu_1 \wedge \mu_2$, $X\mu_1$, and $\mu_1 \mathcal{U}\mu_2$ are formulas, if so are $\mu_1$ and $\mu_2$.

An LTL interpretation is a function $\xi : N \to 2^{\mathcal{P}}$, i.e., an infinite word over the alphabet $2^{\mathcal{P}}$, which maps each instant of time into the propositions holding at such instant. We write $\xi_i$ for denoting the interpretation $\lambda t.\xi(t + i)$. LTL semantics is then defined inductively as follows:

- $\xi \models p$ iff $p \in \xi(0)$, for $p \in \mathcal{P}$,
- $\xi \models \neg\mu_1$ iff $\xi \not\models \mu_1$,
- $\xi \models \mu_1 \vee \mu_2$ iff $\xi \models \mu_1$ or $\xi \models \mu_2$,
- $\xi \models \mu_1 \wedge \mu_2$ iff $\xi \models \mu_1$ and $\xi \models \mu_2$,
- $\xi \models X\mu_1$ iff $\xi_1 \models \mu_1$,
- $\xi \models \mu_1 \mathcal{U}\mu_2$ iff there exists $i \geq 0$ such that $\xi_i \models \mu_2$ and, for all $0 \leq j < i$, $\xi_j \models \mu_1$.

As usual, we have $\neg\neg\mu \doteq \mu$, $T \doteq p \vee \neg p$ and $F \doteq \neg T$. Moreover, we define $\mu_1 \mathcal{V}\mu_2 \doteq \neg(\neg\mu_1 \mathcal{U}\neg\mu_2)$. This latter operator allows each formula to be turned into *negation normal form*, that is, it allows the pushing of the $\neg$ operator inwards until it occurs only before propositions, without causing an exponential blow up in the size of the translated formula. From now on, each formula is considered to be in negation normal form.

A *literal* is either a proposition or its negation, an *elementary* formula is either T, or F, or a literal, or an $X$-formula. A set of formulas is said to be elementary if all its formulas are. A non-elementary formula $\mu$ can be decomposed, according to the tableau rules of Figure 1, so that $\mu \leftrightarrow \bigwedge_{\beta_1 \in \alpha_1(\mu)} \beta_1 \vee \bigwedge_{\beta_2 \in \alpha_2(\mu)} \beta_2$.

| $\mu$ | $\alpha_1(\mu)$ | $\alpha_2(\mu)$ |
|---|---|---|
| $\mu_1 \wedge \mu_2$ | $\{\mu_1, \mu_2\}$ | $\{F\}$ |
| $\mu_1 \vee \mu_2$ | $\{\mu_1\}$ | $\{\mu_2\}$ |
| $\mu_1 \mathcal{U}\mu_2$ | $\{\mu_2\}$ | $\{\mu_1, X(\mu_1 \mathcal{U}\mu_2)\}$ |
| $\mu_1 \mathcal{V}\mu_2$ | $\{\mu_2, \mu_1\}$ | $\{\mu_2, X(\mu_1 \mathcal{V}\mu_2)\}$ |

**Fig. 1.** Tableau rules.

Finally, a *cover* of a set $A$ of formulas is a, possibly empty, set of sets $C = \{C_i : i \in I\}$ such that $\bigwedge_{\mu \in A} \mu \leftrightarrow \bigvee_{i \in I} \bigwedge_{\eta_i \in C_i} \eta_i$.

We represent formulas via *labeled generalized Büchi automata*. A generalized Büchi automaton is a quadruple $\mathcal{A} = \langle \mathcal{Q}, \mathcal{I}, \delta, \mathcal{F} \rangle$, where $\mathcal{Q}$ is a finite set of *states*, $\mathcal{I} \subseteq \mathcal{Q}$ is the set of *initial states*, $\delta : \mathcal{Q} \to 2^{\mathcal{Q}}$ is the *transition function*, and $\mathcal{F} \subseteq 2^{2^{\mathcal{Q}}}$ is a, possibly empty, set of sets of accepting states $\mathcal{F} = \{F_1, F_2, \ldots, F_n\}$. An *execution* of $\mathcal{A}$ is an infinite sequence $\rho = q_0 q_1 q_2 \ldots$ such that $q_0 \in \mathcal{I}$ and, for each $i \geq 0$, $q_{i+1} \in \delta(q_i)$. $\rho$ is *accepting execution* if, for each $F_i \in \mathcal{F}$, there exists $q_i \in F_i$ that appears infinitely often in $\rho$. A labeled generalized Büchi automaton is a triple $\langle \mathcal{A}, \mathcal{D}, \mathcal{L} \rangle$, where $\mathcal{A}$ is a generalized Büchi automaton, $\mathcal{D}$ is some finite domain, and $\mathcal{L} : \mathcal{Q} \to 2^{\mathcal{D}}$ is the *labeling function*. A labeled generalized Büchi automaton *accepts* a word $\xi = x_0 x_1 x_2 \ldots$ from $\mathcal{D}^\omega$ iff there exists an accepting execution $\rho = q_0 q_1 q_2 \ldots$ of $\mathcal{A}$ such that $x_i \in \mathcal{L}(q_i)$, for each $i \geq 0$.

## 3 The Core

LTL2AUT, GPVW+, and GPVW can be obtained by suitably instantiating the core we are about to present. The instantiation affects some functions that, in what follows, are highlighted through the SMALL CAPITAL font. The central part of the core is the computation of a cover of a set of formulas, which is used for generating states. The propositional information will be used for defining the labeling, while the $X$ information will be used to define the transition function.

### 3.1 Cover Computation

The algorithm for computing covers is defined by extending the propositional tableau in order to allow it to deal with temporal operators. The fundamental rules used for decomposing temporal operators are the identity $\mu \mathcal{U} \eta \equiv \eta \vee (\mu \wedge X(\mu \mathcal{U} \eta))$ and its dual $\mu \mathcal{V} \eta \equiv \eta \wedge (\mu \vee X(\mu \mathcal{V} \eta))$. The line numbers in the following description refer to the algorithm appearing in Figure 2. The algorithm handles the following data structures:

***ToCover*** The set of formulas to be covered but still not processed.
***Current*** The element of the cover currently being computed.
***Covered*** The formulas already processed and covered by *Current*.
***Cover*** The cover so far computed.

When computing the current element of the cover, the algorithm first checks whether all the formulas have been covered (line 4). If so, *Current* is ready to be added to *Cover* (line 5). If a formula $\mu$ has still to be covered (line 6), the algorithm checks whether $\mu$ has to be stored in the current element of the cover (line 8) and, if so, adds it to *Current* (line 9). Processing $\mu$ can be avoided in two cases: If there is a contradiction involving it (line 10) or it is redundant (line 12). In the former case, *Current* is discarded (line 11), while in the latter one $\mu$ is discarded (line 13). Finally, if $\mu$ does need to be covered, it is covered according to its syntactic structure. If $\mu$ is elementary, it is covered simply by itself (line 15). Otherwise, $\mu$ is covered by covering, according to the tableau rules appearing in Figure 1, either $\alpha_1(\mu)$ (line 16) or $\alpha_2(\mu)$ (line 18). This is justified by recalling that $\mu \leftrightarrow \bigwedge_{\beta_1 \in \alpha_1(\mu)} \beta_1 \vee \bigwedge_{\beta_2 \in \alpha_2(\mu)} \beta_2$.

```
1  function Cover(A)
2    return cover(A, ∅, ∅, ∅)

3  function cover(ToCover, Current, Covered, Cover)
4    if ToCover = ∅
5      then return Cover ∪ {Current}
6      else select μ from ToCover
7             remove μ from ToCover and add it to Covered
8             if HAS_TO_BE_STORED(μ)
9               then Current = Current ∪ {μ}
10            if CONTRADICTION(μ, ToCover, Current, Covered)
11              then return Cover
12              else if REDUNDANT(μ, ToCover, Current, Covered)
13                      then return cover(ToCover, Current, Covered, Cover)
14                      else if μ is elementary
15                              then return cover(ToCover, Current ∪ {μ}, Covered, Cover)
16                              else return cover(ToCover ∪ (α₁(μ) \ Current),
17                                               Current, Covered,
18                                      cover(ToCover ∪ (α₂(μ) \ Current),
19                                               Current, Covered, Cover))
```

**Fig. 2.** Cover computation.

## 3.2 The Automaton Construction

Our goal is to build a labeled generalized Büchi automaton recognizing exactly all the models of a linear time temporal logic formula $\psi$. The algorithm is presented in two phases. First, we introduce the automaton structure, i.e., its states, which are obtained as covers, initial states, and transition function. The line numbers in the following description refer to this part of the algorithm, which appears in Figure 3. Then, we complete such structure by defining labeling and acceptance conditions.

The algorithm starts by computing the initial states as cover of $\{\psi\}$ (line 2). A set $U$ of states whose transition function has still to be defined is kept. All the initial states are clearly added to $U$ (line 2). When defining the transition function for the state $s$ (line 4), we first compute its successors as cover of $\{\mu : X\mu \in s\}$ (line 5). For each computed successor $r$, the algorithm checks whether $r$ has been previously generated as a state $r'$ (line 6). If so, it suffices to add $r'$ to $\delta(s)$ (line 7). Otherwise, $r$ is added to $Q$ and $\delta(s)$ (lines 8 and 9). Moreover, $r$ is also added to $U$ (line 10), for $\delta(r)$ to be eventually computed.

The domain $\mathcal{D}$ is $2^{\mathcal{P}}$ and the label of a state $s$ consists of all subsets of $2^{\mathcal{P}}$ that are compatible with the propositional information contained in $s$. More in detail, let $Pos(s)$ be $s \cap \mathcal{P}$ and $Neg(s)$ be $\{p \in \mathcal{P} : \neg p \in s\}$. Then, $\mathcal{L}(s) = \{X : X \subseteq \mathcal{P} \wedge Pos(s) \subseteq X \wedge X \cap Neg(s) = \emptyset\}$. Finally, we have to impose acceptance conditions. Indeed, our construction allows some executions inducing interpretations that are not models of $\psi$. This happens because it is possible to procrastinate forever the

```
1  procedure create_automaton_structure(ψ)
2      U = Q = I = Cover({ψ}), δ = ∅
3      while U ≠ ∅
4          remove s from U
5          for r ∈ Cover({μ : Xμ ∈ s})
6              if ∃r' ∈ Q such that r = r'
7              then δ(s) = δ(s) ∪ {r'}
8              else  Q = Q ∪ {r}
9                    δ(s) = δ(s) ∪ {r}
10                   U = U ∪ {r}
```

**Fig. 3.** The algorithm.

fulfilling of $U$-formulas, and arises because the formula $\mu U \eta$ can be covered by covering $\mu$ and by promising to fulfill it later by covering $X(\mu U \eta)$. The problem is solved by imposing generalized Büchi acceptance conditions. Informally, for each subformula $\mu U \eta$ of $\psi$, we define a set $F_{\mu U \eta} \in \mathcal{F}$ containing states $s$ that either do not promise it or immediately fulfill it. In this way, postponing forever fulfilling a promised $U$-formula gives not rise to accepting executions anymore. Formally, we set $F_{\mu U \eta} \doteq \{s \in Cover : \text{SATISFY}(s, \mu U \eta) \rightarrow \text{SATISFY}(s, \eta)\}$ where, again, SATISFY is a function that will be subject to instantiation.

## 4  GPVW, GPVW+, and LTL2AUT

GPVW is obtained by instantiating the Boolean functions parameterizing the previously described core in the following way. HAS_TO_BE_STORED($\mu$) returns T. CONTRADICTION($\mu$, *ToCover*, *Current*, *Covered*) returns T iff $\mu$ is F or $\mu$ is a literal such that $\neg\mu \in Current$. REDUNDANT($\mu$, *ToCover*, *Current*, *Covered*) returns F. SATISFY($s, \mu$) returns T iff $\mu \in s$.

For GPVW+ we have the following instantiations. HAS_TO_BE_STORED($\mu$) returns T iff $\mu$ is a $U$-formula or $\mu$ is the righthand argument of a $U$-formula. CONTRADICTION($\mu$, *ToCover*, *Current*, *Covered*) returns T iff $\mu$ is F or the negation normal form of $\neg\mu$ is in *Covered*. REDUNDANT($\mu$, *ToCover*, *Current*, *Covered*) returns T iff $\mu$ is $\eta U \nu$ and $\nu \in ToCover \cup Current$, or $\mu$ is $\eta V \nu$ and $\eta$, $\nu \in ToCover \cup Current$. SATISFY($s, \mu$) returns T iff $\mu \in s$.

GPVW+ attempts to generate less states than GPVW by reducing the formulas to store in *Current* and by detecting redundancies and contradictions as soon as possible. Indeed, by reducing the formulas to store in *Current*, GPVW+ increases the possibility of finding matching states, while early detection of contradictions and redundancies avoids producing the part of the automaton for dealing with them. However, GPVW+ still does not solve some basic problems. First, states obtained by dealing with a $U$-formula contain either the $U$-formula or its righthand argument. So, for example, states generated for the righthand argument of $\mu U \eta$ are equivalent to, but do not match, prior existing states generated for $\eta$. Second, redundancy and contradiction checks are performed by explicitly looking for the source of redundancy or contradiction. So, for example, a $\mathcal{U}$-formula whose righthand argument is a conjunction is considered redundant if such conjunction appears among the covered formulas, but it is not if, instead of the conjunction, its conjuncts are present.

LTL2AUT overcomes the above problems in a very simple way: Only the elementary formulas are stored in *Current*, while information about the non-elementary ones is derived from the elementary ones and the ones stored in *ToCover* using quick syntactic techniques. More in detail, we inductively define the set $\mathcal{SI}(A)$ of the formulas *syntactically implied* by the set of formulas $A$ as follows

- $\mathrm{T} \in \mathcal{SI}(A)$,
- $\mu \in \mathcal{SI}(A)$, if $\mu \in A$,
- $\mu \in \mathcal{SI}(A)$, if $\mu$ is non-elementary and either $\alpha_1(\mu) \subseteq \mathcal{SI}(A)$ or $\alpha_2(\mu) \subseteq \mathcal{SI}(A)$.

LTL2AUT requires then the following settings. HAS_TO_BE_STORED($\mu$) returns F. CONTRADICTION($\mu$, *ToCover*, *Current*, *Covered*) returns T iff the negation normal form of $\neg\mu$ belongs to $\mathcal{SI}(ToCover \cup Current)$. REDUNDANT($\mu$, *ToCover*, *Current*, *Covered*) returns T iff $\mu \in \mathcal{SI}(ToCover \cup Current)$ and, if $\mu$ is $\eta\mathcal{U}\nu$, $\nu \in \mathcal{SI}(ToCover \cup Current)$. SATISFY($s, \mu$) returns T iff $\mu \in \mathcal{SI}(s)$. The special attention to the righthand arguments of $\mathcal{U}$-formulas in the redundancy check is for avoiding discarding information required to define the acceptance conditions. The proof of correctness of LTL2AUT is described in [DGV99].

## 5 The Test Method

The existent bibliography on problem sets and testing-generating methods for LTL and model checking is very poor. Indeed, papers usually come along with testing their results over, in the best cases, few instances. The method we have adopted is based on two analyses:

**Average-behavior analysis:** For a fixed number $N$ of propositional variables and for increasing values $L$ of the length of the formulas, a problem set $\mathcal{PS}_{\langle F,N,L\rangle}$ of $F$ random formulas is generated and given in input to the procedures to test. After the computation, a statistical analysis is performed and the results are plotted against $L$. The process can be repeated for different values of $N$.

**Temporal-behavior analysis:** For a fixed number $N$ of propositional variables, a fixed length $L$ of the formulas, and for increasing values $P$ of the probability of generating the temporal operators $\mathcal{U}$ and $\mathcal{V}$, a problem set $\mathcal{PS}_{\langle F,N,L,P\rangle}$ of $F$ random formulas is generated and given in input to the procedures to test. After the computation, a statistical analysis is performed and the results are plotted against $P$. The process can be repeated for different values of $N$ and $L$.

When generating random formulas from a formula space, for example defined by the parameters $N$, $L$, and $P$, our target is to cover such space as uniformly as possible. This requires that, when generating formulas of length $L$, we produce formulas of length exactly $L$, and not up to $L$. Indeed, in the latter way, varying $L$, we give preference to short formulas. Random formulas parameterized by $N$, $L$, and $P$, are then generated as follows. A unit-length random formula is generated by randomly choosing, according to uniform distribution, one variable. From now on, unless otherwise specified, randomly chosen stands for randomly chosen with uniform distribution. A random formula of length 2 is generated by generating $op(p)$, where $op$ is randomly chosen in $\{\neg, X\}$ and $p$ is a randomly chosen variable. Otherwise, with probability $\frac{P}{2}$ of choosing either $\mathcal{U}$ or $\mathcal{V}$ and probability $\frac{1-P}{4}$ of choosing $\neg$, $X$, $\wedge$, or $\vee$, the operator $op$ is randomly chosen. If $op$ is unary, the random formula of length $L$ is generated as $op(\mu)$, for some random formula $\mu$ of length $L-1$. Otherwise, if $op$ is binary, for some randomly chosen $1 \leq S \leq L-2$, two random formulas $\mu_1$ and $\mu_2$ of length $S$ and $L-S-1$ are produced, and the random formula $op(\mu_1, \mu_2)$ of length $L$ is generated. Since the set of operators we use is $\{\neg, X, \wedge, \vee, \mathcal{U}, \mathcal{V}\}$, random formulas for the average-behavior analysis are generated by setting $P = \frac{1}{3}$. Note that parentheses are not considered. Indeed, our definition generates a syntax tree that makes the priority between the operators clear.

In both the above analyses, the parameters we are interested in are the size of the automata, namely states and transitions, and the time required for their generation. When comparing two procedures $\Pi_1$ and $\Pi_2$ with respect to some problem set $\mathcal{PS}_{\langle F,N,L,P \rangle}$ and parameter $\theta$, we perform the following statistical analysis. First, we compute the mean value of the outputs of $\Pi_1$ and $\Pi_2$ separately, and then consider their ratio that, hereafter, is denoted by $\frac{E(\Pi_1, \theta, \mathcal{PS}_{\langle F,N,L,P \rangle})}{E(\Pi_2, \theta, \mathcal{PS}_{\langle F,N,L,P \rangle})}$. A different statistical analysis of the data is described in [DGV99].

## 6 Results

LTL2AUT, GPVW, and GPVW+ have been implemented on the top of the same kernel, and are accessible through command line options. The code consists of 1400 lines of C plus 110 lines for a lex/yacc parser. The code has been compiled through gcc version 2.7.2.3 and executed under the SunOS 5.5.1 operating system on a SUNW UltraSPARC-II/296 1G.

LTL2AUT and GPVW+ have been compared, according to the test method discussed in Section 5, on 5700 randomly generated formulas. The results are shown in Figure 4. For the average behavior analysis, LTL2AUT and GPVW+ have been compared on 3300 random formulas generated, according to our test method, for $F = 100$, $N = 1, 2, 3$, and $L = 5, 10, \ldots, 55$. Formulas have been collected in 3 groups, for $N = 1, 2, 3$, and inside each group partitioned into 11 problem sets of 100 formulas each, for $L = 5, 10, \ldots, 55$. For each group, $\frac{E(\text{LTL2AUT, states }, \mathcal{PS}_{\langle 100,N,L \rangle})}{E(\text{GPVW+, states }, \mathcal{PS}_{\langle 100,N,L \rangle})}$, $\frac{E(\text{LTL2AUT, transitions }, \mathcal{PS}_{\langle 100,N,L \rangle})}{E(\text{GPVW+, transitions }, \mathcal{PS}_{\langle 100,N,L \rangle})}$, and $\frac{E(\text{LTL2AUT, time }, \mathcal{PS}_{\langle 100,N,L \rangle})}{E(\text{GPVW+, time }, \mathcal{PS}_{\langle 100,N,L \rangle})}$ have been plotted against $L$. The results show that

LTL2AUT clearly outperforms GPVW+, with respect to both the size of automata and computation time. Indeed, just considering formulas of length 30, LTL2AUT produces on the average less than 60% of the states of GPVW+

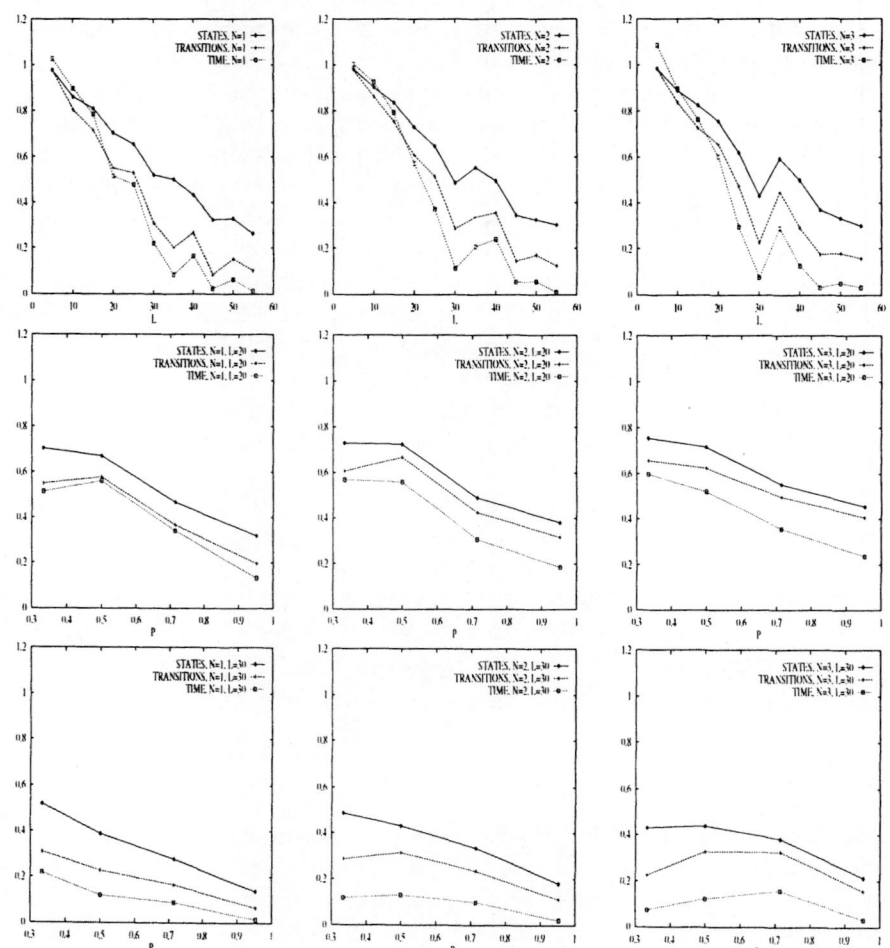

**Fig. 4.** LTL2AUT vs. GPVW+. Upper row: Average-behavior analysis, $F = 100$, $N = 1, 2, 3$, $L = 5, 10, \ldots, 55$. Middle and lower rows: Temporal-behavior analysis, $F = 100$, $N = 1, 2, 3$, $L = 20, 30$, $P = 0.\overline{3}, 0.5, 0.7, 0.95$.

(for transitions situation is even better) spending on the average less than 30% of the time of GPVW+. Moreover, the initial phase, in which LTL2AUT does have a time overhead with respect to GPVW+, affects formulas, for $L = 5$ and $N = 3$, which are solved by LTL2AUT in at most 0.000555 CPU seconds, as opposed to the most demanding sample for $L = 55$ and $N = 3$, which is solved by

LTL2AUT in 6659 CPU seconds. For the temporal-behavior analysis, LTL2AUT and GPVW+ have been compared over 2400 random formulas generated for $F = 100$, $N = 1, 2, 3$, $L = 20, 30$, and $P = 0.\overline{3}, 0.5, 0.7, 0.95$. Note that $P = 0.\overline{3}$

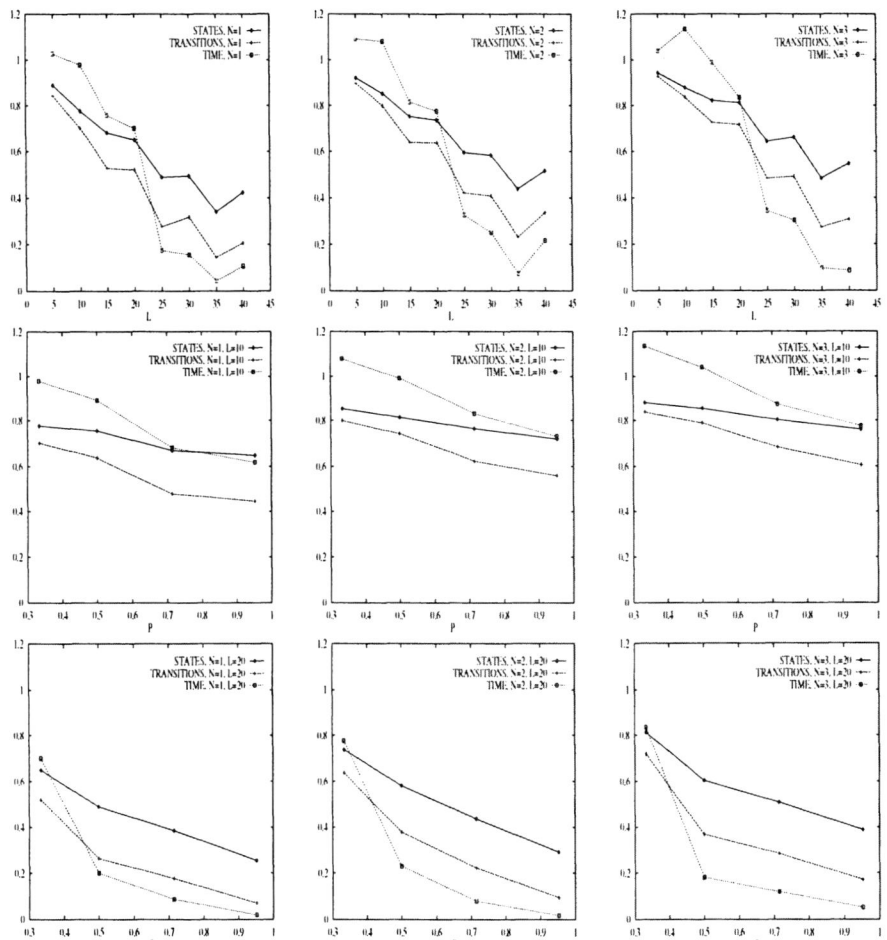

**Fig. 5.** GPVW+ vs. GPVW. Upper row: Average-behavior analysis, $F = 100$, $N = 1, 2, 3$, $L = 5, 10, \ldots, 40$. Middle and lower rows: Temporal-behavior analysis, $F = 100$, $N = 1, 2, 3$, $L = 10, 20$, $P = 0.\overline{3}, 0.5, 0.7, 0.95$.

is the probability we have assumed for the average-behavior analysis. Formulas have been collected in 3 groups, for $N = 1, 2, 3$, and inside each group partitioned into 2 sub-groups, for $L = 20, 30$. Each sub-group has still been partitioned into 4 problem sets, for $P = 0.\overline{3}, 0.5, 0.7, 0.95$. For each sub-group, we have plotted $\dfrac{E(\text{LTL2AUT, states}, \mathcal{PS}_{(100,N,L,P)})}{E(\text{GPVW+, states}, \mathcal{PS}_{(100,N,L,P)})}$, $\dfrac{E(\text{LTL2AUT, transitions}, \mathcal{PS}_{(100,N,L,P)})}{E(\text{GPVW+, transitions}, \mathcal{PS}_{(100,N,L,P)})}$, and

$\dfrac{E(\text{LTL2AUT, time }, \mathcal{PS}_{\langle 100, N, L, P \rangle})}{E(\text{GPVW+, time }, \mathcal{PS}_{\langle 100, N, L, P \rangle})}$ against $P$. Again, the results demonstrate that LTL2AUT clearly outperforms GPVW+.

The comparison between GPVW+ and GPVW, whose results are shown in Figure 5, follows the lines of the previous one, by only changing some parameters for allowing GPVW to compute in reasonable time. The average-behavior analysis has been carried out over 2400 random formulas generated for $F = 100$, $N = 1, 2, 3$, and $L = 5, 10, \ldots, 40$. The temporal-behavior analysis has been performed over 2400 random formulas generated for $F = 100$, $N = 1, 2, 3$, $L = 10, 20$, and $P = 0.\overline{3}, 0.5, 0.7, 0.95$. The results show that GPVW+ clearly outperforms GPVW both in the size of automata and, after an expected initial phase, also in time. The initial phase interests formulas, for $L = 10$ and $N = 3$, which are solved by GPVW+ in at most 0.004226 CPU seconds, as opposed to the hardest sample for $L = 40$ and $N = 3$, which is solved by GPVW+ in 178 CPU seconds.

Finally, a direct comparison between LTL2AUT and GPVW can be found in [DGV99].

## 7 Conclusions

We have demonstrated that the algorithm for building an automaton from a linear temporal logic formula can be significantly improved. Moreover, we have proposed a test methodology that can be also used for evaluating other LTL deciders, and whose underlying concept, namely targeting a uniform coverage of the formula space, can be exported to other logics. Of course, the notion of uniform coverage can be further refined, and this is part of our future work. In particular, we plan to adapt to LTL the probability distributions proposed in [MSL92] for propositional logic and adapted in [GS96] to the modal logic $K$. These distributions assigns equal probabilities to formulas of the same structure (e.g., 3-CNF in the propositional case). We are also planning to extend the concept of syntactic implication to a semantic one and, finally, to explore automata generation in the symbolic framework.

## References

[CVWY91] C. Courcoubetis, M. Vardi, P. Wolper, and M. Yannakakis. Memory efficient algorithms for the verification of temporal properties. In E. M. Clarke and R. P. Kurshan, editors, *Proceedings of Computer-Aided Verification (CAV '90)*, volume 531 of *LNCS*, pages 233–242, Berlin, Germany, June 1991. Springer.

[DGV99] M. Daniele, F. Giunchiglia, and M. Y. Vardi. Improved automata generation for linear time temporal logic. Technical Report 9903-10, ITC-IRST, March 1999.

[GPVW95] R. Gerth, D. Peled, M. Vardi, and P. Wolper. Simple on-the-fly automatic verification of linear temporal logic. In *Protocol Specification Testing and Verification*, pages 3–18, Warsaw, Poland, 1995. Chapman & Hall.

[GS96]    F. Giunchiglia and R. Sebastiani. Building decision procedures for modal logics from propositional decision procedures: the case study of modal K. In M. A. McRobbie and J. K. Slaney, editors, *Proceedings of the Thirteenth International Conference on Automated Deduction (CADE-96)*, volume 1104 of *LNAI*, pages 583–597, Berlin, July30 August–3 1996. Springer.

[Hol97]   G. J. Holzmann. The model checker spin. *IEEE Trans. on Software Engineering*, 23(5):279–295, May 1997. Special issue on Formal Methods in Software Practice.

[KMMP93] Y. Kesten, Z. Manna, H. McGuire, and A. Pnueli. A decision algorithm for full propositional temporal logic. In C. Courcoubertis, editor, *Proceedings of Computer-Aided Verification (CAV'93)*, volume 697 of *LNCS*, pages 97–109, Elounda, Greece, June 1993. Springer.

[MSL92]   D. Mitchell, B. Selman, and H. Levesque. Hard and easy distributions of SAT problems. In W. Swartout, editor, *Proceedings of the 10th National Conference on Artificial Intelligence*, pages 459–465, San Jose, CA, July 1992. MIT Press.

[Sch98]   S. Schwendimann. A new one-pass tableau calculus for PLTL. *Lecture Notes in Computer Science*, 1397:277–291, 1998.

[Tho90]   W. Thomas. Automata on infinite objects. In J. van Leeuwen, editor, *Handbook of Theoretical Computer Science*, chapter 4, pages 133–191. Elsevier Science Publishers B. V., 1990.

[VW86]    M. Y. Vardi and P. Wolper. An automata-theoretic approach to automatic program verification. In *lics86*, pages 332–344, 1986.

[VW94]    M. Y. Vardi and P. Wolper. Reasoning about infinite computations. *Information and Computation*, 115(1):1–37, 15 November 1994.

# On the Representation of Probabilities over Structured Domains[*]

Marius Bozga and Oded Maler

VERIMAG, Centre Equation, 2, av. de Vignate, 38610 Gières, France,
**bozga@imag.fr maler@imag.fr**

**Abstract.** In this paper we extend one of the main tools used in verification of discrete systems, namely Binary Decision Diagrams (BDD), to treat probabilistic transition systems. We show how probabilistic vectors and matrices can be represented canonically and succinctly using probabilistic trees and graphs, and how simulation of large-scale probabilistic systems can be performed. We consider this work as an important contribution of the verification community to numerous domains which need to manipulate very large matrices.

## 1 Introduction

Many problems in discrete verification can be reduced to the the following one: *given a non-deterministic finite-state automaton $\mathcal{A} = (Q, \delta)$ and a set $P \subseteq Q$ of states, find the set $P^*$ of all the states reachable from $P$.* One common way to do this calculation is to let $P^0 = P$ and $P^{i+1} = \delta(P^i)$ until $P^i$ is included in the union $P^0 \cup \ldots \cup P^{i-1}$. Here $P^i$ is the set of states reachable from $P$ after exactly $i$ steps.

This method can be formulated using Boolean state-vectors and transition matrices. Each subset $P$ of an $n$-element set of states can be written as an $n$-dimensional Boolean row vector $p$ (a function from $Q$ to $\{0, 1\}$) and any transition relation $\delta$ as an $n \times n$ Boolean matrix $A_\delta$ (a function from $Q \times Q$ to $\{0, 1\}$). Thus, the calculation step $P^{i+1} = \delta(P^i)$ is equivalent to the multiplication of a vector by a matrix: $p^{i+1} = p^i \cdot A_\delta$. For example, consider Figure 1 where a 5-state automaton is depicted along with its corresponding $5 \times 5$ matrix $A_\delta$. The reader can verify that calculating the states reachable in one step from $P = \{1, 2\}$ is done via the multiplication $[1, 1, 0, 0, 0] \cdot A_\delta = [0, 1, 1, 0, 1]$ where logical conjunction and disjunction replace multiplication and addition, respectively.

Probabilistic transition systems, such as *discrete Markov chains*, operate in a similar but different fashion. At any given stage of the system's evolution the state is given by a probability function $p : Q \to [0, 1]$ such that $\sum_{q \in Q} p(q) = 1$. The transition structure is probabilistic as well and is represented by a function

---

[*] This work was partially supported by the European Community Esprit-LTR Project 26270 VHS (Verification of Hybrid systems) and the French-Israeli collaboration project 970MAEFUT5 (Hybrid Models of Industrial Plants).

262

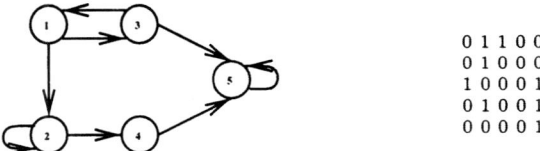

$$
\begin{array}{ccccc}
0 & 1 & 1 & 0 & 0 \\
0 & 1 & 0 & 0 & 0 \\
1 & 0 & 0 & 0 & 1 \\
0 & 1 & 0 & 0 & 1 \\
0 & 0 & 0 & 0 & 1
\end{array}
$$

**Fig. 1.** A non-deterministic automaton and its transition matrix.

$\delta : Q \times Q \to [0,1]$ where $\delta(q,q')$ denotes the *conditional probability* of being in $q'$ in the next-state *given* that the current state is $q$. The evolution from one probabilistic state vector to another is captured by the vector by matrix multiplication $p^{i+1} = p^i \cdot A_\delta$, this time over the reals.

The *state-explosion problem*, also known as *the curse of dimensionality*, arises when the system under consideration is composed of many sub-systems. The size of the global state-space is exponential in the number of components and verification by explicit enumeration of states and transitions becomes impossible. Symbolic methods provide an alternative to explicit state enumeration. They are based on the following observation: the global state-space of a composed system can be encoded naturally using *state-variables* (a variable for the local state of each component). The evolution of each variable usually depends on a small subset of the other variables and the corresponding transition law can be written concisely as a formula in some adequate formalism (e.g. propositional logic when the variables are Boolean) and the global transition relation is a conjunction of such formulae. Similarly, sets of states can be written down as formulae. With the aid of appropriate data-structures, a symbolic version of the basic computation $P^{i+1} = \delta(P^i)$ can be performed, calculating a (hopefully concise) representation of $P^{i+1}$ from a representation of $P^i$ and $\delta$.

In verification of systems modeled as automata this technique is called *symbolic model-checking* [McM93,BCM+93] and it had a great success. In fact it can be seen as one of the breakthroughs in verification, facilitating the analysis of systems with hundreds of state variables, far beyond the capabilities of explicit enumeration on current and future computers. The most popular representation scheme used in symbolic verification is the *binary decision diagram* (BDD), which is a formalism for representing Boolean functions, admitting the following properties [B86,MT98]:

1. It is canonic – given an ordering of the variables, a unique BDD corresponds to every Boolean function.
2. There are relatively-efficient algorithms for manipulating BDDs, in particular for the operations needed to compute $P^{i+1} = \delta(P^i)$.
3. It performs well in the analysis of many structured systems: the size of the BDD remains small relative to the size of the state-space.

The goal of the paper is to apply this recipe to probabilistic systems, that is, to define a representation formalism for probabilistic vectors and transition functions such that the operation $p^{i+1} = p^i \cdot A_\delta$ could be performed for systems for which it is impossible to do so using currently existing methods. To this end we define *probabilistic decision graphs* (PDG)[1] , a data-structure for representing probabilities over structured domains which enjoys the nice properties of BDDs.

The rest of the paper is organized as follows. In section 2 we present probabilistic decision trees and graphs and show they constitute a canonic representation for probabilities. In section 3 we rephrase the basic definitions of Markov chains. Section 4 is devoted to the representation of probabilistic transition functions by *conditional* probabilistic graphs and sketch the PDG structure of some generic classes of probabilistic systems. The calculation of next-state probabilities on PDGs via the projection operation described in section 5 and some preliminary experimental results are reported in section 6. Finally we discuss the significance of this work and mention some of the previous relevant applications of BDD technology outside the Boolean realm.

## 2  Probabilistic Decision Graphs

Let $\mathbb{B} = \{0, 1\}$. We assume an underlying set $Q = \mathbb{B}^n$, and a probability distribution on $Q$, i.e. a function $p : Q \to [0, 1]$ such that $\sum_{q \in Q} p(q) = 1$. Such a function can be extended naturally to subsets of $Q$ by letting $p(Q') = \sum_{q \in Q'} p(q)$ for every $Q' \subseteq Q$. We will abuse strings from $\mathbb{B}^{\leq n}$ (the set of binary strings of length not greater than $n$) to denote certain subsets of $\mathbb{B}^n$. A string $u = x_1 x_2 \cdots x_n$ will stand for the singleton $\{(x_1, \ldots, x_n)\}$ while a string $x_1 x_2 \cdots x_i$, $i < n$ will stand for the set $\{(x_1, \ldots, x_i, x_{i+1}, \ldots, x_n) : (x_{i+1}, \ldots, x_n) \in \mathbb{B}^{n-i}\}$. This can be defined recursively by associating with $u$ the union of the sets associated with $u0$ and $u1$. Note that the empty string $\varepsilon$ denotes the whole $\mathbb{B}^n$. To avoid additional symbols we use the same notation for a string and for the set it denotes. The set $\mathbb{B}^{\leq n}$ has a binary tree structure and every level $\mathbb{B}^i$ corresponds to a partition of $\mathbb{B}^n$. The next definition is the essence of this paper.

**Definition 1 (Probabilistic Decision Trees).** *A probabilistic decision tree* (PDT) *of depth $n$ is a tuple $P = (S, 0, 1, v)$ where $S = \mathbb{B}^{\leq n}$, 0 and 1 are respectively the* left-successor *and* right-successor *partial functions on $S$, and $v : S \to [0, 1]$ is a function satisfying $v(\varepsilon) = 1$ and for every non-leaf node $s$, $v(s0) + v(s1) = 1$.*

**Theorem 1 (Unique Representation).** *There is a one-to-one[2] correspondence between probabilities on $\mathbb{B}^n$ and PDTs.*

**Proof:** First we assign probabilities to nodes by letting $p(\varepsilon) = 1$ and

$$p(sx) = p(s) \cdot v(sx) \qquad x \in \mathbb{B} \qquad (1)$$

It is not hard to see that all $p$ values are in $[0, 1]$ and that their sum at each level of the tree is 1. Conversely, given a probability on the leaves, it is straightforward to

---

[1] We say "graphs" instead of "diagrams" to avoid yet another xDD acronym.
[2] In our definition there is an implicit ordering on the "variables".

calculate the probability of the sets associated with the upper nodes by letting $p(s) = p(s0) + p(s1)$ and then compute $v$ via normalization, i.e. the inverse of (1): $v(sx) = p(sx)/p(s)$. In the case when $p(s) = 0$ we can put any number in $v(sx) = 0/0$, and a convention such as $1/2$ can be used.

PDTs are nothing but the presentation of probabilities using the so-called "chain-rule", the probabilistic analogue of Shannon factorization of Boolean functions which underlies BDDs:

$$p(x_1 x_2 \cdots x_n) = p(x_1) \cdot p(x_1 x_2 | x_1) \cdots p(x_1 x_2 \cdots x_n | x_1 \cdots x_{n-1})$$

where $p(r|s)$ is the conditional probability of $r$ given $s$. We will replace this unfortunate (but very common) notation with $p_s(r)$ such that the above rule will be written as

$$p(x_1 x_2 \cdots x_n) = p(x_1) \cdot p_{x_1}(x_1 x_2) \cdots p_{x_1 \cdots x_{n-1}}(x_1 \cdots x_n).$$

Decision trees are exponential in the number of variables and, by themselves, do not solve the state explosion problems. However, when there is some structure in the objects they represent, different nodes may have identical sub-trees and the tree can be represented concisely by a directed acyclic graph (DAG) carrying the same information. The transformation of a tree into a DAG is a variation of the classical procedure for minimizing automata, and can be phrased as follows.

**Definition 2 (Probabilistic Decision Graphs).** *Let $P = (S, 0, 1, v)$ be a PDT and let $\sim$ be a congruence relation[3] on $S$ defined as $s \sim s'$ if $v(s) = v(s')$ and both $s0 \sim s'0$ and $s1 \sim s'1$. The associated probabilistic decision graph (PDG) is $G = (S/\sim, 0, 1, v)$.*

In other words, the nodes of G are the equivalence classes of $\sim$. Graphically speaking, the process starts from the bottom of the tree by merging leaves $sx$ and $s'x'$ which have identical $v$'s. Then the edge from $s$ labeled by $x$ and the edge from $s'$ labeled by $x'$ are redirected toward the merged node and the process continues recursively upward. Note that $sx = \bot$ for a leaf $s$, hence $s \sim s'$ only if both belong to the same level of the tree.

**Example**: Consider the following probability function over $\mathbb{B}^3$:

| 000 | 001 | 010 | 011 | 100 | 101 | 110 | 111 |
|-----|-----|-----|-----|-----|-----|-----|-----|
| $\frac{1}{6}$ | $0$ | $\frac{2}{15}$ | $\frac{1}{30}$ | $\frac{4}{15}$ | $\frac{1}{15}$ | $\frac{1}{15}$ | $\frac{4}{15}$ |

Figure 2-(a) shows the probabilities of all subsets in $\mathbb{B}^{\leq 3}$. The PDT in Figure 2-(b) is obtained via the normalization $v(sx) = p(sx)/p(s)$. The reduction modulo $\sim$ into a PDG starts in Figure 2-(c) by merging identical leaves and terminates in Figure 2-(d) by merging some of their parents.[4] Like in BDDs, when there is

---

[3] Congruence with respect to the 0 and 1 operations.

[4] Unlike BDDs we do not go further and eliminate nodes whose left and right successors are identical: we restrict ourselves to *balanced* DAGs where all paths from the root to the leaves are of the same length, otherwise we cannot satisfy the requirement that the sum of the leaves at every level is 1.

a lot of independence between the variables, the size of the PDG is much smaller than the size of $Q$. In the rest of the paper we describe algorithms in terms of full trees, bearing in mind that the actual implementation reduces every tree into its corresponding minimal DAG.

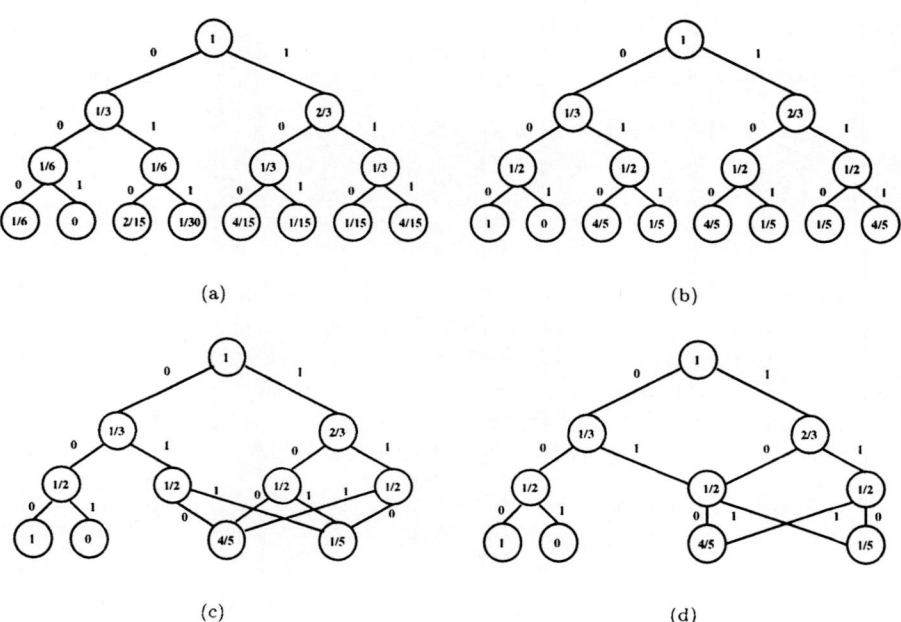

**Fig. 2.** Transforming a probability function (a) into a PDT (b) and successively via (c) into a PDG (d).

## 3 Markov Transition Functions

Having defined a canonical representation for probabilistic state vectors, we now move to the representation of transition matrices. In a non-probabilistic setting there is not much difference between sets (subsets of $\mathbb{B}^n$) and relations (subsets of $\mathbb{B}^{2n}$) and both can be represented by BDDs of the same type. For probabilistic systems, we must be more careful.

**Definition 3 (Markov Transition Function).** *A Markov transition function on $Q$ is a function $\delta : Q \to (Q \to [0,1])$ such that for every $q \in Q$, $\delta_q : Q \to [0,1]$ is a probability function on $Q$.*

In 20th century mathematics, such functions used to be written as $|Q| \times |Q|$ matrices such as

$$A_\delta = \begin{matrix} \delta_1(1) & \delta_1(2) & \ldots & \delta_1(n) \\ \delta_2(1) & \delta_2(2) & \ldots & \delta_2(n) \\ \ldots & \ldots & \ldots\ldots \\ \delta_n(1) & \delta_n(2) & \ldots & \delta_n(n) \end{matrix}$$

where each line represents a particular $\delta_q$. The action of $\delta$ on a probabilistic state-vector $p$ can be decomposed into two stages. The first can be viewed as applying a function $\hat{\delta} : (Q \to [0,1]) \to (Q \times Q \to [0,1])$ where $\hat{p} = \hat{\delta}(p)$ if for every $q, q' \in Q$, $\hat{p}(q, q') = p(q) \cdot \delta_q(q')$. In other words, given that the current state probability is $p$, $\hat{\delta}(p)$ denotes the probability of any *transition* to happen. Matrix-wise, when $p$ is written as a vector $[p_1, \ldots, p_n]$, calculating $\hat{\delta}(p)$ amounts to multiplying every element of $p$ by the elements of its corresponding row in $\delta$ to obtain

$$A_{\hat{\delta}(p)} = \begin{matrix} p_1 \cdot \delta_1(1) & p_1 \cdot \delta_1(2) & \ldots & p_1 \cdot \delta_1(n) \\ p_2 \cdot \delta_2(1) & p_2 \cdot \delta_2(2) & \ldots & p_2 \cdot \delta_2(n) \\ \ldots & \ldots & \ldots\ldots \\ p_n \cdot \delta_n(1) & p_n \cdot \delta_n(2) & \ldots & p_n \cdot \delta_n(n) \end{matrix}$$

Note that unlike $\delta$, $\hat{\delta}(p)$ *is* a probability function on $Q \times Q$.

The probability of being in the next step at a state $q'$ is then the sum of the probabilities of the form $\hat{p}(q, q')$, i.e. those leading to $q'$. This can be captured by a function: $w : (Q \times Q \to [0,1]) \to (Q \to [0,1])$ defined as $w(\hat{\delta}) = \sum_i \hat{\delta}_i$. Matrixly speaking, this is equivalent to summing up every column of $A_{\hat{\delta}(p)}$ to obtain a vector $p'$. Hence the composition $w \circ \hat{\delta} : (Q \to [0,1]) \to (Q \to [0,1])$ gives the evolution of the system as the action of a probabilistic transition matrix on a probabilistic state vector.[5]

Next we define a data-structure for representing $\delta$ when $Q = \mathbb{B}^n$ and a natural way to transform it, given a PDG-represented probability $p$, into a PDG of depth $2n$ for $\hat{\delta}(p)$. After that we define the basic operation on PDGs, the *projection* which is used in the calculation of $w$.

## 4    Conditional Probabilistic Decision Graphs

The basic idea is to extend PDTs such that nodes at certain levels of the tree are empty (with $v$ undefined) to denote undetermined variables.[6] To this end we will use somewhat more elaborate notations.

Let $X = \{1^x, 2^x, \ldots, n^x\}$ and $Y = \{1^y, 2^y, \ldots, n^y\}$ be two copies of $\{1, \ldots, n\}$. An order relation $\prec$ on $X \cup Y$ can be written as a bijection $J : \{1, 2, \ldots, 2n\} \to$

---

[5] For those familiar with BDDs, we mention that these operations resemble the non-probabilistic ones: $\hat{\delta}(q, q') = p(q) \wedge \delta(q, q')$ and $w(q') = \exists q\ \hat{\delta}(q, q') = \bigvee_q \hat{\delta}(q, q')$.

[6] In fact we could have started the paper by defining data-structures for conditional probability functions, with a partition of variables into two types. This way we could obtain probability functions as the special case where all the variables are determined, and Markov transition functions as a special case where the sizes of the two sets of variables are the same and certain restrictions are imposed on variable dependencies. However, we prefer clarity over generality.

$X \cup Y$. Without loss of generality we assume that $\prec$ is compatible with the natural ordering of $X$ and of $Y$, i.e. $1^x \prec 2^x \prec \ldots \prec n^x$. Given $J$, any binary string $s \in \mathbb{B}^{\leq 2n}$ can be mapped into a pair of strings $J^x(s)$ and $J^y(s)$ from $\mathbb{B}^{\leq n}$. For example, if $J = 1^x \prec 2^x \prec 1^y \prec 3^x \prec 2^y \prec 3^y$ then for a string $s = x_1 x_2 y_1 x_3 y_2 y_3$, $J^x(s) = x_1 x_2 x_3$ and $J^y(s) = y_1 y_2$. We also extend our string notation for sets: a string of the form $x_{i_1} x_{i_1} \cdots x_{i_m}$ with $0 < i_1 < i_2 < \ldots < i_m \leq n$ will denote a subset of $\mathbb{B}^n$ with the obvious meaning, i.e. the set of $n$-tuples such that the value of every $i_j$-coordinate is $x_{i_j}$.

A Markov transition function over $\mathbb{B}^n$ is a function $\delta : \mathbb{B}^n \to (\mathbb{B}^n \to [0,1])$ whose instances are written as $\delta_{x_1 \cdots x_n}(y_1 \cdots y_n)$. For every $x_1 \cdots x_n$, $\delta_{x_1 \cdots x_n}$ is a probability function which can be written using the chain rule just as as any other probability:

$$\delta_{x_1 \cdots x_n}(y_1 \cdots y_n) = \delta_{x_1 \cdots x_n}(y_1) \cdot \delta_{x_1 \cdots x_n y_1}(y_1 y_2) \cdots \delta_{x_1 \cdots x_n y_1 \cdots y_{n-1}}(y_1 \cdots y_n).$$

We restrict our attention to Markov chains in which every coordinate of the state-space behaves *causally*, i.e. it depends only on the *previous* values of the state variables.[7] This means that for every $x_1 \ldots x_n$ and every $y_i$, $y_j$ we have $\delta_{x_1 \cdots x_n y_i}(y_j) = \delta_{x_1 \cdots x_n}(y_j)$. Hence $\delta$ can be written as:

$$\delta_{x_1 \cdots x_n}(y_1 \cdots y_n) = \delta_{x_1 \cdots x_n}(y_1) \cdot \delta_{x_1 \cdots x_n}(y_2) \cdots \delta_{x_1 \cdots x_n}(y_n). \tag{2}$$

We say that $j^y$ is *independent* of $i^x$ if for every $x_1, \ldots, x_{i-1}, x_{i+1}, \ldots x_n$,

$$\delta_{x_1 \cdots x_{i-1} 0 x_{i+1} \cdots x_n}(y_j) = \delta_{x_1 \cdots x_{i-1} 1 x_{i+1} \cdots x_n}(y_j).$$

In this case we can use the notation $\delta_{x_1 \cdots x_{i-1} x_{i+1} \cdots x_n}(y_j)$. When this is not the case we say that $i^x$ *influences* $j^y$ and denote it by $i^x \to j^y$.

An order relation $\prec$ on $X \cup Y$ is *compatible* with a Markov transition function $\delta$ iff for every $i^x \in X, j^y \in Y$, $i^x \to j^y$ implies $i^x \prec j^y$. The *default ordering* $1^x \prec \ldots \prec n^x \prec 1^y \prec \ldots \prec n^y$ is compatible with *any* $\delta$ and is the only one compatible with a $\delta$ for which every $j^y$ depends on all $X$.

**Definition 4 (Conditional PDT and PDG).**  *A conditional probabilistic decision tree (CPDT) of depth $n$ is a tuple $P = (S, 0, 1, J, v)$ where $S = \mathbb{B}^{\leq 2n}$, $0$ and $1$ are as in a PDT, $J$ is the ordering bijection and $v : S \to [0,1]$ is a partial function, defined only on nodes $s$ such that $J(|s|) \in Y$, satisfying $v(\varepsilon) = 1$ and for every node $s$, $v(s0) + v(s1) = 1$ whenever it is defined. A conditional probabilistic decision graph (CPDG) is $G = (S/\sim, 0, 1, J, v)$ where $\sim$ is the congruence relation of Definition 2.*

**Theorem 2 (CPDT=Markov Transition Function).**  *There is a one-to-one correspondence between Markov transition functions and CPDTs.*

---

[7] Note that one can write Markov transition functions over $Q$ which *do not* admit such a causal decomposition, and this observation might be a source of interesting investigations in the theory of stochastic processes. In fact, the above implies that every $m$-state Markov chain which admits a causal decomposition can be represented in space $O(m \log m)$ instead of $O(m^2)$.

**Sketch of Proof:** Similar to that of Theorem 1. We assume a fixed ordering bijection $J$ compatible with $\delta$. For every $Y$-node $sy_i$ of the CPDT we associate $v(sy_i)$ with the conditional probability $\delta_{J^x(s)}(y_i)$, for example $v(x_1 x_2 y_1 x_3 y_2) = \delta_{x_1 x_2 x_3}(y_2)$. To reconstruct $\delta$ from a tree we go down the tree until we calculate $\delta$ for the lowest $Y$-nodes. To build à CPDT from $\delta$ we climb-up starting from the $Y$-leaves and construct the tree. ⌐

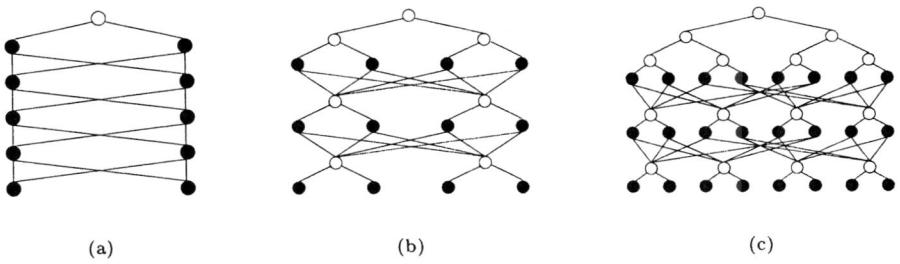

(a)                    (b)                    (c)

**Fig. 3.** Schematic CPDGs for Markov transition function which consist of: (a) Independent Bernoulli trials (b) Independent Markov chains (c) A cascade with $k = 2$. The dark nodes indicate $Y$-nodes.

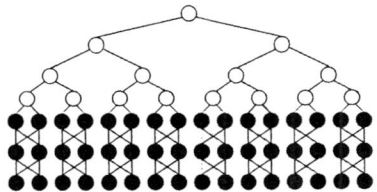

**Fig. 4.** A schematic CPDG for an arbitrary (but causal) Markov transition function.

We mention some classes of probabilistic transition systems such that the pattern of interaction between their components alone suffices for giving an upper-bound on the size of their CPDGs. Consider first the degenerate case of $n$ independent Bernoulli trials. It can be modeled as a direct product of $n$ memory-less automata, for which the probability of the next state is independent of the current state. Thus, $\delta_{x_1 \ldots x_n}(y_1 \ldots y_n)$ can be written as $\delta(y_1) \cdots \delta(y_n)$ and represented by a CPDG without empty nodes, which is in fact a PDG, like in Figure 3-(a).

As a slightly less trivial example consider a direct product of $n$ independent 2-state Markov chains. In this case each $i^y$ depends only on $i^x$ and the transition function can be represented by the CPDG of Figure 3-(b). More generally, consider a *cascade* $\mathcal{A}_1, \ldots, \mathcal{A}_n$ of probabilistic automata where the transition probabilities of each automaton $\mathcal{A}_i$ depends on the states of its $k$ predecessors (including itself) $\mathcal{A}_{i-k+1}, \ldots, \mathcal{A}_{i-1}, \mathcal{A}_i$. Such systems will have a CPDG of size $O(n2^k)$ similar to the one appearing in Figure 3-c for $k = 2$.

When there are no such constraints on variable dependencies, the default order needs to be used and no a-priori lower-bound better than $n2^n$ can be stated (although some independencies might make the corresponding CPDG smaller). We repeat that even this bound is better than the $2^{2n}$ size implied by a straightforward encoding of the transition matrix. The general structure of such a CPDG is depicted in Figure 4.

Going from $p$ and $\delta$ to $\hat{\delta}(p)$ is straightforward: take $v(s)$ from the PDT for $p$ and put it in any nodes $s'$ of the CPDT of $\delta$ such that $J^x(s') = s$. This way the whole tree becomes full and represents the probability $\hat{\delta}(p)$ over $\mathbb{B}^{2n}$.

## 5 Projection

The basic operation on probabilities (and PDGs) is the probabilistic analogue of the elimination of a quantified variable in Boolean functions (and BDDs). This is what is needed to transform $\hat{\delta}(p)$ into $\delta(p)$.

**Definition 5 (Projection).** *Let* $p : \mathbb{B}^n \to [0,1]$ *be a probability. The $k$-projection of $p$, is a function* $p_{\downarrow k} : \mathbb{B}^{n-1} \to [0,1]$ *defined as*

$$p_{\downarrow k}(x_1 \cdots x_{k-1} x_{k+1} \cdots x_n) = \begin{array}{c} p(x_1 \cdots x_{k-1} 0 x_{k+1} \cdots x_n) \\ + \\ p(x_1 \cdots x_{k-1} 1 x_{k+1} \cdots x_n) \end{array} \qquad (3)$$

Using conditional probabilities, (3) can be rewritten as

$$p(x_1 \ldots x_{k-1}) \cdot \begin{bmatrix} p_{x_1 \cdots x_{k-1}}(0 x_{k+1} \cdots x_n) \\ + \\ p_{x_1 \cdots x_{k-1}}(1 x_{k+1} \ldots x_n) \end{bmatrix}$$

and further as

$$p(x_1 \cdots x_{k-1}) \cdot \begin{bmatrix} v(x_1 \cdots x_{k-1} 0) \cdot p_{x_1 \cdots x_{k-1} 0}(x_{k+1} \cdots x_n) \\ + \\ v(x_1 \cdots x_{k-1} 1) \cdot p_{x_1 \cdots x_{k-1} 1}(x_{k+1} \cdots x_n) \end{bmatrix}$$

As one can see, performing a $k$-projection on the PDT representation of $p$ consists of copying the first $k - 1$ levels of the tree and then plugging at each branch $x_1 \cdots x_{k-1}$ a sub-tree which encodes the *weighted sum* of the functions $p_{x_1 \cdots x_{k-1} 0}$ and $p_{x_1 \cdots x_{k-1} 1}$. This is the main computational burden in the manipulation of PDGs. The transformation of a PDT $P = (S, 0, 1, v)$ for $p$ with $S = \mathbb{B}^n$ into a PDT $P_{\downarrow k} = (S_{\downarrow k}, 0, 1, v_{\downarrow k})$ for $p_{\downarrow k}$ with $S_{\downarrow k} = \mathbb{B}^{n-1}$ is performed as follows. For any node $s \in \mathbb{B}^{\leq k-1}$ we have $p_{\downarrow k}(s) = p(s)$. For the other nodes we have

$$p_{\downarrow k}(x_1 \cdots x_{k-1} s) = p(x_1 \cdots x_{k-1} 0 s) + p(x_1 \cdots x_{k-1} 1 s)$$

These values are calculated from the top down and every calculation of $p_{\downarrow k}(sx)$ is followed by calculating $v_{\downarrow k}(sx)$ as $v_{\downarrow k}(sx) = p_{\downarrow k}(sx)/p_{\downarrow k}(s)$, which in the first $k-1$ levels reduces simply to $v_{\downarrow k}(s) = v(s)$. Aplying this procedure $n$ times[8] we transform a probability on $\mathbb{B}^{2n}$ to a probability on $\mathbb{B}^n$ and complete the computation of $p' = p \cdot A_\delta$. While working with PDGs, one can avoid part of the computation whenever there is an equivalence of the form $p_{s0} = p_{s1}$. In that case the weighted sum $r \cdot p_{s0} + (1 - r)p_{s1}$ is equal to both.

# 6  Implementation and Experimental Results

The treatment of the mathematical *real* numbers by computer involves an additional dimension of problematics absent from traditional applications of verification methodology. The continuum is approximated by a very large (but finite) subset of the rationals, the *floating point* numbers. Practitioners seem to be satisfied with this approximation. It turns out that for exploiting the advantages of PDGs we had to go further and round node values to multiples of $2^{-m}$ (for $m$ ranging between 3 to 10), otherwise the size of non-trivial PDGs becomes exponential after few iterations because of the low probability of two nodes having *exactly* the same floating-point value. With this discretization, systems with limited interaction among variables usually converge to vectors with a small PDG description. As for the semantic price of the approximation, if we reflect a bit on the empirical source of probability estimations in models, we realize that these numbers are not sacred and an initial "imprecision" of $2^{-m}$ does not make any difference.

We have implemented these data-structures and algorithms and tested their performance on some generic examples. The implementation is preliminary and does not yet employ all the optimizations one can find in BDD packages. Let us first mention the trivial cases. For $n$ randomly-generated mutually-independent Markov chains we can treat almost any $n$. This is, of course, not so impressive if one realizes that each chain could be simulated separately. Yet someone unaware of BDDs will be rather surprised to see how fast you can multiply a $2^{15} \times 2^{15}$ transition matrix void of any apparent structure or sparseness (see table 1). A slightly less trivial example is a chain of noisy communication channels where each component copies the value of its predecessor with probability $1 - \epsilon$. Such a chain converges to a uniform probability vector where $p(q) = 1/2^n$ for every state. Here again we could iterate for very large $n$ with a linear growth in the size of the PDGs.

Next, we have tested randomly-generated cascades of communication depth 2, which using the previously mentioned discretization, usually converge to vectors with small PDGs, although exponential ones are, of course, still possible. We demonstrate the time and space behavior of the algorithm on a family consisting of a cascade of noisy AND gates such that each component becomes the conjunction of its previous value and that of its predecessors (Figure 5) with

---

[8] Like in BDDS, this procedure can be extended naturally to a procedure that eliminates several variables in a single pass.

```
0.000564 0.000093 0.000412 0.000068 0.000094 0.000015 0.000068 0.000011 0.000727 0.000120 ...
0.000653 0.000003 0.000477 0.000002 0.000108 0.000001 0.000079 0.000000 0.000842 0.000004 ...
0.000823 0.000135 0.000153 0.000025 0.000137 0.000022 0.000025 0.000004 0.001061 0.000175 ...
0.000953 0.000005 0.000177 0.000001 0.000158 0.000001 0.000029 0.000000 0.001229 0.000006 ...
   ...      ...      ...      ...      ...      ...      ...      ...      ...      ...
```

**Table 1.** An initial fragment of a $2^{15} \times 2^{15}$ matrix which can be iterated until convergence within less than a second.

probability 0.9. The performance results are depicted in Figure 6 and although space behaves nicely, computation time still grows exponentially, reaching almost 4 hours for $n = 54$. The reason lies in the fundamental difference between BDDs and PDGs: in the former, when an algorithms encounters a node, it does not need to remember via which branch the node is reached, and thus the hashing mechanism prevents duplicate calls. On the other hand, in PDGs, each time the projection procedure is called with a node, it has, as an additional parameter, the probability associated with its parent. Hence procedure calls with identical arguments are rather rare and the current implementation needs to do exponential work on linear-sized PDGs. We are currently investigating improvements of the implementation.

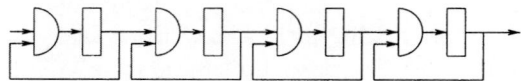

**Fig. 5.** A chain of noisy AND gates.

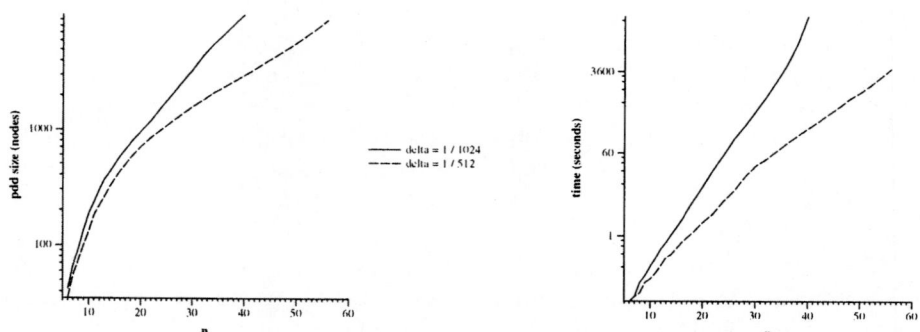

**Fig. 6.** The PDG size and time until convergence as a function of the number of variables, for discretizations of 1/1024 and 1/512.

# 7 Discussion

We have introduced and implemented a new method for manipulating large probabilistic transition systems. We hope that this technique will improve the performance of probabilistic simulation tools. In addition, the investigation of the structure of PDGs might contribute to a better understanding of the structure of probabilistic functions. The application domains which might benefit from such a technique are numerous and include performance and reliability analysis, probabilistic verification, planning under uncertainty [P94,BDH99], calculation of equilibria in economics, statistical mechanics and more.

This work is built on what we consider to be the main insight of the BDD experience: in many situations the indices of rows and columns in matrices are the outcome of "flattenning" of much more structured domains. This flattenning, which is unavoidable if one wants to draw a matrix on a two-dimensional sheet of paper, hides the structure of the problem, or at least makes it very hard to retrieve.[9] BDDs and PDGs suggest a way of maintaining this structural information and exploiting it in efficient computations.

Among previous extensions of BDD technology to represent functions from $\mathbb{B}^n$ to $\mathbb{N}$ (motivated chiefly by arithmetical circuits), $\mathbb{R}$ and other domains we mention the structure called Multi-terminal BDDs (MTBDD) in [CFM+93] and Algebraic Decision Diagrams (ADD) in [BFG+93]. This is a straightforward extension of BDDs with leaves having values in non-Boolean domains. Algorithms for performing matrix multiplications and other operations on these representations have been proposed and applied, for example, to probabilistic verification [BCG+97]. The main drawback of MTBDDs/ADDs is that they yield a succint representation only if the corresponding vectors and matrices have a lot of *identical* entries, e.g. sparse matrices having many zeros. In contrast many generic examples of functions with no interaction between the variables will lead to exponential MTBDDs: for example it is not hard to create probabilities on $\mathbb{B}^n$ with all variables mutually-independent, and yet no two elements will have the same probability. In fact, the ability to represent functions concisely as decision graphs *without* putting any information on the non-leaf nodes is a special property of Boolean algebra.

The above observation has led some researchers in the hardware verification community [VPL96,TP97] to consider extending BDD with values on their edges (which is practically the same as putting values on the nodes, as we do here). This structure is called Edge-valued BDD (EVBDD) and it has been used to encode the so-called Pseudo-Boolean functions which are essentially functions from $\{0,1\}^n$ to $\mathbb{N}$. EVBDDs contain both additive and multiplicative constants and in some cases overcome the limitations of MTBDDs. However, since the class of functions treated by EVBDDs is much less constrained than the class of

---

[9] Just compare the non-intuitive definition of the Kronecker product (also known as Tensor product) of two matrices with the straightforward Cartesian product of automata.

probabilistic functions, normalization and matrix multiplication are much more complicated than the ones reported in this paper.

Finally, let us mention another formalism, related to PDGs, the *Bayesian Networks* which are used extensively in AI [P88,J96]. Like PDGs, Bayesian networks consist of a graphical representation of variables and their probabilistic dependencies. The comparison between the two formalisms is outside the scope of this paper, but it seems that PDGs can be viewed as a constrained and well-behaving sub-class of networks, with a special emphasis on the *dynamic* aspects (next-state probabilities) which makes them, perhaps, more suitable for treating large-scale Markov decision processes.

**Acknowledgements**: We are grateful to Moshe Tennenholz for raising the possibility of applying some verification techniques to AI problems of planning under uncertainty. His visit in Grenoble, in fact, triggered this work. We thank Amir Pnueli for many fruitful discussions at various stages of this work, and in particular for the observations concerning causal Markov chains and weighted sum of identical sub-trees. Eugene Asarin reminded us of certain facts concerning the convergence of probabilistic matrix multiplications.

# References

[B86]     R.E. Bryant, Graph-based Algorithms for Boolean Function Manipulation, *IEEE Trans. on Computers* C-35, 677-691, 1986.

[BCM+93] J.R. Burch, E.M. Clarke, K.L. McMillan, D.L. Dill, and L.J. Hwang, Symbolic Model-Checking: $10^{20}$ States and Beyond, *Information and Computation* 98, 142-70, 1992.

[BDH99]   C. Boutilier, T. Dean and S. Hanks, Decision Theoretic Planning: Structural Assumptions and Computational Leverage, *J. of AI Research* (to appear).

[BFG+93]  R.I. Bahar, E.A. Frohm, C.M. Ganoa, G.D. Hachtel, E. Macii, A. Pardo and F. Somenzi, Algebraic Decision Diagrams and their Applications, *Proc. ICCAD'93*, 188-191, 1993.

[BCG+97]  C. Baier, E. Clarke, V. Garmhausen-Hartonas, M. Kwiatkowska and M. Ryan, Symbolic Model Checking for Probabilistic Processes, in P. Degano, R. Gorrieri and A. Marchetti-Spaccamela (Eds.), *Proc. ICALP'97*, 430-440, LNCS 1256, Springer, 1997.

[CFM+93]  E. M. Clarke, M. Fujita, P. C. McGeer, K. L. Mcmillan and J. C.-Y. Yang, Multi-terminal Binary decision Diagrams: An Efficient Data-structure for Matrix Representation, *Proc. ILWS'93*, 1-15, 1993.

[J96]     F.V. Jensen, *An Introduction to Bayesian Networks*, Springer, 1996.

[McM93]   K.L. McMillan, *Symbolic Model-Checking: an Approach to the State-Explosion problem*, Kluwer, 1993.

[MT98]    C. Meinel and T. Theobald, *Algorithms and Data Structures in VLSI Design: OBDD - Foundations and Applications*, Springer, 1998.

[P88]     J. Pearl, *Probabilistic Reasoning in Intelligent Systems*, Morgan Kaufmann, 1988.

[P94]     M.L. Puterman, *Markov Decision Processes*, Wiley, 1994.

[TP97]    P. Tafertshofer and M. Pedram, Factored Edge-Valued Binary Decision Diagrams, *Formal Methods in system Design* 10, 137-164, 1997.

[VPL96]   S. B. K. Vrudhula, M. Pedram and Y.-T. Lai, Edge-valued Binary Decision Diagrams, in T. Sasao and M. Fujita (Eds.), *Representations of Discrete Functions*, 109-132, Kluwer, 1996.

# Model Checking Partial State Spaces
# with 3-Valued Temporal Logics
# (Extended Abstract)

Glenn Bruns and Patrice Godefroid

Bell Laboratories, Lucent Technologies
{grb,god}@bell-labs.com

**Abstract.** We address the problem of relating the result of model checking a partial state space of a system to the properties actually possessed by the system. We represent incomplete state spaces as partial Kripke structures, and give a 3-valued interpretation to modal logic formulas on these structures. The third truth value ⊥ means "unknown whether true or false". We define a preorder on partial Kripke structures that reflects their degree of completeness. We then provide a logical characterization of this preorder. This characterization thus relates properties of less complete structures to properties of more complete structures. We present similar results for labeled transition systems and show a connection to intuitionistic modal logic. We also present a 3-valued CTL model checking algorithm, which returns ⊥ only when the partial state space lacks information needed for a definite answer about the complete state space.

## 1 Introduction

The theory and engineering of model checking has led to tools that can analyze systems with millions of states. However, many systems we would like to analyze have state spaces that are still often orders of magnitude larger than these tools can handle. In this case a common approach is simply to explore just a part of the state space; unexplored states and transitions are then absent in the incomplete or "partial" state space.

In model checking a partial state space, the main issue is how answers obtained in checking the partial state space relate to properties of the full state space. Obviously, one cannot assume that all answers apply to the full state space. The partial state space may be lacking "bad" states one is interested in avoiding, or "good" states that one is interested in reaching. Naively, one could work only with simple safety properties such as "all reachable states satisfy proposition $p$", with the understanding that if the answer is false in the partial state space then it is also false in the complete state space. But this approach too strongly restricts the properties we can check.

Clearly a more systematic understanding is needed. We can work logically and ask: which class of properties will hold of the complete state space just if they hold of the partial state space? Or we can work operationally and ask: how should we describe the relationship between a partial state space and a more complete one? For example, we might consider that a partial state space is *simulated* by a more complete one. Then we know that box-free modal mu-calculus formulas that hold of the partial state space will hold of the complete state space [BBLS92]. A problem with using the simulation relation for this purpose is that it limits the kinds of properties we can check of the partial state space, and does not tell us that if a property fails to hold of a partial state space then it also fails to hold of more complete state spaces.

Our solution to this problem is to use models that capture explicitly the incompleteness of state spaces, and to use 3-valued logics to capture the possibility that we may not know whether a property is true or not in a partial state space. In this approach every formula of the logic can be checked of the partial state space. If the answer true or false is obtained then the answer also holds of the complete state space. If the answer $\perp$ (meaning "unknown") is obtained then the partial state space lacks information needed for a definite answer about the complete state space.

A state-based framework is adopted for most of the paper. In the next section we review Kripke structures and propositional modal logic. In Section 3 we define partial Kripke structures and the interpretation of modal logic on these structures. We also define a preorder on partial Kripke structures that reflects their degree of completeness and show that propositional modal logic (under our 3-valued interpretation) characterizes this preorder. In Section 4 we present a model checker for 3-valued CTL. In Section 5 we show how our results can be applied to the problem of model-checking partial state space. In Section 6 the main results of Section 3 are reworked in an action-based framework. In Section 7 we present our conclusions and discuss related work.

## 2 Kripke Structures and Modal Logic

Let $P$ be a nonempty finite set of *atomic propositions*.

**Definition 1.** *A Kripke structure $M$ is a tuple $(S, L, \mathcal{R})$, where $S$ is a set of states, $L : S \times P \to \{true, false\}$ is an* interpretation *that associates a truth value in $\{true, false\}$ with each atomic proposition in $P$ for each state in $S$, and $\mathcal{R} \subseteq S \times S$ is a* transition *relation on $S$.*

For technical convenience, we assume that a Kripke structure has no terminating state by requiring that $\mathcal{R}$ be *total*, i.e., that every state has an outgoing $\mathcal{R}$-transition. This assumption does not restrict the modeling power of the formalism, since we can model a terminated execution as repeating forever its last state by adding a self-loop to that state. Note that Kripke structures can be *nondeterministic*: a state can have more than one outgoing $\mathcal{R}$-transition. We also assume that the number of outgoing transitions from a state is finite.

Temporal logics are modal logics geared towards the description of the temporal ordering of events [Eme90]. Propositional modal logic (e.g, see [Var97]) is propositional logic extended with the modal operator $\Diamond$. Propositional modal logic can itself be extended with a fixpoint operator to form a modal fixpoint logic, also referred to as the propositional $\mu$-calculus [Koz83]. This very expressive logic includes as fragments linear-time temporal logic (LTL) [MP92] and computation-tree logic (CTL) [CE81].

For the sake of simplicity, let us first consider propositional modal logic. More expressive logics will be discussed later. We now recall the syntax and semantics of propositional modal logic.

**Definition 2.** *Given a nonempty finite set $P$ of atomic propositions, formulas of propositional modal logic have the following abstract syntax, where $p$ ranges over $P$:*

$$\phi ::= p \mid \neg\phi \mid \phi_1 \wedge \phi_2 \mid \Diamond\phi$$

**Definition 3.** *The satisfaction of a formula $\phi$ of propositional modal logic in a state $s$ of a Kripke structure $M = (S, L, \mathcal{R})$, written $(M, s) \models \phi$, is defined inductively as follows:*

$$
\begin{aligned}
(M, s) &\models p & &\text{if } L(s, p) = true \\
(M, s) &\models \neg\phi & &\text{if } (M, s) \not\models \phi \\
(M, s) &\models \phi_1 \wedge \phi_2 & &\text{if } (M, s) \models \phi_1 \text{ and } (M, s) \models \phi_2 \\
(M, s) &\models \Diamond\phi & &\text{if } (M, t) \models \phi \text{ for some } t \text{ such that } (s, t) \in \mathcal{R}
\end{aligned}
$$

The derived modal operator $\Box$ is the dual of $\Diamond$, i.e., $\neg\Diamond\neg$. Thus, we have $(M, s) \models \Box\phi$ if $(M, t) \models \phi$ for all $t$ such that $(s, t) \in \mathcal{R}$. When $M$ is understood, we write $s \models \phi$ instead of $(M, s) \models \phi$.

Propositional modal logic can be used to define an equivalence relation on states of Kripke structures: two states are equivalent if they satisfy the same set of formulas of the logic. It is well known [HM85] that the equivalence relation induced in this way by propositional modal logic coincides with the notion of bisimulation relation [Mil89,Par81] (or more accurately, with that of zig-zag relation [vB84], since propositions are mentioned in the relation).

**Definition 4.** *Let $M_1 = (S_1, L_1, \mathcal{R}_1)$ and $M_2 = (S_2, L_2, \mathcal{R}_2)$ be Kripke structures. A binary relation $\mathcal{B} \subseteq S_1 \times S_2$ is a bisimulation relation if $(s_1, s_2) \in \mathcal{B}$ implies:*

- *$\forall p \in P : L_1(s_1, p) = L_2(s_2, p)$,*
- *if $(s_1, s_1') \in \mathcal{R}_1$, then there is some $s_2' \in S_2$ such that $(s_2, s_2') \in \mathcal{R}_2$ and $(s_1', s_2') \in \mathcal{B}$, and*
- *if $(s_2, s_2') \in \mathcal{R}_2$, then there is some $s_1' \in S_1$ such that $(s_1, s_1') \in \mathcal{R}_1$ and $(s_1', s_2') \in \mathcal{B}$.*

*Two states $s_1$ and $s_2$ are bisimilar, denoted $s_1 \sim s_2$, if they are related by some bisimulation relation.*

**Theorem 1.** *[HM85] Let $M_1 = (S_1, L_1, \mathcal{R}_1)$ and $M_2 = (S_2, L_2, \mathcal{R}_2)$ be Kripke structures such that $s_1 \in S_1$ and $s_2 \in S_2$, and let $\Phi$ denote the set of all formulas of propositional modal logic. Then*

$$(\forall\phi \in \Phi : [(M_1, s_1) \models \phi] = [(M_2, s_2) \models \phi]) \text{ iff } s_1 \sim s_2.$$

Propositional modal logic is then called a *logical characterization* of $\sim$. This means that propositional modal logic cannot distinguish between bisimilar states, and that states satisfying exactly the same set of propositional modal logic formulas are bisimilar.

# 3 Partial Kripke Structures and 3-Valued Modal Logic

To model check partial state spaces, we need a way to model the absence of information about the missing parts of the full state space, both operationally (in terms of Kripke structures) and logically (in terms of modal logics). A natural approach to the operational modeling of incompleteness is to model an incomplete state space with a kind of partially-defined Kripke structure. We show that a compatible approach in the logical modeling of incompleteness is to interpret modal logic with a third truth value $\perp$, which is understood as "unknown". More precisely, we model partial state spaces as partial Kripke structures. We then define a 3-valued modal logic whose semantics is defined with respect to partial Kripke structures. We proceed by studying an equivalence relation and preorder implicitly defined by this logic. As before, let $P$ be a nonempty finite set of atomic propositions.

**Definition 5.** *A partial Kripke structure $M$ is a tuple $(S, L, \mathcal{R})$, where $S$ is a set of states, $L : S \times P \to \{true, \perp, false\}$ is an interpretation that associates a truth value in $\{true, \perp, false\}$ with each atomic proposition in $P$ for each state in $S$, and $\mathcal{R} \subseteq S \times S$ is a transition relation on $S$.*

In interpreting propositional modal logic on partial Kripke structures, we interpret the operators $\wedge$ and $\neg$ using Kleene's strongest regular 3-valued propositional logic [Kle87]. In this logic $\perp$ is understood as "unknown whether true or false". A simple way to define conjunction (resp. disjunction) in this logic is as the minimum (resp. maximum) of its arguments, under the order $false < \perp < true$. We write min and max for these functions, and extend them to sets in the obvious way, with $min(\emptyset) = true$ and $max(\emptyset) = false$. We define negation using the function neg that maps $true$ to $false$, $false$ to $true$, and $\perp$ to $\perp$. Notice that these functions give the usual meaning of the propositional operators when applied to values $true$ and $false$.

We now consider a 3-valued propositional modal logic having the same syntax as propositional modal logic, and the following semantics.

**Definition 6.** *The truth value of a formula $\phi$ of 3-valued propositional modal logic in a state $s$ of a partial Kripke structure $M = (S, L, \mathcal{R})$, written $[(M, s) \models \phi]$, is defined inductively as follows:*

$$[(M, s) \models p] = L(s, p)$$
$$[(M, s) \models \neg\phi] = neg([(M, s) \models \phi])$$
$$[(M, s) \models \phi_1 \wedge \phi_2] = min([(M, s) \models \phi_1], [(M, s) \models \phi_2])$$
$$[(M, s) \models \Diamond\phi] = max(\{[(M, t) \models \phi] \mid (s, t) \in \mathcal{R}\})$$

We again define $\Box$ as the dual of $\Diamond$, so $[(M, s) \models \Box\phi] = min(\{[(M, t) \models \phi] \mid (s, t) \in \mathcal{R}\})$. This semantics gives the usual meaning of the propositional and modal operators when applied to complete Kripke structures.

This 3-valued propositional modal logic can be used to define a preorder on partial Kripke structures that reflects their degree of completeness. Let $\leq$ be the ordering on truth values such that $\perp \leq true$, $\perp \leq false$, $x \leq x$ (for all $x \in \{true, \perp, false\}$), and $x \not\leq y$ otherwise. Note that the operators neg, min and max are monotonic with respect to $\leq$: if $x \leq x'$ and $y \leq y'$, we have $neg(x) \leq neg(x')$, $min(x, y) \leq min(x', y')$, and $max(x, y) \leq max(x', y')$. This property is important to prove the results that follow.

**Definition 7.** *Let* $M_1 = (S_1, L_1, \mathcal{R}_1)$ *and* $M_2 = (S_2, L_2, \mathcal{R}_2)$ *be partial Kripke structures. The* completeness preorder *is the greatest relation* $\preceq \subseteq S_1 \times S_2$ *such that* $s_1 \preceq s_2$ *implies the following:*

- $\forall p \in P : L_1(s_1, p) \leq L_2(s_2, p)$,
- *if* $(s_1, s_1') \in \mathcal{R}_1$, *then there is some* $s_2' \in S_2$ *such that* $(s_2, s_2') \in \mathcal{R}_2$ *and* $s_1' \preceq s_2'$, *and*
- *if* $(s_2, s_2') \in \mathcal{R}_2$, *then there is some* $s_1' \in S_1$ *such that* $(s_1, s_1') \in \mathcal{R}_1$ *and* $s_1' \preceq s_2'$.

Intuitively, $s_1 \preceq s_2$ means that $s_1$ and $s_2$ are "nearly bisimilar" except that the atomic propositions in state $s_1$ may be less defined than in state $s_2$. Obviously, $s_1 \sim s_2$ implies $s_1 \preceq s_2$.

The following theorem shows how the completeness preorder can be logically characterized with 3-valued propositional modal logic.

**Theorem 2.** *Let* $M_1 = (S_1, L_1, \mathcal{R}_1)$ *and* $M_2 = (S_2, L_2, \mathcal{R}_2)$ *be partial Kripke structures such that* $s_1 \in S_1$ *and* $s_2 \in S_2$, *and let* $\Phi$ *denote the set of all formulas of 3-valued propositional modal logic. Then*

$$(\forall \phi \in \Phi : [(M_1, s_1) \models \phi] \leq [(M_2, s_2) \models \phi]) \text{ iff } s_1 \preceq s_2.$$

*Proof.* Proofs of theorems are omitted in this extended abstract because of space constraints.

In other words, partial Kripke structures that are "more complete" with respect to $\preceq$ have more definite properties with respect to $\leq$, i.e., have more properties that are either *true* or *false*. Moreover, any formula $\phi$ of 3-valued propositional modal logic that evaluates to *true* or *false* on a partial Kripke structure has the same truth value when evaluated on every more complete structure.

Formulas that evaluate to $\perp$ on a partial Kripke structure must be evaluated on a more complete structure to get a definite answer. Obviously, any partial Kripke structure can be completed to obtain a traditional fully-defined Kripke structure, where $\phi$ always evaluates to either *true* or *false*. Some partial Kripke structures can only be completed to form Kripke structures that all satisfy the property $\phi$, or to form Kripke structures that all violate $\phi$ (this is the case, for instance but not exclusively, when $\phi$ is a tautology or is unsatisfiable with a 2-valued interpretation). Some other partial Kripke structures can be completed to form Kripke structures that satisfy $\phi$ as well as Kripke structures that violate $\phi$. Note that checking a formula $\phi$ on a partial Kripke structure may return $\perp$ even if $\phi$ is a tautology or is unsatisfiable in the 2-valued interpretation.

The following theorem states that 3-valued propositional modal logic logically characterizes the equivalence relation induced by the completeness preorder $\preceq$.

**Theorem 3.** *Let $M_1 = (S_1, L_1, \mathcal{R}_1)$ and $M_2 = (S_2, L_2, \mathcal{R}_2)$ be partial Kripke structures such that $s_1 \in S_1$ and $s_2 \in S_2$, and let $\Phi$ denote the set of all formulas of 3-valued propositional modal logic. Then*

$$(\forall \phi \in \Phi : [(M_1, s_1) \models \phi] = [(M_2, s_2) \models \phi]) \text{ iff } (s_1 \preceq s_2 \text{ and } s_2 \preceq s_1).$$

The bisimulation relation of Definition 4 can be applied directly to partial Kripke structures. Two states $s_1$ and $s_2$ of partial Kripke structures are *bisimilar*, denoted $s_1 \sim s_2$, if they are related by some bisimulation relation. Since $\sim$ is a stronger relation than $\preceq$, $s_1 \sim s_2$ implies both $s_1 \preceq s_2$ and $s_2 \preceq s_1$, and that 3-valued propositional modal logic cannot distinguish between bisimilar states.

However, the converse is not true: $s_1 \preceq s_2$ and $s_2 \preceq s_1$ does not imply $s_1 \sim s_2$. This is illustrated by the example below. The existence of such an example proves that, in contrast with 2-valued propositional modal logic, 3-valued propositional modal logic is *not* a logical characterization of bisimulation as defined in Definition 4.

*Example 1.* Here is an example of two non-bisimilar states that cannot be distinguished by any formula of 3-valued propositional modal logic.

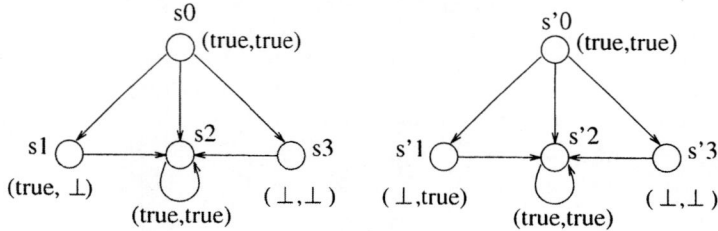

These two partial Kripke structures have two atomic propositions $p$ and $q$, whose truth value is defined in each state as indicated in the figure by a pair of the form $(p, q)$. We have the following relations:

- $s_2 \preceq s_2'$ and $s_2' \preceq s_2$,
- $s_3 \preceq s_3'$ and $s_3' \preceq s_3$,
- $s_1 \preceq s_2'$ and $s_3' \preceq s_1$, $s_1' \preceq s_2$ and $s_3 \preceq s_1'$,
- $s_0 \preceq s_0'$ and $s_0' \preceq s_0$.

We have that $s_0 \preceq s_0'$ and $s_0' \preceq s_0$, but $s_0 \not\sim s_0'$ since $s_1$ is not bisimilar to any state in the second partial Kripke structure.

## 4   A Model Checker for 3-Valued CTL

We have so far focused on modal propositional logic because it is a simple context in which to present our ideas. However, this logic cannot express even simple safety properties. In this section we present a 3-valued semantics for computation-tree logic (CTL) [CE81] as well as a model-checking algorithm. We consider CTL because it extends the expressiveness of modal propositional logic, the model-checking algorithm for the standard 2-valued interpretation is well known, and because it is expressive enough to specify many interesting properties.

Our algorithm is based on the algorithm of [CES86]. We focus here, as in [CES86], on formulas of the form $A(f_1 \, \mathcal{U} \, f_2)$, since the model checking of other CTL formulas is either similar or much simpler. Formula $A(f_1 \, \mathcal{U} \, f_2)$ holds of a state in a Kripke structure if, along all paths from the state, there exists a state in the path for which $f_2$ holds and for which $f_1$ holds of all previous states in the path.

The semantics of CTL is given as an inductive definition of the satisfaction relation $\models$ between a Kripke structure $M = (S, L, \mathcal{R})$ and a CTL formula. The clause of the definition of $\models$ for formula $A(f_1 \, \mathcal{U} \, f_2)$ reads

$$s_0 \models A(f_1 \, \mathcal{U} \, f_2) \quad \text{iff} \quad \text{for all paths } (s_0, s_1, \ldots),$$
$$\exists i \geq 0 : s_i \models f_2 \wedge \forall j : 0 \leq j < i \Rightarrow s_j \models f_1$$

(Here the Kripke structure $M$ is understood.) To see if a state satisfies $A(f_1 \, \mathcal{U} \, f_2)$, the procedure $au$ of the CTL model checker of [CES86] works roughly as follows. It is called with a formula $f$ of the form $A(f_1 \, \mathcal{U} \, f_2)$, a state $s_0$, and a result variable $b$. It is assumed that when $au$ is called a state is $labeled$ with $f_1$ just if it satisfies $f_1$, and similarly for $f_2$. A depth-first search of the states reachable from $s_0$ is then made, with states $marked$ as they are visited. Initially, if $s_0$ is labeled with $f_2$, then $s_0$ is labeled with $A(f_1 \, \mathcal{U} \, f_2)$ and the procedure terminates with $b$ set to $true$. Otherwise if $s_0$ is not labeled with $f_1$, then the procedure terminates with $b$ set to $false$. Otherwise procedure $au$ is called recursively on all successors of $s_0$. If a recursive call is made to a state that is already marked, the procedure terminates with $b$ set to $false$.

For 3-valued CTL we define $A(f_1 \, \mathcal{U} \, f_2)$ as follows:

$$[s_0 \models A(f_1 \, \mathcal{U} \, f_2)] = \min(\{[(s_0, s_1, \ldots) \models f_1 \, \mathcal{U} \, f_2] \mid (s_0, s_1, \ldots) \text{ a path}\})$$
$$[(s_0, s_1, \ldots) \models f_1 \, \mathcal{U} \, f_2] = \max(\{[(s_0, s_1, \ldots) \models f_1 \, \mathcal{U}_k \, f_2] \mid k \geq 0\})$$
$$[(s_0, s_1, \ldots) \models f_1 \, \mathcal{U}_k \, f_2] = \min(\min(\{[s_i \models f_1] \mid i < k\}), \{[s_k \models f_2]\})$$

The min operators in this definition correspond to conjunction and universal quantification in the definition for 2-valued CTL above, and similarly the max operator in this definition corresponds to existential quantification in the definition above. The two definitions agree on complete Kripke structures.

Consider the problem of adapting the procedure $au$ of the CTL model checker of [CES86] to the 3-valued case. One way in which the algorithm becomes more complicated is in checking a state for the first time. Suppose our partial Kripke structure has only a single path, and that the value of formulas $f_1$ and $f_2$ for the first three states on the path are as follows:

$$s_0 : (f_1 = true, f_2 = \perp), s_1 : (f_1 = true, f_2 = false), s_2 : (f_1 = \perp, f_2 = true)$$

We see that $f_2$ is $\perp$ at $s_0$, but we cannot conclude immediately that $A(f_1 \, \mathcal{U} \, f_2)$ is $\perp$ at $s_0$ because we may find (and do, in this example) that $f_2$ is $true$ at a later state. However, if $f_1$ were $\perp$ or $false$ at state $s_1$, then we could conclude that $A(f_1 \, \mathcal{U} \, f_2)$ is $\perp$ at $s_0$.

Determining the result when a cycle is detected also becomes more complicated. In the 2-valued algorithm we know that $f_1$ holds but $f_2$ does not along all states in a cycle. In the 3-valued case, for states in a cycle it may be that $f_2$ is *true* and $f_2$ is *false*, or $f_2$ is *true* and $f_2$ is $\perp$, or $f_2$ is $\perp$ and $f_2$ if *false*.

Figure 1 shows our modified version of the procedure *au* of [CES86]. The idea behind the algorithm is to check the partial Kripke structure twice. First check the structure under a *pessimistic* interpretation, in which the value $\perp$ is understood as *false*. If the result of the check is *true* then return *true* as the 3-valued result. Then check the structure under an *optimistic* interpretation, in which the value $\perp$ is understood as *true*. If the result of this check is *false* then return *false*. Otherwise return $\perp$.

Our algorithm merges these two checks so that they can be run at the same time. Procedure *au* now takes an additional argument $mode \subseteq \{p, o\}$ and returns a pair $(v_p, v_o)$. If *mode* contains constant $p$ (resp. $o$) then value $v_p$ ($v_o$) is the result of the pessimistic search. If *mode* does not contain $p$ (resp. $o$) then $v_p$ ($v_o$) is *false*. When $mode = \{p, o\}$ we interpret the returned pairs $(false, false)$, $(false, true)$, and $(true, true)$ in a 3-valued sense as *false*, $\perp$, and *true*, respectively. Notice that an optimistic check must give *true* if a pessimistic one does, so result $(true, false)$ is impossible.

In our algorithm states have distinct optimistic and pessimistic labelings. Function $labeled(s, f, i)$ returns *true* just if state $s$ has label $i \in \{p, o\}$ for formula $f$. Function $add\_label\_i(s, f, i)$ gives state $s$ label $i$ for formula $f$. Function $label(s, f, mode)$ returns a pair $(v_p, v_o)$ where $v_i$ is *false* if $i \notin mode$ and $labeled(s, f, i)$ otherwise. The operator $\vee$ on pairs of truth values is defined by $(x, y) \vee (u, w) = (x \vee u, y \vee w)$. The order $<$ on pairs of truth values is defined by $(false, false) < (false, true) < (true, false) < (true, true)$.

States have distinct optimistic and pessimistic markings as well. Function $marked(s)$ returns the set of interpretations for which state $s$ is marked. Function $add\_mark(s, A)$, where $A \subseteq \{p, o\}$, marks $s$ with each interpretation in $A$.

The proof of correctness of our model-checking algorithm is omitted in this extended abstract. Our modified procedure, like the original one, requires time $O(\text{card}(S) + \text{card}(\mathcal{R}))$, and thus the overall complexity of the resulting 3-valued CTL model-checking algorithm is still $O(\text{length}(\phi) \times (\text{card}(S) + \text{card}(\mathcal{R})))$.

# 5 Applications

We now discuss how to exploit the results of the previous sections in practice. Consider a (possibly infinite) complete state space modeled as a Kripke structure $M = (S, L, \mathcal{R})$. Imagine that this state space is so large that only part of it can be explored. We now present a simple construction to define a partial Kripke structure $M' = (S', L', \mathcal{R}')$ representing only the explored states and transitions of this state space.

Let $S_E \subseteq S$ be the set of explored states and $\mathcal{R}_E \subseteq \mathcal{R}$ be the set of explored transitions. For this application, we can assign the value $\perp$ to all the atomic propositions in each unexplored state $s \in S \setminus S_E$. Since unexplored states are indistinguishable with this model, a single state $s_\perp$ of $M'$ is enough to model all of them. For every unexplored transition $(s, t) \in \mathcal{R} \setminus \mathcal{R}_E$ such that $s \in S_E$,

```
1   procedure au(f,s,b,mode)
2   begin
3       parent_mode := mode;
4       mode := mode - marked(s);

5       add_mark(s,mode);
6       temp_mode := mode;
7       for all i in temp_mode do
8           begin
9               if labeled(s,f2,i) then
10                  begin add_label_i(s,f,i); mode := mode - {i} end;
11              else if ¬labeled(s,f1,i) then
12                  mode := mode - {i}
13          end;
14      if mode = ∅ then
15          begin b := label(s,f,parent_mode); return end;

16      push(s,ST);
17      min := (true, true);
18      for all s1 ∈ successors(s) do
19          begin
20              au(f,s1,b1,mode);
21              if b1 < min then min := b1;
22              if min = (false, false) then break
23          end;

24      pop(ST);
25      b := min ∨ label(s,f,parent_mode - mode);
26      add_label(s,f,b);
27      return
28  end
```

**Fig. 1.** Procedure *au* of model-checking algorithm for 3-valued CTL

we add a transition $(s, s_\perp)$ in $\mathcal{R}'$ to model that we do not know where this unexplored transition leads. To preserve our assumption that $\mathcal{R}'$ is total, we also assume there is a transition $(s_\perp, s_\perp)$ in $\mathcal{R}'$. However, this is the only outgoing $\mathcal{R}'$-transition of $s_\perp$, modeling that unexplored states cannot lead back to explored states. In summary, we have the following:

- $S' = S_E \cup \{s_\perp\}$
- $L'(s,p) = \begin{cases} L(s,p) \text{ if } s \in S_E \\ \perp \qquad \text{if } s = s_\perp \end{cases}$
- $\mathcal{R}' = \mathcal{R}_E \cup \{(s, s_\perp) \mid s \in S_E \text{ and } (s,t) \in \mathcal{R} \setminus \mathcal{R}_E\} \cup \{(s_\perp, s_\perp)\}$

Let us assume that $M$ has initial state $s_0$, and that $s_0$ is explored and denoted by $s_0'$ in $S'$. It is easy to prove the following.

**Theorem 4.** Let Kripke structure $M = (S, L, \mathcal{R})$ with initial state $s_0$ represent a complete state space, and let $M' = (S', L', \mathcal{R}')$ be a partial Kripke structure *built from M by the construction above. Then*

$$s_0' \preceq s_0.$$

Theorems 2 and 4 together guarantee that any formula $\phi$ of 3-valued propositional modal logic that evaluates to *true* or *false* on a partial state space defined with the construction above has the same truth value when evaluated on the corresponding complete state space.

*Example 2.* Consider the three following partial Kripke structures with a single atomic proposition $p$, whose truth value is defined in each state as indicated in the figure.

The formula $A(true\,\mathcal{U}\,p)$ of 3-valued CTL has a different truth value in each of the top states of these partial Kripke structures: $[s_1 \models A(true\,\mathcal{U}\,p)] = true$, $[s_2 \models A(true\,\mathcal{U}\,p)] = \perp$, and $[s_3 \models A(true\,\mathcal{U}\,p)] = false$.

An important application of our framework is thus to make it possible to cope with missing parts of the state space during model checking and still obtain a definite answer when this is possible. In the case of CTL properties, the algorithm of the previous section captures exactly when this is possible and how do it, for any CTL formula and any partial Kripke structure.

Other possible applications for our framework include the evaluation of heuristics for guiding the search and pruning state spaces (one can determine which heuristics more often give definite answers for which properties), and the analysis of systems containing state variables whose values cannot be read (and hence are unknown) at some points during the execution of the system.

## 6   An Action-Based Approach to Partial State Spaces

In this section we revisit the main results of Section 3 in an *action-based* framework, where system behavior is modeled as a labeled transition system rather than a Kripke structure. Here the focus is how a system responds to events (or *actions*), which are modeled as transition labels, rather than on the propositions that hold of system states.

To capture the incompleteness of a state space, a transition system can be labeled with a divergence predicate $\uparrow$ [Mil81]. If the divergence predicate holds for label $a$ at state $p$ then intuitively some of the $a$ transitions from $p$ in the full state space may be missing at $p$ in the partial state space. Note that this predicate takes a value of either *true* or *false* for each state and label, while the atomic propositions of partial Kripke structures are 3-valued.

**Definition 8.** *An* extended transition system *is a structure* $(S, A, \{\overset{a}{\to} \mid a \in A\}, \uparrow)$ *where $S$ is a set of states, $A$ is a set of labels, $\{\overset{a}{\to} \mid a \in A\}$ is a family of transition relations, and $\uparrow \subseteq S \times A$ is a* divergence *relation.*

We write $p \overset{a}{\to} q$ if $(p, q) \in \overset{a}{\to}$. We write $p \uparrow a$ if $(p, a) \in \uparrow$ and say that $p$ *diverges* for $a$. Also, we write $p \downarrow a$ if not $p \uparrow a$ and say that $p$ *converges* for $a$.

The degree to which a state space is complete is modeled here by the *divergence preorder* [Mil81,Wal90] (also known as the *partial bisimulation preorder*), which is a generalization of the simulation and bisimulation relations. If a pair $(p, q)$ is in this relation, then $q$ must be able to match every transition of $p$. Furthermore, if $p$ is convergent for label $a$, then $p$ must be able to match every transition of $q$.

**Definition 9.** *The* divergence preorder $\sqsubseteq$ *is the greatest binary relation on states of an extended transition system such that $p \sqsubseteq q$ implies:*

- *whenever $p \overset{a}{\to} p'$ there exists a $q'$ such that $q \overset{a}{\to} q'$ and $p' \sqsubseteq q'$, and*
- *if $p \downarrow a$, then $q \downarrow a$ and whenever $q \overset{a}{\to} q'$ there exists a $p'$ such that $p \overset{a}{\to} p'$ and $p' \sqsubseteq q'$.*

This preorder differs from the completeness preorder of Section 3 because the divergence predicate specifically captures the possibility that transitions are missing at a state, while in partial Kripke structures an atomic proposition with value $\perp$ may not represent this possibility.

Hennessy-Milner Logic (HML) [HM85] is a propositional modal logic for labeled transition systems. Formulas of HML have the following abstract syntax:

$$\phi ::= \mathtt{tt} \mid \neg\phi \mid \phi_1 \wedge \phi_2 \mid \langle a \rangle \phi$$

where $a$ ranges over $A$. We use the standard propositional abbreviations, including $\mathtt{ff}$ and $\vee$, plus the derived modal operator $[a]$, defined by $[a]\phi = \neg\langle a \rangle \neg\phi$.

We give the following 3-valued interpretation of HML formulas. The truth value of an HML formula $\phi$ for a state $p$, written $[p \models \phi]$, is defined inductively as follows:

$$[p \models \mathtt{tt}] = true$$
$$[p \models \neg\phi] = \mathrm{neg}([p \models \phi])$$
$$[p \models \phi_1 \wedge \phi_2] = \min([p \models \phi_1], [p \models \phi_2])$$
$$[p \models \langle a \rangle \phi] = \begin{cases} \max(\{[p' \models \phi] \mid p \overset{a}{\to} p'\}) & \text{if } p \downarrow a \\ \max(\{[p' \models \phi] \mid p \overset{a}{\to} p'\} \cup \{\perp\}) & \text{otherwise} \end{cases}$$

HML, under our 3-valued interpretation, characterizes the divergence preorder on extended transition systems.

**Theorem 5.** *Let $(S, A, \{\overset{a}{\to} \mid a \in A\}, \uparrow)$ be an extended transition system such that the set $\{p' \mid p \overset{a}{\to} p'\}$ is finite for all $p$ in $S$ and $a$ in $A$. Let $p$ and $q$ be states in $S$. Then*

$$(\forall\phi : [p \models \phi] \le [q \models \phi]) \text{ iff } p \sqsubseteq q.$$

Our 3-valued interpretation of HML has a close connection to the intuitionistic interpretation by Plotkin. In [Sti87] Plotkin's interpretation is presented and it is shown that the logic characterizes the divergence preorder. A positive form of HML is used there, with syntax

$$\phi ::= \texttt{tt} \mid \texttt{ff} \mid \phi_1 \wedge \phi_2 \mid \phi_1 \vee \phi_2 \mid \langle a \rangle \phi \mid [a]\phi$$

Negation is not present, but the complementary forms of tt, $\wedge$, and $\langle a \rangle$ are included. The intuitionistic semantics of this logic is like that of standard 2-valued HML, except for the $[a]$ operator. The intuitionistic semantics of the two modal operators are:

$$p \models_I \langle a \rangle \phi \text{ if } \exists p' : p \xrightarrow{a} p' \text{ and } p' \models_I \phi$$
$$p \models_I [a]\phi \text{ if } p \downarrow a \text{ and } \forall p' : p \xrightarrow{a} p' \Rightarrow p' \models_I \phi$$

These two operators are no longer duals, unlike the standard 2-valued interpretation and our 3-valued interpretation. For example, if process $p$ has no $a$ transitions and $p \uparrow a$ then $p \not\models [a]\texttt{ff}$ and $p \not\models \langle a \rangle \texttt{tt}$.

The precise connection between this interpretation and our 3-valued interpretation is as follows. We define the syntactic complement $\text{comp}(\phi)$ of a positive HML formula $\phi$ as follows: $\text{comp}(\texttt{tt}) = \texttt{ff}$, $\text{comp}(\texttt{ff}) = \texttt{tt}$, $\text{comp}(\phi_1 \wedge \phi_2) = \text{comp}(\phi_1) \vee \text{comp}(\phi_2)$, $\text{comp}(\phi_1 \vee \phi_2) = \text{comp}(\phi_1) \wedge \text{comp}(\phi_2)$, $\text{comp}(\langle a \rangle \phi) = [a]\text{comp}(\phi)$, and $\text{comp}([a]\phi) = \langle a \rangle \text{comp}(\phi)$. Then our 3-valued interpretation gives the result $\perp$ for $p$ and $\phi$ just if both $\phi$ and $\text{comp}(\phi)$ fail to hold for $p$.

**Theorem 6.** *Let $\phi$ be a formula of positive HML and let $p$ be a state of an extended transition system. Then the following all hold:*

1. *$[p \models \phi] = \text{true iff } p \models_I \phi$*
2. *$[p \models \phi] = \text{false iff } p \models_I \text{comp}(\phi)$*
3. *$[p \models \phi] = \perp \text{ iff } p \not\models_I \phi \text{ and } p \not\models_I \text{comp}(\phi)$*

In [Sti87] the divergence preorder is characterized by intuitionistic HML as follows. Let $p$ and $q$ be processes in extended transition systems. Then $p \sqsubseteq q$ just if, for all $\phi$ of positive HML, $p \models_I \phi \Rightarrow q \models_I \phi$. From Theorem 6 the equivalent condition in 3-valued HML is $([p \models \phi] = \text{true}) \Rightarrow ([p \models \phi] = \text{true})$. Clearly $\forall \phi : ([p \models \phi] = \text{true}) \Rightarrow ([q \models \phi] = \text{true})$ is equivalent to the condition $\forall \phi : [p \models \phi] \leq [q \models \phi]$ used in Theorem 5 above. Thus, in this action-based framework, we could have defined 3-valued HML in terms of intuitionistic HML, and then derived our characterization result from the characterization result of [Sti87].

An advantage of 3-valued modal logic over intuitionistic modal logic is that it more naturally captures the problem of model-checking partial state spaces. For example, a 3-valued modal logic leads directly to a model checker that, given a state and a formula, returns *true*, *false*, or $\perp$. In contrast, a model checker directly based on intuitionistic modal logic would return either *true* or *false*. The value $\perp$ could only be inferred from the results of multiple checks.

# 7 Conclusions

We developed a simple framework for reasoning about partially-known behaviors of a system. We showed that the use of 3-valued temporal logics nicely models the absence of information about unknown parts of the state space of a system. We then precisely determined, both operationally and logically, the relationship between a partial state space and a more complete one. We also presented a model-checking algorithm for 3-valued CTL. This model checker can check any CTL formula on any partial state space, and returns either a definite answer of *true* or *false* concerning the full state space, or ⊥ ("I don't know") if the partial state space lacks information needed for a definite answer.

We also compared our results on partial Kripke structures with existing work on extended transition systems. In the latter framework, we showed that Hennessy-Milner Logic with our 3-valued interpretation provides an alternative characterization of the divergence preorder in addition to the intuitionistic interpretation of Plotkin. Further work on divergence preorders and logics to characterize them can be found in [Sti87,Wal90]. Verification techniques based on the divergence preorder are described in [Wal90,CS90]. In all this work logical formulas are interpreted normally in the 2-valued sense. To our knowledge none of the work on 3-valued modal logics (e.g., [Seg67,Mor89,Fit92]) shows how these logics can be used to characterize relations like our completeness preorder.

The model-checking framework developed in this paper could be extended so it can be performed "symbolically" following the ideas of [BCM+90]. This would require the use of data structures and algorithms for representing and manipulating 3-valued formulas, such as Ternary Decision Diagrams [Sas97].

## Acknowledgments

We thank Michael Benedikt and the anonymous referees for helpful comments on this paper.

## References

[BBLS92] S. Bensalem, A. Bouajjani, C. Loiseaux, and J. Sifakis. Property preserving simulations. In *Proceedings of CAV '92, LNCS 663*, pages 260–273, 1992.

[BCM+90] J.R. Burch, E.M. Clarke, K.L. McMillan, D.L. Dill, and L.J. Hwang. Symbolic model checking: $10^{20}$ states and beyond. In *Proceedings of the 5th Symposium on Logic in Computer Science*, pages 428–439, Philadelphia, June 1990.

[CE81] E. M. Clarke and E. A. Emerson. Design and Synthesis of Synchronization Skeletons using Branching-Time Temporal Logic. In D. Kozen, editor, *Proceedings of the Workshop on Logic of Programs, Yorktown Heights*, volume 131 of *Lecture Notes in Computer Science*, pages 52–71. Springer-Verlag, 1981.

[CES86] E.M. Clarke, E.A. Emerson, and A.P. Sistla. Automatic verification of finite-state concurrent systems using temporal logic specifications. *ACM Transactions on Programming Languages and Systems*, 8(2):244–263, January 1986.

[CS90]     Rance Cleaveland and Bernhard Steffen. When is "partial" adequate? A logic-based proof technique using partial specifications. In *Proceedings of the 5th Annual Symposium on Logic in Computer Science*. IEEE Computer Society Press, 1990.

[Eme90]    E. A. Emerson. Temporal and modal logic. In J. van Leeuwen, editor, *Handbook of Theoretical Computer Science*. Elsevier/MIT Press, Amsterdam/Cambridge, 1990.

[Fit92]    Melvin Fitting. Many-valued modal logics II. *Fundamenta Informaticae*, 17:55–73, 1992.

[HM85]     M. Hennessy and R. Milner. Algebraic laws for nondeterminism and concurrency. *Journal of the ACM*, 32(1):137–161, 1985.

[Kle87]    Stephen Cole Kleene. *Introduction to Metamathematics*. North Holland, 1987.

[Koz83]    D. Kozen. Results on the Propositional Mu-Calculus. *Theoretical Computer Science*, 27:333–354, 1983.

[Mil81]    R. Milner. A Modal Characterization of Observable Machine Behavior. In *Proc. CAAP'81*, volume 112 of *Lecture Notes in Computer Science*, pages 25–34. Springer-Verlag, 1981.

[Mil89]    R. Milner. *Communication and Concurrency*. Prentice Hall, 1989.

[Mor89]    Osamu Morikawa. Some modal logics based on a three-valued logic. *Notre Dame Journal of Formal Logic*, 30(1):130–137, 1989.

[MP92]     Z. Manna and A. Pnueli. *The Temporal Logic of Reactive and Concurrent Systems: Specification*. Springer-Verlag, 1992.

[Par81]    D. M. R. Park. Concurrency and automata on infinite sequences. In P. Deussen, editor, $5^{th}$ *GI Conference*, volume 104 of *Lecture Notes in Computer Science*, pages 167–183. Springer-Verlag, 1981.

[Sas97]    T. Sasao. Ternary Decision Diagrams – A Survey. In *Proc. IEEE International Symposium on Multiple-Valued Logic*, pages 241–250, Nova Scotia, May 1997.

[Seg67]    Krister Segerberg. Some modal logics based on a three-valued logic. *Theoria*, 33:53–71, 1967.

[Sti87]    Colin Stirling. Modal logics for communicating systems. *Theoretical Computer Science*, 49:331–347, 1987.

[Var97]    M.Y. Vardi. Why is modal logic so robustly decidable? In *Proceedings of DIMACS Workshop on Descriptive Complexity and Finite Models*. AMS, 1997.

[vB84]     J. van Bentham. Correspondence theory. In D. Gabbay and F. Guenthner, editors, *Handbook of Philosophical Logic Vol. II*. Reidel, 1984.

[Wal90]    D. J. Walker. Bisimulation and divergence. *Information and Computation*, 85(2):202–241, 1990.

# Elementary Microarchitecture Algebra

John Matthews and John Launchbury

Oregon Graduate Institute,
P.O. Box 91000, Portland OR 97291-1000, USA
{johnm,jl}@cse.ogi.edu
http://www.cse.ogi.edu/PacSoft/Hawk

**Abstract.** We describe a set of remarkably simple algebraic laws governing microarchitectural components. We apply these laws to incrementally transform a pipeline containing forwarding, branch speculation and hazard detection so that all pipeline stages and forwarding logic are removed. The resulting unpipelined machine is much closer to the reference architecture, and presumably easier to verify.

## 1  Introduction

Transformational laws are well known in digital hardware, and form the basis of logic simplification and minimization, and of many retiming algorithms. Traditionally, these laws occur the gate level: de Morgan's law being a classic example. In this paper, we examine whether corresponding transformational laws hold at the microarchitectural level.

A priori, there is no reason to think that large microarchitectural components should satisfy any interesting algebraic laws, as they are constructed from thousands of individual gates. Boundary cases could easily remove any uniformity that has to exist for simple laws to be present. Yet we have found that when microarchitectural units are presented in a particular way, many powerful laws appear. Moreover, as we demonstrate in this paper, these laws *by themselves* are powerful enough to allow us to show equivalence of pipelined and non-pipelined microarchitectures.

We have used this algebraic approach to simplify a pipelined microarchitecture that uses forwarding, branch speculation and pipeline stalling for hazards. The resulting pipeline is very similar to the reference machine specification (i.e. no forwarding logic), while still retaining cycle-accurate behavior with the original implementation pipeline. The top-level transformation proof is simple enough to be carried out on paper, but we have mechanized enough of the theory in the Isabelle theorem prover [20] to have verified it semi-automatically, using Isabelle's powerful rewriting engine.

Interestingly, both circuits and laws can be expressed diagrammatically. A paper proof (transformation using equivalence laws) proceeds as a series of microarchitecture block diagrams, each an incrementally transformed version of the last. The laws often have a geometric flavor to them, such as laws to swap two components with each other, or laws to absorb one component into another. We find this diagrammatic approach an excellent way to communicate proofs.

For us, the most time-consuming part of this technique has been discovering the local behavior-preserving laws. It is our experience that these laws are much easier to discover when one uses the right level of abstraction. In particular, we encapsulate all control and dataflow information concerning a given instruction in the pipeline into an abstract data type called a *transaction* [1, 17]. We have found that not only do transactions reduce the size of microarchitecture specifications, they also provide enough "auxiliary" state information to make law-discovery practical.

The rest of the paper gives a brief introduction to our specification language, and then discusses many of the laws we have discovered. We then show their use by applying the laws in a proof of equivalence between two microarchitectures. While space constraints prohibit us from giving the complete proof, the top-level proof is sketched diagrammatically in [16].

## 2  Specifying a Pipelined Microarchitecture

We specify microarchitectures using the *Hawk* language [4, 17]. Hawk allows us to express modern microarchitectures clearly and concisely, to simulate the microarchitectures, either directly with concrete values, or symbolically, and provides a formal basis for reasoning about their behavior at source-code level. Currently Hawk is a set of libraries built on top of the pure functional language Haskell, which is strongly typed, supports first-class functions, and infinite data structures, such as streams [8, 21]. It is this legacy that led us to look for transformation laws in the first place: one often-cited benefit of purely functional programs is that they are amenable to verification through equational reasoning. We wanted to see if such algebraic techniques scaled up to microarchitectural verification.

### 2.1  Hawk Signals

Hawk is a purely declarative synchronous specification language, sharing a semantic base similar to Lustre[7]. The basic data structure underlying Hawk is the *signal*, which can be thought of as an infinite sequence of values, one per clock cycle, and circuits are pure functions from input signals to output signals. The elements of a signal must belong to the same type.

We use a notion of *transactions* to specify the immediate state of an entire instruction as it travels through the microprocessor [1]. A transaction is a record with fields containing the instruction's opcode, source register names and values, and the destination register name and its value, plus any additional information, like the speculative branch target PC for each branching instruction. A microarchitecture is a network of components, each of which processes signals of transactions.

290

Figure 1 shows the diagram of a simple one-stage microarchitecture, built out of transaction signal processors. Each component incrementally assigns values to various transaction fields, based on the component's internal state (if any) and the values of transaction fields assigned by earlier components. A textual Hawk specification of this circuit consists of set of mutually-recursive stream equations between the components. However, in this paper we will represent Hawk circuits as diagrams.

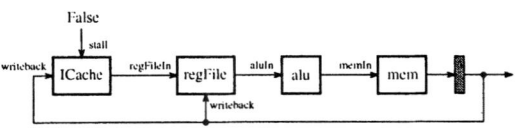

**Fig. 1.** One-stage pipeline.

For example, the `regFile` component has two transaction signal inputs and one transaction signal output. At a given clock cycle, the first input (called `regFileIn` in Figure 1) contains a transaction whose opcode and register name fields have been initialized, but whose value fields have all been zeroed out. The second input (called `writeback`) contains the completed transaction from the previous clock cycle. The `regFile` component first updates its internal register file state, based on the destination register name and value fields of the `writeback` input. It then fills in the source operand value fields of the `regFileIn` transaction based on the corresponding operand register names and the updated register file, and outputs the filled in transaction, all within the same clock cycle.

The `alu` component examines the opcode and source operand value fields of the transaction output by `regFile`. If the opcode is an ALU operation (which include branch instructions), the `alu` component computes the appropriate result, assigns the result to the destination operand value field of the transaction, and outputs the transaction along the `memIn` wire, again within the same (long) clock cycle. If the opcode is not an ALU operation, the `alu` component outputs the transaction unchanged.

The `mem` component behaves similarly for memory load and store operations. Like the `regFile` component, the `mem` component has internal state, representing the contents of data memory at each clock cycle. This state is updated and referenced based on the transactions sent to the `mem` component. Just as with the `alu` component, all memory and transaction updating occurs within the same clock cycle. The `mem` component sends the completed transaction to a `delay` component (represented in our diagrams as a shaded box), to make it available to the `ICache` and `regFile` components in the next clock cycle. These transactions also become the output of the entire microarchitecture, as is shown by the right-most arrow. The initial value output by the `delay` component is the default transaction `nopTrans`, which represents an "inert" transaction which behaves like a NOP instruction, but does not affect the `ICache`'s program counter.

The `ICache` component produces new transactions, based on the value of the current program counter and the contents of program memory (the instruction-set architectures we consider have separate address spaces for instructions and data). Both the current PC and the instruction memory contents are internal to `ICache`. The ICache takes on its `writeback` input the completed transaction from the previous clock cycle. The ICache examines the transaction for branches that have been taken. When it finds such an instruction, it modifies its internal PC accordingly and starts fetching transactions from the branch target address. The ICache has as output a signal of transactions representing the newly-fetched instructions. Each transaction's source and destination operand values are initialized to zero, since the ICache doesn't know what values they should have. The other pipeline components will fill in these fields with their correct values. The ICache has a second input, called `stall`, which is a signal of Boolean values. On clock cycles where `stall` is asserted, the ICache will output the same transaction as it did on the previous clock cycle. In this simple microarchitecture, `stall` is always false. In more complex pipelines, the `stall` signal is typically asserted when the pipeline needs to stall due to a branch misprediction.

For more complex pipelines, we also allow the ICache to perform branch prediction, based on an internal branch target buffer. When performing branch prediction, the ICache will also annotate branch instruction transactions with the predicted branch target PC. A `branch_misp` component (not shown in Figure 1) can locally compare the predicted branch target with the actual branch target to determine if a branch misprediction has occurred.

## 3 Microarchitecture Laws

With any algebraic reasoning there need to be some ground rules. We take as fundamental the notion of *referential transparency* or, in hardware terms, a *circuit duplication law*. Any circuit whose output is used in multiple places is equivalent to duplicating the circuit

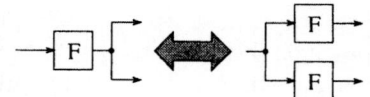

**Fig. 2.** Universal circuit-duplication law

itself, and using each output once. This law is shown graphically in Figure 2. Because of the declarative nature of our specification language, every circuit satisfies this law. That is, it is impossible within Hawk for a specification of a component to cause hidden side-effects observable to any other component specification. In many specification languages this law does not hold universally. For example, duplicating a circuit that incremented a global variable on every clock cycle would cause the global variable to be incremented multiple times per clock period, breaking behavioral equivalence. Hawk circuits can still be stateful, but all stateful behavior must be local and/or expressed using feedback.

The next few sections introduce many other laws, some of which are specific to particular combinations of components, while others are quite widely applicable. Each instantiation of a law needs to be proved with respect to the specification of the circuit components involved. We have found induction and bisimulation to be the most useful ways of proving the laws in this paper, expressed as proofs in Isabelle.

## 3.1 Delay Laws

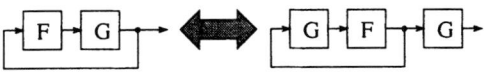

**Fig. 3.** feedback rotation law

The delay circuit is a fundamental building block of clocked circuits, especially when combined with feedback. A feedback variant of the circuit duplication law shown in Figure 3, called the *feedback rotation* law, allows circuits to be split along feedback wires. This law is not universal, but it is valid for any circuit that does not contain zero-delay cycles (amongst others). Happily, all of the laws we discuss, including the feedback rotation law itself, preserve a well-formedness property: if a circuit contains no zero-delay cycles, then any transformed circuit will also have no zero-delay cycles.

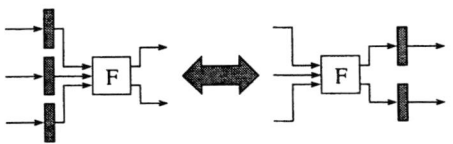

**Fig. 4.** time-invariance law.

The *time-invariance* law (Figure 4) is also nearly universal. A circuit is *time-invariant* if one can retime the circuit by removing the delays from all the inputs of the circuit and placing new delays on the circuit's outputs. Any combinatorial circuit that preserves default values is automatically time-invariant, but so are stateful circuits like the register file and memory cache. Interestingly, the ICache is not.

We use the above laws extensively to remove pipeline stages. If a pipeline stage is time-invariant, then we can move the pipeline registers (represented as delay circuits) from before the pipeline stage to afterwards. If subsequent pipeline stage are also time-invariant, then we can repeat the process, eventually moving all of the delay circuits to the end of the pipeline. However, forwarding logic between pipeline stages must still access the appropriate time-delayed outputs of later pipeline stages. The feedback-rotation law polices this, and ensures that the appropriate time-delay is kept by forcing delays to be inserted on all feedback wires to the forwarding circuits.

## 3.2 Bypasses and Bypass Laws

The purpose of forwarding logic in a pipeline is to ensure that results computed in later pipeline stages are available to earlier pipeline stages in time to be used. Conceptually, the forwarding logic at each pipeline stage examines its current instruction's source operand register names to see if they match a later stage's destination operand register name. For every matching source operand, the operand value is replaced with the result value computed by the later pipeline stage. Non-matching source operands continue to use operand values given by the preceding pipeline stage.

This conceptual logic can be implemented concisely using transactions. A *bypass* circuit (Figure 5) has two inputs, each a signal of transactions: The first input (`inp`) contains the transactions from the preceding pipeline stage. The second input (`update`) contains the transactions from a subsequent pipeline stage. The `bypass` circuit at each clock cycle compares the source operand names of the current `inp` transaction with the destination operand names of the current `update` transaction. The output of `bypass` is identical to `inp`, except that source operands matching `update`'s destination operand are updated. Bypasses arise frequently enough in pipeline specifications that we draw them specially, as diamonds with the `update` input connected to either the top or the bottom.

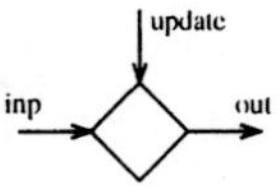

**Fig. 5.** bypass circuit

Bypass circuits have many nice properties. Not only are they time-invariant and obey a kind of idempotence (Figure 6), but they also interact closely with register files and various execution units.

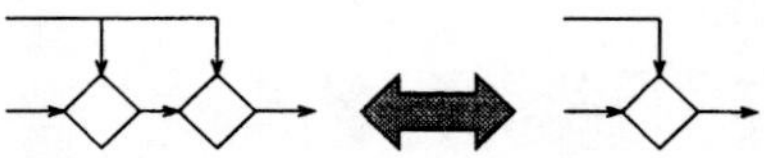

**Fig. 6.** bypass circuit idempotence law

The fundamental interaction between a bypass and register file is shown in Figure 7. We call this the *register-bypass law*, and it is used repeatedly in eliminating forwarding logic when simplifying pipelines. The law states that we can delay writing a value into the register file, so long as we also forward the value to be written, in case that register was being read on the same clock cycle.

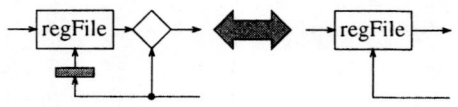

**Fig. 7.** register-bypass law

Initially we considered this law to be a theorem about register files, and accordingly we proved that it held for a number of different implementations. However, it is also tempting to view this law as an *axiom* of register files. In effect, by using the law repeatedly from right to left, we obtain a specification for how the register file must behave for any time prefix.

**Hazard - Bypass Law** Another bypass law permits the removal of bypasses between execution units. It is often the case that after retiming all delay circuits to the end of a pipeline, two execution units in a pipeline (such as an ALU unit and a Load/Store unit) are connected with one-cycle feedback loops. Each bypass circuit is forwarding the outputs of an execution unit to the inputs of that same execution unit, one clock cycle later.

If the upstream pipeline stages can guarantee that there is no hazard between successive transactions, then the double feedback is equivalent to the single feedback circuit shown at the bottom of Figure 8. This (conditional) identity is called the *hazard-bypass* law.

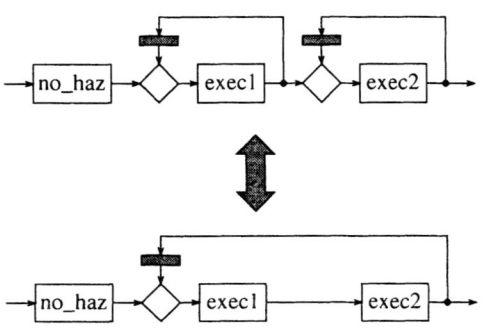

**Fig. 8.** hazard-bypass law

To be more concrete, suppose exec1 is the ALU and exec2 the memory cache. Then an ALU-mem hazard arises if a transaction which loads a register value from memory is immediately followed by an ALU operation which requires that register's value. Under these circumstances the two feedback loops would give different results. Under all other circumstances the two circuits are equivalent. We express this conditional equivalence using the no_haz component. It is an example of a projection component and is discussed in the next section.

### 3.3 Projection Laws

Many laws, like the hazard-bypass law above, require that the input signals satisfy certain properties, and commonly, we may know that the output signal of a given component always satisfies a particular property. We can capture this knowledge of properties using signal *projections*.

A signal projection is a component with one input and one output. As long as the input signal satisfies the property of interest, the component acts like an identity function, returning the input signal unchanged. However, if the input does not satisfy the property we are interested in, the projection component modifies the input signal in some arbitrary way so that the property is satisfied.

Let us consider an example. For the hazard-bypass law we are interested in expressing the absence of ALU-mem hazards in a transaction signal. We reify this property as a no_haz projection. On each clock cycle, the no_haz component compares the current input transaction with the previous input transaction. If there is no ALU-mem hazard between the two transactions, then the current transaction is output unchanged. If a hazard does exist, then no_haz will instead output nopTrans, which is guaranteed not to generate a hazard (since nopTrans contains no source operands).

Where do projections come from? After all, they are not the sort of component that microarchitectural designers introduce just for fun.

Fig 9 provides an example of a law which "generates" a projection. The hazard-squashing logic guarantees that its output contains no hazards, and this is expressed in that the circuit is unchanged when the no_haz component is inserted on its output.

(The hazard component outputs a Boolean on each clock cycle stating whether its two input transactions constitute a hazard. The kill component takes a transaction signal and a Boolean signal as inputs. On each clock cycle, if the

Boolean input is false, then `kill` outputs its input transaction unchanged. If the Boolean input is true, then `kill` outputs a `nopTrans`, effectively "killing" the input transaction.)

To be useful, a projection component needs to be able to migrate from a source circuit that produces it (such as the circuit in Figure 9) to a target circuit that needs the projection to enable an algebraic law (such as the

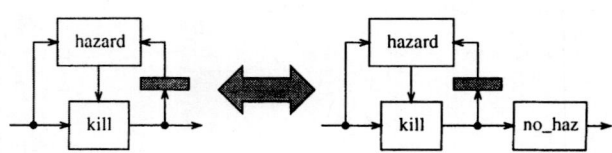

**Fig. 9.** Hazard-squashing logic guarantees no hazards

hazard-bypass law). Thus a projection component must be able to commute with the intervening circuits between the source and the target circuit. Well-designed projections commute with many circuits. For instance, the `no_haz` projection commutes with `bypass`, `alu`, `mem`, and `regFile` components. It also commutes with `delay` components (that is, `no_haz` is time-invariant).

Projections are also convenient for expressing the fact that a component only uses some of the fields of an input transaction. For instance, the `hazard` component only looks at the opcode, source, and destination register name fields of its two input transactions. We can create a projection called `proj_ctrl` that sets every other field of a transaction to a default value, and prove a law stating that the `hazard` component is unchanged when `proj_ctrl` is added to any of its inputs. We can then show that `proj_ctrl` commutes with other components, such as bypasses and delays. This allows us to move the input wires to `hazard` across these other components, which is sometimes necessary to enable other laws. Similarly, the `proj_branch_info` projection allows us to move `ICache` and `branch_misp` component inputs.

## 4    Transforming the Microarchitecture

The laws we have been discussing can be used for aggressively restructuring microarchitectures while retaining equivalence. We have used them to simplify several pipelined microarchitectures with a view to verification. The example we present here contains three levels of forwarding logic, resolves hazards by stalling the pipeline, and performs branch speculation. The block diagram for this microarchitecture is shown in Figure 10.

By using just algebraic laws, we have been able to reduce most of the complexity, leaving essentially an unpipelined microarchitecture. We are currently implementing the algebraic laws as a rewrite system in Isabelle. For this paper we describe our top-level rewrite strategy informally.

**Retiming** We first remove all delay circuits from the main pipeline path. We accomplish this by repeatedly applying the time-invariance law, and by splitting delays along wires through the circuit duplication and feedback rotation laws.

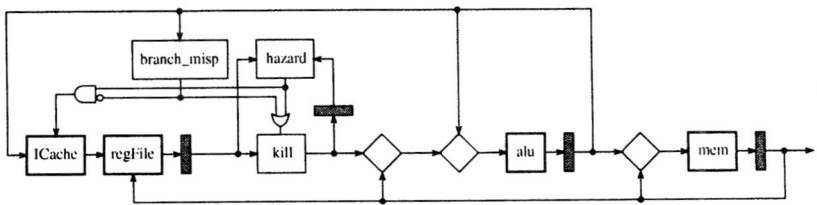

**Fig. 10.** Microarchitecture before simplification

**Move control wires** Next, we move all wires not directly involved with forwarding logic to either before or after all of the **bypass** circuits. This is to enable the hazard-bypass laws, which we apply in a later step. We move the wires by inserting projection circuits and using the corresponding projection-commutativity laws.

**Propagate hazard information** The hazard-bypass laws can only be applied when there are no hazards between the affected stages. So we generate a no-hazard projection at the end of the dispatch stage (which is justified by a projection-absorption law applicable to the kill-circuit complex in that stage), and then move it between the first and second bypass circuits. We also use additional properties of the **proj_ctrl**, **kill**, and **regFile** circuits (discussed in [16]) to swap the hazard/kill complex with the register file, so that the register-bypass law can be used more readily in the next step of the simplification. The circuit in Figure 11 shows the microarchitecture after this step has been completed. Notice that the ALU and memory units are now connected exactly as required for an application of the hazard-bypass law.

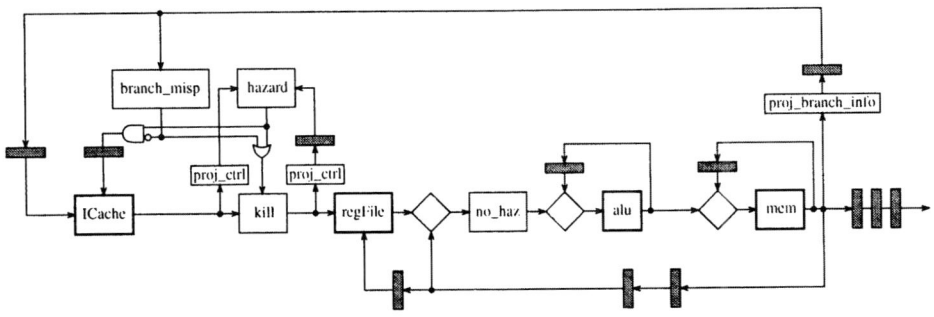

**Fig. 11.** Microarchitecture after the "propagate hazard information" step

**Remove forwarding logic** We can now apply the hazard-bypass law to remove the bypass circuit just prior to the memory unit. We eliminate the other two bypass circuits by applying the register-bypass law twice.

**Cleanup** The pipeline has now been simplified as much as possible, except that there are still some extra delay components as well as several unnecessary projection circuits. We merge delay components, then move the projection circuits back to their places of origin and remove them using the projection laws in the opposite direction.

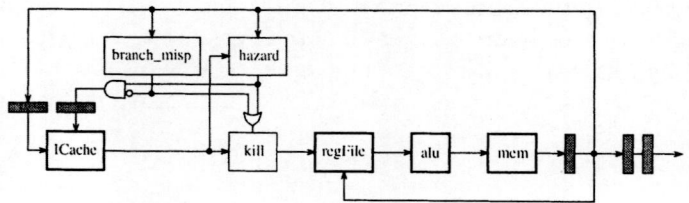

**Fig. 12.** Microarchitecture after simplification

The final microarchitecture is shown in Figure 12. This circuit still outputs exactly the same transaction values, cycle-for-cycle, as the microarchitecture in Figure 10, but is considerably less complex. We can now apply conventional techniques to verify that this microarchitecture is a valid implementation of the ISA.

## 5    Discussion

### 5.1    Related work

Hawk is built on top of the pure functional language Haskell, where algebraic techniques for transforming functional programs are routinely used for equivalence checking and verification [2, 3, 13] and for compilation and optimization [5, 12]. Much of our work can be seen as an extension of these ideas. Hawk itself is very similar in flavor to Lustre [6] except that in Lustre signals are accompanied by additional clock information. The Hawk specification style follows from the work of Johnson[9], O'Donnell[18], and Sheeran[25].

We have also been influenced by the algebraic techniques used in the relational hardware-description language Ruby [24]. Sizeable Ruby circuits have been successfully derived and verified through algebraic manipulation [10, 11]. What distinguishes our work is our focus on microarchitectural units as objects of study in their own right. The Ruby research has emphasized circuits at the gate level.

In terms of verification, our approach is most similar to two known techniques, called retiming [14, 23, 26] and unpipelining [15]. A circuit is *retimed* when the delay components of the circuit are repositioned, while the functional components are left unchanged, effectively through repeated applications of the time-invariance law. Typically, circuits are retimed to reduce the clock cycle time. In contrast, we retime circuits as part of a simplification process. In fact, we often use the time invariance law to increase cycle time!

*Unpipelining* [15] is a verification technique where a pipelined microarchitecture, specified as a state machine, is incrementally transformed into a functionally-equivalent unpipelined microarchitecture. Unpipelining proceeds by repeatedly merging the last stage of a pipeline into the next to last stage, producing a microarchitecture with one less stage on each iteration. On each iteration, the two microarchitectures are proven equivalent by induction over time. This is similar to our approach, except that we use transactions to encapsulate and reuse many of the verification steps, and we only need to prove the equivalence of the portion of the microarchitecture being transformed, rather than the entire microarchitecture, on each iteration. On the other hand, Levitt and Olukotun's implementation of unpipelining is much more automated than our work up to now.

Transactions were a key concept in allowing us to discover and formulate many of the algebraic laws of microarchitectural components. Unsurprisingly, the usefulness of transactions has been noticed before. Aagaard and Leeser used transactions to specify and verify hierarchical networks of pipelines [1], and Önder and Gupta have used a similar concept of *instruction contexts* as a core datatype in UPFAST, an imperative microarchitecture simulation language [19]. Further, Sawada and Hunt use an extended form of transactions in their verification of a speculative out-of-order microarchitecture [22]. Each transaction records two snapshots of the entire ISA state, before and after the instruction is executed. In their work, however, transactions are not part of the microarchitecture itself, but are constructed separately for verification purposes.

## 5.2 Next steps in microarchitecture algebra

As we have come to see it, the main principle of applying algebraic techniques to microarchitectures is to use geometric reasoning to move and absorb circuits, and to express that reasoning as local equalities whenever possible. Conditional equalities can be expressed using projections.

Some care is required in the definition of basic components. We have striven to design the component circuits to satisfy as rich a variety of algebraic laws as possible, such as preserving default values, satisfying time-invariance, and so on. Sometimes we hit on the correct definitions immediately, but more commonly adapted the definitions over time admitting more and more laws. One example of this is in pipeline registers. Initially, we used conditional delays to act as pipeline registers, but since then have found it useful to separate clocked behavior from functional behavior, enabling the two dimensions to be manipulated separately.

In some sense the components we now manipulate are not optimal in terms of transistor counts. In particular, many units receive and propagate information they are not interested in. However, much of this overhead can be removed automatically through a similar set of rewrite laws built around more primitive components than those presented in this paper. We plan to write this up in a subsequent paper.

## 6 Acknowledgements

We wish to thank Borislav Agapiev, Carl Seger, Byron Cook, Sava Krstic, and Thomas Nordin for their valuable contributions to this research. The authors are supported by Intel Strategic CAD Labs and Air Force Material Command (F19628-93-C-0069). John Matthews receives support from a graduate research fellowship with the NSF.

## References

1. AAGAARD, M., AND LEESER, M. Reasoning about pipelines with structural hazards. In *Second International Conference on Theorem Provers in Circuit Design* (Bad Herrenalb, Germany, Sept. 1994).
2. BIRD, R., AND WADLER, P. *Introduction to Functional Programming*. Prentice Hall International Series in Computer Science. Prentice Hall, 1988.
3. BIRD, R. S., AND MOOR, O. D. *Algebra of Programming*. Prentice Hall, 1996.
4. COOK, B., LAUNCHBURY, J., AND MATTHEWS, J. Specifying superscalar microprocessors in Hawk. In *FTH'98, Workshop on Formal Techniques for Hardware and Hardware-like Systems* (Marstrand, Sweden, June 1998).
5. GILL, A., LAUNCHBURY, J., AND PEYTON JONES, S. L. A Short Cut to Deforestation. In *FPCA'93, Conference on Functional Programming Languages and Computer Architecture* (Copenhagen, Denmark, June 1993), ACM Press, pp. 223–232.
6. HALBWACHS, N. *Synchronous programming of reactive systems*. Kluwer Academic Pub., 1993.
7. HALBWACHS, N., LAGNIER, F., AND RATEL, C. Programming and verifying real-time systems by means of the synchronous data-flow programming language Lustre. *IEEE Transactions on Software Engineering, Special Issue on the Specification and Analysis of Real-Time Systems* (September 1992).
8. HUDAK, P., PETERSON, J., AND FASEL, J. A gentle introduction to Haskell. Available at www.haskell.org, Dec. 1997.
9. JOHNSON, S. D. *Synthesis of Digital Systems from Recursive Equations*. ACM Distinguished Dissertation Series. MIT Press, 1984.
10. JONES, G., AND SHEERAN, M. Collecting butterflies. Tech. rep., Oxford University Computing Laboratory, 1991.
11. JONES, G., AND SHEERAN, M. Designing arithmetic circuits by refinement in ruby. In *Mathematics of Program Construction* (1993), vol. 669 of *LNCS*, Springer Verlag.
12. JONES, S. L. P., AND SANTOS, A. L. M. A transformation-based optimiser for Haskell. *Science of Computer Programming 32*, 1–3 (Sept. 1998), 3–47.
13. LAUNCHBURY, J. Graph algorithms with a functional flavour. *Lecture Notes in Computer Science 925* (1995).
14. LEISERSON, C. E., AND SAXE, J. B. Retiming synchronous circuitry. *Algorithmica 6* (1991), 5–35.

15. LEVITT, J., AND OLUKOTUN, K. A scalable formal verification methodology for pipelined microprocessors. In *33rd Design Automation Conference (DAC'96)* (New York, June 1996), Association for Computing Machinery, pp. 558–563.

16. MATTHEWS, J., AND LAUNCHBURY, J. Elementary microarchitecture algebra: Top-level proof of pipelined microarchitecture. Tech. Rep. CSE-99-002, Oregon Graduate Institute, Computer Science Department, Portland, Oregon, Mar. 1999.

17. MATTHEWS, J., LAUNCHBURY, J., AND COOK, B. Specifying microprocessors in Hawk. In *IEEE International Conference on Computer Languages* (Chicago, Illinois, May 1998), pp. 90–101.

18. O'DONNELL, J. From transistors to computer architecture: Teaching functional circuit specification in Hydra. In *Symposium on Functional Programming Languages in Education* (July 1995).

19. ÖNDER, S., AND GUPTA, R. Automatic generation of microarchitecture simulators. In *IEEE International Conference on Computer Languages* (Chicago, Illinois, May 1998), pp. 80–89.

20. PAULSON, L. *Isabelle: A Generic Theorem Prover*. Springer-Verlag, 1994.

21. PETERSON, J., ET AL. Report on the programming language Haskell: A non-strict, purely functional language, version 1.4. Available at www.haskell.org, Apr. 1997.

22. SAWADA, J., AND HUNT, W. A. Processor verification with precise exceptions and speculative execution. *Lecture Notes in Computer Science 1427* (1998), 135–146.

23. SAXE, J., AND GARLAND, S. Using Transformations and Verifications in Circuit Design. *Formal Methods in System Design 4*, 1 (1994), 181–210.

24. SHARP, R., AND RASMUSSEN, O. An introduction to Ruby. Teaching Notes ID–U: 1995-80, Dept. of Computer Science, Technical University of Denmark, October 1995.

25. SHEERAN, M. *μFP, an Algebraic VLSI Design Language*. PhD thesis, Programming Research Group, University of Oxford, 1983.

26. SHEERAN, M. Retiming and slowdown in Ruby. In *The Fusion of Hardware Design and Verification* (Glasgow, Scotland, July 1988), G.J. Milne, Ed., IFIP WG 10.2, North-Holland, pp. 289–308.

# Verifying Sequential Consistency
# on Shared-Memory Multiprocessor Systems

Thomas A. Henzinger**    Shaz Qadeer    Sriram K. Rajamani

EECS Department, University of California, Berkeley, CA 94720, USA
{tah,shaz,sriramr}@eecs.berkeley.edu

**Abstract.** In shared-memory multiprocessors *sequential consistency* offers a natural tradeoff between the flexibility afforded to the implementor and the complexity of the programmer's view of the memory. Sequential consistency requires that some interleaving of the local temporal orders of read/write events at different processors be a trace of serial memory. We develop a systematic methodology for proving sequential consistency for memory systems with three parameters —number of processors, number of memory locations, and number of data values. From the definition of sequential consistency it suffices to construct a non-interfering observer that watches and reorders read/write events so that a trace of serial memory is obtained. While in general such an observer must be unbounded even for fixed values of the parameters —checking sequential consistency is undecidable!— we show that for two paradigmatic protocol classes —*lazy caching* and *snoopy cache coherence*— there exist finite-state observers. In these cases, sequential consistency for fixed parameter values can thus be checked by language inclusion between finite automata.

In order to reduce the arbitrary-parameter problem to the fixed-parameter problem, we develop a novel framework for induction over the number of processors. Classical induction schemas, which are based on process invariants that are inductive with respect to an implementation preorder that preserves the temporal sequence of events, are inadequate for our purposes, because proving sequential consistency requires the reordering of events. Hence we introduce *merge invariants*, which permit certain reorderings of read/write events. We show that under certain reasonable assumptions about the memory system, it is possible to conclude sequential consistency for any number of processors, memory locations, and data values by model checking two finite-state lemmas about process and merge invariants: they involve two processors each accessing a maximum of three locations, where each location stores at most two data values. For both lazy caching and snoopy cache coherence we are able to discharge the two lemmas using the model checker MOCHA.

## 1 Introduction

Shared-memory multiprocessors are an important class of supercomputing systems. In recent years a number of such systems have been designed in both academia and industry. The design of a correct and efficient shared memory is one of the most difficult tasks in the design of such systems. The shared-memory interface is a contract between the designer and the programmer of the multiprocessor. In general, there is a

---

* This research was supported in part by the DARPA/NASA grant NAG2-1214, by the SRC contract 97-DC-324.041, by the NSF CAREER award CCR-9501708, by the ARO MURI grant DAAH-04-96-1-0341, and by an SRC fellowship of the third author.
** Also at the Max-Planck Institute for Computer Science, Saarbrücken, Germany.

tradeoff between the ease of programming and the flexibility of shared-memory semantics necessary for an efficient implementation. Not surprisingly, a number of abstract shared-memory models have been developed.

All abstract memory models can be understood in terms of the fundamental *serial-memory* model. A serial memory behaves as if there is a centralized memory that services read and write requests atomically such that a read to a location returns the latest value written to that location. *Coherence*[1] requires that the global temporal order of events (reads and writes) at different processors be a trace of serial memory. *Sequential consistency* [Lam79] ignores the global temporal order and requires only that some interleaving of the local temporal orders of events at different processors be a trace of serial memory. Although sequential consistency is a strictly weaker property than coherence, the absence of a synchronizing global clock between the different processors in a multiprocessor makes a sequentially consistent memory indistinguishable from a serial memory. Compared to coherence, sequential consistency clearly offers more flexibility for an efficient implementation; yet, most real systems that claim to be sequentially consistent actually end up implementing coherence. In an effort to get more flexibility for implementation, memory models that relax local temporal order of events at each processor have been developed in recent years. This has been achieved at the cost of complicating the programmer's interface. These memory models such as weak ordering, partial store ordering, total store ordering, and release consistency [AG96] relax the processor order of events in different ways and provide fence or synchronization operations across which sequentially consistent behavior is guaranteed.

We focus on the verification of sequential consistency for two reasons. First, the interface provided by sequential consistency is clear, easy to understand, and widely believed to be the correct tradeoff between implementation flexibility and complexity of the programmer's view of shared memory. In fact, there is a trend of thought [Hil98] that considers the performance gains achieved by relaxed semantics not worth the added complexity of the programmer's interface and advocates sequential consistency as the shared-memory interface for future multiprocessors. Second, even relaxed memory models have fence operations across which sequentially consistent behavior should be observed. Hence, the techniques developed in this paper will be useful for their verification also.

High-level descriptions of shared-memory systems are typically parameterized by the number $n$ of processors, the number $m$ of memory locations, and the number $v$ of data values that can be written in a memory location. A parameterized memory systems consists of a central-control part $C$ and a processor part $P$. Both $C$ and $P$ are functions that take values for $m$ and $v$ and return a finite-state process. An instantiation of the system containing $n$ processors, $m$ memory locations, and $v$ data values is constructed by composing $C(m, v)$ with $n$ copies of $P(m, v)$. We would like to verify sequential consistency for all values of the parameters. However, sequential consistency is not a *local* property; correctness for $m$ processors (locations, values) cannot be deduced by reasoning about individual processors (locations, values). The following observations about real shared-memory systems, which we assume in our modeling, are crucial for

---

[1] Implementors of cache-based shared-memory systems have used the notion of cache coherence for a long time but the definition of coherence as stated here was first given in [ABM93].

our results. We assume that the memory system is *monotonic* and *symmetric* with respect to both the set of locations, and the set of data values. Monotonicity in locations means that every run of the system projected onto a subset of locations is a run of the system with just that subset of locations. Monotonicity in data values means that a sequence is a run of the system with some set of possible data values if and only if it is a run of the system with a larger set of data values. Symmetry in locations means that, if $\sigma$ is a run of the memory system, and $\lambda_l$ is a permutation on the set of locations, then $\lambda_l(\sigma)$ is also a run of the memory system. Finally, symmetry in data values means that, if $\sigma$ is a run of the memory system, and $\lambda_v$ is any function from data values to data values, then $\lambda_v(\sigma)$ is also a run of the memory system.

Even for fixed values of the parameters, checking if a memory system is sequentially consistent is undecidable [AMP96]. The main reason for the problem being undecidable is that the specification of sequential consistency allows a processor to read the value at a location after an unbounded number of succeeding writes to that location by other processors. In real systems, finite resources such as buffers and queues bound the number of writes that can be pending. It is sufficient to construct a witness that observes the reads and writes occurring in the system (without interfering with it) and reorders them while preserving the order of events in each processor such that a trace of serial memory is obtained. We call such a witness an *observer*. If a finite-state observer exists, then it can be composed with a fixed-parameter instantiation of the memory system and the problem of deciding sequential consistency is reduced to a language-containment check between two finite-state automata which can be discharged by model checking. In the concrete examples we have looked at (see below), we have indeed seen that a finite-state observer exists for fixed values of the parameters.

However, our goal is to verify sequential consistency for arbitrary values of the parameters. Towards this end, we first develop a novel inductive proof framework for proving sequential consistency for any number $n$ of processors, given fixed $m$ and $v$. Inductive proofs on parameterized systems [KM89] use an implementation preorder and show the existence of a *process invariant* such that the composition of the invariant with an additional process is smaller than the process invariant in the preorder. The preorders typically used —for instance, trace containment and simulation— preserve the temporal sequence of events. Since we check a sufficient condition for sequential consistency by the mechanism of an observer that reorders the read/write events of the processors in the system, preorders that preserve the temporal sequence of events do not suffice for our purpose. Our inductive proof strategy first determines a process invariant $I_1$ of the memory system with respect to the trace-containment preorder to get a finite-state abstraction that can generate all sequences of observable actions for any number of processes. We then find a *merge invariant* $I_2$ such that (1) the single-process memory system containing $I_2$ is sequentially consistent, and (2) there is an observer that maps every run $\sigma$ of $I_2\|P$ that can be produced in an environment of $I_1$ to a run $\sigma'$ of $I_2$, such that the read/write events in $\sigma'$ are an interleaving of the read/write events of $I_2$ and $P$ in $\sigma$, and the traces obtained from $\sigma$ and $\sigma'$ are identical. Given a run $\gamma$ of the memory system with $n > 1$ processors, we use the observer to create a run $\gamma'$ of the memory system with $n - 1$ processors, such that $\gamma$ and $\gamma'$ are identical when projected to the events of the first $n - 2$ processors, and the read/write events of the $(n - 1)$-st processor in $\gamma'$ are an interleaving of the read/write events of the $(n - 1)$-st and $n$-th processors in $\gamma$. By doing this $n$ times, we generate a run of the memory system with a single processor, which is sequentially consistent by the base case of the induction.

The induction demonstrates sequential consistency for any number of processors, but given $m$ and $v$. We would like sufficient conditions under which using fixed values for $m$ and $v$ lets us conclude sequential consistency for all $m$ and $v$. To that end, we impose three requirements on the process and merge invariants. The first two requirements —symmetry and monotonicity on memory locations— are identical to the corresponding assumptions on the memory system. The third requirement is called *location independence*. A process is location independent if it has the property that a sequence of events is a run of the process with $m$ locations if the $m$ sequences obtained by projecting onto individual memory locations are runs of the process with a single location. We show that if the two invariants satisfy location symmetry, location monotonicity, and location independence, and the observer is location and data independent, then it suffices to do the induction for three memory locations and two data values. As a result, the correctness of the memory system can be proved by discharging two finite-state lemmas using a model checker —one that proves the correctness of the process invariant, and another that proves the correctness of the merge invariant.

Our proof framework can be applied to a variety of protocols; in particular, all cache-coherence protocols described in [AB86] fall into its domain. We demonstrate the method by verifying two example protocols —lazy caching [ABM93] and a snoopy cache-coherence protocol [HP96]. The correctness of lazy caching has been established before by manual proofs [ABM93,Gra94,LLOR99]. The correctness of the snoopy cache-coherence protocol is argued informally in [HP96]. Finite-state observers exist for both these examples. In both cases, the proof of a parameterized system was reduced to finite-state lemmas in the way described above, and discharged by our model checker MOCHA [AHM+98]. Manual effort was required to construct the process and merge invariants, and the observer, and to verify that the assumptions on the memory system and the requirements on the invariants and observer are indeed satisfied.

**Related work.** We use process induction for the verification of an abstract memory model. We list related work along two axes —work that verifies abstract memory models, and work that verifies systems with an arbitrary number of processes. [MS91,CGH+93,EM95] verify finite instantiations of parameterized memory systems using automatic techniques. [PD95] automatically proves correctness for an arbitrary number of processors but is limited to coherence. [LD92,LLOR99,PD96,PSCH98] verify abstract shared-memory models for all values of parameters but the proofs are not automatic. [GMG91,Gra94,NGMG98] offer sufficient conditions for the satisfaction of sequential consistency that can then be checked on the memory system. [KM89] gives an inductive proof framework for proving the correctness of parameterized systems. [BCG89,WL89,ID96,GS97,EN98] verify parameterized systems but they are not concerned with the specific problem of verifying memory models.

## 2 Parameterized Memory Systems

### 2.1 I/O-processes

We use I/O-processes that synchronize on observable actions to model memory systems. Formally, an *I/O-process* $A$ is a 5-tuple $\langle Priv(A), Obs(A), S(A), S_I(A), T(A) \rangle$ with the following components:

- A set $Priv(A)$ of *private actions* and a set $Obs(A)$ of *observable actions*, such that $Priv(A) \cap Obs(A) = \emptyset$. The set $Act(A)$ is the union of $Priv(A)$ and $Obs(A)$. Private actions are outputs, whereas observable actions can be both inputs and outputs. The set of *extended actions* $\Pi(A)$ is given by $Priv(A) \times \{out\} \cup Obs(A) \times \{in, out\}$.
- A finite set $S(A)$ of *states*.
- A set $S_I(A) \subseteq S(A)$ of *initial states*.
- A *transition relation* $T(A) \subseteq S(A) \times \Pi(A) \times S(A)$ satisfying the property that for all $s \in S(A)$ and $\pi \in Obs(A) \times \{in\}$, there is a state $s' \in S(A)$ such that $\langle s, \pi, s' \rangle \in T(A)$.

For all $\pi \in \Pi(A)$, the first component is denoted by $First(\pi)$ and the second component by $Second(\pi)$. A sequence of extended actions $\pi_1, \pi_2, \ldots, \pi_k$ of $A$ is a *run* if there exist states $s_0, s_1, s_2, \ldots, s_k$ such that $s_0 \in S_I(A)$ and $\langle s_i, \pi_i, s_{i+1} \rangle \in T(A)$ for all $0 \leq i < k$. The projection operators $First$ and $Second$ are extended to runs in the natural way. The set of all runs of the I/O-process $A$ is denoted by $\Sigma(A)$. A run is *closed* if $Second(\pi_i) = out$ for all actions $\pi_i$ in the run. For any set $\beta \subseteq Act(A)$, the *restriction* of the run $\sigma$ to $\beta$ is the subsequence obtained by considering the elements from $\beta \times \{in, out\}$ in $\sigma$, and is denoted by $[\sigma]_\beta$. For any run $\sigma$ of I/O-process $A$, the restriction of $\sigma$ to $Obs(A)$ is called a *trace*. We say that $tr(\sigma)$ is the trace obtained from the run $\sigma$. The set of all traces of the I/O-process $A$ is denoted by $\Gamma(A)$.

Let $A_1$ and $A_2$ be two I/O-processes. We say that $A_1$ *refines* $A_2$, denoted by $A_1 \preceq A_2$, if (1) $Obs(A_1) \subseteq Obs(A_2)$, and (2) every trace of $A_1$ is a trace of $A_2$. The I/O-processes $A_1$ and $A_2$ are *compatible* if (1) $Priv(A_1) \cap Act(A_2) = \emptyset$ and (2) $Priv(A_2) \cap Act(A_1) = \emptyset$. The *composition* $A = A_1 \| A_2$ of two compatible I/O-processes $A_1$ and $A_2$ is the I/O-process $A$ such that

- $Priv(A) = Priv(A_1) \cup Priv(A_2)$, and $Obs(A) = Obs(A_1) \cup Obs(A_2)$.
- $S(A) = S(A_1) \times S(A_2)$, and $S_I(A) = S_I(A_1) \times S_I(A_2)$.
- $(\langle s_1, s_2 \rangle, \pi, \langle t_1, t_2 \rangle) \in T(A)$ iff one of the following three conditions holds:
  1. $\pi = \langle a, in \rangle$ and for $k = 1, 2$, if $a \in Act(A_k)$ then $(s_k, \langle a, in \rangle, t_k) \in T(A_k)$ otherwise $s_k = t_k$.
  2. $\pi = \langle a, out \rangle$ and $(s_1, \langle a, out \rangle, t_1) \in T(A_1)$, and if $a \in Act(A_2)$ then $(s_2, \langle a, in \rangle, t_2) \in T(A_2)$ otherwise $s_2 = t_2$.
  3. $\pi = \langle a, out \rangle$ and $(s_2, \langle a, out \rangle, t_2) \in T(A_2)$, and if $a \in Act(A_1)$ then $(s_1, \langle a, in \rangle, t_1) \in T(A_1)$ otherwise $s_1 = t_1$.

Suppose that $A_1$ and $A_2$ are compatible I/O-processes. A run $\sigma = \pi_1, \pi_2, \ldots, \pi_k$ of $A_1$ *can be closed* by $A_2$ if there is closed run $\sigma'$ of $A_1 \| A_2$ such that $First(\sigma) = First([\sigma']_{Act(A_1)})$.

## 2.2 Parameterized memory systems

A parameterized memory system $M$ has three parameters —the number $n$ of processors, the number $m$ of memory locations, and the number $v$ of data values. The parameterized memory system $M$ is built from two parameterized I/O-processes $C$ and $P$ which have two parameters —the number $m$ of memory locations, and the number $v$ of data values. Intuitively, the I/O-process $P$ represents a single processor in the system and $C$ represents a central controller. The I/O-process $M(n, m, v)$ is built from the I/O-processes $C(m, v)$ and $P(m, v)$ by composing $C(m, v)$ and $n$ copies of $P(m, v)$. Given $n > 0, m > 0$, and $v > 0$, the memory system $M(n, m, v)$ is an I/O-process that has processors numbered from $1 \ldots n$, memory locations numbered from $0 \ldots m - 1$, and data values numbered from $0 \ldots v - 1$.

We now formally define a parameterized memory system. Let $\mathbb{N}$ be the set of all non-negative integers. For any $k > 0$, let $\mathbb{N}_k$ denote the set of all non-negative integers less than $k$. A *parameterized memory system* is a pair $\langle C, P \rangle$ such that both $C$ and $P$ are functions that map $\mathbb{N} \setminus \{0\} \times \mathbb{N} \setminus \{0\}$ to I/O-processes such that for all $m > 0$ and $v > 0$, we have that $Priv(C(m, v)) = PrivNames_C \times \mathbb{N}_m \times (\mathbb{N}_v \cup \{\bot\}), Obs(C(m, v)) = ObsNames_C \times \mathbb{N}_m \times (\mathbb{N}_v \cup \{\bot\}), Priv(P(m, v)) = PrivNames_P \times \mathbb{N}_m \times (\mathbb{N}_v \cup \{\bot\})$, and $Obs(P(m, v)) = ObsNames_P \times \mathbb{N}_m \times (\mathbb{N}_v \cup \{\bot\})$, where $PrivNames_C, ObsNames_C, PrivNames_P$, and $ObsNames_P$ are finite sets that satisfy the following properties:

1. $PrivNames_C \cap ObsNames_C = \emptyset$, and $PrivNames_P \cap ObsNames_P = \emptyset$.
2. $PrivNames_C \cap (ObsNames_P \cup PrivNames_P \times \mathbb{N}) = \emptyset$, and $ObsNames_C \cap (PrivNames_P \times \mathbb{N}) = \emptyset$.
3. $R \in PrivNames_P$ and $W \in PrivNames_P$.

The functions $name, loc$, and $val$ are defined on $Act(C(m, v)) \cup Act(P(m, v))$, and extract respectively the first, second, and third components of the actions. Given some $m$ and $v$, let $RdWr(m, v)$ be the union of the set of *read* actions $\{\langle R, j, k \rangle | j < m \text{ and } k < v\}$ and the set of *write* actions $\{\langle W, j, k \rangle | j < m \text{ and } k < v\}$.

For all $m$ and $v$ and for all $k > 0$, let $P_k(m, v)$ denote the I/O-process that is obtained from $P(m, v)$ by renaming every private action $a$ to action $a'$, such that (1) $name(a')$ is the pair $\langle name(a), k \rangle$, (2) $loc(a') = loc(a)$, and (3) $val(a') = val(a)$. A parameterized memory system defines a function that maps $\mathbb{N} \times \mathbb{N} \setminus \{0\} \times \mathbb{N} \setminus \{0\}$ to I/O-processes as follows:

$$M(0, m, v) \quad = C(m, v)$$
$$M(n + 1, m, v) = M(n, m, v) \| P_{n+1}(m, v)$$

For particular $n, m, v$, we say that $M(n, m, v)$ is a *memory system*. Note that $M(n, m, v)$ is compatible with $P_{n+1}(m, v)$, due to the renaming of private actions in $P_{n+1}(m, v)$, and the conditions on the names of private and observable actions of $C$ and $P$ described above. The observable actions of $M(n, m, v)$ are the same for all $n > 0$. We define a function $proc$ on the set of actions $\bigcup_{k,m,v} Priv(P_k(m, v))$ such that if $a$ is a private action of $P_k(m, v)$, then $proc(a) = k$.

## 2.3 Sequential consistency

Let $Memop(n, m, v)$ be the union of the sets $\{\langle\langle R, i\rangle, j, k\rangle | 0 < i \leq n$ and $j <$ $m$ and $k < v\}$ and $\{\langle\langle W, i\rangle, j, k\rangle | 0 < i \leq n$ and $j < m$ and $k < v\}$. Thus $Memop(n, m, v)$ denotes the set of read and write operations of $M(n, m, v)$. The functions $name$, $loc$, and $val$, which were originally defined on actions of $P(m, v)$ and $C(m, v)$, can be defined analogously on actions of $M(n, m, v)$. Thus, the four functions $name$, $loc$, $val$, and $proc$ are defined on all members of $Memop(n, m, v)$. We use $Memop$ to denote the set $\bigcup_{n,m,v} Memop(n, m, v)$.

Let $\sigma = \pi_1, \pi_2, \ldots, \pi_k$ be a sequence in $Memop^*$, the set of finite sequences with elements from $Memop$. The *abstraction* of $\sigma$, denoted by $\Lambda(\sigma)$, is a labeled directed graph $\langle V, E, L \rangle$, where $V$ is a finite set of vertices, $E \subseteq V \times V$, and $L$ is a function from $V$ to $Memop(n, m, v)$, such that (1) $V = \{1, 2, ..., k\}$, (2) for all $i \in V$, we have that $L(i) = \pi_i$, and (3) for all $x, y \in V$, we have that $\langle x, y \rangle \in E$ iff $proc(L(x)) = proc(L(y))$ and $x < y$. We observe that for every sequence $\sigma \in Memop^*$, the abstraction $\Lambda(\sigma)$ is an acyclic graph. Thus, we can obtain total orderings of the vertices in $\Lambda(\sigma)$ that respect the dependencies specified by its edges. Since the edges form a partial order, several such total orders, which are called linearizations of $\sigma$, may exist. Formally, a one-to-one mapping $f : V \rightarrow V$ is a *total order* of $\Lambda(\sigma) = \langle V, E, L \rangle$ if for all $x, y \in V$, whenever $\langle x, y \rangle \in E$ we have that $f^{-1}(x) < f^{-1}(y)$. If $f$ is a total order of $\Lambda(\sigma)$, then the sequence $L(f(1)), L(f(2)), \ldots, L(f(|V|))$ of actions in $Memop(n, m, v)$ is a *linearization* of $\sigma$.

We are interested in defining which sequences from $Memop^*$ are serial. Intuitively, a sequence from $Memop^*$ is serial if it can be produced by serial memory where each read from a location returns the value written by the last write to that location. We state this formally below. Let $\sigma = \pi_1, \pi_2, \ldots, \pi_k$ be a sequence in $Memop^*$. We define $lastwrite_\sigma$ as a function that associates with each position $i$ in $\sigma$, the position $j$ in $\sigma$ where the most recent write to the location $loc(\pi_i)$ was done. Formally, $lastwrite_\sigma$ is a mapping from the from the set $\{1, 2, ..., k\}$ to $\{1, 2, ..., k\} \cup \{\bot\}$ such that $lastwrite_\sigma(i) = j$ if there exists a $j$ such that $j \leq i$, $loc(\pi_i) = loc(\pi_j)$, $name(\pi_j) = \langle W, n_1 \rangle$ for some $n_1$, and there does not exist any $j'$ with $j < j' \leq i$, $name(\pi_{j'}) = \langle W, n_2 \rangle$ for some $n_2$, and $loc(\pi_{j'}) = loc(\pi_i)$; otherwise $lastwrite_\sigma(i) = \bot$. The sequence $\sigma$ is *serial* if for all $i \leq k$, if $lastwrite_\sigma(i) \neq \bot$, then $val(\pi_i) = val(\pi_{lastwrite_\sigma(i)})$.

For the following definitions, we extend the abstraction function $\Lambda$ to operate on arbitrary sequences $\sigma$ by first restricting it to actions in $Memop$. Formally, for any $\sigma$, we have that $\Lambda(\sigma) = \Lambda([\sigma]_{Memop})$. We extend $\Lambda$ to operate on sequences of extended actions by operating it on the first component of each extended action. Formally, if $\sigma$ is a sequence of extended actions, then $\Lambda(\sigma) = \Lambda(First(\sigma))$. Let $\Sigma_M = \bigcup_{n,m,v} \Sigma(M(n, m, v))$. Then $\Lambda$ is defined for all sequences in $\Sigma_M$.

**Definition 1 (Observer).** *Let $M$ be a parameterized memory system. A function $\Omega$ from $\Sigma_M$ to $Memop^*$ is an observer for the memory system $M(n, m, v)$ if for every run $\sigma \in \Sigma(M(n, m, v))$, the sequence $\Omega(\sigma)$ is a linearization of $\sigma$. The observer $\Omega$ is a serializer for $M(n, m, v)$ if for every run $\sigma \in \Sigma(M(n, m, v))$, the sequence $\Omega(\sigma)$ is serial.*

**Definition 2 (Sequential consistency [Lam79]).** *Let $M$ be a parameterized memory system. The memory system $M(n, m, v)$ is sequentially consistent if it has a serializer. The parameterized memory system $M$ is sequentially consistent if $M(n, m, v)$ is sequentially consistent for all $n > 0$, $m > 0$, and $v > 0$.*

### 2.4 Assumptions on parameterized memory systems

In order to reduce the proof of sequential consistency of the parameterized memory system to finite state model checking obligations, we make some assumptions about memory systems. We first state a few additional definitions. Let $\sigma$ be a run of the memory system $M(n, m, v)$. We denote by $\sigma|_j$ the run $\sigma$ restricted to the $j$th memory location. Formally, we have $\sigma|_j = [\sigma]_\beta$, where $\beta = \{a \mid a \in Act(M(n, m, v)) \text{ and } loc(a) = j\}$. For $j > 0$, we denote by $\sigma_{<j}$ the run $\sigma$ restricted to memory locations numbered less than $j$; that is, $\sigma|_{<j} = [\sigma]_\beta$, where $\beta = \{a \mid a \in Act(M(n, m, v)) \text{ and } loc(a) < j\}$.

**Assumption 1 (Location symmetry)** *Let $\lambda : \mathbb{N}_m \to \mathbb{N}_m$ be a permutation function on the set of memory locations. Extend $\lambda$ to actions, extended actions and extended action sequences in the natural way. Then,*

*1. for all $\sigma \in \Sigma(C(m, v))$, we have that $\lambda(\sigma) \in \Sigma(C(m, v))$, and*
*2. for all $\sigma \in \Sigma(P(m, v))$, we have that $\lambda(\sigma) \in \Sigma(P(m, v))$.*

**Assumption 2 (Location monotonicity)**

*1. If $\sigma \in \Sigma(C(m, v))$, then for all $j \leq m$, we have $\sigma|_{<j} \in \Sigma(C(j, v))$.*
*2. If $\sigma \in \Sigma(P(m, v))$, then for all $j \leq m$, we have $\sigma|_{<j} \in \Sigma(P(j, v))$.*

**Assumption 3 (Data symmetry)** *Let $\lambda : \mathbb{N}_v \cup \{\bot\} \to \mathbb{N}_v \cup \{\bot\}$ be any function on the set of data values, such that $\lambda(x) = \bot$ iff $x = \bot$. Extend $\lambda$ to actions, extended actions and extended action sequences in the natural way. Then,*

*1. for all $\sigma \in \Sigma(C(m, v))$, we have that $\lambda(\sigma) \in \Sigma(C(m, v))$, and*
*2. for all $\sigma \in \Sigma(P(m, v))$, we have that $\lambda(\sigma) \in \Sigma(P(m, v))$.*

**Assumption 4 (Data monotonicity)** *For all $m$, $n$, $v_1$, $v_2$, if $v_1 \leq v_2$, then*

*1. for all $\sigma \in Act(C(m, v_1))^*$, we have $\sigma \in \Sigma(C(m, v_1))$ iff $\sigma \in \Sigma(C(m, v_2))$, and*
*2. for all $\sigma \in Act(P(m, v_1))^*$, we have $\sigma \in \Sigma(P(m, v_1))$ iff $\sigma \in \Sigma(P(m, v_2))$.*

Note that the function $\lambda$ in assumption 1 above is a permutation on the set of locations, whereas the function $\lambda$ in assumption 3 could be any arbitrary function on the set of data values. Let $\lambda_0$ be the function from $Act(M(n, m, v))$ to $Act(M(m, n, v))$, which changes the location attribute to 0. Formally, $\lambda_0(a) = a'$ such that $name(a') = name(a)$, $loc(a') = 0$, and $val(a') = val(a)$. We extend $\lambda_0$ to extended action sequences in the natural way. The observer $\Omega$ is *location independent* if for all $j$, we have that $\Omega(\lambda_0(\sigma|_j)) = \lambda_0(\Omega(\sigma)|_j)$. The observer $\Omega$ is *data independent* if for every function $\lambda : \mathbb{N}_v \cup \{\bot\} \to \mathbb{N}_v \cup \{\bot\}$ such that $\lambda(x) = \bot$ iff $x = \bot$, we have that $\Omega(\lambda(\sigma)) = \lambda(\Omega(\sigma))$.

**Proposition 1.** *Suppose the parameterized memory system M satisfies assumptions 1– 4. For all n > 0, the following two statements are equivalent:*

1. *There is a location and data independent serializer for $M(n, n, 2)$.*
2. *There is a location and data independent serializer for $M(n, m, v)$ for all $m > 0$ and $v > 0$.*

Suppose we fix the number of processors to $n$. Due to the above proposition it suffices to consider only $n$ locations and 2 data values, if the serializer we design is location and data independent. Since our objective is to prove sequential consistency for an arbitrary number of processors, we give a method based on induction over the number of processors for this. The inductive step in the method considers two processors and designs a serializer-like function for them. Then an argument similar to the one used in proving Proposition 1 will let us show that it is enough to perform the inductive step for fixed numbers of memory locations and data values.

## 3  Reducing Sequential Consistency to Finite-state Proof Obligations

### 3.1  Induction on the set of processors

We show how to check sequential consistency of $M(n, m, v)$ for all $n > 0$ by induction over the number of processors. We do not need any of the assumptions 1–4 for the results in this section.

We note that every trace of $\Gamma(M(n, m, v))$ can be obtained by a run in $M(n + 1, m, v)$ in which the $(n + 1)$-st processor does not perform any output action. Hence $\Gamma(M(n, m, v))$ is contained in $\Gamma(M(n + 1, m, v))$ for all $n$. We would like to analyze a processor in an environment consisting of an arbitrary number of processors. Hence, we would like an upper bound on the trace set $\Gamma(M(n, m, v))$ for all $n$. A sufficient condition for this upper bound is captured by process invariants [KM89]. A function $I_1$ with two arguments $m$ and $v$ is a *possible process invariant* for the parameterized memory system $M$ if for all $m$ and $v$, we have that $I_1(m, v)$ is a I/O-process such that that (1) $Obs(I_1(m, v)) = Obs(M(n, m, v))$ for all $n > 0$ (recall that the set of observable actions of $M(n, m, v)$ is the same for all $n > 0$), and (2) $I_1(m, v)$ is compatible with $P(m, v)$.

**Definition 3** (**Process invariant**). *Let $I_1$ be a possible process invariant for the parameterized memory system $M$. The function $I_1$ is a process invariant of $M$ if the following condition is true for all $m$ and $v$:*

$$[A_{I_1}(m, v)] \quad \begin{array}{ll} 1. & C(m, v) \preceq I_1(m, v) \\ 2. & I_1(m, v) \| P(m, v) \preceq I_1(m, v) \end{array}$$

**Proposition 2.** *Suppose $I_1$ is a process invariant of the parameterized memory system $M$. Then, for all $n > 0$, $m > 0$, and $v > 0$, we have that $M(n, m, v) \preceq I_1(m, v)$.*

If the parameterized memory system $M$ is sequentially consistent, then by our definition, there exists an observer $\Omega$ for $M$ such that for every sequence $\sigma$ of memory operations of $M(n, m, v)$, the function $\Omega$ produces a rearranged sequence $\sigma'$ such that (1) $\sigma'$ is serial, and (2) $\sigma$ and $\sigma'$ agree on the ordering of the memory operations of each individual processor. We wish to provide an inductive construction that produces such an observer for arbitrary $n$. The construction uses the notion of a generalized processor called a merge invariant, and a witness function that works like an observer for a two-processor system consisting of the merge invariant and $P(m, v)$.

Recall that $RdWr(m, v)$ is the set of private actions of $P(m, v)$ that represent read and write operations. For technical reasons, we want the memory operations of the merge invariant to be named differently than those of $P(m, v)$. Let $Rd'(m, v) = \{\langle R', j, k\rangle | j < m \text{ and } k < v\}$, and let $Wr'(m, v) = \{\langle W', j, k\rangle | j < m \text{ and } k < v\}$. Let $RdWr'(m, v)$ denote the union of $Rd'(m, v)$ and $Wr'(m, v)$. We define the function $prime$ on $RdWr(m, v)$ by $prime(\langle R, j, k\rangle) = \langle R', j, k\rangle$ and $prime(\langle W, j, k\rangle) = \langle W', j, k\rangle$. We define the function $unprime$ on $RdWr'(m, v)$ by $unprime(\langle R', j, k\rangle) = \langle R, j, k\rangle$ and $unprime(\langle W', j, k\rangle) = \langle W, j, k\rangle$. We extend $prime$ and $unprime$ to sequences of actions in the natural way. We say that the sequence $\sigma' \in RdWr'(m, v)^*$ $rearranges$ the sequence $\sigma \in (RdWr(m, v) \cup RdWr'(m, v))^*$ if $\sigma'$ is an interleaving of $prime([\sigma]_{RdWr(m,v)})$ and $[\sigma]_{RdWr'(m,v)}$.

A function $I_2$ with two integer arguments $m$ and $v$ is a $possible$ $merge$ $invariant$ for the parameterized memory system $M$ if for all $m$ and $v$, we have that $I_2(m, v)$ is an I/O-process such that (1) $Obs(I_2(m, v)) = Obs(P(m, v))$, (2) $RdWr'(m, v) \subseteq Priv(I_2(m, v))$ and $RdWr(m, v) \cap Priv(I_2(m, v)) = \emptyset$, and (3) $I_2(m, v)$ is compatible with both $P(m, v)$ and $C(m, v)$. Let $I_1$ be a process invariant of $M$ and $I_2$ be a possible merge invariant of $M$. A function $\Theta$ from $\bigcup_{m,v} \Sigma(I_2(m, v) \| P(m, v))$ to $\bigcup_{m,v} \Sigma(I_2(m, v))$ is a $merging$ $function$ if $\sigma \in \Sigma(I_2(m, v) \| P(m, v))$ implies $\Theta(\sigma) \in \Sigma(I_2(m, v))$.

**Definition 4 (Merge invariant).** Let $I_1$ be a process invariant and let $I_2$ be a possible merge invariant for the parameterized memory system $M$. The function $I_2$ is a merge invariant of $M$ with respect to $I_1$ if there exists a merging function $\Theta$ such that the following two conditions are true for all $m$ and $v$:

[$B1_{I_2}(m, v)$] For every closed run $\sigma$ of $I_2(m, v) \| C(m, v)$, the sequence $unprime([\sigma]_{RdWr'(m,v)})$ is serial.

[$B2_{I_2,I_1,\Theta}(m, v)$] For every run $\sigma$ of $I_2(m, v) \| P(m, v)$ that can be closed by $I_1(m, v)$, we have that $\Theta(\sigma)$ rearranges $\sigma$, and $[\sigma]_{Obs(I_2(m,v))} = [\Theta(\sigma)]_{Obs(I_2(m,v))}$.

Note that the I/O-process $I_2(m, v) \| C(m, v)$ is a single-processor memory system. We say that the merging function $\Theta$ is a $witness$ for $B2_{I_2,I_1,\Theta}(m, v)$ if $\Theta$ makes condition $B2_{I_2,I_1,\Theta}(m, v)$ true.

Let $I_1$ be a process invariant of $M$. Suppose $I_2$ is a possible merge invariant of $M$, and $\Theta$ is a merging function such that $B1_{I_2}(m, v)$ and $B2_{I_2,I_1,\Theta}(m, v)$ are true for some $m$ and $v$. For some $n > 0$, consider the process $I_2(m, v) \| M(n, m, v)$, which can be written as $I_2(m, v) \| P_n(m, v) \| M(n - 1, m, v)$. Consider any closed run $\sigma$ of $I_2(m, v) \| M(n, m, v)$. Clearly there is a run $\sigma'$ of $I_2(m, v) \| P_n(m, v)$ that is closed by a run of $M(n - 1, m, v)$ to produce $\sigma$. Since $I_1$ is a process invariant of $M$, we have that $\sigma'$ is closed by a run of $I_1(m, v)$. Therefore, using $\Theta$ we can rearrange $\sigma'$ to obtain a run $\Theta(\sigma')$ of $I_2(m, v)$ which is closed by a run of $M(n - 1, m, v)$. Thus we have managed to rearrange a closed run of $I_2(m,v)\|M(n,m,v)$ into a closed run of $I_2(m,v)\|M(n-1,m,v)$. By repeating this procedure we eventually obtain a run of $I_2(m,v)\|C(m,v)$, which is sequentially consistent by condition $B1_{I_2}(m,v)$. Since every run of $M(n,m,v)$ is also run of $I_2(m,v)\|M(n,m,v)$, it follows that $n$ applications of $\Theta$ effectively produce an observer $\Omega$ which is a serializer for $M(n,m,v)$. The existence of such an observer implies the sequential consistency of $M(n,m,v)$.

**Theorem 1.** *Let $M$ be a parameterized memory system. If $I_1$ is a process invariant of $M$ and $I_2$ a merge invariant of $M$ with respect to $I_1$, then $M$ is sequentially consistent.*

Suppose that we manage to come up with possible invariants $I_1$ and $I_2$, and a merging function $\Theta$. How do we verify for all $m$ and $v$ that $A_{I_1}(m,v)$, $B1_{I_2}(m,v)$, and $B2_{I_2,I_1,\Theta}(m,v)$ hold? In the following two sections, we describe sufficient conditions whereby proving these obligations for fixed values of $m$ and $v$ will let us conclude that they hold for all $m$ and $v$.

### 3.2 Reduction to a fixed number of memory locations

In this section, we use assumptions 1 and 2 on the parameterized memory system. Further, we impose requirements on the process and merge invariants and the merging function that will reduce the verification problem to one on a fixed number of memory locations. The first two requirements are identical to assumptions 1 and 2 on the parameterized memory system.

**Requirement 1 (Location symmetry)** *Let $\lambda : \mathbb{N}_m \to \mathbb{N}_m$ be a permutation function on the set of memory locations. Extend $\lambda$ to actions, extended actions and extended action sequences in the natural way. We require for the possible process invariant $I_1$ and the possible merge invariant $I_2$ that*

*1. for all $\sigma \in \Sigma(I_1(m,v))$, we have that $\lambda(\sigma) \in \Sigma(I_1(m,v))$, and*
*2. for all $\sigma \in \Sigma(I_2(m,v))$, we have that $\lambda(\sigma) \in \Sigma(I_2(m,v))$.*

**Requirement 2 (Location monotonicity)** *We require for the possible process invariant $I_1$ and the possible merge invariant $I_2$ that*

*1. if $\sigma \in \Sigma(I_1(m,v))$ then for all $j \leq m$, we have $\sigma|_{<j} \in \Sigma(I_1(j,v))$, and*
*2. if $\sigma \in \Sigma(I_2(m,v))$ then for all $j \leq m$, we have $\sigma|_{<j} \in \Sigma(I_2(j,v))$.*

For any run $\sigma$ of $I_2(m,v)$, we define $tr'(\sigma)$ as the restriction of $\sigma$ to $Obs(I_2(m,v)) \cup RdWr'(m,v)$. Let $\Gamma'(I_2(m,v))$ be the set $\{tr'(\sigma)|\sigma \in \Sigma(I_2(m,v))\}$. Recall that $\lambda_0$ is a function that changes the location attribute of an action to 0.

**Requirement 3 (Location independence)** *We require for the possible process invariant $I_1$ and the possible merge invariant $I_2$ that*

*1. $\sigma \in \Gamma(I_1(m,v))$ if $\sigma \in Act(I_1(m,v))^*$, and for all $0 \leq j < m$, we have $\lambda_0(\sigma|_j) \in \Gamma(I_1(1,v))$, and*
*2. $\sigma \in \Gamma'(I_2(m,v))$ if $\sigma \in Act(I_2(m,v))^*$, and for all $0 \leq j < m$, we have $\lambda_0(\sigma|_j) \in \Gamma'(I_2(1,v))$.*

Consider a merging function $\Theta$. We say that $\Theta$ is *location independent* if whenever $\sigma \in \Sigma(I_2(m,v)\|P(m,v))$, then $\Theta(\lambda_0(\sigma|_j)) = \lambda_0(\Theta(\sigma)|_j)$ for all $j < m$.

**Theorem 2.** *Let $M$ be a parameterized memory system satisfying assumptions 1 and 2. Let $I_1$ be a possible process invariant and let $I_2$ be a possible merge invariant for $M$ satisfying requirements 1–3. Then the following conditions hold for all $v > 0$:*

1. *$A_{I_1}(1,v)$ is true iff $A_{I_1}(m,v)$ is true for all $m > 0$.*
2. *$B1_{I_2}(1,v)$ is true iff $B1_{I_2}(m,v)$ is true for all $m > 0$.*
3. *There is a location-independent witness $\Theta$ satisfying $B2_{I_2,I_1,\Theta}(l,v)$ for $l \leq 3$ iff there is a location-independent witness $\Theta'$ satisfying $B2_{I_2,I_1,\Theta'}(m,v)$ for all $m > 0$.*

The condition $l \leq 3$ in the last item of the above theorem comes from the fact that a witness $\Theta$ needs to preserve three orderings while rearranging a run of $I_2(m,v)\|P(m,v)$ —(1) the order of memory operations in $I_2(m,v)$, (2) the order of memory operations in $P(m,v)$, and (3) the order of observable actions in $I_2(m,v)\|P(m,v)$. If $\Theta$ does not preserve these orderings, and if $\Theta$ is location independent, we can prove that there exists a run $\sigma$ of $I_2(3,v)\|P(3,v)$ such that either $\Theta(\sigma)$ does not rearrange $\sigma$, or $[\sigma]_{Obs(I_2(3,v))} \neq [\Theta(\sigma)]_{Obs(I_2(3,v))}$.

### 3.3 Reduction to a fixed number of data values

In this section, we assume that the memory system satisfies assumptions 3 and 4. Recall the definition of a data-independent observer.

**Theorem 3.** *Let $M$ be a parameterized memory system satisfying assumptions 3 and 4. For all $n > 0$, $m > 0$, and $v > 0$, if $\Omega$ is a data-independent observer for the memory system $M(n,m,v)$, then $\Omega$ is a serializer for $M(n,m,2)$ iff $\Omega$ is a serializer for $M(n,m,v)$.*

Consider a merging function $\Theta$. We say that $\Theta$ is *data independent* if for all $v$, and for every function $\lambda : \mathbb{N}_v \cup \{\bot\} \to \mathbb{N}_v \cup \{\bot\}$ such that $\lambda(x) = \bot$ iff $x = \bot$, we have that $\Theta(\lambda(\sigma)) = \lambda(\Theta(\sigma))$. Suppose that the witness for $B2_{I_2,I_1,\Theta}(m,v)$ is data independent. Then the implicit observer function that is produced for $M(n,m,v)$ as a result of $n$ applications of the witness is also data independent.

**Corollary 1.** *Let $M$ be a parameterized memory system satisfying assumptions 1–4. Let $I_1$ be a possible process invariant and let $I_2$ be a possible merge invariant for $M$ satisfying requirements 1–3. Let $\Theta$ be a location and data independent merging function. Suppose $A_{I_1}(1,2)$ and $B1_{I_2}(1,2)$ are true, and $\Theta$ is a witness for $B2_{I_2,I_1,\Theta}(3,2)$. Then $M(n,m,v)$ is sequentially consistent for all $n > 0$, $m > 0$, and $v > 0$; that is, $M$ is sequentially consistent.*

## 4 Two Applications: Lazy Caching and Snoopy Coherence

We show how the theory developed in the previous section can be used to verify sequential consistency of memory systems with an arbitrary number of processors, locations and data values using a model checker. We consider two specific memory protocols, namely the lazy caching protocol from [ABM93] and a snoopy cache-coherence protocol from [HP96].

For each of these protocols, we first argue that assumptions 1–4 are satisfied by the memory system, and that requirements 1–3 are satisfied by the process and merge invariants. Then, we design a witness $\Theta$ and argue that it is location and data independent. The following observations provide justification for our informal arguments:

- The invariants and the witness have the property that they never base their decisions on data values. Thus, they are data independent by design.
- The memory system inherently enforces a total order on the writes to every location. In fact, every memory system we know of has this property. Our merge witness respects this total order for every location. Let $M$ be a parameterized memory system and let $\Theta$ be a merging function. Let $\sigma$ be a run of $M$ and let $j$ be any location. The order of writes in $\Theta(\sigma)|_j$ is the same as the total order of writes to location $j$ in $\sigma$. Every read to a location reads the value written to that location by some earlier write. The witness also respects this causal relationship between the writes and the reads. If two reads of location $j$ access the value written by the same write, then the witness places them in their temporal order of occurrence in $\Theta(\sigma)|_j$. Thus, the ordering of events to a location $j$ is independent of the events to other memory locations and determined solely by the temporal sequence of events to location $j$. Hence, our witness is naturally location independent.

We finally discharge the three proof obligations of Corollary 1 using our model checker MOCHA.

**Lazy Caching.** The lazy caching protocol allows a processor to complete a write in its local cache and proceed even while other processors continue to access the "old" value of the data in their local caches. Each cache has an output queue in which writes are buffered and an input queue in which reads are buffered. In order to satisfy sequential consistency, some restrictions are placed on read accesses to a cache when either writes or updates are buffered. A complete description of the protocol can be found in [ABM93].

The I/O-process $C(m, v)$ for this protocol is the trivial process with a single state that accepts all input actions. The I/O-process $P(m, v)$ is a description of one processor and cache in the system. The set $Priv(P(m, v))$ has actions with three different names: *read*, *write*, and *update*. An *update* action occurs when a write gets updated to a local cache from the head of its input queue. There is one action for each combination of these names with locations, processors and data values —a total of $3 \times n \times m \times v$ private actions. The set $Obs(P(m, v))$ has actions with one name: *serialize*. A *serialize* action occurs when a processor takes the result of a local write from the head of its output queue and transmits it on the bus. The *serialize* action does not identify the processor which did the action. Thus, a processor has $m \times v$ different observable actions.

The process invariant $I_1$ is such that for all $m$ and $v$, the I/O-process $I_1(m, v)$ simply generates all possible sequences of *serialize* actions. It is trivial to see that $I_1$ is a process invariant. The merge invariant $I_2$ is exactly the same as $P$. The merging function $\Theta$ is non-trivial. It queues *write* actions and delays them until the corresponding *update* action is seen by all processors. It also delays *read* actions until the corresponding *write* has been made visible. The witness preserves processor order, never bases decisions on data values, and respects the total order of writes that is inherent to the lazy-caching protocol. By design, the witness is location and data independent.

We used MOCHA [AHM$^+$98] to verify that the merging function $\Theta$ is a witness for the merge invariant for three locations and two data values. This obligation had about 60 latches and required MOCHA about 4 hours to check on a 625 MHz DEC Alpha 21164.

**Snoopy Cache Coherence.** The snoopy coherence protocol has a bus on which all caches send messages, as well as "snoop" and react to messages. Each location has a state machine which is in one of three states: **read-shared**, **write-exclusive**, or **invalid**. If a location is in **read-shared** state, then a cache has permission to read the value. If a location is in **write-exclusive** state, then a cache has permission to both read and write the value. In order to transition to **read-shared** or **write-exclusive** states, the cache sends messages over the bus, and other caches respond to these messages. There is also a central memory attached to the bus. When a location is not held in **write-exclusive** by any cache, the memory owns that location and responds to read requests for that location.

The I/O-process $C(m, v)$ for this protocol models the central memory, and $P(m, v)$ models one processor with a local cache. The process $C(m, v)$ has no private actions. It has observable actions with four different names: *read-request*, *write-request*, *read-response*, and *write-response*. The process $P(m, v)$ has private actions with two different names: *read* and *write*, and the same set of observable actions as $C(m, v)$. None of the observable actions identify the processor that did the action.

The process invariant is such that for all $m$ and $v$, we have that $I_1(m, v)$ is a generalization of the processor $P(m, v)$. The processor is generalized so that it can send a *read-request* for a location even if it already has the location in **read-shared**, and a *write-request* even if it already has the location in **write-exclusive**. The merge invariant $I_2$ is identical to $I_1$ with the additional capability to execute private *read* and *write* actions. The merging function $\Theta$ preserves temporal order of occurrence of reads and writes. This simple witness works because the snoopy protocol implements coherence. Again, by design the witness is data and location independent. We used MOCHA to verify that $I_1(1, v)$ is a process invariant and $I_1(3, v)$ is a merge invariant. MOCHA required less than 15 minutes to check these.

# References

[AB86] J. Archibald, J.-L. Baer. Cache coherence protocols: evaluation using a multiprocessor simulation model. *ACM Trans. Computer Systems*, 4(4):273–298, 1986.

[ABM93] Y. Afek, G. Brown, M. Merritt. Lazy caching. *ACM Trans. Programming Languages and Systems*, 15(1):182–205, 1993.

[AG96] S.V. Adve, K. Gharachorloo. Shared memory consistency models: a tutorial. *IEEE Computer*, 29(12):66–76, 1996.

[AHM$^+$98] R. Alur, T.A. Henzinger, F.Y.C. Mang, S. Qadeer, S.K. Rajamani, S. Tasiran. MOCHA: Modularity in model checking. In *CAV 98: Computer Aided Verification*, LNCS, pp. 521–525. Springer-Verlag, 1998.

[AMP96] R. Alur, K.L. McMillan, D. Peled. Model-checking of correctness conditions for concurrent objects. In *Proc. 11th IEEE Symp. Logic in Computer Science*, pp. 219–228, 1996.

[BCG89] M.C. Browne, E.M. Clarke, O. Grumberg. Reasoning about networks with many identical finite state processes. *Information and Computation*, 81(1):13–31, 1989.

[CGH+93] E.M. Clarke, O. Grumberg, H. Hiraishi, S. Jha, D.E Long, K.L. McMillan, and L.A. Ness. Verification of the Futurebus+ cache coherence protocol. In *Proc. 11th IFIP WG10.2 Conf. Computer Hardware Description Languages and their Applications*, pp. 15–30, 1993.

[EM95] A.T. Eiriksson, K.L. McMillan. Using formal verification/analysis methods on the critical path in system design: a case study. In *CAV 95: Computer Aided Verification*, LNCS 939, pp. 367–380. Springer-Verlag, 1995.

[EN98] E.A. Emerson, K.S. Namjoshi. Verification of a parameterized bus arbitration protocol. In *CAV 98: Computer Aided Verification*, LNCS 1427, pp. 452–463. Springer-Verlag, 1998.

[GMG91] P.B. Gibbons, M. Merritt, K. Gharachorloo. Proving sequential consistency of high-performance shared memories. In *Proc. 3rd ACM Symp. Parallel Algorithms and Architectures*, pp. 292–303, 1991.

[Gra94] S. Graf. Verification of a distributed cache memory by using abstractions. In *CAV 94: Computer Aided Verification*, LNCS 818, pp. 207–219. Springer-Verlag, 1994.

[GS97] S. Graf, H. Saidi. Construction of abstract state graphs with PVS. In *CAV 97: Computer Aided Verification*, LNCS 1254, pp. 72–83. Springer-Verlag, 1997.

[Hil98] M.D. Hill. Multiprocessors should support simple memory consistency models. *IEEE Computer*, 31(8):28–34, 1998.

[HP96] J.L. Hennessy, D.A. Patterson. *Computer Architecture: A Quantitative Approach*. Morgan-Kaufmann, 1996.

[ID96] C. N. Ip, D. L. Dill. Better verification through symmetry. *Formal Methods in System Design*, 9(1–2):41–75, 1996.

[KM89] R.P. Kurshan, K.L. McMillan. A structural induction theorem for processes. In *Proc. 8th ACM Symp. Principles of Distributed Computing*, pp. 239–247, 1989.

[Lam79] L. Lamport. How to make a multiprocessor computer that correctly executes multiprocess programs. *IEEE Trans. Computers*, C-28(9):690–691, 1979.

[LD92] P. Loewenstein, D.L. Dill. Verification of a multiprocessor cache protocol using simulation relations and higher-order logic. *Formal Methods in System Design*, 1(4):355–383, 1992.

[LLOR99] P. Ladkin, L. Lamport, B. Olivier, D. Roegel. Lazy caching in TLA. To appear in *Distributed Computing*.

[MS91] K. L. McMillan, J. Schwalbe. Formal verification of the Encore Gigamax cache consistency protocol. In *Proc. Symp. Shared Memory Multiprocessors*, Inf. Process. Soc. Japan, pp. 242–251, 1991.

[NGMG98] R. Nalumasu, R. Ghughal, A. Mokkedem, G. Gopalakrishnan. The 'test model-checking' approach to the verification of formal memory models of multiprocessors. In *CAV 98: Computer Aided Verification*, LNCS 1427, pp. 464–476. Springer-Verlag, 1998.

[PD95] F. Pong, M. Dubois. A new approach for the verification of cache coherence protocols. *IEEE Trans. Parallel and Distributed Systems*, 6(8):773–787, 1995.

[PD96] S. Park, D.L. Dill. Protocol verification by aggregation of distributed transactions. In *CAV 96: Computer Aided Verification*, LNCS 1102, pp. 300–310. Springer-Verlag, 1996.

[PSCH98] M. Plakal, D.J. Sorin, A.E. Condon, M.D. Hill. Lamport clocks: verifying a directory cache-coherence protocol. In *Proc. 10th ACM Symp. Parallel Algorithms and Architectures*, pp. 67–76, 1998.

[WL89] P. Wolper, V. Lovinfosse. Verifying properties of large sets of processes with network invariants. In *CAV 89: Computer Aided Verification*, LNCS 407, pp. 68–80. Springer-Verlag, 1989.

# Stepwise CTL Model Checking of State/Event Systems

Jørn Lind-Nielsen and Henrik Reif Andersen

Department of Information Technology, Technical University of Denmark
e-mail: {jl,hra}@it.dtu.dk

**Abstract.** In this paper we present an efficient technique for symbolic model checking of any CTL formula with respect to a state/event system. Such a system is a concurrent version of a Mealy machine and is used to describe embedded reactive systems. The technique uses compositionality to find increasingly better upper and lower bounds of the solution to a CTL formula until an exact answer is found. Experiments show this approach to succeed on examples larger than the standard backwards traversal can handle, and even in many cases where both methods succeed it is shown to be faster.

## 1 Introduction

The range of systems that can be formally verified has improved drastically since the introduction of symbolic model checking [7, 8] with the use of reduced and ordered binary decision diagrams (ROBDD) in the eighties [3, 2]. Since then many people have improved on the basic algorithms by introducing more efficient techniques, more compact representations and new methods for simplifying the models.

One way to do simplifications on the model is by abstraction, where subcomponents of the system considered are removed to yield a smaller and simpler model on which the verification can be done. The technique described here is based on one such incremental abstraction of the system, where first an initially small subset of the system is used as an abstraction. If this set is not enough to prove or disprove the requirements then the set is incrementally extended until a point where it is possible to give an exact positive or negative answer.

The experimental results are promising and show that the iterative approach can be used with success on larger systems than the usual backwards traversal can handle, and it is still faster even when the usual method is feasible.

This work is a direct extension of the work presented at TACAS'98 [11]. Now the technique covers full CTL model checking and calculates simultaneously both an upper and a lower approximation to the solution of the CTL formula.

We apply this technique to the *state/event model* used in the commercial tool visualSTATE™ [13]. This model is a concurrent version of Mealy machines, that is, it consists of a fixed number of concurrent finite state machines that have pairs of input events and output actions associated with the transitions of the machines. The model is synchronous: each input event is reacted upon by all machines in lock-step; the total output is the multi-set union of the output actions of the individual machines. Further synchronization between the machines is achieved by associating a guard with the transitions. Guards are Boolean combinations of conditions on the local states of the other machines.

Both the state space and the transition relation of the state/event system is represented using ROBDDs with a partitioned transition relation, exactly as described in [11].

## 1.1 Related Work

Another similar technique for exploiting the structure of the system to be verified is described in [9]. This technique also computes increasingly better approximations to the exact solution of a CTL formula, but it differs from our approach in several ways. Instead of reusing the previously found states as shown in section 6, this technique has to recalculate the approximation from scratch each time a new component is added to the system. It may also have to include all components in the system, whereas we restrict our inclusion to only the dependency closure (cone of influence) of the formula used. Finally the technique is restricted to ACTL(ECTL) formulae, whereas our technique can be used with any CTL formula.

Pardo and Hachtel describes an abstraction technique in [14] where the approximations are done using ROBDD reduction techniques. This technique is based on the $\mu$-calculus (and so includes CTL). It utilizes the structure of a given formula to find appropriate abstractions, whereas our technique depends on the structure of the model.

The technique for showing language containment of L-processes described in [1], also maintains a subset of processes used in the verification and analyzes error traces from the verifier to find new processes in order to extend this set. Although the overall goal of finding the result through an abstract, simplified model is the same as our, the properties verified are different and the L-processes have properties quite different from ours.

Abstraction as in [5] is similar to ours when the full dependency closure is included from the beginning, and thus it discards the idea of an iterative approach.

The idea of abstraction and compositionality is explored in more detail in David Longs' thesis [12].

## 2 State/Event Systems

A state/event system $S$ consists of $n$ machines $M_1, \ldots, M_n$, an alphabet $E$ of input events and an alphabet $O$ of outputs. Each machine $M_i$ is a triple $(S_i, s_i^0, T_i)$ of local states $S_i$, an initial state $s_i^0 \in S_i$, and a set of transitions $T_i$. The set of transitions is a relation

$$T_i \subseteq S_i \times E \times G_i \times \mathcal{M}(O) \times S_i,$$

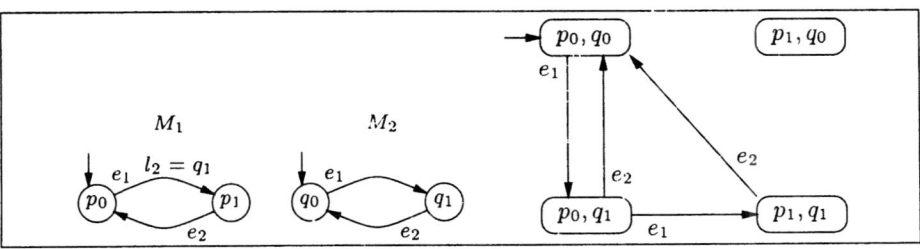

**Fig. 1.** Two state/event machines and the corresponding parallel combination. The small arrows indicate the initial states.

where $\mathcal{M}(O)$ is a multi-set of outputs, and $G_i$ is the set of guards not containing references to machine $i$. These guards are generated from the following simple grammar for Boolean expressions:

$$g \quad ::= \quad l_j = p \mid \neg g \mid g \wedge g \mid tt.$$

The atomic predicate $l_j = p$ is read as "machine $j$ is at local state $p$" and $tt$ denotes a true guard. The global state set $S$ of the state/event system is the product of the local state sets: $S = S_1 \times S_2 \times \cdots \times S_n$. The guards are interpreted straightforwardly over $S$ as given by a satisfaction relation $s \models g$. The expression $l_j = p$ holds for any $s \in S$ exactly when the $j$'th component of $s$ is $p$, i.e., $s_j = p$. The interpretation of the other cases is as usual. The transition relation is total, by assuming that the system stays in its current state when no transitions are enabled for a given input event.

Considering a global state $s$, all guards in the transition relation can be evaluated. We define a version of the transition relation in which the guards have been evaluated. This relation is denoted $s \xrightarrow{e\ o}_i s'_i$ expressing that machine $i$ when receiving input event $e$ makes a transition from $s_i$ to $s'_i$ and generates output $o$ (here $s_i$ is the $i$'th component of $s$). Formally,

$$s \xrightarrow{e\ o}_i s'_i \iff_{def} \exists g.\ (s_i, e, g, o, s'_i) \in T_i \text{ and } s \models g.$$

The transition relation of the whole system is defined as:

$$s \xrightarrow{e\ o} s' \iff_{def} \forall i.\ s \xrightarrow{e\ o_i}_i s'_i \quad \text{where} \quad s' = (s'_1, \ldots, s'_n) \text{ and } o = o_1 \uplus \ldots \uplus o_n$$

Where $\uplus$ denotes multi set union. The example in figure 1 shows a system with two state/event machines and the corresponding parallel combination. Machine $M_2$ starts in state $q_0$ and goes to state $q_1$ on the receipt of event $e_1$. Machine $M_1$ can not move on $e_1$ because of the guard. After this $M_2$ may go back on event $e_2$ or $M_1$ may enter state $p_1$ on event $e_1$. At last both $M_1$ and $M_2$ can return to their initial states on event $e_2$.

## 3   CTL Specifications

CTL [6] is a temporal logic used to specify formal requirements to finite state machines like the state/event systems presented here. Such specifications consist of the Boolean constant true $tt$, conjunction $\wedge$, negation $\neg$, state predicates and temporal operators. We use a state predicate variant where the location of a machine is stated: $l_i = s$ meaning that machine $i$ should be in state $s$, similar to the guards.

The temporal operators are the *next* operator $\mathbf{X}(\phi)$, the *future* operator $\mathbf{F}(\phi)$, the *globally* operator $\mathbf{G}(\phi)$ and the *until* operator $(\phi_1 \, \mathbf{U} \, \phi_2)$. Each of these operators must be directly preceded with a path quantifier to state whether the formula should hold for all possible execution paths of the system ($\mathbf{A}$) or only for at least one execution path ($\mathbf{E}$).

The solution to a CTL formula $\phi$ is the set of states $[\![\phi]\!]$ that satisfy the formula $\phi$. A state/event system $S$ is said to satisfy the property $\phi$, $S \models \phi$ if the initial state $s^0$ is in the solution to $\phi$, $s^0 \in [\![\phi]\!]$.

To describe the exact semantics of the operators we use an additional function $[\![\mathbf{EX}]\!]$ that operates on a set of states $P$. This function returns all the states that may reach at least one of the states in $P$ in exactly one step and is defined as $[\![\mathbf{EX}]\!] \, P = \{s \in S \mid \exists e, o, s'. \ s \xrightarrow{e \ o} s' \wedge s' \in P\}$. The operators are then defined, for a State/Event system with the transition relation $s \xrightarrow{e \ o} s'$, as:

$$
\begin{array}{ll}
[\![tt]\!] = S & [\![l_i = s]\!] = \{s' \in S \mid s'_i = s\} \\
[\![\neg \phi]\!] = S \backslash [\![\phi]\!] & [\![\phi_1 \wedge \phi_2]\!] = [\![\phi_1]\!] \cap [\![\phi_2]\!] \\
[\![\mathbf{EX} \ \phi]\!] = [\![\mathbf{EX}]\!][\![\phi]\!] & [\![\mathbf{EG} \ \phi]\!] = \nu U \subseteq S. \ [\![\phi]\!] \cap [\![\mathbf{EX}]\!]U
\end{array}
$$

$$
[\![\mathbf{E}(\phi_1 \ \mathbf{U} \ \phi_2)]\!] = \mu U \subseteq S. \ [\![\phi_2]\!] \cup ([\![\phi_1]\!] \cap [\![\mathbf{EX}]\!]U)
$$

Here we use $\nu x. f(x)$ and $\mu x. f(x)$ as the maximal and minimal fixed points of a monotone function $f$ on a complete lattice, as given by Tarski's fixed point theorem [16]. The rest of the operators can be defined using the above operators [8].

## 4  Bounded CTL Solutions

In this section we introduce the *bounded* CTL solution. A bounded CTL solution consists of two sets of states, namely $\mathcal{L}[\![\phi]\!]_I$ and $\mathcal{U}[\![\phi]\!]_I$ which are lower- and upper-approximations to the solution of the formula. The idea is to test for inclusion of the initial state in $\mathcal{L}[\![\phi]\!]_I$ and exclusion from $\mathcal{U}[\![\phi]\!]_I$. In the first case we know that the formula holds and in the second that it does not.

To describe bounded CTL solutions we need to formalize the concept of *dependency* between machines in a state/event system. We choose the notion that one machine $M_i$ depends on another machine $M_j$ if there exists at least one guard in $M_i$ that has a syntactic reference to a state in $M_j$. These dependencies form a directed graph, which we call the *dependency graph*. In this graph each vertex represent a machine and an edge from a vertex $i$ to a vertex $j$ represents a dependency in machine $M_i$ on a state in machine $M_j$. Note that we can ignore any dependencies introduced by the global synchronization of the input events.

A formula $\phi$ depends on a machine $M_i$ if $\phi$ contains a sub-formula of the form $l_i = s$, and the *sort* of $\phi$ is all the machines $\phi$ depends on. The *dependency closure* of a machine $M_i$ is all the machines that are reachable from $M_i$ in the dependency graph, including $M_i$. This is also sometimes refered to as the *cone of influence*. The dependency closure of a formula $\phi$ is the union of all the dependency closures of the machines in the sort of $\phi$.

Assume (for the time being) that we have an efficient way to calculate a bounded solution to a CTL formula $\phi$ using only the machines in an index set $I$. The result should be two sets of states $\mathcal{L}[\![\phi]\!]_I$ and $\mathcal{U}[\![\phi]\!]_I$ with the following properties:

$$\mathcal{L}[\![\phi]\!]_I \subseteq [\![\phi]\!] \subseteq \mathcal{U}[\![\phi]\!]_I. \tag{1}$$
$$\mathcal{L}[\![\phi]\!]_{I_1} \subseteq \mathcal{L}[\![\phi]\!]_{I_2} \text{ if } I_1 \subseteq I_2. \tag{2}$$
$$\mathcal{U}[\![\phi]\!]_{I_1} \supseteq \mathcal{U}[\![\phi]\!]_{I_2} \text{ if } I_1 \subseteq I_2. \tag{3}$$
$$\mathcal{L}[\![\phi]\!]_I = [\![\phi]\!] = \mathcal{U}[\![\phi]\!]_I \text{ if } I \text{ is dependency closed.} \tag{4}$$

Both $\mathcal{L}[\![\phi]\!]_I$ and $\mathcal{U}[\![\phi]\!]_I$ are only defined for sets $I$ that include the sort of $\phi$. Property (1) means that $\mathcal{L}[\![\phi]\!]_I$ is a lower approximation of $[\![\phi]\!]$ and $\mathcal{U}[\![\phi]\!]_I$ is an upper approximation of $[\![\phi]\!]$. Property (2) and (3) mean that the approximations converge monotonically towards the correct solution of $\phi$ and property (4) states that we get the correct solution to $\phi$ when $I$ contains all the machines found in the dependency closure of $\phi$.

In section 5 we will show an algorithm that efficiently computes the bounded solution to any CTL formulae. With this, it is possible to make a serious improvement to the usual algorithm for finding CTL solutions. The algorithm utilizes the fact that we may be able to prove or disprove the property $\phi$ using only a (hopefully) small subset of all the machines in the system.

Our algorithm for verifying a CTL property is as follows

**Algorithm** *CTL verifier*
**Input:** A CTL formula $\phi$ and a state/event system $S$ and it's dependency graph $G$
**Output: true** if $s^0 \in [\![\phi]\!]$ and **false** otherwise
1.   $I = \text{sort}(\phi)$; result = **unknown**
2.   **repeat**
3.       calculate $\mathcal{L}[\![\phi]\!]_I$ and $\mathcal{U}[\![\phi]\!]_I$
4.       **if** $s^0 \in \mathcal{L}[\![\phi]\!]_I$ **then** result = **true**
5.       **if** $s^0 \notin \mathcal{U}[\![\phi]\!]_I$ **then** result = **false**
6.       $I = I \cup extend(I, G)$
7.   **until** result $\neq$ **unknown**

First we set $I$ to be the sort of $\phi$ and use this to calculate $\mathcal{L}[\![\phi]\!]_I$ and $\mathcal{U}[\![\phi]\!]_I$. If $s^0 \in \mathcal{L}[\![\phi]\!]_I$, then we know, from property (2), that $\phi$ holds for the system, and if $s^0 \notin \mathcal{U}[\![\phi]\!]_I$ then we know, from property (3), that $\phi$ does not hold. If neither is the case then we add more machines to $I$ and try again. This continues until $\phi$ is either proved or disproved. The algorithm is guaranteed to stop with either a false or a true result when $I$ is the dependency closure of $\phi$, in which case we have $\mathcal{L}[\![\phi]\!]_I = \mathcal{U}[\![\phi]\!]_I$, from property (4), and thus either $s^0 \in \mathcal{L}[\![\phi]\!]_I$ or $s^0 \notin \mathcal{U}[\![\phi]\!]_I$.

The function *extend* selects a new set of machines to be included in $I$. We have chosen to include new machines in a breadth-first manner, so that *extend* returns all machines reachable in $G$ from $I$ in one step.

## 5  Bounded CTL Calculation

In section 4 we showed how to verify a CTL formula $\phi$, by using only a minimal set of machines $I$ from a state/event system and using an efficient algorithm for the calculation of lower and upper approximations of $[\![\phi]\!]$. In this section we will show one such algorithm, and for this we need some more definitions. Relating to an index set $I$ of machines, two states $s, s' \in S$ are *I-equivalent*, written as $s =_I s'$, if for all $i \in I$, $s_i = s'_i$. A set of states $P$ is *I-sorted* if the following predicate is true

$$I\text{-sorted}(P) \Leftrightarrow_{def} \forall s, s' \in S. \ (s \in P \land s =_I s') \Rightarrow s' \in P.$$

This means that if a state $s$ is in $P$ then all other states $s'$, which are $I$-equivalent to $s$, must also be in the set $P$. This is equivalent to say that a set $P$ is $I$-sorted if it is independent of the machines in the complement $\overline{I} = \{1, \dots, n\} \setminus I$.

Consider as an example two machines with the sets of states $S_0 = \{p_0, p_1\}$, $S_1 = \{q_0, q_1, q_2\}$ and a sort $I = \{0\}$. Now the two pairs of states $(p_0, q_1)$ and $(p_0, q_2)$ are $I$-equivalent because their first states match. The set $P = \{(p_0, q_0), (p_0, q_1), (p_0, q_2)\}$ is $I$-sorted because it is independent of the states in $S_1$.

The bounded calculation of the constants $tt$ and $l_i = s$, negation and conjunction is straight forward as shown in figure 2. The results are clearly $I$-sorted and satisfies the properties in section 4, if the sub-expressions $\phi, \phi_1$ and $\phi_2$ does so.

**Next State Operator:** To show how to find $\mathcal{L}[\![\mathbf{EX}\ \phi]\!]_I$ and $\mathcal{U}[\![\mathbf{EX}\ \phi]\!]_I$ we introduce two new operators: $[\![\mathbf{E}_\forall \mathbf{X}]\!]_I$ and $[\![\mathbf{E}_\exists \mathbf{X}]\!]_I$. The lower approximation $[\![\mathbf{E}_\forall \mathbf{X}]\!]_I\ P$ is a conservative approximation to $[\![\mathbf{EX}]\!]$ that only includes states that are guaranteed to reach $P$ in one step, regardless of the states of the machines in $\overline{I}$. The upper approximation $[\![\mathbf{E}_\exists \mathbf{X}]\!]_I\ P$ is an optimistic approximation that includes all states that just might reach $P$. These two operators are defined as:

$$[\![\mathbf{E}_\forall \mathbf{X}]\!]_I\ P = \{s \in S \mid \forall s' \in S. \ s =_I s' \Rightarrow s' \in [\![\mathbf{EX}]\!]_I\ P\}$$
$$[\![\mathbf{E}_\exists \mathbf{X}]\!]_I\ P = \{s \in S \mid \exists s' \in S. \ s =_I s' \land s' \in [\![\mathbf{EX}]\!]_I\ P\}$$

where the results of both operators are $I$-sorted when $[\![\mathbf{EX}]\!]_I\ P$ is $I$-sorted, as a result of the extra quantifiers. The calculation of $[\![\mathbf{EX}]\!]_I\ P$ can be done efficiently *when $P$ is I-sorted*, using a partitioned transition relation [4]. The definition of $[\![\mathbf{EX}]\!]_I$ is

$$[\![\mathbf{EX}]\!]_I\ P = \{s \in S \mid \exists e, o, s'. \ s \xrightarrow{e\ o} s' \land s' \in P\}.$$

This seems to depend on all $n$ machines in $S$, but as a result of $P$ being $I$-sorted, it can be reduced to

$$[\mathbf{EX}]_I\ P = \{s \in S \mid \exists e, o.\ \exists s'_{\overline{I}}.\ \exists s'_I.\ s \xrightarrow{e\ o}_I s'_I \wedge (s'_1, \ldots, s'_N) \in P\}$$

where $\exists s'_I.\ s \xrightarrow{e\ o}_I s'_I$ means $\bigwedge_{i \in I} \exists s'_i.\ s \xrightarrow{e\ o}_i s'_i$. This clearly depends on only the transition relations for the machines in $I$.

Now we can define $\mathcal{L}[\mathbf{EX}\ \phi]_I$ and $\mathcal{U}[\mathbf{EX}\ \phi]_I$ as

$$\mathcal{L}[\mathbf{EX}\ \phi]_I\ = [\mathbf{E}_\forall \mathbf{X}]_I\ \mathcal{L}[\phi]_I$$
$$\mathcal{U}[\mathbf{EX}\ \phi]_I\ = [\mathbf{E}_\exists \mathbf{X}]_I\ \mathcal{U}[\phi]_I.$$

Both $\mathcal{L}[\mathbf{EX}\ \phi]_I$ and $\mathcal{U}[\mathbf{EX}\ \phi]_I$ are clearly $I$-sorted because both $[\mathbf{E}_\forall \mathbf{X}]_I$ and $[\mathbf{E}_\exists \mathbf{X}]_I$ are so, and if $\phi$ satisfies the properties in section 4 then so does $\mathcal{L}[\mathbf{EX}\ \phi]_I$ and $\mathcal{U}[\mathbf{EX}\ \phi]_I$.

**Globally and Until operators:** The semantics for $\mathbf{EG}\ \phi$ is defined in the same manner as $\mathbf{EX}\ \phi$, with an added fixed point calculation:

$$\mathcal{L}[\mathbf{EG}\ \phi]_I = \nu U.\ \mathcal{L}[\phi]_I \cap [\mathbf{E}_\forall \mathbf{X}]_I U$$
$$\mathcal{U}[\mathbf{EG}\ \phi]_I = \nu U.\ \mathcal{U}[\phi]_I \cap [\mathbf{E}_\exists \mathbf{X}]_I U.$$

The result is also $I$-sorted and satisfies the properties in section 4 if $\phi$ does. For $\mathbf{E}(\phi_1\ \mathbf{U}\ \phi_2)$ we take

$$\mathcal{L}[\mathbf{E}(\phi_1\ \mathbf{U}\ \phi_2)]_I = \mu U.\ \mathcal{L}[\phi_2]_I \cup (\mathcal{L}[\phi_1]_I \cap [\mathbf{E}_\forall \mathbf{X}]_I\ U)$$
$$\mathcal{U}[\mathbf{E}(\phi_1\ \mathbf{U}\ \phi_2)]_I = \mu U.\ \mathcal{U}[\phi_2]_I \cup (\mathcal{U}[\phi_1]_I \cap [\mathbf{E}_\exists \mathbf{X}]_I\ U).$$

## 6  Reusing Bounded CTL Calculations

One problem with the operators $\mathcal{L}[\phi]_I$ and $\mathcal{U}[\phi]_I$ from section 5, when used in the bounded CTL verifier, is that all previously found states have to be rediscovered whenever a new set of machines $I$ is introduced. In this section we will show how to avoid this problem for the $\mathbf{EG}$ operator and sketch how to do it for the $\mathbf{E}(\phi_1 \mathbf{U}\ \phi_2)$ operator. The final algorithm is shown in figure 2.

First we show how the calculation of $\mathcal{U}[\mathbf{EG}\ \phi]_{I_2}$ can be improved by reusing the previous calculation of $\mathcal{U}[\mathbf{EG}\ \phi]_{I_1}$ when $I_1 \subseteq I_2$. From the definition of $\mathcal{U}[\mathbf{EG}\ \phi]_I$ we get the following:

$$\mathcal{U}[\mathbf{EG}\ \phi]_{I_2} \subseteq \mathcal{U}[\mathbf{EG}\ \phi]_{I_1} \subseteq \mathcal{U}[\phi]_{I_1}\ and$$
$$\mathcal{U}[\mathbf{EG}\ \phi]_{I_2} \subseteq \mathcal{U}[\phi]_{I_2}\qquad \subseteq \mathcal{U}[\phi]_{I_1}$$

and from this we know that

$$\mathcal{U}[\mathbf{EG}\ \phi]_{I_2} \subseteq \mathcal{U}[\mathbf{EG}\ \phi]_{I_1} \cap \mathcal{U}[\phi]_{I_2}.$$

We also know, from Tarski's fixed point theorem, that $\nu f \subseteq x \Rightarrow \nu f = \bigcap_i f^i(x)$, which means the maximum fixed point calculation of $f$ can be started from any

$$\mathcal{B}[tt]_{I_k} \quad\quad\quad = \quad (S\,,\,S)$$

$$\mathcal{B}[l_i = s]_{I_k} \quad\quad = \text{let } L = \{s' \in S \mid s'_i = s\}$$
$$U = \{s' \in S \mid s'_i = s\}$$
$$\text{in } (L, U)$$

$$\mathcal{B}[\neg\phi]_{I_k} \quad\quad\quad = \text{let } (L, U) = \mathcal{B}[\phi]_{I_k}$$
$$\text{in } (S \setminus U\,,\,S \setminus L)$$

$$\mathcal{B}[\phi_1 \wedge \phi_2]_{I_k} \quad = \text{let } (L_1, U_1) = \mathcal{B}[\phi_1]_{I_k}$$
$$(L_2, U_2) = \mathcal{B}[\phi_2]_{I_k}$$
$$\text{in } (L_1 \cap L_2\,,\,U_1 \cap U_2)$$

$$\mathcal{B}[\mathbf{EX}\ \phi]_{I_k} \quad\quad = \text{let } (L, U) = \mathcal{B}[\phi]_{I_k}$$
$$\text{in } ([\mathbf{E_\forall X}]_{I_k}\ L\,,\,[\mathbf{E_\exists X}]_{I_k}\ U)$$

$$\mathcal{B}[\mathbf{EG}\ \phi]_{I_k} \quad\quad = \text{let } (L_1, U_1) = \mathcal{B}[\phi]_{I_k}$$
$$(\_\,, U_2) = \mathcal{B}[\mathbf{EG}\ \phi]_{I_{k-1}}$$
$$U = \nu V.\,(U_1 \cap U_2) \cap [\mathbf{E_\exists X}]_{I_k} V \quad\quad \text{(a)}$$
$$L = \nu V.\,(L_1 \cap U) \cap [\mathbf{E_\forall X}]_{I_k} V \quad\quad \text{(b)}$$
$$\text{in } (L\,,\,U)$$

$$\mathcal{B}[\mathbf{E}\ (\phi_1 \mathbf{U}\ \phi_2)]_{I_k} = \text{let } (L_1, U_1) = \mathcal{B}[\phi_1]_{I_k}$$
$$(L_2, U_2) = \mathcal{B}[\phi_2]_{I_k}$$
$$(L_3, \_\,) = \mathcal{B}[\mathbf{E}\ (\phi_1 \mathbf{U}\ \phi_2)]_{I_{k-1}}$$
$$L = \mu V.\,(L_2 \cup L_3) \cup (L_1 \cap [\mathbf{E_\exists X}]_{I_k} V) \quad \text{(c)}$$
$$U = \mu V.\,(U_2 \cup L) \cup (U_1 \cap [\mathbf{E_\exists X}]_{I_k} V) \quad \text{(d)}$$
$$\text{in } (L\,,\,U)$$

**Fig. 2.** Full description of how the lower and upper approximations $(\mathcal{L}[\phi]_I, \mathcal{U}[\phi]_I) = \mathcal{B}[\phi]_I$ are calculated for a state/event system $S$. The sorts are $I_k$ for the current sort and $I_{k-1}$ for the previous sort. Initially we have $\mathcal{B}[\phi]_{I_0} = (\emptyset, S)$ and $I_0$ is the sort of the expression. We use $L$ for a lower approximation and $U$ for an upper approximation. The lines (a)–(d) show where we reuse previously found states.

$x$ as long as $x$ includes the maximal fixed point of $f$. Here we use $f^i(x)$ as the $i$'th application of $f$ on itself. From this it is clear that the fixed point calculation of $\mathcal{U}[\mathbf{EG}\ \phi]_{I_2}$ can be started from the intersection of the two sets $\mathcal{U}[\mathbf{EG}\ \phi]_{I_1}$ and $\mathcal{U}[\phi]_{I_2}$. Normally this fixed point calculation would have been started from $\mathcal{U}[\phi]_{I_2}$, but in this way we reuse the calculation of $\mathcal{U}[\mathbf{EG}\ \phi]_{I_1}$ to speed up the calculation of $\mathcal{U}[\mathbf{EG}\ \phi]_{I_2}$.

The same idea can be used for the lower approximation $\mathcal{L}[\mathbf{EG}\ \phi]_{I_2}$, where the fixed point iteration can be started from the intersection of $\mathcal{L}[\phi]_{I_2}$ and $\mathcal{U}[\mathbf{EG}\ \phi]_{I_2}$, so that we reuse the calculation of the upper approximation. The algorithm in figure 2 utilizes this in line (a) for the upper approximation and in line (b) for the lower approximation.

Exactly the same can be done for $\mathcal{L}[\mathbf{E}(\phi_1 \mathbf{U}\ \phi_2)]_I$ and $\mathcal{U}[\mathbf{E}(\phi_1 \mathbf{U}\ \phi_2)]_I$, except that the previous *lower* approximations should be used to restart the calculation, as shown in line c and d in figure 2.

| System | Machines | Local states | Declared | Reachable |
|--------|---------:|-------------:|:--------:|----------:|
| INTERVM | 6 | 182 | $10^6$ | 15144 |
| VCR | 7 | 46 | $10^5$ | 1279 |
| DKVM | 9 | 55 | $10^6$ | 377568 |
| HI-FI | 9 | 59 | $10^7$ | 1416384 |
| FLOW | 10 | 232 | $10^5$ | 17040 |
| MOTOR | 12 | 41 | $10^6$ | 34560 |
| AVS | 12 | 66 | $10^7$ | 1438416 |
| VIDEO | 13 | 74 | $10^8$ | 1219440 |
| ATC | 14 | 194 | $10^{10}$ | 6399552 |
| OIL | 24 | 96 | $10^{13}$ | 237230192 |
| TRAIN1 | 373 | 931 | $10^{136}$ | – |
| TRAIN2 | 1421 | 3204 | $10^{476}$ | – |

**Table 1.** The state/event systems used in the experiments. The last two columns show the size of the declared and reachable state space. The size of the declared state space is the product of the number of local states of each machine. The reachable state space is only known for those systems where a forward iteration of the state space can complete.

## 7  Examples

The technique presented here has been tested on ten industrial state/event systems and two systems constructed by students in a course on embedded systems. The examples are all constructed using visualSTATE™ [13] and cover a large range of different applications. The examples are HI-FI, AVS, ATC, FLOW, MOTOR, INTERVM, DKVM, OIL, TRAIN1 and TRAIN2 which are industrial examples and VCR and VIDEO which are constructed by students. In table 1 we have listed some characteristics for these examples.

The experiments were carried out on a pentium 166MHz PC with 32Mb of memory, running Linux. For the ROBDD encoding we used BuDDy [10], a locally produced ROBDD package which is comparable in efficiency to other state of the art ROBDD packages, such as CUDD [15].

For each example we tested three different sets of CTL formulae. One set of formulae for detecting non-determinism in the system, one set for detecting local deadlocks and one for finding homestates.

Non-determinism occurs when two transitions leading out of a state depends on the same event and has guards that are enabled at the same time in a reachable global state. That is, the intersection of the two guards $g = g_1 \wedge g_2$ should be non-empty and reachable. Every combination of guards were then checked for reachability using the formula **EF** $g$.

Locally deadlocked states are local states from which there can never be enabled any outgoing transition, no matter how the rest of the system behaves. So for each local state $s$ in the system we check for absence of local deadlocks using the formula **AG** $(s \Rightarrow \textbf{EF} \, \neg s)$

Homestates are states that can be reached from any point in the reachable state space. So for each local state $s$ of the system we get the formula $\mathbf{AG}$ ($\mathbf{EF}$ $s$).

We have unfortunately only access to the examples in an anonymous form, so we have no way of generating more specialized properties.

In table 2 we have listed the time it takes to complete checking a whole set of CTL formulae using the standard backwards traversal with either *all* machines in the system or only the machines in the dependency closure, and the time used with stepwise traversal. For the largest system it is only the stepwise traversal that succeeds and with the exception of one system (ATC) the stepwise traversal is also faster or comparable in speed to the standard backwards traversal.

We have also shown the number of tests that can be verified using fewer machines than in the dependency closure, how much of the dependency closure there was needed to do it, how many tests that had to include the full dependency closure and the average size of that dependency closure. From this we can see that in the TRAIN2 example we can verify most of the formulae using only a small fraction $(3 - 15\%)$ of the dependency closure and when the full dependency closure has to be included then the average size of it is only as little as 1 ( although we know that some tests includes more than 200 machines in the dependency closure). This indicates that TRAIN2 is a *loosely coupled* system i.e. a system with few dependencies among the state machines.

We also see that ATC and OIL are more strongly coupled, as the average dependency closure is larger than for the other examples. This property is also mirrored in the time needed to verify the two examples.

# 8   Conclusion

We have extended the successful model checking technique presented in [11] with the ability to do full CTL model checking and not only reachability and deadlock detection. We have also added the calculation of both upper *and* lower approximations to the result and in this way making it possible to stop earlier in the verification process with either a negative or a positive answer.

Test examples have shown the stepwise traversal of the state space to be more efficient, than the normal backwards traversal, in terms of both time and space for a range of industrial examples. We have also shown that the stepwise technique may succeed in cases where the standard techniques fails.

The examples also indicates that the stepwise traversal works best on loosely coupled systems, that is; systems with few dependencies among the involved state machines.

### Acknowledgement

Thanks to the colleagues of the VVS project for numerous fruitful discussions on the verification of state/event models.

| Test Data | | | Run times | | | | Dependencies | | | | |
|---|---|---|---|---|---|---|---|---|---|---|---|
| Example | Test | Num | Full | DC. | Step | Red. | Part. DC. | | Full DC. | | |
| | | | | | | | Ok | Err | Ok | Err | Size |
| INTERVM | D | 182 | 6.7 | **6.2** | 6.8 | | 150 41% | 0 0% | 32 | 0 | 4.5 |
| (6) | H | 182 | 50.3 | 47.3 | **40.6** | +19% | 96 57% | 0 0% | 86 | 0 | 4.8 |
| VCR | C | 1 | 0.3 | **0.2** | 0.2 | | 0 0% | 0 0% | 1 | 0 | 6.0 |
| (7) | D | 46 | 0.6 | **0.4** | 0.8 | | 2 40% | 0 0% | 44 | 0 | 5.4 |
| | H | 46 | 2.2 | **1.3** | 1.5 | | 2 40% | 0 0% | 44 | 0 | 5.4 |
| DKVM | D | 55 | 0.5 | **0.4** | 0.4 | | 46 20% | 0 0% | 9 | 0 | 1.0 |
| (9) | H | 55 | 8.7 | 8.7 | **6.7** | | 27 45% | 1 11% | 27 | 0 | 1.7 |
| HI-FI | D | 59 | 0.8 | 0.7 | **0.5** | | 56 18% | 0 0% | 3 | 0 | 3.0 |
| (9) | H | 59 | 3.5 | 3.1 | **2.3** | | 52 56% | 0 0% | 7 | 0 | 5.3 |
| FLOW | C | 2 | 0.6 | 0.6 | 0.6 | | 2 75% | 0 0% | 0 | 0 | - |
| (10) | D | 232 | 1.4 | **1.1** | **1.1** | | 224 49% | 0 0% | 8 | 0 | 1.0 |
| | H | 232 | 3.6 | 2.4 | **2.1** | | 223 49% | 0 0% | 9 | 0 | 1.2 |
| MOTOR | D | 41 | 0.9 | 0.9 | **0.6** | | 32 21% | 0 0% | 9 | 0 | 1.0 |
| (12) | H | 41 | 1.2 | 1.2 | **0.7** | | 32 24% | 0 0% | 9 | 0 | 1.0 |
| AVS | C | 5 | 1.2 | 1.2 | **1.1** | | 4 27% | 0 0% | 1 | 0 | 3.0 |
| (12) | D | 66 | 2.0 | 1.7 | **1.5** | | 57 34% | 0 0% | 8 | 1 | 1.3 |
| | H | 66 | 6.0 | 5.2 | **4.0** | | 42 64% | 3 76% | 20 | 1 | 3.2 |
| VIDEO | D | 74 | 0.9 | 0.7 | **0.6** | | 70 30% | 0 0% | 4 | 0 | 2.0 |
| (13) | H | 74 | 2.6 | **1.3** | **1.3** | | 57 54% | 0 0% | 17 | 0 | 4.3 |
| ATC | C | 122 | 153.5 | 140.4 | **138.6** | +10% | 11 92% | 0 0% | 111 | 0 | 12.0 |
| (14) | D | 194 | 119.0 | **110.2** | 135.3 | -14% | 3 8% | 63 75% | 6 | 122 | 11.6 |
| | H | 194 | 495.3 | 461.2 | **443.7** | +10% | 3 8% | 63 75% | 6 | 122 | 11.6 |
| OIL | C | 114 | 242.8 | 177.4 | **163.8** | +33% | 2 25% | 29 25% | 83 | 0 | 12.0 |
| (24) | D | 96 | 15.0 | 9.6 | **7.3** | +51% | 58 19% | 6 17% | 26 | 6 | 6.6 |
| | H | 96 | 35.5 | 23.8 | **15.5** | +56% | 22 22% | 33 9% | 31 | 10 | 7.8 |
| TRAIN1 | C | 99 | 76.1 | 3.7 | **3.6** | +95% | 82 57% | 0 0% | 17 | 0 | 4.5 |
| (373) | D | 931 | 449.7 | **5.0** | 5.3 | +99% | 388 41% | 9 58% | 502 | 32 | 1.0 |
| | H | 931 | 478.8 | **4.9** | 4.9 | +99% | 354 41% | 42 50% | 500 | 35 | 1.0 |
| TRAIN2 | C | 1245 | - | - | **265.4** | +100% | 912 8% | 30 6% | 303 | 0 | 1.1 |
| (1421) | D | 3204 | - | - | **199.0** | +100% | 1569 3% | 16 8% | 1583 | 36 | 1.0 |
| | H | 3204 | - | - | **197.1** | +100% | 1521 3% | 58 15% | 1585 | 40 | 1.0 |

**Table 2.** Test examples for runtime and dependency analysis. All times are in seconds. The tests are C-Conflicts, D-Deadlock and H-Homestates. The Num column shows the number of tests, the Full column is the time used with all machines included from the beginning (and still using a partitioned transition relation), the DC. column is the time used with only the dependency closure included from the beginning and the Step column is the time used with stepwise traversal. A dash means timeout after one hour or spaceout around 20Mb, all other tests were done with less than 250k ROBDD nodes in memory at one time. The Red column is the reduction in runtime $= (Full - Step)/Full$. Some systems have no conflicts and we have left out the data for these. The Part.DC. column shows the number of tests that could be verified using fewer state machines than in the full dependency closure, whether the result was true (Ok) or false (Err) and how much of the dependency closure was included. The Full DC. column shows the number of tests that needed the full dependency closure to be proven true (Ok) or false (Err) and the average size of the dependency closure (Size).

# References

1. F. Balarin and A.L. Sangiovanni-Vincentelli. An iterative approach to language containment. In C. Courcoubetis, editor, *CAV'93. 5th International Conference on Computer Aided Verification*, volume 697 of *LNCS*, pages 29–40, Berlin, 1993. Springer-Verlag.

2. Randal E. Bryant. Graph-Based Algorithms for Boolean Function Manipulation. *IEEE Transactions on Computers*, C-35(8):677–691, August 1986.

3. Randal E. Bryant. Symbolic Boolean manipulation with ordered binary decision diagrams. *ACM Computing Surveys*, 24(3):293–318, September 1992.

4. J. R. Burch, E. M. Clarke, and D. E. Long. Symbolic model checking with partitioned transition relations. In A. Halaas and P. B. Denyer, editors, *Proc. 1991 Int. Conf. on VLSI*, August 1991.

5. William Chan, Richard J. Anderson, Paul Beame, and David Notkin. Improving efficiency of symbolic model checking for state-based system requirements. In *Proceedings of the ACM SIGSOFT International Symposium on Software Testing and Analysis (ISSTA-98)*, volume 23,2 of *ACM Software Engineering Notes*, pages 102–112, New York, March2–5 1998. ACM Press.

6. E. M. Clarke, E. A. Emerson, and A. P. Sistla. Automatic verification of finite-state concurrent systems using temporal logic specifications. *ACM Transactions on Programming Languages and Systems*, 8(2):244–263, April 1986.

7. J.R. Burch, E.M. Clarke, D.E. Long, K.L. MacMillan, and D.L. Dill. Symbolic model checking for sequential circuit verification. *IEEE Transactions on Computer-Aided Design of Integrated Circuits and Systems*, 13(4):401–424, April 1994.

8. J.R. Burch, E.M. Clarke, K.L. McMillan, and D.L. Dill. Sequential Circuit Verification Using Symbolic Model Checking. In *Proceedings of the 27th ACM/IEEE Design Automation Conference*, pages 46–51, Los Alamitos, CA, June 1990. ACM/IEEE, IEEE Society Press.

9. W. Lee, A. Pardo, J.-Y. Jang, G. Hachtel, and F. Somenzi. Tearing based automatic abstraction for CTL model checking. In *Proceedings of the IEEE/ACM International Conference on Computer-Aided Design*, pages 76–81, Washington, November10–14 1996. IEEE Computer Society Press.

10. Jørn Lind-Nielsen. *BuDDy - A Binary Decision Diagram Package*. Technical University of Denmark, 1997. http://britta.it.dtu.dk/~jl/buddy.

11. Jørn Lind-Nielsen, Henrik Reif Andersen, Gerd Behrmann, Henrik Hulgaard, Kåre Kristoffersen, and Kim G. Larsen. Verification of Large State/Event Systems using Compositionality and Dependency Analysis. In *TACAS'98 Tools and Algorithms for the Construction and Analysis of Systems*. Lecture Notes in Computer Science, 1998.

12. David E. Long. *Model Checking, Abstraction and Compositional Verification*. PhD thesis, Carnegie Mellon, 1993.

13. Beologic® A/S. *visualSTATE™ 3.0 User's Guide*, 1996.

14. Abelardo Pardo and Gary D. Hachtel. Automatic abstraction techniques for propositional $\mu$-calculus model checking. In *Computer Aided Verification, CAV'97*. Springer Verlag, 1997.

15. Fabio Somenzi. *CUDD: CU Decision Diagram Package*. University of Colorado at Boulder, 1997.

16. A. Tarski. A lattice-theoretical fixpoint theorem and its application. *Pacific J.Math.*, 5:285–309, 1955.

# Optimizing Symbolic Model Checking for Constraint-Rich Models

Bwolen Yang, Reid Simmons, Randal E. Bryant, and David R. O'Hallaron

School of Computer Science
Carnegie Mellon University
Pittsburgh, PA 15213
{bwolen, reids, bryant, droh}@cs.cmu.edu

**Abstract.** This paper presents optimizations for verifying systems with complex time-invariant constraints. These constraints arise naturally from modeling physical systems, e.g., in establishing the relationship between different components in a system. To verify constraint-rich systems, we propose two new optimizations. The first optimization is a simple, yet powerful, extension of the conjunctive-partitioning algorithm. The second is a collection of BDD-based macro-extraction and macro-expansion algorithms to remove state variables. We show that these two optimizations are essential in verifying constraint-rich problems; in particular, this work has enabled the verification of fault diagnosis models of the Nomad robot (an Antarctic meteorite explorer) and of the NASA Deep Space One spacecraft.

## 1 Introduction

This paper presents techniques for using symbolic model checking to automatically verify a class of real-world applications that have many time-invariant constraints. An example of constraint-rich systems is the symbolic models developed by NASA for on-line fault diagnosis [15]. These models describe the operation of components in complex electro-mechanical systems, such as autonomous spacecraft or robot explorers. The models consist of interconnected components (e.g., thrusters, sensors, motors, computers, and valves) and describe how the *mode* of each component changes over time. Based on these models, the Livingstone diagnostic engine [15] monitors sensor values and detects, diagnoses, and tries to recover from inconsistencies between the observed sensor values and the predicted modes of the components. The relationships between the modes and sensor values are encoded using symbolic constraints. Constraints

Effort sponsored in part by the Advanced Research Projects Agency and Rome Laboratory, Air Force Materiel Command, USAF, under agreement number F30602-96-1-0287, in part by the National Science Foundation under Grant CMS-9318163, and in part by grants from the Intel Corporation and NASA Ames Research Center. The U.S. Government is authorized to reproduce and distribute reprints for Governmental purposes notwithstanding any copyright annotation thereon. The views and conclusions contained herein are those of the authors and should not be interpreted as necessarily representing the official policies or endorsements, either expressed or implied, of the Advanced Research Projects Agency, Rome Laboratory, or the U.S. Government.

between state variables are also used to encode interconnections between components. We have developed an automatic translator from such fault models to SMV (Symbolic Model Verifier) [10], where mode transitions are encoded as transition relations and state-variable constraints are translated into sets of time-invariant constraints.

To verify constraint-rich systems, we introduce two new optimizations. The first optimization is a simple extension of the conjunctive-partitioning algorithm. The other is a collection of BDD-based macro-extraction and macro-expansion algorithms to remove redundant state variables. We show that these two optimizations are essential in verifying constraint-rich problems. In particular, these optimizations have enabled the verification of fault diagnosis models for the Nomad robot (an Antarctic meteorite explorer) [1] and the NASA Deep Space One (DS1) spacecraft [2]. These models can be quite large, with up to 1200 state bits.

The rest of this paper is organized as follows. We first briefly describe symbolic model checking and how time-invariant constraints arise naturally from modeling (Section 2). We then present our new optimizations: an extension to conjunctive partitioning (Section 3), and BDD-based algorithms for eliminating redundant state variables (Section 4). We then show the results of a performance evaluation on the effects of each optimization (Section 5). Finally, we present a comparison to prior work (Section 6) and some concluding remarks (Section 7).

## 2 Background

Symbolic model checking [5, 6, 10] is a fully automatic verification paradigm that checks temporal properties (e.g., safety, liveness, fairness, etc.) of finite state systems by symbolic state traversal. The core enabling technology for symbolic model checking is the use of the Binary Decision Diagram (BDD) representation [4] for state sets and state transitions. BDDs represent Boolean formulas canonically as directed acyclic graphs such that equivalent sub-formulas are uniquely represented as a single subgraph. This uniqueness property makes BDDs compact and enables dynamic programming to be used for computing Boolean operations symbolically.

To use BDDs in model checking, we need to map sets of states, state transitions, and state traversal to the Boolean domain. In this section, we briefly describe this mapping and motivate how time-invariant constraints arise. We then finish with definitions of some additional terminology to be used in the rest of the paper.

### 2.1 Representing State Sets and Transitions

In the symbolic model checking of finite state systems, a state typically describes the values of many components (e.g., latches in digital circuits) and each component is represented by a *state variable*. Let $V = \{v_1, ..., v_n\}$ be the set of state variables in a system, then a state can be described by assigning values to all the variables in $V$. This valuation can in term be written as a Boolean formula that is true exactly for the valuation as $\bigwedge_{i=0}^{n}(v_i == c_i)$, where $c_i$ is the value assigned to the variable $v_i$, and the "$==$" represents the equality operator in a predicate (similar to the C programming language). A set of states can be represented as a disjunction of the Boolean formulas that represent the states. We denote the BDD representation for a set of states $S$ by $S(V)$.

In addition to the set of states, we also need to map the system's state transitions to the Boolean domain. We extend the above concept of representing a set of states to representing a set of ordered-pairs of states. To represent a pair of states, we need two sets of state variables: $V$ the set of *present-state variables* for the first tuple and $V'$ the set of *next-state variables* for the second tuple. Each variable $v$ in $V$ has a corresponding next-state variable $v'$ in $V'$. A valuation of variables in $V$ and $V'$ can be viewed as a state transition from one state to another. A transition relation can then be represented as a set of these valuations. We denote the BDD representation of a transition relation $T$ as $T(V, V')$.

In modeling finite state systems, the overall state transitions are generally specified by defining the valid transitions for each state variable. To support non-deterministic transitions of a state variable, the expression that defines the transitions evaluates to a set, and the next-state value of the state variable is non-deterministically chosen from the elements in the set. Hereafter, we refer to an expression that evaluates to a set either as a *set expression* or as a *non-deterministic expression* depending on the context, and we use the bold font type, as in $\mathbf{f}$, to represent such expression. Let $\mathbf{f}_i$ be the set expression representing state transitions of the state variable $v_i$. Then the BDD representation for $v_i$'s transition relation $T_i$ can be defined as $T_i(V, V') := (v'_i \in \mathbf{f}_i(V))$. For synchronous systems, the BDD for the overall state transition relation $T$ is $T(V, V') := \bigwedge_{i=0}^{n} T_i(V, V')$. Detailed descriptions on this formulation, including mapping of asynchronous systems, can be found in [5].

## 2.2 Time-Invariant Constraints and Their Common Usages

In symbolic model checking, time-invariant constraints specify the conditions that must always hold. More formally, let $C_1, \ldots, C_l$ be the time-invariant constraints and let $C := C_1 \wedge C_2 \wedge \ldots \wedge C_l$. Then, in symbolic state traversal, we consider only states where $C$ is true. We refer to $C$ as the *constrained space*.

To motivate how time-invariant constraints arise naturally in modeling complex systems, we describe three common usages. One common usage is to make the same non-deterministic choice across multiple expressions in transition relations. For example, in a master-slave model, the master can non-deterministically choose which set of idle slaves to assign the pending jobs, and the slaves' next-state values will depend on the choice made. To model this, let $\mathbf{f}$ be a non-deterministic expression representing how the master makes its choice. If $\mathbf{f}$ is used multiple times, then each use makes a non-deterministic choice independently of other uses. Thus, to ensure that the same non-deterministic choice is seen by the slaves, a new state variable $u$ is introduced to record the choice made, and $u$ is then used to define the slaves' transition relations. This recording process is expressed as the time-invariant constraint $u \in \mathbf{f}$.

Another common usage is for establishing the interface between different components in a system. For example, suppose two components are connected with a pipe of a fixed capacity. Then, the input of one component is the minimum of the pipe's capacity and the output of the other component. This relationship is described as a time-invariant constraint between the input and the output of these two components.

Third common usage is specific uses of generic parts. For example, a bi-directional fuel pipe may be used to connect two components. If we want to make sure the fuel flows only one way, we need to constrain the valves in the fuel pipe. These constraints are specified as time-invariant constraints. In general, specific uses of generic parts arise naturally in both the software and the hardware domain as we often use generic building blocks in constructing a complex system.

In the examples above, the use of time-invariant constraints is not always necessary because some these constraints can be directly expressed as a part of the transition relation and the associated state variables can be removed. However, these constraints are used to facilitate the description of the system or to reflect the way complex systems are built. Without these constraints, multiple expressions will need to be combined into possibly a very complicated expression. Performing this transformation manually can be error-prone. Thus it is up to the verification tool to automatically perform these transformations and remove unnecessary state variables. Our optimizations for constraint-rich models is to automatically eliminate redundant state variables (Section 4) and partition the remaining constraints (Section 3).

## 2.3 Symbolic State Traversal

To reason about temporal properties, the *pre-image* and the *image* of the transition relation are used for symbolic state traversal, and time-invariant constraints are used to restrict the valid state space. Based on the BDD representations of a state set $S$ and the transition relation $T$, we can compute the *pre-image* and the *image* of $S$, while restricting the computations to the constrained space $C$, as follows:

$$pre\text{-}image(S)(V) := C(V) \land \exists V'.[T(V,V') \land (S(V') \land C(V'))] \qquad (1)$$

$$image(S)(V') := C(V') \land \exists V.[T(V,V') \land (S(V) \land C(V))] \qquad (2)$$

One limitation of the BDD representation is that the monolithic BDD for the transition relation $T$ is often too large to build. A solution to this problem is the *conjunctive partitioning* [5] of the transition relation. In conjunctive partitioning, the transition relation is represented as a conjunction $P_1 \land P_2 \land ... \land P_k$ with each conjunct $P_i$ represented by a BDD. Then, the pre-image can be computed by conjuncting with one $P_i$ at a time, and by using *early quantification* to quantify out variables as soon as possible. The early-quantification optimization is based on the property that sub-formulas can be moved out of the scope of an existential quantification if they do not depend on any of the variables being quantified. Formally, let $V_i'$, a subset of $V'$, be the set of variables that do not appear in any of the subsequent $P_j$'s, where $1 \leq i \leq k$ and $i < j \leq k$. Then the pre-image can be computed as

$$p_1 := \exists V_1'.[P_1(V,V') \land (S(V') \land C(V'))] \qquad (3)$$

$$p_2 := \exists V_2'.[P_2(V,V') \land p_1]$$

$$\vdots$$

$$p_k := \exists V_k'.[P_k(V,V') \land p_{k-1}]$$

$$pre\text{-}image(S)(V) := C(V) \land p_k$$

The determination and ordering of partitions (the $P_i$'s in above) can have significant performance impact. Commonly used heuristics [7, 11] treat the state variables' transition relations ($T_i$'s) as conjuncts. The ordering step then greedily schedules the partitions to quantify out more variables as soon as possible, while introducing fewer new variables. Finally, the ordered partitions are tentatively merged with their predecessors to reduce the number of intermediate results. Each merged result is kept only if the resulting graph size is less than a pre-determined limit.

The conjunctive partitioning for the image computation is performed similarly with present-state variables in $V$ being the quantifying variables instead of next-state variables in $V'$. However, since the quantifying variables are different between the image and the pre-image computation, the resulting conjuncts for image computation is typically very different from those for pre-image computation.

## 2.4 Additional Terminology

We define the *ITE* operator (if-then-else) as follows: given arbitrary expressions $f$ and $g$ where $f$ and $g$ may both be set expressions, and Boolean expression $p$, then

$$ITE(p, f, g)(X) := \begin{cases} f(X) \text{ if } p(X); \\ g(X) \text{ otherwise;} \end{cases}$$

where $X$ is the set of variables used in expressions $p$, $f$, and $g$. We define a *care-space optimization* as any algorithm *care-opt* that has following properties: given an arbitrary function $f$ where $f$ may be a set expression, and a Boolean formula $c$, then

$$care\text{-}opt(f, c) := ITE(c, f, d),$$

where $d$ is defined by the particular algorithm used. The usual interpretation of this is that we only *care* about the values of $f$ when $c$ is true. We will refer to $c$ as the *care space* and $\neg c$ as the *don't-care space*. The goal of care-space optimizations is to heuristically minimize the representation for $f$ by choosing a suitable $d$ in the don't-care space. Descriptions and a study of some care-space optimizations, including the commonly used *restrict* algorithm [6], can be found in [13].

## 3 Extended Conjunctive Partitioning

The first optimization is the application of the conjunctive-partitioning algorithm on the time-invariant constraints. This extension is derived based on two observations. First, as with the transition relations, the BDD representation for time-invariant constraints can be too large to be represented as a monolithic graph. Thus, it is crucial to represent the constraints as a set of conjuncts rather than a monolithic graph.

Second, in constraint-rich models, many *quantifying variables* (variables being quantified) do not appear in the transition relation. There are two common causes for this. First, when time-invariant constraints are used to make the same non-deterministic choices, new variables are introduced to record these choices (described as the first example in Section 2.2). In the transition relation, these new variables are used only in their present-state form. Thus, their corresponding next-state variables do not appear in the transition relation, and for the pre-image computation, these next-state variables are parts of the quantifying variables. The other cause is that many state variables are used only to establish time-invariant constraints. Thus, both the present- and the next-state version of these variables do not appear in the transition relations.

Based on this observation, we can improve the early-quantification optimization by pulling out the quantifying variables $(V_0')$ that do not appear in any of the transition relations. Then, these quantifying variables $(V_0')$ can be used for early quantification in conjunctive partitioning of the constrained space $(C)$ where the time-invariant constraints hold. Formally, let $Q_1, Q_2, ..., Q_m$ be the partitions produced by the conjunctive partitioning of the constrained space $C$, where $C = Q_1 \wedge Q_2 \wedge ... \wedge Q_m$. For the pre-image computation, Equation 3 is replaced by

$$q_1 := \exists W_1'.[Q_1(V') \wedge S(V')]$$
$$q_2 := \exists W_2'.[Q_2(V') \wedge q_1]$$
$$\vdots$$
$$q_m := \exists W_m'.[Q_m(V') \wedge q_{m-1}]$$
$$p_1 := \exists V_1'.[P_1(V, V') \wedge q_m]$$

where $W_i'$, a subset of $V_0'$, is the set of variables that do not appear in any of the subsequent $Q_j$'s, where $1 \leq i \leq m$ and $i < j \leq m$. Similarly, this extension also applies to the image computation.

## 4 Elimination of Redundant State Variables

Our second optimization for constraint-rich models is targeted at reducing the state space by removing unnecessary state variables. This optimization is a set of BDD-based algorithms that compute an equivalent expression for each variable used in the time-invariant constraints (*macro extraction*) and then globally replace a suitable subset of variables with their equivalent expressions (*macro expansion*) to reduce the total number of variables.

The use of macros is traditionally supported by language constructs (e.g., DEFINE in the SMV language [10]) and by simple syntactic analyses such as detecting deterministic assignments (e.g., $a == f$ where $a$ is a state variable and $f$ is an expression) in the specifications. However, in constraint-rich models, the constraints are often specified in a more complex manner such as *conditional* dependencies on other state variables (e.g., $p \Rightarrow (a == f)$ as conditional assignment of expression $f$ to variable $a$ when $p$ is true). To identify the set of valid macros in such models, we need to combine the effects of multiple constraints. For these models, one drawback of syntactic analysis is that, for each type of expression, syntactic analysis will need to add a template to pattern match these expressions. Another more severe drawback is that it is difficult for syntactic analysis to estimate the actual cost of instantiating a macro. Estimating this cost is important because reducing the number of variables by macro expansion can sometimes result in significant performance degradation caused by large increases in other BDD sizes. These two drawbacks make the syntactic approach unsuitable for models with complex time-invariant constraints.

Our approach uses BDD-based algorithms to analyze time-invariant constraints and to derive the set of possible macros. The core algorithm is a new assignment-extraction algorithm that extracts assignments from arbitrary Boolean expressions (Section 4.1). For each variable, by extracting its assignment form, we can determine the variable's corresponding equivalent expression, and when appropriate, globally replace the variable with its equivalent expression (Section 4.2). The strength of this algorithm is that by using BDDs, the cost of macro expansion can be better characterized since the actual model checking computation is performed using BDDs.

Note that there have been a number of research efforts on BDD-based redundant variable removal. To better compare our approach to these previous research efforts, we postpone the discussion of this prior work until Section 6, after describing our algorithms and the performance evaluation.

## 4.1 BDD-Based Assignment Extraction

The assignment-extraction problem can be stated as follows: given an arbitrary Boolean formula $f$ and a variable $v$ (where $v$ can be non-Boolean), find $\mathbf{g}$ and $h$ such that

- $f = (v \in \mathbf{g}) \wedge h$,
- $\mathbf{g}$ does not depend on $v$, and
- $h$ is a Boolean formula and does not depend on $v$.

The expression $(v \in \mathbf{g})$ represents a non-deterministic assignment to variable $v$. In the case that $\mathbf{g}$ always returns a singleton set, the assignment $(v \in \mathbf{g})$ is deterministic. A solution to this assignment-extraction problem is as follows:

$$h = \exists v.f$$
$$\mathbf{t} = \bigcup_{k \in K_v} ITE(f|_{v \leftarrow k}, \{k\}, \emptyset) \qquad (4)$$
$$\mathbf{g} = restrict(\mathbf{t}, h)$$

where $K_v$ is the set of all possible values of variable $v$, and $restrict$ [6] is a care-space optimization algorithm that tries to reduce the BDD graph size (of $\mathbf{t}$) by collapsing the don't-care space ($\neg h$). The BDD algorithm for the $\bigcup_{k \in K_v}$ operator is similar to the BDD algorithm for the existential quantification with the $\vee$ operator replaced by the $\cup$ operator for variable quantification. A correctness proof of this algorithm can be found in the technical-report version of this paper [17].

## 4.2 Macro Extraction and Expansion

In this section, we describe the elimination of state variables based on macro extraction and macro expansion. The first step is to extract macros with the algorithm shown in Figure 1. This algorithm extracts macros from the constrained space ($C$), which is represented as a set of conjuncts. It first uses the assignment-extraction algorithm to extract assignment expressions (line 5). It then identifies the deterministic assignments as candidate macros (line 6). For each candidate, the algorithm tests to see if applying the macro may be beneficial (line 7). This test is based on the heuristic that if the BDD graph size of a macro is not too large and its instantiation does not cause excessive increase in other BDDs' graph sizes, then instantiating this macro may be beneficial. If the resulting right-hand-side **g** is not a singleton set, it is kept separately (line 9). These **g**'s are combined later (line 10) to determine if the intersection of these sets would result in a macro (lines 11-13).

```
extract_macros(C, V)
     /* Extract macros for variables in V from
        the set C of conjuncts representing the constrained space */
1     M ← ∅    /* initialize the set of macros found so far */
2     for each v ∈ V
3         N ← ∅    /* initialize the set of non-singletons found so far */
4         for each f ∈ C such that f depends on v
5             (g, h) ← assignment-extraction (f, v)    /* f = (v ∈ g) ∧ h */
6             if (g always returns a singleton set)    /* macro found */
7                 if (is-this-result-good(g))
8                     M ← {(v, g)} ∪ M
9                 else N ← {g} ∪ N
10        g' ← ∩_{g∈N} g
11        if (g' always returns a singleton set)    /* macro found */
12            if ((is-this-result-good(g')))
13                M ← {(v, g')} ∪ M
14    return M
```

**Fig. 1.** Macro-extraction algorithm. In lines 7 and 12, "is-this-result-good" uses BDD properties (such as graph sizes) to determine if the result should be kept.

After the macros are extracted, the next step is to determine the instantiation order. The main purpose of this algorithm (in Figure 2) is to remove circular dependencies. For example, if one macro defines variable $v_1$ to be $(v_2 \wedge v_3)$ and a second macro defines $v_2$ to be $(v_1 \vee v_4)$, then instantiating the first macro results in a circular definition in the second macro $(v_2 = (v_1 \wedge v_3) \vee v_4)$ and thus invalidates this second macro. Similarly, the reverse is also true. To determine the set of macros to remove, the algorithm builds a dependence graph (line 1) and breaks circular dependencies based on graph sizes (lines 2-4). It then determines the ordering of the remaining macros based on the topological order (line 4) of the dependence graph.

Finally, in the topological order, each macro $(v, \mathbf{g})$ is instantiated in the remaining macros and in all other expressions (represented by BDDs) in the system, by substituting the variable $v$ with its equivalent expression **g**.

order_macros($M$)

    /* Determine the instantiation order of the macros in set $M$ */

    /* first build the dependence graph $G = (M, E)$ */

1   $E = \{(x, y) | x = (v_x, \mathbf{g}_x) \in M, y = (v_y, \mathbf{g}_y) \in M, \mathbf{g}_y \text{ depends on } v_x\}$

    /* then remove circular dependences */

2   while there are cycles in $G$,

3      $M_C \leftarrow$ set of macros that are in some cycle

4      remove the macro with largest BDD size in $M_C$

5   return a topological ordering of the remaining macros in $G$

**Fig. 2.** Macro-ordering algorithm.

## 5 Evaluation

### 5.1 Experimental Setup

The benchmark suite used is a collection of 58 SMV models gathered from a wide variety of sources, including the 16 models used in a BDD performance study [16]. Out of these 58 models, 37 models have no time-invariant constraints, and thus our optimizations do not get triggered and have no influence on the overall verification time. Out of the remaining 21 models, 10 very small models ($< 10$ seconds) are eliminated. On the remaining 11 models, our optimizations have made non-negligible performance impact on 7 models. In Figure 3, we briefly describe these 7 models. Note that some of these models are quite large, with up to 1200 state bits.

| Model | # of State Bits | Description |
|---|---|---|
| acs | 497 | the altitude-control module of the NASA DS1 spacecraft |
| ds1-b | 657 | a buggy fault diagnosis model for the NASA DS1 spacecraft |
| ds1 | 657 | corrected version of *ds1-b* |
| futurebus | 174 | FutureBus cache coherency protocol |
| nomad | 1273 | fault diagnosis model for an Antarctic meteorite explorer |
| v-gate | 86 | reactor-system model |
| xavier | 100 | fault diagnosis model for the Xavier robot |

**Fig. 3.** Description of models whose performance results are affected by our optimizations.

We performed the evaluation using the Symbolic Model Verifier (SMV) model checker [10] from Carnegie Mellon University. Conjunctive partitioning was used only when it was necessary to complete the verification. In these cases (including *acs, nomad, ds1-b,* and *ds1*), the size limit for each partition was set to 10,000 BDD nodes. For the remaining cases, the transition relations were represented as monolithic BDDs. The performance of all the benchmark models were measured in the following four settings:

**Base:** no new optimizations except that the constrained space $C$ is represented as a conjunction with each conjunct's BDD graph size limited to 10,000

nodes (i.e., optimizations in Section 3 are used without the "early quantification on the constrained space $C$" optimization). Without this partitioning, the BDD representation of the constrained space could not be constructed for 4 models.

**Quan:** same as the **Base** case with the addition of the "early quantification on the constrained space" optimization (Section 3).

**SynMacro:** same as the **Quan** case with the addition of a syntactic analysis that pattern matches deterministic assignment expressions ($v == f$, where $v$ is a state variable and $f$ is an expression) as macros and expands these macros.

**BDDMacro:** all the optimizations are turned on; i.e., same as the **SynMacro** case with the addition of BDD-based assignment extraction to extract macros.

The evaluation was performed on a 200MHz Pentium-Pro with 1 GB of memory running Linux. Each run was limited to 6 hours of CPU time and 900 MB of memory.

## 5.2  Results

Figure 4 shows the impact of our optimizations for the 7 models whose results changed by more than 10 CPU seconds and 10% from the **Base** case. For all benchmarks, the time spent by our optimizations is very small ($< 5$ seconds or $< 5\%$ of total time) and is included in the running time reported.

The overall impact of our optimizations is shown in the rightmost column of Figure 4. These results demonstrate that our optimizations have significantly improved the performance for 2 cases (with speedups up to 74) and have enabled the verification of 4 cases. For the *v-gates* model, the performance degradation (speedup $= 0.7$) is in the computation of the reachable states from the initial states. Upon further investigation, we believe that it is caused by the macro instantiation, which increases the graph size of the transition relation from 122-thousand to 476-thousand nodes. This case demonstrates that reducing the number of state variables does not always improve performance.

| Model | Base sec | Quan sec | SynMacro sec | BDDMacro sec | Base / BDDMacro speedup |
|---|---|---|---|---|---|
| acs | *m.o.* | 32 | 76 | 7 | *enabled* |
| ds1-b | *m.o.* | 321 | 138 | 54 | *enabled* |
| ds1 | *m.o.* | *m.o.* | *t.o.* | 37 | *enabled* |
| futurebus | 1410 | 53 | 35 | 19 | 74.2 |
| nomad | *m.o.* | *t.o.* | 7801 | 633 | *enabled* |
| v-gates | 36 | 35 | 53 | 50 | 0.7 |
| xavier | 16 | 5 | 1 | 2 | 8.0 |

**Fig. 4.** Performance impact of each optimization. The *m.o.*'s and *t.o.*'s are the results that exceeded the 900-MB memory limit and the 6-hour time limit, respectively.

The remaining columns of Figure 4 show the impact of each optimization. The results show that by simply performing early quantification on the constraints (the **Quan** column), we have enabled the verification of *acs* and *ds1-b*, and achieved significant performance improvement on *futurebus* (speedup > 20). This is mostly due to the fact that a large number of variables can be pulled out of the transition relations and applied to conjunctive partitioning and early quantification of the time-invariant constraints (Figure 5(a)). With the addition of syntactic analysis for macro extraction (the **SynMacro** column), we are able to verify *nomad*. Finally, by adding BDD-based macro extraction (the **BDDMacro** column), we are able to verify *ds1*. The results in Figure 5(b) show that BDD-based macro extraction (**BDDMacro**) can be rather effective in reducing the number of variables, especially for the *acs, nomad, ds1-b, and ds1* models where > 150 additional BDD variables (i.e., > 75 state bits) are removed in comparison to using syntactic analysis (**SynMacro**).

| Model | Total # of BDD Variables | CP Optimization # of BDD vars extracted | | Macro Optimization # of BDD vars removed | |
|---|---|---|---|---|---|
| | | image | pre-image | SynMacro | BDDMacro |
| acs | 994 | 439 | 449 | 82 | 352 |
| ds1-b | 1314 | 550 | 566 | 148 | 492 |
| ds1 | 1314 | 550 | 566 | 220 | 496 |
| futurebus | 348 | 58 | 110 | 12 | 18 |
| nomad | 2546 | 1121 | 1174 | 688 | 844 |
| v-gates | 172 | 0 | 17 | 16 | 16 |
| xavier | 200 | 69 | 86 | 64 | 116 |

(a)                                            (b)

**Fig. 5.** Effectiveness of each optimization. (a) Number of quantifying BDD variables that are pulled out of the transition relation for early quantification of the time-invariant constraints. These results are measured without macro optimizations. With macro optimizations, the corresponding results are basically the same as subtracting off the number of state variables removed. (b) The number of BDD variables removed by macro expansion. **Note:** the number of BDD variables is twice the number of state variables—one copy for the present state and one copy for the next state.

# 6 Related Work

There have been many research efforts on BDD-based redundant state-variable removal in both logic synthesis and verification. These research efforts all use the reachable state space (set of states reachable from initial states) to determine functional dependencies for Boolean variables (macro extraction). The reachable state space effectively plays the same role as a time-invariant constraint, because the verification process only needs to check specifications in the reachable state space,

Berthet et al. propose the first redundant state-variable removal algorithm in [3]. In [9], Lin and Newton describe a branch-and-bound algorithm to identify the maximum set of redundant state variables. In [12], Sentovich et al. propose new algorithms for latch removal and latch replacement in logic synthesis. There is also some work on detecting and removing redundant state variables while the reachable state space is being computed [8, 14].

From the algorithmic point of view, our approach is different from prior work in two ways. First, in determining the relationship between variables, the algorithms used to extract functional dependencies in previous work can be viewed as direct extraction of deterministic assignments to Boolean variables. In comparison, our assignment extraction algorithm is more general because it can also handle non-Boolean variables and extract non-deterministic assignments. Second, in performing the redundant state-variable removal, the approach used in the previous work would need to combine all the constraints first and then extract the macros directly from the combined result. However, for constraint-rich models, it may not be possible to combine all the constraints because the resulting BDD is too large to build. Our approach addresses this issue by first applying the assignment extraction algorithm to each constraint separately and then combining the results to determine if a macro can be extracted (see Figure 1).

Another difference is that in previous work, the goal is to remove as many variables as possible. However, we have empirically observed that in some cases, removing additional variables can result in significant performance degradation in overall verification time (slowdown over 4). To address this issue, we use simple heuristics (size of the macro and the growth in graph sizes) to choose the set of macros to expand. This simple heuristic works well in the test cases we tried. However, in order to fully evaluate the impact of different heuristics, we need to gather a larger set of constraint-rich models from a wider range of applications.

## 7 Conclusions and Future Work

The two optimizations we proposed are crucial in verifying this new class of constraint-rich applications. In particular, they have enabled the verification of real-world applications such as the Nomad robot and the NASA Deep Space One spacecraft.

We have shown that the BDD-based assignment-extraction algorithm is effective in identifying macros. We plan to use this algorithm to perform a more precise cone-of-influence analysis with the assignment expressions providing the exact dependence information between the variables. In general, we plan to study how BDDs can be use to further help other compile-time optimizations in symbolic model checking.

## Acknowledgement

We thank Ken McMillan for discussions on the effects of macro expansion. We thank Olivier Coudert, Fabio Somenzi and reviewers for comments on this work. We are grateful to Intel Corporation for donating the machines used in this work.

# References

1. BAPNA, D., ROLLINS, E., MURPHY, J., AND MAIMONE, M. The Atacama Desert trek - outcomes. In *Proc. of the 1998 International Conference on Robotics and Automation* (May 1998), pp. 597–604.

2. BERNARD, D. E., DORAIS, G. A., FRY, C., JR., E. B. G., KANEFSKY, B., KURIEN, J., MILLAR, W., MUSCETTOLA, N., NAYAK, P. P., PELL, B., RAJAN, K., ROUQUETT, N., SMITH, B., AND WILLIAMS, B. Design of the remote agent experiment for spacecraft autonomy. In *Proc. of the 1998 IEEE Aerospace Conference* (March 1998), pp. 259–281.

3. BERTHET, C., COUDERT, O., AND MADRE, J. C. New ideas on symbolic manipulations of finite state machines. In *1990 IEEE Proc. of the International Conference on Computer Design* (September 1990), pp. 224–227.

4. BRYANT, R. E. Graph-based algorithms for Boolean function manipulation. *IEEE Transactions on Computers C-35*, 8 (August 1986), 677–691.

5. BURCH, J. R., CLARKE, E. M., LONG, D. E., MCMILLAN, K. L., AND DILL, D. L. Symbolic model checking for sequential circuit verification. *IEEE Transactions on Computer-Aided Design of Integrated Circuits and Systems 13*, 4 (April 1994), 401–424.

6. COUDERT, O., AND MADRE, J. C. A unified framework for the formal verification of circuits. In *Proc. of the International Conference on Computer-Aided Design* (Feb 1990), pp. 126–129.

7. GEIST, D., AND BEER, I. Efficient model checking by automated ordering of transition relation partitions. In *Proc. of the Computer Aided Verification* (June 1994), pp. 299–310.

8. HU, A. J., AND DILL, D. L. Reducing BDD size by exploiting functional dependencies. In *Proc. of the 30th ACM/IEEE Design Automation Conference* (June 1993), pp. 266–71.

9. LIN, B., AND NEWTON, A. R. Exact redundant state registers removal based on binary decision diagrams. *IFIP Transactions A, Computer Science and Technology A*, 1 (August 1991), 277–86.

10. MCMILLAN, K. L. *Symbolic Model Checking*. Kluwer Academic Publishers, 1993.

11. RANJAN, R. K., AZIZ, A., BRAYTON, R. K., PLESSIER, B., AND PIXLEY, C. Efficient BDD algorithms for FSM synthesis and verification. Presented in the IEEE/ACM International Workshop on Logic Synthesis, May 1995.

12. SENTOVICH, E. M., AND HORIA TOMA, G. B. Latch optimization in circuits generated from high-level descriptions. In *Proc. of the International Conference on Computer-Aided Design* (November 1996), pp. 428–35.

13. SHIPLE, T. R., HOJATI, R., SANGIOVANNI-VINCENTELLI, A. L., AND BRAYTON, R. K. Heuristic minimization of BDDs using don't cares. In *Proc. of the 31st ACM/IEEE Design Automation Conference* (June 1994), pp. 225–231.

14. VAN EIJK, C. A. J., AND JESS, J. A. G. Exploiting functional dependencies in finite state machine verification. In *Proc. of European Design and Test Conference* (March 1996), pp. 266–71.

15. WILLIAMS, B. C., AND NAYAK, P. P. A model-based approach to reactive self-configuring systems. In *Proc. of the Thirteenth National Conference on Artificial Intelligence and the Eighth Innovative Applications of Artificial Intelligence Conference* (August 1996), pp. 971–978.

16. YANG, B., BRYANT, R. E., O'HALLARON, D. R., BIERE, A., COUDERT, O., JANSSEN, G., RANJAN, R. K., AND SOMENZI, F. A performance study of BDD-based model checking. In *Proc. of the Formal Methods on Computer-Aided Design* (November 1998), pp. 255–289.

17. YANG, B., SIMMONS, R., BRYANT, R. E., AND O'HALLARON, D. R. Optimizing symbolic model checking for constraint-rich models. Tech. Rep. CMU-CS-99-118, School of Computer Science, Carnegie Mellon University, March 1999.

# Efficient Timed Reachability Analysis Using Clock Difference Diagrams

G. Behrmann[1], K.G. Larsen[1], J. Pearson[2], C. Weise[1], and W. Yi[2]

[1] BRICS[***], Aalborg University, Denmark, (behrmann|kgl|cweise)@cs.auc.dk
[2] Dept. of Computer Systems, Uppsala University, Sweden, (justin|yi)@docs.uu.se

**Abstract.** One of the major problems in applying automatic verification tools to industrial-size systems is the excessive amount of memory required during the state-space exploration of a model. In the setting of real-time, this problem of state-explosion requires extra attention as information must be kept not only on the discrete control structure but also on the values of continuous clock variables.

In this paper, we exploit Clock Difference Diagrams, CDD's, a BDD-like data-structure for representing and effectively manipulating certain non-convex subsets of the Euclidean space, notably those encountered during verification of timed automata.

A version of the real-time verification tool UPPAAL using CDD's as a compact data-structure for storing explored symbolic states has been implemented. Our experimental results demonstrate significant space-savings: for eight industrial examples, the savings are in average 42% with moderate increase in runtime.

We further report on how the symbolic state-space exploration itself may be carried out using CDD's.

## 1 Motivation

In the last few years a number of verification tools have been developed for real-time systems (e.g. [HHW95,DY95,BLLPW96]). The verification engines of most tools in this category are based on reachability analysis of timed automata following the pioneering work of Alur and Dill [AD94]. A timed automaton is an extension of a finite automaton with a finite set of real-valued clock-variables. Whereas the initial decidability results are based on a partitioning of the infinite state-space of a timed automaton into finitely many equivalence classes (so-called *regions*), tools such as KRONOS and UPPAAL are based on more efficient data structures and algorithms for representing and manipulating timing constraints over clock variables. The abstract reachability algorithm applied in these tools is shown in Figure 1. The algorithm checks whether a timed automaton may reach a state satisfying a given state formula $\phi$. It explores the state space of the automaton in terms of *symbolic states* of the form $(l, D)$, where $l$ is a

---

[***] BRICS: Basic Research in Computer Science, Centre of the Danish National Research Foundation

```
PASSED:= {}
WAIT:= {(l₀, D₀)}
repeat
      begin
      get (l, D) from WAIT
      if (l, D) ⊨ φ then return "YES"
      else if D ⊈ D' for all (l, D') ∈ PASSED then
            begin
            add (l, D) to PASSED            (*)
            NEXT:={(lₛ, Dₛ) : (l, D) ⤳ (lₛ, Dₛ) ∧ Dₛ ≠ ∅}
            for all (lₛ', Dₛ') in NEXT do
                  put (lₛ', Dₛ') to WAIT
            end
      end
until WAIT={}
return "NO"
```

Fig. 1. An algorithm for symbolic reachability analysis.

control–node and $D$ is a constraint system over clock variables $\{X_1, \dots, X_n\}$. More precisely, $D$ consists of a conjunction of simple clock constraints of the form $X_i \, op \, c$, $-X_i \, op \, c$ and $X_i - X_j \, op \, c$, where $c$ is an integer constant and $op \in \{<, \leq\}$. The subsets of $\mathbb{R}^n$ which may be described by clock constraint systems are called *zones*. Zones are among those convex polyhedra, where all edge-points are integer valued, and where border lines may or may not belong to the set (depending on a constraint being strict or not).

We observe that several operations of the algorithm are critical for efficient implementation. In particular the algorithm depends heavily on operations for checking set inclusion and emptiness. In the computation of the set NEXT, operations for intersection, forward time projection (future) and projection in one dimension (clock reset) are required. A well-known data-structure for representing clock constraint systems is that of *Difference Bounded Matrices*, DBM, [Dill87], giving for each pair of clocks[1] the upper bound on their difference. All operations required in the reachability analysis in Figure 1 can be easily implemented on DBM's with satisfactory efficiency. In particular, the various operations may benefit from a *canonical* DBM representation with tightest bounds on all clock differences computed by solving a shortest path problem. However, computation of this canonical form should be postponed as much as possible, as it is the most costly operation on DBM's with time-complexity $O(n^3)$ ($n$ being the number of clocks).

DBM's obviously consume space of order $O(n^2)$. Alternatively, one may represent a clock constraint system by choosing a minimal subset from the constraints of the DBM in canonical form. This *minimal form* [LPW95] is preferable

---

[1] For uniformity, we assume a special clock $X_0$ which is always zero. Thus $X_i \, op \, c$ and $-X_i \, op \, c$ can be rewritten as the differences $X_i - X_0 \, op \, c$ and $X_0 - X_i \, op \, c$.

when adding a symbolic state to the main global data-structure PASSED, as in practice the space-requirement is only linear in the number of clocks.

Considering once again the reachability algorithm in Figure 1, we see that a symbolic state $(l, D)$ from the waiting-list WAIT is freed from being explored (the inner box) provided some symbolic state $(l, D')$ already in PASSED 'covers' it (i.e. $D \subseteq D'$). Though clearly a sound rule and provably sufficient for termination of the algorithm, exploration of $(l, D)$ may be avoided under less strict conditions. In particular, it suffices for $(l, D)$ to be 'covered' collectively by the symbolic states in PASSED with location $l$, i.e.:

$$D \subseteq \bigcup \{D' \mid (l, D') \in \text{PASSED}\} \tag{1}$$

However, this requires handling of unions of zones, which complicates things considerably. Using DBM's, finite unions of zones – which we will call *federations* in the following – may be represented by a list of all the DBM's of the union. However, the more "non-convex" the zone becomes, the more DBM's will be needed. In particular, this representation makes the inclusion-check of (1) computational expensive.

In this paper, we introduce a more efficient BDD-like data-structure for federations, *Clock Difference Diagrams*, CDD's. A CDD is a directed acyclic graph, where inner nodes are associated with a given pair of clocks and outgoing arcs state bounds on their difference. This data-structure contains DBM's as a special case and offers simple boolean set-operations and easy inclusion- and emptiness-checking. Using CDD's, the PASSED-list may be implemented as a collection of symbolic states of the form $(l, F)$, where $F$ is a CDD representing the union of all zones for which the location $l$ has been explored[2]. Thus, the more liberal termination condition of (1) may be applied, potentially leading to faster termination of the reachability algorithm. As any BDD-like data-structure, CDD's eliminate redundancies via sharing of substructures. Thus, the CDD representation of $F$ is likely to be much smaller than the explicit DBM-list representation. Furthermore, sharing of identical substructures between CDD's from *different* symbolic states may be obtained for free, opening for even more efficient storage-usage.

Having implemented a CDD-package and used it in modifying UPPAAL, we report on some very encouraging experimental results. For eight industrial examples found in the literature, significant space-savings are obtained: the savings are in average 42% with moderate increase in run-time (in average an increase of 7%).

To make the reachability algorithm of Figure 1 fully symbolic, it remains to show how to compute the successor set NEXT based on CDD's. In particular, algorithms are needed for computing forward projection in time and clock-reset for this data-structure. Similar to the canonical form for DBM's these operation are obtained via a *canonical* CDD form, where bounds on all arcs are as tight as possible.

---

[2] Thus $D$ is simply unioned with $F$, when a new symbolic state $(l, D)$ is added to the PASSED-list (cf. Fig. 1, line (*)).

**Related Work.** The work in [Bal96] and [WTD95] represent early attempts of applying BDD-technology to the verification of continuous real-time systems. In [Bal96], DBM's themselves are coded as BDD's. However, unions of DBM's are avoided and replaced by convex hulls leading to an approximation algorithm. In [WTD95], BDD's are applied to a symbolic representation of the discrete control part, whereas the continuous part is dealt with using DBM's.

The Numerical Decision Diagrams of [ABKMPR97,BMPY97] offer a canonical representation of unions of zones, essentially via a BDD-encoding of the collection of regions covered by the union. [CC95] offers a similar BDD-encoding in the simple case of one-clock automata. In both cases, the encodings are extremely sensitive to the size of the in-going constants. As we will indicate, NDD's may be seen as degenerate CDD's requiring very fine granularity.

CDD's are in the spirit of Interval Decision Diagrams of [ST98]. In [Strehl'98], IDD's are used for analysis in a discrete, one-clock setting. Whereas IDD's nodes are associated with independent real-valued variables, CDD-nodes – being associated with differences – are highly dependent. Thus, the subset- and emptiness checking algorithms for CDD's are substantially different. Also, the canonical form requires additional attention, as bounds on different arcs along a path may interact.

The CDD datastructure was first introduced in [LPWW98], where a thorough study of various possible normalforms is given. A similar datastructure has recently been introduced in [MLAH99a,MLAH99b].

## 2 Timed Automata

Timed automata were first introduced in [AD94] and have since then established themselves as a standard model for real–time systems. We assume familiarity with this model and only give a brief review in order to fix the terminology and notation used in this paper.

A timed automaton is a standard finite-state automaton extended with a finite collection of real-valued clocks. The nodes (often called *(control) nodes*) are labelled with an *invariant*. Transitions are labelled with a *guard*, a *clock reset* and a *synchronisation*. Guards and invariants are clock constraints. Intuitively, a timed automaton starts execution with all clocks set to zero. Clocks increase uniformly with time while the automaton is within a node. The automaton can only stay within a node while the clocks fulfill the node's invariant. A transition can be taken if the clocks fulfill the guard. By taking the transition, all clocks in the clock reset will be set to zero, while the remaining keep their values. Thus transitions occur instantaneously. Semantically, a state of an automaton is a pair of a control node and a *clock valuation*, i.e. the current setting of the clocks. Transitions in the semantic interpretation are either labelled with a synchronisation (if it is an instantaneous switch from the current node to another) or with a positive time delay (if the automaton stays within a node letting time pass).

For the formal definition, we denote the clocks by $C = \{X_1, \ldots, X_n\}$, and use $\mathcal{B}(C)$ ranged over by $g$ and $D$ to denote the set of clock constraint systems over $C$.

**Definition 1.** *A timed automaton $A$ over clocks $C$ is a tuple $\langle N, l_0, E, I \rangle$ where $N$ is a finite set of nodes (control-nodes), $l_0$ is the initial node, $E \subseteq N \times \mathcal{B}(C) \times 2^C \times C$ corresponds to the set of edges, and finally, $I : N \to \mathcal{B}(C)$ assigns invariants to nodes. In the case, $\langle l, g, r, l' \rangle \in E$, we write $l \xrightarrow{g,r} l'$.*

Formally, we represent the values of clocks as functions (called clock assignments) from $C$ to the non–negative reals $\mathbb{R}_\geq$. We denote by $\mathcal{V}$ the set of clock assignments for $C$. A semantical *state* of an automaton $A$ is now a pair $(l, u)$, where $l$ is a node of $A$ and $u$ is a clock assignment for $C$, and the semantics of $A$ is given by a transition system with the following two types of transitions (corresponding to delay–transitions and edge–transitions):

- $(l, u) \longrightarrow (l, u + d)$ if $I(l)(u)$ and $I(l)(u + d)$
- $(l, u) \longrightarrow (l', u')$ if there exist $g, r$ such that $l \xrightarrow{g,r} l'$, $u \in g$, $u' = [r \mapsto 0]u$, $I(l)(u)$ and $I(l')(u')$

where for $d \in \mathbb{R}_\geq$, $u + d$ denotes the time assignment which maps each clock $X$ in $C$ to the value $u(X) + d$, and for $r \subseteq C$, $[r \mapsto 0]u$ denotes the assignment for $C$ which maps each clock in $r$ to the value 0 and agrees with $u$ over $C \backslash r$. By $u \in g$ we denote that the clock assignment $u$ satisfies the constraint $g$ (in the obvious manner).

Clearly, the semantics of a timed automaton yields an infinite transition system, and is thus not an appropriate basis for decision algorithms. However, efficient algorithms may be obtained using a finite–state *symbolic* semantics based on *symbolic states* of the form $(l, D)$, where $D \in \mathcal{B}(C)$ [HNSY94,YPD94]. The symbolic counterpart to the standard semantics is given by the following two (fairly obvious) types of symbolic transitions:

- $(l, D) \rightsquigarrow (l, (D \wedge I(l))^\uparrow \wedge I(l))$ • $(l, D) \rightsquigarrow (l', r(g \wedge D \wedge I(l)) \wedge I(l'))$ if $l \xrightarrow{g,r} l'$

where time progress $D^\uparrow = \{u + d \mid u \in D \wedge d \in \mathbb{R}_\geq\}$ and clock reset $r(D) = \{[r \mapsto 0]u \mid u \in D\}$. It may be shown that $\mathcal{B}(C)$ (the set of constraint systems) is closed under these two operations ensuring the well–definedness of the semantics. Moreover, the symbolic semantics corresponds closely to the standard semantics in the sense that, whenever $u \in D$ and $(l, D) \rightsquigarrow (l', D')$ then $(l, u) \longrightarrow (l', u')$ for some $u' \in D'$.

## 3 Clock Difference Diagrams

While in principle DBM's are an efficient implementation for clock constraint systems, especially when using canonical form only when necessary and minimal form when suitable, they are not very good at handling unions of zones. In this section we will introduce a more efficient data structure for federations: *clock difference diagrams* or short CDD's. A CDD is a directed acyclic graph with two kinds of nodes: inner nodes and terminal nodes. Terminal nodes represent the constants true and false, while inner nodes are associated with a *type* (i.e. a clock pair) and arcs labeled with intervals giving bounds on the clock pair's difference. Figure 2 shows examples of CDD's.

A CDD is a compact representation of a decision tree for federations: take a valuation, and follow the unique path along which the constraints given by type and interval are fulfilled by the valuation. If this process ends at a true node, the valuation belongs to the federation represented by this CDD, otherwise not. A CDD itself is not a tree, but a DAG due to sharing of isomorphic subtrees.

A *type* is a pair $(i, j)$ where $1 \leq i < j \leq n$. The set of all types is written $\mathcal{T}$, with typical element $t$. We assume that $\mathcal{T}$ is equipped with a linear ordering $\sqsubseteq$ and a special bottom element $(0, 0) \in \mathcal{T}$, in the same way as BDD's assume a given ordering on the boolean variables. By $\mathcal{I}$ we denote the set of all non-empty, convex, integer-bounded subsets of the real line. Note that the integer bound may or may not be within the interval. A typical element of $\mathcal{I}$ is denoted $I$. We write $\mathcal{I}_\emptyset$ for the set $\mathcal{I} \cup \{\emptyset\}$.

In order to relate intervals and types to constraint, we introduce the following notation: $(i)$ given a type $(i, j)$ and an interval $I$ of the reals, by $I(i, j)$ we denote the clock constraint having type $(i, j)$ which restricts the value of $X_i - X_j$ to the interval $I$, $(ii)$ given a clock constraint $D$ and a valuation $v$, by $D(v)$ we denote the application of $D$ to $v$, i.e. the boolean value derived from replacing the clocks in $D$ by the values given in $v$.

Note that typically we will use the notation jointly, i.e. $I(i, j)(v)$ expresses the fact that $v$ fulfills the constraint given by the interval $I$ and the type $(i, j)$.

This allows us to give the definition of a CDD:

**Definition 2 (Clock Difference Diagram).** *A Clock Difference Diagram (CDD) is a directed acyclic graph consisting of a set of nodes $V$ and two functions* type : $V \rightarrow \mathcal{T}$ *and* succ : $V \rightarrow 2^{\mathcal{I} \times V}$ *such that*

- *$V$ has exactly two terminal nodes called* True *and* False, *where* type(True) $=$ type(False) $= (0, 0)$ *and* succ(True) $=$ succ(False) $= \emptyset$.
- *all other nodes $n \in V$ are inner nodes, which have attributed a type* type($n$) $\in$ $\mathcal{T}$ *and a finite set of successors* succ($n$) $= \{(I_1, n_1), \ldots, (I_k, n_K)\}$, *where $(I_i, n_i) \in \mathcal{I} \times V$.*

*We shall write $n \xrightarrow{I} m$ to indicate that $(I, m) \in$ succ($n$). For each inner node $n$, the following must hold:*

- *the successors are disjoint: for $(I, m), (I', m') \in$ succ($n$) either $(I, m) = (I', m')$ or $I \cap I' = \emptyset$,*
- *the successor set is an $\mathbb{R}$-cover: $\bigcup \{I \mid \exists m.n \xrightarrow{I} m\} = \mathbb{R}$,*
- *the CDD is ordered: for all $m$, whenever $n \xrightarrow{I} m$ then* type($m$) $\sqsubseteq$ type($n$)

*Further, the CDD is assumed to be reduced, i.e.*

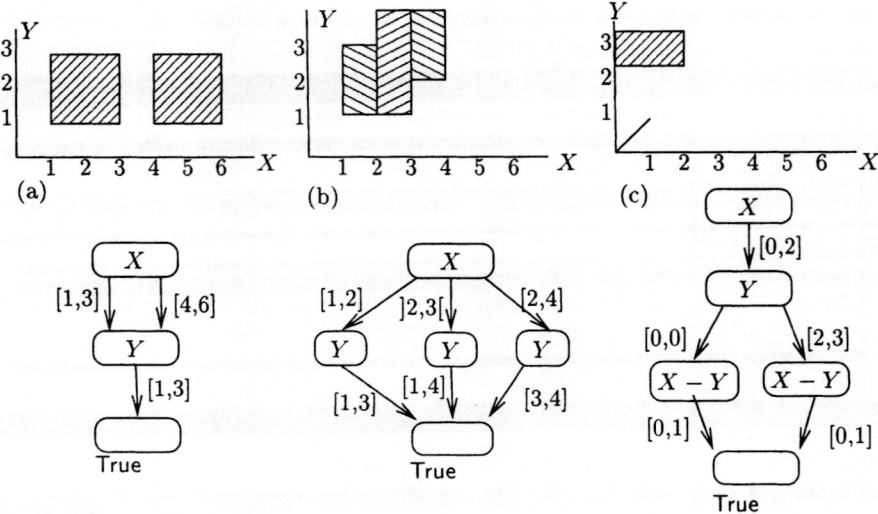

**Fig. 2.** Three example CDD's. Intervals not shown lead implicitly to False

- *it has maximal sharing: for all* $n, m \in V$, $\mathsf{succ}(n) = \mathsf{succ}(m)$ *implies* $n = m$,
- *it has no trivial edges: whenever* $n \xrightarrow{I} m$ *then* $I \neq \mathbb{R}$,
- *all intervals are maximal: whenever* $n \xrightarrow{I_1} m, n \xrightarrow{I_2} m$ *then* $I_1 = I_2$ *or* $I_1 \cup I_2 \notin \mathcal{I}$

Note that we do not require a special root node. Instead each node can be chosen as the root node, and the sub-DAG underneath this node is interpreted as describing a (possibly non-convex) set of clock valuations. This allows for sharing not only within a representation of one set of valuations, but between all representations. Figure 2 gives some examples of CDD's. The following definition makes precise how to interpret such a DAG:

**Definition 3.** *Given a CDD* $(V, \mathsf{type}, \mathsf{succ})$, *each node* $n \in V$ *is assigned a semantics* $[\![n]\!] \subseteq \mathcal{V}$, *recursively defined by*

- $[\![\mathsf{False}]\!] := \emptyset$, $[\![\mathsf{True}]\!] := \mathcal{V}$,
- $[\![n]\!] := \{v \in \mathcal{V} \mid n \xrightarrow{I} m, I(\mathsf{type}(n))(v) = \mathsf{true}, v \in [\![m]\!]\}$ $n$ *an inner node*

For BDD's and IDD's, testing for equality can be achieved easily due to their canonicity: the test is reduced to a pure syntactical comparison. However, in the case of CDD's canonicity is not achieved in the same straightforward manner.

To see this, we give an example of two reduced CDD's in Figure 3(a) describing the same set. The two CDD's are however not isomorphic. The problem with CDD's – in contrast to IDD's – is that the different types of constraints in the nodes are not independent, but influence each other. In the above example obviously $1 \leq X \leq 3$ and $X = Y$ already imply $1 \leq Y \leq 3$. The constraint on $Y$

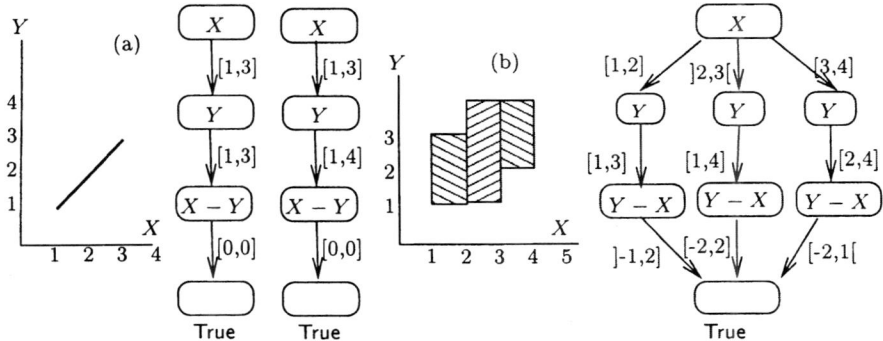

**Fig. 3.** (a) Two reduced CDD's for the same zone, (b) A tightened CDD

in the CDD on the right hand side is simply too loose. Therefore a step towards an improved normal form is to require that on all paths, the constraints should be the tightest possible. We turn back to this issue in the final section.

## 4  Operation on CDD's

**Simple Operations.** Three important operations on CDD's, namely union, intersection and complement, can be defined analogously to IDD's. All use a function makenode which for a given type $t$ and a successor set $S = \{(I_1, n_1), \ldots, (I_k, n_K)\}$ will either return the unique node in the given CDD $C = (V, \text{type}, \text{succ})$ having these attributes or, in case no such exists, add a new node to the CDD with the given attributes. This operation – shown in Figure 4 – is important in order to keep reducedness of the CDD. Note that using a hashtable to identify nodes already in $V$, makenode can be implemented to run in constant time. Note further that makenode itself uses an operation reduce – not given in this paper – which ensures that $S$ itself is reduced, i.e. it has maximal sharing, no trivial edges and all intervals are maximal. Additionally, $S$ is required to be well-formed, i.e. all intervals must be disjoint and form an $\mathbb{R}$-cover.

Then union can be defined as in Figure 4. Intersection is computed by replacing "union" by "intersect" everywhere in the definition of the union operation, and additionally adjusting the base cases. The complement is computed by essentially swapping True and False nodes.[3]

**From constraint systems to CDD's.** The reachability algorithm of UPPAAL currently works with constraint systems (represented either as canonical DBM's or in the minimal form). The desired reachability algorithm will need to combine

---

[3] As for the BDD apply-operator, using a hashed operation-cache is needed to avoid recomputation of the same operation for the same arguments.

```
makenode(t, S):   reduce(S)
                  if (∃n ∈ V.type(n) = t ∧ succ(n) = S) return n
                  else V := V ∪ {n} // where n is a fresh node
                      type := type ∪ {n ↦ t}; succ := succ ∪ {n ↦ S}
                      return n
                  endif
union(n₁, n₂):if n₁ = True or n₂ = True then return True
             elseif n₁ = False then return n₂
             elseif n₂ = False then return n₁
             else if type(n₁) = type(n₂) then
                     return makenode(type(n₁), {(I₁ ∩ I₂,union(n′₁, n′₂)) |
                         n₁ --I₁--> n′₁, n₂ --I₂--> n′₂, I₁ ∩ I₂ ≠ ∅})
                  elseif type(n₁) ⊑ type(n₂) then
                         return makenode(type(n₁), {(I₁, union(n′₁, n₂)) | n₁ --I₁--> n′₁})
                  elseif type(n₂) ⊑ type(n₁) then
                         return makenode(type(n₂), {(I₂, union(n₁, n′₂)) | n₂ --I₂--> n′₂})
                  endif
             endif
makeCDD(D):   n := True
              for t ∈ 𝒯 \ {(0, 0)} do // use ordering ⊑
                  I := I_{D(t)}
                  if I ≠ ℝ then
                      if lo(I) = ∅ then n := makenode(t, {(I, n), (hi(I), False)})
                      elseif hi(I) = ∅ then n := makenode(t, {(I, n), (lo(I), False)})
                      else n := makenode(t, {(I, n), (hi(I), False), (lo(I), False)})
                      endif
                  endif
              endfor
              return n
subset(D, n):  if D = false or n = True then return true
               elseif n = False then return false
               else return ⋀_{n --I--> m} subset(D ∧ I(type(n)), m)
               endif
```

**Fig. 4.** Algorithms

and compare DBM's obtained from exploration of the timed automaton with CDD's used as a compact representation of the PASSED-list.

For the following we assume that a constraint system $D$ holds at most one simple constraint for each pair of clocks $X_i, X_j$ (which is obviously true for DBM's and the minimal form). Let $D(i, j)$ be the set of all simple constraints of type $(i, j)$, i.e. those for $X_i - X_j$ and $X_j - X_i$. The constraint system $D(i, j)$ gives an upper and/or a lower bound for $X_i - X_j$. If not present, choose $-\infty$ as lower and $+\infty$ as upper bound. Denote the interval defined thus by $I_{D(i,j)}$.

Further, given an interval $I \in \mathcal{I}$, let $lo(I) := \{r \in \mathbb{R} \mid \forall r' \in I.r < r'\}$ be the set of lower bounds and $hi(I) := \{r \in \mathbb{R} \mid \forall r' \in I.r > r'\}$ the set of upper bounds. Note that always $lo(I), hi(I) \in \mathcal{I}_\emptyset$. Using this notation, a simple algorithm makeCDD for constructing a CDD from a constraint system can be given as in Figure 4. Using this, we can easily union zones to a CDD as required in the modified reachability algorithm of UPPAAL (cf. footnote 2). Note that for this asymmetric union it is advisable to use the minimal form representation for the zone, as this will lead to a smaller CDD, and subsequently to a faster and less space-consuming union-operation.

**Crucial Operations.** Testing for equality and set-inclusion of CDD's is not easy without utilizing a normal form. Looking at the test given in (1) it is however evident that all we need is to test for inclusion between a zone and a CDD. Such an asymmetric test for a zone $Z$ and a CDD $n$ can be implemented as shown in Figure 4 without need for canonicity.

Note that when testing for emptiness of a DBM as in the first if-statement, we need to compute its canonical form. If we know that the DBM is already in canonical form, the algorithm can be improved by passing $D \wedge I(\text{type}(n))$ in canonical form. As $D \wedge I(\text{type}(n))$ adds no more than two constraints to the zone, computation of the canonical form can be done faster than in the general case, which would be necessary in the test $D = \text{true}$.

The above algorithm can also be used to test for emptiness of a CDD using $\text{empty}(n) := \text{subset}(\text{true}, \text{complement}(n))$, where true is the empty set of constraints, fulfilled by every valuation.

As testing for set inclusion $C_1 \subseteq C_2$ of two CDD's $C_1, C_2$ is equivalent to testing for emptiness of $C_1 \cap \overline{C_2}$, also this check can be done without needing canonicity.

## 5  Implementation and Experimental Results

This section presents the results of an experiment where both the current[4] and an experimental CDD-based version of UPPAAL were used to verify eight industrial examples found in the literature – including a gearbox controller [LPY98], various communication protocols used in Philips audio equipment (see [BPV94], [DKRT97], [BGK+96]), and in B&O audio/video equipment [HSLL97,HLS98], and the start-up algorithm of the DACAPO protocol [LPY97] – as well as Fischer's protocol for mutual exclusion.

In Table 1 we present the space requirements and runtime of the examples on a Sun UltraSPARC 2 equipped with 512 MB of primary memory and two 170 MHz processors. Each example was verified using the current purely DBM-based algorithm of UPPAAL (Current), and three different CDD-based algorithms. The first (CDD) uses CDD's to represent the continuous part of the PASSED-list, the second (Reduced) is identical to CDD except that all inconsistent paths – i.e.

---

[4] More precisely UPPAAL version 2.19.2, which is the most recent version of UPPAAL currently used in-house.

**Table 1.** Performance statistics for a number of systems. **P** is the number of processes, **V** the number of discrete variables, and **C** the number of clocks in the system. All times are in seconds and space usage in kilobytes. Space usage only includes memory required to store the PASSED-list.

| System | P | V | C | Current Time | Space | CDD Time | Space | Reduced Time | Space | CDD+BDD Time | Space |
|---|---|---|---|---|---|---|---|---|---|---|---|
| PHILIPS | 4 | 4 | 2 | 0.2 | 25 | 0.2 | 23 | 0.2 | 23 | 0.35 | 94 |
| PHILIPS COL | 7 | 13 | 3 | 21.8 | 2,889 | 23.0 | 1,506 | 28.8 | 1,318 | 70.6 | 5,809 |
| B&O | 9 | 22 | 3 | 56.0 | 5,793 | 55.9 | 2,248 | 63.4 | 2,240 | 300.2 | 4,221 |
| BRP | 6 | 7 | 4 | 22.1 | 3,509 | 21.3 | 465 | 46.5 | 448 | 68.9 | 873 |
| POWERDOWN1 | 10 | 20 | 2 | 81.3 | 4,129 | 79.2 | 1,539 | 82.6 | 1,467 | 164.7 | 4,553 |
| POWERDOWN2 | 8 | 20 | 1 | 19.3 | 4,420 | 19.8 | 4,207 | 19.7 | 4,207 | 79.5 | 5,574 |
| DACAPO | 6 | 12 | 5 | 55.1 | 4,474 | 57.1 | 2,950 | 64.5 | 2,053 | 256.1 | 6,845 |
| GEARBOX | 5 | 4 | 5 | 10.5 | 1,849 | 11.2 | 888 | 12.35 | 862 | 29.9 | 7,788 |
| FISCHER4 | 4 | 1 | 4 | 1.14 | 129 | 1.36 | 96 | 2.52 | 48 | 2.3 | 107 |
| FISCHER5 | 5 | 1 | 5 | 40.6 | 1,976 | 61.5 | 3,095 | 154.4 | 396 | 107.3 | 3,130 |

those representing the empty set – are removed from the CDD's, and the third (CDD+BDD) extends CDD's with a BDD-based representation of the discrete part in order to achieve a fully symbolic representation of the PASSED-list. As can be seen, our CDD-based modification of UPPAAL leads to truly significant space-savings (in average 42%) with only moderate increase in run-time (in average 7%). When inconsistent paths are eliminated the average space-saving increases to 55% at the cost of an average increase in run-time of 54%. If we only consider the industrial examples the average space-savings of CDD are 49% while the average increase in run-time is below 0.5%. Maybe unexpectedly, CDD+BDD when compared with Current leads to a degraded performance in both time and space. Additionally, a closer look at the usage of the WAIT-list reveals that the less strict termination condition of (1) only in a few cases leads to faster termination. This offers a good explanation for the lack in runtime-improvement.

## 6 Towards a fully symbolic timed reachability analysis

The presented CDD-version of UPPAAL uses CDD's to store the PASSED-list, but zones (i.e. DBM's) in the exploration of the timed automata. The next goal is to use CDD's in the exploration as well, thus treating the continuous part fully symbolic. In combination with the suggested BDD-based approach for the discrete part, this would result in a fully symbolic timed reachability analysis, saving even more space and time.

The central operations when exploring a timed automaton are time progress and clock reset. Using *tightened CDD's*, these operations can be defined along the same lines as for DBM's. A tightened CDD is one where along each path to True all constraints are the the tightest possible. In [LPWW98] we have shown how to effectively transform any given CDD into an equivalent tightened one.

Figure 3(b) shows the tightened CDD-representation for example (b) from Figure 2. Given this tightened version, the time progress operation is obtained by simply removing all upper bounds on the individual clocks. In general, this gives a CDD with overlapping intervals, which however can easily be turned into a CDD obeying our definition. More details on these operations can be found in [LPWW98].

CDD's come equipped with an obvious notion of being *equally fine partitioned*. For equally fine partitioned CDD's we have the following normal form theorem [LPWW98]:

**Theorem 1.** *Let $C_1, C_2$ be two CDD's which are tightened and equally fine partitioned. Then $[\![C_1]\!] = [\![C_2]\!]$ iff $C_1$ and $C_2$ are graph-isomorphic.*

A drastic way of achieving equally fine partitioned CDD's is to allow only atomic integer-bounded intervals, i.e. intervals of the form $[n, n]$ or $(n, n+1)$. This approach has been taken in [ABKMPR97,BMPY97] demonstrating canonicity. However, this approach is extremely sensitive to the size of the constants in the analyzed model. In contrast, for models with large constants our notion of CDD allows for coarser, and hence more space-efficient, representations.

## 7  Conclusion

In this paper, we have presented Clock Difference Diagrams, CDD's, a BDD-like data-structure for effective representation and manipulation of finite unions of zones. A version of the real-time verification tool UPPAAL using CDD's to store explored symbolic states has been implemented. Our experimental results on eight industrial examples found in the literature demonstrate significant space-savings (in average 42%) with a moderate increase in run-time (in average 7%). Currently, we are pursuing realization of the fully symbolic state-space exploration of the last section and [LPWW98], extending UPPAAL from pure reachability checking to checking for general real-time properties.

## References

[ABKMPR97] Asarain, Bozga, Kerbrat, Maler, Pnueli, Rasse. Data-Structures for the Verification of Timed Automata. In Proc. HART'97, LNCS 1201, pp. 346–360.

[AD94] Alur, Dill. Automata for Modelling Real-Time Systems. In *Proc. of ICALP'90*, LNCS 443, 1990.

[Bal96] Felice Balarin. *Approximate Reachability Analysis of Timed Automata*. Proc. Real-Time Systems Symposium, Washington, DC, December 1996, pp. 52–61.

[BGK+96] Bengtsson, Griffioen, Kristoffersen, Larsen, Larsson, Pettersson, Yi. Verification of an audio protocol with bus collision using uppaal. CAV'96, LNCS 1102, 1996.

[BLLPW96] Bengtsson, Larsen, Larsson, Pettersson, Yi. UPPAAL in 1995. In *Proc. TACAS'96*, LNCS 1055, pp. 431–434. Springer March 1996.

[BMPY97] Bozga, Maler, Pnueli, Yovine. Some progress in the symbolic verification of timed automata. *Proc. CAV'97*, LNCS 1254, pp. 179–190, 1997.

[BPV94] Bosscher, Polak, Vaandrager. Verification of an Audio-control Protocol. In *Proc. FTRTFT*, LNCS 863, 1994.

[CC95] Campos, Clarke. Real-time symbolic model checking for discrete time models. In C. Rattray T. Rus, Eds., *AMAST Series in Computing: Theories and Experiences for Real-Time System Development*, 1995.

[Dill87] Dill. *Timing Assumptions and Verification of Finite-State Concurrent Systems*. in: LNCS 407, Springer Berlin 1989, pp. 197-212.

[DKRT97] D'Arginio, Katoen, Ruys, Tretmans. Bounded retransmission protocol must be on time ! In *Proc. TACAS'97*, LNCS 1217, 1997.

[DY95] Daws, Yovine. Two examples of verification of multirate timed automata with KRONOS. In *Proc. 16th IEEE Real-Time Systems Symposium*, pp 66–75, Dec 95.

[HNSY94] Henzinger, Nicollin, Sifakis, Yovine. Symbolic Model Checking for Real-Time Systems. *Information and Computation*, 111(2):193–244, 1994.

[HHW95] Henzinger, Ho, Wong-Toi. A Users Guide to HYTECH. Technical report, Department of Computer Science, Cornell University, 1995.

[HLS98] Havelund, Larsen, Skou. Formal Verification of an Audio/Video Power Controller using the Real-Time Model Checker UPPAAL. Technical report made for Bang& Olufsen, 1998.

[HSLL97] Havelund, Skou, Larsen, Lund. Formal Modelling and Analysis of an Audio/Video Protocol: An Industrial Case Study using UPPAAL. In *In Proc. 18th IEEE Real-Time System Symposium*, 1997.

[LPW95] Larsen, Pettersson, Yi. *Compositional and Symbolic Model-Checking of Real-Time Systems*. In Proc. 16th IEEE Real-Time Systems Symposium, December 1995.

[LPWW98] Larsen, Weise, Yi, Pearson. *Clock Difference Diagrams*. DoCS Technical Report No.98/99, Uppsala University, Sweden, presented at the Nordic Workshop on Programming Theory, Turku, Finland, November 1998.

[LPY97] Lönn, Pettersson, Yi. Formal Verification of a TDMA Protocol Start-Up Mechanism. In *Proc. 1997 IEEE Pacific Rim International Symposium on Fault-Tolerant Systems*, pp. 235–242, 1997.

[LPY98] Lindahl, Pettersson, Yi. Formal design and analysis of a gear controller. In Bernhard Steffen (Ed.), *Proc. TACAS'98*, LNCS 1384, pp. 281–297. Springer 1998.

[MLAH99a] Møller, Lichtenberg, Andersen, Hulgaard. *Difference decision diagrams*. Technical report IT-TR-1999-023, Technical University of Denmark, February 1999.

[MLAH99b] Møller, Lichtenberg, Andersen, Hulgaard. *On the symbolic verification of timed systems*. Technical report IT-TR-1999-024, Technical University of Denmark, February 1999.

[ST98] Strehl, Thiele. Symbolic Model Checking of Process Networks Using Interval Diagram Techniques. ICCAD-98, San Jose, California, pp. 686–692, 1998.

[Strehl'98] Strehl. Using Interval Diagram Techniques for the Symbolic Verification of Timed Automata. Technical Report TIK-53, ETH Zürich, July 1998.

[WTD95] Wong-Toi, Dill. Verification of real-time systems by successive over and under approximation. CAV'95, July 1995.

[YPD94] Yi, Pettersson, Daniels. Automatic Verification of Real-Time Communicating Systems By Constraint-Solving. In *Proc. 7th International Conference on Formal Description Techniques*, 1994.

# Mechanizing Proofs of Computation Equivalence

Marcelo Glusman    Shmuel Katz

Department of Computer Science
The Technion, Haifa, Israel
{marce, katz}@cs.technion.ac.il

**Abstract.** A proof-theoretic mechanized verification environment that allows taking advantage of the "convenient computations" method is presented. The $PVS$ theories encapsulating this method reduce the conceptual difficulty of proving a safety or liveness property for all the possible interleavings of a parallel computation by separating two different concerns: proving that certain *convenient* computations satisfy the property, and proving that every computation is related to a convenient one by a relation which preserves the property. We define one such relation, the equivalence of computations which differ only in the order of independent operations. We also introduce the computation as an explicit semantic object. The application of the method requires the definition of a "measure" function from computations into a well-founded set. We supply two possible default measures, which can be applied in many cases, together with examples of their use. The work is done in $PVS$, and a clear separation is made between "infrastructural" theories to be supplied as a *proof environment* library to users, and the specification and proof of particular examples.

## 1  Introduction

This paper presents a proof environment for $PVS$ [13, 17, 12] that supports convenient computations and exploits partial order based on the independence of operations in different processes, for the first time in a mechanized theorem-proving context. Thus theoretic work defining this approach [8, 9, 11] is turned into a *proof environment* for theorem-proving that can be used without having to rejustify basic principles. Besides making convenient computations practical in a theorem-proving tool, we demonstrate what is involved in packaging such a framework into a proof environment for use by nonexperts in the particular theory. The modular structure of the theories (the units of PVS code that contain definitions and theorems) should encourage using parts of the environment whenever convenient computations are natural to the problem statement or proof.

In the continuation, basic theories are described in which computation sequences are viewed as 'first-class' objects that can be specified, equivalence of computations based on independence of operations is precisely defined, and a proof method using measure induction over well-founded sets is encapsulated. Two possible default measures are provided to aid the user in completing the proof obligations, one involving the distance between matching pairs of events, and one for computations that have *layers* of events. As an example among those classes of properties that can be proven with the convenient computations method, (those properties preserved by the chosen reduction relation), we show a subclass of the stable properties: final-state properties.

We summarize how a user can exploit the environment and describe two generic examples. The first demonstrates ideas of *virtual atomicity* for sequences of events local to a single process, and the second shows the use of the layers measure for a pipelined implementation of insertion sorting. In this and the other examples we have done, the proof environment (infrastructural theories) contains over half of the lines in the *PVS* specification files and also of the interactive PVS prover commands, taken as a rough indication of the proof effort.

## Convenient computations and the need for mechanization

Methods that exploit the partial order among independent operations have been used both for model checking and for general theorem proving (see [16] for a variety of approaches). In particular, ideas of the independence of operations that lead to partial order reductions have either been used for (usually linear) temporal logic based model checking reductions [14, 18, 7], or for theoretical work on general correctness proofs in unbounded domains. [11, 15, 8]. For general correctness (as opposed to model checking) no mechanization has been implemented until now, and sample proofs have been hand simulated.

The intuitive idea behind convenient computations is simple. A system defines a collection of linear sequences of the events and/or states (where each sequence is called a *computation*). We often convince ourselves of the correctness of a concurrent system by considering some "convenient" computations in which events occur in an orderly fashion even though they may be in different processes. It is usually easier to prove properties for these well-chosen computations than for all the possible interleavings of parallel processes. Two computations are called *equivalent* if they differ only in that independent (potentially concurrent) events appear in a different order. There are classes of safety and liveness properties which are satisfied equally by any two equivalent computations (i.e., either both satisfy the property, or neither does). If we show that any non-convenient computation is equivalent to some convenient one, then we can conclude that any properties of this kind verified for the convenient computations must also be satisfied by the non-convenient ones.

In certain contexts, like sequential consistency of memory models and serializability of database transaction protocols, where the convenient computations' behavior is taken as the correct one by definition, the computation equivalence itself is the goal of the verification effort. Even when the goal is to prove certain properties of a system, if we attempt to reduce the problem to verification of the convenient computations, we might find flaws in our intuitive belief that they "represent" all possible computations. Finding that some computations are *not* equivalent to any convenient one can have as much practical value as finding a counterexample to a property expressed by a logical formula.

The availability of general purpose theorem proving tools such as $PVS$ opens the way for a mechanized application of the convenient computations technique. Usually, attempts to carry out mechanized proofs in such tools raise issues that might be overlooked when using "intuitive" formal reasoning. Moreover, proofs can be saved and later, in the face of change, adjusted and rerun rather than just discarded. The down side of mechanized theorem proving methods is the need to prove many facts that are easily understood and believed to be correct by human intuition. Many of these facts are common to all applications of a proof approach. General definitions and powerful lemmas can be packed in theories that provide a comfortable proof environment. These theories also clarify the new approach, and generate the needed proof obligations for any particular application. The proof obligations arise as "importing assumptions" of generic theories, as "type checking conditions" when defining objects of the provided types, or as antecedents (preconditions) in the provided theorems that have the form of a logical implication.

## Existing versus proposed verification styles

The $PVS$ tool is a general-purpose theorem prover with a higher-order logic designed to verify and challenge specifications, and is not tailored to any computation model or programming language. It does provide a *prelude* of theories about arithmetic, inequalities, sets, and other common mathematical structures, and some additional useful libraries. Decidable fragments of logic are treated by a collection of decision procedures that replace many tedious subproofs. However, it has no inherent concept of states, operations, or computations. Usual verification examples, like proving an invariant in a transition system, involve the definition of states, initial conditions (initial-state functions), and transitions (next-state functions) by the user. To prove invariance of a state property P, one just writes and proves an induction theorem of the form:

$$(initial(s) \Rightarrow P(s)) \wedge (P(s) \Rightarrow P(next(s)))$$

The computations themselves are not mentioned directly, and the property "in every state, P" ($\Box P$ of linear temporal logic) is justified (usually implicitly) by such an induction theorem.

As part of the proof environment presented here, we provide precise definitions for computations, conditional independence of operations, computation equivalence, and verification of properties based on computation equivalence and convenient computations using well-founded sets.

We define a "computation" type as a function from discrete time into "steps" (a state paired with an operation), and specify temporal properties as arbitrary predicates over computations. Thus, if $c : comps$ is a function from $t : time$ to steps, and $st$ is a projection function from a step to its *state* component, then

$$\Box P = global\_P?(c : comps) : bool = \forall t \in time : P(st(c(t)))$$

This style is needed so we can reason about computations and their relationships. Note that we are not limited to linear-time properties by this style of expression. The higher-order logic of $PVS$ allows us for example, to express a $CTL^*$ formula like "GEFp" by means of a predicate on computations:

$$GEFp(c : comps) : boolean =$$
$$\forall(t : time) : \exists(d : comps) : \quad \forall(tp : time | tp < t) : d(tp) = c(tp)$$
$$\wedge \exists(tf : time | tf \geq t) : p(st(d(tf)))$$

or in words, "for every time point $t$ there exists a computation (called $d$) which is identical to $c$ before time $t$ and, at time $t$ or later, has a state that satisfies p"

## 2   The theories

In this section we describe a hierarchy of theories, whose IMPORTING relationships can be seen in Figure 1. They provide the foundation for reasoning about equivalence among computations. The top level of the hierarchy contains three main components: the *computation model*, the *equivalence* notion, and the *proof method*. An additional *default measure* component uses the other theories in specific contexts that hide some of the proof obligations in an application.

In the computation model component, transition systems and computations over them are defined. The option of providing global restrictions on possible sequences of transitions (for example, in order to introduce various notions of *fairness* [6, 2]) is also provided. In the equivalence component, theories are presented that encode when transitions are independent, and when computations are defined to be equivalent (in that independent transitions occur in a different order). The proof method component shows how to prove that for an arbitrary set and subset, every element of the set is related to some element of the subset, using well-foundedness. Here the elements are arbitrary, and the relation is given as a parameter. When instantiated with the equivalence relation from the equivalence component, the needed proof rule and its justification are provided. As an example of the classes of properties relevant to this method, we include a theory that defines the "final-state properties" and proves that they are preserved by the defined computation equivalence relation.

After presenting these theories in somewhat more detail, two default measures are described, for matching pairs of operations and for layered computations. We then summarize how a user should apply the theories to an application, and describe two examples.

(Note: The $PVS$ files for the proof environment and the examples are available from the Web page at http://www.cs.technion.ac.il/~marce).

### 2.1   Computation model

Our model of computation is defined by three parameterized theories: step_sequences, execution_sequences, and computations. Each application using these theories must define types for the specific states and the operations as

358

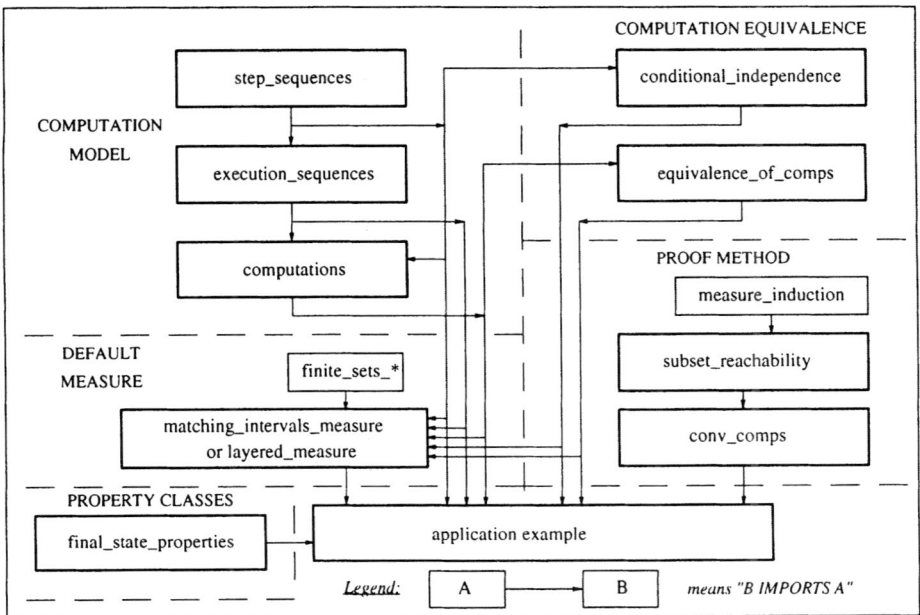

**Fig. 1.** The hierarchy of theories.

actual parameters upon instantiation of the theories. The theory `step_sequences`, based on these two types, defines function types needed to build a transition system: `initial_conditions`, `enabling_conditions`, and `next_state_functions`. It also defines the types `time`, `steps` (records with two fields: `st: states` and `op: ops`), and `step_seqs` (functions from time to steps).

In an application, the user defines the initial states, the enabling conditions and the next-state functions for each operation, and then instantiates the theory `execution_sequences`. This theory defines the subtype of the well-built `execution_sequences`: the ones that start in an initial state, and whose steps are consecutive, i.e., the operations are enabled on the corresponding state, and the state in the following step is their next-state value.

The theory `computations` has an additional parameter to be provided by a user, namely, a predicate on `execution_sequences` called `relevant?` which is used to define the subtype `comps`. This includes only those `execution_sequences` which satisfy the added predicate. This restriction can be used to focus on a special subset of all the possible execution sequences, for example to express fairness assumptions or to analyze just a part of the system's behavior (such as a finite collection of transactions).

## 2.2 Computation equivalence

Equivalence between computations and independence of operations is formalized by the theories `conditional_independence` and `equivalence_of_comps`.

The functional independence defined in the first of these theories is over pairs of operations and states, expressing when two operations are independent in a given state. It requires that the execution of either of the two operations doesn't interfere with the other's enabledness, and that the result of applying both operations from the given state must be the same regardless of their ordering.

Though this functional independence expresses commutativity of operations, it is not practical to prove it each time we need to show that a pair of consecutive operations can be exchanged. To separate this (local) consideration and make later proofs simpler, we allow the user to define a separate conditional independence relation also over pairs of operations and states. This predicate must be symmetric and it must imply the functional independence of the two operations from the given state. (These conditions will appear as proof obligations when the theory is instantiated.) This arrangement allows the user to choose how much independence is to be considered for a particular application.

The theory `equivalence_of_comps` first defines the result of swapping two independent operations on a given state in an execution sequence. If the need arises to prove that the result is a legal computation (a `relevant?` execution sequence), it is passed as a proof obligation to the application since `relevant?`is only defined there. The rest of the theory deals only with legal computations that are identical up to the swapping of independent operations, defining:

- `one_swap_equiv?(c1,c2)`: c1 and c2 are different and differ by a single swap, i.e., c2 is the result of swapping consecutive independent operations in c1 at some time t.
- `swap_equiv_n?(c1, c2, n)`: c1 and c2 differ by up to $n$ single swaps.
- `swap_equiv?(c1,c2)`: this is the transitive closure of `one_swap_equiv?` and is true iff there is an $n$ s.t. `swap_equiv_n?(c1, c2, n)`.

In the theory, the relation `swap_equiv?` is proven to be an equivalence relation. This relation is the formalization of the intuitive notion of equivalent computations, and the equivalence classes that it generates in the set of all computations are called *interleaving sets* in the context of partial order reductions and the temporal logic $ISTL^*$[9, 10].

## 2.3  Proof method

Consider an arbitrary set (or data type) T, with a preorder relation `path_to?` over its elements, and choose a subset of T - those elements which satisfy a given predicate. We want to prove that from each element in T we can reach one in the chosen subset. We first pick a "measure function" which maps elements from T into elements of a well-founded structure $(M, <)$. In the theory `subset_reachability` we show that it suffices to prove that each element *outside* the chosen subset has a path to one with a strictly smaller measure.

The theory `conv_comps` has parameters that define a computation model, a `reduces_to?` preorder, a predicate for choosing the conv?enient computations, and a measure function into a well-founded set. These are used with the subset_reachability theory to provide a sufficient condition:

$$\forall c : \neg conv?(c) \implies \exists d : reduces\_to?(c, d) \wedge m(d) < m(c) \qquad (1)$$

from which reduction to convenient computations is proved:

$$\forall c : \exists d : conv?(d) \wedge reduces\_to?(c, d)$$

It also provides a theorem defining the two added proof obligations that must be discharged in an application to verify *any* property p? for all computations:

$$\forall c : conv?(c) \implies p?(c)$$

$$\forall c, d : reduces\_to?(c, d) \implies (p?(d) \implies p?(c)) \qquad (2)$$

In other words, p? must be true for the convenient computations, and must respect the preorder used in the theory. In a wider context, the theory of convenient computations can be used to reduce the verification of properties of general computations to the simpler problem of verification over the convenient computations. The reduces_to? relation can be any preorder for which the required premises ((1) and (2)) can be proven. Since the theory is parametric, other computation models and notions of equivalence can be used, besides those seen here.

## 2.4 Property classes

Any property preserved by the relation (preorder) chosen as a reduction to convenient computations, is a candidate to be verified by this method. A common example is that of stable properties. The theory final_state_properties exemplifies a special case of stable properties. It defines a final state of a computation as any point in time after which the computation remains quiescent i.e. every operation-state pair is the same as the next one. A function is defined that, given a state property, generates a computation predicate that enforces that state property on all final states. The "final-state properties" thus generated are proven invariant under the swap-equivalence relation.

## 2.5 Default measures

The choice of measure functions should address the intuitive notion of "how close" a computation is to a convenient one. (e.g. how many independent operation pairs should be swapped). Only then will the proof obligations generated be easy (if not trivial) to discharge. We provide theories with two measures that widen the support given to the user of the method.

**Matching intervals measure:** In [8] the convenient computations method was applied (manually) to the sequential consistency problem. The measure involved intervals of selected events (computation steps) and their length. The measure value was lowered by moving unrelated events out of the interval until all the selected events happened consecutively. We provide a simpler version which can be applied to achieve the same effect. An *interval* is defined as a pair of points in time $(t1, t2)$, and its distance (length) is $t2 - t1 - 1$ (thus a consecutive pair $(t, t + 1)$ has distance zero). The measure value for a computation is defined as the sum of all the distances of its matching intervals.

To use this measure, the application must supply a predicate `match?(c,i)` that defines the "matching" intervals i (pairs of points) in a given computation c. In a matching interval we want two events to ideally happen immediately one after the other, in a certain order, even if in many computations there are intervening events. Typical cases are sending and receiving a value over an empty communication channel, or performing a series of local steps in a process. The minimum value is attained when all the matching intervals have zero distance. In a reasonable application of the method, the definition of the matching intervals should make it easy to prove that nonconvenient computations have a nonzero measure. The `match?` predicate must satisfy the following requirements:

- Every computation has finitely many matching intervals. This is to make the measure finite. (An alternative would be to require that the set of nonzero-distance matching intervals be finite, and sum distances only over that set.)
- The matching intervals in two one-swap-equivalent computations are the same, up to the exchange of the end-points affected by the swap.
- No two matching intervals start in the same time point and no two end together. This is used to simplify the number of cases.
- Swappable (i.e., independent consecutive) operations cannot appear at the ends of a (zero-distance) matching interval.

These requirements mainly restrain the choice of the `match?` function to a usable one. Again, for reasonable choices their proof is straightforward.

The theory also provides and proves a heuristic for finding a computation d which is equivalent to a given computation c and has a smaller measure. Such a d exists if c satisfies that for some $t$:

$$(only\_starts\_interval?(c, t) \ \land \ \neg only\_starts\_interval?(c, t + 1)) \ \lor$$
$$(only\_ends\_interval?(c, t + 1) \ \land \ \neg only\_ends\_interval?(c, t))$$

where $only\_starts\_interval?(c, t) = starts\_interval?(c, t) \land \neg ends\_interval?(c, t)$ (and $only\_ends\_interval?$ is defined similarly).

The predicates `starts_interval?(c,t)` and `ends_interval?(c,t)` state that there is a matching interval in c that starts(ends) at time t. This means that either an event only starting an interval is followed by one *not* only starting an interval, or an event only ending an interval is preceded by one not only ending an interval. Due to the other assumptions, if this holds, the relevant pair can be exchanged, yielding a computation with a smaller measure.

**Layered measure** Another way of thinking of convenient computations of a program is to define ordered phases or layers of execution [5,4]. Each event is associated with a layer. If the events in every layer appear contiguously in the computation, without events from a layer getting mixed with events from an earlier layer, the computation is considered convenient. Examples where this approach seems natural are programs with communication-closed layers and distributed snapshot algorithms [3]. In contrast to some of those previous works, however, we do not focus on syntactic layers: the same program instruction occurring more than once might produce events belonging to different execution layers.

The `layered_measure` theory considers programs with a finite number of layers, where all but the last one must be finite and eventually finish, i.e., for each computation and for each layer in it, there is a time after which all the events belong to other layers. If infinite computations are considered, this can be achieved by applying some sort of fairness assumption.

For each event (computation step) except those associated with the last layer, we count the number of previous events that belong to a (strictly) later layer than the layer of that event. The measure value of a computation is the sum of those counts. Clearly, computations with a zero measure value should be convenient in an application, since no event is preceded by an event from a later layer.

The application must define a natural number `lastlayer` and function (`layer`) that maps a computation and a time point into a natural number less than or equal to `lastlayer`. This function must meet the following requirements:

- As mentioned before, for every layer below `lastlayer` there is a time after which there are no more time points belonging to it. Proofs of this requirement are based on basic progress of the computation, which can be supported by fairness assumptions from the `relevant?` predicate.
- The `layer` function is the same for one-swap-equivalent computations, except at the two time points involved in the swap, where the layer values are interchanged. This is trivial for reasonable definitions of the `layer` function.
- For any time $t$ where $layer(t) > layer(t+1)$, the operations at $t$ and $t+1$ must be independent, i.e. a swap must be possible. This seemingly strong requirement is easy to prove if layering is appropriate for the application.

In this theory, it is proven that any assignment of layers satisfying these conditions guarantees that any computation in which a later-layer event comes before a previous-layer event (and thus having a non-zero measure) is equivalent to one with a smaller measure. Thus, showing a drop in the measure value is hidden from a user, if the three conditions above can be shown.

## 3   Using the method: a summary

### 3.1   The user's problem description

First, the **computation model** must be described by defining the types of the states and operations, the initial states, the operations' enabling conditions, and their next-state functions. Any necessary global restrictions such as fairness or finiteness are then added to define the relevant computations.

Second, the user must define the conditional independence relation between the operations at given states. This is used to instantiate the **computation equivalence** theory which will provide the `swap-equiv` relation. The theory will generate proof obligations to show that the user's suggested relation is a valid independence relation. Finally, in the **proof method** theories, the convenient computations must be provided in the instantiation of the theory `conv-comps`, and a measure function must be defined (either by the user, or using one of the two provided).

These are all the definitions needed to prove computation equivalence. Aside from the importing assumptions of the theories used, the user is left to prove that for every non-convenient computation there is a reduction to a computation with a lower measure (for the two default measures provided there is a sufficient condition that makes that proof much easier).

To prove any property (predicate over computations) for all the computations of an application, the theorem provided in `conv_comps` leaves the user to prove that the property holds for convenient computations and that equivalence over the user's independence relation preserves the property.

## 3.2 The user's design decisions and tradeoffs

As in any proof method, experience is essential in successfully applying the elements of this method. Choosing the *relevant* computations can be critical, especially in proving the importing assumptions of the theories that define measure functions.

When proving that the reduction preserves the property to be verified, and also when proving that the independence relation implies functional independence, it helps to have as small an independence relation as possible. This conflicts with the interest of having more opportunities to swap operations in order to find a computation with a smaller measure.

If we include more computations in the class of convenient computations, it may be easier to show a reduction to a smaller measure for the remaining nonconvenient computations. On the other hand, we reduce the benefit of the use of equivalence by having to prove the desired properties directly for a larger class of convenient computations.

As seen in the proof obligation (2), the properties that can be verified when the theories are combined in an application are those which are preserved by the reduction relation. A lemma in the theory `equivalence_of_comps` simplifies this requirement: it suffices to show that two computations which differ only in the order of *one* pair of independent operations, must satisfy p? equally:

$$\forall c, d : one\_swap\_equiv?(c, d) \implies p?(d) \implies p?(c) \qquad (3)$$

This requirement is easy to prove for large classes of properties, e.g., those defined in the theory `final_state_properties`.

In certain cases, one might need to add "history" variables to the state, (without affecting the behavior of the rest of the state components) to support property verification. For example, in order to verify mutual exclusion, a flag that records a violation of the mutual exclusion should be added. This is done so that two computations which differ only by the order of a pair of operations are not considered equivalent if one of them violates the mutual exclusion requirement and the other does not. The original system variables might not suffice to make those operations functionally dependent.

The characterization of the properties which can be proven by this method is a subject worth further research. In this paper we have focused on the proofs that computations are equivalent, and particularly on showing that every computation is equivalent to one of the convenient computations.

## 4 Example 1: Using the matching intervals measure

Our first example (a full listing is at the Web page given earlier) shows how a sequence of local actions in a process can be considered atomic. It is typical of many situations where a sequence of local actions can be viewed as virtually atomic [1].

```
%       flag: bool=FALSE       tl,tm,x: nat
% PL:   10: tl=1       % local || PM:  m0: tm=2                % local
%       11: x=tl       % global||       m1: await flag=TRUE
%       12: flag=TRUE          ||       m2: x=x+tm             % global
%       13: STOP              ||       m3: STOP
```

Here the operation l2 must occur before m1, so in fact we observe all the possible interleavings of the operation m0 (PM's initialization) with the operations l0-l2. The **states** type contains the two program counters explicitly. The **ops** type is {l0,l1,l2, m0,m1,m2, stop}. The **initial?** predicate on states is straightforward. The **en?** enabling condition, and the **next** next-state-function are defined in table format to enhance readability.

In this example we define two operations as independent if they are both **stop** or if they belong to different processes and satisfy **indep_l_m?**, a predicate given in tabular form. The table's rows and columns represent operations which belong to different processes, and the entries are state predicates, though in this particular case they are not state-dependent (always TRUE or FALSE). This table was filled based on our understanding of the semantics of the programming language. The independence relation must be proved to imply functional equivalence and to be symmetric, as a type-correctness requirement. After that is done, to decide if two operations can be swapped, we only need to look them up in the table. The convenient computations are chosen as those in which m0 is executed immediately before m1 (and after l0–l2). We choose to use the default measure with matching pairs. Here we can define the **match?** predicate so that only the pair (m0,m1) matches. Clearly, when the measure is zero, the computation is convenient.

The proof that for any nonconvenient computation there is an equivalent one with a smaller measure was accomplished by using the theorem provided in the matching_intervals_measure theory. Note that if the instructions in question were in a loop, the definition of "matching intervals" would have to guarantee that the proper occurrences of the instructions are matched, e.g., by using a loop counter as well as the operations. There is another condition: computations must have a finite number of matching intervals. In the present example, this is easy to show since each operation is done exactly once. In general, this would be proven by using some kind of finiteness constraint, typically from the relevant? predicate.

Although our main concern is proving computation equivalence, we show the remaining proof obligations for a final-state property. The proof obligation (conv_implies_p) shows that $p$ holds for the convenient computations and is not completed here. The other obligation (one_swap_equiv_preserves_p) is easily discharged by invoking a theorem from the theory final_state_properties.

## 5   Example 2: Using the layered measure

Our second example (also available at the Web page) is a typical representative of the pipelined processing paradigm. In our example, all computations are equivalent to those that execute "one wave at a time," i.e., in which a new input is entered only when all the operations related to the previous inputs have been finished. The program is a pipelined insertion-sort algorithm in which the buffers between the processors can hold a single value. We assume that each processor does its local actions atomically: taking its input, comparing it with the value it holds, and sending the maximum between them to the next processor in the pipeline. To understand why it is complicated to prove that the algorithm correctly sorts the inserted values without the convenient computations approach, consider a general computation. In a typical state, the $k$ first processors already have a value, and some of them have a nonempty incoming buffer. There could be several such processors whose successor has room in its buffer, so many different operations would be enabled in such a state. To verify the sorting algorithm we need a general invariant, much harder to find than the one needed if we only have to consider convenient computations in which there is at most one possible continuation at a time.

The example is described in the theory pipeline_sort, parametric on the type of the values being sorted, their total-ordering relation, the number of input values (and of processors) NUM, and an array from 0 to NUM-1 holding those values.

The processors' indices range from 1 up to NUM. Since we choose to use the layers approach, we augment the state variables and next-state functions to allow defining the layer value of each computation step. The system state includes a counter of the number of inputs already inserted, and an array of processor states. Each such processor state includes a locally held value, an input buffer, and an integer (`input_layer`) that holds the *layer* associated with that input. This number is taken from the global counter when inputting a new value into the first processor in the pipeline, and is copied to the next processor when a value is propagated forward, regardless of the result of the comparison between the input and the locally held value.

The layer value of an "input-new-value" operation is the value of the global input counter. For a normal computation step by any processor, the layer value is the `input_layer` stored in that processor's state. Since it originated from the global counter's value when the layer began, this value ranges from 0 up to `NUM-1`. The idling operation, enabled only at the end of the whole computation, has a layer value `NUM`.

The initial states, enabling conditions and next-state-functions are coded in a straightforward way. In this case, we imposed no added restrictions when describing the `relevant?` computations.

The independence relation is defined as TRUE only between operations done by non-adjacent processors (and for two idling steps). This simplified relation is much easier to use during the proofs than the functional independence relation.

These are the (nontrivial) proof obligations generated after instantiating all the needed infrastructural theories with the above mentioned definitions:

- The user's independence relation implies functional independence and is symmetric. Proving this requires only local reasoning.
- Each layer eventually ends. To prove this we used sublemmas that show eventual progress by simple induction.
- The layering function is consistent for one-swap-equivalent computations. This is easily proven because the `layer` function's definition is local.
- Consecutive events whose layer values are not in ascending order can be swapped. To prove this, we show that any two such events can only involve non-contiguous processors, whose operations are independent by definition.

To prove computation equivalence using the theorem from `conv_comps`, we need to prove that each nonconvenient computation is equivalent to one with a smaller measure. Using the theorem from the `layered_measure` theory, we only need to prove that in each non-convenient computation there is an event $a$ that precedes an event $b$ where $b$'s layer value is strictly smaller than $a$'s. To prove this we show that the layer value of an input operation is bigger than that of any operation belonging to a processing "wave" that started with a previous input.

Note that none of the proof obligations involve the specification (sorting is not mentioned, the values sorted are not relevant) and all are local or structural in nature. Since the layer measure is appropriate to the structure of the system, any difficulty in the proofs is technical, not conceptual.

## Acknowledgment

This research was supported by the Bar-Nir Bergreen Software Technology Center of Excellence at the Technion.

# References

1. K. Apt and E. R. Olderog. *Verification of Sequential and Concurrent Programs.* Springer-Verlag, 1991.
2. K. R. Apt, N. Francez, and S. Katz. Appraising fairness in languages for distributed programming. *Distributed Computing,* 2:226–241, 1988.
3. K.M. Chandy and L. Lamport. Distributed snapshots: determining global states of distributed systems. *ACM Trans. on Computer Systems,* 3(1):63–75, Feb 1985.
4. C. Chou and E. Gafni. Understanding and verifying distributed algorithms using stratified decomposition. In *Proceedings of 7th ACM PODC,* pages 44–65, 1988.
5. T. Elrad and N. Francez. Decompositions of distributed programs into communication closed layers. *Science of Computer Programming,* 2(3):155–173, 1982.
6. N. Francez. *Fairness.* Springer-Verlag, 1986.
7. P. Godefroid. On the costs and benefits of using partial-order methods for the verification of concurrent systems. In D. Peled, V. Pratt, and G. Holzmann, editors, *Partial Order Methods in Verification,* pages 289–303. American Mathematical Society, 1997. DIMACS Series in Discrete Mathematics and Theoretical Computer Science, vol. 29.
8. S. Katz. Refinement with global equivalence proofs in temporal logic. In D. Peled, V. Pratt, and G. Holzmann, editors, *Partial Order Methods in Verification,* pages 59–78. American Mathematical Society, 1997. DIMACS Series in Discrete Mathematics and Theoretical Computer Science, vol. 29.
9. S. Katz and D. Peled. Interleaving set temporal logic. *Theoretical Computer Science,* 75:263–287, 1990. Preliminary version was in the 6th ACM-PODC, 1987.
10. S. Katz and D. Peled. Defining conditional independence using collapses. *Theoretical Computer Science,* 101:337–359, 1992.
11. S. Katz and D. Peled. Verification of distributed programs using representative interleaving sequences. *Distributed Computing,* 6:107–120, 1992.
12. S. Owre, N. Shankar, J. M. Rushby, and D. W. J. Stringer-Calvert. *PVS Language Reference.* Computer Science Lab, SRI International, Menlo Park, CA, 1998.
13. Sam Owre, John Rushby, Natarajan Shankar, and Friedrich von Henke. Formal verification for fault-tolerant architectures: Prolegomena to the design of PVS. *IEEE Transactions on Software Engineering,* 21(2):107–125, February 1995.
14. D. Peled. Combining partial order reductions with on-the-fly model checking. *Journal of Formal Methods in System Design,* 8:39–64, 1996.
15. D. Peled and A. Pnueli. Proving partial order properties. *Theoretical Computer Science,* 126:143–182, 1994.
16. D. Peled, V. Pratt, and G. Holzmann(eds.). *Partial Order Methods in Verification.* American Mathematical Society, 1997. DIMACS Series in Discrete Mathematics and Theoretical Computer Science, vol. 29.
17. John Rushby, Sam Owre, and N. Shankar. Subtypes for specifications: Predicate subtyping in PVS. *IEEE Transactions on Software Engineering,* 24(9):709–720, September 1998.
18. P. Wolper and P. Godefroid. Partial-order methods for temporal verification. In *Proceedings of CONCUR'93 (Eike Best, ed.), LNCS 715,* 1993.

# Linking Theorem Proving and Model-Checking with Well-Founded Bisimulation *

Panagiotis Manolios[1], Kedar Namjoshi[2], and Robert Sumners[3]

[1] Department of Computer Sciences, University of Texas at Austin
pete@cs.utexas.edu
[2] Bell Laboratories, Lucent Technologies
kedar@research.bell-labs.com
[3] Department of Electrical and Computer Engineering
University of Texas at Austin
sumners@cerc.utexas.edu

**Abstract.** We present an approach to verification that combines the strengths of model-checking and theorem proving. We use theorem proving to show a bisimulation up to stuttering on a—potentially infinite-state—system. Our characterization of stuttering bisimulation allows us to do such proofs by reasoning only about single steps of the system. We present an on-the-fly method that extracts the reachable quotient structure induced by the bisimulation, if the structure is finite. If our specification is a temporal logic formula, we model-check the quotient structure. If our specification is a simpler system, we use an equivalence checker to show that the quotient structure is stuttering bisimilar to the simpler system. The results obtained on the quotient structure lift to the original system, because the quotient, by construction, is refined by the original system.
We demonstrate our methodology by verifying the alternating bit protocol. This protocol cannot be directly model-checked because it has an infinite-state space; however, using the theorem prover ACL2, we show that the protocol is stuttering bisimilar to a small finite-state system, which we model-check. We also show that the alternating bit protocol is a refinement of a non-lossy system.

## 1 Introduction

We propose an approach to verification that combines the strengths of the model-checking [CE81,QS82,CES86] and the automated theorem proving (*e.g.*, [BM79,GM93]) approaches. We use a theorem prover to reduce an infinite-state (or large finite-state) system to a finite-state system, which we then handle using automatic methods.

The reduction amounts to proving a stuttering bisimulation [BCG88] that preserves properties of interest. Two states are stuttering bisimilar if they are equivalent up to next-time free $CTL^*$ properties ($CTL^* \backslash X$). $CTL^* \backslash X$ can be used to state most properties of asynchronous systems (including fairness) and many timing-independent properties of synchronous hardware. Bisimulation—the usual notion of branching-time equivalence—is not appropriate when comparing systems at different levels of abstraction because a single step of the abstract system may correspond to many steps of the concrete system. Weak bisimulation [Mil90] allows such comparisons, but does not preserve $CTL^* \backslash X$ properties.

* Manolios's research was supported in part by the Admiral B.R. Inman Centennial Chair in Computing Theory. Namjoshi's research was supported in part by NSF Grant CCR-9415496 and SRC Grant 97-DP-388. Sumners's research was supported in part by an AMD/SRC fellowship.

We introduce well-founded equivalence bisimulation (WEB), a characterization of stuttering bisimulation that is based on well-founded bisimulation [Nam97]. A proof that a relation is a WEB involves checking that each action of the program preserves the relation. Such single step proofs can be checked by theorem provers more readily than proofs based on the original definition of stuttering bisimulation.

A WEB induces a quotient structure that is equivalent (up to stuttering) with the original system. The idea is to check the quotient structure, but constructing the quotient structure can be difficult because determining if there is a transition between states in the quotient structure depends on whether there is a transition between some pair of related states in the original system (the number of such pairs may be infinite). Moreover, the quotient structure may be infinite-state, but the set of its reachable states may be finite. To address these two concerns, we introduce an on-the-fly algorithm that for a large class of systems automatically extracts the quotient structure. Once the quotient structure is extracted, we can model-check it or we can use a WEB equivalence checker to compare it with another system.

We are interested in *mechanical verification*; by this we mean that every step in the proof of correctness (except for meta-theory and mechanical tools) is checked mechanically. The theorem prover we use is ACL2 [KM97]. ACL2 is an extended version of the Boyer-Moore theorem prover [BM79]. ACL2 is based on a first-order, executable logic of total recursive functions with induction. We have implemented a $\mu$-calculus model checker with Büchi automata, a WEB equivalence checker, and the quotient extraction algorithm in ACL2; this allows us to perform all of the verification in ACL2 (this is possible because ACL2 is executable). The ACL2 files used are available upon request from the first author.

We demonstrate our approach by verifying the alternating bit protocol [BSW69]. We chose the alternating bit protocol because it has been used as a benchmark for verification efforts, and since this is the first paper to use WEBs for verifying systems, it makes sense to compare our results with existing work. The alternating bit protocol has a simple description but lengthy hand proofs of correctness (*e.g.*, [BG94]), it is infinite-state, and its specification involves a complex fairness property. We have found it to be surprisingly difficult to verify mechanically; many previous papers verify various versions of the protocol (*e.g.*, [Mil90,CE81,HS96,BG96,MN95]), but all make simplifying assumptions, either by restricting channels to be bounded buffers, by ignoring data, or by ignoring fairness issues.

In the next section, we discuss notation and present the theoretical background, including the definitions of WEB, quotient structure, and refinement; related theorems are also presented. Due to space limitations, proofs of the theorems are omitted; they will appear in a future paper. We assume that the reader is familiar with the temporal logic $CTL^*$ [EH86]. In Section 3, we present the ACL2 formalization of the alternating bit protocol. In Section 4, we present the proof of correctness and in Section 5, we present concluding remarks and comparisons to other work.

## 2  Theoretical Background

### 2.1  Preliminaries

IN denotes the natural numbers, *i.e.*, $\{0, 1, \ldots\}$. Function application is denoted by an infix dot "." and is right associative. $\langle Qx : r : b \rangle$ denotes a quantified expression, where $Q$ is the quantifier, $x$ the dummy, $r$ the range of $x$ (true if omitted), and $b$ the body. "Such that" and "with respect to" are abbreviated by "s.t." and "w.r.t.", respectively. The cardinality of a set $S$ is denoted by $|S|$. For a relation $R$, we write $sRw$ instead of $\langle s, w \rangle \in R$. We write $R(S)$ for the image of $S$ under $R$, *i.e.*, $R(S) = \{y : \langle \exists x : x \in S : xRy \rangle\}$ and $R|_A$ for $R$ left-restricted to the set $A$, i.e., $R|_A = \{\langle a, b \rangle : (aRb) \;\land\; (a \in A)\}$. A *well-founded structure* is a pair $\langle W, \prec \rangle$ where $W$ is a set and $\prec$ is a binary relation on $W$ s.t. there are no infinitely decreasing sequences on $W$ w.r.t. $\prec$. We abbreviate $((s \prec w) \;\lor\; (s = w))$ by $s \preccurlyeq w$. From highest to lowest binding power, we have: parentheses, function application, binary relations (*e.g.*, $sBw$), equality ($=$) and membership ($\in$), conjunction ($\land$) and disjunction ($\lor$), implication ($\Rightarrow$), and finally, binary equivalence ($\equiv$). Spacing is used to reinforce binding: more space indicates lower binding.

**Definition 1** *(Transition System)*
A Transition System (TS) is a structure $\langle S, \dashrightarrow, L, I, AP \rangle$, where $S$ is a non-empty set of states, $\dashrightarrow \;\subseteq S \times S$ is the *transition relation* (which must be left total), $AP$ is the set of *atomic propositions*, $L : S \to 2^{AP}$ is the *labeling function* which maps each state to the subset of atomic propositions that hold at that state, and $I$ is the (non-empty) set of *initial states*. We only consider transition systems with countable branching.

**Definition 2** *(Well-Founded Equivalence Bisimulation (WEB))*
$B$ is a well-founded equivalence bisimulation on TS $M = \langle S, \dashrightarrow, L, I, AP \rangle$ iff:

1. $B$ is an equivalence relation on $S$; and
2. $\langle \forall s, w \in S : sBw : L.s = L.w \rangle$; and
3. There exists a function, $rank : S \times S \to W$, s.t. $\langle W, \prec \rangle$ is well-founded, and
$\langle \forall s, u, w \in S : sBw \;\land\; s \dashrightarrow u :$
$\qquad (\exists v : w \dashrightarrow v : uBv) \quad\lor$
$\qquad (uBw \;\land\; rank.(u, u) \prec rank.(s, s)) \quad\lor$
$\qquad (\exists v : w \dashrightarrow v : sBv \;\land\; rank.(u, v) \prec rank.(u, w)) \rangle$

We will call a pair $\langle rank, \langle W, \prec \rangle \rangle$ satisfying condition 3 in the above definition, a *well-founded witness*. Note that to prove a relation is a WEB, reasoning about single steps of $\dashrightarrow$ suffices, whereas, to prove a stuttering bisimulation, one has to reason about infinite paths (the definition of stuttering bisimulation [BCG88] is essentially the same as the above definition except for 3, which states that for any $s, w$ s.t. $sBw$, any infinite path from $s$ can be "matched" by an infinite path from $w$.). It is much simpler to use a theorem prover to reason about single steps of $\dashrightarrow$ than it is to reason about infinite paths; this is the motivation for the above definition.

**Theorem 1** (cf. [BCG88,Nam97]) *If $B$ is a WEB on TS $M$ and $sBw$, then for any $CTL^* \backslash X$ formula $f$, $M, s \models f$ iff $M, w \models f$.*

For an equivalence relation $B$ on TS $M$, a *quotient structure* $M/B$ (read $M$ "mod" $B$) can be defined, whose states are the equivalence classes of $B$ and whose transition relation is derived from the transition relation of $M$. Quotient structures can be much smaller than the original: an equivalence relation with finitely many classes induces a finite quotient structure (of a possibly infinite-state system).

**Definition 3** *(Quotient Structure)*
Let $M = \langle S, \dashrightarrow, L, I, AP \rangle$ be a TS and let $B$ be a WEB on $M$. The class of state $s$ is denoted by $[s]$. The quotient structure $M/B$ is the TS $\langle \mathcal{S}, \rightsquigarrow, \mathcal{L}, \mathcal{I}, AP \rangle$, where:

1. $\mathcal{S} = \{[s] \;:\; s \in S\}$; and
2. $\mathcal{L}.C = L.s$, for some $s$ in $C$ (equivalent states have the same label); and
3. $\mathcal{I} = \{[s] \;:\; s \in I\}$; and
4. The transition relation is given by: For $C, D \in \mathcal{S}$, $C \rightsquigarrow D$ iff either

(a) $C \neq D$ and $\langle \exists s, w : s \in C \wedge w \in D : s \dashrightarrow w \rangle$, or

(b) $C = D$ and $\langle \forall s : s \in C : \langle \exists w : w \in C : s \dashrightarrow w \rangle \rangle$

(The case distinction is needed to prevent spurious self loops in the quotient structure, arising from stuttering steps in the original structure.)

**Theorem 2** (cf. [Nam97]) *If $B$ is a WEB on TS $M$, then there is a WEB on the union of $M$ and $M/B$ that relates states from $M$ with their equivalence classes.*

**Corollary 1** *For any $CTL^*\backslash X$ formula $f$, $M, s \models f$ iff $M/B, [s] \models f$.*

## 2.2 Quotient Extraction

We define a class of functions which we call "representative" functions. As we will see, representative functions allow us to extract finite quotient structures automatically.

**Definition 4** *(Representative Function)*
Let $M = \langle S, \dashrightarrow, L, I, AP \rangle$ be a TS and let $B$ be a WEB on $M$, with well-founded witness $\langle rank, \langle W, \prec \rangle \rangle$. Let $rep : S \to S$; then $rep$ is a representative function for $M$ w.r.t. $B$ if for all $s, w \in S$:

1. $sBw \equiv rep.s = rep.w$; and
2. $rep.rep.s = rep.s$; and
3. $rank.(w, rep.s) \preccurlyeq rank.(w, s)$; and
4. $rank.(rep.s, rep.s) \preccurlyeq rank.(s, s)$

**Theorem 3** *Let $rep$ be a representative function for TS $M = \langle S, \dashrightarrow, L, I, AP \rangle$ w.r.t. WEB $B$. Let $S' = rep(S)$, and let $M' = \langle S', \rightrightarrows, L|_{S'}, rep(I), AP \rangle$, where $s \rightrightarrows u$ iff $\langle \exists v : s \dashrightarrow v : rep.v = u \rangle$. Then $M'$ is $M/B$, up to a renaming of states.*

Representative functions are very useful (when they exist) because they identify states that have all of the branching behavior of their class. They allow one to view the quotient structure as a submodel of the original structure, and they are used in the following on-the-fly algorithm for constructing quotient structures.

**Algorithm 1** *Quotient Construction*
Given a representative function, $rep$, for $M = \langle S, \dashrightarrow, L, I, AP \rangle$ w.r.t. $B$, one can construct the reachable quotient structure induced by $B$ if $rep(I)$ is finite and computable, and if for all $s \in S$, $rep(\dashrightarrow (s))$ is finite and computable. We start by mapping $I$ to $rep(I)$ and then explore the state space, e.g., by a breadth first traversal. Given a state, $s$, in the induced quotient structure (recall that $s$ is also a state in the original structure), we compute the set $rep(\dashrightarrow (s))$, which is the set of next states of $s$ in the quotient structure. This process is repeated until no new states are generated. If the set of reachable quotient structure states is finite, the process will terminate.

## 2.3 Refinement

In this section, $M = \langle S, \dashrightarrow, L, I, AP \rangle$ and $M' = \langle S', \dashrightarrow', L', I', AP' \rangle$. $M$ and $M'$ are *isomorphic* if there is a bijection $f : S \to S'$ s.t. $s \dashrightarrow w$ iff $f.s \dashrightarrow' f.w$, and $f(I) = I'$. $M$ and $M'$ are *$\beta$-isomorphic* if they are isomorphic, $\beta$ is a subset of both $AP$ and $AP'$, and $L$ and $L'$ agree when restricted to $\beta$, i.e., for any $p \in \beta, p \in L.s$ iff $p \in L'.f.s$ for all $s$. We say $M$ and $M'$ are WEB if $AP = AP'$ and there are WEBs on $M$ and $M'$ s.t. the quotient structures induced are $AP$-isomorphic. $M$ and $M'$ are *$\beta$-WEB* if $\beta$ is a subset of both $AP$ and $AP'$ and the structures obtained from $M$ and $M'$ by restricting $L$ and $L'$ to $\beta$ are WEB. If $M$ and $M'$ are $AP'$-WEB, then we say that $M$ is a *refinement* of $M'$.

**Theorem 4** *(Refinement)*

1. *If $M$ is a refinement of $M'$, then any $CTL^*\backslash X$ formula that holds in $M'$ holds in $M$.*
2. *If $M$ and $M''$ are $\beta$-isomorphic, $M''$ is a refinement of $M'$, and $AP'$ is a subset of $\beta$, $M$ is a refinement of $M'$.*

Note that the converse of the first part of the theorem does not hold because $AP$ may be a proper superset of $AP'$. Refinement in a branching-time framework corresponds to refining atomicity in such a way that when the variables introduced for the refinement are hidden, the resulting system and the original system are WEB. Refinement depends crucially on stuttering [Lam80] because we are comparing systems at differing levels of abstraction and any reasonable correctness condition will not make assumptions about how long it takes for something to happen, *i.e.*, the condition should be stuttering insensitive (*i.e.*, the condition will not use $X$, the next-time temporal operator).

## 3  Protocol

The alternating bit protocol is used to implement reliable communication over faulty channels. We present the protocol from the view of the sender and receiver first and then in complete detail. The sender interacts with the communication system via the register *smsg* and the flag *svalid*. The sender can assign a message to *smsg* provided it is invalid, *i.e.*, *svalid* is false. The receiver interacts with the communication system via the register *rmsg* and the flag *rvalid*. The receiver can read *rmsg* provided it is valid, *i.e.*, *rvalid* is

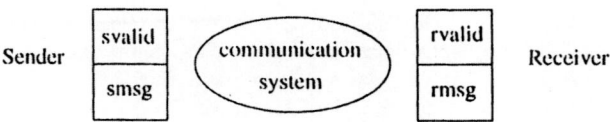

**Fig. 1.** Protocol from sender's and receiver's view

not false; when read, *rmsg* is invalidated. Figure 1 depicts the protocol from this point of view.

The communication system consists of the flags *sflag* and *rflag* as well as the two lossy, unbounded, and FIFO channels *s2r* and *r2s*. The idea behind the protocol is that the contents of *smsg* are sent across *s2r* until an acknowledgment for the message is received on *r2s*, at which point a new message can be transmitted. Similarly, acknowledgments for a received message are sent across *r2s* until a new message is received. In order for the receiving end to distinguish between copies of the same message and copies of different messages, each message is tagged with *sflag* before being placed on *s2r*. When a new message is received, *rflag* is assigned the value of the message tag and gets sent across *r2s*; this also allows the sending end to distinguish acknowledgments. There may be an arbitrary number of copies of a message (or an acknowledgment) on the channels, and it turns out that there are at most two distinct messages (or acknowledgments) on the channels, hence binary flags suffice. Figure 2 depicts the protocol.

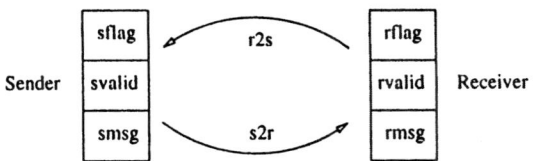

**Fig. 2.** Alternating Bit Protocol

The above discussion is informal; a formal description follows, but first we discuss notation. We have formalized the protocol and its proof in ACL2, however, for presentation purposes we describe the formalization using standard notation. We remain faithful to the ACL2 formalization, *e.g.*, we do not use types: functions that appear typed are really under-specified, but total. The concatenation operator on sequences is denoted by ":", but sometimes we use juxtaposition; "$\epsilon$" denotes the empty sequence; *head.s* is the first element of sequence *s*; *tail.s* is the sequence resulting from removing the first element from *s*; $|s|$ is the size of the sequence. Messages are pairs; *info* returns the first component of a message and *flag* returns the second.

A state is an eight-tuple $\langle sflag, svalid, smsg, s2r, r2s, rflag, rvalid, rmsg \rangle$; *state* is a predicate that recognizes states. The *sflag* of state $s$ is denoted *sflag.s* and similarly for the other fields. Rules are functions from states into states; they are listed in Table 1 and are of the form $G \to A$; if $A$ is used as a rule, it abbreviates true $\to A$. Rule $G \to A$ defines the function ($\lambda s$ : $\underline{\text{if}}\ G.s\ \underline{\text{then}}\ A.s\ \underline{\text{else}}\ s$). We now define the transition relation, $R$ (corresponding to $\dashrightarrow$ in the previous section): $sRw$ iff $s$ is a state and $w$ can be obtained by applying some rule to $s$.

We have defined the states and transition relation of the alternating bit protocol. The states are labeled with an eight-tuple, as mentioned above. It should be clear that we can convert this type of labeling into a labeling over atomic propositions (boolean variables) by introducing enough—in this case an infinite number of—atomic propositions, therefore, the alternating bit protocol defines a TS, *ABP*.

| Rule | Definition |
|---|---|
| Skip | skip |
| Accept.m | $\neg svalid \to smsg, svalid := m, \text{true}$ |
| Send-msg | $svalid \to s2r := s2r : \langle smsg, sflag \rangle$ |
| Drop-msg | $s2r \neq \epsilon \to s2r := tail.s2r$ |
| Get-msg | $s2r \neq \epsilon \wedge \neg rvalid \to$ |
|  | $\underline{\text{if}}\ flag.head.s2r = rflag$ |
|  | $\quad\underline{\text{then}}\ s2r := tail.s2r$ |
|  | $\quad\underline{\text{else}}\ s2r, rmsg, rvalid, rflag := tail.s2r, info.head.s2r, \text{true}, flag.head.s2r$ |
| Send-ack | $r2s := r2s : rflag$ |
| Drop-ack | $r2s \neq \epsilon \to r2s := tail.r2s$ |
| Get-ack | $r2s \neq \epsilon \to$ |
|  | $\underline{\text{if}}\ head.r2s = sflag$ |
|  | $\quad\underline{\text{then}}\ r2s, svalid, sflag := tail.r2s, \text{false}, \neg sflag$ |
|  | $\quad\underline{\text{else}}\ r2s := tail.r2s$ |
| Reply | $rvalid := \text{false}$ |

**Table 1.** Rules defining the transition relation

# 4 Protocol Verification

We give an overview of the verification of the alternating bit protocol. $ABP''$ is the alternating bit protocol, with some variables distorted. Let $\beta$ be the set of variables that are not distorted; then $ABP$ and $ABP''$ are $\beta$-isomorphic. We define a relation $B$ and prove that $B$ is a WEB on $ABP''$. We define $rep$, a representative function on $ABP''$ w.r.t. $B$. We use our extraction procedure to extract the structure defined by $rep$. $ABP'$ is this structure, restricted to $\beta$. We model-check $ABP'$; by Theorem 4, $ABP$ is a refinement of $ABP'$ and any $CTL^*\backslash X$ formulae that hold on $ABP'$ also hold on $ABP$.

We also show that $ABP'$ is WEB to a non-lossy protocol; in many cases such a check is more convincing than model-checking because it shows that one system is a refinement of another.

## 4.1 Well-Founded Equivalence Bisimulation

In this subsection we define a relation $B$ and outline the ACL2 proof that $B$ is a WEB. We start with some definitions.

For the following definitions, $a$ and $b$ are sequences of length 1, $a \neq b$, and $x$ is an arbitrary finite sequence. The function $compress$ acts on sequences to remove adjacent duplicates. Formally,

$$compress.\epsilon = \epsilon \qquad\qquad\qquad compress.a = a$$
$$compress.aax = compress.ax \qquad compress.abx = a : compress.bx$$

The predicate $good\text{-}s2r$ recognizes sequences that define valid channel contents. Formally,

$$good\text{-}s2r.\epsilon = \text{true} \qquad good\text{-}s2r.ax = (a = \langle info.a, flag.a\rangle) \wedge good\text{-}s2r.x$$

The function $s2r\text{-}state$ compresses the $s2r$ field of a state, except that already received messages at the head of $s2r$ are ignored. Formally,

$$s2r\text{-}state.s = compress.relevant\text{-}s2r.(s2r.s, \langle rmsg.s, rflag.s\rangle)$$

where the function $relevant\text{-}s2r$ is defined by:

$$relevant\text{-}s2r.(\epsilon, a) = \epsilon \qquad\qquad relevant\text{-}s2r.(bx, a) = bx$$
$$relevant\text{-}s2r.(ax, a) = relevant\text{-}s2r.(x, a)$$

The function $r2s\text{-}state$ compresses the $r2s$ field of a state, except that acknowledgements at the head of $r2s$ with a flag different from $sflag$ are ignored. Formally,

$$r2s\text{-}state.s = compress.relevant\text{-}r2s.(r2s.s, sflag.s)$$

where the function $relevant\text{-}r2s$ is defined by:

$$relevant\text{-}r2s.(\epsilon, a) = \epsilon \qquad\qquad relevant\text{-}r2s.(ax, a) = ax$$
$$relevant\text{-}r2s.(bx, a) = relevant\text{-}r2s.(x, a)$$

The main idea behind the bisimulation is to relate states that have similar compressed channels—i.e., are equivalent under $s2r\text{-}state$ and $r2s\text{-}state$—and are otherwise identical. We define the bisimulation in terms of rule

$$rep: \quad good\text{-}s2r.s2r \quad\rightarrow\quad s2r, r2s := s2r\text{-}state, r2s\text{-}state$$

We now define our proposed WEB $B$: $sBu$  iff  $rep.s = rep.u$. It is easy to see that $B$ is an equivalence relation that, except for $s2r$ and $r2s$, preserves the labeling of states. We define $rank$, a function on states as follows: $rank.s = |s2r.s| + |r2s.s|$.

We will show that $\langle rank, \langle \mathbb{N}, < \rangle \rangle$ is a well-founded witness (to be pedantic we can define $rank$ so that it has two arguments, as follows: $rank.(u, s) = |s2r.s| + |r2s.s|$) Note that if $sBw$, $sRu$, and $sBu$, then $uBw$ and by rule $Skip$, $wRw$, therefore, we need only concern ourselves with the case where $\neg sBu$. To show $B$ is a WEB, it suffices to show:

$$sBw \wedge sRu \wedge \neg sBu \;\Rightarrow\; \langle \exists v : wRv : uBv \vee (sBv \wedge rank.v < rank.w) \rangle$$

We break up the proof (that $B$ is a WEB) into the eight cases in Table 2 by expanding $R$, i.e., by considering all the ways in which $s$ can be related to $u$. The cases have the

| Rule | Lemma |
|------|-------|
| $Accept.m$ | $sBw \;\Rightarrow\; uBv$ |
| $Send\text{-}msg$ | $sBw \wedge \neg sBu \;\Rightarrow\; uBv$ |
| $Drop\text{-}msg$ | $sBw \wedge \neg sBu \;\Rightarrow\; (uBv) \vee (sBv \wedge rank.v < rank.w)$ |
| $Get\text{-}msg$ | $sBw \wedge \neg sBu \wedge u \neq Drop\text{-}msg.s \;\Rightarrow\; (uBv) \vee (sBv \wedge rank.v < rank.w)$ |
| $Send\text{-}ack$ | $sBw \wedge \neg sBu \;\Rightarrow\; uBv$ |
| $Drop\text{-}ack$ | $sBw \wedge \neg sBu \;\Rightarrow\; (uBv) \vee (sBv \wedge rank.v < rank.w)$ |
| $Get\text{-}ack$ | $sBw \wedge \neg sBu \wedge u \neq Drop\text{-}ack.s \;\Rightarrow\; (uBv) \vee (sBv \wedge rank.v < rank.w)$ |
| $Reply$ | $sBw \;\Rightarrow\; uBv$ |

**Table 2.** WEB case analysis

form: Rule Lemma; when $u$ or $v$ appear in Lemma they abbreviate the terms Rule.$s$ and Rule.$w$, respectively. We prove the cases in ACL2.

In order to tie up the case analysis, we define a function $step$ that takes three states, $s, u$, and $w$, as arguments. If $sBu$, $step$ returns $w$, else if $u = A.s$, for $A$, a rule from Table 1, $step$ returns $A.w$, else $step$ returns $w$. Since we proved that $B$ is an equivalence relation, the following theorem implies that $B$ is a WEB (existential quantification is replaced by the witness function $step$):

$$sBw \wedge sRu \wedge v = step.(s, u, w) \;\Rightarrow\; wRv \wedge (uBv \vee (sBv \wedge rank.v < rank.w))$$

## 4.2  Quotient Extraction

In this subsection we prove the following ACL2 theorems which show that $rep$ is a representative function satisfying the requirements of Theorem 3; hence, the quotient structure induced by $rep$ is isomorphic to the quotient structure w.r.t. $B$: $sBw \equiv rep.s = rep.w$, $rep.rep.s = rep.s$, and $rank.rep.s \leq rank.s$. We extract the quotient structure (induced by $rep$) of the alternating bit protocol restricted to binary messages. In the following subsections, we describe the use of model-checking and WEB equivalence checking to analyze this structure.

We now have enough machinery to describe how refinement is used in the verification of the alternating bit protocol. $ABP$ is the model of the alternating bit protocol in ACL2. $ABP''$ is $ABP$ with $s2r$, $r2s$ relabeled by $s2r\text{-}state$ and $r2s\text{-}state$, respectively. $B$ is a bisimulation on $ABP''$ with well-founded witness $\langle rank, \langle \mathbb{N}, < \rangle \rangle$, s.t. $rank.(u, s) = |s2r.f^{-1}.s| + |r2s.f^{-1}.s|$ ($f$ is the bijection between $ABP$ and $ABP''$; recall that $rank$ is defined on states of $ABP''$). The quotient structure of $ABP''$ w.r.t. $B$ is isomorphic to the structure induced by $rep$. $ABP'$ is this structure, with $s2r$ and $r2s$

hidden. It is $ABP'$ that we analyze in the next two subsections. By Theorem 4, $ABP$ is a refinement of $ABP'$ and properties of $ABP'$ can be lifted to $ABP$.

## 4.3  Model-Checking

We model-check the quotient structure extracted by the above mentioned procedure, using a $\mu$-calculus model-checker and a fair-$CTL$ to $\mu$-calculus translator, both written in ACL2. We check the following formulae (written in $CTL^*\backslash X$):

1. $AG(sending1 \Rightarrow A(sending1\ W\ rmsg = 1))$
2. $AG(receiving1 \Rightarrow A(receiving1\ W\ delivered1))$
3. $AGEF svalid$ (acceptance of a new message is always eventually possible)

where *sending1*, *receiving1*, and *delivered1* are abbreviations for *svalid* $\wedge$ *smsg* $= 1$, *rvalid* $\wedge$ *rmsg* $= 1$, and $\neg rvalid$ $\wedge$ *rmsg* $= 1$, respectively; formulae analogous to 1 and 2 are proved for message 0. All of the above formulae hold on the extracted structure, which is what one would expect. The property $AGAF svalid$ (acceptance of a new message is always eventually guaranteed), however, does not hold without further fairness assumptions.

The liveness properties are as follows. Each property is shown under a set of fairness assumptions on the actions of the process. These are either weak fairness (infinitely often disabled or infinitely often executed) or strong fairness (infinitely often enabled implies infinitely often executed).

1. $AG(sendingNew1 \Rightarrow A(sending1\ U\ rmsg = 1))$ (*sendingNew1* represents the sending of a new copy of message 1): This holds under weak fairness on the Send-msg and Reply actions, and strong fairness on the receipt of a new message by the action Get-msg. A similar property holds for message 0.
2. $AGAF svalid$: This holds under the fairness assumptions for the previous property, along with weak fairness on the Send-ack action and strong fairness on the receipt of a new acknowledgment by the action Get-ack.

Since the fairness conditions mention actions, we compose Büchi automata accepting fair paths with the quotient structure and model-check the resulting structure on fair-$CTL$ formulae which refer both to the propositions of the quotient structure and the accepting states of the automata.

We use an argument based on bisimulation to derive sufficient conditions for data-independence [Wol86] of the protocol. These are verified in ACL2; as a consequence, the properties shown above for the data domain $\{0, 1\}$ suffice to show similar properties for *arbitrary* data domains.

## 4.4  Bisimulation Checking

In many cases, the correctness proof is more convincing if we can show that the extracted model is bisimilar to a model that is so simple, it is correct by inspection. In the case of the alternating bit protocol, we can show that the extracted model is bisimilar to a simple, non-lossy version of the protocol, presented in Table 3.

We use a WEB equivalence checker (based on the description in [BCG88]) written in ACL2 to verify that the non-lossy protocol in Table 3 and the extracted protocol are WEB. The main idea is that we create the disjoint union of the transition systems corresponding to the extracted protocol and the non-lossy protocol. The algorithm will compute the coarsest WEB on a structure; hence, if the initial states of the two systems are in the same class, the two systems are WEB. In computing the coarsest WEB, we examine only *svalid*, *smsg*, *rvalid*, and *rmsg*. Notice that this view is exactly the one presented in Figure 1.

| Rule | Definition |
|------|------------|
| Accept.m | $\neg svalid \rightarrow smsg, svalid := m, \text{true}$ |
| Send-msg | $svalid \wedge \neg rvalid \wedge \neg sent \rightarrow rvalid, sent, rmsg := \text{true}, \text{true}, smsg$ |
| Ready | $sent \rightarrow svalid, sent := \text{false}, \text{false}$ |
| Reply | $rvalid := \text{false}$ |

**Table 3.** Rules defining the transition relation of the non-lossy protocol

## 5 Related Work and Conclusions

Among related work, [MN95] prove safety properties of the alternating bit protocol by using Isabelle/HOL to prove that a manually constructed finite-state system contains all of the traces of the alternating bit protocol and then model-check the finite-state system. [HS96] show the correctness of an infinite-state system by using PVS to verify that a simple manually constructed finite-state system is a conservative approximation of the infinite-state system. The work described in this paper improves upon such methods by (i) using a (verified) representative function to *automatically* construct a quotient structure, and (ii) using WEBs instead of simulations or trace containment: this allows us to check properties *exactly*, *i.e.*, if a property holds (fails) on the simple system, then it holds (fails) on the original system.

There are several known types of infinite-state systems (*e.g.*, [ACD90,GS92,AJ96,EN95]) for which the model-checking problem is decidable, but these types of systems often turn out to be too specialized for many cases where it is possible to devise finite abstractions. There have been several approaches to automatically verifying the alternating bit protocol: safety properties of such lossy channel systems are decidable [AJ96]; however, in order to construct automatic abstractions that demonstrate liveness properties, most other verifications of the alternating bit protocol (*e.g.*, [GS97]) consider channels to be bounded.

Mechanical verification is necessary. In our case, we managed to convince ourselves that a candidate relation was a WEB for the alternating bit protocol, even though it was not; this became clear only when we tried to prove it mechanically.

An interesting direction for future work is to apply the methodology presented here to the verification of other infinite-state systems (*e.g.*, pipelined and out-of-order execution machines and memory coherence protocols).

### Acknowledgments

J Moore was always available to discuss ACL2; he also read and commented on substantial parts of the proof script. Jun Sawada and Richard Trefler were involved in the early stages of the project; along with Rajeev Joshi, they have read this paper and have made many useful suggestions.

### References

[ACD90] R. Alur, C. Courcoubetis, and D. Dill. Model checking for real time systems. In *5th IEEE Symp. on Logic in Computer Science*, 1990.

[AJ96]     P.A. Abdulla and B. Jonsson. Verifying programs with unreliable channels. *Information and Computation*, 127(2), 1996.

[BCG88]    M. Browne, E.M. Clarke, and O. Grumberg. Characterizing finite Kripke structures in propositional temporal logic. *Theoretical Computer Science*, 59, 1988.

[BG94]     M.A. Bezem and J.F. Groote. A correctness proof of a one bit sliding window protocol in mCRL. *The Computer Journal*, 1994.

[BG96]     B. Boigelot and P. Godefroid. Symbolic verification of communication protocols with infinite state spaces using QDD's. In *Conference on Computer Aided Verification*, volume 1102 of *LNCS*, 1996.

[BM79]     R. Boyer and J. Moore. *A Computational Logic*. Kluwer Academic Publishers, 1979.

[BSW69]    K.A. Barlett, R.A. Scantlebury, and P.C. Wilkinson. A note on reliable full duplex transmission over half duplex links. In *Communications of the ACM*, volume 12, 1969.

[CE81]     E.M. Clarke and E. A. Emerson. Design and synthesis of synchronization skeletons using branching time temporal logic. In *Workshop on Logics of Programs*, volume 131 of *LNCS*. Springer-Verlag, 1981.

[CES86]    E.M. Clarke, E.A. Emerson, and A.P. Sistla. Automatic verification of finite-state concurrent systems using temporal logic. *ACM Transactions on Programming Languages and Systems*, 8(2), 1986.

[EH86]     E. A. Emerson and J. Y. Halpern. "Sometimes" and "not never" revisited: on branching versus linear time temporal logic. *JACM*, 33(1):151–178, January 1986.

[EN95]     E.A. Emerson and K.S. Namjoshi. Reasoning about rings. In *ACM Symposium on Principles of Programming Languages*, 1995.

[GM93]     M. J. C. Gordon and T. F. Melham, editors. *Introduction to HOL: A theorem proving environment for higher order logic*. Cambridge University Press, 1993.

[GS92]     S. German and A.P. Sistla. Reasoning about systems with many processes. *Journal of the ACM*, 1992.

[GS97]     S. Graf and H. Saidi. Construction of abstract state graphs with PVS. In *Conference on Computer Aided Verification*, volume 1254 of *LNCS*, 1997.

[HS96]     K. Havelund and N. Shankar. Experiments in theorem proving and model checking for protocol verification. In *Formal Methods Europe (FME)*, volume 1051 of *LNCS*. Springer-Verlag, 1996.

[KM97]     M. Kaufmann and J S. Moore. An industrial strength theorem prover for a logic based on Common Lisp. *IEEE Transactions on Software Engineering*, 23(4):203–213, April 1997.

[Lam80]    L. Lamport. "Sometimes" is sometimes "not never". In *ACM Symposium on Principles of Programming Languages*, 1980.

[Mil90]    R. Milner. *Communication and Concurrency*. Prentice-Hall, 1990.

[MN95]     O. Müller and T. Nipkow. Combining model checking and deduction for I/O-Automata. In *Proceedings of TACAS*, 1995.

[Nam97]    K. S. Namjoshi. A simple characterization of stuttering bisimulation. In *17th Conference on Foundations of Software Technology and Theoretical Computer Science*, volume 1346 of *LNCS*, pages 284–296, 1997.

[QS82]     J.P. Queille and J. Sifakis. Specification and verification of concurrent systems in CESAR. In *Proc. of the 5th International Symposium on Programming*, volume 137 of *LNCS*, 1982.

[Wol86]    P. Wolper. Expressing interesting properties of programs in propositional temporal logic. In *Proceedings of the 13th ACM Symposium on Principles of Programming Languages*, pages 184–193. ACM Press, 1986.

# Automatic Verification of Combinatorial and Pipelined FFT Circuits

Per Bjesse

Chalmers University of Technology, Sweden

bjesse@cs.chalmers.se

**Abstract.** We describe how three hardware components (two combinational and one pipelined) for computing the Fast Fourier Transform have been proved equivalent using an automatic combination of symbolic simulation, rewriting techniques, induction and theorem proving. We also give some advice on how to verify circuits operating on complex data, and present a general purpose proof strategy for equivalence checking between combinational and pipelined circuits.

## 1 Introduction

FFT components are a challenge to verify as they compute complex functions involving many arithmetic operations. Bit-level correctness proofs for such circuits are not within the reach of today's technology; an appropriate level of modelling is therefore on the level of individual arithmetic operations on signals carrying numerical data.

In order to make verification techniques industrially interesting, it is generally agreed that a high degree of automation is desirable. Unfortunately classical automatic methods such as propositional logic tautology checking or model checking can not be immediately applied at this level of abstraction. Different extensions of model checking with uninterpreted functions encoded in BDDs have been proposed [VB98]; we instead use theorem proving, but in such a way that no user guidance is needed during the proofs.

As we aim for verification at the arithmetic level, it is imperative to structure the proofs to be as simple as possible; we therefore devise heuristics for the particular class of circuits we verify and apply automatic analyses that aim to reduce the work that has to be done in the theorem prover. For this end we use the Lava hardware development platform that has a powerful language in which we can implement our analyses and write parametrisable scripts that control complex theorem prover interactions [BCSS98].

The work described is an industrial case study with Ericsson Cadlab, Stockholm.

## 2 The Lava hardware development platform

Lava is a hardware description language and a framework for hardware verification developed at Chalmers and Xilinx [BCSS98]. One of the principal uses of Lava is as a platform for hardware verification experiments.

Lava is embedded in the functional language Haskell; all aspects of the development of hardware from descriptions down to the interfacing to layout tools are expressed in the same language. The use of a polymorphic high level language that supports higher order functions gives very concise hardware descriptions and allows us to devise combinators that capture common design patterns.

The circuit descriptions can be interpreted by symbolic evaluation in a number of different ways; examples of built in standard analyses are circuit simulation, generation of logical formulas in formats suitable for external theorem provers and generation of VHDL. The verification interpretation is parametrised over the proof procedure and allows the passing of optional proof parameters; a user can therefore quickly retarget from one proof procedure to another without losing fine grain control.

## 3  The Fast Fourier Transforms

The Fast Fourier Transforms (FFTs) are efficient algorithms for computing a length $N$ sequence of complex numbers $X$ given an initial sequence $x$ and a constant $W_N$ defined as $e^{-j2\pi/N}$:

$$X(k) = \sum_{n=0}^{N-1} x(n) \cdot W_N^{kn}, \qquad k \in \{0 \dots N{-}1\}$$

The FFTs exploit symmetries in the *twiddle factors* $W_N^k$ together with restrictions of sequence lengths (for example to powers of two) to reduce the number of necessary computations. Examples of twiddle factor laws that express useful symmetries are

$$W_N^0 = 1$$
$$W_N^N = 1$$
$$W_n^k \cdot W_n^m = W_n^{k+m}$$
$$W_n^k = W_{2n}^{2k}, \qquad (n, k \leq N)$$

The FFT algorithms are often implemented in combinational hardware, and are key building blocks in signal processing applications; the FFTs are rumoured to be the worlds most implemented algorithms in hardware.

The reference FFT is the *decimation in time* Radix-2 algorithm, which operates on input sequences whose length is a power of two [PM92]. If the input length also is a power of four, the *decimation in frequency* Radix-$2^2$ FFT can be applied [He95]. From a designer's point of view the question is whether the combinational circuits that implement these algorithms are equivalent. As the networks are fundamentally different, verification of equivalence is a non-trivial undertaking.

Combinational implementations are not the only ones possible; pipelined sequential designs can use less circuit area by trading space for time. A pipelined implementation of a size $2^n$ Radix-$2^2$ FFT (see figure 1) consists of two simple

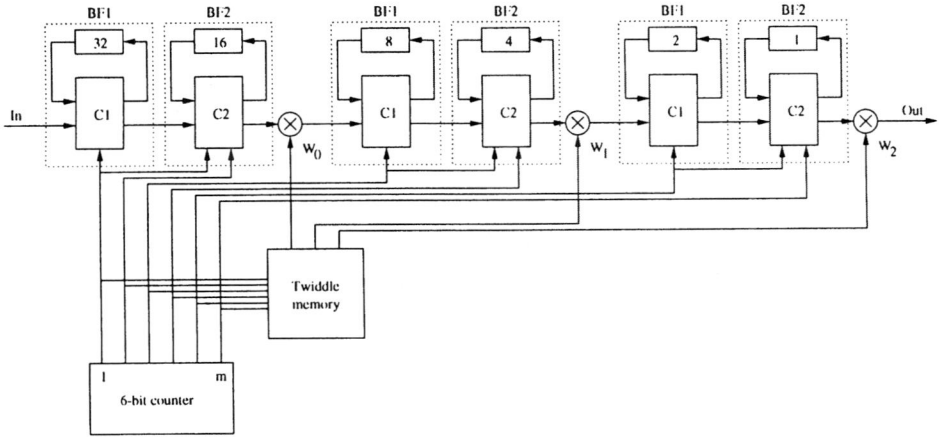

**Fig. 1.** Structure of pipelined implementation of a size 64 Radix-$2^2$ FFT

kinds of combinational components ($C1$ and $C2$) that together form a stage; a whole circuit consists of $n/2$ stages. Each primitive block is controlled by synchronisation signals generated by an $n$-bit counter. This counter also addresses a multi port memory that outputs streams of twiddle factors that are multiplied together with the outputs of each stage.

Figure 2 shows how the pipelined FFT circuit simulates the corresponding combinational circuit over time by reading the inputs in the first sequence of input values $IF(0)$ while spitting out undefined outputs until time $lag$ $(2^n - 1$ for a size $2^n$ FFT) when the first element of the output sequence $OF(0)$ is generated; the lag time is always constant. At the same time as the outputs are produced, inputs from a new input sequence are read so that the circuit continuously processes data.

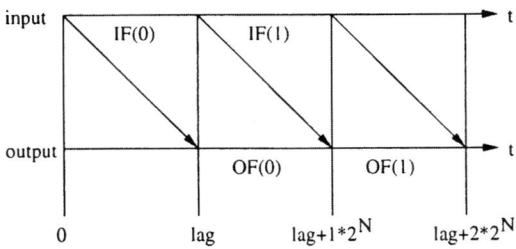

**Fig. 2.** Operation of the pipelined circuit

# 4 FFT low-level descriptions

The FFT descriptions are parameterised by the circuit size and are formulated using a number of simple circuits and combinators that are useful for signal processing applications.

A key point is that the regularity of the combinational networks makes the circuits very easy to describe in Lava; the description of the Radix-2 FFT in terms of the signal processing combinators is just 3 lines long (see appendix A).

The Lava circuit descriptions can be used to automatically generate structural VHDL for all parts of the implementations with the exception of the multi port memory component.

# 5 Verification of components

As we want automatic proofs, we will only be concerned with equivalence checking for fixed size circuits. We will also exploit designer knowledge and use Lava analyses in order to make the proofs tractable for the external proof procedure. The circuits are modelled on the level of operations on infinite precision complex numbers; this modelling is appropriate as finite representations of complex numbers only can be used for approximate calculation of the FFT. A reasonable notion of implementation equivalence must therefore be defined in terms of infinite precision complex arithmetic.

As a shorthand, we adopt the convention that

$$F(x,y) \equiv F(x(0)..x(i-1), y(0)..y(i-1))$$

if $F \in Form$ (the set of first order logic formulas) and $x, y \in S^i$ where $S$ is any non-empty set.

## 5.1 Theoretical basis of the verifications

Combinational circuits can be viewed as functions $f$ from input to output. Lava's symbolic evaluation can generate formulas $\delta_f$ that define the functions we are concerned with in the sense that $T \vdash \delta_f(I, O) \Rightarrow f(I) = O$ if $T$ is a theory containing theorems that are true in a standard interpretation of complex arithmetic.

The formulas that are constructed in the following verifications are expressed in first order logic with equality, and contain variables and two-place function symbols *plus*, *sub*, *tim* and $W$. The circuit equivalence checking problem is reduced to showing that certain formulas that capture implementation equivalence are members of the theory $T$ which we give axioms for. The axioms are well-known properties of complex arithmetic and some twiddle factor identities. We know that the axioms hold in the interpretation $\Im$ that complies with the following conditions

– The domain is the set of complex numbers

- *plus* designates complex addition
- *sub* designates complex subtraction
- *tim* designates complex multiplication
- $W$ designates the function $f_w(k, N) = e^{-j2\pi k/N}$

All formulas that are derivable from the axioms in a sound proof system are therefore also true in $\mathfrak{I}$.

## 5.2 Combinational FFT verification

Are the abstract implementations of the Radix-2 and the Radix-$2^2$ FFT equivalent for sizes that are an exponent of four?

The fixed size FFT circuits are functions $F_1(I)$ and $F_2(I)$ from complex input sequences to complex output sequences. Lava's symbolic evaluation can generate formulas $\delta_1$ and $\delta_2$ that define these functions. Our criterion for equivalence of the combinational FFT is that

$$\delta_1(I, O_1) \wedge \delta_2(I, O_2) \ \rightarrow \ O_1 = O_2$$

Instead of generating the two defining formulas individually and then combining them together to a resulting formula, we can construct a test bench circuit that directly generates the correctness formula when interpreted symbolically:

```
fftSame n =
  do inp <- newCmplxVector (4^n)
     out1 <- radix2 (2*n) inp
     out2 <- radix22 n inp
     equals (out1,out2)
```

The test bench builds a vector of unrestricted complex variables, which are given to both FFT implementations. The resulting output sequences are then pointwise compared to each other for equality. If the formula describing this system is derivable by the theorem prover using the axioms for the theory $T$, then it is true in the model $\mathfrak{I}$ and the implementations are equivalent.

Lava's verification interpretation takes a test bench circuit and a proof procedure with some arguments, and automatically generates formulas and runs the proof. The manual step that has to be taken is to choose a prover and possibly give proof options. In this case, we have to choose a first order logic theorem prover, and specify some axioms. These include some simple algebraic laws for the arithmetic operators, such as distributivity of multiplication over addition and that 1 is a unit element for multiplication. The twiddle factor identities from section 3 are also necessary.

Although these axioms with any first order logic prover are in theory sufficient to prove the circuits equivalent, the number of consequences grows very quickly if the rules are applied mindlessly. This combined with the fact that the FFT circuits generate formulas that for larger sizes grow to be megabytes big means that we must give extra proof options in order to make the proofs tractable. Symbolic evaluation of the FFTs for 4 abstract inputs reveals some interesting circuit properties (the input and output vectors are indexed backwards):

```
Lava> symbolic_eval (radix2 2)
[(x3 - W(2, 0) * x1) - W(4, 1) * (x2 - W(2, 0) * x0),
 (W(2, 0) * x1 + x3) - W(4, 0) * (W(2, 0) * x0 + x2),
 W(4, 1) * (x2 - W(2, 0) * x0) + (x3 - W(2, 0) * x1),
 W(4, 0) * (W(2, 0) * x0 + x2) + (W(2, 0) * x1 + x3)
]

Lava> symbolic_eval (radix22 1)
[W(4, 0) * ((x3 - x1) - W(4, 1) * (x2 - x0)),
 W(4, 0) * ((x1 + x3) - (x0 + x2)),
 W(4, 0) * (W(4, 1) * (x2 - x0) + (x3 - x1)),
 W(4, 0) * ((x0 + x2) + (x1 + x3))
]
```

The lack of control logic in the combinational FFT components causes the circuit outputs to be polynomials in the inputs and twiddle factors only. Rewriting of the expressions by simplifying away twiddle factors that are equal to 0 or 1, conversion of the remaining twiddle factors to the form $W_N^x$ and restructuring of arithmetic expressions to sum of products form makes it possible to show the two results equal by syntactic equality alone.

The rewriting has to be done in a particular way for it to be applicable to the larger circuits. If the axioms are given as standard equalities, they can be used in both directions. This is not how the most efficient proof would proceed, as it suffices to use all the rules in one direction only: expand out the polynomials, take away trivial twiddle factors and rewrite the others.

Unidirectional rules are therefore more suitable for our purposes. The theorem prover Otter has efficient such rules that are called demodulators [MW97]; the use of a demodulation rule can be unconditional or restricted by predicates on terms. An important property of these rules is that they are used as often as possible *without accumulating intermediate results*. This reduces the number of consequences and makes normalisation of large expressions tractable.

The demodulation proof rules are specified inside Lava and passed to Otter as two theories. The actual proofs are done by calling the verification interpretation on the test bench and the proof configuration:

```
options = [Prover otter, Theory arithmetic, Theory (twiddle 4)]

Lava> verify options (fftSame 1)
Valid
```

In this way the equivalence of circuits up to size 256 is proven automatically. Statistics for the resulting proofs and some system formula measures such as the number of primitive logical and arithmetic operations are given in table 1. The running times are measured on a 300 MHz Sun Enterprise 450.

| FFT size | Verification time (s) | Formula size (Bytes) | # of variables | # of formula operations |
|----------|----------------------|----------------------|----------------|-------------------------|
| 4 | 0.09 | 1179 | 33 | 59 |
| 16 | 0.39 | 10 761 | 233 | 433 |
| 64 | 10.31 | 172 088 | 1334 | 2529 |
| 256 | 827 | 2 886 561 | 6939 | 13 313 |

**Table 1.** Statistics for verification of equivalence between combinational FFTs

## 5.3 Pipelined FFT verification

We would now like to verify that the sequential pipelined implementation of the Radix-$2^2$ is equivalent to the combinational circuit. We employ a strategy that is optimised for equivalence checking of combinational and constant delay ("lag") pipelined circuits.

The presentation is divided into two parts: The first part describes the strategy and the second demonstrates how it applies to the particular case of our FFT verification.

**A strategy for pipeline equivalence proofs** If we observe the pipelined circuit for a single clock period, it is a function from a starting state $S$ and input $I$ to a finishing state $S'$ and a resulting output $O$.

$$(O, S') = ppl(I, S)$$

We use the term "frame" to refer to a complete in- or output data sequence for the combinational or pipelined circuit. Lava can generate a defining formula $\delta_{ppl}(I, S, O, S')$ for the $ppl(I, S)$ transition function that captures how the circuit behaves over a single clock tick. The objective is to show equivalence between the two implementations for any number of successive frames starting from a (partially) specified initial state, using the following verification strategy which we refer to as $Equiv_\omega$:

1. Generate the defining formula $\delta_{ppl}(I, S, O, S')$ of the pipelined circuit.
2. Define $l$ to be the number of inputs that the pipelined circuit has to consume before it can read the first input of the second frame.
3. Define $m$ as the least number of time steps that the pipelined circuit has to run to allow an observer to deduce that the output from the sequential circuit matches a single frame of output from the combinational implementation.
4. Let $k = max(l, m)$.
5. Let $\delta_{ppl}^k$ be the following formula that expresses what behaviour a length $k$ trace of the sequential circuit exhibits

$$\delta_{ppl}(I_0, S_0, O_0, S_1) \wedge \delta_{ppl}(I_1, S_1, O_1, S_2) \wedge \ldots \wedge \delta_{ppl}(I_{k-1}, S_{k-1}, O_{k-1}, S_k)$$

This is the $k$-step unrolling of the pipelined transition function.

We refer to a trace that is a model for $\delta_{ppl}^k$ as a $T$ trace, and observe the following:

- If we define an initialisation state as a state that immediately precedes the processing of a new frame, both $S_0$ and $S_l$ are initialisation states on all $T$ traces. Furthermore, $S_l$ is the closest initialisation state to $S_0$.
  - Any infinite trace of the system is made up from infinitely many concatenated $T$ traces; given that $l < k$ successive traces $tr_n$ and $tr_{n+1}$ also overlap with $tr_n(l \ldots k-1) = tr_{n+1}(0 \ldots k-l-1)$.
6. Generate a defining formula for the combinational circuit, $\delta_{cmb}(I, O)$.
7. From $\delta^k_{ppl}$ and $\delta_{cmb}$, construct a formula $\lambda$ that expresses implementation equivalence for a single frame of inputs
8. A proof of $\lambda$ without any assumptions at all on the initialisation state $S_0$ implies $\forall S_0.\lambda$. This corresponds to equivalence for any number of time frames as the circuits will behave in the same way regardless of the initialisation state values before a new frame is processed; a direct proof of $\lambda$ is hence not realistic. Therefore strengthen the assumptions on $S_0$ by a formula $\phi$ that restricts some of the $S_0$ variables to the initial values given in the pipelined circuit description. If now

$$\phi(S_0) \;\rightarrow\; \lambda$$

is provable, the circuits are equivalent for any number of time frames under the assumption that $\phi$ is always true in initialisation states. Refer to this assumption as assumption $A$
9. Try to prove assumption $A$ valid by a proof of

$$\phi(S_0) \wedge \lambda \;\rightarrow\; \phi(S_l)$$

As $\phi$ holds in the initial state of the circuit, this formula implies $A$ as it asserts that $\phi$ will hold in the state $S_l$ (that is reached immediately before a new processing cycle is initiated) if $\phi$ is true in $S_0$ (that was reached immediately before this frame was processed); $A$ is therefore entailed by induction.
10. If step 8 and step 9 were successful, deduce multi frame equivalence

A valid question is, of course, "Why is it reasonable to assume that a part of the pipelined circuit always is in a state where $\phi$ holds before a new frame is read?". This is probable as the pipelined circuit is supposed to repeat the frame processing behaviour again; the registers in the control logic should therefore have similar contents in the initialisation states as in the specified initial circuit state.

By having reduced the problem to two simple proofs we have devised a simple strategy for showing pipelined circuits with a fixed lag equivalent to combinational implementations. This strategy is implemented in an automatic Lava proof script that is parameterised over circuit descriptions, frame length, the constant lag and a proof configuration for the frame equivalence proof. This script automatically generates and reduces all formulas as much as possible before calling the theorem prover specified in the proof configuration; the only manual steps are to choose which state variables to restrict and to select a proof procedure. Any prover and extra proof options can be specified in the proof configuration; the pipelined circuit description can also have as many or as few initial values given as desired.

**Application to the pipelined Radix-$2^2$ FFT** The script that implements *Equiv$_\omega$* proves pipeline equivalence for the FFT circuits with the automatically generated equivalence formula $\lambda$ defined as

$$\delta_{ppl}^{k}(I_0..I_{k-1}, S_0..S_k, O_0..O_{k-1}) \wedge \delta_{cmb}(I_0..I_{i-1}, O_0'..O_{i-1}') \rightarrow O_{lag}..O_{k-1} = O_0'..O_{i-1}'$$

where $lag = 2^N - 1$, $i = 2^N$ and $k = 2^N + lag$.

A sufficient restriction $\phi$ on the initial state of the pipelined FFT circuit is that the $n$-bit counter is initialised to 0. The reason why this simple assertion is strong enough to prove the FFT implementations equivalent is that at re-initialisation the rest of the pipeline state is unimportant, new values have to be read for processing anyway. This is likely to hold for most pipelined implementations of combinational circuits.

The initialisation information $\phi$ is always used by the Lava script to reduce the generated formulas as much as possible while they are produced. This reduction computes the values of logical expressions whenever possible and propagates the resulting new information. As a consequence, the formulas that specify the behaviour of the control logic inside the pipelined FFT are evaluated away and the re-initialisation invariant in step 9 of *Equiv$_\omega$* is proved by syntactic equality. The equivalence checking problem for the pipelined FFT is therefore reduced back to a proof of an equivalence formula that turns out to be amenable to normalisation with the theories used for the combinational equivalence checking. The complexity of the resulting proofs are indicated in table 2.

| FFT size | Verification time (s) | Formula size (Bytes) |
|----------|----------------------|---------------------|
| 4        | 0.05                 | 1227                |
| 16       | 0.61                 | 10 045              |
| 64       | 22.26                | 162 862             |
| 256      | 1361                 | 2 797 617           |

**Table 2.** Statistics for verification of pipelined equivalence

## 5.4 Manual preparation

Approximately two weeks was spent on studying the FFT implementations, devising signal processing combinators and writing circuit descriptions. The addition of support in Lava's interpretations for complex numbers and the writing of the symbolic simulation interpretation with automatic formula reduction took one week of work each.

Finding the proof procedure was the creative step for the combinational FFT verification. Two other theorem provers, Prover [Stå89] and Gandalf [Tam97], was tried before Otter. Prover lacked crucial arithmetic laws, and Gandalf did not support the unidirectional rules that were needed to make the proofs scale up. A correct set of rewrite rules took some hours work by two users, Koen Claessen and Tanel Tammet, who were unfamiliar with the FFT but knew Otter well. Any other applicable proof procedure would also have needed rewrite rules for the twiddle factors, so we believe that this degree of manual work is unavoidable.

Once the symbolic simulation interpretation with formula reduction was written, a first (more involved) pipeline proof script could be constructed in half an hour. This strategy was successful the first time it was tried; we later simplified the heuristic to the presented form. The only non-reusable steps of the combinational and pipelined verifications were to choose Otter with rewrite rules as the proof procedure and to restrict the synchronisation counter state to the initial state 0.

# 6   Lessons learned

The FFT circuits are representatives for a general class of circuits that compute complex functions without using a large amount of boolean control logic. In general, a few guidelines for proofs of circuit equivalence for such circuits can be drawn out of the FFT work:

- For each problem domain, it might be possible to find a small number of generalised proof scripts that can be powerful enough for a particular class of problems to make proofs automatic in most cases. These scripts should be parametrisable by proof options so that they not are too blunt to be reusable.
- As the proofs that have to be done when operations like arithmetic are involved are relatively complex, the prover's job must be simplified as much as possible. The use of automatic partial evaluation and formula reduction can in some cases lessen the need for prover inferences drastically. A tool like Lava that supports analyses like simplification of formulas by propositional reasoning and cone-of-influence analysis can help the designer simplify the problem at hand.
- It is not always necessary to explore the state space of a design. Ordinary induction can sometimes avoid very complex or intractable computations, and make for uncomplicated proofs.
- Normal form rewriting is a powerful technique that can be implemented very efficiently using modern rewrite engines. However, the use of unidirectional rules is crucial to make the strategy applicable to larger circuits.

# 7   Related work

The Radix-2 FFT algorithm has previously been verified against the DFT using the ACL2 theorem prover [Gam98]. The level of abstraction in this verification was high and the proof thus required substantial user interaction. In contrast, we have aimed for fully automatic proofs, and verified the hardware FFTs at the netlist level. Our proofs are only for equivalence of fixed size circuits, but are not reliant on circuit regularity.

The pipeline proof principle bears some resemblance to the refinement mapping approach to pipelined microprocessor control verification [BD94,Cyr93]. However, as we are comparing a pipelined circuit against a combinational one, we cannot directly associate a single sequential step with the combinational implementation; we instead correlate whole frames. We also exploit the fact that constant lag pipelined circuits are targeted.

There are alternatives to Otter as a proof procedure: the Stanford validity checker decides quantifier free first order logic with linear arithmetic and uninterpreted functions by boolean case splitting (backtracking), rewrites and congruence closure [BDL96]. SVC has been used extensively in hardware verification, and is used as the decision procedure in the Burch and Dill approach to microprocessor verification [BD94]. Multiway decision graphs are a variation on the ROBDD theme that accommodates abstract data types, uninterpreted function symbols and rewrite rules [ZSC+95]; this data structure has been used to verify non-pipelined microprocessors and an ATM switch [TZS+96]. MDGs give a canonical representation for a fragment of quantifier free first-order formulas and support exploration of abstract state spaces (but do not guarantee convergence of fixpoint computations). As we have demonstrated, it is not always necessary to do such expensive computations; induction and normalising can be both sufficient and efficient.

Both MDGs and SVC need the user to provide rewrite rules or a normaliser for new theories. This means that the manual step of finding a normal form for twiddle factors is also necessary with these proof procedures.

## 8 Conclusions

This paper has shown how some FFT circuits have been verified from within the hardware development tool Lava after the existing system was extended with complex numbers and a general purpose strategy for equivalence checking of combinational and fixed lag pipelined circuits. The verification has been automatic in the sense that the only manual proof steps has been to select the proof procedure, rewrite rules and the initial state variables to restrict. The proofs are at a relatively low level, which should give a high confidence in the correctness of the modelled circuits; the logical formulas has been generated by symbolic evaluation of the hardware descriptions. No part of the verification has relied on the specific way that the arithmetic operators are implemented, or the representation of complex numbers. However, the proofs are not general in the size of the FFT; different instances have to be proved separately.

We have also presented an induction principle that exploits the problem structure of equivalence checking between a pipelined circuit and a combinational reference circuit, and contributed some suggestions for verification of circuits that contain little control logic but do complicated computations expressed in abstract operations.

# 9 Future work

Lava is optimised for developing and verifying hardware. We pay for the strength we gain by limiting the problem domain, however, by presently being unable to reason internally about the proof strategies. Instead we have to go outside the system to a general purpose interactive theorem prover and do high level proofs there. We would like to have Lava integrated with a proof system that would allow us to do this kind of reasoning.

The counter examples that are produced by proof procedures are formatted and passed back to the user by Lava; unfortunately many first order logic theorem provers (including Otter) lack such capabilities. For verification with normal form rewriting to be smooth, it must be easy to find a rewriting theory quickly. It is therefore imperative to have some tool that analyses the output of a failed proof and allows the user to deduce what rules are missing, or gives the user good clues to why the two formulas are not equivalent. This is something that should (and will) be implemented in Lava as a proof analysis.

## Acknowledgements

Thanks to Koen Claessen and Tanel Tammet for finding the Otter rewriting theory, and to Mary Sheeran and Byron Cook for careful readings of earlier drafts.

# References

[BCSS98] Per Bjesse, Koen Claessen, Mary Sheeran, and Satnam Singh. Lava: Hardware Design in Haskell. In *Proceedings of the third International Conference on Functional Programming*. ACM SIGPLAN, acm press, September 1998.

[BD94] Jerry Burch and David Dill. Automatic Verification of Microprocessor Control. In *Proceedings of the Computer Aided Verification Conference*, July 1994.

[BDL96] Clark Barrett, David Dill, and Jeremy Levitt. Validity checking for combinations of theories with equality. In Mandayam Srivas and Albert Camilleri, editors, *Formal Methods In Computer-Aided Design*, volume 1166 of *Lecture Notes in Computer Science*, pages 187–201. Springer Verlag, November 1996. Palo Alto, California, November 6–8.

[Cyr93] David Cyrluk. Microprocessor verification in PVS. Technical Report SRI-CSL-93-12, SRI Computer Science Laboratory, December 1993.

[Gam98] Ruben Gamboa. Mechanically verifying the correctness of the Fast Fourier Transform in ACL2. In *Third International Workshop on Formal Methods for Parallel Programming: Theory and Applications*, 1998.

[He95] Shousheng He. *Concurrent VLSI Architectures for DFT Computing and Algorithms for Multi-output Logic Decomposition*. PhD thesis, Lund Institute of Technology, 1995.

[MW97] William W. McCune and L. Wos. Otter: The CADE-13 competition incarnations. *Journal of Automated Reasoning*, 18(2):211–220, 1997.

[PM92] John Proakis and Dimitris Manolakis. *Digital Signal Processing*. Macmillan, 1992.

[Stå89]    Gunnar Stålmarck. A System for Determining Propositional Logic Theorems by Applying Values and Rules to Triplets that are Generated from a Formula, 1989. Swedish Patent No. 467 076 (approved 1992), U.S. Patent No. 5 276 897 (1994), European Patent No. 0403 454 (1995).

[Tam97]    Tanel Tammet. Gandalf. *Journal of Automated Reasoning*, 18(2):199–204, 1997.

[TZS⁺96]   Sofiène Tahar, Zijian Zhou, Xiaoyu Song, Eduard Cerny, and Michel Langevin. Formal verification of an ATM switch fabric using Multiway Decision Graphs. In *IEEE Proceedings of Sixth Great Lakes Symposium on VLSI*, March 1996.

[VB98]     Miroslav Velev and Randal Bryant. Bit-Level Abstraction in the Verification of Pipelined Microprocessors by Correspondence Checking. In *Formal Methods in Computer-Aided Design*, volume 1522 of *LNCS*, pages 18–35, Palo Alto, November 1998. Springer Verlag.

[ZSC⁺95]   Zijian Zhou, Xiaoyu Song, Fransisco Corella, Eduard Cerny, and Michel Langevin. Description and Verification of RTL Designs Using Multiway Decision Graphs. In *Proceedings of the Conference on Hardware Description Languages and their applications*, August 1995.

# A   Appendix

## A.1   The Radix-2 FFT description

Figure 3 shows a size 16 Radix-2 FFT network, where merging arrows indicate addition and constants under a wire indicate multiplication. The Lava description of the size $2^n$ Radix-2 FFT circuit follows the network structure closely, and is parametrised by $n$:

```
radix2 n =
  bitRev n >-> compose [ stage i | i <- [1..n] ]
  where
    stage i = raised (n-i) two (twid i >-> bflys (i-1))
    twid  i = one (decmap (2^(i-1)) (wMult (2^i)))
```

The FFT circuit is made up from the sequential composition of an initial bit reversal permutation network (not shown in the picture) and $n$ circuit stages. Stage $i$ is a column of $2^{n-i}$ components that each contains a twiddle factor multiplication stage sequentially composed with a butterfly network. Given that $x = 2^{i-1}$, a size $i$ multiplication stage performs multiplications with $W_{2^i}^0 ... W_{2^i}^{x-1}$ on the respective wires of one half of a bus, while passing the other half through unchanged.

More information on the signal processing building blocks and the descriptions of the combinational circuits can be found in [BCSS98].

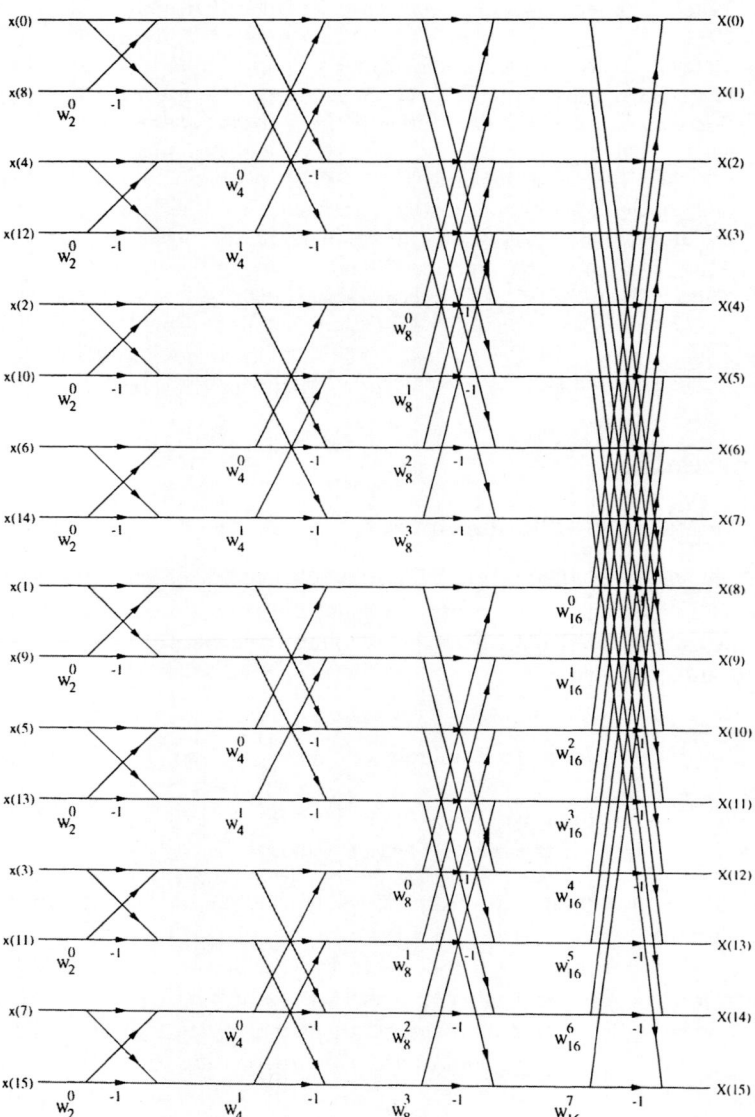

**Fig. 3.** The structure of a size 16 Radix-2 FFT

# Efficient Analysis of Cyclic Definitions

Kedar S. Namjoshi and Robert P. Kurshan

Bell Laboratories
Lucent Technologies
{kedar,k}@research.bell-labs.com
URL : http://cm.bell-labs.com/cm/cs/who/{kedar,k}

**Abstract.** We present a new algorithm for detecting semantic combinational cycles that is simpler and more efficient than earlier algorithms found in the literature. Combinational circuits with syntactic cycles often arise in processor and bus-based designs. The intention is that external inputs and delay elements such as latches break these cycles, so that no "semantic" cycles remain. Unbroken semantic cycles are considered a design error in this context. Such unbroken cycles may also occur inadvertently in compositions of Mealy machines.

Verification systems that accept semantically cyclic definitions run the risk of certifying systems that have electrically bad or unexpected behavior, while those that prohibit all cyclic definitions constrain the types of systems that can be subjected to formal verification. Earlier work on this issue has led to a reasonable condition, called *Constructivity*, that guarantees the absence of semantic cycles. This formulation is, however, computational in nature, and existing algorithms to decide constructivity are somewhat inefficient. Moreover, they do not apply naturally to circuit definitions in high-level languages that allow variables with non-Boolean types. We propose a new formulation of constructivity, formulated as a satisfiability question, that does not have these limitations. We have implemented the new algorithm in the verification tool COSPAN/FormalCheck. Our experience indicates that the algorithm is simple to implement and usually incurs negligible overhead.

## 1 Introduction

A circuit may be described as a set of definitions, one for each gate of the circuit. For most circuits, the induced syntactic dependency graph of such a definition is acyclic. Syntactically cyclic definitions, however, occur in many contexts in digital design: Malik [9] points out that it is often desirable to re-use functional units by connecting them in a cyclic fashion through a routing mechanism, and Stok [13] notes that such definitions often arise in the output of synthesis programs. In these cases, the intention is that the routing mechanism can be controlled through external inputs, so that any "semantically" cyclic paths are broken for each valuation of the external "free" inputs and delay elements such as latches. Semantically cyclic definitions may also occur inadvertently in systems composed of several Mealy machines, from feedback connections between the combinational inputs and outputs. Verification systems that accept semantically cyclic definitions run the risk of certifying systems that have behavior that is unexpected or electrically bad, while those that prohibit syntactically cyclic definitions constrain the types of systems that can be subjected to formal verification.

Most current design and verification systems either prohibit all syntactically cyclic definitions, or accept only some of the semantically acyclic definitions. The Esterel compiler is the only existing system we know of that analyzes definitions for semantic cyclicity using the notion of "*Constructivity*" proposed by Berry [2], which considers a circuit to be semantically acyclic iff for every external input, a unique value can be derived for each internal wire by a series of inferences on the definition of the circuit (a precise statement is given in Section 2). Shiple [11] shows that constructive definitions are precisely those that are well-behaved electrically, for any assignment of delay values, in the up-bounded inertial delay model [4].

It is inefficient to check constructivity by enumerating all possible external valuations. Symbolic algorithms for checking constructivity [2, 12, 11] manipulate *sets* of input valuations, representing them with BDD's [3]. This manipulation is based on simultaneous fixpoint equations derived from the circuit definitions and the types of the variables. For variables with $k$ values in their type, these algorithms require $k$ sets of valuations for each variable. Moreover, for arithmetic operations, the fixpoint equations are constructed from partitions (for $+$) or factorizations (for $*$) of all numbers in the type. Thus, these algorithms are somewhat inefficient and difficult to implement for variables with non-Boolean types.

We show in this paper that, by a simple transformation, one can reformulate constructivity as the satisfiability of a set of equations derived from the definitions, over variable types extended with a value $\perp$ (read as "bottom"). This formulation is non-computational and easily extensible to variables with any finite type. The formulation also handles definitions of indexed variables in the same manner. We have implemented this constructivity check in the verification tool COSPAN [7], which is the verification engine for the commercial verification tool FormalCheck; the implementation is simple, and our experience indicates that it usually incurs negligible overhead.

Section 2 motivates and precisely defines constructivity. The new formulation is derived in Section 3. Section 4 describes the implementation of this idea in the COSPAN/FormalCheck verification system. The paper concludes with a discussion of related work and future directions in Section 5.

## 2   Cyclic Definitions

**Notation**: The notation generally follows the style in [6]. Function application is represented with a "." and is right-associative; for instance, $f.g.a$ is parsed as $f.(g.a)$. Quantified expressions and those involving associative operators are written in the format $(Q\ x : r.x : g.x)$, where $Q$ is either a quantifier (e.g., $\forall, \exists$) or an associative operator (e.g., $+, *, min, max, lub, glb$), $x$ is the "dummy" variable,

$r.x$ is the range of $x$, and $g.x$ is the expression. For instance, $(\forall x\ r(x) \Rightarrow g(x))$ is expressed as $(\forall x : r.x : g.x)$, $(\exists x\ r(x) \land g(x))$ is expressed as $(\exists x : r.x : g.x)$, and $\sum_{i=0}^{i=n} x_i$ is expressed as $(+i : i \in [0, n] : x.i)$. When the range $r$ is *true* or understood from the context, we drop it and write $(Q\ x :: g.x)$. Proofs are presented as a chain of equivalences or implications, with a hint for each link of the chain. □

For simplicity, we consider all variables to be defined over a single finite type $T$. The vocabulary of operator symbols is given by a finite set $F$. Each symbol in $F$ has an associated "arity", which is a natural number. A symbol $f$ with arity $n$ corresponds to a function $f^* : T^n \to T$; symbols with arity 0 correspond to values of $T$. Terms over $F$ and a set of variables $X$ are built as follows : a variable $x$ in $X$ is a term, and for terms $t.i$ $(i \in [0, n))$ and a function symbol $f$ of arity $n$, $f.(t.0, \ldots, t.(n-1))$ is a term.

**Definition 0 (Simultaneous definition).** *A simultaneous definition is specified by a triple* $(E, X, Y)$, *where* $X$ *and* $Y$ *are disjoint finite sets of variables,* $E$ *is a set of expressions of the form* $y\ ::=\ t$, *where* $y \in Y$ *and* $t$ *is a term in* $X \cup Y$, *such that there is exactly one expression in* $E$ *for each variable in* $Y$.

In terms of the earlier informal description of a circuit as a set of definitions, $X$ is the set of "external" variables (the free inputs and latches) and $Y$ is the set of "internal" variables (the internal gate outputs); notice that a simultaneous definition contains definitions only for the internal variables. A simultaneous definition induces a *dependency relation* among the variables in $Y$; for each expression $y\ ::=\ t$, $y$ "depends on" each of the variables appearing in $t$. A simultaneous definition is *syntactically cyclic* iff this dependency relation contains a cycle. We illustrate some of the subtleties in formulating a correct notion of *semantic acyclicity* with a few examples.

**Example 0 :** Syntactic Acyclicity

The external variable set is $\{x, y\}$ and the internal variable set is $\{p, q\}$.

$$p\ ::=\ x \land \neg y$$
$$q\ ::=\ x \lor y$$

This is syntactically acyclic; hence, for every valuation of $x$ and $y$, $p$ and $q$ have uniquely defined values. □

**Example 1 :** Syntactic Cyclicity, Semantic Acyclicity

The external variable set is $\{x, y\}$ and the internal variable set is $\{p, q\}$.

$$p\ ::=\ \text{if } x \text{ then } y \text{ else } q$$
$$q\ ::=\ \text{if } x \text{ then } p \text{ else } x$$

This is syntactically cyclic; however, notice that if $x$ is *true*, the definition simplifies to the acyclic definition:

$$p\ ::=\ y$$
$$q\ ::=\ p$$

Similarly, the simplified definition is acyclic when $x$ is *false*. Thus, each setting of the external variable $x$ breaks syntactic cycles. $\square$

**Example 2 :** Semantic Cyclicity

The external variable set is $\{x\}$ and the internal variable set is $\{p, q\}$.

$$p ::= q \wedge x$$
$$q ::= p$$

This is syntactically cyclic. If $x$ is *false*, the simplified definition is acyclic; however, when $x$ is *true*, it simplifies to one that presents a semantic cycle:

$$p ::= q$$
$$q ::= p$$

$\square$

A plausible semantics for a simultaneous definition is to interpret each expression $y ::= t$ as an equation $y = t$, and declare the definition to be semantically acyclic if this set of simultaneous equations has a solution for each valuation of the external variables. With this semantics, Examples 0 and 1 are semantically acyclic, but so is Example 2. One may attempt to rectify this situation by requiring there to be a *unique* solution for each input valuation; the following example illustrates that this is also incorrect.

**Example 3**: Incorrectness of the "unique solution" criterion.

The external variable set is $\{x\}$ and the internal variable set is $\{p, q\}$.

$$p ::= p \wedge x$$
$$q ::= \text{if } p \text{ then } \neg q \text{ else } false$$

This is syntactically cyclic. If $x$ is *false*, the simplified definition is acyclic, and hence has a unique solution. If $x$ is *true*, the simplified definition is the following.

$$p ::= p$$
$$q ::= \text{if } p \text{ then } \neg q \text{ else } false$$

This has the unique solution $p = false, q = false$. Hence, the definition has a unique solution for each valuation of $x$ ! The "unique solution" criterion thus leaves the cycles $p ::= p, q ::= \neg q$ undetected. $\square$

The examples suggest that a straightforward formulation in terms of solutions to the simultaneous equations may not exist. Berry [2], strengthening a formulation of Malik [9], proposed a condition called *Constructivity*. Constructivity is based on the simplification process that was carried out informally in the examples above : for each valuation of the external variables, one attempts to simplify the right hand sides of the definitions. If a term $t$ in a definition $y ::= t$ simplifies to a constant $a$, the current valuation is extended with $y = a$, and the definition $y ::= t$ is removed. The simplifications are restricted to cases where the result is defined by the current valuation irrespective of the values of variables that are currently undefined. For instance, with $\{x = false\}$ as the current valuation, if $x$ then $y$ else $z$ simplifies to $z$; $x \wedge y$ simplifies to *false*; but $y \vee \neg y$ *does not* simplify to *true*. Berry [2] shows that this process produces a unique result, *independent* of the order in which simplification steps are applied. The appropriateness of constructivity is shown by Shiple [11], who demonstrates that constructive definitions are precisely those that are well-behaved electrically, for any assignment of delay values, in the up-bounded inertial delay model [4]. Malik [9] shows that the problem of detecting semantic cyclicity is NP-complete.

**Definition 1 (Constructivity).** *A simultaneous definition is semantically acyclic iff for each valuation of the external variables, the simplification process leads to an empty set of definitions.*

## 3 Constructivity as Satisfiability

There is another way of viewing the simplification process that leads to our new formulation. Simplification is seen as a fixpoint process that computes the "maximal" extension of the original valuation of external variables (maximal in the sense that the set of definitions cannot be simplified further with this valuation). The algorithms for checking constructivity proposed in [9, 12] use this fixpoint formulation. We show (Theorem 1 below) that it is possible to re-cast the fixpoint formulation as a satisfiability question. This observation lets us develop a simple algorithm for constructivity that extends easily to non-Boolean types.

### 3.1 Background

To formulate simplification as a fixpoint process, we need some well-known concepts from Scott's theory of Complete Partial Orders (CPO's) [10]. The type $T$ is extended with a new element $\bot$ (read as "bottom") to form the type $T_\bot$. $T_\bot$ is equipped with the partial order $\preceq$, defined by $a \preceq b$ iff $a = b$ or $a = \bot$. Note that $\preceq$ is a CPO (every sequence of elements that is monotonically increasing w.r.t. $\preceq$ has a least upper bound). The greatest lower bound (*glb*) of two elements $a, b$ is defined as : $glb.(a, b) = if\ a \neq b\ then\ \bot\ else\ a$. The ordering $\preceq$ is extended point-wise to vectors on $T_\bot$ by $u \sqsubseteq v$ iff $|u| = |v| \ \wedge\ (\forall i :: u.i \preceq v.i)$. This ordering is a CPO on the set of vectors on $T_\bot$. The greatest lower bound is also defined point-wise over vectors of the same length: $glb.(u, v) = w$, where for every $i$, $w.i = glb.(u.i, v.i)$.

For each function symbol $f$ in $F$, $f_\bot$ is a symbol of the same arity that indicates application to $T_\bot$ rather than to $T$. The interpretation $f_\bot^*$ of $f_\bot$ over $T_\bot$ should be a function that extends $f^*$ and is monotone w.r.t. the order $\sqsubseteq$; i.e., for vectors $u, v$ of length the arity of $f_\bot$, $u \sqsubseteq v$ implies $f_\bot^*.u \sqsubseteq f_\bot^*.v$. The ordering $\sqsubseteq$ and the monotonicity condition encodes the informal description of $\bot$ as the "undefined" value: if $v$ is "more defined" than $u$, then $f_\bot^*.v$ should also be "more defined" than $f_\bot^*.u$. The extension of a term $t$ is represented by $t_\bot$ and is defined recursively based on the structure of the term: $(x)_\bot = x$; $(f.(t.0, \ldots, t.(n-1)))_\bot = f_\bot.(t_\bot.0, \ldots, t_\bot.(n-1))$. It is straightforward to show that the interpretation of an extended term is also monotonic w.r.t. $\sqsubseteq$. Every monotonic function on a CPO has a least fixpoint.

## 3.2 Constructivity as a Fixpoint Process

A partial valuation constructed during the simplification process can now be represented as total function from $X \cup Y$ to $T_\perp$, where currently undefined variables are given the value $\perp$. An initial valuation $V$ is a function that maps $X$ into $T$ and $Y$ to $\{\perp\}$. At each step, for some non-deterministically chosen definition $y \ ::= \ t$, the current valuation $V$ is updated to $V.[y \leftarrow t_\perp^*.V]$. By an argument [1] (cf. [5]) based on monotonicity, this non-deterministic process terminates with a valuation that is the simultaneous least fixpoint of the derived set of equations $\{y = t_\perp^* \mid (y \ ::= \ t) \in E\}$. For a simultaneous definition $C = (E, X, Y)$, let $(lfp \ Y : \ E^*.(X, Y))$ denote this least fixpoint. The fixpoint depends on, and is defined for, each valuation of $X$. The constructivity definition can now be re-stated as follows.

**Definition 2 (Constructivity-FIX).** *A simultaneous definition $(E, X, Y)$ is semantically acyclic iff for each initial valuation $V$, the vector $(lfp \ Y : \ E^*.(V, Y))$ has no $\perp$-components.*

For a vector $v$ over $T_\perp$, let $\perp free.v$ be the predicate $(\forall \ i :: v.i \neq \perp)$. The constructivity condition is precisely $(\forall \ v : \ \perp free.v : \ \perp free.(lfp \ Y : \ E^*.(v, Y)))$. Malik [9] checks a weaker condition in which the set of internal variables $Y$ has a subset of "output" variables $W$. Let $output\perp free.v$ be the predicate $(\forall \ i : i \in W : v.i \neq \perp)$. Malik's condition can be phrased as : $(\forall \ v : \ \perp free.v : output\perp free.(lfp \ Y : \ E^*.(v, Y)))$.

Checking the Constructivity-FIX condition independently for each initial valuation is inefficient. Malik, Berry, Touati and Shiple [9, 2, 12, 11] use a derived scheme that operates on sets of external valuations. If the type $T$ has $k$ elements, the scheme associates $k$ subsets with each variable $y$ in $Y$: the set $y.i$, $i \in [0, k)$, contains external valuations for which the variable $y$ evaluates to $i$. These subsets are updated by set operations derived from the semantics of the basic operators. For instance, for the definition "$x \ ::= \ y \wedge z$", the updates are given by $x.false = y.false \cup z.false$, and $x.true = y.true \cap z.true$.

This scheme has two limitations that arise for non-Boolean types: (i) the algorithm has to maintain $k$ sets for each variable, and (ii) the set operations needed can be quite complex when the basic operators include (bounded) arithmetic. For example, for the definition $x \ ::= \ y + z$, $x.k$ would be defined as $y.l + z.m$, for various partitions of $k$ as $l + m$; similarly, for $x \ ::= \ y * z$, $x.k$ would be defined as $y.l * z.m$, for various factorizations of $k$ as $l * m$. Our new formulation, Constructivity-SAT, changes Constructivity-FIX to a satisfiability question and avoids these difficulties.

## 3.3 Constructivity as Satisfiability

The new formulation (apparently) strengthens the Constructivity-FIX definition to require that *every* fixpoint of $E^*$ is $\perp$-free. The equivalence of the two formulations is shown in Theorem 1.

**Definition 3 (Constructivity-SAT).** *A simultaneous definition* $(E, X, Y)$ *is semantically acyclic iff* $(\forall\, v, u : \bot free.v \,\wedge\, u = E^*.(v, u) : \bot free.u)$.

**Lemma 0.** *For a monotone property $P$ and a monotone function $f$ on a CPO $\sqsubseteq$, $P.(lfp\ X : f.X)$ iff $(\forall\, u : u = f.u : P.u)$.*

*Proof.* The implication from right to left is trivially true, as $(lfp\ X : f.X)$ satisfies the condition $u = f.u$. For the other direction, note that the fixpoints of $f$ are partially ordered by $\sqsubseteq$, with the least fixpoint below any other fixpoint. By the monotonicity of $P$, if $P$ holds of the least fixpoint, it holds of every fixpoint. $\square$

**Theorem 1.** *Constructivity-FIX and Constructivity-SAT are equivalent.*

*Proof.* For any simultaneous definition $C = (E, X, Y)$,

$\qquad\quad C$ satisfies Constructivity-FIX
$\equiv\qquad$ { by definition }
$\qquad (\forall\, v : \bot free.v : \bot free.(lfp\ Y : E^*.(v, Y)))$
$\equiv\qquad$ { $\bot free$ is monotone w.r.t. $\sqsubseteq$; Lemma 0 }
$\qquad (\forall\, v : \bot free.v : (\forall\, u : u = E^*.(v, u) : \bot free.u))$
$\equiv\qquad$ { rearranging }
$\qquad (\forall\, v, u : \bot free.v \,\wedge\, u = E^*.(v, u) : \bot free.u)$
$\equiv\qquad$ { by definition }
$\qquad C$ satisfies Constructivity-SAT
$\square$

The extension of a function $f$ from $T^n$ to $T^n_\bot$ can be defined in general as follows: the value of the extension at a vector $v$ is the greatest lower bound of the function values at $\bot$-free vectors above $v$ in the order. Formally, $f^*_\bot.v = (glb\ w : \bot free.w \,\wedge\, v \sqsubseteq w : f^*.w)$. It is straightforward to show that this is a monotone extension of $f$. The extensions of basic arithmetic and Boolean functions are easily determined by this formula. For example, the extension of $\wedge$ is given by:

$$u \wedge_\bot v = \quad\begin{array}{ll} false & \text{if } u = false \text{ or } v = false; \text{ otherwise,} \\ \bot & \text{if } u = \bot \text{ or } v = \bot; \qquad \text{otherwise,} \\ u \wedge v \end{array}$$

To illustrate the use of the general formulation, we can check that

$\qquad u \wedge_\bot false$
$=\qquad$ { by the general formulation }
$\qquad (glb\ x, y : x \neq \bot \,\wedge\, y \neq \bot \,\wedge\, u \preceq x \,\wedge\, false \preceq y : x \wedge y)$
$=\qquad$ { definition of $\preceq$ }
$\qquad (glb\ x : x \neq \bot \,\wedge\, u \preceq x : x \wedge false)$
$=\qquad$ { definition of $\wedge$ }
$\qquad (glb\ x : x \neq \bot \,\wedge\, u \preceq x : false)$
$=\qquad$ { definition of $glb$ }
$\qquad false$

The extension of $*$ is similar to that for $\wedge$, with 0 substituted for *false*. The extension of $+$ is given below :

$$u +_\perp v = \quad \perp \quad \text{if } u = \perp \text{ or } v = \perp; \quad \text{otherwise,}$$
$$u + v$$

The extensions of other basic operators can be defined equally easily. The new formulation thus overcomes both the limitations of the earlier one: the extensions are easy to define and compute, and we do not need to maintain sets of valuations for each variable; the only changes required are to extend both the types of variables and the definitions of the basic operators.

### 3.4 Indexed Variables

In many input languages, including the S/R language of the COSPAN system, it is possible to declare arrays of variables. If $z$ is such an array variable, definitions of the form $z[c] ::= t$, where $c$ is a constant, can be handled with the machinery presented earlier, by treating $z[c]$ as an ordinary variable. A definition of the form $z[e] ::= t$, however, where $e$ is a non-constant term, cannot be handled with the earlier machinery, as it corresponds to the set of definitions $\{z[c] ::= \underline{\text{if }} (e = c) \underline{\text{ then }} t \mid c \in indices(z)\}$. Notice that the term $\underline{\text{if }} (e = c) \underline{\text{ then }} t$ is a *partial* function. As a typical instance, consider the following definition, where $z$ is an array indexed by $\{0, 1\}$, and $x$ and $y$ are variables.

$$z[x] ::= a$$
$$z[y] ::= b$$

The semantics of S/R requires that the valuations of $x$ and $y$ be distinct. The defining term for $z[0]$ is the partial function *if $x = 0$ then $a$ else if $y = 0$ then $b$*. This term may itself be considered as a partial function on $T_\perp$, defined only for $x = 0$ and $y = 0$. With this interpretation, it is monotonic [1] w.r.t. $\sqsubseteq$. Recombining the terms for $z[0]$ and $z[1]$, one obtains the following modification (for $T_\perp$) of the original definitions for $z[x]$ and $z[y]$:

$$z[x] ::= \underline{\text{if }} x \neq \perp \underline{\text{ then }} a$$
$$z[y] ::= \underline{\text{if }} y \neq \perp \underline{\text{ then }} b$$

These definitions contribute in the following way to the induced "equations":

$$(x \neq \perp) \Rightarrow (z[x] = a)$$
$$(y \neq \perp) \Rightarrow (z[y] = b)$$

## 4 Implementation

We have implemented this new formulation in the COSPAN/FormalCheck verification system [7]. The input language for the COSPAN system is S/R ("selection/resolution") [8]. An S/R program consists of a number of processes,

---

[1] A partial function $f$ is monotonic w.r.t. a partial order $\preceq$ iff whenever $x \preceq y$ and $f$ is defined at $x$, $f$ is defined at $y$ and $f.x \preceq f.y$.

which may be viewed as Mealy machines with Rabin/Streett-type acceptance conditions. The variables of each process are either state or selection variables. Selection variables, in turn, are either free (unconstrained) inputs or combinational variables used to determine the next-state relation of the system [8]. In the terminology of the earlier sections, the state variables together with the free input variables form the "external" variables, since the inputs and state variables do not change value for the duration of the selection cycle; the other selection variables form the "internal variables".

There are no restrictions in S/R on the dependencies between selection variables: selection variables declared within a process may be mutually interdependent and may be used as inputs to other processes, thus potentially introducing syntactic cycles that span process boundaries. In addition, the presence of *semantic* cycles may depend on the valuation of the state variables. For instance, a semantic cycle may be "unreachable", if the particular states in which it is induced are unreachable. The question, then, is to identify whether any semantic cycles are present in reachable states of the program for some free-input valuation (this problem is shown to be PSPACE-complete in [11]).

The S/R compiler parses the program and analyzes syntactic dependencies among internal variables. If there is a syntactic cycle, it identifies a set of internal variables whose elimination would break each syntactic cycle; such a set is commonly called a "feedback vertex set". The parser retains the variables in the feedback vertex set, and macro-expands the other variables, so that the variables in the feedback vertex set are defined in terms of themselves and the input and state variables. In the terminology used earlier, these remaining internal variables and their defining terms form the simultaneous definition that is to be analyzed. We will refer to these internal variables as the "relevant" variables. Each relevant variable is treated as a state variable for reachability analysis.

Our implementation uses a single MTBDD terminal to represent $\perp$. While MTBDD's for multiplication are exponential in the number of bits, they represent most other operations efficiently and are therefore used in COSPAN. The types of the relevant variables are extended to include the $\perp$-terminal. The types of input and state variables are not extended. The implementation includes a library of extended basic operators, defined as described in Section 2. These extend the basic operators of S/R, including Boolean operators, arithmetic operators such as $+, *, div, exp, mod$, and conditional operators such as if then else .

Each definition $x ::= t$ of a relevant non-indexed variable is converted to the equation $x = t^*_\perp$, while a definition $z[e] ::= t$ of an indexed variable is converted to $(e^*_\perp \neq \perp) \Rightarrow (z[e^*_\perp] = t^*_\perp)$, as described in Section 3.4. The conjunction of these formulae forms the simultaneous fixpoint term $Y = E^*.(S, X, Y)$, where $S$ is the set of state variables, $X$ is the set of free input variables, and $Y$ is the set of relevant variables. The Constructivity-SAT formula determines (by negation) the following predicate on state variables:

$$Cyclic.S = (\exists X, Y : Y = E^*.(S, X, Y) \wedge \neg\perp free.Y).$$

The predicate $\neg Cyclic$ is checked for invariance during reachability analysis; if it fails, the system automatically generates an error-track leading from an initial state to a state $s$ such that *Cyclic.s* is true. It is not difficult to recover the set of variables involved in a semantic cycle for a particular input $k$ at state $s$ by inspecting the BDD for $(Y = E^*.(s, k, Y) \land \neg\bot free.Y)$ – every path to a 1-node includes variables that have value $\bot$; these variables are involved in a semantic cycle.

The description above should indicate that implementing the constructivity check with the new formulation is a fairly simple process. We have experimented with this implementation on a test suite for COSPAN formed of several large programs that represent real designs. While syntactic cycles are usually short, some of our examples had cycles of length greater than 20. Our experience has been that, in most cases, the run-time and BDD sizes increase, if at all, by a negligible amount. There are a few cases where the BDD sizes increase by a large amount, and even some where the sizes decrease – this seems to be attributable to the irregular behavior of the dynamic reordering algorithms. We have not conducted a thorough comparison with the algorithm in [12], but it is reasonable to expect that our algorithm will be more efficient for non-Boolean variables, as it avoids both the large number of BDD's and the fixpoint computation. It is less certain whether our algorithm offers a large improvement on the earlier one in the case when all variables are Boolean; this would require experimental comparison. In any case, the potential benefits of detecting semantic cycles before circuit fabrication far outweigh the disadvantage of the (usually small) time and memory increases that we have observed for our detection process.

## 5    Related Work and Conclusions

The work most related to ours is by Berry [2] and Shiple [11]. Berry proposed the original operational formulation of constructivity (Constructivity) and the denotational formulation (Constructivity-FIX), based on work by Malik [9]. These definitions are based on computational processes – one would prefer a non-computational definition of the concept of "semantic acyclicity". Shiple, Berry and Touati [12, 2, 11] and Malik [9] propose symbolic, fixpoint-based algorithms to check constructivity. These algorithms are difficult to implement and somewhat inefficient for variables with non-Boolean types.

Our new formulation overcomes both limitations, by presenting a simple, non-computational definition of constructivity (Constructivity-SAT) and a symbolic algorithm based on the new formulation that is simple to implement for variables with arbitrary finite types. Our initial experiments with the implementation of this algorithm in the formal verification system COSPAN/FormalCheck indicate that in most cases it has minimal, if any, adverse impact on the execution time and BDD sizes. It should be quite easy to incorporate this algorithm into other verification and synthesis tools. As in [11], one can also determine the set of input values for which a circuit is constructive, by not quantifying over $v$ in the Constructivity-SAT definition.

In [11] Shiple considers a class of cyclic combinational circuits whose behavior is based on the assumption that the circuit retains "state" across clock cycles (for example, a flip-flop implemented by a pair of cross-connected NAND gates). It would be interesting to see if our formulation of constructivity can be modified to analyze such sequential behavior.

**Acknowledgements:** Thanks to Tom Szymanski for providing references to work on constructivity, and to Kousha Etessami, Mihalis Yannakakis, and Jon Riecke for useful comments and discussions about this work.

# References

1. H. Bekič. Definable operations in general algebras, and the theory of automata and flowcharts. Technical report, IBM, 1969. Reprinted in Programming Languages and Their Definition, LNCS 177, 1984.
2. G. Berry. *The Constructive Semantics of Esterel.* Draft book, available at ftp://ftp-sop.inria.fr/meije/esterel/papers/constructiveness.ps.gz, 1995.
3. R. Bryant. Graph based algorithms for boolean function manipulation. *IEEE Transactions on Computers*, 1986.
4. J. A. Brzozowski and C-J. H. Seger. *Asynchronous Circuits.* Springer-Verlag, 1994.
5. P. Cousot. Asynchronous iterative methods for solving a fixed point system of monotone equations in a complete lattice (rapport de recherche r.r. 88). Technical report, Laboratoire IMAG, Universite' scientifique et me'dicale de Grenoble, 1978.
6. E. W. Dijkstra and C. S. Scholten. *Predicate Calculus and Program Semantics.* Springer-Verlag, 1990.
7. R. H. Hardin, Z. Har'El, and R. P. Kurshan. COSPAN. In *Proc. CAV'96*, volume 1102, pages 423–427. LNCS, 1996.
8. J. Katzenelson and R. P. Kurshan. S/R: A language for specifying protocols and other coordinating processes. In *Proc. IEEE Conf. Comput. Comm.*, pages 286–292, 1986.
9. S. Malik. Analysis of cyclic combinational circuits. *IEEE Transactions on Computer-Aided Design*, 1994.
10. D. S. Scott. A type-theoretical alternative to CUCH, ISWIM, OWHY. Unpublished notes, Oxford, 1969. Published in *Theoretical Computer Science*, 1993.
11. T. Shiple. *Formal Analysis of Synchronous Circuits.* PhD thesis, Univerisity of California, Berkeley, 1996.
12. T. Shiple, G. Berry, and H. Touati. Constructive analysis of cyclic circuits. In *European Design and Test Conference*, 1996.
13. L. Stok. False loops through resource sharing. In *International Conference on Computer-Aided Design*, 1992.

# 6 Appendix

This appendix contains the definitions of the extended basic operators of S/R.

**Boolean Operators:**

$$
\begin{array}{llll}
u \wedge_\perp v = & \mathit{false} & \text{if } u = \mathit{false} \text{ or } v = \mathit{false}; & \text{otherwise,} \\
& \perp & \text{if } u = \perp \text{ or } v = \perp; & \text{otherwise,} \\
& u \wedge v & & \\
u \vee_\perp v = & \mathit{true} & \text{if } u = \mathit{true} \text{ or } v = \mathit{true}; & \text{otherwise,} \\
& \perp & \text{if } u = \perp \text{ or } v = \perp; & \text{otherwise,} \\
& u \vee v & & \\
\neg_\perp u = & \perp & \text{if } u = \perp; & \text{otherwise,} \\
& \neg u & &
\end{array}
$$

**Arithmetic Operators:**

$$
\begin{array}{llll}
u +_\perp v = & \perp & \text{if } u = \perp \text{ or } v = \perp; & \text{otherwise,} \\
& u + v & & \\
u *_\perp v = & 0 & \text{if } u = 0 \text{ or } v = 0; & \text{otherwise,} \\
& \perp & \text{if } u = \perp \text{ or } v = \perp; & \text{otherwise,} \\
& u * v & & \\
u \; div_\perp \; v = & 0 & \text{if } u = 0; & \text{otherwise,} \\
& \perp & \text{if } (u = \perp \text{ and } v \neq 0) \text{ or } v = \perp; & \text{otherwise,} \\
& u \; div \; v & & \\
u \; mod_\perp \; v = & 0 & \text{if } u = 0 \text{ or } v = 1; & \text{otherwise,} \\
& \perp & \text{if } (u = \perp \text{ and } v \neq 0) \text{ or } v = \perp; & \text{otherwise,} \\
& u \; mod \; v & & \\
u \; exp_\perp \; v = & 0 & \text{if } u = 0; & \text{otherwise,} \\
& 1 & \text{if } u = 1 \text{ or } v = 0; & \text{otherwise,} \\
& \perp & \text{if } u = \perp \text{ or } v = \perp; & \text{otherwise,} \\
& u \; exp \; v & &
\end{array}
$$

**Comparison Operators:**

$$
\begin{array}{llll}
u <_\perp v = & \perp & \text{if } u = \perp \text{ or } v = \perp; & \text{otherwise,} \\
& u < v & & \\
u \leq_\perp v = & \perp & \text{if } u = \perp \text{ or } v = \perp; & \text{otherwise,} \\
& u \leq v & & \\
u =_\perp v = & \perp & \text{if } u = \perp \text{ or } v = \perp; & \text{otherwise,} \\
& u = v & &
\end{array}
$$

**Conditional Operators:**

$$
\begin{array}{llll}
(\underline{if} \; c \; \underline{then} \; u \; \underline{else} \; v)_\perp = & u & \text{if } c = \mathit{true}; & \text{otherwise,} \\
& v & \text{if } c = \mathit{false}; & \text{otherwise,} \\
& u & \text{if } c = \perp \text{ and } u = v; & \text{otherwise,} \\
& \perp & \text{if } c = \perp \text{ and } u \neq v & \\
(\underline{if} \; c \; \underline{then} \; u)_\perp = & u & \text{if } c = \mathit{true} &
\end{array}
$$

# A Theory of Restrictions for Logics and Automata

Nils Klarlund

AT&T Labs–Research (klarlund@research.att.com)

**Abstract.** BDDs and their algorithms implement a decision procedure for Quantified Propositional Logic. BDDs are a kind of acyclic automata. Unrestricted automata (recognizing unbounded strings of bit vectors) can be used to decide more expressive monadic second-order logics. Prime examples are WS1S, a number-theoretic logic, or a string-based notation such as those proposed in some introductory texts. It is not clear which one is to be preferred. Also, the inclusion of first-order variables in either version is problematic since their automata-theoretic semantics depends on restrictions.

In this paper, we provide a mathematical framework to address these problems. We introduce three and six-valued characterizations of regular languages under restrictions. From properties of the resulting congruences, we are able to carry out detailed state space analyses that allows us to solve the two problems in WS1S in a way that require no extra normalization calculations compared to a naive decision procedure for string-oriented logic.

We report briefly on the practical experiments that support our results. We conclude that WS1S with first-order variables is the superior choice among monadic second-order logics.

## 1 Motivation

Büchi[2] and Elgot[4], and independently Trakhtenbrot[13], argued almost forty years ago that a logical notation, now called the Weak Second-order theory of 1 Successor or WS1S, would be a more natural alternative to what already was known as regular expressions. WS1S has an extremely simple syntax and semantics: it is variation of predicate logic with first-order variables that denote natural numbers and second-order variables that denote finite sets of natural numbers; it has a single function symbol, which denotes the successor function, and has usual comparison operators such as $\leq, =, \in$ and $\supseteq$. Büchi, Elgot, and Trakhtenbrot showed that a decision procedure exists for this logic. The idea is to view interpretations as finite strings over bit vectors and then to show by explicit constructions of automata that the set of satisfying interpretations for any subformula is a regular language. A distinguishing feature of this *number-theoretic* approach is that the semantics refer to *all* the natural numbers or *all* of finite subsets.

In contrast, the logical semantics often suggested in explanations of the logic-automaton connection, such as in [11, 12], is tied to the finiteness of the strings of a regular language. Here, the notation is interpreted over a string, which is fixed for the purpose of the semantics. The string defines a set of positions from 0 to the length of the string minus 1; then, first-order variables range over this set, and second-order variables over its subsets. This *string-theoretic* approach is appealing for certain applications, for example in the description and verification of parameterized hardware[1]. Among other names, these logics have been called MSO(S)[12], SOM[+][11], and M2L(Str)[5, 7]. They vary slightly, but we will identify them as M2L(Str) in this paper.

There are at least three important reasons for preferring the number-theoretic approach. (1) Its mathematical semantics is simpler. (2) WS1S appears to be the stronger logic: it is easy to encode Presburger arithmetic in WS1S, but no similar encoding is known for the string-theoretic formulation. Presburger arithmetic by itself is a promising verification technique, see [3, 10]. (3) There are semantic problems in the string-theoretic formulation as pointed out in [7]; for example, what does a first-order variable denote if the string is empty and thus define no positions?

Even so, it is not obvious that any string-theoretic problem solved by a decision procedure for M2L(Str) can be effectively encoded in WS1S. More precisely, we desire an *efficient translation algorithm*, which we define to be one that in linear time transforms any formula $\phi$ in M2L(Str) to a formula in WS1S $\phi'$ such that $\phi'$ is decided in time linear in the time that $\phi$ is decided. Let us call the question of finding such an algorithm the *translation problem*. In practice, of course, we want something stronger: the total running time of going around WS1S should be no longer than using the M2L(Str) decision procedure directly.

Another problem with monadic second-order logics is that first-order variables and terms are handled by formula rewritings transforming them into second-order variables subjected to logical restrictions. Consequently, automata corresponding to subformulas are not simply determined by the mathematical semantics, but also by details of the rewritings. Alternatively, extra automata product operations can be used to *normalize* these intermediate automata with automata corresponding to the restrictions. The *first-order semantics problem* is to find a representation that is no bigger than a normalized representation, while not requiring extra normalization steps.

## Contributions of this paper

In this paper, we propose solutions to the translation problem and the first-order semantics problem. Our solutions are based on a theory of restrictions that we develop as follows.

We formulate a syntax for WS1S, where restrictions are made explicit, and we provide initially three different semantics: (1) the *ad hoc* semantics that correspond to the usual treatment of first-order variables, (2) the *conjunctive semantics*, where *all* the intermediate automata are conjoined with restrictions, and (3) the *three-valued semantics*. We explain why the ad hoc semantics must be rejected, and why the conjunctive semantics would slow down the decision procedure. We show that the three-valued semantics makes most normalizations unnecessary. Also, we indicate how the three-valued semantics can be realized using an automata-theoretic approach adapted from the standard WS1S decision procedure.

To study the question of automata sizes, we give a detailed congruence-theoretic analysis of a regular language under restrictions. We introduce a notion of a *thin* language, and we show that the restrictions occurring in the treatment of first-order variables and in the translation problem are thin. We prove that languages under thin restrictions make comparisons of the conjunctive semantics and the the three-valued semantics easy: the latter are the same as the former except for some extra equivalence classes that we characterize. We show that if the automata of restrictions are bounded, then the sizes of intermediate automata occurring under the three-valued semantics are, to within a constant factor, the same as the sizes of automata of the conjunctive semantics.

We strengthen this result by exhibiting congruences based on a *six-valued semantics* that are no bigger (to an additive constant of 3) than those of the conjunctive semantics. Our main result is that the resulting decision procedure, while requiring only few normalizations, involve intermediate automata that are up to exponentially smaller than the ones occurring under the conjunctive semantics.

Finally, we report on our integration of the theory presented here into the tool Mona[9], which implements a decision procedure for WS1S. We conclude that WS1S, and not a string-oriented logic, is the superior logical interface to automata calculations.

## 2 WS1S: review and issues

*Nutshell WS1S* can be presented as follows. A formula $\phi$ is *composite* and of the form $\tilde{\phi}'$, $\phi'$ & $\phi''$, or ex2 $P^i : \phi'$, or *atomic* and of the form $P^i$ sub $P^j$, $P^i$ <= $P^j$, $P^i$ =$P^j$ \ $P^k$, or $P^i$ =$P^j$ +1. Here, we have assumed that variables are all second-order and named $P^i$, where $i \geq 1$. Other comparison operators, second-order terms with set-theoretic operators, and Boolean connectives can be introduced by trivial syntactic abbreviations, see [9, 12]. The treatment of first-order terms is discussed later.

**Semantics of WS1S** Given a fixed main formula $\phi_0$, which we sometimes regard as an abstract syntax tree (with its root facing up), we define its semantics inductively relative to a string $w$ over the alphabet $\mathbb{B}^k$, where $\mathbb{B} = \{0, 1\}$ and $k$ is the number of variables in $\phi_0$. We assume that $\phi_0$ is closed and that each variable is bound in at most one occurrence of an existential quantifier. Generally, we assume that all formulas are subformulas of $\phi_0$. We now regard a string $w = a_0 \cdots a_{\ell-1}$, where $\ell = |w|$ is the length of $w$, to be of the form:

$$
\begin{matrix}
P^1 \\
\cdots \\
P^k
\end{matrix}
\qquad
\begin{pmatrix} a_0^1 \\ \cdots \\ a_0^k \end{pmatrix} \cdots \begin{pmatrix} a_{\ell-1}^1 \\ \cdots \\ a_{\ell-1}^k \end{pmatrix}
$$

where we have indicated that if the string is viewed as a matrix, then row $i$ is called the $P^i$-*track*. Each letter $a$ is sometimes written in a transposed notation as $(a^1, \ldots, a^k)^t$. The interpretation of $P^i$ defined by $w$ is the finite set $\{j \mid \text{the } j\text{th bit in the } P^i\text{-track is } 1\}$. Note that suffixing $w$ with any string consisting of letters of the form $(0, \ldots, 0)^t$ does not change the interpretation of any variable. Therefore, we will say that $w$ is *minimum* if it possesses no such non-empty suffix.

The semantics of a formula $\phi$ can now be defined inductively relative to an interpretation $w$. We use the notation $w \vDash \phi$ (which is read: $w$ satisfies $\phi$) if the interpretation defined by $w$ makes $\phi$ true:

$$
\begin{array}{ll}
w \vDash \,\tilde{}\,\phi' & \text{iff } w \nvDash \phi' \\
w \vDash \phi' \,\&\, \phi'' & \text{iff } w \vDash \phi' \text{ and } w \vDash \phi'' \\
w \vDash \text{ex2 } P^i : \phi' & \text{iff } \exists \text{ finite } M \subseteq \mathbb{N} : w[P^i \mapsto M] \vDash \phi' \\
w \vDash P^i \text{ sub } P^j & \text{iff } w(P^i) \subseteq w(P^j) \\
w \vDash P^i \text{ <= } P^j & \text{iff } \forall h \in w(P^i) : \exists k \in w(P^j) : h \leq k \\
w \vDash P^i = P^j \backslash P^k & \text{iff } w(P^i) = w(P^j) \backslash w(P^k) \\
w \vDash P^i = P^j \text{ +1} & \text{iff } w(P^i) = \{j + 1 \mid j \in w(P^j)\}
\end{array}
$$

where we use the notation $w[P^i \mapsto M]$ for the shortest string $w'$ that interprets all variables $P^j$, $j \neq i$, as $w$ does, but interprets $P^i$ as $M$. Note that if we here assume that $w$ is minimum, then $w$ is of the form $\tilde{w} \cdot w_0$, where all tracks, except the $P^i$-track, in $w_0$ are all 0s and either $\tilde{w}$ is empty or at least one non-$P^i$ track in $\tilde{w}$ is of the form $\mathbb{B}^* \cdot 1$. Then, $w'$ is of the form $\tilde{w} \cdot w''$, where $w''$ is 0 everywhere except for the $P^i$-track, which is of the form $\mathbb{B}^* \cdot 1$ if non-empty.

Note that the interpretation of $\phi_0$ is independent of $w$, since it is a closed formula. Thus, $\phi_0$ is either true or false, and we write either $\vDash \phi_0$ or $\nvDash \phi_0$. For any formula $\phi$, we associate the *language* $L_\phi = \{w \mid w \vDash \phi\}$.

## 2.1 Automata-theoretic semantics

The automata-theoretic semantics defines a decision procedure that associates to each $\phi$ the minimum automaton $A_\phi$ accepting the language $L_\phi$. For atomic formula, a small automaton (with at most three states) can be directly constructed. For a formula $\phi$ of the form $\tilde{}\,\phi'$, the automaton $A_\phi$ is taken to be the complement of the automaton $A_{\phi'}$, which is calculated by induction. Note that this automata-theoretic semantics of negation is symmetric: the complement automaton is gotten by just reversing final and non-final states. The case of conjunction is handled by an automata-theoretic product construction, followed by a minimization construction. Finally, the case of quantification is slightly more complicated. Consider $\phi = w \vDash \text{ex2 } P^i : \phi'$. We calculate $A_\phi$ from $A_{\phi'}$ by means of an intermediate, nondeterministic automaton $A_{\phi''}$ that is gotten from $A_{\phi'}$ in two steps. First, any state for which a path exists to an accepting state along a string of letters of the form $(0, \ldots, 0, X, 0, \ldots, 0)^t$ (where the $X$ means that the value of the $i$th component is irrelevant) is made accepting. Second, for any transition of the form $(s, a, s')$ from state $s$ to $s'$, we add the transition $(s, a, s'')$, where $s''$ is the state reached according to the unique transition $(s, \bar{a}, s'')$ with $\bar{a}$ being the same letter as $a$ except that the $i$th component is negated. The automaton $A_\phi$ is then calculated by determinizing $A_{\phi''}$, followed by a minimization construction.

## 2.2 Semantics of first-order variables

Adding first-order variables to WS1S can easily be done as follows: a first-order variable $p$ is regarded as a second-order term $P$ that is restricted to take on values that are singleton sets, where the sole element denotes the value of $p$, see [12, 11, 8]. The restriction can be imposed by conjoining a singleton predicate $\texttt{singleton}(P)$ to the formula where $P$ is quantified. This *ad hoc strategy* means that the semantics of a formula containing $p$ is not robust: its meaning on interpretations $w$ not fulfilling $\texttt{singleton}(P)$ is not well-defined. Even if the restriction is imposed whenever $p$ occurs in an atomic formula, the semantics is not closed under complementation. For example, the formula $\phi = p{=}0$, where $p$ is first-order is handled as $\phi' = P{=}\{0\}$, where $P$ is second-order. But the complement of $\phi'$ is $\tilde{\ }(P = \{0\})$, something that is different from the representation of $\tilde{\ }(p = 0)$, namely $\tilde{\ }(P = \{0\})$ & $\texttt{singleton}(P)$. The solution is to conjoin the restriction to every subformula $\phi$ in a procedure we call *normalization*. Then, we would have a simple explanation of the language $L(\phi)$ that we call the *conjunctive semantics*.

The practical problem with the conjunctive semantics is that additional product and minimization calculations would be necessary: for each automaton $A$ representing a subformula $\phi$ and each free variable $P^i$, the automaton representing the singleton property for $P^i$ must be conjoined to $A$. Such extra calculational work slow down the decision procedure, probably by a factor of at least two. (Complementation, which is normally fast since it consists of flipping acceptance statuses of states, now would involve a product and a minimization operation; and product operations would involve at least one additional product and minimization even if the restrictions are calculated separately.) So in practice, the Mona implementation (prior to the one implemented with the results of this article) used the ad hoc strategy: the restriction for variable $p$ is conjoined only to atomic formulas where $p$ occur and to the formula in the existential quantification introducing $p$.

*Ad hoc emulation of string semantics in WS1S* A simplified syntax for the string-theoretic version of monadic second-order logic is the same as nutshell WS1S syntax. The satisfaction relation is denoted $\vDash_{string}$; it is the same as for WS1S except that quantification is changed to:

$$w \vDash_{string} \texttt{ex2 } P^i : \phi' \text{ iff } \exists M \subseteq \{0, \dots, |w| - 1\} : w[P^i \mapsto M] \vDash \phi'$$

where the notation $w[P^i \mapsto M]$ now has a different meaning: it denotes the string $w$ altered so that the $P^i$ track describes $M$. Thus, the witness string $w[P^i \mapsto M]$ for the existential quantification has the same length as $w$. The interpretation of $\phi_0$ on a string of $w$ still does not depend on the individual tracks of $w$, but it *does* depend on the length of $w$. Thus we write $i \vDash_{string} \phi_0$ if $\phi_0$ holds for a string $w$ of length $i$. For example, a closed formula can be written that under this semantics holds if and only if $w$ is of even length.

To emulate $\vDash_{string}$ in $\vDash$, we must restrict all second-order terms to sets of numbers less than or equal to the last position in the string. Thus, we introduce a first-order variable $ that simulates the entity $|w| - 1$. A $-*constraint* for a variable expresses that the variable is a subset of $\{0, \dots, \$\}$. Then, we normalize all formulas by conjoining $-constraints for all free variables. The result is a WS1S formula $\phi'$ with one free variable $ such that $i \vDash_{string} \phi \Leftrightarrow w \vDash \phi'$, where the $-track of $w$ interprets $ as $i$. For example, the formula ex1 $p$: ex1 q: $p = q$ becomes in WS1S

> ex2 $P$: ex2 $Q$:
> $\quad$ singleton$(P)$ & singleton$(Q)$ & singleton$(\$)$
> $\quad$ & $P$<=$ & $Q$<=$ & $P$ sub $Q$ & $Q$ sub $P$

as expressed in nutshell syntax, whereas the M2L(Str) formulation is

> ex2 $P$: ex2 $Q$:
> $\quad$ singleton$(P)$ & singleton$(Q)$
> $\quad$ $P$ sub $Q$ & $Q$ sub $P$

**Proposition 1.** *Under the translation outlined above, the minimized, canonical automata arising during the WS1S decision procedure are essentially the same as the ones arising during the M2L(Str) procedure except for one or two additional states.*

*Proof.* The WS1S automaton can be gotten from the M2L(Str) automaton by considering the $-track as some $P^i$ track and by adding states $s_{accept}$ (an accepting state) and $s_{reject}$ (a rejecting state). The transition relation of the new automaton is the same as for the old one as long as the $-component is 0. When the $-component is 1, corresponding to the end of the string under the M2L(Str) representation, a transition is made to $s_{accept}$ or $s_{reject}$ according to the accept status of the state that would have been reached in the old automaton. From $s_{accept}$, a transition is made to $s_{reject}$ if the $-component is 1 or if any other component corresponding to a first-order variable is 1; otherwise, the transition is made to $s_{accept}$. The $s_{reject}$ state is connected to itself on all letters. The WS1S automaton so described may not be minimum, since the reject state may already have been present in the automaton. All other states of the old automaton are still distinct when considered as part of the new automaton.

Our practical experiments with running string-based examples translated into WS1S were based on this ad hoc strategy. We discovered the following problem.

*Parity example* Consider the formula ex1 $p$: $(p$ in $P^1$ <=> $\cdots$ <=> $p$ in $P^n)$ under the string-theoretic semantics. The formula holds if and only if there is a position

412

contained in an even number of the sets $P^i$. Translated into nutshell WS1S under the ad hoc strategy, the formula becomes:

> ex2  $P$ :  $(P$ in $P^1$ & singleton$(P)$ & singleton$(\$)$ & $P^1$<=$\$)$ <=>
>
> $\cdots$ <=>  (1)
>
> $(P$ in $P^n$ & singleton$(P)$ & singleton$(\$)$ & $P^n$<=$\$)$.

**Proposition 2.** *The parity formula (1) produces intermediate automata whose size is doubly exponential in n. But if the restrictions are conjoined to all subformula, not only the atomic ones, then all intermediate automata have less than 6 states.*

We formalize the ad hoc semantics in the next section; but already here, it is clear that it is inadequate for restrictions.

## 3  WS1S with restrictions and a three-valued semantics

To give a precise understanding of restrictions, we introduce *nutshell WS1S-R*, a variation on WS1S where restrictions are made explicit. Existential quantification becomes **ex2** $P^i$ **where** $\rho\colon \phi'$. Let $\rho(P^i) = \rho$ be the *restriction* of variable $P^i$. Also, we assume that each $P^i$ is restricted, possibly to the formula $P^i=P^i$, i.e., **true**. The semantics we will propose for this syntax rely on an exact understanding of the binding mechanisms in play. We say that in $\rho(P^i)$, variable $P^i$ is *$\rho$-bound*. Variable $P^i$ is *existentially bound* in both $\rho(P^i)$ and $\phi'$. A variable occurrence $P^i$ is *free in the conventional part of* $\phi$ if $P^i$ is free in $\phi$ in the usual sense, where $\phi$ is regarded as an independent formula, and the occurrence is not within a restriction of an existential quantification within $\phi$. The *relevant variables*, RV$(\phi)$, for formula $\phi$ is the least set of variables $P$ such that there is an occurrence of $P$ that is not $\rho$-bound and that is free in the conventional part of $\phi$ or free in the conventional part of $\rho(P')$, where $P' \in$ RV$(\phi)$. We define the *induced restriction* $\rho^*(\phi)$ to be the conjunction of the restrictions of relevant variables, that is, $\bigwedge_{P^i \in \mathrm{RV}(\phi)}$.

To carry out inductive arguments, we define the partial ordering $\trianglelefteq$ among subformulas (regarded as nodes in the abstract syntax tree) as follows: $\phi \trianglelefteq \phi'$ if $\phi$ is a subformula of $\phi'$ or if there is a formula $\psi = $ **ex2** $P^i$ **where** $\rho(P^i)\colon \phi''$ such that $\phi$ is a subformula of $\rho(P^i)$ and $\phi'$ is a subformula of $\phi''$. The partial ordering $\trianglelefteq$ is well-founded (a post-order labeling of nodes with numbers $0, 1, \ldots$ produces an ordering containing $\trianglelefteq$). Note for each $P \in$ RV$(\phi)$, $\rho(P) \triangleleft \phi$. This will ensure that the semantic definitions to follow make sense.

*The ad hoc semantics* We state the ad hoc semantics using a meaning function $[\![\phi]\!]^{ah}$ (anticipating multi-valued semantics):

$$[\![\tilde{}\phi']\!]^{ah}w = \neg[\![\phi']\!]^{ah}w$$

$$[\![\phi' \And \phi'']\!]^{ah}w = [\![\phi']\!]^{ah}w \land [\![\phi'']\!]^{ah}w$$

$$[\![ex2 \ P^i \ \textbf{where} \ \rho\colon \phi']\!]^{ah}w = \begin{cases} 1 & \text{if } \exists M : [\![\phi']\!]^{ah}w[P^i \mapsto M] = 1 \text{ and } [\![\rho^*(P^i)]\!]^{ah} = 1 \\ 0 & \text{if } \forall M : [\![\phi']\!]^{ah}w[P^i \mapsto M] = 0 \text{ or } [\![\rho^*(P^i)]\!]^{ah} = 0 \end{cases}$$

$$[\![P^i \ \textbf{sub} \ P^j]\!]^{ah}w = \begin{cases} 1 & \text{if } w \vDash P^i \ \textbf{sub} \ P^j \text{ and } [\![\rho^*(P^i \ \textbf{sub} \ P^j)]\!]^{ah}w = 1 \\ 0 & \text{if } w \nvDash P^i \ \textbf{sub} \ P^j \text{ or } [\![\rho^*(P^i \ \textbf{sub} \ P^j)]\!]^{ah}w = 0 \end{cases}$$

We have only shown the semantics of one kind of atomic formula; the others are treated similarly. (The normalization of atomic formulas is optional.)

**The conjunction semantics** This semantics is the same as the ad hoc semantics except that the restrictions are also applied to the case of & and ~.

*The three-valued semantics* Let $\mathbb{B}^\perp = \mathbb{B} \cup \{\perp\}$ be the *extended Boolean domain*. We use $\perp$ to denote a "don't care" situation, one where not all the restrictions hold. Boolean operators $\land^3$ and $\neg^3$ are defined on this domain as for the usual case with the added rule that if any argument is $\perp$, then the result is $\perp$.

$$[\![\tilde{}\phi']\!]^3w = \neg^3[\![\phi']\!]^3w$$

$$[\![\phi' \And \phi'']\!]^3w = [\![\phi']\!]^3w \land^3 [\![\phi'']\!]^3w$$

$$[\![ex2 \ P^i \ \textbf{where} \ \rho\colon \phi']\!]^3w = \begin{cases} 1 & \text{if } \exists M : [\![\phi']\!]^3w[P^i \mapsto M] = 1 \\ 0 & \text{if } \forall M : [\![\phi']\!]^3w[P^i \mapsto M] \neq 1 \text{ and } \exists M : [\![\phi']\!]^3w[P^i \mapsto M] = 0 \\ \perp & \text{if } \forall M : [\![\phi']\!]^3w[P^i \mapsto M] = \perp \end{cases}$$

$$[\![P^i \ \textbf{sub} \ P^j]\!]^3w = \begin{cases} 1 & \text{if } w \vDash P^i \ \textbf{sub} \ P^j \text{ and } [\![\rho^*(P^i \ \textbf{sub} \ P^j)]\!]^3w = 1 \\ 0 & \text{if } w \nvDash P^i \ \textbf{sub} \ P^j \text{ and } [\![\rho^*(P^i \ \textbf{sub} \ P^j)]\!]^3 = 1 \\ \perp & \text{if } [\![\rho^*(P^i \ \textbf{sub} \ P^j)]\!]^3 \neq 1 \end{cases}$$

Something seems to be missing in this semantics: the enforcement of a restriction of a variable in an existential quantification. The proposition below shows that the restriction bubbles up automatically if needed. The semantics works only if we require that every restriction is satisfiable given that the restrictions referred to by the restriction are already true. Formally, for subformula $\phi = ex2 \ P^i \ \textbf{where} \ \rho\colon \phi'$ of $\phi_0$, we require

$$\vDash \left( \underset{P \in RV(\phi') \setminus \{P^i\}}{\And} \rho(P) \right) \Rightarrow ex2 \ P^i : \rho \tag{2}$$

The semantics is now justified as:

**Proposition 3.** *Given the requirement (2), the following holds.*

(a) $w \nvDash \rho(P^i)$ *for some* $P^i$ *in* $RV(\phi)$ $\quad \Leftrightarrow \quad w \nvDash \rho^*(\phi) \quad \Leftrightarrow \quad [\![\phi]\!]^3w = \perp.$

(b) $w \vDash \phi \And \rho^*(\phi) \quad \Leftrightarrow \quad [\![\phi]\!]^3w = 1$

(c) $w \vDash \tilde{}\phi \And \rho^*(\phi) \quad \Leftrightarrow \quad [\![\phi]\!]^3w = 0$

**Automata-theoretic realization of the three-valued semantics** The procedure outlined in Section 2.1 can be modified to reflect the three-valued semantics. The case of existential quantification requires a slightly more sophisticated reclassification of the acceptance statuses of states prior to the subset construction. Let us call the resulting algorithm the *three-valued decision procedure*.

# 4 Congruences for restricted languages

All languages considered will be regular and over the alphabet $\Sigma = \mathbb{B}^k$. For a language $L$, the *canonical right-congruence* $\sim_L$ is defined as $u \sim_L v$ iff $\forall w :$ $u{\cdot}w \in L \Leftrightarrow v{\cdot}w \in L$, where $u, v, w \in \Sigma^*$. The set of congruence classes is denoted $\Sigma^*/{\sim_L}$. This set can be regarded as the canonical, finite-state automaton.

Consider languages $L$, sometimes called the *property*, and $R$, assumed nonempty, called a *restriction*. Thus, $L_\phi$ and $L_{\rho^*(\phi)}$ constitute such a pair for any subformula $\phi$ of $\phi_0$. The *conjunction representation* is $L' = L \cap R$, and the *conjunction congruence* is $\sim_{L \cap R}$. The *three-valued representation* is not a language, but a function $\chi^3_{L,R}(u)$, defined to be 1 if $u \in L \cap R$, 0 if $u \in \overline{L} \cap R$, and $\bot$ if $u \notin R$. The *three-valued* congruence $\sim^3_{L,R}$ is then defined by $u \sim^3 v \Leftrightarrow$ for all $w$, $\chi^3_{L,R}(u \cdot w) = \chi^3_{L,R}(v \cdot w)$.

## 4.1 Relating the conjunction and three-valued semantics

A *thin language* $R$ is a non-empty set of strings such that

$$\forall u, v, w : u \not\sim_R v \Rightarrow u \cdot w \notin R \lor v \cdot w \notin R \tag{3}$$

In particular, the canonical automaton for $R$ has exactly one accepting state.

**Proposition 4.** *1. $R_{singleton(i)} = \{u \in \mathbb{B}^k \mid track\ i\ contains\ exactly\ one\ occurrence\ of\ a\ 1\}$ is thin.*

*2. The language*

$$R_{\$\text{-}restrict(i)} = \{u \in \mathbb{B}^k \mid the\ occurrences\ of\ 1\ in\ track\ i\ are\ all\ in\ positions\\ no\ greater\ than\ that\ of\ the\ first\ occurrence\ of\ a\ 1\\ in\ track\ \$\} \ \cap\ R_{singleton(\$)}$$

*is thin.*

*3. If $R$ and $R'$ are thin and $R \cap R' \neq \emptyset$, then $R \cap R'$ is thin.*

*4. Let $R$ be thin, and let $L$ be any language. If $u \sim_{L \cap R} v$ and $u$ has an accepting extension, then $u \sim_R v$ (and, consequently, $u \sim^3_{L,R} v$).*

*5. If $u$ and $v$ both have no accepting extensions, then $u \sim_R v \Leftrightarrow u \sim^3_{L,R} v$.*

*6. Thus, if $R$ is thin, then $|\Sigma^*/{\sim^3_{L,R}}| \leq |\Sigma^*/{\sim_{L \cap R}}| + |\Sigma^*/{\sim_R}|$.*

From this proposition, it follows easily that all $\rho^*(\phi)$ are thin languages if variables are subjected to first-order restrictions or $-restrictions (or both). The proposition also tells us that $\Sigma^*/{\sim^3_{L,R}}$ is pieced together from $\Sigma^*/{\sim_{L \cap R}}$ plus a subset of $\Sigma^*/{\sim_R}$.

**Proposition 5.** *Assume that all restrictions are thin languages. If the automata of restrictions are bounded in size, then the sizes of the intermediate, minimized automata in the three-valued decision procedure are the same, to within an additive constant, as the sizes of corresponding automata under the conjunctive semantics.*

This result is the justification for the practical use of the three-valued semantics since usually the number of first-order variables in simultaneous use is quite small. (The size of the additive constant is exponential in the number of free first-order variables.) And as with the ad hoc semantics, normalizations are not required for most subformulas, and the automata are, apart from the $\Sigma^*/\sim_R$ parts, the same as those that occur when the automaton of every subformula is normalized.

## 4.2 The six-valued representation

We show next how to get rid of the boundedness assumption in Proposition 5. Define a string $u$ to be *interesting* if it has (a) some extension $v$, called an *accepting extension*, such that $u \cdot v$ in $L \cap R$, and (b) some extension $\bar{v}$, called a *rejecting extension*, such that $u \cdot \bar{v}$ in $\overline{L} \cap R$. Also, a *"don't care"* extension is one that makes a string fall outside $R$. Note that all prefixes of an interesting string are also interesting. In other words, an uninteresting string cannot be extended so as to become interesting. The truth-value $\iota(u)$ denotes whether a string is interesting. Let $cut(u)$ be the shortest uninteresting prefix of $u$ if such a prefix exists; otherwise, when all prefixes are interesting, $cut(u)$ is defined to be $u$. The *membership status* $\epsilon(u)$ of uninteresting $u$ is defined by

$$
\epsilon(u) = \begin{cases} 1 & \text{if } cut(u) \text{ has an accepting extension} \\ 0 & \text{if } cut(u)u \text{ has a rejecting extension} \\ \bot & \text{if all extensions of } cut(u) \text{ are "don't care"} \end{cases} \tag{4}
$$

(These three cases are clearly mutually exclusive.) When $u$ is interesting, $\epsilon(u)$ is defined to be $\chi^3_{L,R}(u)$. Define the *sexpartite representation* $\chi^6_{L,R}$ to be $(\iota(u), \epsilon(u))$. The *canonical six-valued congruence* $\sim^6_{L,R}$ is defined from the representation as before. Now, an equivalence class $M$ is either interesting or non-interesting. In the latter case, there is a value $E \in \mathbb{B}_\bot$ such that for all $u \in M$, $\epsilon(u) = E$; moreover, for all $v$, $u \cdot v$ is also in $M$. Thus, the non-interesting equivalence classes are graph-theoretic sinks when $\Sigma/\sim^6_{L,R}$ is regarded as a finite-state automaton. There are between 0 and 3 such classes, depending on $L$ and $R$.

Let $c$ be a natural number and let $\xi : \Sigma^* \Rightarrow \mathbb{B}$ be a Boolean characterization of all strings. We say that $\sim$ *quasi-refines* $\approx$ *up to* $c$ *under* $\xi$ when there are strings $u_1, \ldots, u_c$ such that

$$
\begin{aligned}
&\forall u, u' : \xi(u) \wedge u \sim u' \Rightarrow \xi(u') \wedge u \approx u' \text{ and} \\
&\forall u, u' : \neg\xi(u) \wedge u \sim u' \Rightarrow \neg\xi(u') \wedge \exists i, j : u \approx u_i \wedge u' \approx u_j
\end{aligned} \tag{5}
$$

Thus, $\xi$ respects $\sim$ (that is, it can mapped through $\Sigma^*/\sim$) and $\sim$ is as least as fine as $\approx$ on strings for which $\xi$ holds; but, when $\xi$ doesn't hold, strings are mapped to one of the $c$ designated equivalence classes of $\approx$.

**Proposition 6.** *If $R$ is thin, then $\sim_{L \cap R}$ quasi-refines $\sim_{L,R}^6$ up to 3 under $\xi(u) =$ "there is an accepting extension of $u$."*

Thus, the six-valued congruence squeezes the parts of $\Sigma^*/\sim_{L,R}^3$ that corresponds to $\Sigma^*/\sim_R$ (as explained after Proposition 4) into at most three classes.

### 4.3 Six-valued semantics for WS1S and sexpartite automata

Under the six-valued semantics, the automaton corresponding to $\phi$ calculates $\sim_{L_\phi, L_{\rho^*(\phi)}}^6$ by a six-way partition of the states. For non-interesting strings, it may erroneously calculate a value in $\{0, 1\}$, where the three-valued semantics specifies $\bot$. Consequently, a product with the automaton for the restriction of a variable must be carried out before the qualifier elimination in the WS1S-R decision procedure. However, it can be shown that no minimization is necessary following this step. Let us call the resulting algorithm the *six-valued decision procedure*. Thus, we may improve Proposition 5:

**Theorem 1.** *Assume that all restrictions are thin languages.*

1. *The sizes of the intermediate, minimized automata occurring during the six-valued decision procedure are (to within an additive constant) less than those of the conjunctive semantics.*
2. *The conjunctive automata may be exponentially bigger than the six-valued automata.*
3. *The six-valued decision procedure require no normalization for products and complementations.*

## 5 In practice

We showed experimental evidence in [6] that we had found WS1S to be as fast a way to decide string-theoretic problems as M2L(Str) but only after sometimes solving by hand state explosion problems like the one discussed in Section 2.2.

Since June 1998, the Mona tool has been based on the three-valued semantics for WS1S, and our state explosion problems stemming from running M2L(Str) formulas through WS1S have disappeared. Moreover, with a default restriction mechanism that we have added to Mona, M2L(Str) formulas can be directly embedded in WS1S. The running times under this semantics are in all non-contrived cases the same (to within 5% or so) as for the ad hoc semantics we used before. (In practice, we used first-order restrictions that are not thin languages, but which enjoy similar properties.) We have not yet implemented the six-valued semantics, but there is no reason not to expect that it will run as fast, while sometimes making intermediate automata smaller.

Thus, we believe to have established WS1S as the superior choice for a practical logical notation associated with automata.

*Acknowledgements* Anders Møller implemented the ideas presented here and contributed many useful insights. Jacob Elgaard found exploding Mona code from which the parity example was derived. Ken McMillan kindly discussed restriction issues with me. And thanks to the referees for pointing out some errors in an earlier version.

# References

1. David Basin and Nils Klarlund. Automata based symbolic reasoning in hardware verification. *Formal Methods in System Design*, pages 255–288, 1998. Extended version of "Hardware verification using monadic second-order logic," *Computer aided verification : 7th International Conference, CAV '95*, LNCS 939, 1995.

2. J.R. Büchi. Weak second-order arithmetic and finite automata. *Z. Math. Logik Grundl. Math.*, 6:66–92, 1960.

3. Tevfik Bultan, Richard Gerber, and William Pugh. Symbolic model checking of infinite state systems using presburger arithmetic. In *Proceedings of the 9th International Conference on Computer Aided Verification (CAV '97)*, volume 1254 of *LNCS*, pages 400–411. Springer, 1997.

4. C.C. Elgot. Decision problems of finite automata design and related arithmetics. *Trans. Amer. Math. Soc.*, 98:21–52, 1961.

5. J.G. Henriksen, J. Jensen, M. Jørgensen, N. Klarlund, B. Paige, T. Rauhe, and A. Sandholm. Mona: Monadic second-order logic in practice. In *Tools and Algorithms for the Construction and Analysis of Systems, First International Workshop, TACAS '95, LNCS 1019*, 1996.

6. Anders Møller Jacob Elgaard, Nils Klarlund. Mona 1.x: new techniques for ws1s and ws2s. In *Computer Aided Verification, CAV '98, Proceedings*, volume 1427 of *LNCS*. Springer Verlag, 1998.

7. P. Kelb, T. Margaria, M. Mendler, and C. Gsottberger. Mosel: a flexible toolset for Monadic Second-order Logic. In *Computer Aided Verification, CAV '97, Proceedings*, LNCS 1217, 1997.

8. N. Klarlund. Mona & Fido: the logic-automaton connection in practice. In *CSL '97 Proceedings*. LNCS 1414, Springer-Verlag, 1998.

9. Nils Klarlund and Anders Møller. *MONA Version 1.3 User Manual*. BRICS, 1998. URL: http://www.brics.dk/mona.

10. Thomas R. Shiple, James H. Kukula, and Rajeev K. Ranjan. A comparison of Presburger engines for EFSM reachability. In *Computer Aided Verification, CAV '98, Proceedings*, volume 1427 of *LNCS*. Springer Verlag, 1998.

11. Howard Straubing. *Finite Automata, Formal Logic, and Circuit Complexity*. Birkhäuser, 1994.

12. Wolfgang Thomas. Languages, automata, and logic. In G. Rozenberg and A. Salomaa, editors, *Handbook of Formal Languages*, chapter Languages, automata, and logic. Springer Verlag, 1997.

13. B.A. Trakhtenbrot. Finite automata and the logic of one-place predicates. *Sib. Math. J*, 3:103–131, 1962. In Russian. English translation: *AMS Transl.*, 59 (1966), pp. 23-55.

# Model Checking Based on Sequential ATPG

Vamsi Boppana, Sreeranga P. Rajan, Koichiro Takayama, and Masahiro Fujita

Fujitsu Laboratories of America, Inc., 595 Lawrence Expressway, Sunnyvale, CA 94086,

{vboppana,sree,ktakayam,fujita}@fla.fujitsu.com

**Abstract.** State-space explosion remains to be a significant challenge for Finite State Machine (FSM) exploration techniques in model checking and sequential verification. In this work, we study the use of sequential ATPG (Automatic Test-Pattern Generation) as a solution to overcome the problem for a useful class of temporal logic properties. We also develop techniques to exploit the existence of synchronizing sequences to reduce some temporal logic properties to simpler properties that can be efficiently checked using an ATPG algorithm . We show that the method has the potential to scale up to large, industrial-strength, hardware designs for which current model checking techniques fail.

## 1 Introduction

The state-space explosion problem that challenges Finite State Machine (FSM) exploration techniques such as CTL temporal logic model checking [McM93] for automatic formal verification has been intensively studied from various angles. There have been numerous efforts to tackle the state-space explosion problem [CGL94]. Techniques such as compact data structures to represent the state-space [Bry95], on-the-fly model checking [Pel96], state-space reduction techniques such as localization reduction [Kur94], and navigated model checking [TSNH98] have improved the applicability of model checking towards increasingly large designs.

However, past efforts in alleviating the state-space explosion problem fall short of making model checking scale up for efficient automatic verification of current, industrial, hardware designs. Current model checking techniques could fail in several ways including failure to extract state-transition relation information from the design structure and requiring excessive storage for functional representations of the state-space during computation.

In this work, we study the use of sequential ATPG (Automatic Test-Pattern Generation) algorithms [ABF90] for model checking a simple class of CTL formulae. The approach involves the construction, based on the CTL formula, of a new circuit structure from the circuit to be verified. Model checking is then cast into *detecting* a *stuck-at-fault* on the output line of the constructed circuit. The method avoids building elaborate functional information such as a complete state transition relation and benefits from a directed, on-the-fly, structural exploration of the design under verification. Experiments are performed on benchmark circuits with simple formulae of the form **AG EF** $P$ to study the efficiency of state space exploration with a state-of-the-art sequential ATPG. Furthermore, we show reductions of the form **AG EF** $P$ to **EF** $P$ based on verifying the existence of *synchronizing* sequences [Koh78,Hen68], whose application causes an FSM to reach a specific state regardless of the starting state. The motivation for these reductions stems from the fact that most machines are synchronizable (atleast partially/weakly) with designer-supplied/ATPG-generated sequences and because they enable efficient ATPG problem formulations. The reduction results have been verified and incorporated into the PVS [ORR⁺96] proof checker.

The rest of the paper is organized as follows: Section 2 discusses the reduction of simple CTL formulae for synchronizable machines. A discussion on sequential ATPG algorithms and their application in state-space exploration is given in Section 3. The method of transforming model checking simple CTL formulae to stuck-at-fault testing is explained in Section 4. Experimental results are discussed in Section 5. Finally, conclusions are summarized in Section 6.

## 2 Formula Reduction for Synchronizable FSMs

Synchronizability of a FSM is used to reduce CTL formulae of the form **AG EF** $P$ to **EF** $P$. A formal definition of synchronizable machines is given in Section 2.1 followed by an example illustrating the reduction in Section 2.2. The formalization of the reduction of CTL formulae and their proofs in the PVS proof checker are explained in Section 2.3 and Section 2.4 respectively.

### 2.1 Synchronizable FSMs

**Definition 1 (Synchronizability [Koh78,Hen68])** *A machine $M$ is synchronizable, if there exists an input sequence $Y$, that takes $M$ to a specified final state, regardless of the output or the initial state.*

**Definition 2 (Initializability [CA89,CA93])** *A machine $M$ is initializable with three-valued logic simulation if there exists an input sequence $Y$, such that the resulting state of $M$ (evaluated by three-valued simulation) is fully specified on the application of $Y$, when the initial state is fully unspecified (consisting of all Xs and corresponding to the entire state space). Initializability, is thus synchronizability subject to three-valued logic simulation.*

It is important to note that verifying that a given sequence of test vectors is an initializing sequence is a much simpler task than verifying if the sequence is a synchronizing sequence. The reason is that while checking for initializing sequences can be done on the structure of the circuit (using 3-valued logic simulation on the netlist), checking for synchronizing sequences may often require some form of knowledge and representation of the state space. For large, industrial designs, the only feasible checks possible are based on initializing sequences.

**Table 1.** Example FSM

| PS ↓ | NS x=0 | NS x=1 |
|------|--------|--------|
| A | B | D |
| B | A | B |
| C | D | A |
| D | D | C |

## 2.2 Basic Idea and Example

Consider the FSM shown in Table 1 [Koh78]. The machine has four states $A$, $B$, $C$ and $D$, and one input $x$. The first column in the table represents the present state, the next two columns represent the next states reached up on the application of input $x$.

It is clear that the machine has a synchronizing sequence 01010; this sequence, when applied to the FSM, synchronizes the machine to state $D$, regardless of the output or the initial state. Consider the property $D \models AGEF(C)$. This property can now be reduced to $D \models EF(C)$ based on verifying that there is a synchronizing sequence to the state $D$ (in this example, the sequence 01010 achieves the objective).

An intuitive explanation of the savings possible from this method is presented below. Consider any arbitrary state that is reachable from $D$, say $B$ for illustration. Transferring the machine from state $B$ to state $C$ can be performed in the two distinct steps of transferring the machine from state $B$ to the synchronized state $D$ followed by transferring the machine from state $D$ to state $C$. Symbolically, this can be represented by the following:

$$B \xrightarrow{EF} C \Leftarrow (B \xrightarrow{Syn.seq.} D : D \xrightarrow{EF} C).$$

The key is to note that checking for the validity of a given initializing sequence (for example, from designers or from ATPG vectors), incurs only the cost of logic simulation. We also note the important difference between the use of a synchronizing sequence and a reset sequence that is potentially derived from a reset signal in the circuit. While the use of reset signals is equally applicable for our result, it may be entirely uninteresting to apply a reduction in the formula based on the use of such signals. However, synchronizing sequences (which are more general than reset sequences), when available, can be used to simplify the properties as illustrated. Further, checking of multiple properties of the kind illustrated can benefit from a single check for the validity of a synchronizing sequence.

## 2.3 Reduction of CTL Formulae: Formalization

Synchronizability can be formally expressed as a CTL formula: **AG EF** $(s_0)$, where $s_0$ is the specific state to which the FSM is synchronizable. Using the above CTL formula to represent synchronizability, we state the following result that if there exists a synchronizing sequence for the FSM, then checking for the existence of at least one path from the synchronized state on which a property holds eventually is equivalent to checking for the property to hold eventually along at least one path from every state. Formally,

**Result 1** *AG-EF Reduction*

$$\text{AG EF}(s = s_0) \wedge \text{EF}_{s_0}(\text{p}) \implies \text{AG EF}(\text{p})$$

where $s_0$ is the specific state to which the FSM is synchronizable, $p$ is the predicate to be checked. The reduction of the formula into the form **EF**(*p*) is critically helpful in embedding the predicate $p$ directly into the state justification engine of the sequential ATPG algorithm. A brief description of the main phases in a sequential ATPG algorithm and the proposed transformation procedure for obtaining a sequential ATPG problem are discussed later in the paper.

### 2.4 Proof Mechanization of the CTL Formula Reduction

In this section, we verify and incorporate the model checking reduction results stated in Section 2.3 into a mechanical theorem prover PVS [ORR+96]. PVS provides an integrated environment for the development and analysis of formal specifications and has a powerful theorem prover with a high-degree of automation together with a Binary Decision Diagram (BDD)-based model checker. The verification of properties is performed by invoking appropriate built-in proof strategies. The proof strategies consist of a combination of induction, rewriting, and special purpose decision procedures such as for linear arithmetic and model checking using BDDs.

The proof of Result 1 proceeds by first lifting the CTL operator AG to a general universal quantification on states in PVS and then expanding the EF operator first into a mu-calculus formula which is then expanded into least/greatest fixpoints definitions. Using definitions and theorems of least/greatest fixpoints theory the proof is completed. The proof is fully automatic using PVS after lifting the AG operator to a general universal quantification on states. It takes a few seconds on SPARCstation20 with 32M.

## 3 Sequential ATPG algorithms and State Space Exploration

The objective of sequential ATPG algorithms is to generate test sequences that detect all the detectable stuck-at faults in a sequential circuit [ABF90]. There is a large body of literature available in the area of algorithms to solve the sequential ATPG problem. A brief summary of the main steps in a typical sequential ATPG algorithm is now presented. A detailed discussion of these algorithms is beyond the scope of this paper.

A *stuck-at-0(1)* fault refers to the value of a line in the circuit being held to a constant 0(1) value. A sequential ATPG algorithm attempts to detect every such fault (two faults per each line in the sequential circuit) in the circuit. A fault is said to be detected if there exists a sequence that produces different responses on the good machine and faulty machines. Varying requirements on the start states sequential circuit are possible (the machine may be assumed to start either from a completely unknown state or a from a given start state).

Typical sequential ATPG algorithms achieve this objective of detecting a fault by solving three sub-problems, *excitation, propagation, and (state) justification. Excitation* refers to the process of identifying an input vector (on a single time-frame) that can either produce a difference between the two circuits at a primary output or a flip-flop. The objective of *propagation* is to then produce a test sequence that can take a difference value (good/faulty equal to 1/0 or 0/1) from a flip-flop and propagate it to a primary output. *(State) justification* is the process of taking any requirements at the state lines (flip-flops) that were produced at the excitation phase and justify them either to the starting state or the all-unknowns state. Efficient methods to solve each of these problems are available in literature. Current methods are capable of handling designs with thousands of latches.

The main benefits of using a sequential ATPG algorithm are that there is no explicit storage of states required at each time-frame; time-frame expansion is on-the-fly and is restricted only to those parts of the design that truly need to expanded (this is a way to perform on-the-fly abstraction). The algorithms overcome the need to store all the states at each step of navigation through the state space by using decision trees that keep track of variables being assigned at specific stages in the program (for example, a latch may be given a value of 1 at a time-frame and if that value assignment results in no solution to the problem, a value of 0 is reached by backtracking). Hence, this method of searching for a requirement in the state space achieves a balance between a purely breadth-first state exploration method (as in conventional model checkers) and a purely depth-first exploration method (not efficient to explore large state spaces). The state-tuples that the method explores at each time frame are usually decided based on effective heuristics to determine easily *controllable* or *observable* state elements.

## 3.1 Distinguishing Sequence Generation

Results demonstrating the ability of state-of-the-art sequential ATPG algorithms to justify and efficiently handle large state spaces (over 1700 latches) have been reported in academic literature. In addition, commercial sequential ATPG tools are frequently applied to designs consisting of several thousand latches. We first present the results from a state-of-the-art, deterministic, test generation algorithm [NP91] (capable of proving the indistinguishability of the faulty machine from the good machine) and then present results obtained by using a genetic algorithm-based sequential ATPG [HRP97] that is *extremely efficient for obtaining distinguishing sequences but is incapable of proving undetectable faults.* The fault detection results reported in that work achieved the highest known detection coverages at that time.

These results are presented in Tables 2 and 3. For the data in Table 2, the time limit and backtrack limit for each fault were set to be 20 seconds and 100,000 respectively in each of the circuits except for s35932. because of the large number of faults in it. For this circuit, a two second time limit and a backtrack limit of 10,000 were placed.

The columns in the table indicate the circuit name, the number of detected faults, the number of faults proven to be undetectable by the test generator, the number of aborted faults, the time taken in seconds, and the number of vectors respectively. For the data in Table 3, the columns represent the circuit, checkpoint, number of detected faults, number of vectors produced and the time taken, respectively. The checkpoints refer to varying stages during execution of the genetic algorithm where computation could be stopped. The entries in bold represented the highest reported fault coverages at the time. It is clear from the data in these two tables that sequential ATPG algorithms have the ability to navigate through large state spaces efficiently to achieve the desired objectives.

**Table 2.** Sequential ATPG results

| Circuit | Detected | Undetectable | Aborted | Time (sec.) | Vectors |
|---|---|---|---|---|---|
| s298 | 265 | 26 | 17 | 389 | 306 |
| s344 | 314 | 8 | 20 | 489 | 117 |
| s400 | 336 | 9 | 81 | 1888 | 1644 |
| s420 | 28 | 152 | 275 | 6235 | 16 |
| s526 | 51 | 17 | 487 | 10883 | 34 |
| s641 | 404 | 61 | 2 | 89 | 219 |
| s713 | 476 | 105 | 0 | 23 | 177 |
| s820 | 812 | 31 | 7 | 433 | 928 |
| s832 | 816 | 46 | 8 | 500 | 967 |
| s953 | 89 | 990 | 0 | 147 | 14 |
| s1238 | 1283 | 72 | 0 | 14 | 478 |
| s1423 | 555 | 11 | 949 | 20359 | 88 |
| s1488 | 1439 | 27 | 20 | 1238 | 1124 |
| s1494 | 1439 | 27 | 20 | 1238 | 1124 |
| s5378 | 3152 | 148 | 1303 | 27078 | 949 |
| s35932 | 34719 | 3856 | 519 | 7172 | 317 |

# 4 Model Checking using Sequential ATPG

The transformation of model checking to stuck-at-fault detection can be performed based on an automata-theoretic approach as illustrated in Figure 1. Given a temporal logic formula, the transformation constructs monitor automata and a test network realizing a function that evaluates to "1" iff the monitor automaton/automata reaches a *bad* state/states. After generating the network, a sequential ATPG algorithm can be invoked on the new circuit with the stuck-at fault to be tested as its objective. Note that transforming model checking to stuck-at-fault detection in this manner may not be the most efficient. It is usually more efficient to build the model-checking objectives such

**Table 3.** Sequential ATPG results

| Circuit | Ckpt | Det | Vec | Time | Circuit | Ckpt | Det | Vec | Time |
|---------|------|------|------|------------|---------|------|-------|-------|-----------|
| s382 | 1 | 361 | 601 | 1.07 min | s1423 | 1 | **1410** | 2065 | 13.2 min |
|  | 2 | 362 | 1285 | 5.9 min |  | 2 | **1410** | 2965 | 40.1 min |
|  | 3 | **364** | 1486 | 8.1 min |  | 3 | **1414** | 3943 | 1.27 hr |
| s444 | 1 | 408 | 354 | 38.5 sec | s1494 | 1 | 1393 | 295 | 5.34 min |
|  | 2 | **420** | 753 | 2.3 min |  | 2 | **1453** | 540 | 7.50 min |
|  | 3 | **424** | 1945 | 20.1 min |  | 3 | **1453** | 540 | 7.60 min |
| s526 | 1 | **431** | 486 | 1.37 sec | s5378 | 1 | **3562** | 2175 | 4.60 hr |
|  | 2 | **442** | 1098 | 8.3 min |  | 2 | **3607** | 4461 | 25.1 hr |
|  | 3 | **454** | 2642 | 54.5 min |  | 3 | **3639** | 11571 | 37.8 hr |
| s713 | 1 | 475 | 157 | 1.1 min | s35932 | 1 | **35100** | 257 | 2.1 hr |
|  | 2 | **476** | 176 | 1.30 min |  | 2 | **35100** | 257 | 10.2 hr |
|  | 3 | **476** | 176 | 1.31 min |  | 3 | **35100** | 257 | 10.9 hr |
| s820 | 1 | 812 | 572 | 3.07 min | am2910 | 1 | **2190** | 953 | 6.25 min |
|  | 2 | **814** | 590 | 3.60 min |  | 2 | **2197** | 1761 | 13.5 min |
|  | 3 | **814** | 590 | 3.63 min |  | 3 | **2198** | 2509 | 29.4 min |
| s1196 | 1 | 1235 | 521 | 1.12 min | div16 | 1 | 1727 | 352 | 32.0 min |
|  | 2 | 1237 | 536 | 1.21 min |  | 2 | **1810** | 1168 | 2.62 hr |
|  | 3 | **1239** | 574 | 1.49 min |  | 3 | **1814** | 3476 | 8.1 hr |

as checking for the reachability of a bad state in the monitor automaton into the implementation of the ATPG algorithm as state justification objectives. We note again that reducing formulae to forms that permit passing of objectives directly to the state-justification engine is critically helpful in the efficiency of this procedure.

Any property for which a monitor automaton can be constructed to result in a test network of manageable size can be checked by such a transformation. Intuitively, this approach seems ideally suited for checking *safety* properties i.e., those properties every violation of which occurs after a finite execution of the system. A theoretical characterization of the exact class of properties that can be transformed effectively into sequential ATPG problems was not attempted in this paper. Our paper is targeted at studying the efficiency of sequential ATPG algorithms for state space exploration. Specifically, we have restricted the properties to be of the form **EF** $P$. The general reduction approach would be based on techniques for constructing monitor automata for more general properties [Wol82,FTMo83,FTMo85,NFKT87] and may be able to exploit recent results on constructing smaller automata based on a classification of safety properties [KV99].

### 4.1 Example

The transformation of a property of the form **EF** $P$, where $P$ is a conjunction of value assignments to some signals in the circuit is shown in Figure 2. The property checked

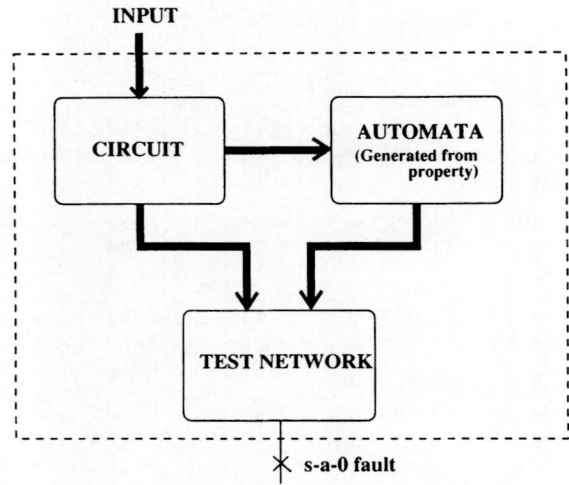

INPUT

**Fig. 1.** Transformation of model checking to sequential ATPG: resulting circuit structure

in the example is **EF (y1 = 1 AND y2 = 1)**. In the example, an AND gate tying the signals **y1** and **y2** is added to the original circuit under verification. Note that no monitor automata are needed to be constructed for this example.

## 4.2 Three-valued testability and overspecification

It is important to note that various definitions of untestability have been discussed in literature [PR92,PR93,CM93,Bop97]. A detailed discussion of these definitions is beyond the scope of this paper. However, two of the most important issues involved in the definition of untestability are briefly discussed.

First, we consider the notion of three-valued testability. A fault is three-valued testable iff there exists a test sequence that can produce a difference (0/1 or 1/0) at a primary output when the good and the faulty machines are started from the all-unknowns (all Xs) states and three-valued logic simulation is used to evaluate the output responses. This is the notion of untestability used by most practical gate-level ATPG algorithms operating with three-valued logic. The set of three-valued testable faults was shown to be a subset of all testable faults [PR92,PR93]..

Secondly, we consider the problem of overspecification [CM92,CM93] present in **some** sequential ATPG algorithms. The problem occurs because most gate-level test generation algorithms for sequential circuits are based on the use of the time frame expansion technique [ABF90] and the use of combinational test generation algorithms such as PODEM [Goe90] within each time frame. Some underlying combinational test generation algorithms, unfortunately, may overspecify the requirements at present state

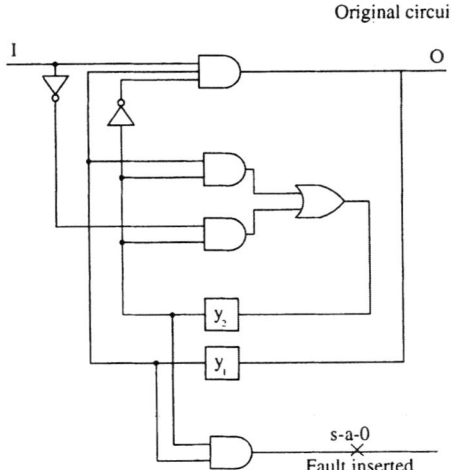

Original circuit

**Fig. 2.** Transformation of model checking to sequential ATPG: example

lines while processing a time frame (PODEM, for instance, may overspecify the requirements). This, of course, does not create a problem for combinational circuits, because overspecifying primary inputs does not affect the applicability of a test vector to the circuit. However, for sequential circuits, whenever this occurs, the objectives on the previous time frame may be more specified than necessary and may result in an incorrect claim by the test generation algorithm regarding the three-valued testability of the fault.

While the loss of accuracy caused by the use of three-valued logic and overspecification have not been much of a concern to the test generation problem itself (because it was shown that they cause only a small loss of fault coverage in the test generation process), it has potentially serious implications as far as using some ATPG algorithms for verification is concerned. Untestability characterization and several techniques for improving the accuracy of the test generation process (for example, based on verifying the existence of initializing sequences) have been presented earlier [PR93,CM93,Bop97]. The design verification application must be carefully analyzed before choosing the appropriate sequential ATPG algorithm.

## 5  Experimental Results

**Results on state justification experiments for some *hard-to-test* ISCAS circuits**

Four circuits have been chosen for our experiments on property checking because of the difficulty posed by them to sequential ATPG algorithms. Each of these circuits has

**Table 4.** Number of properties successfully checked using VIS and ATPG

| Circuit | Number of signal assignments per property (5 properties for each case) | | | | | |
|---------|-----|------|-----|------|-----|---------|
| | 2 | | 3 | | 5 | |
| | VIS | ATPG | VIS | ATPG | VIS | ATPG |
| s526 | 5 | 5 | 5 | 4 | 5 | 5 (4+1) |
| s1423 | 0 | 4 | 0 | 0 | 0 | 0 |
| s5378 | 0 | 5 (2+3) | 0 | 4 | 0 | 0 |
| s35932 | 0 | 4 | 0 | 1 | 0 | 1 |

been checked to be initializable using ATPG-generated test sequences. The sequential ATPG algorithm being used in our experiments is HITEC [NP91]. Our experiments on the ISCAS circuits were run on a SPARCstation 20 with 64MB of memory. A time limit of 20 seconds and a backtrack limit of 100,000 where set in the ATPG algorithm for each of the formulae checked.

Table 4 shows the experimental results comparing the performance of the ATPG-based approach with VIS [Gro96]. For each circuit, fifteen properties of the form **AG EF**( $P_i$ ) were generated and verified against the circuit. For each formula, $P_i$ was generated by choosing a specific number of internal signals (five properties generated for each case with two, three and five signals), specifying Boolean values for them randomly, and **AND**ing them together. For example, a case with two signal assignments could consist of a $P_i$ with (a=1 AND b=0). The table lists the number of cases out of the five chosen cases that the formula was successfully proven/disproved. For entries where numbers are provided in parantheses, the first number in the paranthesis indicates the number of cases for which vectors were obtained and the second number indicates the number of cases for which no test sequence was available (proven untestable). As can be clearly seen from the Table, the ATPG-based approach is capable of providing results for certain formulae even for very large circuits.

It is also interesting to note the differences in the state space exploration strategy in the two approaches. Results are shown on the small circuit s526 for which VIS could successfully complete the model-checking experiment to compare it with the state space exploration strategy in the ATPG-based approach. These results are presented in Table 5. Five signals were chosen from the circuit, random Boolean values were assigned to these signals and they were tied together by an **AND** as before. The numbers of vectors produced to achieve the required assignment of internal signals and the times required for generating these sequences are shown. The number of vectors produced by the ATPG-based approach indicates the performance of the structural search (somewhere between a DFS and a BFS) as opposed to the BFS-like search (for these types of formulae) involved in VIS. We emphasize again, of course, that the ATPG-based approach does not need to build the state transition relation and extensive functional representations and hence is memory efficient. Even the largest benchmark circuit tried (with 1728 flip-flops) required less than 20MB of memory.

**Table 5.** Differences in state space exploration strategy

| Circuit | VIS | | ATPG | |
|---|---|---|---|---|
| | Vectors | Time (sec.) | Vectors | Time (sec.) |
| s526 | 21 | 0.9 | 132 | 880.8 |
| s526 | 48 | 1.8 | 240 | 41.4 |
| s526 | 1 | 0.6 | 3 | 0.03 |
| s526 | 8 | 0.8 | 50 | 3.6 |
| s526 | 1 | 0.8 | 3 | 0.02 |

**Results on property checking experiments on an industrial circuit**

Experiments were also performed on a large industrial circuit to verify the effectiveness of the proposed sequential ATPG-based property checking system. The design used was that of an IO controller consisting of five modules: ADDRESS_DECODER, OUT_CONTROL, READ_CONTROL, IRQ_CONTROL and REG_BANK. The circuit consisted of 148 flip-flops, 51 primary inputs, 51 primary outputs and 1753 basic cells.

Experiments were performed to identify load sequences for obtaining specific values at registers embedded deep in the design. The ATPG approach was compared against a state-of-the-art, model checking tool BINGO [INH96,IN97]. The ATPG approach was successful in obtaining a sequence for *every* register tried while BINGO could not produce any sequence more than 6 vectors long. BINGO was terminated in each of these cases because the memory requirement exceeded 500 MB. The ATPG approach required no more than 20 MB for each of the cases and produced vector sequences of length upto 22.

## 6 Conclusions

In this paper we have given an efficient method based on stuck-at-fault testing techniques for automatic verification for a useful subclass of properties of synchronizable FSMs, typical of hardware designs. We have presented reduction of CTL formulae of the form **AG EF** $P$ to **EF** $P$ based on the existence of synchronization sequences and proven the reductions in the PVS proof-checker. Model checking the reduced formulae is transformed to stuck-at-fault testing and solved by sequential ATPG.

We have shown that the method has the potential to scale up to large hardware designs for which current model checking methods fail. The reason our method scales up is because it does not involve extracting and computing expensive functional information such as the complete state-transition relation. Instead, the approach relies on efficient fault-testing that exploits the circuit structure of the hardware design to be verified. As part of future work, we plan to characterize and experiment with more general properties that can be reduced to the stuck-at-fault testing problem and to investigate methods to incorporate the advantages of BDD-based model checking and the ATPG-based approach into a unified framework.

# References

[ABF90]  M. Abramovici, M. A. Breuer, and A. D. Friedman. *Digital System Testing and Testable Design*. New York, NY: Computer Science Press, 1990.

[AH96]  R. Alur and T. A. Henzinger, editors. *Computer-Aided Verification, CAV '96*, volume 1102 of *Lecture Notes in Computer Science*, New Brunswick, NJ, July/August 1996. Springer-Verlag.

[Bop97]  V. Boppana. State information-based solutions for sequential circuit diagnosis and testing. Technical Report CRHC-97-20, Ph.D. thesis, Center for Reliable and High-Performance Computing, University of Illinois at Urbana-Champaign, July 1997.

[Bry95]  R.E. Bryant. Binary decision diagrams and beyond: Enabling technologies for formal verification. In *Proceedings of the International Conference on Computer-Aided Design*, pages 236–243, November 1995.

[CA89]  K. T. Cheng and V. Agrawal. State Assignment for Initialilzable Synthesis. In *Proc. Intl. Conf. Computer-Aided Design*, pages 212–215, November 1989.

[CA93]  K. T. Cheng and V. Agrawal. Initializability consideration in sequential machine synthesis. *IEEE Trans. Computers*, 41(3):374–379, March 1993.

[CGL94]  E. Clarke, O. Grumberg, and D. Long. Verification tools for finite-state concurrent systems. In *A Decade of concurrency–Reflections and Perspectives*, volume 803 of *Lecture Notes in Computer Science*. Springer-Verlag, 1994.

[CM92]  K. T. Cheng and H. K. T. Ma. On the over-specification problem in sequential ATPG algorithms. In *Proc. Design Automation Conf.*, pages 16–21, June 1992.

[CM93]  K. T. Cheng and H. K. T. Ma. On the over-specification problem in sequential ATPG algorithms. *IEEE Trans. Computer-Aided Design*, 12(10):1599–1604, October 1993.

[FTMo83]  M. Fujita, H. Tanaka, and T. Moto-oka. Verification with prolog and temporal logic. In *Proc. of IFIP WG10.2 International Conference on Hardware Description Languages and their Applications*, May 1983.

[FTMo85]  M. Fujita, H. Tanaka, and T. Moto-oka. Logic design assistance with temporal logic. In *Proc. of IFIP WG10.2 International Conference on Hardware Description Languages and their Applications*, Aug. 1985.

[Goe90]  P. Goel. An implicit enumeration algorithm to generate tests for combinational logic circuits. *IEEE Trans. Computers*, C-30(3):215–222, March 1990.

[Gro96]  The VIS Group. VIS: A system for verification and synthesis. In Alur and Henzinger [AH96], pages 428–432.

[Hen68]  F. C. Hennie. *Finite-State Models for Logical Machines*. New York, NY: John Wiley & Sons, Inc., 1968.

[HRP97]  M. S. Hsiao, E. M. Rudnick, and J. H. Patel. Sequential circuit test generation using dynamic state traversal. In *Proc. European Design and Test Conf.*, pages 22–28, March 1997.

[IN97]  H. Iwashita and T. Nakata. Forward model checking techniques oriented to buggy designs. In *Proc. Intl. Conf. Computer-Aided Design*, pages 400–404, November 1997.

[INH96]  H. Iwashita, T. Nakata, and F. Hirose. Ctl model checking based on forward state traversal. In *Proc. Intl. Conf. Computer-Aided Design*, pages 82–87, November 1996.

[Koh78]  Z. Kohavi. *Switching and Finite Automata Theory*. New York, NY: McGraw-Hill, 1978.

[Kur94]  R. P. Kurshan. *Computer-Aided Verification of Coordinating Processes—The Automata-Theoretic Approach*. Princeton University Press, Princeton, NJ, 1994.

[KV99]  O. Kupferman and Moshe Y. Vardi. Model checking of safety properties. In *CAV99*, 1999.

[McM93]  Kenneth L. McMillan. *Symbolic Model Checking*. Kluwer Academic Pub., Boston, MA, 1993.

[NFKT87]  H. Nakamura, M. Fujita, S. Kono, and H. Tanaka. Temporal logic based fast verification systems using cover expressions. In *Proc. of IFIP WG10.5 International Conference on VLSI*, Aug. 1987.

[NP91]  T. Niermann and J. H. Patel. HITEC: A test generation package for sequential circuits. In *Proc. European Design Automation Conf.*, pages 214–218, February 1991.

[ORR$^+$96]  S. Owre, S. Rajan, J.M. Rushby, N. Shankar, and M.K. Srivas. PVS: Combining specification, proof checking, and model checking. In Alur and Henzinger [AH96], pages 411–414.

[Pel96]  Doron Peled. Combining partial order reductions with on-the-fly model-checking. *Formal Methods in System Design*, 8(1):39–64, 1996.

[PR92]  I. Pomeranz and S. M. Reddy. The multiple observation time test strategy. *IEEE Trans. Computer-Aided Design*, 40(5):627–637, May 1992.

[PR93]  I. Pomeranz and S. M. Reddy. Classification of faults in synchronous sequential circuits. *IEEE Trans. Computers*, 42(9):1066–1077, September 1993.

[TSNH98]  K. Takayama, T. Satoh, T. Nakata, and F. Hirose. An approach to verify a large scale system-on-a-chip using symbolic model checking. In *Proceedings of the International Conference on Computer Design*, pages 308–313, October 1998.

[Wol82]  P. Wolper. "synthesis of communicating processes from temporal logic specifications". Technical Report STAN-CS-82-925, Dept. of Computer Science, Stanford University, 1982.

# Automatic Verification of Abstract State Machines

## (Extended Abstract)

Marc Spielmann

LuFG MGdI, RWTH Aachen, D-52056 Aachen, Germany
spielmann@informatik.rwth-aachen.de

**Abstract.** Abstract state machines (ASMs) provide the basis of a successful methodology for specification and verification of software and hardware systems. Nevertheless, computer aided verification of ASM-programs has not yet been well-developed. In this paper we try to shed some light on the limits of automatic verifiability of ASM-programs.

We introduce a class of restricted ASM-programs, which are called nullary programs, and provide an algorithm that decides whether a given nullary program satisfies a given correctness property (expressible in a CTL*-like temporal logic) on all inputs. Our decision algorithm runs in PSPACE and we show that this is optimal. We also show that straightforward generalizations of nullary programs cannot be verified algorithmically, as some basic verification problems become undecidable.

## 1 Introduction

*Abstract state machines* (ASMs) [Gur95,Gur97], formerly known as *evolving algebras,* provide the formal foundation of a method to design and analyze complex hardware and software systems. When designing such a system one usually starts with a high-level description of the system and, by stepwise refining intermediate stages, eventually obtains a low-level description which is close to executable code. The *ASM-method* proposes to describe each stage of the refinement process in terms of ASM-programs. (That ASM-programs really suffice to express all levels of abstraction of a dynamic system is witnessed by many large-scale applications of the ASM-method [BH98].) The advantage of this approach is that ASM-programs are close to logic (see Theorem 5 in Section 3), which makes them easily accessible for well-understood mathematical methods. Essentially this mathematical foundation of ASM-programs supports the formal verification of systems designed by means of the ASM-method. For an introduction to the ASM-method the reader is referred to [Bör95]. Although there do exist numerous verification examples in the ASM-literature [BH98], one can hardly find an example where all or part of the verification process is mechanized. That is, computer aided verification of ASM-programs has not yet been well-developed. In this paper we investigate the problem of verifying ASM-programs automatically.

In its full generality, *automatic verification of programs* (not necessarily in ASM-syntax) is the following decision problem. Given a program $\Pi$ and a correctness property $\varphi$ (expressed in some appropriate specification formalism), decide whether for every input $I$ the computation of $\Pi$ on $I$ satisfies $\varphi$. Obviously, decidability of this problem crucially depends on the expressiveness of the programming language and the specification formalism one has in mind.

Here, we present a class of restricted ASM-programs and a specification formalism resembling the branching-time logic CTL* [CES86,Eme90] for which the above decision problem is decidable, i.e., which can be verified automatically. We call our programs *nullary programs* because the main restriction we impose on ASM-programs is that every dynamic function must have arity 0. (Roughly speaking, a nullary dynamic function $v$ is nothing but a program variable in the usual sense. During a computation step the value of $v$, i.e., the interpretation of the function symbol $v$, may change. This corresponds to assigning a new value to the 'program variable' $v$.) As a possible field of application for nullary programs we suggest the high-level ASM-descriptions that naturally occur when designing a complex dynamic system via the ASM-method. The decision algorithm we provide can then be used to verify such high-level ASM-descriptions.

Aside from possible applications we think that the technique underlying our decision algorithm is also of independent interest, as in some sense our algorithm performs symbolic model checking of software. By software we here mean programs that get a priori unbounded input and whose computations depend on a 'non-trivial' part of the input. Nullary programs are software in this sense. For example, one can write a nullary program $\Pi_R$ that solves the reachability problem for all finite graphs. Given an arbitrary finite graph with two distinguished nodes *source* and *target* as input, $\Pi_R$ decides whether *target* is reachable from *source* (see Example 3 in Section 3). $\Pi_R$ also indicates that nullary programs go beyond the scope of finite state systems. One can hardly imagine a finite state system which 'faithfully' represents all computations of a reachability algorithm on *all* possible input graphs.

To make our verification technique more precise let us reconsider model checking. Can we use model checking for automatic verification of programs (again, not necessarily in ASM-syntax)? That is, is it possible to model-check whether a given program $\Pi$ satisfies a given correctness property $\varphi$ for all possible inputs? The answer is yes if there are only finitely many inputs to be checked and the space (or time) complexity of $\Pi$ is bounded by some function in the size of the input. For instance, repeat the following steps for each input $I$. First run $\Pi$ on $I$ and this way obtain the *computation graph of $\Pi$ on $I$*, i.e., the graph whose nodes are the reachable configurations of $\Pi$ on $I$ and whose edges represent transitions from one configuration to a successor configuration. This graph is clearly finite and can be viewed as a Kripke structure whose labels are complete descriptions of configurations of $\Pi$. Using standard techniques one can (model-) check whether $\Pi$ satisfies $\varphi$ on $I$. Since there are only finitely many inputs we can indeed decide whether $\Pi$ satisfies $\varphi$ on every input. From the theoretical point of view there is no principle difference between finite states systems and resource-bounded programs running on a finite number of inputs.

'Real' programs, however, are supposed to be correct for infinitely many inputs, e.g., for all finite graphs. In this case a naive application of model checking fails simply because one cannot construct for all inputs the corresponding computation graphs. The main idea in this paper is to avoid an explicit construction of the computation graphs by translating a given program $\Pi$ into a logical formula which can be seen as a symbolic representation of *all* computation graphs of $\Pi$ (independent of a particular input). Combining this formula with the correctness property $\varphi$ to be checked, one can reduce the problem of (model-) checking whether $\Pi$ satisfies $\varphi$ on *all* inputs to the problem of deciding finite validity of a logical formula.

We demonstrate the new technique for nullary programs and correctness properties definable in a specification logic called CGL* – a straightforward adaption of CTL* for reasoning about computation graphs. It turns out that the one-step semantics of a given nullary program $\Pi$ can be expressed in terms of an existential first-order formula. Employing a translation of CTL* into transitive closure logic (FO+TC) by Immerman and Vardi [IV97], one can combine this existential formula with an arbitrary CGL*-formula $\varphi$ so that the resulting (FO+TC)-formula is finitely valid iff all computation graphs of $\Pi$ satisfy $\varphi$. The latter means that $\Pi$ satisfies $\varphi$ on all inputs. We then observe that finite validity (resp. finite satisfiability) of the obtained (FO+TC)-formula is decidable in PSPACE if $\Pi$ takes relational input and $\varphi$ is an existential (resp. universal) CGL*-formula. Hence, in order to decide whether $\Pi$ satisfies $\varphi$ on all inputs our algorithm first turns the instance $(\Pi, \varphi)$ of the verification problem into a (FO+TC)-formula and then decides finite validity of this formula.

After showing this positive result about nullary programs with relational input we prove that for nullary programs with functions in their input most basic verification problems (like reachability of a safe state and being constantly in safe states) become undecidable. This even holds for very simple nullary programs. Also, the situation does not change when we restrict attention to relational input and instead increase the computational power of nullary programs (e.g., by allowing first-order quantifiers in guards or dynamic functions of arity $> 0$).

## 2 Preliminaries

A *vocabulary* is a set $\Upsilon$ of relation and function symbols each associated with an arity. Nullary function symbols are usually referred to as constant symbols. All vocabularies we consider here are finite and contain at least the two constant symbols 0 and 1 (which we usually do not include explicitly). A $\Upsilon$-*structure* $\mathcal{A}$ consists of a set $A$, called the *universe* of $\mathcal{A}$, an interpretation $R^{\mathcal{A}} \subseteq A^k$ for each $k$-ary relation symbol $R \in \Upsilon$, and an interpretation $f^{\mathcal{A}} : A^k \to A$ for each $k$-ary function symbol $f \in \Upsilon$. We will always assume that $0^{\mathcal{A}} \neq 1^{\mathcal{A}}$. $\mathrm{Fin}(\Upsilon)$ denotes the set of all finite $\Upsilon$-structures.

A $k$-*ary query* on $\mathrm{Fin}(\Upsilon)$ is a mapping $Q$ that assigns to every $\mathcal{A} \in \mathrm{Fin}(\Upsilon)$ a $k$-ary relation $Q^{\mathcal{A}} \subseteq A^k$ such that the following holds: every isomorphism between $\mathcal{A}$ and $\mathcal{B}$, $\mathcal{A}, \mathcal{B} \in \mathrm{Fin}(\Upsilon)$, is also an isomorphism between $(A, Q^{\mathcal{A}})$ and $(B, Q^{\mathcal{B}})$. In the special case $k = 0$ we call $Q$ a *boolean query* and view $Q$ as a subset of $\mathrm{Fin}(\Upsilon)$ closed under isomorphism. As an example, recall that every first-order formula $\varphi(x_1, \ldots, x_k)$ over $\Upsilon$ (where all free variables of $\varphi$ occur among $x_1, \ldots, x_k$) defines a $k$-ary query on $\mathrm{Fin}(\Upsilon)$ mapping $\mathcal{A} \in \mathrm{Fin}(\Upsilon)$ to $\varphi^{\mathcal{A}} := \{(a_1, \ldots, a_k) \in A^k : \mathcal{A} \models \varphi[a_1, \ldots, a_k]\}$.

*Transitive closure logic*, (FO+TC), is the closure of first-order logic under the transitive closure operator TC. More formally, (FO+TC)$(\Upsilon)$ is the set of all $\Upsilon$-formulas derivable from the usual formula-formation rules of first-order logic (with equality) and the following rule.

**(TC)** If $\varphi$ is a formula, $\bar{x}$ and $\bar{x}'$ are two $k$-tuples of variables, and $\bar{t}$ and $\bar{t}'$ are two $k$-tuples of terms, then $[\mathrm{TC}_{\bar{x}, \bar{x}'}\, \varphi](\bar{t}, \bar{t}')$ is a formula.

The meaning of $[\mathrm{TC}_{\bar{x}, \bar{x}'}\, \varphi](\bar{t}, \bar{t}')$ is as follows. Regard $[\mathrm{TC}_{\bar{x}, \bar{x}'}\, \varphi]$ as a new $2k$-ary relation symbol whose interpretation is the transitive, reflexive closure of the image of the $2k$-ary query defined by $\varphi(\bar{x}, \bar{x}')$. If, e.g., $\varphi(x, y) := Exy \vee Eyx$ and $G = (V, E)$ is a directed graph with two distinguished nodes $s$ and $t$, then $(G, s, t) \models [\mathrm{TC}_{x,y}\, \varphi](s, t)$ iff there is an undirected path in $G$ connecting $s$ and $t$. For a formal definition of the semantics of (FO+TC) see, e.g., [EF95].

The *existential fragment* of (FO+TC), (E+TC), is the set of all (FO+TC)-formulas without occurrence of a universal quantifier and where all negated subformulas are quantifier-free.

Deciding *finite validity* and *finite satisfiability* of (E+TC)-formulas over a fixed vocabulary will be of particular interest for us. For every vocabulary $\Upsilon$, FINVAL$_\Upsilon$(E+TC) (resp. FINSAT$_\Upsilon$(E+TC)) is the following decision problem. Given a sentence $\varphi \in$(E+TC)$(\Upsilon)$, decide whether $\mathcal{A} \models \varphi$ for every $\mathcal{A} \in \mathrm{Fin}(\Upsilon)$ (resp. for some $\mathcal{A} \in \mathrm{Fin}(\Upsilon)$).

**Theorem 1.** *Let $\Upsilon$ be a vocabulary that contains relation and constant symbols only. Then both* FINVAL$_\Upsilon$(E+TC) *and* FINSAT$_\Upsilon$(E+TC) *are* PSPACE-*complete.*

# 3 Nullary Programs

In this section we introduce *nullary programs*. Basically, a nullary program is a *nondeterministic basic ASM-program* (in the sense of [Gur97]) where every dynamic function (i.e., a function that can be redefined during a computation) is nullary. We show that nullary programs have the same expressive power as the logic (E+TC). An immediate consequence is that on ordered input structures they compute exactly all NLOGSPACE computable functions.

Let $\Upsilon$ be a finite vocabulary. A *program vocabulary that extends $\Upsilon$*, denoted $\Upsilon_\mathrm{P}$, is obtained from $\Upsilon$ by adding some new constant symbols $v_1, \ldots, v_k$ to $\Upsilon$. Nullary programs over $\Upsilon_\mathrm{P}$ (which we will define below) take finite $\Upsilon$-structures as input; we frequently refer to $\Upsilon$ as the *input vocabulary*. Each $v_i$ will play the role of a program variable. The value, i.e., the interpretation, of $v_i$ may change during a computation step of a nullary program. We call $v_i$ a *dynamic* (abbreviating the official ASM-term "nullary dynamic function symbol").

**Definition 2.** Let $\Upsilon_\mathrm{P} = \Upsilon \,\dot\cup\, \{v_1, \ldots, v_k\}$ be a program vocabulary. *Nullary programs over $\Upsilon_\mathrm{P}$* are defined inductively:

1. **Update:** For every dynamic $v_i$ and every $\Upsilon_P$-term $t$ the assignment $v_i := t$ is a nullary program.
2. **Conditional:** If $\varphi$ is a quantifier-free $\Upsilon_P$-formula and $\Pi$ a nullary program, then $(\texttt{if } \varphi \texttt{ then } \Pi)$ is a nullary program (with *guard* $\varphi$).
3. **Parallel execution:** If $\Pi_0$ and $\Pi_1$ are nullary programs, then $\Pi_0 || \Pi_1$ is a nullary program. (For readability, $\Pi_0 || \Pi_1$ is sometimes written as $\frac{\Pi_0}{\Pi_1}$).
4. **Choice:** Let $\bar{z}$ be a tuple of variables, $\varphi$ a quantifier-free $\Upsilon_P$-formula, and $\Pi$ a nullary program. If $\exists \bar{z} \varphi$ is finitely valid, i.e., if it holds in all finite $\Upsilon_P$-structures for all interpretations of the free variables of $\exists \bar{z} \varphi$, then $(\texttt{choose } \bar{z} : \varphi \ \Pi)$ is a nullary program (with *guard* $\varphi$).

(Intuitively, the semantics of $(\texttt{choose } \bar{z} : \varphi \ \Pi)$ is as follows. Choose nondeterministically values for the variables in $\bar{z}$ so that the guard $\varphi$ is satisfied. Finite validity of $\exists \bar{z} \varphi$ guarantees the existence of such values. The actual program to be executed is then obtained from $\Pi$ by replacing every occurrence of $z_i$ in $\Pi$ with the value chosen for $z_i$. Note that in many cases $\varphi := true$ suffices as guard. However, if for your favorite guard $\varphi$, $\exists \bar{z} \varphi$ is not finitely valid, you can often replace $\varphi$ with $\varphi' := \varphi \vee \bar{z} = \bar{0}$ and sort out 'invalid' choices of $\bar{0}$ inside $\Pi$.)

A nullary program is *deterministic* if it is derivable from the above rules without using the choice rule. $\qquad\qquad\square$

The free and bound variables of a nullary program are defined in the obvious way. For instance, in the nullary program $(\texttt{choose } \bar{z} : \varphi \ \Pi)$ each variable in $\bar{z}$ occurs bounded. We can restrict attention to nullary programs without free variables if we substitute every free variable by a new constant symbol. For simplicity we will do so from now on.

The semantics of ASM-programs is usually given by means of *update sets* [Gur97,Gur95]. We define the semantics of nullary programs in a different way, which will be more convenient for our purposes. Nevertheless, our semantics coincide with the standard semantics.

**Semantics of Nullary Programs.** Consider a nullary program $\Pi$ over $\Upsilon_P$, $\Upsilon_P = \Upsilon \,\dot{\cup}\, \{v_1, \ldots, v_k\}$. $\Pi$ takes finite $\Upsilon$-structures as *input*. A *state* of $\Pi$ on an input $\mathcal{A} \in \text{Fin}(\Upsilon)$ is a finite $\Upsilon_P$-structure $(\mathcal{A}, a_1, \ldots, a_k)$, where $a_1, \ldots, a_k$ are the interpretations (or values) of the dynamics $v_1, \ldots, v_k$, respectively. The *initial state* of $\Pi$ on $\mathcal{A}$ is $(\mathcal{A}, 0, \ldots, 0)$. As with a Turing machine program, the 'program text' $\Pi$ is viewed as a description of how to modify the current state of $\Pi$ in order to obtain a possible successor state. Formally, $\Pi$ induces a $2k$-ary relation $\Pi^{\mathcal{A}} \subseteq A^k \times A^k$ so that $(\bar{a}, \bar{a}') \in \Pi^{\mathcal{A}}$ means that if $\Pi$ is currently in state $(\mathcal{A}, \bar{a})$ then in the next step it may change to state $(\mathcal{A}, \bar{a}')$.

To the definition of $\Pi^{\mathcal{A}}$. By induction on the construction of $\Pi$, we define an existential $\Upsilon$-formula $\varphi_\Pi(\bar{x}, \bar{x}')$, all of whose free variables occur among $\bar{x} = x_1, \ldots, x_k$ and $\bar{x}' = x_1', \ldots, x_k'$. For a better understanding assume that the interpretation of $x_i$ (resp. $x_i'$) equals the current value of $v_i$ (resp. the value of $v_i$ in a successor state). We write $[\bar{v}/\bar{x}]$ to denote the substitution of every occurrence of $v_i$ by $x_i$.

If $\Pi = v_i := t$       let $\varphi_\Pi := x_i' = t[\bar{v}/\bar{x}]$.

If $\Pi = \text{if } \varphi \text{ then } \Pi_0$    let $\varphi_\Pi := \varphi[\bar{v}/\bar{x}] \to \varphi_{\Pi_0}$.

If $\Pi = \Pi_0 \| \Pi_1$       let $\varphi_\Pi := \varphi_{\Pi_0} \wedge \varphi_{\Pi_1}$.

If $\Pi = \text{choose } \bar{z} : \varphi \ \Pi_0$ let $\varphi_\Pi := \exists \bar{z}(\varphi[\bar{v}/\bar{x}] \wedge \varphi_{\Pi_0})$.

Consider two states $(\mathcal{A}, \bar{a})$ and $(\mathcal{A}, \bar{a}')$ of $\Pi$. Intuitively, $\mathcal{A} \models \varphi_\Pi[\bar{a}, \bar{a}']$ means that, if $\Pi$ is currently in state $(\mathcal{A}, \bar{a})$ and $(v_i := t)$ is an update in $\Pi$ (possibly occurring in the scope of guards all of which are satisfied in $(\mathcal{A}, \bar{a})$), then $a_i' = t^{(\mathcal{A}, \bar{a})}$ is the new value of $v_i$ in successor state $(\mathcal{A}, \bar{a}')$. $\varphi_\Pi$ describes all those updates which *must* be performed in the next step.

$\varphi_\Pi$ is not yet the desired definition of $\Pi^{\mathcal{A}}$. This is because $\varphi_\Pi$ does not say that dynamics not effected by any update *must not* change – which is the intended meaning of $\Pi$. (Suppose, e.g., that $v_i$ does not occur in $\Pi$. Then $\mathcal{A} \models \varphi_\Pi[\bar{a}, \bar{a}']$ may hold even when $a_i \neq a_i'$.) We fix this as follows. For every $\Gamma \subseteq \{x_1' = x_1, \ldots, x_k' = x_k\}$ let $\varphi_{\Pi, \Gamma}(\bar{x}, \bar{x}') := \varphi_\Pi \wedge \bigwedge \Gamma$ (where, by convention, $\bigwedge \varnothing \equiv true$). Call $\Gamma$ *maximal w.r.t. to state* $(\mathcal{A}, \bar{a})$ if $\mathcal{A} \models \exists \bar{x}' \varphi_{\Pi, \Gamma}[\bar{a}, \bar{x}']$ and there is no $\Gamma^*$, $\Gamma \subsetneq \Gamma^*$, such that $\mathcal{A} \models \exists \bar{x}' \varphi_{\Pi, \Gamma^*}[\bar{a}, \bar{x}']$. Finally, let $(\bar{a}, \bar{a}') \in \Pi^{\mathcal{A}}$ iff either

- there exists a $\Gamma$ maximal w.r.t. $(\mathcal{A}, \bar{a})$ such that $\mathcal{A} \models \varphi_{\Pi, \Gamma}[\bar{a}, \bar{a}']$, or
- $\bar{a} = \bar{a}'$ and $\mathcal{A} \not\models \exists \bar{x}' \varphi_\Pi[\bar{a}, \bar{x}']$.

In the latter case we say that $\Pi$ is *inconsistent* in state $(\mathcal{A}, \bar{a})$. If $(\bar{a}, \bar{a}') \in \Pi^{\mathcal{A}}$ then $(\mathcal{A}, \bar{a}')$ is called a *successor state* of $(\mathcal{A}, \bar{a})$. Notice that every state has at least one successor state. If $\Pi$ is deterministic then every state has a unique successor state.

A *run of $\Pi$ on $\mathcal{A}$* is an infinite sequence of states such that the first state in the sequence is the initial state of $\Pi$ on $\mathcal{A}$ and the $(i + 1)^{\text{th}}$ state is a successor of the $i^{\text{th}}$ state. Every run of $\Pi$ on $\mathcal{A}$ can be embedded in the *computation graph of $\Pi$ on $\mathcal{A}$*, denoted $C_\Pi(\mathcal{A})$, which is the finite graph $(S, R, s_0)$ consisting of

- state set $S := \{(\mathcal{A}, \bar{a}) : \bar{a} \in A^k\}$,
- reachability relation $R := \{((\mathcal{A}, \bar{a}), (\mathcal{A}, \bar{a}')) : (\bar{a}, \bar{a}') \in \Pi^{\mathcal{A}}\}$, and
- initial state $s_0 := (\mathcal{A}, \bar{0})$.

Assume that $\Upsilon_P$ contains the distinguished dynamic *accept*. We say that $\Pi$ *accepts $\mathcal{A}$* if in $C_\Pi(\mathcal{A})$ there exists a path from $s_0$ to a state where the value of the dynamic *accept* is 1. $\Pi$ *computes a boolean query* $Q \subseteq \text{Fin}(\Upsilon)$ if for every $\mathcal{A} \in \text{Fin}(\Upsilon)$, $\Pi$ accepts $\mathcal{A}$ iff $\mathcal{A} \in Q$.

*Example 3.* Consider the following decision problem known as REACHABILITY. Given a finite directed graph $G = (V, E)$ and two nodes $s$ and $t$ in $G$, decide whether there exists a path from source $s$ to target $t$ in $G$. REACHABILITY can be seen as a boolean query on finite structures of the from $(G, s, t)$. We present a nullary program $\Pi_R$ that computes this boolean query.

The input vocabulary of $\Pi_R$ is $\Upsilon := \{E, s, t\}$, where $E$ denotes the binary edge relation of the input graph and $s$ and $t$ the source and the target, respectively. (Recall that by our general assumption we also have $0, 1 \in \Upsilon$.)

$\Pi_R$ as defined below is a nullary program over the program vocabulary $\Upsilon_P :=$ $\Upsilon \,\dot{\cup}\, \{mode, pebble, accept\}$; it employs the three dynamics $mode$, $pebble$, and $accept$. (For readability we use a slightly relaxed syntax and omit parentheses.)

$$
\begin{aligned}
\Pi_R \;:=\; &\texttt{if } mode = 0 \texttt{ then}\\
&\quad pebble := s\\
&\quad mode := 1\\[4pt]
&\texttt{if } mode = 1 \texttt{ then}\\
&\quad \texttt{if } pebble \neq t \texttt{ then}\\
&\qquad \texttt{choose } z : true\\
&\qquad\quad \texttt{if } E(pebble, z) \texttt{ then } pebble := z\\
&\quad \texttt{else}\\
&\qquad accept := 1
\end{aligned}
$$

On an input $\mathcal{A} = (G, s, t)$, the states of $\Pi_R$ are $\Upsilon_P$-structures of the form $(\mathcal{A}, a_m, a_p, a_a)$, where $a_m, a_p$, and $a_a$ are the values of $mode, pebble$, and $accept$, respectively. Initially, $\Pi_R$ is in state $(\mathcal{A}, 0, 0, 0)$. In the first step, $\Pi_R$ moves to state $(\mathcal{A}, 1, s, 0)$. Then, as long as the value of $pebble$ does not equal $t$, $\Pi_R$ chooses a node $a$ in $G$, checks whether $(pebble, a)$ is an edge in $G$, and updates $pebble$ with $a$ if so; otherwise it performs no update. If $pebble$ is ever updated with $t$, $\Pi_R$ accepts by updating $accept$ with 1. In this case $\Pi_R$ becomes idle; it repeats the accepting state infinitely often. $\qquad\square$

**Lemma 4.** *For every nullary program $\Pi$ over $\Upsilon_P$, $\Upsilon_P = \Upsilon \,\dot{\cup}\, \{v_1, \dots, v_k\}$, there is an existential first-order formula $\chi_\Pi(\bar{x}, \bar{x}')$ over $\Upsilon$ with $2k$ free variables $\bar{x}, \bar{x}'$ such that for every $\mathcal{A} \in \mathrm{Fin}(\Upsilon)$ and all $\bar{a}, \bar{a}' \in A^k$, $\mathcal{A} \models \chi_\Pi[\bar{a}, \bar{a}']$ iff $(\bar{a}, \bar{a}') \in \Pi^{\mathcal{A}}$. $\chi_\Pi$ can be obtained from $\Pi$ in time polynomial in the size of $\Pi$.*

One can view $\chi_\Pi$ in the previous lemma as a symbolic representation of the reachability relations of all possible computation graphs of $\Pi$ (independent of a specific input). In fact, for every input $\mathcal{A}$, there exists a path from $s_0$ to $(\mathcal{A}, \bar{a})$ in $C_\Pi(\mathcal{A})$ iff $\mathcal{A} \models [\mathrm{TC}_{\bar{x}, \bar{x}'} \, \chi_\Pi(\bar{x}, \bar{x}')][\bar{0}, \bar{a}]$.

**Theorem 5.** *A boolean query $Q$ is computable by a nullary program iff $Q$ is definable in the logic (E+TC).*

*Proof.* (Sketch.) Suppose $\Pi$ computes $Q$. Let $\chi_\Pi(\bar{x}, \bar{x}')$ be obtained from $\Pi$ according to Lemma 4, where $x_i$ (resp. $x_i'$) represent the value of $accept$. Then $\exists \bar{x}'([\mathrm{TC}_{\bar{x}, \bar{x}'} \, \chi_\Pi(\bar{x}, \bar{x}')](\bar{0}, \bar{x}') \wedge x_i' = 1)$ defines $Q$. For the other direction assume that the sentence $\varphi \in (\mathrm{E+TC})(\Upsilon)$ defines $Q$. There exists a quantifier-free formula $\psi(\bar{x}, \bar{x}')$ such that $\varphi$ is equivalent to $[\mathrm{TC}_{\bar{x}, \bar{x}'} \, \psi(\bar{x}, \bar{x}')](\bar{0}, \bar{1})$ (see, e.g., [GM96]). Redefine $\Pi_R$ in Example 3 by replacing $pebble$, $z$, $s$, $t$, and $E(pebble, z)$ with $\bar{p}$, $\bar{z}$, $\bar{0}$, $\bar{1}$, and $\psi(\bar{p}, \bar{z})$, respectively, where $\bar{p}$ is now a sequence of dynamics. The obtained program is a nullary program over $\Upsilon \,\dot{\cup}\, \{mode, \bar{p}, accept\}$ and computes $Q$. $\qquad\square$

Immerman [Imm87] showed that on ordered structures a boolean query $Q$ is NLogspace computable iff $Q$ is definable in (E+TC). This gives us the first part of the next corollary. The second part follows from a result in [GS99].

**Corollary 6.** *Let $Q$ be a boolean query on ordered structures. (1) $Q$ is computable by a nullary program iff $Q$ is NLOGSPACE computable. (2) $Q$ is computable by a deterministic nullary program iff $Q$ is LOGSPACE computable.*

## 4 Verifying Nullary Programs

Verification of nullary programs only makes sense in the context of a specification formalism suitable to express correctness properties of nullary programs. Since all runs of a nullary program $\Pi$ on an input $\mathcal{A}$ are embedded in $C_\Pi(\mathcal{A})$ it is reasonable to express correctness properties of nullary programs as properties of their computation graphs. Below we present a straightforward adaption of the branching-time logic CTL* [CES86,Eme90] to the computation graph setting. The new logic is called CGL* (*computation graph logic 'star'*), alluding to CTL*.

**Definition 7.** Let $\Upsilon_P$ be a program vocabulary. *State formulas over $\Upsilon_P$ and path formulas over $\Upsilon_P$* are defined by simultaneous induction:

**(S1)** Every sentence in $(E+TC)(\Upsilon_P)$ is a state formula.
**(S2)** If $\alpha$ is a path formula, then $\mathbf{E}\alpha$ is a state formula.
**(P1)** Every state formula is also a path formula.
**(P2)** If $\alpha$ and $\beta$ are path formulas, then so are $\alpha \vee \beta$, $\alpha \wedge \beta$, and $\neg\alpha$.
**(P3)** If $\alpha$ and $\beta$ are path formulas, then so are $\mathbf{X}\alpha$, $\alpha\mathbf{U}\beta$, and $\alpha\mathbf{B}\beta$.

An *existential state formula* is a state formula which can derived from the above rules without using in rule **(P2)** the clause to form negated formulas.

CGL*($\Upsilon_P$) (resp. ECGL*($\Upsilon_P$)) is the set of all state formulas (resp. existential state formula) over $\Upsilon_P$. □

The intuitive meaning of the existential path quantifier $\mathbf{E}$ and the temporal operators $\mathbf{X}$ and $\mathbf{U}$ is as in CTL*. $\alpha\mathbf{B}\beta$ stands for "$\alpha$ holds *before* $\beta$ fails" [IV97]. A formal definition of the semantics of CGL* follows. Let $C = (S, R, s_0)$ be the computation graph of some nullary program over $\Upsilon_P$. A *run in $C$* is a mapping $\rho$ from the natural numbers to $S$ such that $(\rho(i), \rho(i+1)) \in R$ for all $i$. Let $\rho|i$ denote the run $\rho'$ defined by $\rho'(j) := \rho(i+j)$. Consider a state formula $\varphi$ and a path formula $\alpha$, both over $\Upsilon_P$. Similar to CTL* one defines $(C, \mathcal{A}) \models \varphi$ for every state $\mathcal{A} \in S$ and $(C, \rho) \models \alpha$ for every run $\rho$ in $C$ by simultaneous induction on the construction of $\varphi$ and $\alpha$. The only new cases are

**(S1)** $(C, \mathcal{A}) \models \varphi \quad :\Leftrightarrow \quad \mathcal{A} \models \varphi$
**(P3)** $(C, \rho) \models \alpha\mathbf{B}\beta \quad :\Leftrightarrow \quad \forall i((C, \rho|i) \models \neg\beta \Rightarrow \exists j(j < i \wedge (C, \rho|j) \models \alpha))$.

For every $\varphi \in$ CGL*($\Upsilon_P$) let $C \models \varphi$ iff $(C, s_0) \models \varphi$.

To give an example of a meaningful CGL*-formula, let us express correctness of the nullary program $\Pi_R$ in Example 3 in terms of CGL*. More precisely, we will display a state formula $\varphi_R$ over the program vocabulary of $\Pi_R$, such that $\Pi_R$ is correct (i.e., $\Pi_R$ computes the boolean query REACHABILITY) iff $C_{\Pi_R}(\mathcal{A}) \models \varphi_R$ for every input $\mathcal{A}$. The following definition of $\varphi_R$ is justified by two observations: (1) $\Pi_R$ is correct iff for every input $\mathcal{A}$, $\mathcal{A} \in$ REACHABILITY iff $C_{\Pi_R}(\mathcal{A}) \models \mathbf{EF}(accept = 1)$ (where $\mathbf{F}\beta := true\mathbf{U}\beta$). (2) $\mathcal{A} \in$ REACHABILITY iff $\mathcal{A} \models [\mathrm{TC}_{x,x'} \, E(x,x')](s,t)$ iff $C_{\Pi_R}(\mathcal{A}) \models \mathbf{E}([\mathrm{TC}_{x,x'} \, E(x,x')](s,t))$.

$$\varphi_R := \mathbf{E}([\mathrm{TC}_{x,x'} \, E(x,x')](s,t)) \leftrightarrow \mathbf{EF}(accept = 1).$$

Hence, one can prove correctness of $\Pi_R$ by verifying $C_{\Pi_R}(\mathcal{A}) \models \varphi_R$ for every input $\mathcal{A}$.

**Verifying Nullary Programs w.r.t. CGL\*-Properties.** Let $L$ be a sublogic of CGL\*. *Verifying nullary programs w.r.t.* $L$ means solving the decision problem:

VERIFY($L$): Given a nullary program $\Pi$ and a state formula $\varphi \in L$, both over the same program vocabulary $\Upsilon_P$ (that extends some input vocabulary $\Upsilon$), does $C_\Pi(\mathcal{A}) \models \varphi$ hold for every $\mathcal{A} \in \mathrm{Fin}(\Upsilon)$?

Let VERIFY$_\Upsilon(L)$ denote the corresponding problem where the input vocabulary $\Upsilon$ is a priori fixed (the program vocabulary $\Upsilon_P$, however, may still vary).

The complexity of the latter problem is more significant for applications than that of VERIFY($L$). For instance, assume that in order to solve a computational problem a nullary program $\Pi$ was put forward which happens not to satisfy some correctness property $\varphi \in L$. In that case, one usually has to rewrite $\Pi$ (and possibly modify some correctness properties), rather than changing the computational problem itself (and thus the input vocabulary $\Upsilon$).

Notice that deciding VERIFY$_\Upsilon$(CGL\*) subsumes symbolic model checking of CTL\*-properties. Every Kripke structure $\mathcal{K}$ (given symbolically in terms of boolean formulas) and every CTL\*-formula $p$ (appropriate for $\mathcal{K}$) can easily be turned into a nullary program $\Pi_\mathcal{K}$ and a CGL\*-formula $\varphi_p$ such that $\mathcal{K} \models p$ iff $(\Pi_\mathcal{K}, \varphi_p) \in$ VERIFY$_{\{0,1\}}$(CGL\*).

Recall that ECGL\* denotes the existential fragment of CGL\* and let ACGL\* be the set of all negated ECGL\*-formulas. Our main positive result is:

**Theorem 8.** *Let $\Upsilon$ be a vocabulary that contains relation and constant symbols only. Then both* VERIFY$_\Upsilon$(ECGL\*) *and* VERIFY$_\Upsilon$(ACGL\*) *are* PSPACE-*complete. In other words, given a nullary program $\Pi$ and a correctness property $\varphi \in$ ECGL\*, both over the same program vocabulary that extends the fixed $\Upsilon$, deciding whether $\Pi$ satisfies $\varphi$ (or $\neg\varphi$) for all inputs is a* PSPACE-*complete problem.*

The restriction to relational input vocabularies in the theorem is essential. In the next section we will see that neither of the two verification problems is decidable if the input vocabulary contains a unary function symbol.

*Proof.* (Sketch.) PSPACE-hardness of both problems is shown via a reduction from the satisfiability problem for quantified boolean formulas. To prove containment we reduce VERIFY$_\Upsilon$(ECGL\*) to FINVAL$_\Upsilon$(E+TC) and VERIFY$_\Upsilon$(ACGL\*) to FINSAT$_\Upsilon$(E+TC). The assertion is then implied by Theorem 1. Most of the reduction work has already been done by Immerman and Vardi ([IV97], Theorem 9) who defined a translation of CTL\* into (FO+TC). If we replace in this translation $R(y, y')$ (the reachability relation of a given Kripke structure) with $\chi_\Pi(\bar{y}, \bar{y}')$ (the 'reachability relation' induced by $\Pi$ according to Lemma 4) and replace every variable $y$ (representing a state of the Kripke structure) with a tuple $\bar{y}$ of variables (representing the dynamic part of a state of $\Pi$), then we immediately obtain:

**Fact 9 ([IV97]).** *For every nullary program $\Pi$ and every $\varphi \in$ ECGL\*, both over same program vocabulary $\Upsilon_P$, $\Upsilon_P = \Upsilon \,\dot{\cup}\, \{v_1, \dots, v_k\}$, there exists a formula $\chi_{\Pi,\varphi}(\bar{y}) \in$ (E+TC)$(\Upsilon)$ such that for every $\mathcal{A} \in \mathrm{Fin}(\Upsilon)$ and all $\bar{a} \in A^k$, $\mathcal{A} \models \chi_{\Pi,\varphi}[\bar{a}]$ iff $(C_\Pi(\mathcal{A}), (\mathcal{A}, \bar{a})) \models \varphi$.*

It follows that $(\Pi, \varphi) \in \mathrm{VERIFY}_\Upsilon(\mathrm{ECGL}^*)$ iff $\chi_{\Pi,\varphi}(\bar{0}) \in \mathrm{FINVAL}_\Upsilon(\mathrm{E+TC})$ and that $(\Pi, \varphi) \notin \mathrm{VERIFY}_\Upsilon(\mathrm{ACGL}^*)$ iff $\chi_{\Pi,\neg\varphi}(\bar{0}) \in \mathrm{FINSAT}_\Upsilon(\mathrm{E+TC})$. One can modify the translation by Immerman and Vardi (by introducing new variables) so that it becomes polynomial-time computable. $\square$

The space complexity of $\mathrm{VERIFY}_\Upsilon(\mathrm{ECGL}^*)$ and $\mathrm{VERIFY}_\Upsilon(\mathrm{ACGL}^*)$ grows exponentially in the sum of the arities of relation symbols in $\Upsilon$. In particular, $\mathrm{VERIFY}(\mathrm{ECGL}^*)$ and $\mathrm{VERIFY}(\mathrm{ACGL}^*)$ are in EXPSPACE for (non-fixed) relational input vocabularies with constants. As already pointed out, this complexity bound is more of theoretical interest since for most applications the number of input relations as well as their arities will be fixed.

Although ECGL\* and ACGL\* are only small fragments of CGL\*, they still suffice to express many useful correctness properties. For example, for every linear-time formula $\alpha$ (i.e, a path-formula without path-quantifiers) we have $\mathbf{E}\alpha \in$ ECGL\* and $\mathbf{A}\alpha \in$ ACGL\*. Especially common fairness properties like "impartiality", "weak fairness", and "strong fairness" can be expressed in these fragments (see, e.g., [EL87] and references there). Observe though that the formula $\varphi_R$ expressing correctness of $\Pi_R$ in Example 3 is neither in ECGL\* nor in ACGL\*. Nevertheless, there are formulas definable in ACGL\* which imply partial correctness of $\Pi_R$.

## 5 On Input with Functions

A minimal requirement on any automatic verifier for nullary programs is that, when given a nullary program $\Pi$, it should be able to decide whether $\Pi$ *reaches only 'safe' states* on every input, or, equally desirable, whether $\Pi$ *can reach a 'safe' state* on every input. Here, safety for a state could mean that a designated dynamic in $\Pi$ does or does not assume a particular value. This motivates the definition of two simple verification problems which any automatic verifier for nullary programs should be able to solve:

ALWAYS SAFE: Given a nullary program $\Pi$ and a dynamic $v$ in $\Pi$, does $C_\Pi(\mathcal{A}) \models$ $\mathbf{AG}(v = 0)$ hold for every input $\mathcal{A}$?

SOMETIMES SAFE: Given a nullary program $\Pi$ and a dynamic $v$ in $\Pi$, does $C_\Pi(\mathcal{A}) \models \mathbf{EF}(v \neq 0)$ hold for every input $\mathcal{A}$?

The next theorem states our main negative result. We call a dynamic $v$ in a nullary program $\Pi$ *boolean* if every update of $v$ in $\Pi$ has either the form $v := 0$ or $v := 1$.

**Theorem 10.** *For nullary programs whose input vocabulary contains two non-nullary symbols, one of which is a function symbol,* ALWAYS SAFE *and* SOMETIMES SAFE *are undecidable.* ALWAYS SAFE *is already undecidable for deterministic such programs with two non-boolean dynamics.*

*Proof.* (Sketch.) Consider a sentence $\varphi \in (\text{E+TC})(\Upsilon)$ and let $Q_\varphi$ denote the boolean query defined by $\varphi$. By Theorem 5 there exists a nullary program $\Pi_\varphi$ computing $Q_\varphi$. Obviously, $\varphi$ is finitely valid iff $Q_\varphi = \text{Fin}(\Upsilon)$ iff $\Pi_\varphi$ accepts every $\mathcal{A} \in \text{Fin}(\Upsilon)$ iff $(\Pi_\varphi, accept) \in$ SOMETIMES SAFE. This establishes a reduction of FINVAL$_\Upsilon$(E+TC) to SOMETIMES SAFE. A similar argument reduces FINSAT$_\Upsilon$(E+TC) to ALWAYS SAFE. The first assertion is now implied by:

**Lemma 11.** *If $\Upsilon$ contains two non-nullary symbols, one of which is a function symbol, then both* FINSAT$_\Upsilon$(E+TC) *and* FINVAL$_\Upsilon$(E+TC) *are undecidable.*

The proof of Lemma 11 is by reduction of two undecidable problems for deterministic finite automata with two input heads (namely the emptiness problem and its dual – the totality problem) to FINSAT$_\Upsilon$(E+TC) and FINVAL$_\Upsilon$(E+TC), respectively. A straightforward adaption of the first reduction yields the second assertion of the theorem. □

Theorem 10 essentially says that nullary programs which assume (arbitrarily defined) functions in their input cannot be verified algorithmically. But what if we stick to relational input and increase the computational power of nullary programs? Following the general ASM-framework we may allow first-order quantifiers in guards or dynamic functions of arity $> 0$. (A unary dynamic function $f$, e.g., can occur in an update of the form $f(t) := s$, meaning that in the next state the value of $f$ at argument $t$ will be updated to $s$.) The proof of the next corollary is similar to that of the second assertion of Theorem 10.

**Corollary 12.** *If the definition of nullary programs is relaxed in one of the following two ways and the input vocabulary contains a relation symbol of arity $\geq 2$, then* ALWAYS SAFE *is undecidable. (1) Allow a single first-order quantifier to occur in one guard. (2) Allow the usage of one unary dynamic function.*

## 6 Conclusions and Future Work

We have introduced nullary programs – a class of restricted abstract state machine programs – and investigated the problem of verifying them automatically. On the one hand, automatic verification of nullary programs with relational input (against CTL*-like correctness properties) is PSPACE-complete. On the other hand, most basic verification problems become undecidable when we admit arbitrarily defined functions in the input or increase the computational power of nullary programs in a straightforward manner. Altogether this might suggest that with nullary programs we are approaching the limit of automatic verifiability of ASM-programs.

There are several directions for future work. (1) The decision procedures underlying Theorem 1 form the core of our verification algorithm. Both procedures perform a semi-naive exhaustive search and hence are not efficient. The question is whether they can be improved so that we obtain a reasonable performance in realistic settings. (2) Identify other fragments $L$ of CGL* for which VERIFY($L$) is decidable. To this end investigate finite validity and finite satisfiability of formulas obtained by Fact 9 when $\varphi$ varies in $L$. (3) Extend CGL* with counting constructs. Notice that properties like "$\varphi$ holds in all even moments" are expressible in (E+TC).

**Acknowledgements.** I am grateful to Erich Grädel for bringing the subject of model checking ASMs to my attention and to Eric Rosen for many fruitful discussions and valuable suggestions.

# References

[BH98] E. Börger and J. Huggins. Abstract State Machines 1988–1998: Commented ASM Bibliography. *Bulletin of the EATCS*, 64:105–127, February 1998.

[Bör95] E. Börger. Why Use Evolving Algebras for Hardware and Software Engineering? In *Proceedings of SOFSEM '95*, volume 1012 of *LNCS*, pages 236–271. Springer Verlag, 1995.

[CES86] E.M. Clarke, E.A. Emerson, and A.P. Sistla. Automatic Verification of Finite State Concurrent Systems Using Temporal Logic. *ACM Trans. on Prog. Lang. and Sys.*, 8(2):244–263, April 1986.

[EF95] H. D. Ebbinghaus and J. Flum. *Finite Model Theory*. Springer-Verlag, 1995.

[EL87] E.A. Emerson and C.L. Lei. Modalities for model checking: branching time logic strikes back. *Science of Computer Programming*, 8:275–306, 1987.

[Eme90] E.A. Emerson. Temporal and Modal Logic. In J. van Leeuwen, editor, *Handbook of Theoretical Computer Science*, volume B, pages 995–11072. Elsevier Science Publishers B.V., 1990.

[GM96] E. Grädel and G. McColm. Hierarchies in Transitive Closure Logic, Stratified Datalog and Infinitary Logic. *Annals of Pure and Applied Logic*, 77:166–199, 1996.

[GS99] E. Grädel and M. Spielmann. Logspace Reducibility via Abstract State Machines. Submitted for publication, 1999.

[Gur95] Y. Gurevich. Evolving Algebras 1993: Lipari Guide. In E. Börger, editor, *Specification and Validation Methods*, pages 9–36. Oxford University Press, 1995.

[Gur97] Y. Gurevich. May 1997 Draft of the ASM Guide. Technical Report CSE-TR-336-97, University of Michigan, May 1997.

[Imm87] N. Immerman. Languages that capture complexity classes. *SIAM Journal of Computing*, 16:760–778, 1987.

[IV97] N. Immerman and M.Y. Vardi. Model Checking and Transitive Closure Logic. In *Proceedings of CAV '97*, volume 1254 of *LNCS*, pages 291–302. Springer-Verlag, 1997.

# Abstract and Model Check While You Prove[*]

Hassen Saïdi and Natarajan Shankar

Computer Science Laboratory
SRI International
Menlo Park, CA 94025, USA
{saidi,shankar}@csl.sri.com

**Abstract.** The construction of abstractions is essential for reducing large or infinite state systems to small or finite state systems. Boolean abstractions, where boolean variables replace concrete predicates, are an important class that subsume several abstraction schemes. We show how boolean abstractions can be constructed simply, efficiently, and precisely for infinite state systems while preserving properties in the full $\mu$-calculus. We also propose an automatic refinement algorithm which refines the abstraction until the property is verified or a counterexample is found. Our algorithm is implemented as a proof rule in the PVS verification system. With the abstraction proof rule, proof strategies combining deductive proof construction, model checking, and abstraction can be defined entirely within the PVS framework.

## 1 Introduction

When verifying temporal properties of reactive systems, algorithmic methods are used when the problem is decidable, and deductive methods are employed, otherwise. Algorithmic methods such as model checking are limited by the state space explosion problem. State space reduction techniques such as symbolic representations, symmetry, and partial order reductions have yielded good results but the state spaces that can be handled in this manner are still quite modest. Deductive methods using theorem proving continue to require a considerable amount of manual guidance. While it is clear that any way out of this impasse must rely on a combination of theorem proving and model checking, specific methodologies are needed to make such a combination work with a reasonable degree of automation. It is known that abstraction is a key methodology in combining deductive and algorithmic techniques. Abstraction can be used to reduce problems to model-checkable form, where deductive tools are used to construct valid abstract descriptions or to justify that a given abstraction is valid. In this

[*] This research was supported by the National Science Foundation under Grant Nos. CCR-9509931 and CCR-9712383, and by the Air Force Office of Scientific Research Contract No. F49620-95-C0044. We thank our colleagues John Rushby and Sam Owre for their helpful comments on earlier versions of this paper.

paper, we propose a practical verification methodology that is, based on a simple, efficient, and precise form of boolean abstraction generation that preserves properties in the $\mu$-calculus. We extend the boolean abstraction scheme defined in [GS97] that uses predicates over concrete variables as abstract variables, to abstract assertions in the rich assertional language of PVS [OSRSC98]. The PVS language admits the definition of a fixed point operator that is used to define the $\mu$-calculus in PVS [RSS95]. With this definition of the $\mu$-calculus in PVS, model checking implemented as a PVS proof rule can be used as a decision procedure.

Our conservative abstraction scheme is implemented as a proof rule that abstracts any PVS formula over concrete state variables and produces a PVS formula over abstract state variables. Any assertion expressing a general or temporal property of a concrete PVS specification is abstracted into a *stronger* assertion expressing a property over the corresponding abstract specification. The resulting abstract assertion is in a decidable logic, and decision procedures such as model checking can be used to discharge it.

Unlike previous work for the automatic abstraction of infinite state systems using decision procedures [GS97,CU98,BLO98], our algorithm does not always over-approximate the transition relation as is done to preserve only universally quantified path temporal formulas in logics such as ∀CTL. Extensions of the preservation results [DGG94,CGL94] to the more expressive logic CTL* are defined using the notion of mixed abstraction which involves multiple next-state relations. Our algorithm abstracts a $\mu$-calculus formula which is not tied to a single transition system. Thus, no distinction is made between universal and existential fragments. The integration of our abstraction algorithm as a PVS proof rule allows us to design powerful proof strategies combining abstract interpretation, model checking and proof checking. We also propose an automatic abstraction refinement algorithm that is applied when model checking fails. This is done by automatically enriching the abstract state with new relevant predicates until the property is proved or a counterexample is found.

The paper is organized as follows. In Section 2 we show how boolean abstractions can be defined in PVS. In Section 3, we present an efficient abstraction algorithm for the computation of the "most precise" abstraction of a given boolean abstraction of a predicate over concrete state variables. In Section 4, we generalize this algorithm to abstract any PVS assertion, including $\mu$-calculus formulas over concrete state variables into assertions over abstract state variables. In Section 5, we present the refinement algorithm.

## 2 Boolean Abstractions in PVS

Propositional $\mu$-calculus is an extension of propositional calculus that includes predicates defined by means of least and greatest fixed point operators, $\mu$ and $\nu$, respectively. It is strictly more expressive than CTL* which includes both linear and branching time temporal logics such as LTL and CTL. In [RSS95] a detailed description of the encoding of the propositional $\mu$-calculus in PVS is presented.

The least fixed point operator is defined as $\mu(F) = \bigcap\{x \mid F(x) \subseteq x\}$, the predicate that is the greatest lower bound of the pre-fixed points of a monotone predicate transformer $F$. The temporal operators of CTL, such as **AG**, **AF**, **EG**, and **EF**, can be easily defined using their fixed-point characterizations. When the state space is finite, the predicates can be coded in boolean form and model checking of $\mu$-calculus formulas can be done using binary decision diagrams (BDDs).

As a simple example, we consider a simple protocol where two processes are competing to enter a critical section in mutual exclusion using a semaphore. The PVS theory describing the protocol is given as follows.

```
semaphore : THEORY
  BEGIN
IMPORTING  MU@ctlops
 location : TYPE = {idle, wait, critical}
 state : TYPE = [# pc1,pc2:location , sem: int #]
  s,s1,s2 : VAR state

 init(s) : bool= pc1(s)=idle and pc2(s)=idle and sem(s)=1

 N(s1,s2) : bool = ...

  safe: THEOREM
   init(s) IMPLIES
     AG(N, LAMBDA s: NOT (critical?(pc1(s)) AND
                           critical?(pc2(s))))(s)
END semaphore
```

The state is given as a record consisting of two program counters and a semaphore `sem`. The expression `N(s1,s2)` is transition relation of the protocol. We are interested in proving that both processes have mutually exclusive access to the critical section. The property `safe` is expressed as a CTL property using the usual operator **AG**, which is translated into a $\mu$-calculus property. When the state type is finite, the property can be verified using model checking[RSS95]. In this simple example, `sem` is of type integer and cannot be encoded with a finite number of boolean variables and hence the property cannot be directly model checked. We propose to extend the capabilities of PVS with a boolean abstraction mechanism that can conservatively reduce a $\mu$-calculus property of an infinite state system to model checkable form. In this abstraction, certain predicates at the concrete level (that might be used in guards, expressions, or properties) can be replaced by abstract boolean variables. This gives us a general method for constructing abstractions by evaluating any predicate over the variables of the program. Since the set of boolean variables is finite, so is the set of abstract states. Boolean abstraction is defined using a set of predicates of the form $\lambda(s : \text{state}) : \varphi(s)$ over the concrete state type `state`. An abstraction of the mutual exclusion protocol can be defined using two predicates

446

$\lambda(s) : sem(s) \leq 0$ and $\lambda(s) : sem(s) > 0$. These predicates define an abstract state type

$$\text{abs\_state}: \text{TYPE} = [\# \text{ pc1}, \text{pc2}: \text{location}, \text{B1}, \text{B2}: \text{boolean}\#]$$

where the state components pc1 and pc2 are of finite type and therefore are not abstracted, and the state component sem referenced by the two predicates defining the abstraction is encoded with two boolean components B1 and B2 corresponding to the two predicates. In this particular example, these two predicates happen to be exclusive, but boolean abstractions can be defined more generally with an arbitrary set of predicates over the concrete state type.

## 3 Efficient Computation of Boolean Abstractions

Abstract interpretation [CC77] is the general framework for defining abstractions using Galois connections[1]. The domain of the abstraction function $\alpha$ consists of sets of concrete states, represented by predicates, and ordered by implication. The range of the abstraction consists of boolean formulas constructed using the boolean variables $B_1, \cdots, B_k$, ordered by implication. If $X$ ranges over sets of concrete states and $Y$ ranges over boolean formulas in $B_1, \cdots, B_k$, then the abstraction and concretization function $\alpha$ and $\gamma$ have the following properties:

- $\alpha(X) = \bigwedge\{Y \mid X \Rightarrow \gamma(Y)\}$,

- $\gamma(Y) = \bigvee\{X \mid \alpha(X) \Rightarrow Y\}$.

However, we use a simpler and precise concretization function $\gamma$ which consists simply in substituting each abstract variable $B_i$ by its corresponding predicate $\varphi_i$, and each abstract state variable abs_s by the corresponding concrete state variable s. That is

$$\gamma(Y) = Y[\varphi_i(s)/B_i(abs\_s)].$$

We propose to apply boolean abstractions to any predicate (assertion or transition relation) written in a rich assertional language.

*Abstraction of assertions.* For any predicate $P$ over the concrete variables, the abstraction $\alpha(P)$ of $P$ can be computed as the conjunction of all boolean expressions $b$ satisfying the condition:

$$P \Rightarrow \gamma(b) \tag{1}$$

---

[1] A Galois connection is a pair $(\alpha, \gamma)$ defining a mapping between a concrete domain lattice $\wp(Q)$ and an abstract domain lattice $\wp(Q^A)$, where $\alpha$ and $\gamma$ are two monotonic functions such that $\forall(P_1, P_2) \in \wp(Q) \times \wp(Q^A). \ \alpha(P_1) \subseteq P_2 \Leftrightarrow P_1 \subseteq \gamma(P_2)$.

Note that there are $2^{2^k}$ distinct boolean truth functions in $k$ variables, and testing all of these could become very expensive. This set is designated as the set of *test points*. An abstraction is *precise* with respect to the considered abstract lattice, if the set of test points is the entire set of the boolean expressions forming the abstract lattice. Any over-approximation of the $\alpha(P)$ can be computed with a smaller set of test points for which the implication (1) must be valid. For example, in [GS97], the abstract lattice considered is the lattice of monomials[2] over the set of boolean variables. In this case, it is not necessary to prove (1) for all the monomials over the set $\{B_1, \cdots, B_k\}$, but only for the atoms $B_1, \cdots, B_k$ and their negations. We can efficiently compute $\alpha(P)$ for any predicate $P$ by choosing the abstract space as the whole boolean algebra over $B$ or by choosing a sub-lattice of $B$ and the corresponding test points, using the following fact:

**Theorem 1.** *Let $B = \{B_1, \cdots, B_k\}$ be a set of boolean variables, and let $\mathcal{B}_A$ be the boolean algebra defined by the structure $< B, \wedge, \vee, \neg, true, false >$. Let $\mathcal{D}_B$ be the subset of $\mathcal{B}_A$ containing only literals[3] and disjunctions of literals. To compute the most precise image by $\alpha$ of any set of concrete states $P$ (given as a predicate), it is sufficient to consider as a set of test points, the set $\mathcal{D}_B$ instead of the whole set $\mathcal{B}_A$ of boolean expressions. That is, testing*

$$P \Rightarrow \gamma(b)$$

*for all boolean expressions in $\mathcal{B}_A$ is equivalent to test this implication only for $b$ in $\mathcal{D}_B$. That is, $2^{2^k}$ tests can be reduced to at most only $3^k - 1$ tests.*

**Proof.** We consider the fact that each boolean expression $b$ can be written in a conjunctive normal form $d_1 \wedge \cdots \wedge d_j$, where each $d_i$ is a disjunction of literals. Thus, the proof of the implication (1) for each element $b$ can be first decomposed to simpler proofs $P \Rightarrow \gamma(d_i)$. This implication can be proved for each $d_i$ by first testing one disjunct, that is a literal, or more than one disjunct if necessary. That is, only for disjunctions in $\mathcal{D}_B$. ∎

This theorem gives us an efficient way of computing precise abstractions by reducing the set of proof obligations from $2^{2^K}$, the number of elements of $\mathcal{B}_A$, to only $3^k - 1$, the number of elements of the smaller set $\mathcal{D}_B$, and also gives us an order in which the proof obligations should be generated and proved. In fact, when the set of predicates $\{\varphi_1, \cdots, \varphi_k\}$ is properly chosen, the actual number of tests is far fewer than $3^k - 1$. When a proof for any element $b_i$ of the set $\mathcal{D}_B$ succeeds or fails, then the number of tests will decrease due to the fact that for many elements $b_j$ of $\mathcal{D}_B$, the test is redundant due to subsumption. Figure 1(a) shows how the image by $\alpha$ of a set $P(s)$ of concrete states is computed. The variable $\alpha$ is initialized to *true*. The variable *fail* consists of the set of elements of $\mathcal{D}_B$ that have not been proved to be in the abstraction of $P$. The set *fail* is

---

[2] Monomial are the expressions $\bigwedge\limits_{i \in \{1 \cdots k\}} b_i$ where each $b_i$ is either $B_i$ or $\neg B_i$.

[3] A literal is either a boolean variable $B_i$ or its negation $\neg B_i$

$\alpha_+(P(s), C)$
**Initialization**
   $\alpha := TRUE$;
   $fail := \emptyset$;
   $i := 1$;
**Iteration**
   while $i < k$ do
    $\mathcal{D} := disjuncts(i, \alpha)$;
    while $\mathcal{D} \neq \emptyset$ do
     let $b = choose\_in\ \mathcal{D}$   in
     remove $b$ from $\mathcal{D}$
     If $\neg(\alpha \wedge b \in fail)$
      Then
        If $\vdash P(s) \wedge C \Rightarrow \gamma(b)$
         Then $\alpha := \alpha \wedge b$
         Else $fail := fail \cup b$
      Else $skip$
    od
    $i := i + 1$
   od
   return $\alpha$

(a)

$\alpha_+(P(s_1, s_2), C)$
**Initialization**
   $\alpha := TRUE$;
   $fail := \{FALSE\}$;
   $i := 1;\ j := 1$;
**Iteration**
   while $j < k$ do
   $\mathcal{C} := conjuncts(j, \alpha)$;
   while $i < k$ do
   $\mathcal{D} := disjuncts(i, \alpha)$;
   while $\mathcal{D} \neq \emptyset\ \wedge\ \mathcal{C} \neq \emptyset$ do
    let $(b_1, b_2) = choose\_in\ \mathcal{C} \times \mathcal{D}$   in
    If $\neg(\alpha \wedge (b_1 \Rightarrow b_2) \in fail)$
     Then
       If $\vdash P(s_1, s_2) \wedge C \wedge \gamma(b_1) \Rightarrow \gamma(b_2)$
        Then $\alpha := \alpha \wedge (b_1 \Rightarrow b_2)$
        Else $fail := fail \cup (b_1 \Rightarrow b_2)$
      Else $skip$
    ...
   return $\alpha$

(b)

**Fig. 1.** Efficient computation of $\alpha(P)$

initially just the singleton $\{FALSE\}$. It is assumed that there has already been a prior check to ensure that $P(s) \wedge C$ is not equivalent to $FALSE$. The construction starts by using disjunctions of length 1, i.e., the literals $B_i$ and $\neg B_i$ for $b$. The literals $b$ for which the proof obligation $P(s) \Rightarrow \gamma(b)$ succeeds, are added to $\alpha$. At each iteration, when such a proof succeeds, it is possible to eliminate from the current set of test points the elements for which the test is no longer necessary. This is done by the test $\alpha \wedge b \in fail$. For instance, in the first iteration when we consider only literals, if the proof succeeds for $B_i$, it is not necessary to test $\neg B_i$. The test for $\neg B_i$ can only fail, otherwise, both $\neg B_i$ and $B_i$ would be added to $\alpha$, and $\alpha(P)$ would be equivalent to $FALSE$. In the next iteration, the test points that are disjunctions of two literals and not already subsumed by the disjunctions in $\alpha$, are considered. Once again, the successful test points are added to $\alpha$, $i$ is incremented and the iteration is repeated for disjunctions of length $i$. The image $\alpha$ of a set of concrete states is computed incrementally and can be interrupted at any moment, providing an over-approximation of the precise image. Furthermore, we use additional heuristics to avoid unnecessary tests. For instance, if the intersection of the set of free variables of $P$ and those of $\gamma(B_i)$ is empty, it is not necessary to consider the boolean expressions constructed using $B_i$.

*Abstraction of a Transition Relation.* Transitions are expressed as general assertions over a pair of concrete states $(s_1, s_2)$. The abstraction of a predicate $P(s_1, s_2)$ describing such a transition relation is defined as a predicate $B(abs\_s_1, abs\_s_2)$ over the abstract pair $(abs\_s_1, abs\_s_2)$. Figure 1(b) shows how a concrete predicate $P(s_1, s_2)$ representing a transition relation is abstracted. The algorithm constructs a transition relation over the variables $\{B_1, \cdots, B_{2k}\}$ by constraining the current and the next abstract states. This is done by considering as set of test points the set of implications $b_1 \Rightarrow b_2$, where $b_1$ and $b_2$ represent formulas in the current and the next abstract state variables, respectively. Again, the abstraction of $P$ is computed incrementally by first constraining the next state, that is by enumerating the disjunctions $b_2$. When all the proofs fail for a given choice of $b_1$, the current state is constrained by considering a longer conjunction for $b_1$. Consider for instance the expression

$$s_2 = s_1 \text{WITH } [\text{sem} := \text{sem}(s_1) + 1].$$

This assertion over a pair of concrete state variables $(s_2, s_2)$ of type `state` is abstracted with respect to the predicates $\lambda(s) : sem(s) \le 0$ and $\lambda(s) : sem(s) > 0$ to the following assertion over a pair of abstract state variables $(abs\_s_1, abs\_s_2)$ of type `abs_state`:

$$(B_1(abs\_s_1) \Rightarrow (B_1(abs\_s_2) \vee B_2(abs\_s_2)))$$
$$\wedge (B_2(abs\_s_1) \Rightarrow B_2(abs\_s_2))$$
$$\wedge (\neg B_2(abs\_s_1) \Rightarrow (\neg B_2(abs\_s_2) \vee \neg B_1(abs\_s_2)) \wedge (B_1(abs\_s_2) \vee B_2(abs\_s_2)))$$
$$\wedge (\neg B_1(abs\_s_1) \Rightarrow B_2(abs\_s_2) \wedge \neg B_1(abs\_s_2)).$$

## 4 Abstract Interpretation as a Proof Rule

Our abstraction algorithm computes the most precise over-approximation of an assertion over concrete states, using a validity checker for the generated assertions. We implemented this algorithm in the PVS verification system as a primitive proof rule. Our goal is to approximate a PVS formula over concrete state variables, that is a PVS boolean expression, by a formula over abstract state variables. This generated theorem is stronger than the original one. However, it is expressed in a decidable theory that can be handled by model-checking, BDD simplification, or the ground decision procedures available in PVS. To do so, we generalize the abstraction algorithm defined in [PH97] for the $\mu$-calculus to the PVS assertion language and we use our abstraction algorithm to approximate assertions. This algorithm abstracts propositional $\mu$-calculus formulas using over-approximation of predicates and under-approximation of negated predicates. Under-approximation of an assertion is defined as follows:

$$\alpha_-(P(s)) = \bigvee \{b \mid \gamma(b) \Rightarrow P(s)\}$$

We use only the over-approximation algorithm relying on the following lemma.

**Lemma 1.** *Let $\varphi$ a predicate defining a set of states. For all predicate $\varphi$*

$$\alpha_+(\neg\varphi(s)) \Leftrightarrow \neg\alpha_-(\varphi(s)).$$

We now formally define the abstraction function $[\![\ ]\!]^\sigma$ which approximates a PVS boolean expression $f$ such that, $[\![\ f\ ]\!]^+$ denotes an *over* approximation of $f$, and $[\![\ f\ ]\!]^-$ an *under* approximation of $f$. We also use a context $c$ consisting of a PVS formula that is valid at the PVS subformula that is being approximated. The intuition behind using such a context expression is that when an expression $e_1 \wedge e_2$ is being abstracted, one can assume that $e_1$ is valid when abstracting $e_2$ and vice-versa. The context when omitted is just the boolean constant *TRUE*. $[\![\ f\ ]\!]^\sigma_c$ denotes the approximation of $f$ under the context $c$.

*Approximation of PVS assertions.* The abstraction function $[\![\ ]\!]$ is defined recursively on the structure of the PVS assertion language as follows.

$$
\begin{aligned}
\textit{propositions}: \quad & [\![e_1 \wedge e_2]\!]^\sigma_c && \longrightarrow [\![e_1]\!]^\sigma_{c\wedge e_2} \wedge [\![e_2]\!]^\sigma_{c\wedge e_1} \\
& [\![\neg e]\!]^\sigma_c && \longrightarrow \neg[\![e]\!]^{-\sigma}_c \\[6pt]
\textit{quantifiers}: \quad & [\![\exists(s):e]\!]^\sigma_c && \longrightarrow \exists(abs\_s):[\![e]\!]^\sigma_c \\
& [\![\forall(s):e]\!]^\sigma_c && \longrightarrow \forall(abs\_s):[\![e]\!]^\sigma_c \\
& [\![\lambda(s):e]\!]^\sigma_c && \longrightarrow \lambda(abs\_s):[\![e]\!]^\sigma_c \\[6pt]
\textit{fixpoints}: \quad & [\![\mu/\nu(\lambda(Q):\mathrm{F}(Q))]\!]^\sigma_c && \longrightarrow \mu/\nu(\lambda(abs\_Q):[\![\mathrm{F}(Q)]\!]^\sigma_c) \\[6pt]
\textit{atoms}: \quad & [\![e(s)]\!]^+_c && \longrightarrow \alpha_+(e(s),c) \\
& [\![e(s_1,s_2)]\!]^+_c && \longrightarrow \alpha_+(e(s_1,s_2),c) \\
& [\![e(s)]\!]^-_c && \longrightarrow \alpha_-(e(s),c) \\
& [\![e(s_1,s_2)]\!]^-_c && \longrightarrow \alpha_-(e(s_1,s_2),c) \\
& [\![\varphi_i(s)]\!]^\sigma_c && \longrightarrow B_i(abs\_s) \\[6pt]
\textit{constants}: \quad & [\![\ e\ ]\!]^\sigma_c && \longrightarrow e \quad \textit{if free variables}(e) = \emptyset
\end{aligned}
$$

The following theorem establishes the fact that the abstraction provides, respectively, an over and under approximation of any PVS boolean expression.

**Theorem 2.** *Let $f$ be a PVS assertion, $[\![\ ]\!]$ an abstraction function. We have:*

$$\vdash f \Rightarrow \gamma([\![\ f\ ]\!]^+) \quad \textit{and} \quad \vdash \gamma([\![\ f\ ]\!]^-) \Rightarrow f$$

**Proof.** The proof is established by induction on the structure of the assertion $f$. It is easy to show that by the definitions of $\alpha_+$ and $\alpha_-$, both implications hold when $f$ is an atom. The other cases can be deduced by monotonicity of the logical connectives, and the fixed point operators. ∎

The soundness of the abstraction function is established by the following theorem.

**Theorem 3 (preservation).** *Let* $[\![\ ]\!]$ *be the abstraction function defined above as a boolean abstraction, and let* $f$ *be any PVS boolean formula. Then*

$$\vdash\ [\![\ f\ ]\!]^{-}\quad implies\quad \vdash\ f$$

Theorem 2 ensures that for an assertion $f$, the abstraction algorithm produces a stronger assertion $\gamma([\![\ f\ ]\!]^{-})$. Note that $\vdash [\![\ f\ ]\!]^{-}$ trivially implies $\vdash \gamma([\![\ f\ ]\!]^{-})$, which then justifies the preservation result of Theorem 3.

The abstraction algorithm where a formula $f$ is under-approximated is implemented as a PVS proof rule abstract. This atomic proof rule takes a goal given by a PVS formula (a $\mu$-calculus formula) and a set of state predicates, and translates this to a propositional formula (a propositional $\mu$-calculus formula) which is returned as a new goal. This goal can be discharged using any other PVS proof command including BDD simplification and model checking.

We have defined a PVS proof strategy that carries out a sequence of inference steps that simplify goal formulas by rewriting all definitions, including constant definitions such as the temporal operators of the logic CTL in terms of the $\mu$ and $\nu$ operators, and applies the abstraction function on the resulting goal.

$\forall\ (s:\ \text{state}):$
  $\text{init}(s) \supset$
    $\neg\mu.\lambda\ (Q:\ \text{pred[state]}):$
      $(\lambda\ (u:\ \text{state}):$
        $(\neg\lambda\ s:$
          $\neg(\text{critical?}(\text{pc1}(s))\wedge$
            $\text{critical?}(\text{pc2}(s))))$
        $(u)\vee$
      $\exists\ (v:\ \text{state}):$
        $(Q(v) \wedge N(u,v)))(s)$

$\forall\ (abs\_s:\ \text{abs\_state}):$
  $\neg[\![\text{init}(s)]\!]^{+}\vee$
    $\neg\mu.\lambda\ (abs\_Q:\ \text{pred[abs\_state]}):$
      $(\lambda\ (abs\_u:\ \text{abs\_state}):$
        $(\neg\lambda\ abs\_s:$
          $\neg(\text{critical?}(\text{pc1}(abs\_s))\wedge$
            $\text{critical?}(\text{pc2}(abs\_s))))$
        $(abs\_u)\vee$
      $\exists\ (abs\_v:\ \text{abs\_state}):$
        $(abs\_Q(abs\_v) \wedge [\![N(u,v)]\!]^{+}))(abs\_s)$

**Fig. 2.** An example of abstraction for a PVS assertion

Figure 2 shows how the $\mu$-calculus formula corresponding to the theorem safe presented in the PVS theory semaphore in Section 2 is approximated. The property of mutual exclusion $\lambda(s)\ :\ \neg(\text{critical?}(\text{pc1}(s)) \wedge \text{critical?}(\text{pc2}(s)))$ is expressed as an invariance property. As expected for such properties, the initial state and the transition relation are over-approximated. For instance, we have

$$[\![\text{init}(s)]\!]^{+}\ \longrightarrow\ \text{idle?}(\text{pc1}(abs\_s)) \wedge \text{idle?}(\text{pc2}(abs\_s)) \wedge \neg B_1(abs\_s) \wedge B_2(abs\_s)$$

We have tried other examples including a simple snoopy cache-coherence protocol with an arbitrary number of processes [Rus97] and a variant of the alternating-bit communication protocol called the bounded retransmission protocol [HS96]. The main invariant of the cache coherence protocol is proved by an abstraction defined in terms of five predicates. The preservation of the invariant is then proved by abstraction and BDD-based propositional simplification.

The bounded retransmission protocol is verified using an abstraction also defined in terms of five predicates. The construction of the abstract description takes about 100 seconds in PVS. The resulting abstract assertion is discharged using model checking. In contrast, Havelund and Shankar's verification [HS96] of this example required 57 invariants to justify the validity of a manually derived abstraction.

## 5 Refining an Abstraction

The abstraction proof rule is used in PVS to generate new goals that depend only on finite state variables. Such goals can be discharged using a PVS proof rule such as the BDD simplifier or the $\mu$-calculus simplifier. However model checking on the new goal can fail because the abstraction is too coarse. It is then necessary to refine the abstraction using a richer abstract domain. Since our abstraction algorithm presented in Section 4 allows us to compute the most precise abstraction with respect the predicates $\varphi_1, \cdots, \varphi_k$, refining the abstraction requires additional predicates. The refinement algorithm takes as arguments the original PVS assertion $f$, a new list of predicates $\varphi_{k+1}, \cdots, \varphi_l$, and a context $\Gamma_\alpha$ computed previously. The context $\Gamma_\alpha$ is a hash-table which associates to each atom the BDD representing its abstraction, that is the BDD $\alpha$, and the set $fail$ of BDDs. The refinement algorithm descends through the structure of $f$ and refines each sub-formula with the new predicates. The refinement algorithm is similar to the algorithm computing $\alpha_+(P)$ of Figure 1. However the variables $\alpha$ and $fail$ are initialized with their already computed values. This allows us to take advantage of the success or failure of already executed proofs. The new set of test points is defined as the disjunctions formed using the literals $B_{k+1}, \cdots, B_l$ and their negation. This set is augmented with the boolean expressions over the old variables $B_1, \cdots, B_k$ for which the proof previously failed. The algorithm returns a more precise approximation of $P$.

We implemented our abstraction and refinement algorithms as a proof strategy defining a semi-decision procedure that abstracts an original PVS formula and then applies model checking. If model checking fails, the abstraction is refined until model checking succeeds. This strategy is expressed as follows in the PVS strategies language

```
(TRY (THEN (abstract (phi_1...phi_k)) (model-check))
     (skip)
     (REPEAT
      (LET ((Φ (new-list-of-predicates)))
      (THEN (refine Φ) (model-check)))))
```

Our refinement algorithm tries to eliminate as much of the nondeterminism created by the over-approximation of the transition relation as possible. Absence of nondeterminism can be easily detected by checking that when the abstraction of a transition $\alpha_+(P(s_1, s_2), C)$ is computed, the index $i$ will never reach a value greater than 1. For instance, the abstraction of the assertion

$$e(s_1, s_2) \equiv s_2 = s_1 \text{WITH } [\text{sem} := \text{sem}(s_1) + 1]$$

presented in Section 3 is nondeterministic since it contains the conjunct

$$(B_1(abs\_s_1) \Rightarrow (B_1(abs\_s_2) \vee B_2(abs\_s_2))).$$

Refining such an abstraction involves translating the predicate characterizing the next state, that is $(B_1(abs\_s_2) \vee B_2(abs\_s_2))$ into a disjunctive normal form. Then, for each disjunct, the pre-image is computed with respect the concrete assertion $e(s_1, s_2)$. In this particular case, the pre-images for $B_1(abs\_s_2)$ and $B_2(abs\_s_2)$ are, respectively, $\exists(s_2) : e(s, s_2) \wedge \varphi_1(s_2)$ and $\exists(s_2) : e(s, s_2) \wedge \varphi_2(s_2)$. Their simplified forms are respectively $sem(s) < 0$ and $sem(s) = 0$.

# 6 Conclusion

We have presented a general abstraction/refinement algorithm that preserves the full $\mu$-calculus as the basis for an integration of abstract interpretation, model checking, and proof checking. We have implemented this boolean abstraction algorithm as an extension to the PVS theorem prover. This allows us to define powerful proof strategies combining deductive proof, induction, abstraction, and model checking within a single framework. It also allows our abstraction algorithm to be used in the framework of a richly expressive specification language encompassing finite, infinite-state, and parametric systems. The computation of the abstraction is completely automatic, and uses the PVS decision procedures to test the generated implications.

We are currently investigating cases where it is possible to detect whether a constructed abstraction *strongly* preserves fragments of the $\mu$-calculus so that abstract counterexamples yield concrete ones. This is done by finding sufficient conditions allowing us to use the various preservation results presented in [LGS+95,DGG94].

The new PVS version includes code generation capabilities, and as future work, we plan to define abstraction construction in the PVS specification language, and to automatically extract the code implementing the abstraction operation. Such experiments are similar to the ones presented in [vHPPR98] where, for instance, the code implementing a BDD simplifier is extracted automatically from its formal specification.

# References

[BLO98]    S. Bensalem, Y. Lakhnech, and S. Owre. Computing abstractions of infinite state systems compositionally and automatically. In *Proceedings of the 9th Conference on Computer-Aided Verification, CAV'98*, LNCS. Springer Verlag, June 1998.

[CC77]     P. Cousot and R. Cousot. Abstract interpretation: a unified lattice model for static analysis of programs by construction or approximation of fixpoints. In *4th POPL*, January 1977.

[CGL94]    E.M. Clarke, O. Grumberg, and D.E. Long. Model checking and abstraction. *ACM Transactions on Programming Languages and Systems*, 16(5):1512–1542, September 1994.

[CU98]     Michael Colon and Thomas Uribe. Generating finite-state abstractions of reactive systems using decision procedures. In *Proceedings of the 9th Conference on Computer-Aided Verification, CAV'98*, LNCS. Springer Verlag, June 1998.

[DGG94]    D. Dams, O. Grumberg, and R. Gerth. Abstract interpretation of reactive systems: Abstractions preserving ∀CTL*, ∃CTL* and CTL*. In Ernst-Rudiger Olderog, editor, *IFIP Conference PROCOMET'94*, pages 561–581, 1994.

[GS97]     S. Graf and H. Saïdi. Construction of abstract state graphs with PVS. In *Conference on Computer Aided Verification CAV'97*, LNCS 1254, Springer Verlag, 1997.

[HS96]     Klaus Havelund and N. Shankar. Experiments in theorem proving and model checking for protocol verification. In *Formal Methods Europe FME '96*, number 1051 in Lecture Notes in Computer Science, pages 662–681, Oxford, UK, March 1996. Springer-Verlag.

[LGS+95]   C. Loiseaux, S. Graf, J. Sifakis, A. Bouajjani, and S. Bensalem. Property preserving abstractions for the verification of concurrent systems. *Formal Methods in System Design, Vol 6, Iss 1, January 1995*, 1995.

[OSRSC98]  S. Owre, N. Shankar, J. M. Rushby, and D. W. J. Stringer-Calvert. *The PVS Specification Language*. Computer Science Laboratory, SRI International, Menlo Park, CA, August 1998.

[PH97]     A. Pardo and G.D. Hachtel. Automatic abstraction techniques for propositional $\mu$-calculus model checking. In *Conference on Computer Aided Verification CAV'97*, LNCS 1254, Springer Verlag, 1997.

[RSS95]    S. Rajan, N. Shankar, and M.K. Srivas. An integration of model checking with automated proof checking. In *Computer-Aided Verification, CAV '95*, number 939 in Lecture Notes in Computer Science, Liège, Belgium, 1995. Springer-Verlag.

[Rus97]    John Rushby. Specification, proof checking, and model checking for protocols and distributed systems with PVS. In *FORTE/PSTV '97*, Osaka, Japan, November 1997.

[vHPPR98]  Friedrich von Henke, Stephan Pfab, Holger Pfeifer, and Harald Rueß. Case studies in meta-level theorem proving. In Jim Grundy and Malcolm Newey, editors, *Theorem Proving in Higher Order Logics: 11th International Conference, TPHOLs '98*, volume 1479 of *Lecture Notes in Computer Science*, pages 461–478, Canberra, Australia, September 1998. Springer-Verlag.

# Deciding Equality Formulas by Small Domains Instantiations *

Amir Pnueli, Yoav Rodeh, Ofer Shtrichman, and Michael Siegel

Dept. of Applied Mathematics and Computer Science, the Weizmann Institute of
Science, Rehovot, Israel, {amir|yrodeh|ofers}@wisdom.weizmann.ac.il

**Abstract.** We introduce an efficient decision procedure for the theory
of equality based on finite instantiations. When using the finite instantiations method, it is a common practice to take a range of $[1..n]$ (where
$n$ is the number of input non-Boolean variables) as the range for all
non-Boolean variables, resulting in a state-space of $n^n$. Although various attempts to minimize this range were made, typically they either
required various restrictions on the investigated formulas or were not
very effective. In many cases, the $n^n$ state-space cannot be handled by
BDD-based tools within a reasonable amount of time. In this paper we
show that significantly smaller domains can be algorithmically found, by
analyzing the structure of the formula. We also show an upper bound for
the state-space based on this analysis. This method enabled us to verify
formulas containing hundreds of integer and floating point variables.

*Keywords:* Finite Instantiation, equality logic, uninterpreted functions, compiler verification, translation validation, Range Allocation.

## 1 Introduction

Automated validation techniques for formulas of the theory of equality become
increasingly important as the advantages of abstraction and the use of uninterpreted functions (UIFs) become more evident. UIFs are mainly useful when
proving equivalence between two models. Proving design equivalence or comparing a specification to an implementation are two typical examples of such
equivalence proofs. In our case, we proved equivalence between source and target code serving as the input and output of a compiler, and thus verified that
the compilation process was correct (see [PSS98b], [PSS99] and [Con95] for more
details about this project).

When verifying equivalence between two formulas, it is often possible to abstract away all functions, except the equality sign and Boolean operators, by
replacing them with UIFs. An abstracted formula holds less information and
therefore can be represented by a significantly smaller BDD. It was Ackerman
[Ack54] who first showed the reduction of such abstracted formulas to function-
free formulas of the theory of equality, while preserving validity. He suggested
doing so by replacing each occurrence of a function with a new variable, and
adding constraints that preserve their functionality as an antecedent of the

---

* This research was supported in part by the Minerva Center for Verification of Reactive Systems, a gift from Intel, a grant from the U.S.-Israel bi-national science
foundation, and an *Infrastructure* grant from the Israeli Ministry of Science and the
Arts.

formula, rewriting the formula $(z = F(x, y) \land u = y) \rightarrow z = F(x, u)$ into $((x = x \land y = u) \rightarrow f_1 = f_2) \rightarrow ((z = f_1 \land u = y) \rightarrow z = f_2)$.

The abstraction process itself does not preserve validity and may transform a valid formula such as $x + y = y + x$ into the invalid formula $F(x, y) = F(y, x)$ which does not hold for all functions $F$. However, in many useful contexts, such as the verification of compilers which do not perform extensive arithmetical optimizations, the process of abstraction is often justified. At least we can rely on the fact that the process of abstraction into UIFs never generates false positives, and that if the abstract version is found valid, this is also the case with the concrete formulas it abstracts.

After performing such an abstraction followed by Ackerman's reduction, the resulting formula is an equality formula, and enjoys the small model property (i.e. it is satisfiable iff it is satisfiable over a finite domain). Therefore, the next step is the calculation of a finite domain, such that the formula is valid iff it is valid over all interpretations of this finite domain. The latter can be checked with a finite state decision procedure. A known 'folk theorem' is that it is enough to give each variable the range $[1..n]$ (where $n$ is the number of non-Boolean input variables), resulting in a state-space of $n^n$. It is not difficult to see that this range is sufficient for preserving the validity or invalidity of the formula. If a formula is not valid, there is at least one assignment that makes the formula false. Any assignment that partitions the variables into the same equivalence classes will also falsify the formula (the absolute values are of no importance). Since there can not be more than $n$ classes, the $[1..n]$ range is sufficient regardless of the formula's structure. In this paper we will show that analyzing the formula's structure can lead to significantly smaller domains. For example, a trivial improvement is to construct a graph whose vertices are the formula's non-Boolean variables, and the edges represent the comparisons between them. Then, instead of giving a range of $[1..n]$ to all variables, give to each variable the range $[1..k]$, where $k$ is the size of the component it belongs to ($k \leq n$). Experiments with 'real-life' problems has shown us that this simple partitioning can be very effective.

Hojati et. al ([HIKB96], [HKGB97]) tried to avoid the $[1..n]$ range by first considering the explicit DNF of the formula. Given the formula in this form, they 'colored' the comparison graph of each clause (a graph based on the disequalities in the formula) and chose the maximal chromatic number (the number of colors needed for coloring the graph) as the range for each variable. As a second step, they tried to approximate the maximum number of disequalities needed to satisfy the formula, in a general formula. Given that number, a uniform range of $[1..k]$ is sufficient, where $k$ is calculated on the basis of this number. It seems that finding a good approximation is very hard. Although several heuristics are suggested, it is unclear how well they work. They also indicated an inherent problem with finding a good BDD ordering in the presence of Ackerman constraints (the *stripping assertions* in the notation of their paper).

Sajid et al [SGZ+98] proposed a different approach. Since non-Boolean variables appear in the formula only when compared to one another, they suggest encoding each such comparison with a new Boolean variable, and ensuring transitivity of equality by restricting the BDD traversing accordingly. Although this traversing procedure is proved by the authors to be worst-case exponential, it proved to be more efficient than finite instantiations with the $[1..n]$ range.

Even with this range, which we show in this paper is not tight, it is not always the case that this kind of encoding results in a smaller state-space (as was mentioned by the authors themselves). Consider, for example, a formula where all variables are compared to each other (graphically, this is a clique of $n$ vertices). In this case, $n \cdot (n - 1)/2$ new Boolean variables will be introduced, each represented by a BDD variable. Finite instantiations with a range of $[1..n]$, on the other hand, will require only $n \cdot \log n$ BDD variables.

In a more recent work, Bryant, German and Velev [BGV99] restricted the logic to formulas that contain positive equalities only, i.e. the outcome of any equality test between terms can only be part of a monotonically positive Boolean formula. This restriction disallows the use of the outcome of equalities in control decisions. Given this restricted logic, they were able to substitute UIFs with unique constants that serve as 'witnesses' in case the formula is false. This replacement naturally reduced the state-space immensely, and made the decision procedure highly efficient. Although they chose the same case study examined by [SGZ+98], the results are not given in a way that they can be compared.

The formulas we consider here are not restricted to positive equalities. They are implications of the form $\bigwedge_{i=1}^{n} \varphi_i \rightarrow \bigwedge_{j=1}^{m} \psi_j$, typically with several thousand clauses on each side, and more than a thousand variables. The abstraction process adds several hundred more variables (hundreds of which are integer and floating-point) and thousands of constraints. Although we decompose the formula, we still have many verification conditions with more than 150 integer variables. Since the size of the domain is crucial to the time required to complete the proof with a BDD-based tool, the $n^n$ state-space (where $n > 150$ in our case) is naturally far too large to handle.

In the next section, we present a precise definition of the problem we consider: deciding validity (satisfiability) of equality formulas, and explain how it naturally arises in the context of translation validation. In Section 3 we outline our general solution strategy, which is a computation of a small set of domains (ranges) $R$ such that the formula is satisfiable iff it is satisfiable over $R$, followed by a test for $R$-satisfiability performed by a standard BDD package. The remaining question is how to find such a set of small domains. To answer this question, we show how it can be reduced to a graph-theoretic problem. The rest of the paper focuses on algorithms, which, in most cases, produce tractably small domains. In Section 4, we describe the basic algorithm. The soundness proof of the algorithm is given in Section 5. In Section 6, we present several improvements to the basic algorithm, and analyze their effect on the upper bound of the resulting state-space. We describe experimental results from an industrial case study in Section 7, and conclude in Section 8 by considering possible directions for future research.

## 2 The Problem: Deciding Equality Formulas

Our interest in the problem of deciding equality formulas arose within the context of the *Code Validation Tool* (CVT) that we developed as part of the European project *Sacres*. The focus in this project is on developing a methodology and a set of tools for the correct construction of safety critical systems.

CVT is intended to ensure the correctness of the code generator incorporated in the *Sacres* tools suite which automatically translates high level specifications into running code in C and Ada (see [PSS98b], [PSS99], [Con95]). Rather than formally verifying the code generator program, CVT verifies the correctness of every individual run of the generator, comparing the source with the produced target language program and checking their compatibility. This approach of *translation validation* seems to be promising in many other contexts, where verification of the operation of a translator or a compiler is called for.

We will illustrate this approach by a representative example. Assume that a source program contained the statement $z := (x_1 + y_1) \cdot (x_2 + y_2)$ which the translator we wish to verify compiled into the following sequence of three assignments:

$$u_1 := x_1 + y_1;\ u_2 := x_2 + y_2;\ z := u_1 \cdot u_2,$$

introducing the two auxiliary variables $u_1$ and $u_2$.

For this translation, CVT first constructs the verification condition

$$u_1 = x_1 + y_1 \wedge u_2 = x_2 + y_2 \wedge z = u_1 \cdot u_2 \quad \to \quad z = (x_1 + y_1) \cdot (x_2 + y_2),$$

whose validity we wish to check.

The second step performed by CVT in handling such a formula is to abstract the concrete functions appearing in the formula, such as addition and multiplication, by abstract (uninterpreted) function symbols. The abstracted version of the above implication is:

$$u_1 = F(x_1, y_1) \wedge u_2 = F(x_2, y_2) \wedge z = G(u_1, u_2) \quad \to \quad z = G(F(x_1, y_1), F(x_2, y_2))$$

Clearly, if the abstracted version is valid then so is the original concrete one.

Next, we perform the Ackerman reduction [Ack54], replacing each functional term by a fresh variable but adding, for each pair of terms with the same function symbol, an extra antecedent which guarantees the functionality of these terms. Namely, that if the two arguments of the original terms were equal, then the terms should be equal. It is not difficult to see that this transformation preserves validity.

Applying the Ackerman reduction to the abstracted formula, we obtain the following equality formula:

$$\varphi: \quad \left( \begin{array}{l} (x_1 = x_2 \wedge y_1 = y_2 \to f_1 = f_2) \wedge \\ (u_1 = f_1 \wedge u_2 = f_2 \to g_1 = g_2) \wedge \\ u_1 = f_1 \wedge u_2 = f_2 \wedge z = g_1 \end{array} \right) \quad \to \quad z = g_2 \qquad (1)$$

Note the extra antecedent ensuring the functionality of $F$ by identifying the conditions under which $f_1$ should equal $f_2$ and the similar requirement for $G$.

This shows how equality formulas such as $\varphi$ of Equation (1) arise in the process of translation validation.

**Equality Formulas:** Even though the variables appearing in an equality formula such as $\varphi$ are assumed to be completely uninterpreted, it is not difficult to see that a formula such as $\varphi$ is generally valid (satisfiable) iff it is valid (respectively, satisfiable) when the variables appearing in the formula range over the integers. This leads to the following definition of the syntax of equality formulas that the method presented in this paper can handle.

Let $x_1, x_2, \ldots$ be a set of *integer variables*, and $b_1, b_2, \ldots$ be a set of *Boolean variables*. We define the set of *terms* $\mathcal{T}$ by

$$\mathcal{T} \quad ::= \quad \textit{integer constant} \mid x_i \mid \textbf{if } \Phi \textbf{ then } \mathcal{T}_1 \textbf{ else } \mathcal{T}_2$$

The set of equality formulas $\Phi$ is defined by

$$\Phi \quad ::= \quad b_j \mid \neg \Phi \mid \Phi_1 \vee \Phi_2 \mid \mathcal{T}_1 = \mathcal{T}_2 \mid \textbf{if } \Phi_0 \textbf{ then } \Phi_1 \textbf{ else } \Phi_2$$

Additional Boolean operators such as $\wedge, \rightarrow, \leftrightarrow$, can be defined in terms of $\neg, \vee$.

For simplicity, we will not consider in this paper the cases of integer constants and Boolean variables. The full algorithm is presented in [PRSS98].

## 3 The Solution: Instantiations over Small Domains

Our solution strategy for checking whether a given equality formula $\varphi$ is satisfiable can be summarized as follows:

1. Determine, in polynomial time, a *range allocation* $R : Vars(\varphi) \mapsto 2^{\mathbb{N}}$, by mapping each integer variable $x_i \in \varphi$ into a small finite set of integers, such that $\varphi$ is satisfiable (valid) iff it is satisfiable (respectively, valid) over some $R$-interpretation.

2. Encode each variable $x_i$ as an enumerated type over its finite domain $R(x_i)$, and use a standard BDD package to construct a BDD $B_\varphi$. Formula $\varphi$ is satisfiable iff $B_\varphi$ is not identical to 0.

We define the complexity of a range allocation $R$ to be the size of the state-space spanned by $R$, that is, if $Vars(\varphi) = \{x_1, \ldots, x_n\}$, then the complexity of $R$ is $|R| = |R(x_1)| \times |R(x_2)| \times \cdots \times |R(x_n)|$. Obviously, the success of our method depends on our ability to find range allocations with small complexity.

### 3.1 Some Simple Bounds

In theory, there always exists a *singleton* range allocation $R^*$, satisfying the above requirements, such that $R^*$ allocates each variable a domain consisting of a single natural, i.e., $|R^*| = 1$. This is supported by the following trivial argument. If $\varphi$ is satisfiable, then there exists an assignment $(x_1, \ldots, x_n) = (z_1, \ldots, z_n)$ satisfying $\varphi$. It is sufficient to take $R^* : x_1 \mapsto \{z_1\}, \ldots x_n \mapsto \{z_n\}$ as the singleton allocation. If $\varphi$ is unsatisfiable, it is sufficient to take $R^* : x_1, \ldots, x_n \mapsto \{0\}$.

However, finding the singleton allocation $R^*$ amounts to a head-on attack on the primary NP-complete problem. Instead, we generalize the problem and attempt to find a small range allocation which is adequate for a *set* of formulas $\Phi$ which are "structurally similar" to the formula $\varphi$, and includes $\varphi$ itself.

Consequently, we say that the range allocation $R$ is *adequate* for the formula set $\Phi$ if, for every equality formula in the set $\varphi \in \Phi$, $\varphi$ is satisfiable iff $\varphi$ is satisfiable over $R$.

First, let us consider $\Phi_n$, the set of all equality formulas with at most $n$ variables.

**Claim 1 (Folk theorem)** *The uniform range allocation* $R : \{x_1, \ldots, x_n\} \mapsto [1..n]$ *with complexity* $n^n$ *is adequate for* $\Phi_n$.

We can do better if we do not insist on a *uniform* range allocation which allocates the same domain to all variables. Thus the range allocation $R : x_i \mapsto [1..i]$ is also adequate for $\Phi_n$ and has the better complexity of $n!$. In fact, we conjecture that $n!$ is also a lower bound on the size of range allocations adequate for $\Phi_n$.

The formula set $\Phi_n$ utilizes only a simple structural characteristic common to all of its members, namely, the number of variables. Focusing on additional structural characteristics of formulas, we obtain much smaller adequate range allocations, which we proceed to describe in the rest of this paper.

## 3.2   An Approach Based on the Set of Atomic Formulas

We assume that $\varphi$ has no constants or Boolean variables, and is given in a positive form, i.e. negations are only allowed within atomic formulas of the form $x_i \neq x_j$. An important property of formulas in positive form is that they are monotonically satisfied, i.e. if $S_1$ and $S_2$ are two subsets of atomic formulas of $\varphi$ (where $\varphi$ is given in positive form), and $S_1 \subseteq S_2$, then $S_1 \models \varphi$ implies $S_2 \models \varphi$. Any equality formula can be brought into a positive form, by expressing all Boolean operations such as $\rightarrow$, $\leftrightarrow$ and the *if-then-else* construct in terms of the basic Boolean operations $\neg$, $\vee$, and $\wedge$, and pushing all negations inside.

Let $At(\varphi)$ be the set of all atomic formulas of the form $x_i = x_j$ or $x_i \neq x_j$ appearing in $\varphi$, and let $\Phi(A)$ be the family of all equality formulas which have $A$ as the set of their atomic formulas. Obviously $\varphi \in \Phi(At(\varphi))$. Note that the family defined by the atomic formula set $\{x_1 = x_2, x_1 \neq x_2\}$ includes both the satisfiable formula $x_1 = x_2 \vee x_1 \neq x_2$ and the unsatisfiable formula $x_1 = x_2 \wedge x_1 \neq x_2$.

For a set of atomic formulas $A$, we say that the subset $B = \{\psi_1, \ldots, \psi_k\} \subseteq A$ is *consistent* if the conjunction $\psi_1 \wedge \cdots \wedge \psi_k$ is satisfiable. Note that a set $B$ is consistent iff it does not contain a chain of the form $x_1 = x_2, x_2 = x_3, \ldots, x_{r-1} = x_r$ together with the formula $x_1 \neq x_r$.

Given a set of atomic formulas $A$, a range allocation $R$ is defined to be *satisfactory* for $A$ if every consistent subset $B \subseteq A$ is $R$-satisfiable.

For example, the range allocation $R \colon x_1, x_2, x_3 \mapsto \{0\}$ is satisfactory for the atomic formula set $\{x_1 = x_2, x_2 = x_3\}$, while the allocation $R \colon x_1 \mapsto \{1\}$, $x_2 \mapsto \{2\}$, $x_3 \mapsto \{3\}$ is satisfactory for the formula set $\{x_1 \neq x_2, x_2 \neq x_3\}$. On the other hand, no singleton allocation is satisfactory for the set $\{x_1 = x_2, x_1 \neq x_2\}$. A minimal satisfactory allocation for this set is $R \colon x_1 \mapsto \{1\}$, $x_2 \mapsto \{1, 2\}$.

**Claim 2** *The range allocation $R$ is satisfactory for the atomic formula set $A$ iff $R$ is adequate for $\Phi(A)$ the set of formulas $\varphi$ such that $At(\varphi) = A$.*

Thus, we concentrate our efforts on finding a small range allocation which is satisfactory for $A = At(\varphi)$ for a given equality formula $\varphi$. In view of the claim, we will continue to use the terms satisfactory and adequate synonymously.

Partition the set $A$ into the two sets $A = A_= \cup A_{\neq}$, $A_=$ containing all the equality formulas in $A$, while $A_{\neq}$ contains the disequalities. Variable $x_i$ is called a *mixed variable* iff $(x_i, x_j) \in A_=$ and $(x_i, x_k) \in A_{\neq}$ for some $x_j, x_k \in Vars(\varphi)$.

Note that the sets $A_=(\varphi)$ and $A_{\neq}(\varphi)$ for a given formula $\varphi$ can be computed without actually carrying out the transformation to positive form. All that is required is to check whether a given atomic formula has a positive or negative *polarity* within $\varphi$. A sub-formula $p$ has a positive polarity within $\varphi$ iff it is nested under an even number of negations.

*Example 1.* Let us illustrate these concepts on the formula $\varphi$ of Equation (1), whose validity we wished to check.

Since our main algorithm checks for satisfiability, we proceed to form the positive form of $\neg\varphi$, which is given by:

$$\neg\varphi: \begin{pmatrix} (x_1 \neq x_2 \vee y_1 \neq y_2 \vee f_1 = f_2) \wedge \\ (u_1 \neq f_1 \vee u_2 \neq f_2 \vee g_1 = g_2) \wedge \\ u_1 = f_1 \wedge u_2 = f_2 \wedge z = g_1 \end{pmatrix} \wedge z \neq g_2,$$

and therefore

$$A_= : \{(f_1 = f_2), (g_1 = g_2), (u_1 = f_1), (u_2 = f_2), (z = g_1)\}$$
$$A_{\neq} : \{(x_1 \neq x_2), (y_1 \neq y_2), (u_1 \neq f_1), (u_2 \neq f_2), (z \neq g_2)\}$$

Note that $u_1, u_2, f_1, f_2, g_2$ and $z$ in this example are mixed variables. □

This example would require a state-space of 11! if we used the range allocation $[1..i]$ ($11^{11}$, using $[1..n]$). As is shown below, our algorithm finds an adequate range allocation of size 16.

### 3.3 A Graph-Theoretic Representation of the Sets $A_=$, $A_{\neq}$

The sets $A_{\neq}$ and $A_=$ can be represented by two graphs, $G_=$ and $G_{\neq}$ defined as follows:

$(x_i, x_j)$ is an edge on $G_=$, the *equalities graph*, iff $(x_i = x_j) \in A_=$.

$(x_i, x_j)$ is an edge on $G_{\neq}$, the *disequalities graph*, iff $(x_i \neq x_j) \in A_{\neq}$.

We refer to the joint graph as $G$. Each vertex in $G$ represents a variable. Vertices representing mixed variables are called *mixed vertices*.

An inconsistent subset $B \subseteq A$ will appear as a *contradictory cycle* i.e. a cycle consisting of a single $G_{\neq}$ edge and any positive number of $G_=$ edges.

In Fig. 1, we present the graph $G$ corresponding to the formula $\neg\varphi$, where $G_=$-edges are represented by dashed lines and $G_{\neq}$-edges are represented by solid lines. Note the three contradictory cycles: $(g_2 - g_1 - z), (u_1 - f_1)$, and $(u_2 - f_2)$.

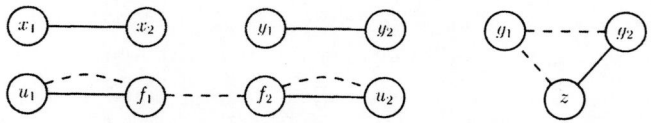

**Fig. 1.** The Graph $G : G_{\neq} \cup G_=$ representing $\neg\varphi$

## 4 The Basic Range Allocation Algorithm

Following is a two-step algorithm for computing an economic range allocation $R$ for the variables in a given formula $\varphi$.

### I. Pre-processing

Initially, $R(x_i) = \emptyset$, for all vertices $x_i \in G$.

A. Remove all $G_{\neq}$ edges which do not lie on a contradictory cycle.
B. For every singleton vertex (a vertex comprising a connected component by itself) $x_i$, add to $R(x_i)$ a fresh value $u_i$, and remove $x_i$ from the graph.

## II. Value Allocation

A. While there are mixed vertices in $G$ do:
   1. Choose a mixed vertex $x_i$. Add $u_i$, a fresh value, to $R(x_i)$.
   2. Assign $R(x_j) := R(x_j) \cup \{u_i\}$ for each vertex $x_j$, s.t. there is a $G_=$-path from $x_i$ to $x_j$.
   3. Remove $x_i$ from the graph.
B. For each (remaining) connected $G_=$ component $C_=$, add a common fresh value $u_{C_=}$ to $R(x_k)$, for every $x_k \in C_=$.

We refer to the fresh values $u_i$ added to $R(x_i)$ in steps I.B and II.A.1, and $u_{C_=}$ added to $R(x_k)$ for $x_k \in C_=$ in step II.B, as the *characteristic* values of these vertices. We write $char(x_i) = u_i$ and $char(x_k) = u_{C_=}$. Note that every vertex is assigned a single characteristic value. Vertices which are assigned their characteristic values in steps I.B and II.A.1 are called *individually assigned vertices*, while the vertices assigned characteristic values in step II.B are called *communally assigned vertices*. Fresh values are assigned in ascending order, so that $char(x_i) < char(x_j)$ implies that $x_i$ was assigned its characteristic value before $x_j$.

The presented description of the algorithm leaves open the order in which vertices are chosen in step II.A, which has a strong impact on the size of the resulting state-space. The set of vertices that are removed in this step can be seen as a *vertex cover* of the $G_{\neq}$ edges, i.e., a set of vertices $V$ such that every $G_{\neq}$ edge has at least one of its ends in $V$. To keep this set as small as possible, we apply the known "greedy" heuristic for the Minimal Vertex Cover problem, and accordingly we denote this set by *mvc*. We choose mixed vertices following a descending degree on $G_{\neq}$. Among vertices with equal degrees on $G_{\neq}$, we choose the one with the highest degree on $G_=$. This heuristic seems not only to find a small vertex cover, it also partitions the graph rather rapidly.

*Example 2.* The following table represents the sequence of steps resulting from the application of the Basic Range Allocation algorithm to the formula $\neg\varphi$:

| Step/ var | $x_1$ | $x_2$ | $y_1$ | $y_2$ | $u_1$ | $f_1$ | $f_2$ | $u_2$ | $g_2$ | $z$ | $g_1$ | Removed |
|---|---|---|---|---|---|---|---|---|---|---|---|---|
| Step I.A | | | | | | | | | | | | Edges: $(x_1 - x_2), (y_1 - y_2)$ |
| Step I.B | 0 | 1 | 2 | 3 | | | | | | | | $x_1, x_2, y_1, y_2$ |
| Step II.A $(f_1)$ | | | | | 4 | 4 | 4 | 4 | | | | $f_1$ |
| Step II.A $(f_2)$ | | | | | | | 4,5 | 4,5 | | | | $f_2$ |
| Step II.A $(g_2)$ | | | | | | | | | 6 | 6 | 6 | $g_2$ |
| Step II.B | | | | | 4,7 | | | | | | | |
| Step II.B | | | | | | | | 4,5,8 | | | | |
| Step II.B | | | | | | | | | | 6,9 | 6,9 | |
| Final $R$-sets | 0 | 1 | 2 | 3 | 4,7 | 4 | 4,5 | 4,5,8 | 6 | 6,9 | 6,9 | Size $= 48$ |

## 5 The Algorithm is Sound

In this section we argue for the soundness of the basic algorithm. We begin by describing a procedure which, given the allocation $R$ produced by the basic algorithm and a consistent subset $B$, assigns to each variable $x_i \in G$ an integer value $a(x_i) \in R(x_i)$. We then continue by proving that this assignment guarantees that every consistent subset is satisfied, and that it is always feasible.

## An Assignment Procedure

Given a consistent subset $B$ and its representative graph $G(B)$, assign to each vertex $x_i \in G(B)$ a value $a(x_i) \in R(x_i)$, according to the following rules:

**1.** If $x_i$ is connected by a (possibly empty) $G_=(B)$-path to an individually assigned vertex $x_j$, assign to $x_i$ the minimal value of $char(x_j)$ among such $x_j$'s.

**2.** Otherwise, assign to $x_i$ its communally assigned value $char(x_i)$.

*Example 3.* Consider the $R$-sets that were computed in example 2. Let us apply the assignment procedure to a subset $B$ that contains all edges excluding both edges between $u_1$ to $f_1$, the dashed edge between $g_1$ and $g_2$, and the solid edge between $f_2$ and $u_2$. The assignment will be as follows:

By rule 1, $f_1, f_2$ and $u_2$ are assigned the value $char(f_1) = $ '4', because $f_1$ was the first mixed vertex in the sub-graph $\{f_1, f_2, u_2\}$ that was removed in step II.A, and consequently it has the minimal characteristic value.

By rule 1, $x_1, x_2, y_1$ and $y_2$ are assigned the characteristic values '0', '1', '2', '3' respectively, which they received in step I.B.

By rule 1, $g_2$ is assigned the value $char(g_2) = $ '6' which it received in II.A.

By rule 2, $z$ and $g_1$ are assigned the value '9' which they received in II.B.

$\square$

**Claim 3** *The assignment procedure satisfies every consistent subset $B$.*

**Proof:** We have to show that all constraints implied by the set $B$ are satisfied by the assignment.

Consider first the case of two variables $x_i$ and $x_j$ which are connected by a $G_=(B)$ edge. We have to show that $a(x_i) = a(x_j)$. Since $x_i$ and $x_j$ are $G_=(B)$-connected, they belong to the same $G_=(B)$-connected component. If they were both assigned a value in step 1, then they were assigned the minimal value of an individually assigned vertex to which they are both $G_=(B)$-connected. If, on the other hand, they were both assigned a value in step 2, then they were assigned the communal value assigned to the $G_=$ component to which they both belong. Thus, in both cases they are assigned the same value.

Next, consider the case of two variables $x_i$ and $x_j$ which are connected by a $G_{\neq}(B)$ edge. To show that $a(x_i) \neq a(x_j)$, we distinguish between three cases:

**A:** If both $x_i$ and $x_j$ were assigned values by rule 1, they must have inherited their values from two distinct individually allocated vertices. Because, otherwise, they are both connected by a $G_=(B)$ path to a common vertex, which together with the $(x_i, x_j)$ $G_{\neq}(B)$-edge closes a contradictory cycle, excluded by the assumption that $B$ is consistent.

**B:** If one of $x_i$, $x_j$ was assigned a value by rule 1 while the other acquired its value by rule 2, then since any communal value is distinct from any individually allocated value, $a(x_i)$ must differ from $a(x_j)$.

**C:** The remaining case is when both $x_i$ and $x_j$ were assigned values by rule 2. The fact that they were not assigned values in step 1 implies that their characteristic values are not individually but communally allocated. If $a(x_i) = $

$a(x_j)$ it means that $x_i$ and $x_j$ were allocated their communal values in the same step II.B of the allocation algorithm, which implies that they had a $G_=$-path between them. Hence, $x_i$ and $x_j$ belong to a contradictory cycle, and the solid edge $(x_i, x_j)$ was therefore still part of $G$ in the beginning of step II.A. By definition of $mvc$, at least one of them was individually assigned in step II.A.1, and consequently, according to the assignment procedure, the component it belongs to is assigned a value by rule 1, in contrast to our assumption. We can therefore conclude that our assumption that $a(x_i) = a(x_j)$ was false. □

**Claim 4** *The assignment procedure is feasible (i.e. the R-sets include the values required by the assignment procedure).*

**Proof:** Consider first the two classes of vertices that are assigned a value by rule 1. The first class includes vertices that are removed in step I.B. These vertices have only one (empty) $G_=(B)$ path to themselves, and are therefore assigned the characteristic value they received in this step. The second class includes vertices that have a (possibly empty) $G_=(B)$ path to a vertex from $mvc$. Let $x_i$ denote such a vertex, and let $x_j$ be the vertex with the minimal characteristic value that $x_i$ can reach on $G_=(B)$. Since $x_i$ and all the vertices on this path were still part of the graph when $x_j$ was removed in step II.A, then according to step II.A.2, $char(x_j)$ was added to $R(x_i)$. Thus, the assignment of $char(x_j)$ to $x_i$ is feasible.

Next, consider the vertices that are assigned a value by rule 2. Every vertex that is removed in step I.B or II.A is clearly assigned a value by rule 1. All the other vertices are communally assigned a value in step II.b. In particular, the vertices that do not have a path to an individually assigned vertex are assigned such a value. Thus, the two steps of the assignment procedure are feasible. □

**Claim 5** $\varphi$ *is satisfiable iff* $\varphi$ *is satisfiable over R.*

**Proof:** By claims 3 and 4, $R$ is satisfactory for $A_= \cup A_{\neq}$. Consequently, by claim 2 $R$ is adequate for $\Phi(At(\varphi))$, and in particular $R$ is adequate for $\Phi(\varphi)$. Thus, by the definition of adequacy, $\varphi$ is satisfiable iff $\varphi$ is satisfiable over $R$. □

## 6 Improvements of the Basic Algorithm

There are several improvements to the basic algorithm, which can significantly decrease the size of the resulting state-space. Here, we present some of them.

### 6.1 Coloring

Step II.A.1 of the basic algorithm calls for allocation of *distinct* characteristic values to the mixed vertices. This is not always necessary, as we demonstrate in the following small example.

*Example 4.* Consider the subgraph $\{u_1, f_1, f_2, u_2\}$ from the graph of Fig. 1. Application of the basic algorithm to this subgraph may yield the following allocation, where the assigned characteristic values are underlined: $R_1 : u_1 \mapsto \{0, \underline{2}\}, f_1 \mapsto \{\underline{0}\}, f_2 \mapsto \{0, \underline{1}\}, u_2 \mapsto \{0, 1, \underline{3}\}$. This allocation leads to a state-space complexity of 12.

By relaxing the requirement that all individually assigned characteristic values should be distinct, we can obtain the allocation $R_2 : u_1 \mapsto \{0, \underline{2}\}, f_1 \mapsto \{\underline{0}\}, f_2 \mapsto \{\underline{0}\}, u_2 \mapsto \{0, \underline{1}\}$ with a state-space complexity of 4. It is not difficult to see that $R_2$ is adequate for the considered subgraph. □

We will now explore some conditions under which the requirement of distinct individually assigned values can be relaxed while maintaining adequacy of the allocation.

Assume that the mixed vertices are assigned their individual characteristic values in the order $x_1, \ldots, x_m$. Assume that we have already assigned individual *char* values to $x_1, \ldots, x_{r-1}$ and are about to assign a *char* value to $x_r$. What may be the reasons for not assigning to $x_r$ the value of $char(x_i)$ for some $i < r$? Examining our assignment procedure, such an assignment may lead to violation of the $B$-constraints only if there exists a path of the form:

$$x_i - - - \cdots - - - x_j \text{———} x_k - - - \cdots - - - x_r$$

where for every individually assigned vertex $x_p$ on the $G_=$-path from $x_i$ to $x_j$ (including $x_j$), $i \leq p$, and equivalently for every vertex $x_q$ on the $G_=$-path from $x_r$ to $x_k$ (including $x_k$), $r \leq q$.

This observation is based on the way the assignment procedure works: it assigns to all vertices in a connected $G_=(B)$ component the characteristic value of the mixed vertex with the lowest index. Thus, if there exists a vertex $x_p$ on the path from $x_i$ to $x_j$ s.t. $p < i$, then $x_j$ will not be assigned the value $char(x_i)$. Consequently, there is no risk that the assignment procedure will assign $x_j$ and $x_k$ the same value, even if the characteristic values of $x_i$ and $x_r$ are equal.

We refer to vertices that have such a path between them as being *incompatible* and assign them different characteristic values.

**Assigning Values to Mixed Vertices with Possible Duplication.**

To allow duplicate characteristic values, we add the following as step I.C of the algorithm.

1. Predetermine the order $x_1, \ldots, x_m$, by which individually assigned variables will be allocated their characteristic values.
2. Construct an *incompatibility graph* $G_{inc}$ whose vertices are $x_1, \ldots, x_m$ and there is an edge connecting $x_i$ to $x_r$ iff $x_i$ and $x_r$ are incompatible.
3. Find a minimal coloring for $G_{inc}$, i.e. assign values ('colors') to the vertices of $G_{inc}$ s.t. no two neighboring vertices receive the same value. Due to the preprocessing step, we require that each connected component is colored with a unique 'pallet' of colors.

Step II.A.1 should be changed as follows:

1. Choose a mixed vertex $x_i$. Add to $R(x_i)$ the color $c_i$ that was determined in step I.C.3 as the characteristic value of $x_i$.

Like the case of minimal vertex covering, step 3 calls for the solution of the NP-hard problem of minimal coloring. In a similar way, we resolve this difficulty by applying one of the approximation algorithms (e.g. one of the "greedy" algorithms) for solving this problem.

*Example 5.* Once more, let us consider the subgraph $\{u_1, f_1, f_2, u_2\}$ of Fig. 1. The modified version of the algorithm identifies the order of choosing the mixed vertices as $f_1, f_2$. The incompatibility graph $G_{inc}$ for this ordering simply consists of the two vertices $f_1$ and $f_2$ with no edges. This means that we can color them by the same color, leading to the allocation $R_2 : u_1 \mapsto \{0, \underline{2}\}, f_1 \mapsto \{\underline{0}\}, f_2 \mapsto \{\underline{0}\}, u_2 \mapsto \{0, \underline{1}\}$, presented in Example 4.

For demonstration purposes, assume that all four vertices in this component were connected by additional edges to other vertices, and that the removal order of step II.A was determined to be : $f_1, f_2, u_2, u_1$. The resulting $G_{inc}$ is depicted in Fig. 2(a). By the definition of $G_{inc}$, every two vertices connected on this graph must have different characteristic values. For example $f_1$ and $u_2$ cannot have the same characteristic value because $G(B)$ can consist of both the solid edge $(f_2, u_2)$ and the dashed edge $(f_1, f_2)$ (in the original graph). Since according to the assignment procedure the value we assign to $f_1$ and $f_2$ is determined by $char(f_1)$, it must be different than $char(u_2)$.

Since this graph can be colored by two colors, say, $f_1$ and $f_2$ colored by 0, while $u_1$ and $u_2$ colored by 1, we obtain the allocation $R_3 : u_1 \mapsto \{0, \underline{1}\}, f_1 \mapsto \{\underline{0}\}, f_2 \mapsto \{\underline{0}\}, u_2 \mapsto \{0, \underline{1}\}$  □

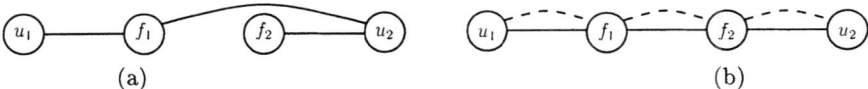

(a)                                    (b)

**Fig. 2.** (a) The Graph $G_{inc}$ (b) Illustrating selective allocation

## 6.2 Selective Assignments of Characteristic Values in step II.B

Step II.B of the basic algorithm requires an unconditional assignment of a fresh characteristic value to each remaining connected $G_=$ component. This is not always necessary, as shown by the following example.

*Example 6.* Consider the graph $G$ presented in Fig. 2(b). Applying the Range Allocation algorithm to this graph can yield the ordering $f_1, f_2$ and consequently the allocation $R_4 : u_1 \mapsto \{0, \underline{3}\}, f_1 \mapsto \{\underline{0}\}, f_2 \mapsto \{0, \underline{1}\}, u_2 \mapsto \{0, 1, \underline{2}\}$ with complexity 12 (although by the coloring procedure suggested in the previous sub-section $u_1$ and $f_2$ can have the same characteristic value, it will not reduce the state-space in this case).

Our suggestion for improvement will identify that, while it is necessary to add the characteristic value '3' to $R(u_1)$, the addition of '2' to $R(u_2)$ is unnecessary, and the allocation $R_5 : u_1 \mapsto \{0, \underline{3}\}, f_1 \mapsto \{\underline{0}\}, f_2 \mapsto \{0, \underline{1}\}, u_2 \mapsto \{0, 1\}$ with complexity 8 is adequate for the graph of Fig. 2(b).  □

Assume that $C_=$ is a remaining connected $G_=$ component with no mixed vertices, and let $K = \bigcap_{x \in C_=} R(x)$ be the set of values that are common to the allocations of all vertices in $C_=$ (in fact, it can be proven that for all $x \in C_=$, $R(x)$ is equal). Let $y_1, \ldots, y_k \notin C_=$ be all the vertices which are $G_{\neq}$-neighbors of vertices in $C_=$. The following condition is sufficient for *not* assigning the vertices of $C_=$ a fresh characteristic value:

Condition *Con*: $k < |K|$, or $K - \bigcup_{i=1}^{k} R(y_i) \neq \emptyset$.

Note that when condition *Con* holds, there is always a value in $K$ which is different from the values $y_1, \ldots, y_k$.

For example, when we consider the component $\{u_2\}$ in the graph of Fig. 2(b), we have that $K = \{0, 1\}$ with $|K| = 2$, while $\{u_2\}$ has only one $G_{\neq}$-neighbor: $f_2$. Consequently, we can skip the assignment of the fresh value '2' to $u_2$.

Therefore, we modify step II.B of the basic algorithm to read as follows:

B. For each (remaining) connected $G_=$ component $C_=$, if condition *Con* does not hold, add a common fresh value $u_{C_=}$ to $R(x_k)$, for every $x_k \in C_=$.

A more general analysis of these situations is based on solving a *set-covering* problem (or approximations thereof) for each invocation of step II.B (more details are provided in [PRSS98]). Experimental results have shown that due to this analysis, in most cases step II.B is not activated. Furthermore, condition *Con* alone identifies almost all of these cases without further analysis.

### 6.3 An Upper Bound

We present an upper bound for the size of the state-space, as computed by our algorithm. For a dashed connected component $G_=^k$, let $n_k = |G_=^k|$ and let $m_k = |mvc_k|$ (the number of individually assigned vertices in $G_=^k$). Also, let $y_k$ denote the number of colors needed for coloring these $m_k$ vertices (obviously, $y_k \le m_k$).

When calculating the maximum state-space for the component $G_=^k$, there are three groups of vertices to consider:

1. For every vertex $x_i$ s.t. $i \le y_k, |R(x_i)| \le i$. Altogether they contribute $y_k!$ or less to the state-space.
2. For every vertex $x_i$ s.t. $y_k < i \le m_k, |R(x_i)| \le y_k$. Altogether they contribute $y_k^{m_k - y_k}$ or less to the state space.
3. For every vertex $x_i$ s.t. $m_k < i \le n_k, |R(x_i)| \le y_k + 1$. Each of these vertices can not have more than $y_k$ values when the $m_k$-th vertex is removed. Then, only one more value can be added to their $R$-set in step II.B (in fact, this additional element is rarely added, as was explained in the previous subsection). Altogether these vertices contribute $(y_k + 1)^{n_k - m_k}$ or less to the state-space.

Combining these three groups, the new upper bound for the state-space is:

$$StateSpace \le \prod_k (y_k!) \cdot y_k^{m_k - y_k} \cdot (y_k + 1)^{n_k - m_k} \tag{2}$$

The worst case, according to formula (2), is when all vertices are mixed ($G_= \equiv G_{\neq}$), there is one connected component ($n_k = n$), the minimal vertex cover is $m_k = m = n - 1$ and the chromatic number $y_k$ is equal to $m_k$. Graphically, this is a 'double clique' (a clique where $G_= \equiv G_{\neq}$) which brings us back to $n!$, the upper bound that was previously derived in Section 3.

## 7 Experimental Results

The Range Allocation algorithm proved to be very effective for the application of *code validation*. One of the reasons for this has to do with the process of *decomposition* (described in [PSS99]) which the CVT tool invokes before range allocation. If the right-hand side of the implication we try to prove is a conjunction of $m$ clauses, then this process decomposes the implication up to $m$ separate formulas. Each of these formulas consists of one clause in the right-hand side, and the *cone of influence* on the left (this is the portion of the formula in the left-hand side that is needed for proving the chosen clause on the right). This process often leads to highly unbalanced comparison graphs: $G_=$ is relatively large (all the comparisons on the left-hand side with positive polarity belong to this graph) and $G_{\neq}$ is very small, resulting in a relatively small number of mixed vertices. These types of graphs result in very small ranges, and many times a large number of variables receive a single value in their range and thus become constants. We have many examples of formulas containing 150 integer variables or more (which, using the $[1..n]$ range, results in a state-space of $150^{150}$), which after performing the Range Allocation algorithm, can be proved in less than a second with a state-space of less than 100. In most cases, these graphs are made of many unconnected $G_=$ components with a very small number of $G_{\neq}$ edges.

We used CVT to validate an industrial size program, a code generated for the case study of a turbine developed by SNECMA[Con95]. The program was partitioned manually (by SNECMA) into 5 modules which were separately compiled. Altogether the specification of this system is a few thousand lines long and contains more than 1000 variables. After the abstraction we had about 2000 variables. Following is a summary of the results achieved by CVT:

| Module | Conjuncts | Time (min.) |
|--------|-----------|-------------|
| M1 | 530 | 1:54 |
| M2 | 533 | 1:30 |
| M3 | 124 | 0:27 |
| M4 | 308 | 2:22 |
| M5 | 860 | 5:55 |
| Total : | 2355 | 12:08 |

The figures for module M5 are only an estimate because the decomposition has been performed manually rather than automatically.

We also tried to conduct a comparative study with [SGZ+98]. Although we had the same input files (the comparison between pipelined and non-pipelined microprocessors, as originally suggested by Burch and Dill [BD94]) as they did, it was nearly impossible to compare the results on this specific example, because of several reasons, the most significant of which were that all the examples considered in [SGZ+98] were solvable in fragments of a second by both methods, and also led to comparable sizes BDD's.

We predict that a comparison on harder problems will reveal that the two methods are complementary. While the Boolean encoding method is efficient when there is a small number of comparisons, the Range Allocation algorithm is more efficient when there is a small number of mixed vertices.

## 8   Conclusions and Directions for Future Research

We presented the Range Allocation method, which can be used as a decision procedure based on finite instantiations, when validating formulas of the theory of equality. This method proved to be highly effective for validating formulas with a large number of integer and float variables.

The method is relatively simple and easy to implement and apply. There is no need to rewrite the verified formula, and any satisfiability checker can be used as a decision procedure.

The algorithm described in this paper is a simplified version of the full Range Allocation algorithm implemented in the CVT tool. The full algorithm includes several issues that were not discussed here mainly due to lack of space. A more comprehensive description of the algorithm can be found in [PRSS98].

The Range Allocation algorithm can be improved in various ways. For example, the $mvc$ set is not unique, and the problem of choosing among $mvc$ sets that have an equal size is still an open question. Furthermore, given an $mvc$ set, the ordering in which the vertices in this set are removed in stage II/a should also be further investigated. Another possible improvement is the identification of special kind of graphs. For example, the range [1..4] is enough for any *planar* graph (where $G_= \equiv G_{\neq}$). It should be rather interesting to investigate whether 'real-life' formulas have any special structure which can then be solved by utilizing various results from graph theory.

Another possibility for future research is to extend the algorithm to formulas with less abstraction, and more specifically to formulas including the $>$ and $\geq$ relations.

# References

[Ack54]   W. Ackerman. *Solvable cases of the Decision Problem*. Studies in Logic and the Foundations of Mathematics. North-Holland, Amsterdam, 1954.

[BD94]    J. R. Burch and D. L. Dill. Automatic verification of pipelined microprocessor control. In *Proc. CAV'94*, lncs 818, pp 68–80.

[BGV99]   R. Bryant, S. German, and M. Velev. Exploiting positive equality in a logic of equality with uninterpreted functions. In *this volume*, 1999.

[Con95]   The Sacres Consortium. Safety critical embedded systems: from requirements to system architecture, 1995. Esprit Project Description EP 20.897, URL http://www.tni.fr/sacres.

[HIKB96]  R. Hojati, A. Isles, D. Kirkpatrick, and R.K. Brayton. Verification using uninterpreted functions and finite instantiations. *FMCAD'96*, pp 218 – 232.

[HKGB97]  R. Hojati, A. Kuehlmann, S. German, and R. Brayton. Validity checking in the theory of equality using finite instantiations. In *Proc. Intl. Workshop on Logic Synthesis*, 1997.

[PRSS98]  A. Pnueli, Y. Rodeh, O. Shtrichman, and M. Siegel. An efficient algorithm for the range minimization problem. *Tech. report*, Weizmann Institute, 1998.

[PSS98b]  A. Pnueli, M. Siegel, and O. Shtrichman. Translation validation for synchronous languages. *ICALP98* lncs 1443, pages 235–246

[PSS99]   A. Pnueli, M. Siegel, and O. Shtrichman. The code validation tool (CVT)-automatic verification of a compilation process. *Intl. journal on Software Tools for Technology Transfer (STTT)*, vol 2, 1999.

[SGZ+98]  K. Sajid, A. Goel, H. Zhou, A. Aziz, S. Barber, and V. Singhal. BDD based procedures for a theory of equality with uninterpreted functions. *CAV'98*, lncs 1427, pp 244–255.

# Exploiting Positive Equality in a Logic of Equality with Uninterpreted Functions [*]

Randal E. Bryant[1], Steven German[2], and Miroslav N. Velev[3]

[1] Computer Science, Carnegie Mellon University, Pittsburgh, PA
Randy.Bryant@cs.cmu.edu
[2] IBM Watson Research Center, Yorktown Hts., NY
german@watson.ibm.com
[3] Electrical and Computer Engineering, Carnegie Mellon University, Pittsburgh, PA
mvelev@ece.cmu.edu

**Abstract.** In using the logic of equality with unininterpreted functions to verify hardware systems, specific characteristics of the formula describing the correctness condition can be exploited when deciding its validity. We distinguish a class of terms we call "p-terms" for which equality comparisons can appear only in monotonically positive formulas. By applying suitable abstractions to the hardware model, we can express the functionality of data values and instruction addresses flowing through an instruction pipeline with p-terms.

A decision procedure can exploit the restricted uses of p-terms by considering only "maximally diverse" interpretations of the associated function symbols, where every function application yields a different value except when constrained by functional consistency. We present a procedure that translates the original formula into one in propositional logic by interpreting the formula over a domain of fixed-length bit vectors and using vectors of propositional variables to encode domain variables. By exploiting maximal diversity, this procedure can greatly reduce the number of propositional variables that must be introduced.

We present experimental results demonstrating the efficiency of this approach when verifying pipelined processors using the method proposed by Burch and Dill. Exploiting positive equality allows us to overcome the exponential blow-up experienced previously [VB98] when verifying microprocessors with load, store, and branch instructions.

## 1 Introduction

For automatically reasoning about pipelined processors, Burch and Dill demonstrated the value of using propositional logic, extended with uninterpreted functions, uninterpreted predicates, and the testing of equality [BD94]. Their approach involves abstracting the data path as a collection of registers and memories storing data, units such as ALUs operating on the data, and various connections and multiplexors providing methods for data to be transferred and selected. The operation of units that transform data is

---

[*] This research was supported at Carnegie Mellon University by SRC Contract 98-DC-068 and by grants from Fujitsu, Motorola, and Intel

abstracted as blocks computing functions with no specified properties other than functional consistency, i.e., that applications of a function to equal arguments yield equal results: $x = y$ implies $f(x) = f(y)$. The state of a register at any point in the computation can be represented by a symbolic term, an expression consisting of a combination of domain variables, function and predicate applications, and Boolean operations.

The correctness of a pipelined processor can be expressed as a formula in this logic that compares for equality the terms describing the results produced by the processor to those produced by an instruction set reference model. In their paper, Burch and Dill also describe a decision procedure for their logic based on theorem proving search methods. It uses combinatorial search coupled with algorithms for maintaining a partitioning of the terms into equivalence classes based on the equalities that hold at a given step of the search.

Burch and Dill's work has generated considerable interest in the use of uninterpreted functions to abstract data operations in processor verification. A common theme has been to adopt Boolean methods, either to allow integration of uninterpreted functions into symbolic model checkers [DPR98,BBCZ98], or to allow the use of Binary Decision Diagrams in the decision procedure [HKGB97,GSZAS98,VB98]. Boolean methods allow a more direct modeling of the control logic of hardware designs and thus can be applied to actual processor designs rather than highly abstracted models. In addition to BDD-based decision procedures, Boolean methods could use some of the recently developed satisfiability procedures for propositional logic. In principle, Boolean methods could outperform decision procedures based on theorem proving search methods, especially when verifying processors with more complex control logic.

Boolean methods can be used to decide the validity of a formula containing terms and uninterpreted functions by exploiting the property that a given formula contains a limited number of function applications and therefore can be proved to be universally valid by considering its interpretation over a sufficiently large, but finite domain [Ack54]. The formula to be verified can be translated into one in propositional logic, using vectors of propositional variables to encode the possible values generated by function applications [HKGB97]. Our implementation of such an approach [VB98] as part of a BDD-based symbolic simulation system was successful at verifying simple pipelined data paths. We found, however, that the computational resources grew exponentially as we increased the pipeline depth. Modeling the interactions between successive instructions flowing through the pipeline, as well as the functional consistency of the ALU results, precludes having an ordering of the variables encoding term values that yields compact BDDs. Similarly, we found that extending the data path to a complete processor by adding either load and store instructions or instruction fetch logic supporting jumps and conditional branches led to impossible BDD variable ordering requirements. Goel *et al* [GSZAS98] presented an alternate approach to using BDDs to decide the validity of formulas in the logic of equality with uninterpreted functions. They use Boolean variables to encode the equality relations between terms, rather than to encode term values. Their experimental results were also somewhat disappointing. To date, the possibility that Boolean methods could outperform theorem proving methods has not been realized.

In this paper, we show that the characteristics of the formulas generated when modeling processor pipelines can be exploited to greatly reduce the number of propositional variables that are introduced when translating the formula into propositional logic. We distinguish a class of terms we call *p-terms* for which equations, i.e., equality comparisons between terms, can appear only in monotonically positive formulas. Such formulas are suitable for describing the top-level correctness condition, but not for modeling any control decisions in the hardware. By applying suitable abstractions to the hardware model, we can express the functionality of data values and instruction addresses with p-terms.

A decision procedure can exploit the restricted uses of p-terms by considering only "maximally diverse" interpretations of the associated "p-function" symbols, where every function application yields a different value except when constrained by functional consistency. In translating the formula into propositional logic, we can then use vectors with fixed bit patterns rather than propositional variables to encode the possible results of function applications. This reduction in variables greatly simplifies the BDDs generated, avoiding the exponential blow-up experienced by other procedures.

Others have recognized the value of restricting the testing of equality when modeling the flow of data in pipelines. Berezin *et al* [BBCZ98] generate a model of an execution unit suitable for symbolic model checking in which the data values and operations are kept abstract. In our terminology, their functional terms are all p-terms. They use fixed bit patterns to represent the initial states of registers, much as we replace p-term domain variables by fixed bit patterns. To model the outcome of each program operation, they generate an entry in a "reference file" and refer to the result by a pointer to this file. These pointers are similar to the bit patterns we generate to denote the p-function application outcomes. Damm *et al* consider an even more restricted logic that allows them to determine the universal validity of a formula by considering only interpretations over the domain $\{0, 1\}$. Verifying an execution unit in which the data path width is reduced to a single bit then suffices to prove its correctness for all possible widths. In comparison to these other efforts, we maintain the full generality of the unrestricted functional terms of Burch and Dill while exploiting the efficiency gains possible with p-terms. In our processor model, we can abstract register identifiers as unrestricted terms, while modeling program data and instruction data as p-terms. In contrast, both [BBCZ98] and [DPR98] used bit encodings of register identifiers and were unable to scale their verifications to a realistic number of registers.

In a different paper in this proceedings, Pnueli, *et al* [PRSS99] also propose a method to exploit the polarity of the equations in a formula containing uninterpreted functions with equality. They describe an algorithm to generate small domains for each domain variable such that the universal validity of the formula can be determined by considering only interpretations in which the variables range over their restricted domains. A key difference of their work is that they examine the equation structure after replacing all function application terms with domain variables and introducing functional consistency constraints as described by Ackermann [Ack54]. These consistency constraints typically contain large numbers of equations—far more than occur in the original formula—that mask the original p-term structure. In addition, we use a new method of replacing function application terms with domain variables. Our scheme allows us to exploit maximal diversity by assigning fixed values to the domain variables generated while expanding p-function application terms.

In the remainder of the paper, we first define the syntax and semantics of our logic by extending that of Burch and Dill's. We prove our central result concerning the need to consider only maximally diverse interpretations when deciding the validity of formulas in our logic. We describe a method of translating formulas into propositional logic. We discuss the abstractions required to model processor pipelines in our logic. Finally, we present experimental results showing our ability to verify a simple, but complete pipelined processor. A more detailed presentation with complete proofs is given in [BGV99].

## 2 Logic of Equality with Uninterpreted Functions (EUF)

The logic of Equality with Uninterpreted Functions (EUF) presented by Burch and Dill [BD94] can be expressed by the following syntax:

$$term ::= ITE(formula, term, term)$$
$$| \; function\text{-}symbol(term, \ldots, term)$$
$$formula ::= \textbf{true} \; | \; \textbf{false} \; | \; (term = term)$$
$$| \; (formula \wedge formula) \; | \; (formula \vee formula) \; | \; \neg formula$$
$$| \; predicate\text{-}symbol(term, \ldots, term)$$

In this logic, *formulas* have truth values while *terms* have values from some arbitrary domain. Terms are formed by applications of uninterpreted function symbols and by applications of the *ITE* (for "if-then-else") operator. The *ITE* operator chooses between two terms based on a Boolean control value, i.e., $ITE(\textbf{true}, x_1, x_2)$ yields $x_1$ while $ITE(\textbf{false}, x_1, x_2)$ yields $x_2$. Formulas are formed by comparing two terms for equality, by applying an uninterpreted predicate symbol to a list of terms, and by combining formulas using Boolean connectives. A formula expressing equality between two terms is called an *equation*. We use *expression* to refer to either a term or a formula.

Every function symbol $f$ has an associated *order*, denoted $ord(f)$, indicating the number of terms it takes as arguments. Function symbols of order zero are referred to as *domain variables*. We use the shortened form $v$ rather than $v()$ to denote an instance of a domain variable. Similarly, every predicate $p$ has an associated order $ord(p)$. Predicates of order zero are referred to as *propositional variables*.

The truth of a formula is defined relative to a nonempty domain $\mathcal{D}$ of values and an interpretation $I$ of the function and predicate symbols. Interpretation $I$ assigns to each function symbol of order $k$ a function from $\mathcal{D}^k$ to $\mathcal{D}$, and to each predicate symbol of order $k$ a function from $\mathcal{D}^k$ to $\{\textbf{true}, \textbf{false}\}$. Given an interpretation $I$ of the function and predicate symbols and an expression $E$, we can define the *valuation* of $E$ under $I$, denoted $I[E]$, according to its syntactic structure. $I[E]$ will be an element of the domain when $E$ is a term, and a truth value when $E$ is a formula.

A formula $F$ is said to be *true under interpretation* $I$ when $I[F]$ equals $\textbf{true}$. It is said to be *valid over domain* $\mathcal{D}$ when it is true for all interpretations over domain $\mathcal{D}$. $F$ is said to be *universally valid* when it is valid over all domains. It can be shown that if a formula is valid over some suitably large domain, then it is universally valid [Ack54]. In particular, it suffices to have a domain as large as the number of syntactically distinct function application terms occurring in $F$.

# 3 Logic of Positive Equality with Uninterpreted Functions (PEUF)

## 3.1 Syntax

PEUF is an extended logic based on EUF given by the following syntax:

$$
\begin{aligned}
\textit{g-term} ::=\ & \textit{ITE}(\textit{formula}, \textit{g-term}, \textit{g-term}) \\
& |\ \textit{g-function-symbol}(\textit{p-term}, \ldots, \textit{p-term}) \\
\textit{p-term} ::=\ & \textit{g-term}\ |\ \textit{ITE}(\textit{formula}, \textit{p-term}, \textit{p-term}) \\
& |\ \textit{p-function-symbol}(\textit{p-term}, \ldots, \textit{p-term}) \\
\textit{formula} ::=\ & \textbf{true}\ |\ \textbf{false}\ |\ (\textit{term} = \textit{term}) \\
& |\ (\textit{formula} \wedge \textit{formula})\ |\ (\textit{formula} \vee \textit{formula})\ |\ \neg \textit{formula} \\
& |\ \textit{predicate-symbol}(\textit{p-term}, \ldots, \textit{p-term}) \\
\textit{p-formula} ::=\ & \textit{formula}\ |\ (\textit{p-term} = \textit{p-term}) \\
& |\ (\textit{p-formula} \wedge \textit{p-formula})\ |\ (\textit{p-formula} \vee \textit{p-formula})
\end{aligned}
$$

This logic has two disjoint classes of function symbols giving two classes of terms. General terms, or *g-terms*, correspond to terms in EUF. Syntactically, a g-term is a g-function application or an *ITE* term in which the two result terms are hereditarily built from g-function applications and *ITE*s.

The new class of terms is called positive terms, or *p-terms*. P-terms may not appear in negative equations, i.e., equations within the scope of a logical negation. The syntax is restricted in a way that prevents p-terms from appearing in negative equations. When two p-terms are compared for equality, the result is a special, restricted kind of formula called a *p-formula*. P-formulas are built up using only the monotonically positive Boolean operations $\wedge$ and $\vee$. P-formulas may not be placed under a negation sign, and cannot be used as the control for an ITE operation.

Note that our syntax allows any g-term to be "promoted" to a p-term. Throughout the syntax definition, we require function and predicate symbols to take p-terms as arguments. However, since g-terms can be promoted, the requirement to use p-terms as arguments does not restrict the use of g-function symbols or g-terms. In essence, g-function symbols may be used as freely in our logic as in EUF, but the p-function symbols are restricted.

Observe that PEUF does not extend the expressive power of EUF—we could translate any PEUF expression into EUF by considering the g-terms and p-terms to be terms and the p-formulas to be formulas. Instead, the benefit of PEUF is that by distinguishing some portion of a formula as satisfying a restricted set of properties, we can radically reduce the number of different interpretations we must consider when proving that a p-formula is universally valid.

## 3.2  Diverse Interpretations

Let $T$ be a set of terms, where a term may be either a g-term or a p-term. We classify terms as either p-function applications, g-function applications, or *ITE* terms, according to their top-level operation. The first two categories are collectively referred to as function application terms. For any formula or p-formula $F$, define $T(F)$ as the set of all function application terms occurring in $F$.

An interpretation $I$ partitions a term set $T$ into a set of equivalence classes, where terms $T_1$ and $T_2$ are equivalent under $I$, written $T_1 \approx_I T_2$ when $I[T_1]$ equals $I[T_2]$. Interpretation $I'$ is said to be a *refinement* of $I$ for term set $T$ when $T_1 \approx_{I'} T_2$ implies $T_1 \approx_I T_2$ for every pair of terms $T_1$ and $T_2$ in $T$. $I'$ is a *proper* refinement of $I$ for $T$ when it is a refinement and there is at least one pair of terms $T_1, T_2 \in T$ such that $T_1 \approx_I T_2$, but $T_1 \not\approx_{I'} T_2$.

Let $\Sigma$ denote a subset of the function symbols in formula $F$. An interpretation $I$ is said to be *diverse* for $F$ with respect to $\Sigma$ when it provides a maximal partitioning of the function application terms in $T(F)$ having a top-level function symbol from $\Sigma$ relative to each other and to the other function application terms, but subject to the constraints of functional consistency. That is, for $T_1$ of the form $f(S_1, \ldots, S_k)$, where $f \in \Sigma$, an interpretation $I$ is diverse with respect to $\Sigma$ if $I$ has $T_1 \approx_I T_2$ only in the case where $T_2$ is also a term of the form $f(U_1, \ldots, U_k)$, and $S_i \approx_I U_i$ for all $i$ such that $1 \leq i \leq k$. If we let $\Sigma_p(F)$ denote the set of all p-function symbols in $F$, then interpretation $I$ is said to be *maximally diverse* when it is diverse with respect to $\Sigma_p(F)$. Note that this property requires the p-function application terms to be in separate equivalence classes from the g-function application terms.

**Theorem 1.** *P-formula $F$ is universally valid if and only if it is true in all maximally diverse interpretations.*

First, it is clear that if $F$ is universally valid, then $F$ is true in all maximally diverse interpretations. We prove via the following lemma that if $F$ is true in all maximally diverse interpretations it is universally valid.

**Lemma 1.** *If interpretation $I$ is not maximally diverse for p-formula $F$, then there is an interpretation $I'$ that is a proper refinement of $I$ such that $I'[F] \Rightarrow I[F]$.*

*Proof Sketch:* Let $T_1$ be a term occurring in $F$ of the form $f_1(S_1, \ldots, S_{k_1})$, where $f_1$ is a p-function symbol. Let $T_2$ be a term occurring in $F$ of the form $f_2(U_1, \ldots, U_{k_2})$, where $f_2$ may be either a p-function or a g-function symbol. Assume furthermore that $I[T_1] = I[T_2] = z$, but that either symbols $f_1$ and $f_2$ differ or $I[S_i] \neq I[U_i]$ for some value of $i$.

Let $z'$ be a value not in $\mathcal{D}$, and define a new domain $\mathcal{D}' \doteq \mathcal{D} \cup \{z'\}$. Our strategy is to construct an interpretation $I'$ over $\mathcal{D}'$ that partitions the terms in $T(F)$ in the same way as $I$, except that it splits the class containing terms $T_1$ and $T_2$ into two parts—one containing $T_1$ and evaluating to $z'$, and the other containing $T_2$ and evaluating to $z$.

Define function $h: \mathcal{D}' \to \mathcal{D}$ to map elements of $\mathcal{D}'$ back to their counterparts in $\mathcal{D}$, i.e., $h(z') = z$, while all other values of $x$ give $h(x) = x$.

For p-function symbol $f_1$, define $I'(f_1)(x_1, \ldots, x_k)$ as $z'$ when $h(x_i) = I[S_i]$ for all $1 \leq i \leq k_1$, and as $I(f_1)(h(x_1), \ldots, h(x_k))$ otherwise. For other function and predicate symbols, $I'$ is defined to preserve the functionality of interpretation $I$, while also treating argument values of $z'$ the same as $z$. That is, $I'(f)$ for function symbol $f$ having $ord(f) = k$ is defined such that $I'(f)(x_1, \ldots, x_k) = I(f)(h(x_1), \ldots, h(x_k))$.

One can show that interpretation $I'$ maintains the values of all formulas and g-terms as occur under interpretation $I$. Some of the p-terms that evaluate to $z$ under $I$, including $T_1$, evaluate to $z'$. Others, including $T_2$, continue to evaluate to $z$. With respect to p-formulas, consider first an equation of the form $S_a = S_b$ where $S_a$ and $S_b$ are p-terms. The equation will yield the same value under both interpretations except under the condition that $S_a$ and $S_b$ are split into different parts of the class that originally evaluated to $z$, in which case the comparison will yield **true** under $I$, but **false** under $I'$. In any case, we maintain the property that $I'[S_a = S_b] \Rightarrow I[S_a = S_b]$. This implication relation is preserved by conjunctions and disjunctions of p-formulas, due to the monotonicity of these operations. By this argument we can see that $I'$ is a proper refinement of $I$ for $\mathcal{T}(F)$ and that $I'[F] \Rightarrow I[F]$. □

Theorem 1 is proved by repeatedly applying Lemma 1. One can show that any interpretation $I$ of a p-formula $F$ can be refined to a maximally diverse interpretation $I^*$ for $F$ such that $I^*[F]$ implies $I[F]$. It follows that the truth of $F$ for all maximally diverse interpretations implies its truth for all possible interpretations.

## 4  Exploiting Positive Equality in a Decision Procedure

A decision procedure for PEUF must determine whether a given p-formula is universally valid. Theorem 1 shows that we can consider only interpretations in which the values produced by the application of any p-function symbol differ from those produced by the applications of any other p-function or g-function symbol. We can therefore consider the different p-function symbols to yield values over domains disjoint from one another and from the domain of g-function values. In addition, we can consider each application of a p-function symbol to yield a distinct value, except when its arguments match those of some other application.

We describe a decision procedure that first transforms an arbitrary EUF formula into one containing only domain and propositional variables. This restricted class of formulas can readily be translated into propositional formulas by using bit vectors as the domain of interpretation. The transformation can exploit positive equality by using fixed bit patterns rather than vectors of propositional variables to encode the domain variables representing p-function application results.

## 4.1 Eliminating Function and Predicate Applications in EUF

We illustrate our method by considering the formula

$$x = y \ \Rightarrow \ g(f(x)) = g(f(y)) \tag{1}$$

Eliminating the implication gives $\neg(x = y) \lor g(f(x)) = g(f(y))$, and hence both $f$ and $g$ are a p-function symbols, while $x$ and $y$ are g-function symbols. We introduce domain variables $vf_1, vf_2$ and replace term $f(x)$ with $vf_1$ and term $f(y)$ with the term $ITE(y = x, vf_1, vf_2)$. Observe that as we consider interpretations with different values for variables $vf_1$ and $vf_2$, we implicitly cover all values that an interpretation of function symbol $f$ may yield for arguments $x$ and $y$. The $ITE$ structure enforces functional consistency—when $I(x) = I(y)$, we will have both terms evaluate to $I(vf_1)$.

These replacements give a formula: $\neg(x = y) \lor g(vf_1) = g(ITE(y = x, vf_1, vf_2))$. We then introduce domain variables $vg_1$ and $vg_2$ and replace the first application of $g$ with $vg_1$, and the second with $ITE(ITE(y = x, vf_1, vf_2) = vf_1, vg_1, vg_2)$. Our final form is then:

$$\neg(x = y) \ \lor \ vg_1 = ITE(ITE(y = x, vf_1, vf_2) = vf_1, vg_1, vg_2) \tag{2}$$

The complete procedure generalizes that shown for the simple example. Suppose formula $F$ contains $n$ syntactically distinct terms $T_1, T_2, \ldots, T_n$ having the application of function symbol $f$ as the top-level operation. We refer to these as $f$-application terms. We introduce domain variables $vf_1, \ldots, vf_n$ and replace each term $T_i$ with a nested $ITE$ structure $U_i$ of the form

$$U_i \doteq ITE(C_{i,1}, vf_1, ITE(C_{i,2}, vf_2, \cdots ITE(C_{i,i-1}, vf_{i-1}, vf_i) \cdots))$$

where the formula $C_{i,j}$ is true iff the arguments to the top-level application of $f$ in the terms $T_i$ and $T_j$ have the same values. The result of replacing every $f$-application term $T_i$ in $F$ by the new term $U_i$ is a formula that we call $F^{(f)}$.

We remove all function symbols of nonzero order from $F$ by repeating this process. A similar process is used to eliminate applications of predicate symbols having nonzero order, except that we introduce propositional variables $pv_1, pv_2, \ldots$, when replacing applications of predicate symbol $p$. We call the final result of this process the formula $F^*$. Complete details are presented in [BGV99].

**Theorem 2.** *For EUF formula $F$, the transformation process yields a formula $F^*$ containing only domain and propositional variables and such that $F$ is universally valid if and only if $F^*$ is universally valid.*

*Proof Sketch:* To prove this theorem, we first show that our procedure for replacing all instances of function symbol $f$ in an arbitrary formula $G$ by nested $ITE$ terms to yield a formula $G^{(f)}$ preserves universal validity. (1) $G^{(f)}$ universally valid $\Rightarrow G$ universally valid. For any interpretation $I$ of the function and predicate symbols in $G$, we can construct an interpretation $\hat{I}$ of the symbols in $G^{(f)}$ such that $\hat{I}[G^{(f)}] = I[G]$. Interpretation $\hat{I}$ is defined by extending $I$ to include interpretations of the domain variables

$vf_1, \ldots, vf_n$. Each such variable $vf_i$ is given the interpretation $\hat{I}(vf_i) \doteq I[T_i]$, i.e., the value of $f$-application term $i$ under $I$.

(2) Conversely, $G$ universally valid $\Rightarrow G^{(f)}$ universally valid. For any interpretation $\hat{I}$ of the function and predicate symbols in $G^{(f)}$, we can define an interpretation $I$ of the symbols in $G$ such that $I[G] = \hat{I}[G^{(f)}]$. This interpretation is defined by introducing an interpretation of function symbol $f$ such that the values yielded when evaluating each $f$-application term $T_i$ under $I$ matches that yielded for the nested *ITE* structure $U_i$ under $\hat{I}$.

By a similar process we show that our procedure for replacing predicate applications preserves universal validity. The theorem is then proved by inducting on the number of function and predicate symbols. □

## 4.2   Using Fixed Values for P-Function Applications

We can exploit the maximal diversity property by using fixed domain values rather than domain variables when replacing p-function applications by nested *ITE* terms. First, consider the effect of replacing all instances of a function symbol $f$ by nested *ITE* terms, as described earlier, yielding a formula $F^{(f)}$ with new domain variables $vf_1, \ldots, vf_n$.

**Lemma 2.** *If $f \in \Sigma$, then for any interpretation $I$ that is diverse for $F$ with respect to $\Sigma$, there is an interpretation $\hat{I}$ that is diverse for $F^{(f)}$ with respect to $\Sigma - \{f\} \cup \{vf_1, \ldots, vf_n\}$ such that $I[F] = \hat{I}[F^{(f)}]$.*

*Proof Sketch:* The proof of this lemma requires a more refined argument than that of Theorem 2. If we were to define $\hat{I}(vf_i)$ to be $I[T_i]$ for each domain variable $vf_i$, we may not have a diverse interpretation with respect to the newly-generated variables. Instead, we define $\hat{I}(vf_i)$ to be $I[T_i]$ only if there is no value $j < i$ such that the arguments of $f$-application terms $T_j$ and $T_i$ have equal valuations under $I$. Otherwise we let $z'$ be a value not in $\mathcal{D}$, define a new domain $\mathcal{D}' \doteq \mathcal{D} \cup \{z'\}$, and let $\hat{I}(vf_i) = z'$. It can readily be seen that the value assigned to this variable will not affect the valuation of nested *ITE* structure $U_i$ under interpretation $\hat{I}$, and hence it can be arbitrary. □

Suppose we apply the transformation process of Theorem 2 to a p-formula $F$ to generate a formula $F^*$, and that in this process, we introduce a set of new domain variables $V$ to replace the applications of the p-function symbols. Let $\Sigma_p^*(F)$ be the union of the set of domain variables in $\Sigma_p(F)$ and $V$. That is, $\Sigma_p^*(F)$ consists of those domain variables in the original formula $F$ that were p-function symbols as well as the domain variables generated when replacing applications of p-function symbols. Let $\Sigma_g^*(F)$ be the domain variables in $F^*$ that are not in $\Sigma_p^*(F)$. These variables were either g-function symbols in $F$ or were generated when replacing g-function applications.

We first observe that we can generate all maximally diverse interpretations of $F$ by considering only interpretations of the variables in $F^*$ that assign distinct values to the variables in $\Sigma_p^*(F)$:

**Theorem 3.** *PEUF formula $F$ is universally valid if and only if its translation $F^*$ is true for every interpretation $I^*$ such that if $v_p$ is a variable in $\Sigma_p^*(F)$ and $v$ is any other domain variable in $F^*$, then $I^*(v_p) \neq I^*(v)$.*

*Proof Sketch:* This theorem follows by inducting on the number of p-function symbols in $F$, using Lemma 2 to prove the induction step. □

Observe that the nested *ITE* structures we generate when replacing function applications involve many equations in the formulas controlling *ITE* operations. These can cause function symbols that appeared as p-function symbols in the original formula to be g-function symbols in $F^*$. In addition, many of the newly-generated variables will not be p-function symbols in $F^*$. For example, variables $vf_1$ and $vf_2$ are g-function symbols in Equation 2. Nonetheless, this theorem shows that we can still restrict our attention to interpretations that are diverse with respect to these variables.

Furthermore, we can choose particular domains of sufficient size and assign fixed interpretations to the variables in $\Sigma_p^*(F)$. Select disjoint domains $\mathcal{D}_p$ and $\mathcal{D}_g$ for the variables in $\Sigma_p^*(F)$ and $\Sigma_g^*(F)$, respectively, such that $|\mathcal{D}_p| \geq |\Sigma_p^*(F)|$ and $|\mathcal{D}_g| \geq |\Sigma_g^*(F)|$. Let $\alpha$ be any 1–1 mapping $\alpha \colon \Sigma_p^*(F) \to \mathcal{D}_p$.

**Corollary 1.** *PEUF formula $F$ is universally valid if and only if its translation $F^*$ is true for every interpretation $I^*$ such that $I^*(v_p) = \alpha(v_p)$ for every variable $v_p$ in $\Sigma_p^*(F)$, and $I^*(v_g)$ is in $\mathcal{D}_g$ for every variable $v_g$ in $\Sigma_g^*(F)$.*

*Proof Sketch:* Any interpretation that is diverse with respect to $\Sigma_p^*(F)$ defines a 1–1 mapping from the variables in $\Sigma_p^*(F)$ to the domain. We can therefore find an isomorphic interpretation satisfying the requirements for $I^*$ listed above. □

As an illustration, consider formula $F^*$ given by Equation 2 resulting from the transformation of formula $F$ given by Equation 1. We have $\Sigma_p^*(F) = \{vf_1, vf_2, vg_1, vg_2\}$ and $\Sigma_g^*(F) = \{x, y\}$. Suppose we use bit vectors of length 3 as the domain of interpretation. Then we could let $\mathcal{D}_g$ be $\{\langle 0,0,0\rangle, \langle 0,0,1\rangle\}$. We assign $x$ the fixed interpretation $\langle 0,0,0\rangle$, and $y$ the interpretation $\langle 0,0,a\rangle$ where $a$ is a propositional variable. Viewing truth values **true** and **false** as representing bit values 1 and 0, respectively, the different interpretations of $a$ will then cover both the case where $x$ and $y$ have equal interpretations as well as where they are distinct. For variables $vf_1$, $vf_2$, $vg_1$, and $vg_2$, we can assign fixed interpretations $\langle 1,0,0\rangle$, $\langle 1,0,1\rangle$, $\langle 1,1,0\rangle$, and $\langle 1,1,1\rangle$, respectively. Thus, we can translate our formula $F$ into a propositional formula having just a single propositional variable.

Ackermann also describes a scheme for replacing function application terms by domain variables [Ack54]. Using his scheme, we simply replace each instance of a function application by a newly-generated domain variable and then introduce constraints expressing functional consistency. For the example formula given by Equation 1 we would get a modified formula:

$$((x = y \Rightarrow vf_1 = vf_2) \wedge (vf_1 = vf_2 \Rightarrow vg_1 = vg_2))$$
$$\Rightarrow (x = y \Rightarrow vg_1 = vg_2)$$

Observe, however, that there is no clear way to exploit the maximal diversity property with this translated form. If we replace $vf_1$ and $vf_2$ by distinct values in the above case, we fail to consider any interpretations in which arguments $x$ and $y$ have equal values.

# 5 Modeling Microprocessors in PEUF

Our interest is in verifying pipelined microprocessors, proving their equivalence to an unpipelined instruction set architecture model. We use the approach pioneered by Burch and Dill [BD94] in which the abstraction function from pipeline state to architectural state is computed by symbolically simulating a flushing of the pipeline state and then projecting away the state of all but the architectural state elements, such as the register file, program counter, and data memory. Operationally, we construct two sets of p-terms describing the final values of the state elements resulting from two different symbolic simulation sequences—one from the pipeline model and one from the instruction set model. The correctness condition is represented by a p-formula expressing the equality of these two sets of p-terms.

Our approach starts with an RTL or gate-level model of the microprocessor and performs a series of abstractions to create a model of the data path using terms that satisfy the restrictions of PEUF. Examining the structure of a pipelined processor, we find that the signals we wish to abstract as terms can be classified as either program data, instruction addresses, or register identifiers. By proper construction of the data path model, both program data and instruction addresses can be represented as p-terms. Register identifiers, on the other hand, must be modeled as g-terms, because their comparisons control the stall and bypass logic. The remaining control logic is kept at the bit level.

In order to generate such a model, we must abstract the operation of some of the processor units. For example, the data path ALU is abstracted as an uninterpreted p-function, generating a data value given its data and control inputs. We model the PC incrementer and the branch target logic as uninterpreted functions generating instruction addresses. We model the branch decision logic as an uninterpreted predicate indicating whether or not to take the branch based on data and control inputs. This allows us to abstract away the data equality test used by the branch-on-equal instruction. The instruction memory can be abstracted as an uninterpreted function, since it is considered to be read-only.

To model the register file, we use the memory model described by Burch and Dill [BD94], creating a nested *ITE* structure to record the history of writes to the memory. This approach requires equations between memory addresses controlling the *ITE* operations. For the register file, such equations are allowed since g-term register identifiers serve as addresses. For the data memory, however, the memory addresses are p-term program data, and hence such equations cannot be used. Instead, we model the data memory as a generic state machine, changing state in some arbitrary way for each write operation, and returning some arbitrary value dependent on the state and the address for each read operation. Such an abstraction technique is sound, but it does not capture all of the properties of a memory. It is satisfactory for modeling processors in which there is no reordering of writes relative to each other or relative to reads.

# 6 Experimental Results

In [VB98], we described the implementation of a symbolic simulator for verifying pipelined systems using vectors of Boolean variables to encode domain variables, effectively treating all terms as g-terms. This simulation is performed directly on a modified gate-level representation of the processor. In this modified version, we replace all state holding elements with behavioral models we call Efficient Memory Models (EMMs). In addition all data-transformation elements (e.g., ALUs, shifters, PC incrementers) are replaced by read-only EMMs, which effectively implement the transformation of function applications into nested *ITE* expressions. Modifying this program to exploit maximal diversity simply involves having the EMMs generate expressions containing fixed bit patterns rather than vectors of Boolean variables. All performance results presented here were measured on a 125 MHz Sun Microsystems SPARC-20.

We constructed several simple pipeline processor designs based on the MIPS instruction set. We abstract register identifiers as g-terms, and hence our verification covers all possible numbers of program registers including the 32 of the MIPS instruction set. The simplest version of the pipeline implements ten different Register-Register and Register-Immediate instructions. Our program could verify this design in 48 seconds of CPU time and just 7 MB of memory using vectors of Boolean variables to encode domain variables. Using fixed bit patterns reduces the complexity of the verification to 6 seconds and 2 MB.

We then added a memory stage to implement load and store instructions. An interlock stalls the processor one cycle when a load instruction is followed by an instruction requiring the loaded result. Treating all terms as g-terms and using vectors of Boolean variables to encode domain variables, we could not verify this data path, despite running for over 2000 seconds. The fact that both addresses and data for the memory come from the register file induces a circular constraint on the ordering of BDD variables encoding the terms. On the other hand, exploiting maximal diversity by using fixed bit patterns for register values eliminates these variable ordering concerns. As a consequence, we could verify the 32-bit version of this design in just 12 CPU seconds using 1.8 MB.

Finally, we verified a complete CPU, with a 5-stage pipeline implementing 10 ALU instructions, load and store, and MIPS instructions j (jump with target computed from instruction word), jr (jump using register value as target), and beq (branch on equal). This design is comparable to the DLX design verified by Burch and Dill in [BD94], although our version is closer to an actual gate-level implementation. We were unable to verify this processor using the scheme of [VB98]. Having instruction addresses dependent on instruction or data values leads to exponential BDD growth when modeling the instruction memory. Modeling instruction addresses as p-terms, on the other hand, makes this verification tractable. We can verify the 32-bit version processor using 169 CPU seconds and 7.5 MB.

# 7 Conclusions

Eliminating Boolean variables in the encoding of terms representing program data and instruction addresses has given us a major breakthrough in our ability to verify pipelined processors. Our BDD variables now only encode control conditions and register identifiers. For classic RISC pipelines, the resulting state space is small and regular enough to be handled readily with BDDs.

We believe that there are many optimizations that will yield further improvements in the performance of Boolean methods for deciding formulas involving uninterpreted functions. We have found that relaxing functional consistency constraints to allow independent functionality of different instructions, as was done in [DPR98], can dramatically improve both memory and time performance. We have devised a variation on the scheme of [GSZAS98] for generating a propositional formula using Boolean variables to encode the relations between terms [BGV99]. Our method exploits maximal diversity to greatly reduce the number of propositional variables in the generated formula. We are also considering the use of satisfiability checkers rather than BDDs for performing our tautology checking

# References

[Ack54]      W. Ackermann, *Solvable Cases of the Decision Problem*, North-Holland, Amsterdam, 1954.

[BBCZ98]    S. Berezin, A. Biere, E. M. Clarke, and Y. Zhu, "Combining symbolic model checking with uninterpreted functions for out of order processor verification," *Formal Methods in Computer-Aided Design FMCAD '98*, G. Gopalakrishnan and P. Windley, *eds.*, LNCS 1522, Springer-Verlag, November, 1998, pp. 187–201.

[BGV99]      R. E. Bryant, S. German, and M. N. Velev, "Processor verification using efficient reductions of the logic of uninterpreted functions to propositional logic," Technical report CMU-CS-99-115, Carnegie Mellon University, 1999. Available as: `http://www.cs.cmu.edu/~bryant/pubdir/cmu-cs-99-115.ps`.

[BD94]        J. R. Burch, and D. L. Dill, "Automated verification of pipelined microprocessor control," *Computer-Aided Verification CAV '94*, D. L. Dill, *ed.*, LNCS 818, Springer-Verlag, June, 1994, pp. 68–80.

[DPR98]      W. Damm, A. Pnueli, and S. Ruah, "Herbrand automata for hardware verification," *9th International Conference on Concurrency Theory CONCUR '98*, Springer-Verlag, September, 1998.

[GSZAS98]  A. Goel, K. Sajid, H. Zhou, A. Aziz, and V. Singhal, "BDD based procedures for a theory of equality with uninterpreted functions," *Computer-Aided Verification CAV '98*, A. J. Hu and M. Y. Vardi, *eds.*, LNCS 1427, Springer-Verlag, June, 1998, pp. 244–255.

[HKGB97]   R. Hojati, A. Kuehlmann, S. German, and R. K. Brayton, "Validity checking in the theory of equality with uinterpreted functions using finite instantiations," Unpublished paper presented at the *International Workshop on Logic Synthesis*, 1997.

[NO80]        G. Nelson, and D. C. Oppen, "Fast decision procedures based on the congruence closure," *J. ACM*, Vol. 27, No. 2 (1980), pp. 356–364.

[PRSS99]    A. Pnueli, Y. Rodeh, O. Shtrichman, and M. Siegel, "Deciding equality formulas by small-domain instantiations," *Computer-Aided Verification CAV '99*, this proceedings, 1999.

[VB98]        M. N. Velev, and R. E. Bryant, "Bit-level abstraction in the verification of pipelined microprocessors by correspondence checking." *Formal Methods in Computer-Aided Design FMCAD '98*, G. Gopalakrishnan and P. Windley, *eds.*, LNCS 1522, Springer-Verlag, November, 1998, pp. 18–35.

# A Toolbox for the Analysis of Discrete Event Dynamic Systems

Peter Buchholz, Peter Kemper*

Informatik IV, Universität Dortmund, D-44221 Dortmund, Germany

**Abstract.** We present a collection of tools for functional and quantitative analysis of discrete event dynamic systems (DEDS). Models can be formulated as a set of automata with synchronous communication or as Petri nets. Analysis takes place with a strong emphasis on state based analysis methods using Kronecker representations and ordered natural decision diagrams. Independent tools provide access to orthogonal techniques from different fields including computation of bisimulation equivalences, modelchecking, numerical analysis of Markov chains, and simulation. Two file formats are defined to provide a simple exchange mechanism between independent tools which allows to build various combinations of tools.

## 1 Introduction

Tools for the specification and analysis of DEDS exist in a rich variety and show a certain combinatorial explosion from the set of modeling formalisms and the set of analysis techniques. Selection of the "best" modeling formalism is a highly emotional topic, but for selection of analysis techniques criteria boil down to availability of implementations and applicability for a given model. We observed severe difficulties in exchanging models between different tools, such that for our toolbox a strong emphasis is on a simple exchange of information between the independent tools it contains. Fig. 1 gives an overview: the tools are arranged around two file formats by which models can be specified as a set of automata with synchronous communication and as a hierarchical, colored Petri net. The Petri net formalism - named *abstract Petri net notation* (APNN) [2] - integrates several kinds of Petri nets, including place/transition nets, colored Petri nets, timed nets with a stochastic timing, hierarchical nets using place and/or transition refinement, superposed nets based on transition fusion.

Networks of automata with synchronous interaction are specified in a different format, using state transition matrices and synchronization via equal labels. This format directly corresponds to a Kronecker representation of the state transition matrix of the composed model. The representation is compositional and uses a Kronecker product to express synchronization and a Kronecker sum for independent state transitions. The state space of the composed model can be represented in a (usually) very space efficient manner by a directed acyclic graph,

---

* This research is supported by Deutsche Forschungsgemeinschaft, SFB 559.

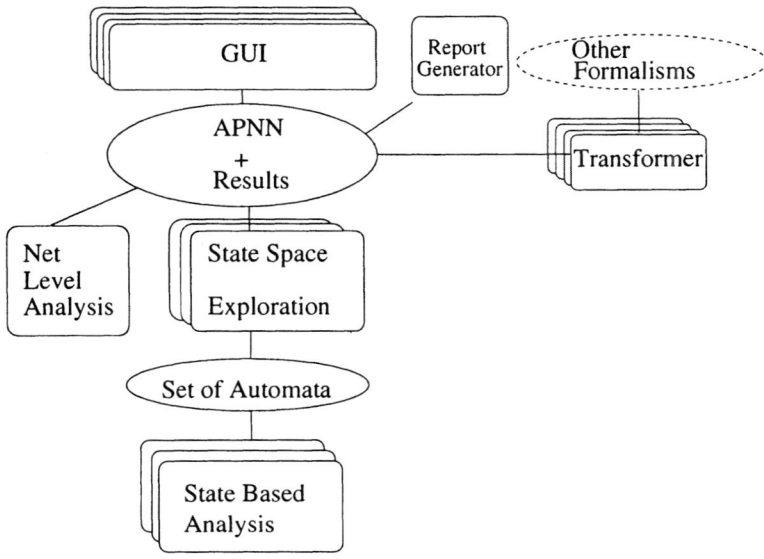

**Fig. 1.** Structural overview of the toolbox

a generalization of ordered binary decision diagrams (OBDDs). The latter allows exchange of state space descriptions among tools with low effort [8, 14]. In the sequel we briefly sketch ways to use the APNN toolbox for modeling and analysis, for details we refer to [1].

## 2 Several ways to obtain a model

Models can be either generated by a the grapical user interface (GUI) contained in the toolbox or translated from other modeling formalisms supported by other tools. A generation by hand, directly editing the textual description at APNN level or the matrix representation at the automata level is possible in principle but not recommended. APNNed [9] provides a GUI for the APNN format. It is a JAVA implementation of a Petri net editor supporting hierarchical nets (based on refinement of places and transitions) and colored nets with finite color sets. APNNed animates the dynamic behavior of a model by the token game in three ways: a) interactive, b) automatic selection of transitions to fire and c) trace-driven by importing a trace generated elsewhere. APNNed also provides functionality to start various analysis tools and to present their results. The analysis tools export results in a specific output format which can be used by the GUI or report generators for result presentation. The toolbox also provides transformers which translate other formats into APNN. These include a translator for generalized stochastic Petri nets (GSPNs) specified by GreatSPN to APNN, a translator for PEP low level nets (which are Place/Transition nets) to APNN and vice versa, and a transformer for Net/Condition Event systems

(NCES) to APNN. The latter is a non-trivial mapping [10, 13] since certain features of NCES have no direct correspondence in the Petri net formalism. A model can also be described at the level of networks of synchronized automata. However, so far no direct user interface is available at this level. A model for a network of automata is automatically generated from a Petri net model in APNN format by the state space exploration tool, cf. Fig. 1. This tool does not necessarily perform an exploration of the overall state space, it is also used to do an exploration by components which maps a set of submodels of a Petri net to a set of automata (provided the Petri net is appropriately structured). Nevertheless, the interface format can be also used to obtain suitable networks of automata from other compositional formalisms, e.g. from CCS-like process algebraic terms, if they are in the form of $(P_1|P_2|\ldots|P_n)\backslash L$ with processes/agents $P_1, \ldots, P_N$ and a set of synchronization labels $L$, however a corresponding tool is currently not available in our toolbox.

## 3  Several ways to analyze a model

The APNN toolbox provides tools for functional and quantitative analysis which apply either at net level or automata level. Only a minority is devoted to Petri nets at the APNN level including computation of invariants and a simulator for quantitative analysis of timed nets. A state space exploration tool transforms an APNN description into the format of the automata level with optional exploration of the overal state space of the composed model as in [12]. A strong emphasis is on tools which exploit the Kronecker structure implicitly given at the automata level. At this level a tool for computation of several equivalences of bisimulation type and subsequent aggregation of automata is available. Especially a weak backward bisimulation preserving reachability is useful in combination with state space exploration of composed automata since a disaggregation module can finally retranslate the resulting state space of an aggregated system into the state space of the original system [7, 8]. A generalization of ordered binary decision diagrams (OBDDs) where nodes are allowed to have a variable number of outgoing arcs (ONDDs) has been successfully applied to represent extremely large states space in space efficient way [8, 7, 14], such that a corresponding file format allows to communicate state spaces between tools. Furthermore a model checker for computational tree logic (CTL) is available at this level [14] implementing classical model checking algorithms adapted to Kronecker algebra. An additional specialized model checker is exclusively devoted to check the liveness property in terms of Petri net theory. In case of (partial) deadlocks it generates a trace of transition firings which can be animated by APNNed. The APNN toolbox also contains a variety of tools for quantitative analysis of stochastic models based on the numerical solution of Markov chains which again profit from the Kronecker structure available at the automata level. These tools can be further distinguished according to hierarchical, block-structured Kronecker representations or modular Kronecker representations, see e.g. [5, 3, 4, 6, 11] for corresponding algorithms. A compositional representation based on

Kronecker algebra is a key advantage of the analysis tools in our toolbox, since this gives a very space efficient data structure for large state transition systems with possibly millions of states.

# References

1. F. Bause, P. Buchholz, and P. Kemper. A toolbox for functional and quantitative analysis of DEDS. Forschungsbericht 680, Fachbereich Informatik, Universität Dortmund (Germany), 1998.
2. F. Bause, P. Kemper, and P. Kritzinger. Abstract Petri net notation. *Petri Net Newsletters*, 49:9–27, Oct 1995.
3. P. Buchholz. Numerical solution methods based on structured descriptions of Markovian models. In G. Balbo and G. Serazzi, editors, *Computer Performance Evaluation - Modelling Techniques and Tools*, pages 251–267. Elsevier, 1992.
4. P. Buchholz. Hierarchical structuring of superposed GSPNs. In *Proc. 7th Int. Workshop Petri Nets and Performance Models (PNPM'97), St-Malo (France), June 1997*, pages 81–90. IEEE CS Press, 1997.
5. P. Buchholz. An adaptive aggregation/disaggregation algorithm for hierarchical Markovian models. *European Journal of Operational Research*, 116(3):85–104, 1999.
6. P. Buchholz, G. Ciardo, S. Donatelli, and P. Kemper. Complexity of Kronecker operations on sparse matrices with applications to the solution of Markov models. Technical report, ICASE Report No. 97-66 NASA/CR-97-206274, 1997. submitted for publication.
7. P. Buchholz and P Kemper. Efficient computation and representation of large reachability sets for composed automata. Forschungsbericht 705, Fachbereich Informatik, Universität Dortmund (Germany), 1999.
8. P Buchholz and P. Kemper. Modular state level analysis of distributed systems - techniques and tool suppport. In *accepted for 5th Int. Conf. on Tools and Algorithms for the Construction and Analysis of Systems (TACAS '99)*, 1999.
9. P. Buchholz, P. Kemper, and the APNNed group. APNNed - a net editor and debugger within the APNN toolbox. In J. Desel, P. Kemper, E. Kindler, and A. Oberweis, editors, *Proc. 5. Workshop Algorithmen und Werkzeuge für Petrinetze*, pages 19–24. Forschungsbericht Nr. 694, FB Informatik, Universität Dortmund, Germany, 1998.
10. H. Hanisch, P. Kemper, and A. Lüder. A modular and compositional approach to modeling and controller verification of manufacturing systems. In *accepted for 14th IFAC Word Congress, July 5-9, 1999, Beijing, China*, 1999.
11. P. Kemper. Numerical analysis of superposed GSPNs. *IEEE Trans. on Software Engineering*, 22(9), Sep 1996.
12. P. Kemper. Reachability analysis based on structured representations. In *Application and Theory of Petri Nets*, LNCS 1091. Springer, 1996.
13. P Kemper. A mapping of autonomous net condition event systems to GSPNs. submitted for publication, 1999.
14. P. Kemper and R. Lübeck. Model checking based on kronecker algebra. Forschungsbericht 669, Fachbereich Informatik, Universität Dortmund (Germany), 1998.

# TIPPtool: Compositional Specification and Analysis of Markovian Performance Models

H. Hermanns[*], V. Mertsiotakis[**], and M. Siegle

*Informatik 7, Universität Erlangen-Nürnberg, Erlangen, Germany*

**Abstract.** In this short paper we briefly describe a tool which is based on a Markovian stochastic process algebra. The tool offers both model specification and quantitative model analysis in a compositional fashion, wrapped in a user-friendly graphical front-end.

## 1 Compositional Performance Modelling

Classical process algebras have been designed as compositional description formalisms for concurrent systems. In *stochastic* process algebras temporal information is attached to actions in the form of continuous random variables representing activity durations, making it possible to specify and analyse both qualitative and quantitative properties. This short paper is about the TIPPtool [5], a tool that emerged from the TIPP project which focussed on a basic framework supporting both functional specification and performance evaluation in a single, process algebraic formalism [6]. The formalism is basically a superset of LOTOS [1], including means to specify exponentially distributed delays. It hence provides a bridge between qualitative and quantitative evaluation, the latter based on Markov chain analysis. More precisely, the underlying semantics of the specification language gives rise to homogeneous continuous time (semi-)Markov chains that can be analysed numerically by means of efficient techniques. Besides some support for analysis of functional aspects, the tool offers algorithms for numerical performance analysis of a given process algebraic specification. Exact and approximate evaluation techniques are provided to calculate various measures of interest. The tool also offers semi-automatic compositional minimisation of complex models based on equivalence-preserving transformations.

## 2 Model specification and analysis

The specification language of the TIPPtool is a superset of LOTOS[1]. In particular, a distinguished type of prefix, $(a, r); P$, is supported, denoting that action $a$ occurs after a delay $\Delta$ which is exponentially distributed with rate parameter $r$ (i.e. $Prob(\Delta \leq t) = 1 - e^{-rt}$); afterwards the process behaves as $P$.

Actions arising from ordinary prefix $a; P$ are called *immediate* actions. They happen as soon as possible if not prevented by the environment, following the *maximal progress* assumption. In particular, internal (or hidden) immediate actions are assumed

---

[*] Current affiliation: *Systems Validation Centre, University of Twente, Enschede, The Netherlands*

[**] Current affiliation: *Development Access, Lucent Technologies, Nürnberg, Germany*

[1] Data types are treated more liberally than in standard LOTOS; integers are a built-in data type.

to happen immediately when enabled. In addition to the basic language elements, *process instantiation*, *parametric processes* and *inter-process communication* can be used to model complex dependences, such as value passing or mobility.

Conservatively extending classical process algebras, a labelled transition system (LTS) is generated from the system specification using structural operational rules [6]. Corresponding to timed and immediate actions there are two types of transitions between states: timed transitions and immediate transitions. The LTS can hence be regarded as a semi-Markov process. Under certain conditions (checked by the tool) the semi-Markov process can be transformed into a continuous time Markov chain. Verifying these properties involves equivalence preserving transformations, based on a stochastic variant of Milner's observational congruence [6]. Since this relation is compositional, it can be applied to minimise the state space of a specification in a componentwise fashion. This minimisation abstracts from internal immediate steps and it aggregates the Markov chain based on the concept of lumpability [10], while preserving functional and stochastic information. For a particular Markov chain, a system of ordinary differential equations needs to be solved in order to obtain the state probabilities at a particular time instant $t$ (transient analysis). Alternatively, solving a linear system of equations leads to the state probabilities in the equilibrium (stationary analysis). These limiting probabilities (where $t \to \infty$) are known to exist for arbitrary finite (homogeneous, continuous time) Markov chains.

## 3  Tool features and structure

In its current version 2.3, the TIPPtool provides the following functionality:

- Model description by means of a LOTOS-based notation,
- Reachability analysis based on the operational semantics,
- Algorithms for deadlock detection and tracing to a given state,
- Algorithms for checking bisimulation-style equivalences and for the minimisation of (sub-)models,
- Stationary and transient analysis of the underlying Markov chain,
- Functions for the calculation of performance and dependability measures,
- Support of experiment series,
- Output of numerical results using the tool PXGRAPH,
- Interfacing with other tools.

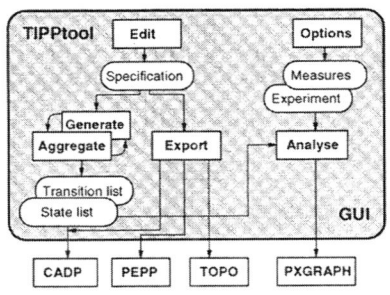

The tool consists of several components whose interaction is shown in the figure on the right. Specifications can be created with an editor (Edit component). The Generate/Aggregate component is responsible for parsing the specification, for the generation of the LTS and for its minimisation according to an equivalence notion. The user may currently choose between four (stochastic variants of) classical congruences. This minimisation is known to be particularly beneficial if it is applied to components of a larger specification in a stepwise, compositional fashion. In the TIPPtool, semi-automatic compositional minimisation is supported in an elegant way: By highlighting a certain fragment of the specification with the mouse, it is possible to invoke compositional minimisation of that fragment. When the minimised representation is computed, a new specification is generated automatically, where the selected fragment has been replaced by its minimised representation.

Via the Options, the user can specify various measures to be calculated, such as the probability of the system being in a certain subset of states, or the throughput (i.e. the mean frequency of occurrence) of some action. An experiment description contains information about model parameters to be varied during analysis. A series of experiments can be carried out automatically in an efficient manner, generating numerical results for different values of a certain model parameter, while the state space only needs to be generated once. Models can be analysed with the Analyse module. This module offers various numerical solution algorithms for the underlying stochastic process, among them two approximate methods [9, 12]. After an experiment series has been carried out, the results are presented graphically with the tool PXGRAPH from UC Berkeley, cf. the screenshot on the right. The

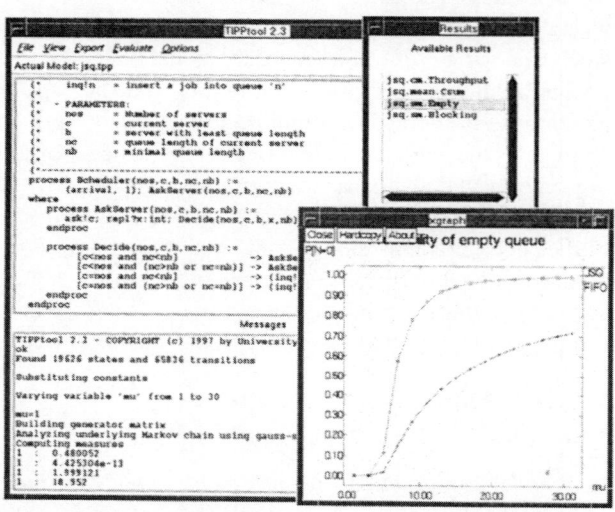

Export module of the tool provides interfaces to three other tools, PEPP [4], TOPO [11], and CADP [2]. The former interface generates stochastic task graphs [8], for which the tool PEPP offers a wide range of both exact and approximate analysis algorithms, some of which work even for general distributions. The second interface provides support for the translation of specifications into a format suitable for the LOTOS tool TOPO. Among other functionalities, TOPO is capable of building C-programs from LOTOS specifications. The third interface can be used to exploit the bisimulation equivalence algorithms of the tool ALDEBARAN, as well as other tools (FC2, AUTOGRAPH), for visualisation or functional verification purposes. Here, the interface is on the level of the state space.

We used the programming language STANDARD ML for implementing the parser, the semantics, the bisimulation algorithms and for the approximate Markov chain solution methods. The numerical analysis part is written in C, on top of a library which provides data structures for sparse matrices (SparseLib1.3 from Kenneth Kundert, UC Berkeley). This library has been extended by iterative solution methods for stationary and transient analysis. The clear interface of the library makes it easy to integrate other solution methods into the tool. The communication with the state space generator is done via ASCII-files. For computing the measures, shell-scripts are used, which are based on standard UNIX-tools such as GREP, AWK and SED. Finally, the graphical user interface has been implemented using the scripting language TCL/TK. The communication between the GUI and the other tools is done via UNIX-pipes.

# 4 Conclusion

In this short paper, we have presented the status quo of the TIPPtool. We have described the particular features of a stochastic process algebra based specification formalism, together with the distinguishing components of the tool. To the best of our knowledge, the TIPPtool is the only existing tool offering compositional minimisation of Markov chain models. TIPPtool is available free of charge for non-commercial institutions, more details can be found at http://www7.informatik.uni-erlangen.de/tipp/. Among others, the tool has been applied to the study of performance and dependability aspects of the plain old telephony system [7], a robot control system [3], and a hospital information system [13]. So far, models with up to $10^7$ states have been tackled compositionally.

# References

1. T. Bolognesi and E. Brinksma. Introduction to the ISO Specification Language LOTOS. In *The Formal Description Technique LOTOS*, pages 23–73, Amsterdam, 1989. North-Holland.
2. Jean-Claude Fernandez, Hubert Garavel, Alain Kerbrat, Radu Mateescu, Laurent Mounier, and Mihaela Sighireanu. Cadp (cæsar/aldebaran development package): A protocol validation and verification toolbox. In *Proceedings of the 8th Conference on Computer-Aided Verification (CAV 96)*, Springer LNCS 1102:437–440. August 1996.
3. S. Gilmore, J. Hillston, R. Holton, and M. Rettelbach. Specifications in Stochastic Process Algebra for a Robot Control Problem. *International Journal of Production Research* 34(4):1065–1080, 1996.
4. F. Hartleb and A. Quick. Performance Evaluation of Parallel Programms — Modeling and Monitoring with the Tool PEPP. In *Proceedings of 7th GI-ITG Fachtagung "Messung, Modellierung und Bewertung von Rechen- und Kommunikationssystemen"*, pages 51–63. Informatik Aktuell, Springer. September 1993.
5. H. Hermanns, U. Herzog, U. Klehmet, V. Mertsiotakis, and M. Siegle. Compositional Performance Modelling with the TIPPtool. In *10th International Conference on Modelling Techniques and Tools for Computer Performance Evaluation (TOOLS 98)*, Springer LNCS 1469:51–62. September 1998.
6. H. Hermanns, U. Herzog, and V. Mertsiotakis. Stochastic Process Algebras – Between LOTOS and Markov Chains. *Computer Networks and ISDN Systems*, 30(9-10):901–924, 1998.
7. H. Hermanns and J.P. Katoen. Automated Compositional Markov Chain Generation for a Plain Old Telephony System. *Science of Computer Programming*. to appear.
8. U. Herzog. A Concept for Graph-Based Stochastic Process Algebras, Generally Distributed Activity Times and Hierarchical Modelling. In *Proc. of the 4th Workshop on Process Algebras and Performance Modelling*, pages 1–20. Universitá di Torino, CLUT, 1996.
9. J. Hillston and V. Mertsiotakis. A Simple Time Scale Decomposition Technique for SPAs. In *The Computer Journal*, 38(7):566–577, 1995.
10. J.G. Kemeny and J.L. Snell. *Finite Markov Chains*. Springer, 1976.
11. J.A. Manas, T. de Miguel, and J. Salvachua. Tool Support to Implement LOTOS Specifications. *Computer Networks and ISDN Systems*, 25(7):815–839, 1993.
12. V. Mertsiotakis and M. Silva. Throughput Approximation of Decision Free Processes Using Decomposition. In *Proc. of the 7th Int. Workshop on Petri Nets and Performance Models*, pages 174–182, St. Malo, June 1997. IEEE CS-Press.
13. M. Siegle, B. Wentz, A. Klingler, and M. Simon. Neue Ansätze zur Planung von Klinikkommunikationssystemen mittels stochastischer Leistungsmodellierung. In *42. Jahrestagung der Deutschen Gesellschaft für Medizinische Informatik, Biometrie und Epidemiologie (GMDS)*, pages 188 – 192, Ulm, September 1997. MMV Medien & Medizin Verlag.

# Java Bytecode Verification by Model Checking[*]
## *System Abstract*

David Basin[1], Stefan Friedrich[1], Joachim Posegga[2], and Harald Vogt[2]

[1] Albert-Ludwigs-Universität Freiburg
Institut für Informatik
Universitätsgelände Flugplatz, D-79110 Freiburg i. Br. Germany.
{basin|friedric}@informatik.uni-freiburg.de

[2] Deutsche Telekom AG,
IT-Research Security (TZ/FE34)
D-64307 Darmstadt, Germany.
{posegga|vogth}@tzd.telekom.de

## 1 Motivation

Verification plays a central role in the security of Java bytecode: the Java bytecode verifier performs a static analysis to ensure that bytecode loaded over a network has certain security related properties. When this is the case, the bytecode can be efficiently interpreted without runtime security checks.

Our research concerns the theoretical foundations of bytecode verification and alternative approaches to specifying and checking security properties. This is important as currently the "security policy" for Java bytecode is given informally by a natural language document [LY96] and the bytecode verifier itself is a closed system (part of the Java virtual machine). We believe that there are advantages to more formal approaches to security. A formal approach can disambiguate the current policy and provide a basis for verification tools. It can also help expose bugs or weaknesses that can corrupt Java security [MF97]. Moreover, when the formal specification is realized in a logic and verification is based on a theorem prover, extensions become possible such as integrating the verification of security properties with other kinds of verification, e.g., proof-carrying code [NL96,NL98].

## 2 Approach

We provide a formal foundation to bytecode verification based on model checking. The idea, which has similarities with data flow analysis and abstract interpretation [Sch98], is as follows. The bytecode for a Java method $M$ constitutes a state transition system where the states are defined by the states of the Java

---

[*] The opinions expressed in this paper are those of the authors and do not necessarily reflect the views of their respective employers.

Virtual Machine (JVM) running $M$, and the transitions are given by the semantics of the JVM instructions used in $M$. From $M$ we can compute an abstraction $M_{fin}$ that abstracts the state-transition system to a simpler one whose states are defined by the values of the JVM's program counter, the operand stack, a stack pointer, and the method's local variables. The actual values of the stack positions and local variables are abstracted away and simply represented by their type information. The transition rules of $M_{fin}$ are defined likewise by the semantics of the JVM machine instructions with respect to our abstraction. Since only finitely many types appears in each method, the resulting abstraction $M_{fin}$ is finite; the size of the state-space is exponential in the number of local variables and the maximal stack height.

After we can apply a model checker to $M_{fin}$. The properties that we model check correspond to the type safety checks performed by the Java bytecode verifier. For example, we specify that each transition in $M_{fin}$ that represents a machine instruction in $M$ finds appropriately typed data in the locations (stack or local variables) it uses. The model checker then either responds that the byte code is secure (with respect to these properties) or provides a counter-example to its security.

## 3   Architectural Description

The overall structure of our system is depicted in Figure 1. As input it takes a Java class file as well as a specification of an abstraction of the Java virtual machine. The specification defines the states of the abstract machine and how each bytecode instruction changes the machine's state. For each instruction, a precondition to its execution is given (e.g. that the operand-stack must contain enough operands of appropriate type) and also invariants are stated (e.g. that the stack may not exceed its maximal size). These are the properties that are model checked.

The core routine (method abstraction) translates bytecode into a finite state transition system using the specification of the abstract machine. Separating the machine spec-

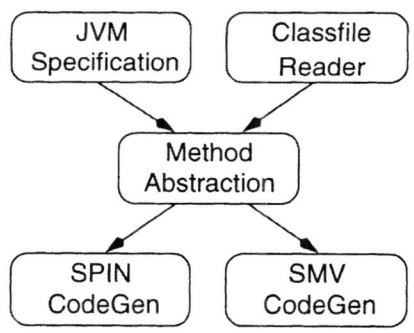

**Fig. 1.** Structure of the compiler

ification from the translation gives us a modular system where we can easily change the virtual machine and the properties checked. Our system is also modular with respect to the model checker used. Currently we have implemented two different back-ends: one that compiles the transition system and properties to the input language of the SMV model checker and a second that generates output in the SPIN language Promela.

# 4  Example Output

As a simple example (even here we must elide details) we give (a) a Java program, (b) the corresponding bytecode, and (c) the output of our system, which is input for the SPIN model checker.

```
#define pc_is_1 (pc == 1)
#define pc_is_2 (pc == 2)

/* Conditions to be checked */
#define cond_1 (locals[0] == INT)
#define cond_2 (st[stp_st - 1] == INT)

[...]

/* State of the abstract machine      */
byte pc;                /* program counter */
byte st[3];             /* operand stack   */
byte stp_st;            /* stack pointer   */
byte locals[1]          /* local variables */
```

```
public static int fac(int a){
      if (a==0)
          return 1;
      else
          return a*fac(a-1);}
```

(a) Java Code

```
.method public static fac(I)I
    .limit stack 3
    .limit locals 1
.line 8
    iload_0
    ifne Label1
.line 9
    iconst_1
    ireturn
.line 11
Label1:
    iload_0
    iload_0
    iconst_1
    isub
    invokestatic Sample/fac(I)I
    imul
    ireturn
.end method
```

(b) Bytecode

```
/* Process that watches if the conditions hold */
proctype asrt_fac() {
    assert( ( !pc_is_1 || cond_1) && [...])}

/* Process that models the transition system */
proctype meth_fac() {
    do
          /* iload_0 */
    :: pc_is_1 -> atomic {
                    pc = pc + 1;
                    st[stp_st] = locals[0];
                    stp_st = stp_st + 1 };

          /* ifne Label1 */
    :: pc_is_2 -> atomic {
                    if
                    :: pc = pc + 5;
                    :: pc = pc + 3
                    fi;
                    stp_st = stp_st - 1 };

    [...]

od }

/* Initialization of the abstract machine */
init {
atomic {
    pc = 1; stp_st = 0; locals[0] = INT;
    run meth_fac(); run asrt_fac() } }
```

(c) $fac_{fin}$ and Properties

The Java program and the bytecode should be clear. We have added by hand some comments to (c). In the process meth_fac, the transitions of the method fac are modeled. For example, the first instruction of the method iload0 loads an integer value from a local variable on the stack; the corresponding condition to be checked (cond_1) requires that the respective variable contains an integer value. The instruction ifne performs a conditional branch, which is modeled by nondeterministically assigning a new value to the program counter. The process asrt_fac runs in parallel to the process meth_fac and checks if all conditions (preconditions and invariants) are fulfilled. SPIN checks this in negligible time (0.03 seconds).

## 5 Future Work

We have completed Version 1 of the system. This formalizes and model-checks the JavaCard subset of Java, which is used for smartcards [Sun98]. We have chosen this particular instance of Java for three reasons: first, JavaCard does not allow for dynamic class loading, therefore there are no "real-time" requirements for bytecode verification. Second, the bytecode verifier for JavaCard lives outside the client platform, so it can easily be replaced/extended without modifying the platform itself. Finally, our aproach can contribute to meeting the high security requirements that smartcard applications usually have.

In a future release we plan to extend this version to the full JVM instruction set. The only significant problems that might occur are run time requirements for the model checker (defined by the time a user is willing to wait when loading a class) and multi-threading, which is not possible in JavaCard and could increase the model checker's search space.

## References

[LY96]   T. Lindholm and F. Yellin. *The Java Virtual Machine Specification*. Addison-Wesley, 1996.

[MF97]   G. McGraw and E.W. Felten. *Java Security: Hostile Applets, Holes, and Antidotes*. Wiley, 1997.

[NL96]   G. Necula and P. Lee. Proof-Carrying Code. Technical Report CMU-CS-96-165, Carnegie Mellon University, School of Computer Science, Pittsburg, PA, September 1996.

[NL98]   G. C. Necula and P. Lee. Safe, untrusted agents using proof-carrying code. In G. Vigna, editor, *Mobile Agents and Security*, volume 1419 of *LNCS*, pages 61–91. Springer, 1998.

[Sch98]  David A. Schmidt. Data flow analysis is model checking of abstract interpretations. In *Conference Record of POPL'98: The 25th ACM SIGPLAN-SIGACT Symposium on Principles of Programming Languages*, pages 38–48, San Diego, California, January 19–21, 1998.

[Sun98]  Sun Microsystems, Inc. Java Card 2.1 Language Subset and Virtual Machine Specification. http://java.sun.com:80/products/javacard/, 1998.

# NuSMV: A New Symbolic Model Verifier

A. Cimatti[1], E. Clarke[2], F. Giunchiglia[1], and M. Roveri[1,3]

[1] ITC-IRST, Via Sommarive 18, 38055 Povo, Trento, Italy,
{cimatti,fausto,roveri}@irst.itc.it

[2] SCS, Carnegie-Mellon University, 5000 Forbes Avenue, Pittsburgh, PA 15213-3891, USA,
Edmund.Clarke@cs.cmu.edu

[3] DSI, University of Milano, Via Comelico 39, 20135 Milano, Italy

## 1 Introduction

This paper describes NuSMV, a new symbolic model checker developed as a joint project between Carnegie Mellon University (CMU) and Istituto per la Ricerca Scientifica e Tecnolgica (IRST). NuSMV is designed to be a well structured, open, flexible and documented platform for model checking. In order to make NuSMV applicable in technology transfer projects, it was designed to be very robust, close to the standards required by industry, and to allow for expressive specification languages.

NuSMV is the result of the reengineering, reimplementation and extension of SMV [6], version 2.4.4 (SMV from now on). With respect to SMV, NuSMV has been extended and upgraded along three dimensions. First, from the point of view of the system functionalities, NuSMV features a textual interaction shell and a graphical interface, extended model partitioning techniques, and allows for LTL model checking. Second, the system architecture of NuSMV has been designed to be highly modular and open. The interdependencies between different modules have been separated, and an external, state of the art BDD package [8] has been integrated in the system kernel. Third, the quality of the implementation has been strongly enhanced. This makes of NuSMV a robust, maintainable and well documented system, with a relatively easy to modify source code. NuSMV is available at http://afrodite.itc.it:1024/~nusmv/.

## 2 System Functionalities

NuSMV can process files written in SMV language [6], and allows for the construction of the model with different modalities, reachability analysis, fair CTL model checking, computation of quantitative characteristics of the model, and generation of counterexamples. In addition, NuSMV features an enhanced partitioning method for synchronous models based on [7], and allows for disjunctive partitioning of asynchronous models, and for the verification of invariant properties in combination with reachability analysis. Furthermore, NuSMV supports LTL model checking. The algorithm is based on the combination of a tableau constructor for the LTL formula with standard CTL model checking, along the lines described in [5].

NuSMV can work in batch mode, just like SMV, processing an input file according to the specified command line options. In addition, NuSMV has an interactive mode: it enters a shell performing a read-eval-print loop, and the user can activate the various computation steps (e.g. parsing, model construction, reachability analysis, model checking) as system commands with different options. (This interaction mode is largely inspired by the VIS interaction mode [2].) These steps can therefore be invoked separately, possibly undone or repeated under different modalities. Each command is associated with an on-line help. Furthermore, the internal parameters of the system can

496

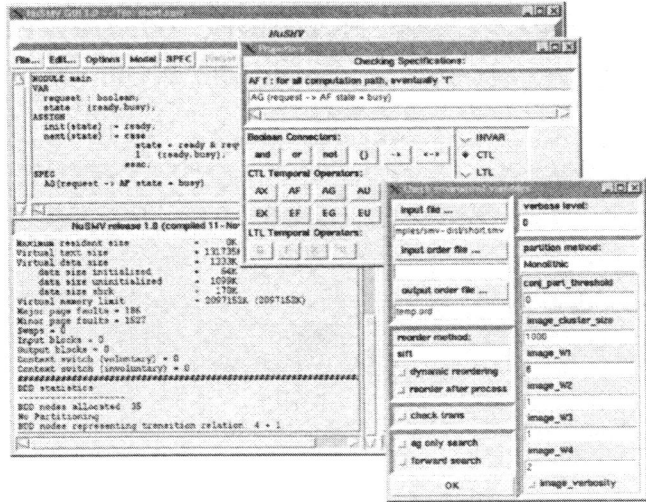

**Fig. 1.** A snapshot of the NuSMV GUI.

be inspected and modified to tune the verification process. For instance, the NuSMV interactive shell provides full access to the configuration options of the underlying BDD package. Thus, it is possible to investigate the effect of different choices (e.g. whether and how to partition the model, the impact of different cache configurations) on the verification process. For instance, it is possible to control the application of BDD variable orderings in a particular phase of the verification (e.g. after the model is built).

On top of the interactive shell, a graphical user interface (GUI from now on) has been developed (Figure 1). The GUI provides an integrated environment to edit and verify the file containing the model description. It provides graphical access to all the commands interpreted by the textual shell of NuSMV, and allows for the modification of the options in a menu driven way. Moreover, the GUI offers a formula editor which helps the user in writing new specifications. Depending on the kind of formula being edited (e.g. propositional, CTL, LTL), various buttons corresponding to modalities and/or boolean connectors are activated and deactivated.

## 3  System Architecture

Model checking is often referred to as "push-button" technology. However, it is very important to be able to customize the model checker according to the system being verified. This is particularly true in technology transfer, when the model checker may act as the kernel for a custom verification tool, to be used for a very specific class of applications. This may require the development of a translator or a compiler for a (possibly proprietary) specification language, and the effective integration of decomposition techniques to tackle the state explosion.

NuSMV has been explicitly designed to be an open system, which can be easily modified, customized or extended. The system architecture of NuSMV has been

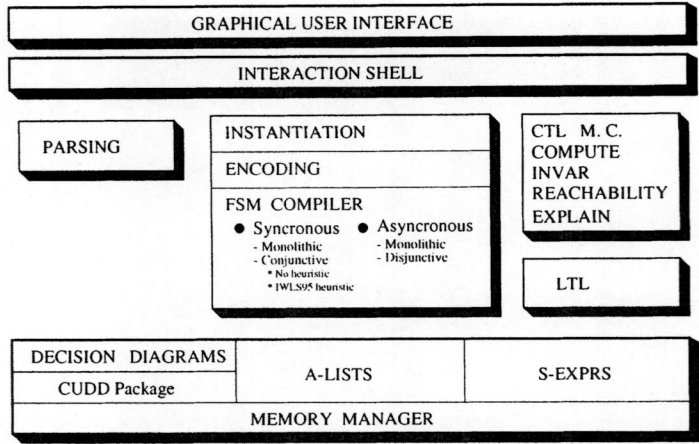

**Fig. 2.** The NuSMV system architecture.

structured and organized in modules. Each module implements a set of functionalities and communicates with the others via a precisely defined interface. A clear distinction between the system back-end and front-end has been enforced, in order to make it possible to reuse the internal components independently of the input language being used to describe the model.

The architecture of NuSMV (see Figure 2) is composed of the following modules:

*Kernel.* The kernel provides the low level functionalities such as dynamic memory allocation, and manipulation of basic data structures (e.g. cons cells, hash tables). The kernel also provides all the basic BDD primitives, directly taken from the CUDD [8] BDD package. The integration of the CUDD package hides the details of the garbage collection. The NuSMV kernel can be used as a black box, following coding standards which have been precisely defined.

*Parser.* This module implements the routines to process a file written in NuSMV language, check its syntactic correctness, and build a parse tree representing the internal format of the input file.

*Compiler.* This module is responsible for the compilation of the parsed model into BDDs. The *Instantiation* submodule processes the parse tree, and performs the instantiation of the declared modules, building a description of the finite state machine (FSM) representing the model. The *Encoding* submodule performs the encoding of data types and finite ranges into boolean domains. Having separated this module makes it possible to have different encoding policies which can be more appropriate for different kind of variables (e.g. data path, control path). The *FSM Compiler* submodule provides the routines for constructing and manipulating FSM's at the BDD level. It is responsible of all the necessary semantic checks on the read model, such as the absence of circular definitions. The FSM's can be represented in monolithic or partitioned form [3]. The heuristics used to perform the conjunctive partitioning of the transition relation and re-ordering of the clusters [7] have been developed to work at the BDD level, independently of the input language. The interface to other modules is given by the primitives for the computation of the image and counter-image of a set of states. These primitives are independent of the method used to represent the transition relation.

*Model Checking.* This module provides the functionalities for reachability, fair CTL model checking, invariant checking, and computation of quantitative characteristics. Moreover, this module provides the routines for counterexample generation and inspection. Counterexamples can be produced with different levels of verbosity, in the form of reusable data structures, and can subsequently be inspected and navigated. All these routines are independent of the particular method used to represent the FSM.

*LTL.* The LTL module is a separated module which calls an external program that translates the LTL formula into a tableau suitable to be loaded into NuSMV. This program also generates a new CTL formula to be verified on the synchronous product of the original system and the generated tableau.

*Interactive shell.* From the interaction shell the user has full access to all the functionalities provided by the system.

*Graphical user interface.* The graphical user interface has been designed on top of the interactive shell. It allows the user to inspect and set the value of the environment variables of the system, and provides full access to all the functionalities.

## 4   Implementation

NuSMV has been designed to be robust, close to the standards required by industry and easy to maintain and modify. NuSMV is written in ANSI C and is POSIX compliant. This makes the system portable to any compliant platform. It has been throughly debugged with Purify (http://www.pureatria.com) to detect memory leaks and runtime memory corruptions errors.

The kernel of NuSMV provides low level functionalities, such as dynamic memory allocation, in a way independent from the underlying operating system. Moreover, it provides routines for the manipulation of basic data structures such as cons cells, hash tables, arrays of generic types, and encapsulates the CUDD BDD package [8].

In order to implement the architecture depicted in Section 3, the source code of NuSMV has been organized in different packages. NuSMV is composed of 11 packages. Each package exports a set of routines which manipulate the data structures defined in the package and which allow to modify the options associated to the functionalities provided by the package itself. Moreover, each package is associated with a set of commands which can be interpreted by the NuSMV interactive shell. We have packages for model checking, FSM compilation, BDD interface, LTL model checking and kernel functionalities. New packages can be added relatively easily, following precisely defined rules.

The GUI has been developed in Tcl/Tk. It runs as a separate process, synchronously communicating with NuSMV by issuing textual commands to the interactive shell, and processing the resulting output to display it graphically.

The code of NuSMV has been documented following the standards of the ext tool (http://alumnus.caltech.edu/~sedwards/ext), which allows for the automatic extraction of the programmer manual from the comments in the system source code. The programmer manual is available in TXT or HTML format, and can be browsed by an HTML viewer. This tool is also used to generate the help on line available through the interactive shell and via the graphical user interface.

The user manual has been written following the TEXINFO standard, from which different formats (i.e. POSTSCRIPT, PDF, DVI, INFO, HTML) can be automatically generated, and accessed via an HTML viewer or in hardcopy.

## 5 Results and Future Directions

NUSMV is a robust, well structured and flexible platform, designed to be applicable in technology transfer projects. The performance of NUSMV have been compared with those of SMV by running a number of SMV examples. Despite the fact that NUSMV gives up some of the optimizations of SMV to simplify the dependencies between modules, an improvement in computation time has been obtained. In most examples NUSMV performs better than SMV, in particular for larger examples. This enhancement in performance is mainly due to the use of CUDD BDD package.

The NUSMV architecture provides a precise distinction between the front-end, specific to the SMV input language, and the back-end (including the heuristics for model partitioning and model checking algorithms), which is independent of the input language. This separation has been used to develop on top of NUSMV the MBP system. MBP is a planner able to synthesize reactive controllers for achieving goals in nondeterministic domains [4].

Functionalities currently under development are a simulator, which is of paramount importance for the user to acquire confidence in the correctness of the model, and a compiler for an imperative style input language, which can often be very convenient in the modeling process. Further developments will include the integration of decomposition techniques (e.g. abstraction and compositional verification), and new and very promising techniques based on the use of efficient procedures for propositional satisfiability, following the ideas reported in [1].

## References

1. A. Biere, A. Cimatti, E. Clarke, and Y. Zhu. Symbolic Model Checking without BDDs. In *Proc. TACAS'99*, March 1999. To appear.
2. R. K. Brayton et al. VIS: A system for Verification and Synthesis. In *Proc. of CAV'96*. LNCS 1102, Springer-Verlag.
3. J. Burch, E. Clarke, and D. Long. Representing Circuits More Efficiently in Symbolic Model Checking. In *Proc. of the 28th ACM/IEEE Design Automation Conference*, pages 403–407, Los Alamitos, CA, June 1991. IEEE Computer Society Press.
4. A. Cimatti, M. Roveri, and P. Traverso. Automatic OBDD-based Generation of Universal Plans in Non-Deterministic Domains. In *Proc. of the 15th National Conference on Artificial Intelligence (AAAI-98)*, Madison, Wisconsin, 1998. AAAI-Press.
5. O. Grumberg E. Clarke and K. Hamaguchi. Another Look at LTL Model Checking. *Formal Methods in System Design*, 10(1):57–71, February 1997.
6. K.L. McMillan. *Symbolic Model Checking*. Kluwer Academic Publ., 1993.
7. R. K. Ranjan, A. Aziz, B. Plessier, C. Pixley, and R. K. Brayton. Efficient BDD algorithms for FSM synthesis and verification. In *IEEE/ACM Proceedings International Workshop on Logic Synthesis*, Lake Tahoe (NV), May 1995.
8. F. Somenzi. CUDD: CU Decision Diagram package — release 2.1.2. Department of Electrical and Computer Engineering — University of Colorado at Boulder, April 1997. ftp://vlsi.colorado.edu/pub/

# PIL/SETHEO: A Tool for the Automatic Analysis of Authentication Protocols*

Johann Schumann

*Institut für Informatik, TU München*
*email:* **schumann@in.tum.de**

## 1 Introduction

Authentication protocols are used in distributed environments ensure the identity of the communication partners and to establish a secure communication between them. With the widespread use of distributed computing (e.g., Internet, electronic commerce), authentication protocols have gained much importance. Because high values can be at stake, such protocols must have extremely high quality and must be resistant with respect to intruders. Therefore, usually formal methods are used for their design and verification. In the literature, a variety of different methods and techniques for protocol analysis have been developed (cf. [Mea94] for an overview). Typically, the methods exhibit their strength in different stages of the development of an authentication protocol: in early design stages, conformance to a development standard [AG98] and absence of major deficiencies of a protocol can be ensured by type checking. As a next step, modal logics of belief are used to model a protocol and its properties. Such logics (e.g., BAN [BAN89], SVO, GNY, or AUTLOG [KW94]) are convenient for the verification of important properties, but are relatively weak with respect to modeling intricate intruder scenarios. Here, model-checking approaches (e.g., [KW96]) can be used. They can efficiently and automatically analyze a protocol. However, they usually cannot provide a positive proof and are limited by the size of the state-space they can explore. Methods for verification which are based on CSP, like [Pau97], avoid this problem by simultaneously modeling a potentially infinite number of interleaving protocol runs, but their degree of automatic processing (e.g., with Isabelle) is still rather small.

The tool PIL/SETHEO addresses the second stage: PIL/SETHEO is capable of automatically proving safety properties of authentication protocols, formalized in the modal belief logics BAN [BAN89] and AUTLOG [KW94]. PIL/SETHEO is based SETHEO, an automated theorem prover for first order predicate logic.

## 2 Requirements and System Architecture

PIL/SETHEO was designed with the goal of practical usability. Therefore, the following important requirements are the basis for PIL/SETHEO's system design:

---

* This work has been supported by the Deutsche Forschungsgemeinschaft (DFG) within Habilitation-grant Schu908/5-1, Schu908/5-2, and SFB 342/A5.

- *automatic processing*: after specifying the protocol and the desired properties the tool should run automatically. Response-times are to be kept below one minute.
- *representation level*: the protocol and its properties are specified in the modal BAN or AUTLOG logic. The transformation into first-order logic must be kept transparent to the user. Thus, no knowledge about first-order theorem proving or SETHEO should be required to use PIL/SETHEO.
- *human readable proofs*: a major benefit of protocol analysis with modal belief logics is that the resulting proofs are relatively short and provide valuable insights to the protocol designer. This is in sharp contrast to model checking techniques (where no proof is provided) and CSP-based techniques which produce rather lengthy and complex proofs. Hence, all proofs are to be presented on the level of the source logic (BAN or AUTLOG) and must be human-readable.
- *feedback on failed conjectures*: during development of a protocol, it is likely that some of the conjectures cannot be proven due to errors in design or formalization. Then, a simple answer "no" (or an endless loop) is rather insufficient. Thus PIL/SETHEO has to offer several ways to provide feedback on what might be wrong in case a proof attempt fails.

These requirements are reflected in PIL/SETHEO's system architecture. Its input is a specification of the protocol's messages, additional assumptions, and the theorems to be proven. The specification language developed for PIL/SETHEO [Wag97] is close to the underlying modal logic (BAN or AUTLOG). An example for a simple protocol (a variant of the RPC-handshake) is shown in Figure 1A.

This input specification in translated into one or more proof tasks in first-order logic (in clausal normal form). PIL/SETHEO uses the approach of meta-interpretation which transforms each BAN (or AUTLOG) formula into a term. A newly introduced predicate symbol holds (abbreviated as ⊢) is true, if and only if its argument (a translated modal formula) can be derived using the inference rules of the resp. modal logic. Thus, all inference rules of the BAN (or AUTLOG) logic are transformed into first-order implications. For details see [Sch97].

These proof tasks form the input of SETHEO, a high performance theorem prover for first-order logic in clausal normal form [Let92]. SETHEO features a wide variety of techniques for pruning the search space which is traversed in a depth-first manner with iterative deepening. When SETHEO finds a proof, a tree-like model elimination tableau is returned. A proof is this form, however, is not readable. Therefore, it is automatically translated into a human-readable form using the tool ILF-SETHEO [WS97]. After a transformation into a sequent-style calculus (block calculus), the proof is syntactically converted into a proof of the original BAN (or AUTLOG) logic and type-set using LaTeX. A short example of the output is shown in Figure 1B. This representation of the proof directly corresponds to the representation level of the input of PIL/SETHEO (left side of Figure). For details on the notation cf. [BAN89,Sch97].

In case, a conjecture cannot be proven, SETHEO usually reaches a run-time limit. In order to increase usability of the tool, PIL/SETHEO features

| A | B |
|---|---|
| Objects:<br>  principal A,B;<br>  sharedkey K_a_b, Kp_a_b;<br>  statement N_a, N_b;<br>Assumptions:<br>  A believes sharedkey K_a_b;<br>  B believes sharedkey K_a_b;<br>  A believes B controls<br>     sharedkey K_a_b;<br>  B believes sharedkey Kp_a_b;<br>  A believes fresh N_a;<br>  B believes fresh N_b;<br>Idealized Protocol:<br>  message 1: A -> B {N_a}(K_a_b);<br>  message 2: A <- B<br>    {f(N_a),N_b}(K_a_b);<br>  message 3: A -> B {N_b}(K_a_b);<br>  message 4: A <- B<br>    {sharedkey Kp_a_b}(K_a_b);<br>Conjectures: after message 4:<br>  B believes A believes N_b; | **Theorem 1.** *conjecture.*<br><br>Proof. We show directly that<br><br>$$conjecture. \qquad (1)$$<br>Because of *Message-Meaning, Assumption$_2$*,<br>and by *Message$_3$*<br>$$\vdash B \models A \hspace{-0.3em}\mid\hspace{-0.3em}\sim N_B. \qquad (2)$$<br>Because of *Theorem*<br>$$conjecture \Leftarrow \vdash B \hspace{-0.2em}\models A \hspace{-0.2em}\models N_B. \qquad (3)$$<br>Because of *Nonce-Verification*: $\forall P, Q, \forall R \;:\;$<br>$P \hspace{-0.2em}\mid\hspace{-0.2em}\equiv\; Q \hspace{-0.2em}\mid\hspace{-0.2em}\equiv\; R \Leftarrow P \hspace{-0.2em}\mid\hspace{-0.2em}\equiv\; Q \mid\sim R \wedge$<br>$P \hspace{-0.2em}\models\; \# R$. Hence by (2) and by *Assumption$_6$*<br>$\neg$ *conjecture*. Hence by (3) *conjecture*. Thus<br>we have completed the proof of (1).    q.e.d. |

**Fig. 1.** Example input (A) and output of PIL/SETHEO (B).

two ways of producing feed-back: *belief-generation* and *abduction*. In the first case, PIL/SETHEO generates all beliefs which are derivable from the given specification and which conform to given syntactic criteria. Let us assume that we had "forgotten" the last assumption (B believes fresh N_b,*Assumption$_6$*) in Figure 1A. Then, our theorem cannot be proven. In that case, the user can ask PIL/SETHEO which kinds of BAN-formulas $B$ believes. PIL/SETHEO, which uses a variant of the DELTA-preprocessor [Sch94] to generate the formulas in a bottom-up way, returns a list of BAN-formulas (in our example 124). PIL/SETHEO's user interface allows to further restrict the focus of the formulas by specifying a syntactic filter. For example, we might ask what $B$ believes to be fresh (freshness is an important issue in protocol analysis with BAN-logic). Now, PIL/SETHEO returns a much shorter list of formulas (8 in our case). From them, it is quite obvious that there are no terms which contain any reference to freshness of time-stamp $N_B$. This is a clear indication that something is wrong with that time-stamp: $B$ does not belief the validity of its own time-stamps. This immediately leads to the missing assumption $B \models \# N_B$ (B believes fresh N_b) which then yields the desired proof.

In the abductive mode, additional assumptions (or patterns, like $B$ believes the freshness of each time-stamp) can be given by the user. PIL/SETHEO then tries to prove the theorem and returns a list of (most specific) instantiations of the additional assumptions which were required to find a proof with given resources. From there, the user can find out those assumptions which might be important for the analysis.

The user interface for PIL/SETHEO is straight forward and easy to use. PIL/SETHEO uses the tool "make" to make sure that for a complete analysis all conjectures have been proven. Upon completion, PIL/SETHEO returns a LaTeX-document containing a full report and all proofs.

## 3 Conclusions

We have used PIL/SETHEO to analyze a number of well-known protocols (Kerberos, Andrew Secure RPC Handshake, Needham Schroeder, Needham Schroeder with pubic keys, Otway Rees, wide-mouthed frog, Yahalom, CCITT-X.509, ISO-10181 and others). All proof tasks arising from the verification of these protocols (with BAN or AUTLOG) could be shown fully automatically within less than one minute per protocol (actual proof times have been below 20 seconds). As far as possible with the formalism of belief logics, we were able to "re-detect" errors in early versions of the protocols. With its fully automatic operation and its capability to generate human-readable proofs in the BAN or AUTLOG logic PIL/SETHEO is a powerful, yet easy to use tool, especially suited for early protocol design phases.

## References

[AG98] M. Abadi and D. Gordon. A calculus for cryptographic protocols: The spi calculus. *Information and Computation*, 1998.

[BAN89] M. Burrows, M. Abadi, and R. Needham. A Logic of Authentication. In *ACM Operating Systems Review 23(5)*, 1989.

[KW94] V. Kessler and G. Wedel. AUTLOG — An Advanced Logic of Authentication. In *Proc. IEEE Computer Security Foundations Workshop IV*, pages 90–99. IEEE, 1994.

[KW96] D. Kindred and J. Wing. Fast, automatic checking of security protocols. In *2nd USENIX Workshop on Electronic Commerce*, pages 41–52, 1996.

[Let92] R. Letz, et al. SETHEO: A High-Performance Theorem Prover. *JAR*, 8(2):183–212, 1992.

[Mea94] C. A. Meadows. Formal verification of Cryptographic Protocols: A Survey. In *Proc. AsiaCrypt*, 1994.

[Pau97] L. Paulson. Proving properties of security protocols by induction. In *PCSFW: Proc. 10th Computer Security Foundations Workshop*. IEEE, 1997.

[Sch94] J. Schumann. DELTA — A Bottom-up Preprocessor for Top-Down Theorem Provers, System Abstract. In *Proc. CADE 12*. Springer, 1994.

[Sch97] J. Schumann. Automatic verification of cryptographic protocols with SETHEO. In *Proc. CADE 14*. Springer, pp. 87–100, 1997.

[Wag97] K. Wagner. PIL: Ein SETHEO-basiertes Werkzeug zur Analyse kryptographischer Protokolle. Fortgeschrittenenpraktikum, TUM, 1997.

[WS97] A. Wolf and J. Schumann. ILF-SETHEO: Processing Model Elimination Proofs for Natural Language Output. In *Proc. CADE 14*. Springer, 1997.

# Author Index

# Lecture Notes in Computer Science

For information about Vols. 1–1548
please contact your bookseller or Springer-Verlag